Surviving
Schizophrenia

ALSO BY E. FULLER TORREY, M.D.

Ethical Issues in Medicine (editor)

Witchdoctors and Psychiatrists

The Death of Psychiatry

International Collaboration in Mental Health (coeditor)

Why Did You Do That?

Schizophrenia and Civilization

The Roots of Treason

Nowhere to Go: The Tragic Odyssey of the Homeless Mentally Ill

Care of the Seriously Mentally Ill (coauthor)

Criminalizing the Seriously Mentally Ill (coauthor)

Frontier Justice: The Rise and Fall of the Loomis Gang

Freudian Fraud

Schizophrenia and Manic-Depressive Disorder (coauthor)

Out of the Shadows

The Invisible Plague (coauthor)

Surviving Manic-Depressive Illness (coauthor)

Surviving Schizophrenia

A Manual for Families, Consumers, and Providers

Fourth Edition

E. Fuller Torrey, M.D.

Quill

An Imprint of HarperCollinsPublishers

First Quill edition published 2001.

Designed by Nancy Singer Olaguera

Library of Congress Cataloging-in-Publication Data

Torrey, E. Fuller (Edwin Fuller).
    Surviving schizophrenia: a manual for families, consumers, and providers / E. Fuller Torrey. — 4th ed.
        p. cm.
    Includes bibliographical references and index.
    ISBN 0-06-095919-3 (pbk.)
        1. Schizophrenia — Popular works. I. Title.

RC514.T633 2001
616.89'82—dc21   00-065348

04   05   RRD   20 19 18 17 16 15 14 13 12 11

I told her the long story about the hospital; how in the beginning it was difficult to get distance from people suffering illnesses that stole their minds for a while or a lifetime, how poignant and painful it was to see them struggle inside schizophrenia. . . . You wonder how it is that they can still work so hard at keeping their spirit, hold to hopes, try to salvage dignity from ruins of lives. Try to even hold on to love. . . . And then there's a day you look around the ward and suddenly understand that it's in here that you've found your heroes.

—Seth Norman, "Saving Grace," 1994

This edition of *Surviving Schizophrenia* is dedicated to Fred Frese, Ed Francell, Jon Stanley, and the many other individuals with severe psychiatric illnesses who, despite their illnesses, work to improve the quality of life for others so afflicted. These individuals are indeed our heroes.

As for me, you must know that I shouldn't precisely have chosen madness if there had been any choice.

Vincent Van Gogh, 1889, in a letter to his brother, written while he was involuntarily confined in the psychiatric hospital at St. Remy

1

One winter day at the lake when
you were small, you went cross country
skiing with your dog. Night came,
and you didn't return. We imagined
you'd broken a leg and lay freezing
in the forest, crying out for us
as we called your name, but we heard
only the crunch of boots along that icy road.
I thought of Hansel, live kindling for a
witch's supper. Fear makes storytellers
of us all. But you returned, red cheeks aglow,
puzzled why we hugged you so hard
for rounding up the errant dog.

2

Now, you recall this memory, as if
it were someone else's story; you are
like the clothes you lose track of. You
do not even know you're gone. Oh Randall!
No use to shout and wail. Cries do not reach
the limbic shores where you float
like a graceful loon whose cries
pierced our summer nights so long ago.
One white morning, you awoke to find
your black feathers rooted in the lake's early freeze.
Your friends had fled. Across the gelid expanse,
I answer your haunting call.
Here I am. Look at me. Talk to me.

Margo Button, "With No Explanation" (Randall Button, afflicted with schizophrenia, committed suicide.)

CONTENTS

ILLUSTRATIONS

PHOTOGRAPHS

Works of art illustrating some symptoms of schizophrenia:

Vincent van Gogh, "Starry Night" (1889)

Joan Miró, "Head of a Catalan Peasant" (1924)

Pablo Picasso, "Nude Woman" (1910)

Marcel Duchamp, "Nude Descending a Staircase" (1912)

Henri Rousseau, "The Dream" (1910)

Edvard Munch, "The Scream" (1895)

MRIs from identical twins, one with schizophrenia and the other well

OTHER

Distribution of the 2.2 Million Persons with Schizophrenia

Inpatients in Public Mental Hospitals per 100,000 Total Population in the United States, 1830–1950

The Magnitude of Deinstitutionalization: Number of Patients in Public Mental Hospitals, 1950–1991

The Course of Schizophrenia

The Location of the Limbic System in the Brain

PREFACE TO THE FOURTH EDITION

When I undertook the initial edition of this book almost 20 years ago, it was with the modest intent of providing some basic information to patients and their families. Ten publishers rejected the manuscript, saying that nobody would buy a book about schizophrenia. The increasingly wide use of this book by individuals affected with schizophrenia, their families, and those who provide psychiatric services, and the book's translation into Italian, Russian, and Japanese, have been a source of great personal gratification. Indeed, I am tempted to do as James Joyce once did and paper my bathroom walls with the original rejection notices!

At the time of the publication of the first edition, the initial CT scans of brains had just been published, the National Alliance for the Mentally Ill (NAMI) had just been formed, and almost no funds were available for schizophrenia research. The contrast with the present is stark. The technology to study the brains of individuals with schizophrenia is light-years ahead of where it was. NAMI is a powerful voice representing those afflicted and their families. And funds to study schizophrenia are much more plentiful, thanks to the advocacy of Senator Pete Domenici and other members of Congress, the National Alliance for Research on Schizophrenia and Affective Disorders (NARSAD), the extraordinary generosity of Ted and Vada Stanley, and others who have contributed to this research.

Despite the progress, however, we still have not unraveled schizophrenia's causes or found truly definitive treatments. The challenges remain. Never have we had better opportunities. Never has there been so much hope.

PREFACE TO THE
FIRST EDITION, 1983

"Your daughter has schizophrenia," I told the woman.

"Oh, my god, anything but that," she replied. "Why couldn't she have leukemia or some other disease instead?"

"But if she had leukemia she might die," I pointed out. "Schizophrenia is a much more treatable disease."

The woman looked sadly at me, then down at the floor. She spoke softly. "I would still prefer that my daughter had leukemia."

This book is a product of a thousand such conversations. Conceived in the darkness of despair, it was fathered by education and mothered by hope. It is written for families whose lives are currently touched by schizophrenia. My sister is afflicted; perhaps your brother, aunt, or son is also. The book provides a scientific framework for understanding its symptoms, causes, and treatment and suggests how families can come to terms with the disease. Above all, the book tries to dispel the multitude of myths and alleviate the millstone of guilt that families have been condemned to carry by mental health professionals; surely this has been Original Psychiatric Sin.

Schizophrenia is a cruel disease. The lives of those affected are often chronicles of constricted experiences, muted emotions, missed opportunities, unfulfilled expectations. It leads to a twilight existence, a twentieth-century underground man. The fate of these patients has been worsened by our propensity to misunderstand, our failure to provide adequate treatment and rehabilitation, our meager research efforts. A disease which should be found, in the phrase of T. S. Eliot, in the "frigid purgatorial fires" has become through our ignorance and neglect a living hell.

Perhaps it is a disease whose time has come. There are rays of hope—research, treatment, the organizations of families and friends. If this book contributes just a little toward bringing schizophrenia out of the Slough of Despond and into the mainstream of American medicine then it will have accomplished its purpose.

ACKNOWLEDGMENTS

I continue to be indebted to many people for this book. Lou AvRutick originally found a home for it at HarperCollins, where Carol Cohen and, more recently, Trena Keating nurtured it to maturity.

The staff of the National Library of Medicine has been unfailingly helpful. Several people contributed useful comments on portions of the manuscript, and I am especially grateful to Dr. Peter Buckley, Camille Callahan, Dr. Faith Dickerson, Dr. John Geddes, Carla Jacobs, D. J. Jaffe, Dr. Michael Knable, Dr. Jeffrey Lieberman, Jon Stanley, Dr. Sidney Wolfe, and Mary Zdanowicz. Katie Petray generously reviewed useful videotapes for appendix C. Ms. Loretta Ostmann, Khoi Nguyen, and Shen Zhong cheerfully provided essential technical support. And my research assistant, Judy Miller, did all of the above and much more; without her attention to detail, the book would not be what it is. Most important, I continue to be indebted to my wife, Barbara, for her support and understanding and the ineffable ingredients that make writing a book possible.

In addition to these, I gratefully acknowledge the following:

Ms. Margo Button for permission to quote a poem from *The Unhinging of Wings.*

Seth Norman for permission to quote from his short story in *Fly Rod and Reel.*

P. J. Kavanagh for permission to quote from the *Collected Poems of Ivor Gurney.*

Joseph H. Berke for permission to reprint excerpts from *Mary Barnes: Two Accounts of a Journey Through Madness.*

Malcolm B. Bowers and Science Press for permission to reprint excerpts from *Retreat from Sanity: The Structure of Emerging Psychosis.*

Andrew McGhie and the British Psychological Society for permission to reprint excerpts from an article in the *British Journal of Medical Psychology.*

British Journal of Psychiatry for permission to reprint excerpts from an article by James Chapman.

Journal of Abnormal and Social Psychology for permission to reprint excerpts from an article by Anonymous.

Anchor Press and Doubleday for permission to reprint excerpts from *These Are My Sisters*, by Lara Jefferson.

Presses Universitaires de France for permission to reprint excerpts from *Autobiography of a Schizophrenic Girl*, by Marguerite Sechehaye.

W. W. Norton and Company for permission to reprint excerpts from *In a Darkness*, by James A. Wechsler.

National Schizophrenia Fellowship for permission to reprint excerpts from *Coping with Schizophrenia*, by H. R. Rollin.

G. P. Putnam and Sons for permission to reprint excerpts from *This Stranger, My Son*, by Louise Wilson.

University Books for permission to reprint excerpts from *The Witnesses*, by Thomas Hennell.

J. G. Hall and *Lancet* for permission to quote from an article.

Nancy J. Hermon and Colin M. Smith for permission to quote from a presentation at the 1986 Alberta Schizophrenia Conference.

Psychological Bulletin and *Schizophrenia Bulletin* for permission to quote from articles.

Mrs. Gilda Nelson for permission to quote from poems by her deceased son, Robert L. Nelson.

The purpose of this book is to make you aware of the progress of schizophrenia and the possible ways in which it may develop. The assessment of symptoms requires an expert. For proper diagnosis and therapy of all symptoms, real or apparent, connected with schizophrenia, please consult your doctor. In my discussion of cases, I have changed all names and identifying details while preserving the integrity of the research findings.

Surviving
Schizophrenia

1

DIMENSIONS OF THE DISASTER

Schizophrenia is to psychiatry what cancer is to medicine: a sentence as well as a diagnosis.

W. Hall, G. Andrews, and G. Goldstein,
Australian and New Zealand Journal of Psychiatry, 1985

Schizophrenia, I said. The word itself is ominous. It has been called "one of the most sinister words in the language." It has a bite to it, a harsh grating sound that evokes visions of madness and asylums. It is not fluid like *démence*, the word from which "dementia" comes. Nor is it a visual word like *écrasé*, the origin of "cracked," meaning that the person is like a cracked pot. Nor is it romantic like "lunatic," meaning fallen under the influence of the moon (which in Latin is *luna*). "Schizophrenia" is a discordant and cruel term, just like the disease it signifies.

Our treatment of individuals with this disease has, all too often, also been discordant and cruel. It is, in fact, the single biggest blemish on the face of contemporary American medicine and social services; when the social history of our era is written, the plight of persons with schizophrenia will be recorded as having been a national scandal. Consider the dimensions of the disaster.

1. *There are at least as many individuals with schizophrenia homeless and living on the streets as there are in all hospitals and related facilities.* Studies of homeless individuals in the United States have estimated their total number to be between 250,000 and 550,000. A median estimate of 400,000 is consistent with the data from most of the studies. Studies have also reported that approximately one-third of homeless individuals are seriously mentally ill, the vast majority of them with schizophrenia. It is likely, therefore, that on any given day

at least 100,000 persons with schizophrenia are living in public shelters and on the streets. As will be described below, there are only approximately 100,000 people with schizophrenia in all hospitals and related facilities at any given time.

2. *There are more individuals with schizophrenia in jails and prisons than there are in all hospitals and related facilities.* A recent Department of Justice survey reported that 16 percent of inmates in local jails and state prisons, or 275,900 individuals, are mentally ill. Based on data from previous jail surveys, it is reasonable to estimate that approximately half of them, or 135,000 individuals, have schizophrenia. Thus, there are more individuals with schizophrenia in jails and prisons than there are in all hospitals and related facilities. Even more shocking is the fact that 29 percent of jails acknowledged holding such individuals *with no charges* against them, often awaiting a bed in a psychiatric hospital. The vast majority of those who do have charges have been charged with misdemeanors such as trespassing. The Los Angeles County Jail is now *de facto* the largest mental institution in the country.

3. *There are increasing episodes of violence committed by individuals with schizophrenia who are not being treated.* Individuals with schizophrenia who take medications are not more violent than the general population. However, as will be discussed in more detail in chapter 11, recent studies have shown that some individuals with schizophrenia who are not taking medication *are* more violent. In one study, 9 percent of individuals with schizophrenia who were living in the community had used a weapon in a fight in the preceding year. In another study, "27 percent of released male and female patients report at least one violent act within a mean of four months after [hospital] discharge." Assaults against family members by individuals with schizophrenia have also risen sharply; a 1991 survey of the members of the National Alliance for the Mentally Ill reported that 11 percent of the seriously mentally ill family members had physically harmed another person within the previous year. A Department of Justice study reported that there are almost 1,000 homicides a year committed by individuals with "a history of mental illness"; media accounts suggest that the majority of these have been diagnosed with schizophrenia. Drug and alcohol abuse and noncompliance with medications both appear to be important factors in increasing violent behavior in this population.

4. *Individuals with schizophrenia are increasingly being victimized by others*. Most crimes against individuals with schizophrenia are not reported; those instances that are reported are often ignored by officials. Purse snatchings and the stealing of disability checks are common, but rapes and even murders are not rare. In Los Angeles, a study of board-and-care home residents, the majority of whom had schizophrenia, reported that one-third of them had been robbed and/or assaulted in the preceding year. In New York, a study of 20 women with schizophrenia reported that half of them had been raped at least once, and 5 had been raped more than once. In Des Moines, Van Mill, a homeless man diagnosed with schizophrenia, was beaten to death by three men, then dumped into a children's wading pool.

5. *Housing for many individuals with schizophrenia is often abysmal.* Because of pressure from state departments of mental health to discharge patients from state hospitals, seriously mentally ill individuals are frequently placed into housing that would not be considered fit for anyone else. For example, in 1979 the police removed 21 "ex-mental patients" living in New York City board-and-care homes "amid broken plumbing, rotting food and roaches. . . . The police found the decaying corpse of a former patient lying undisturbed in one home inhabited by six other residents." Similar reports continued throughout the 1980s, and in 1990 the *New York Times* headlined still another report: "Mental Homes Are Wretched, A Panel Says." In Mississippi "9 ex-patients" were found in a primitive shed with "no toilet or running water" and "guarded by two vicious dogs" to insure that they did not run away.

6. *Many individuals with schizophrenia revolve between hospitals, jails, and shelters.* Because of the failure of mental health professionals to provide medications and insure aftercare for discharged patients, many individuals with schizophrenia undergo a revolving door of admissions and readmissions to hospitals, jails, and public shelters. In Illinois, 30 percent of patients discharged from state psychiatric hospitals are rehospitalized within 30 days. In New York, 60 percent of discharged patients are rehospitalized within a year. A study of readmissions to state psychiatric hospitals found patients with schizophrenia who had been readmitted as many as 121 times. A jail survey identified individuals with schizophrenia who had been jailed as many as 80 times. Between hospitalizations and jailings these

individuals consume inordinate amounts of police and social service time and resources. Studies in Ohio and California in the 1990s reported that law enforcement officials responded to more "mental health crisis" calls than robbery calls. In New York City in 1976 the police responded to approximately 1,000 calls regarding "emotionally disturbed persons"; in 1998 the police responded to 24,787 such calls.

7. *Schizophrenia is remarkably neglected by mental health professionals.* Despite an increase in total psychiatrists, psychologists, and psychiatric social workers from approximately 9,000 in 1940 to over 200,000 in 1998, schizophrenia has been remarkably neglected by these professionals. For example, a study published in 1994 reported that only *3 percent* of all patients seen by psychiatrists in private office practice had a diagnosis of schizophrenia. One major reason for the failure of mental health professionals to treat patients with schizophrenia is the shockingly poor preparation they receive in their training programs. State psychiatric hospitals frequently must fill their positions with poorly trained and/or incompetent professionals; indeed, Wyoming State Hospital in the 1980s went for almost a year without a single psychiatrist on its staff. Many Community Mental Health Centers (CMHCs), originally conceived and funded to provide care for seriously mentally ill individuals being discharged from psychiatric hospitals, merely evolved into counseling centers to do personality polishing for the "worried well." Some CMHCs also built swimming pools with federal funds and paid their administrators handsomely. In 1989 three administrators at a Utah CMHC were charged with 117 counts of felony theft for paying themselves $3.6 million over five years. In 1990 the executive director of a CMHC in Fort Worth was indicted on four counts of felony theft. These stolen funds are but a fraction of the resources that were originally intended for individuals with serious mental illnesses such as schizophrenia but which have been diverted, legally or illegally, to other purposes.

8. *At least 40 percent of all individuals with schizophrenia are receiving no treatment at any given time.* A report from the National Institute of Mental Health Epidemiologic Catchment Area (ECA) survey revealed that only 60 percent of individuals with schizophrenia receive any psychiatric or medical care within a one-year period. At any given time, therefore, at least 40 percent are receiving no treat-

ment. A community survey in Baltimore found that half of all persons with schizophrenia were receiving no treatment for their illness. A major reason for this remarkably low treatment rate has been changes in laws making involuntary hospitalization and treatment more difficult to effect for individuals who, because of their brain dysfunction, have no awareness of their need for treatment. Sadly misguided civil rights lawyers and "patient advocates" regularly defend the individual's right to be psychotic; the thinking of the lawyers and advocates

FACT SHEET ON SCHIZOPHRENIA

- Approximately 2.2 million Americans have schizophrenia in any given year. That is 8 persons out of every 1,000.
- At least 40 percent of them are not receiving treatment at any given time. Thus, there are approximately 900,000 individuals with schizophrenia who are not being treated.
- There are at least as many individuals with schizophrenia who are homeless, living on the streets and in shelters, as there are in all hospitals and related facilities.
- There are more individuals with schizophrenia in jails and state prisons than there are in all hospitals and related facilities.
- There are increasing episodes of violence committed by individuals with schizophrenia who are not being treated. This is the single biggest cause of stigma against individuals with this diagnosis.
- Individuals with schizophrenia are increasingly the victims of crimes, including robberies, assaults, rapes, and murders.
- Public psychiatric treatment services, housing, and rehabilitation services for individuals with schizophrenia are often grossly inadequate and, in many states, getting worse.
- The total direct and indirect costs of schizophrenia in the United States in 2000 were approximately $40 billion. That was more than the entire budgets of the National Institutes of Health and the VA medical system combined.
- Approximately $10 billion of that $40 billion was spent on federal disability payments (SSI and SSDI) for individuals with schizophrenia. Schizophrenia was the single largest diagnosis for individuals receiving both SSI and SSDI.

is more thought-disordered than the people they are defending. For example, in Wisconsin a public defender argued that an individual with schizophrenia who was mute and eating his feces was not a danger to himself; the judge accepted the defense and released the man.

The disastrous care and treatment of individuals with schizophrenia is not unique to the United States, although it is probably worse in this country than in most other developed nations. Many Canadian provinces are proceeding with deinstitutionalization along the same lines as those pioneered by the United States, and conditions in Ontario have especially deteriorated. England has had a series of homicides by discharged patients who were not receiving treatment, and the numbers of mentally ill homeless individuals have increased markedly in Australia and France. Italy passed a law in 1978 prohibiting new admissions to psychiatric hospitals and, except in Verona and Trieste, where community treatment facilities are good, the "Italian experiment" as it is known has been a failure. Japan puts individuals with schizophrenia into private hospitals, which are often owned by the doctors themselves, and keeps them there so that the patients' families will not be embarrassed; this abuse was so widespread that an international commission investigated it in 1986. Nowhere in the world has the treatment of schizophrenia been without major problems, although the Scandinavian nations and the Netherlands probably come closest to achieving a reasonable level of care.

HOW MANY PEOPLE HAVE SCHIZOPHRENIA IN THE UNITED STATES?

Given the fact that the National Institute of Mental Health (NIMH) has been in business for over half a century, one would think that the answer to this fundamental question would be well established. Not so! The number of people who have schizophrenia in the United States is widely debated, with advocates for mentally ill persons using higher numbers and those who are responsible for delivering services using lower numbers.

Much of the problem arose from the NIMH-funded Epidemiologic Catchment Area (ECA) study carried out between 1980 and 1985. That study employed lay interviewers using a questionnaire to ascertain symptoms of mental illness among a sample population at five sites. The ECA study reported that 1.5 percent of the U.S. population ages 18 and over, and 1.2 percent of the population ages 9 to 17, had schizophrenia in a one-year period. Based on the U.S. population of the year 2000, that translates into 3.5 million individuals with schizophrenia in a one-year period, a prevalence rate approximately twice as high as older studies had shown.

The methodology of the ECA study, however, has been seriously criticized for overdiagnosing mental disorders. A study in Baltimore in which psychiatrists interviewed individuals who had been diagnosed as having schizophrenia in the ECA study found remarkably poor agreement with the ECA diagnosis. Data from previous U.S. prevalence studies, data from the Social Security Administration on the number of individuals receiving benefits for severe mental illnesses (2.7 million in 1999), and the 1999 Surgeon General's special report on mental health, which claimed that 1.3 percent of all individuals aged 18 to 54 have schizophrenia, all suggest that 3.5 million individuals with schizophrenia is too high an estimate. Instead, the available data, when taken together, suggests that *the total number of individuals with schizophrenia in the United States in any one-year period is approximately 2.2 million.*

However, 2.2 million people is a lot of people. It is the same number of people as the combined populations of Rhode Island, North Dakota, and Alaska and more than the state population of West Virginia, Nebraska, or Utah. It is also about the same as the number of people who live in the metropolitan areas of Miami, Pittsburgh, Denver, or Seattle. Imagine today that every single person in one of those states or cities has schizophrenia and you will begin to realize the magnitude of this tragedy.

It should be emphasized that the 2.2 million includes *only* people with schizophrenia. It does not include 1.1 million more people who have manic-depressive illness, or an even larger number with severe depression or obsessive-compulsive disorder. But these are just numbers, like the number of people killed in an earthquake in Turkey or a flood in Bangladesh. They fail to convey the human sufferings and personal tragedies that accompany the event both for those affected and for those around them.

Another way to express the prevalence of schizophrenia at any given time is the number of individuals affected per 1,000 total population. In the United States that figure is approximately 8 per 1,000. This means that a town of 3,000 people has approximately 24 cases of schizophrenia, while a city of 3 million people will have over 24,000 cases.

These are just averages, for it appears that there are considerable variations in the prevalence rates in different parts of the United States and among different population groups, as will be discussed below.

WHERE ARE THEY?

If in fact there are 2.2 million Americans with schizophrenia, then why is the disease so invisible? It is invisible because we have become experts in hiding it. Schizophrenia lurks in the closets, hiding behind euphemisms like "nervous breakdown" or "bad case of nerves." It stands quietly behind lace curtains, but nobody bothers to mention it. It is the aunt who used to live with them but then moved; what they don't add is that she moved to the state hospital. It is the son who got in trouble in late adolescence and is now said to be living in Pennsylvania; what they don't add is that he is living in a group home there. It is the sister who tragically committed suicide over, it is rumored, a love affair; what they don't add is that she really committed suicide because she was plagued by voices and chose not to live with her disease. We hide it, hoping nobody will tell, hoping nobody will find out. It is a stigma.

The stigma of schizophrenia makes it all the more tragic, as will be discussed in chapter 14. Not only must persons affected and their families bear the disease itself, but they must bear the stigma of it as well. People with schizophrenia are the lepers of the present day. The aunt, son, or sister hidden in the closet may be discovered at any minute, and then the word will be out. Disaster, Dishonor, Disgrace. The magnitude of schizophrenia as a national calamity is exceeded only by the magnitude of our ignorance in dealing with it.

There is remarkably little hard information on where many of the 2.2 million persons with schizophrenia in the United States are living or receiving care. The Director of the National Institute of Mental Health (NIMH), testifying before the Senate Committee on Appropriations in late 1986, said that NIMH could account for only 42 percent of such individuals; for the other 58 percent their living and care arrangements were unknown. This shocking admission, by the federal agency responsible for maintaining such information, marks one more indication of the neglect this disease has suffered.

If all current sources of information on persons with schizophrenia are synthesized, however, it is possible to construct a reasonably accurate picture of where they are living on any given day. The chart shows the whereabouts of the 2.2 million persons currently diagnosed with this disorder.

Institutionalized: 500,000. On any given day approximately 500,000 of the 2.2 million individuals with schizophrenia are living in various institutions or on the streets. These institutions include:

1. *Hospitals and semihospitals: 100,000.*

State psychiatric hospitals	40,000
Private psychiatric hospitals	4,000
Psychiatric wards of general hospitals	10,000
VA hospitals	5,000
Inpatient units of mental health centers and similar institutions	2,000
"Semihospitals" such as crisis beds, respite beds, institutions for mental disease, etc.	39,000
	100,000

"Semihospitals" are a new and rapidly growing type of hospital in which seriously mentally ill individuals are maintained in a house or other structure in the community with 24-hour nursing coverage. They function essentially as small psychiatric hospitals even though they are technically not classified as hospitals. They have become increasingly popular because states can be reimbursed by the federal Medicaid program for individuals in such institutions, whereas they cannot be so reimbursed if the same person is in a state hospital. This rule is called the Institutions for Mental Disease (IMD) exclusion, and it is the driving force causing states to empty out the state hospitals and transfer the patients to "semihospitals," basically the same kind of institution but called by a different name. It will be discussed later in this chapter.

2. *Nursing homes: 165,000.* There are estimated to be approximately 2.2 million individuals living in nursing homes in the United States. A 1988 survey of nursing homes in four cities reported that 5 percent of the residents had schizophrenia as a primary diagnosis. A 1993 random sampling of nursing home residents in Rochester, New York, found that 7.5 percent of them had a diagnosis of schizophrenia. These findings are consistent with older studies showing

that approximately 8 percent of nursing home residents were "chronic mental patients, formerly residents of long-term psychiatric hospitals." Among nursing home residents under the age of 65, the percentage who have schizophrenia is approximately 33 percent. Some states utilize nursing homes very heavily in place of state psychiatric hospitals. Illinois, for example, is reported to have over 12,000 seriously mentally ill individuals in nursing homes, including facilities of over 400 beds that are exclusively for mentally ill patients. Like many semihospitals, these are really just state hospitals that are now being called by another name.

3. *Jails and prisons: 135,000*. This is discussed above.

4. *Public shelters and living on the streets: 100,000*. This is discussed above.

Supervised living: 400,000. Supervised living arrangements for mentally ill individuals go by a variety of names including foster homes, family care homes, halfway houses, board-and-care homes, county homes, etc. The common denominator of them all is that the individual pays several hundred dollars a month (usually from their SSI or SSDI payments) and receives a room (often shared), three meals a day, and varying degrees of supervision for medication, keeping appointments, etc. As will be discussed in chapter 10, the quality of their facilities varies widely. Nobody knows precisely how many individuals with schizophrenia live in such facilities, but there are estimated to be approximately 600,000 individuals with all diagnoses living in such homes. Based on the rapidly increasing SSI and SSDI payments in recent years and on surveys of families with a seriously mentally ill relative, an estimate of 400,000 individuals with schizophrenia living in these facilities seems reasonable.

Living with family members: 550,000. A recent survey of NAMI members reported that 42 percent of the seriously mentally ill family members were living with a family member. It seems likely that NAMI members are somewhat self-selected in having their ill family member live at home, and that the percentage of all individuals who live with family members is lower than this. An estimate of 550,000 seems reasonable.

Distribution of the 2.2 Million Persons with Schizophrenia

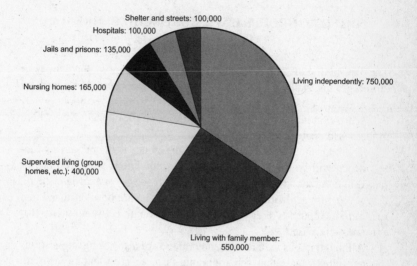

Shelter and streets: 100,000
Hospitals: 100,000
Jails and prisons: 135,000
Nursing homes: 165,000
Living independently: 750,000
Supervised living (group homes, etc.): 400,000
Living with family member: 550,000

Living independently: 750,000. The survey of NAMI members referred to above reported that 31 percent of the seriously mentally ill family members were living independently. It seems likely that NAMI members may include disproportionately few families of mentally ill individuals who are doing well and able to live independently, so an estimate of 750,000 such individuals seems reasonable. It should be added, however, that living "independently" may include a broad range of individuals, from those who are fully self-supporting and completely independent to individuals who live in their own apartment but whose family brings them food and provides care for them at least daily.

It should also be emphasized that this distribution of individuals with schizophrenia is a snapshot taken at a single point in time. Many of these individuals are almost constantly in motion from one venue to another. For example, it would not be unusual for an individual with schizophrenia who had stopped taking his/her medicine and was therefore clinically deteriorating to move from a supervised group home to the family home to a public shelter to jail to the psychiatric ward of a general hospital and back again to the group home, all within a period of six months.

DO SOME GROUPS HAVE MORE SCHIZOPHRENIA THAN OTHERS?

The distribution of schizophrenia among different geographical areas or ethnic groups, both in the United States and elsewhere, has intrigued researchers for almost two centuries. Although most textbooks assert that schizophrenia has approximately the same prevalence everywhere in the world, that is clearly not the case.

The best-documented geographical difference is the urban risk factor, which will be discussed in chapter 6. Individuals who are born or raised in an urban area have approximately twice the risk of later being diagnosed with schizophrenia as individuals who are born or raised in a rural area. Suburban areas and small towns fall between these two extremes risk-wise.

Although not as well documented, there are also strong suggestions in the United States that schizophrenia is more prevalent in northern states and less prevalent in southern states. How much of that difference is attributable to the urban risk factor is not known.

Since a large proportion of the African American population lives in large cities, it is not surprising to find that African Americans as a whole have a higher rate of schizophrenia than whites. Five separate studies have confirmed this in highly urbanized states such as New York, Maryland, and Ohio. The higher rate of schizophrenia among African Americans holds up even when corrections are made for the age distribution of the population; thus, in a very careful study in Rochester, New York, African Americans still had a schizophrenia rate one and one-half times that of whites.

When African Americans who live in rural areas are compared with whites who live in rural areas, however, the results are different. Studies were done in Texas and in Louisiana, and no differences were found. This argues strongly against race being the cause of the difference. Rather, it suggests that it is because a higher proportion of African Americans lives in the inner city that they have a higher schizophrenia rate. Others have claimed that African Americans appear to have a higher rate of schizophrenia because most psychiatrists are white and unconsciously (or consciously) racist and would more readily label an

African American patient than a white patient as having schizophrenia. This may well be so but is impossible to measure. Even if it were so, however, it would explain only a small portion of the differences, and we are left with the fact that people in inner cities, whatever their race, have a disproportionately high schizophrenia rate.

Hispanic Americans, on the other hand, appear to have a lower schizophrenia prevalence rate than the general population. In the ECA study discussed above, the prevalence of schizophrenia among Hispanic residents of Los Angeles was less than half that of non-Hispanic residents, confirming the comparatively low prevalence of schizophrenia found in a previous study of Mexican-American residents of Texas.

There are other groups in America that also appear to have a low prevalence of schizophrenia. An extensive study of the rural, communal-living Hutterites published in 1955 reported a schizophrenia prevalence of only 1.1 per 1,000; a recent follow-up study found that the Hutterites have continued to have a very low rate of schizophrenia. Studies of the rural Amish have also reported few cases of schizophrenia but a higher rate of manic-depressive illness. There have also been impressions reported for over a hundred years that American Indians have a comparatively low prevalence of schizophrenia, but this has yet to be verified by a careful study.

Studies comparing the prevalence of schizophrenia elsewhere in the world have provoked lively controversy among researchers. On one side are those who believe that most reported differences are methodological artifacts or of minor consequence; on the other side are those (including myself) who believe that the differences are real and may provide important clues regarding the causes of the disease. It should be pointed out that all major diseases in which both genetic and nongenetic factors are thought to play a role show significant differences in geographic distribution. Heart disease varies approximately sixfold, rheumatoid arthritis tenfold, insulin-dependent diabetes thirtyfold, and multiple sclerosis fiftyfold; some cancers show even greater differences. Schizophrenia would be a unique disease if its prevalence were approximately the same everywhere in the world. The surprising finding, then, would be not that such differences exist, but rather that they do not exist.

By world standards, the United States' schizophrenia prevalence rate of 8 per 1,000 is comparatively high. At the lower end of the spectrum are studies from countries such as Ghana, Botswana, Papua New Guinea, and Taiwan, with prevalence rates of less than 2 per 1,000. Studies from Canada and from most European and Asian nations fall into the

3 to 6 per 1,000 prevalence range. In addition to the United States, countries that have reported schizophrenia prevalence rates higher than 7 per 1,000 are Ireland, Finland, and Sweden, with a study from northern Sweden reporting the highest rate (17 per 1,000).

Several studies of schizophrenia's prevalence have yielded especially interesting results. Careful studies in Croatia, for example, have shown that villages on the Istrian peninsula have a schizophrenia prevalence rate of 7.3 per 1,000 compared with villages 100 miles away that have a rate of only 2.9 per 1,000. In Micronesia, two surveys found a fourfold difference among various islands, from a low of 4.2 per 1,000 in the Marshall Islands to a high of 16.7 per 1,000 on Palau. In India, nine separate studies have reported that the prevalence of schizophrenia is significantly higher among higher castes than among lower castes.

Ireland is another nation in which schizophrenia has been extensively studied because of reports dating to the last century of a high prevalence both among people who emigrated to other countries and among those who remained in Ireland. As early as 1808, it was claimed that in Ireland "insanity is a disease of as frequent occurrence as in any other country in Europe." Studies in the 1960s and 1970s established that Ireland had more hospitalized patients with schizophrenia per capita than any country in the world, and a three-county community case register reported a schizophrenia prevalence rate of 7.1 per 1,000 in one of the western counties. In 1982 I spent six months in western Ireland studying a small region thought to have an especially high prevalence of schizophrenia; its rate of 12.6 per 1,000 was more than twice that of the surrounding area. This 1982 study also indicated that the high schizophrenia rate in Ireland existed only in older people and not among younger people; subsequent studies have since confirmed that the Irish schizophrenia prevalence rate is lower for individuals born after 1940, suggesting that a change in prevalence, for some unknown reason, took place at approximately that time.

In recent years much interest has been generated by studies of schizophrenia among Caribbean immigrants to England. Such immigrants have been found to have a high schizophrenia prevalence rate that exists not only in the immigrants themselves but also in their offspring born in England. Studies in Jamaica, the country of origin of the largest number of Caribbean immigrants, indicate that the schizophrenia rate there is not especially high. Recent studies in the Netherlands and in Sweden have also reported unusually high rates of schizophrenia among some, but not all, immigrant groups, and the high prevalence rate does not appear to be due to stress.

These are intriguing observations and, in my opinion, may offer important clues to the causes of schizophrenia. If we can understand why the Caribbean immigrants or the western Irish or the Croatian villagers have more than their share of schizophrenia, or why the Hutterites have less than their share, then we may better understand its causes. Sadly, however, this research area has been relatively neglected, especially in the United States.

IS SCHIZOPHRENIA INCREASING OR DECREASING?

As noted above, there is evidence in Ireland that the prevalence rate of schizophrenia decreased in recent decades. Since 1985 similar results have been published from studies in Scotland, England, Denmark, Australia, and New Zealand. The average decrease in schizophrenia in these studies is 35 percent over a 10- to 20-year period. Such studies have been criticized, however, because changing definitions and diagnostic standards make comparisons problematic. Therefore, at this time it can only be said that there is a *suggestion* of a decreasing prevalence of schizophrenia in these countries but that it remains to be confirmed by methodologically careful studies.

Studies in the United States suggest the possibility of a different story. Although no study comparable to the 1980–1984 five-site ECA study was done in the past, independent studies were done at two of the same sites. In Baltimore, a study in 1936 reported a one-year schizophrenia prevalence rate of 2.9 per 1,000. The ECA study, carried out in the same part of Baltimore in 1980–1984, found a six-month rate more than three times as high. Similarly, in New Haven the 1958 study by Hollingshead and Redlich found a six-month schizophrenia prevalence rate of 3.6 per 1,000, whereas the six-month rate for the ECA study was more than twice as high. Case-finding was more complete in the ECA study because a random sampling technique was used, and this would tend to elevate the ECA prevalence rates. However, a narrower definition of schizophrenia was used in the ECA study, which would tend to lower its prevalence rates compared to the two earlier studies. These differences should at least partially cancel each other out.

Despite the numerous methodological problems of the above studies, one is left with an impression that the prevalence of schizophrenia may have increased in the United States in recent decades. This impression is further strengthened by the very high incidence of *new* cases of schizophrenia reported from the ECA study sites. In summary, in the United States schizophrenia may have recently increased, and may still be increasing, in prevalence; this would stand in contrast to several other countries in which schizophrenia may possibly be decreasing in prevalence.

IS SCHIZOPHRENIA OF RECENT ORIGIN?

The history of schizophrenia is a curious one that has provoked a lively debate among scholars. On one side are those who claim that "schizophrenia has existed throughout history. . . . There is definite evidence in support of the view that schizophrenia is an ancient illness." Advocates of this view cite early Sanskrit, Babylonian, and biblical figures such as Nebuchadnezzar (who ate "grass as oxen" for seven years) and Ezekiel (who had visual and auditory hallucinations) to support their claims. They also argue that individuals with schizophrenia were kept at home or were considered to be divinely inspired and so were not defined as sick. The other side (which includes myself) acknowledges that there were indeed occasional people who had brain damage (e.g., from birth injuries or traumas) or brain diseases (e.g., epilepsy, syphilis, or viral encephalitis) that may have produced psychotic symptoms, but that schizophrenia with its hallmark auditory hallucinations and onset in early adulthood was virtually never described.

A stronger argument can be made for the existence of occasional cases of schizophrenia beginning in the late Middle Ages. A few small psychiatric hospitals were opened, such as the Hospital of St. Mary of Bethlehem (which gave birth to the term "bedlam") in London. King Henry VI, who lived from 1421 to 1471, appears to have had a schizophrenia-like disorder. William Shakespeare selected Henry VI as the subject for his first play in 1591. In *Hamlet* (1601), Shakespeare had Hamlet feign lunacy and Ophelia become insane when she discovered that her father had been killed by the man she loved. Nigel Bark makes a strong case that Poor Mad Tom in *King Lear* (1605) had schizophrenia but also concedes it is possible that he was merely feigning madness. One schizophrenia expert claims that the autobiography of George Trosse, an English minister who, as a young man in 1656, developed delusions, auditory hallucinations, and catatonic behavior, is a description of schizophrenia, but another asserts that alcoholic psychosis was the more likely cause for Trosse's symptoms.

Sporadic cases of what may have been schizophrenia continued to appear in the early 1700s but were remarkably few in number. They increased in the latter 1700s and then, suddenly, at the turn of the century, schizophrenia appeared in unmistakable form. Simultaneously (and apparently independently), John Haslam in England and Philippe Pinel in France in the early 1800s both described cases that were certainly schizophrenia. These cases were followed by a veritable outpouring of descriptions continuing throughout the nineteenth century and also by evidence that schizophrenia was increasing in frequency. It was a dramatic entrance for a disease. Haslam's publication in 1809 was an enlarged second edition of his 1798 book, *Observations on Insanity*. It is a remarkable book, with descriptions of delusions, hallucinations, disorders of thinking, and even autopsy accounts of abnormalities in the brains of some of the patients. His descriptions of patients leave no doubt that he was describing what we now call schizophrenia. In 1810 Haslam published an extended description of one patient with schizophrenia, entitling it "Illustrations of Madness: Exhibiting a Singular Case of Insanity," which suggested that such cases were very unusual at that time.

From the observations of John Haslam and Philippe Pinel until the end of the nineteenth century there were continuing arguments in Europe about whether insanity was increasing and, if so, why. As early as 1829, Sir Andrew Halliday warned that "the numbers of the afflicted have more than tripled during the last twenty years," and in 1835 J. C. Prichard added that "the apparent increase is everywhere so striking . . . cases of insanity are far more numerous than formerly." In 1856 in France, E. Renaudin published extensive data demonstrating an increase in insanity, especially among young adults and in urban areas, and the following year in England, John Hawkes wrote: "I doubt if ever the history of the world, or the experience of past ages, could show a larger amount of insanity than that of the present day." By 1873, Harrington Tuke warned that "a great wave of insanity is slowly advancing," and three years later Robert Jamieson added that "the most remarkable phenomenon of our time has been the alarming increase of insanity."

Those who believed that the increase in insanity was real offered a variety of possible explanations, ranging from genetics (e.g., increasing consanguineous marriages) and the increasing complexity of civilization to increased masturbation, use of alcohol, or train travel. Those who argued that the increase was not real claimed that it was a statistical artifact due to increased life expectancy of individuals with mental illnesses, part of a social movement to confine troublesome persons to institutions, or the product of increasing industrialization whereby families left home to work and so could no longer maintain their sick relative at home. Dr. Edward Hare in England analyzed these arguments in detail and concluded that the nineteenth-century increase in insanity was most probably real. More recently, I coauthored a book, *The Invisible Plague*, on this subject and also concluded that insanity really did increase.

In the United States an awareness of a possible increase in insanity appears to have taken place somewhat later than in Europe. The first American hospital exclusively for mentally ill individuals opened in Williamsburg, Virginia, in 1773 with 24 beds, but it was not full for over 30 years. Not a single hospital was opened in the 43-year period between 1773 and 1816, but 22 hospitals were added between 1816 and 1846.

The accompanying graph illustrates the per capita increase in patients in public mental hospitals in the United States from 1830 to 1950. The initial alarm about increasing insanity in America was sounded in 1852 by Pliny Earle, one of the founders of the American Psychiatric Association,

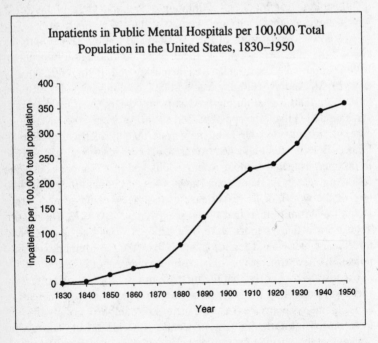

Inpatients in Public Mental Hospitals per 100,000 Total Population in the United States, 1830–1950

who warned that "insanity is an increasing disease." In 1854 Edward Jarvis undertook an extensive census of insane persons in Massachusetts and became convinced that their numbers were increasing; in 1871 Jarvis wrote that "the successive reports, upon whatever source or means of information procured, all tend to show an increasing number of the insane." In 1894 the superintendent of one Massachusetts state psychiatric hospital added that "the insane have increased twice as fast as the whole people. . . . We find this insane accumulation going on as fast as 50 years ago."

DEINSTITUTIONALIZATION:
A CRADLE FOR CATASTROPHE

During the first half of the twentieth century the number of patients in public psychiatric hospitals in the United States increased three-and-one-half-fold, from 144,653 in 1903 to 512,501 in 1950. The per capita increase based on population was almost twofold. The largest single diagnostic group was patients with schizophrenia. The problem of increasing numbers of persons with schizophrenia received remarkably little public attention, however, until World War II, when two events conspired to bring mental illness to center stage.

The first event was the extraordinarily high number of young men who were rejected for induction into military service because of mental illness. General Lewis B. Hershey, testifying before House and Senate hearings after the war, asserted that 856,000 men, representing 18 percent of all possible draftees, had been rejected because of mental illness. The second event was the assignment of approximately 3,000 conscientious objectors, who refused to take up arms, to alternate duty in state psychiatric hospitals. These "conchies," as they were popularly called, included many idealistic young Quakers, Mennonites, and Methodists who were appalled by the inhumane conditions they found in the hospitals. They went to the press, organized reports, and testified before Congress regarding these conditions. Kentucky, for example, was said to be spending only $146.11 per hospitalized psychiatric patient *per year*. And during a 12-year period at St. Elizabeth's Hospital in Washington, D.C., 20 patients were said to have been killed by hospital staff members but "no convictions were had in respect of any such cases."

On May 6, 1946, *Life* magazine published a 13-page exposé of conditions in state psychiatric hospitals entitled "Bedlam 1946: Most U.S. Mental Hospitals Are a Shame and a Disgrace." It was based on the reports of the conscientious objectors and included pictures of naked patients living in filthy conditions. That same month *Reader's Digest* included a condensation of a new novel by Mary Jane Ward entitled *The Snake Pit*, which detailed the terrifying experiences of a woman confined to a psychiatric hospital. In September 1946, Mike Gorman, a young reporter with the *Daily Oklahoman*, published a scathing series of articles about Oklahoma's state psychiatric hospitals (e.g., "the dining room made Dante's *Inferno* seem like a country club"), which was published as a book the following year. In 1948 Albert Deutsch published *The Shame of the States*, based on visits to psychiatric hospitals in 12 states. Deutsch claimed that "in some of the wards there were scenes that rivaled the horrors of the Nazi concentration camps—hundreds of naked mental patients herded into huge, barnlike, filth-infested wards" and included pictures to prove his point. The problem of the mentally ill in America had been etched into the nation's consciousness and conscience as nothing had previously done.

The stage was set for deinstitutionalization, and the introduction in the 1950s of chlorpromazine and reserpine, the first effective antipsychotic drugs, made it more feasible. The election of John F. Kennedy as president in 1960 provided the impetus and funds for emptying the hospitals. Kennedy's younger sister had been publicly identified as mentally retarded but, as will be discussed in chapter 4, had also developed schizophrenia and undergone a lobotomy. Kennedy therefore championed the mentally retarded and the mentally ill and proposed a series of federally funded Community Mental Health Centers (CMHCs) that, it was said, would function as alternatives to state psychiatric hospitals. In his introduction of the CMHC proposal, Kennedy specifically noted that "it has been demonstrated that two out of three schizophrenics—our largest category of mentally ill—can be treated and released within six months." It was to be the launching of a psychiatric *Titanic,* the largest failed social experiment of twentieth-century America.

The magnitude of deinstitutionalization is difficult to comprehend. In 1955, there were 559,000 seriously mentally ill individuals in state psychiatric hospitals. Today there are fewer than 60,000. Based on the nation's population increase between 1955 and 2000 from 166 million to 276 million, if there were the same number of patients per capita in the hospitals today as there were in 1955, their total number today would be 930,000. This means that there are approximately 870,000 individuals who would have been in state psychiatric hospitals in 1955 but who are in the community today. This also means that *almost 90 percent of the people who would have been in those hospitals 45 years ago are not in any hospital today.*

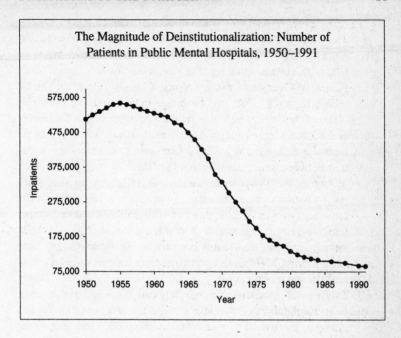

The Magnitude of Deinstitutionalization: Number of
Patients in Public Mental Hospitals, 1950–1991

The vast majority of these individuals can live successfully outside
the hospital if medication and aftercare services are provided. In that
sense deinstitutionalization was and is a humane and reasonable idea.
Why, then, has it been such a disaster? There are six major reasons:

1. *Misunderstanding about causes of serious mental illnesses.*
   When deinstitutionalization got under way in the early 1960s,
   Thomas Szasz's *Myth of Mental Illness* (1961) and Ken Kesey's
   One Flew Over the Cuckoo's Nest (1962) held sway. The belief
   became widespread that psychiatric hospitalization *caused* mental illness; that as soon as you released the patients they would
   live happily ever after. It was a romantic view but in retrospect
   incorrect and remarkably naive.

2. *Failure to shift resources from hospitals to community programs.*
   Despite the massive shift of patients from hospitals to the community, personnel and fiscal resources did not follow them. In
   New York, for example, the state hospital patient population was
   reduced from 93,000 to 24,000 over 25 years, yet during the
   same period not a single hospital was closed and the total num-

ber of state hospital employees *increased* from 23,800 to 37,000.
The main impediments to shifting resources were unions and
powerful members of state legislatures from rural districts in
which the state hospital was the largest employer.

3. *Failure of Community Mental Health Centers (CMHCs).* The $3
billion federal CMHC program was a failure from the start. The
National Institute of Mental Health provided vague guidelines
and virtually no oversight and bypassed state departments of
mental health, thereby ensuring that there would be no coopera-
tion between state hospitals and the CMHCs. Approximately 5
percent of the 789 federally funded CMHCs took responsibility
for the patients being discharged from the hospitals, whereas the
remainder evolved into being counseling and psychotherapy centers for family and personal problems. Some CMHCs built
swimming pools and tennis courts with the federal funds, and
one Florida CMHC even hired swimming instructors with a federal staffing grant.

4. *Lawyers as destructive forces.* Between 1965 and 1990, when
deinstitutionalization was taking place, the number of lawyers in
America increased from 296,000 to 800,000, more than four
times faster than the general population. Some of the lawyers
read Szasz's *Myth of Mental Illness* and dedicated their careers
to bringing lawsuits against states to get mental patients released
from state hospitals, making it more difficult to involuntarily
hospitalize or treat them, and passing state legislation to effectively hasten deinstitutionalization. Through organizations such
as the American Civil Liberties Union and the Bazelon Center
for Mental Health Law (previously known as the Mental Health
Law Project), these lawyers accomplished their goals. The numbers of mentally ill homeless persons, with freedom to be perpet-
ually psychotic, are a living testimony to their success.

5. *Mental health professionals as unavailable.* Federal subsidies
for the training of psychiatrists, psychologists, and psychiatric
social workers began in 1948 and 20 years later had reached
$119 million per year. State subsidies were even more generous.
The professionals, however, were trained to be mental *health*,
not mental *illness*, professionals. No service payback was
required in exchange for their publicly subsidized training, so the
vast majority of them went immediately to the private practice of
psychotherapy. A 1980 survey of private practitioners found that

only 6 percent of patients seen by psychiatrists and 3 percent of patients seen by psychologists had ever been hospitalized for mental illness. For most deinstitutionalized individuals with schizophrenia and other serious mental illnesses the professionals were unavailable.

6. *Federal incentives to empty the hospitals and the IMD exclusion.* Following passage of the federal CMHC legislation, seriously mentally ill individuals being discharged from the hospitals were made eligible for federal Medicaid, Medicare, Supplemental Security Income (SSI), Social Security Disability Insurance (SSDI), food stamps, special housing, and other programs. In effect, this meant that as long as such individuals were in state mental hospitals, they were the fiscal responsibility of the states; once discharged, however, the majority of the fiscal responsibility for their care was shifted to the federal government. The largest federal incentive to empty state hospitals, as noted above, was the Institutions for Mental Disease (IMD) exclusion, whereby federal Medicaid does not reimburse states for patients in state hospitals but does pay for the patients' care once they are transferred to "semihospitals" not run by the state.

Here is how the IMD exclusion works. In 2000, an individual with schizophrenia in Portland, Oregon, might have been hospitalized in the Oregon State Hospital. The cost was $314.70 per day, or $114,865 per year. The federal government would have reimbursed Oregon for *none* of the costs because of the IMD exclusion, so the state would have paid the entire cost. However, if the state denied that person with schizophrenia admission to the state hospital and insisted instead on admitting him to a "semihosptal" that cost $228.69 per day, the federal government would have reimbursed Oregon $93 per day, thereby saving the state $65,590 per year compared to the state hospital. And if the state instead admitted the person to a residential facility that cost $125.98 per day, the federal government would have reimbursed Oregon $76 per day, thereby saving the state $96,472 per year compared to the state hospital. States had, and continue to have, a huge fiscal incentive to shut down state hospitals and hospitalize individuals with schizophrenia anywhere else, regardless of the clinical needs of the patient. The fiscal incentives come entirely from denying intensive hospitalization and emptying the state hospitals; there is no fiscal incentive whatever to provide aftercare. It did not take the states long to learn how to game the system, and this has been a major contributor to the failure of deinstitutionalization.

Given these mistakes, it is no wonder that deinstitutionalization has been a massive failure. Homelessness, jails, violence, victimization, abysmal housing, revolving doors, few professionals, minimal treatment—these consequences were entirely predictable. I could ask the most thought-disordered individual with schizophrenia to set up a scheme for deinstitutionalization and the product would be better than what we have.

Who should be blamed? Blaming conservative politicians, especially former President Reagan, has become the politically correct but factually incorrect answer frequently given by mental health professionals. In fact, the debacle of deinstitutionalization has taken place under four Democratic (Kennedy, Johnson, Carter, and Clinton) and four Republican (Nixon, Ford, Reagan, and Bush) presidents. The *real* blame for the failure of deinstitutionalization rests squarely on the shoulders of the psychiatrists, psychologists, psychiatric social workers, lawyers, and federal and state officials who were, and continue to be, responsible for it.

WHAT IS THE COST OF SCHIZOPHRENIA?

To ask a question about the cost of schizophrenia is, in one sense, meaningless. Anyone who is familiar with schizophrenia knows that its magnitude and tragedy are light-years beyond calculation in dollars and cents. At the same time we live in a society with finite resources and, whether we like it or not, cost–benefit thinking is part of the allocation of those resources. The decision-making process is a political one in which—either explicitly or implicitly—questions are asked such as the following: How much does the disease cost? How much money can be saved by finding better treatments? What is the cost–benefit ratio of spending more research funds on this disease? Because such questions arise, it is important to ascertain the cost of schizophrenia.

The cost of schizophrenia, like any disease, can be calculated in a variety of ways. The economic cost for treating a single case of the disease can be assessed. Or the cost of treating all known cases can be added together. Lost wages because of the disease can be added, as well as the cost of social support (e.g., room and board, rehabilitation programs) needed to keep the person functioning over many years. The cost for treating schizophrenia can also be compared with the cost for treating other diseases, such as heart disease. Finally, but most difficult, the noneconomic cost of schizophrenia can be considered.

The cost for treating schizophrenia in cases in which the person recovers completely is not unreasonable compared with other serious diseases. The person usually requires hospitalization for a few weeks and then medication for several months. However, if the person is not among the fortunate one-quarter of patients who recover completely (see chapter 5), then the costs multiply rapidly.

Estimates have been made of the cost of direct care for treating a single case, for example, Sylvia Frumkin, the woman described in Susan Sheehan's *Is There No Place On Earth For Me?* Over 18 years, she had 27 different admissions to hospitals for schizophrenia. The total cost of her care in 1984 was estimated to be $636,000, which included only hospitalizations, halfway houses, and foster homes. It did not include outpatient medication costs, emergency room services, general health care, social services, law enforcement services needed to return her to the hospital, legal services, court costs, lost wages, or even the direct care costs incurred by Ms. Frumkin's family. I have made a similar approximation of direct care costs for my sister, who has had schizophrenia for over 40 years and has required hospitalization for much of that time; the direct care costs for her hospitalization alone in New York State mental hospitals during that time total over $1.5 million. Such costs, I would submit, are not unusual for persons with severe schizophrenia.

Another approach to calculating disease cost is to examine federal disease disability payments under the Supplemental Security Income (SSI) and Social Security Disability Insurance (SSDI) programs (see chapter 10 for a more detailed description of these). As noted in the accompanying table, in 1999 a total of 9.2 million Americans under age 65 received federal SSI or SSDI medical disability payments. When examined by diagnostic groups, it was found that 31.4 percent of SSI recipients and 26.6 percent of SSDI recipients were categorized as having "mental disorders other than mental retardation" and that this was the single largest category of disability for both SSI and SSDI. Thus, 2.7 million Americans were receiving federal disability payments because of mental disorders, and the total federal cost was $19.5 billion. The Social Security Administration does not provide a diagnostic breakdown within the "mental disorders" category, but other studies suggest that more than half would have been diagnosed with some form of schizophrenia. *Thus, it seems reasonable to assume that federal disability* *payments for individuals with schizophrenia totaled over $10 billion in 1999, and that schizophrenia was the single largest cause of disability for both SSI and SSDI.*

FEDERAL DISABILITY PAYMENTS TO INDIVIDUALS UNDER AGE 65 WITH "MENTAL DISORDERS OTHER THAN MENTAL RETARDATION," 1999

	Total Number of Disabled Recipients Under Age 65	Percent with "Mental Disorders Other Than Mental Retardation"	Total Number of Disabled Individuals with Mental Disorders	Total Federal Payments to These Individuals with Mental Disorders
SSI	4.5 million	31.4 %	1.4 million	$8.5 billion
SSDI	4.7 million	26.6%	1.3 million	$11.0 billion
Totals	9.2 million		2.7 million	$19.5 billion

Two other studies have been carried out to calculate the direct costs (e.g., hospitalization costs, medication) as well as the indirect costs (e.g., lost wages) for everyone in the United States who has schizophrenia. One study, done by Drs. Dorothy Rice and Leonard Miller at the University of California, calculated the total cost of schizophrenia for 1990 at $32.5 billion. The other study, done by Dr. Richard Wyatt and colleagues at the National Institute of Mental Health, calculated the cost for 1991 at $65 billion. The two studies were similar in their estimates of direct costs ($19.5 and $18.6 billion, respectively) but differed substantially in estimates of indirect costs such as family caregiving, lost wages, and the losses due to suicides. Remarkably little hard data are available on which to base estimates of indirect costs.

Assuming for the moment that the total annual cost of schizophrenia in 1990 was $32.5 billion, the lower of these two estimates, given inflation in general and the sharp increases in medical care and pharmaceutical costs during the 1990s, the cost of schizophrenia in 2000 would probably be approximately $40 billion. Of this amount, at least $10 billion would be for federal disability (SSI and SSDI) payments for the subset of individuals with "mental disorders other than mental retardation" who were diagnosed with schizophrenia.

What *is* $40 billion, other than a long string of zeroes that most of us cannot comprehend? In relationship to other expenditures in 2000 by the United States government, $40 billion was more than twice the entire budget of the National Institutes of Health ($15.5 billion) or the Veterans Administration hospitals and medical care system ($18.2 billion). It was also more than three times the annual cost of the space program ($12.6 billion), and more than four times the cost of all foreign aid programs ($8.7 billion). It was more than 10 times the cost of the federal prison service ($3.6 billion), and more than 70 times the budget of the Smithsonian Institution ($0.55 billion). In short, $40 billion is a lot of money.

A major reason why schizophrenia is such an expensive disease is that it usually begins in early adulthood and often lasts until death 50 or more years later. People who get the disease have been raised and educated through childhood and adolescence, with all the costs associated, only to become disabled at precisely the time they are supposed to become economically contributing members of society. Most of the 2.2 million persons with this disease continue to require services such as occasional hospitalization, foster homes, subsidized income, court costs, social services, outpatient psychiatric services, etc. People with schizophrenia are not beyond their economically most productive years when they become sick, as are patients with Alzheimer's disease. Nor do they die relatively quickly, as happens to many patients with cancer. If a fiendish economist from another planet were trying to devise a disease that would force our society to incur the maximum costs, then he (or she) could not do better than schizophrenia. Schizophrenia is economically a three-time loser: Society must raise and educate the person destined to become afflicted, most people with the disease are unable to contribute economically to society, and at the same time many of them require costly services from society for the rest of their lives.

The cost of schizophrenia has also been compared with other diseases. In Australia, the direct and indirect costs for schizophrenia were compared with heart attacks. Despite the fact that heart attacks affect 12 times more people than schizophrenia does in Australia, the overall direct and indirect costs per case of schizophrenia are six times greater than those for heart attacks. These costs did not include pension or social security costs that, since persons with schizophrenia live much longer than persons with heart attacks, would make the disparity even greater.

The huge economic cost of schizophrenia leads directly to the question of economic benefits of research on this disease. As will be discussed in chapter 15, schizophrenia is one of the most under-researched diseases in the western world. In the Australian study referred to above, for example, it was found that research on schizophrenia received only one-fourteenth the funds spent on research on heart attacks. In terms of the relative cost of these diseases to society, this is a foolish allocation of research funds on economic grounds alone. In the United States, a calculation was made in 1984 that if research discoveries could have reduced the cost of schizophrenia by only 10 percent by 1998, the savings that would have accrued over the following decade would have totaled $180 billion.

From a public policy viewpoint, therefore, it would be wise to spend more research money on the causes and treatment of schizophrenia. The burden of schizophrenia to taxpayers is substantial; this was noted as early as 1855 by the Massachusetts Commission on Lunacy, which said:

> In whatever way we look at them, these lunatics are a burden upon the Commonwealth. The curable during their limited period of disease, and the incurable during the remainder of their lives, not only cease to produce, but they must eat the bread they do not earn, and consume the substance they do not create, receiving their sustenance from the treasury of the Commonwealth.

The greatest cost of schizophrenia, however, is the noneconomic costs to those who have it and their families. These costs are incalculable. They include the effects of growing up normally until early adulthood, then being diagnosed with a brain disease that may last for the rest of your life. Hopes, plans, expectations, and dreams are abruptly put on hold. Cerebral palsy and Down's syndrome are tragedies for families of newborns; cancer and Alzheimer's disease are tragedies for families of the elderly. There is no known disease, however, with noneconomic costs so great as for schizophrenia. It is the costliest disease of all.

RECOMMENDED FURTHER READING

Hare, E. "Was Insanity on the Increase?" *British Journal of Psychiatry* 142 (1983): 439–55.

Isaac, R. J., and V. C. Armat. *Madness in the Streets*. New York: Free Press, 1990.

Rice, D. P. "The Economic Impact of Schizophrenia." *Journal of Clinical Psychiatry* 60 (suppl. 1) (1999): 4–6.

Torrey, E. F. *Schizophrenia and Civilization*. New York: Jason Aronson, 1980.

Torrey, E. F. *Nowhere to Go: The Tragic Odyssey of the Homeless Mentally Ill*. New York: Harper and Row, 1988.

Torrey, E. F. *Out of the Shadows: Confronting America's Mental Illness Crisis*. New York: John Wiley, 1997.

Torrey, E. F., and J. Miller. *The Invisible Plague: The Rise of Mental Illness from 1750 to the Present*. New Brunswick, N.J.: Rutgers University Press, 2001.

2

THE INNER WORLD OF MADNESS: VIEW FROM THE INSIDE

What then does schizophrenia mean to me? It means fatigue and confusion, it means trying to separate every experience into the real and the unreal and not sometimes being aware of where the edges overlap. It means trying to think straight when there is a maze of experiences getting in the way, and when thoughts are continually being sucked out of your head so that you become embarrassed to speak at meetings. It means feeling sometimes that you are inside your head and visualising yourself walking over your brain, or watching another girl wearing your clothes and carrying out actions as you think them. It means knowing that you are continually "watched," that you can never succeed in life because the laws are all against you and knowing that your ultimate destruction is never far away.

> Patient with schizophrenia, quoted in Henry R. Rollin,
> *Coping with Schizophrenia*

When tragedy strikes, one of the things that make life bearable for people is the sympathy of friends and relatives. This can be seen, for example, in a natural disaster like a flood and with a chronic disease like cancer. Those closest to the person afflicted offer help, extend their sympathy, and generally provide important solace and support in the person's time of need. "Sympathy," said Emerson, "is a supporting atmosphere, and in it we unfold easily and well." A prerequisite for sympathy is an ability to put oneself in the place of the person afflicted. One must be able to imagine oneself in a flood or getting cancer. Without this ability to put oneself in the place of the person afflicted, there can be abstract pity but not true sympathy.

Sympathy for those afflicted with schizophrenia is sparse because it is difficult to put oneself in the place of the sufferer. The whole disease process is mysterious, foreign, and frightening to most people. As noted by Roy Porter in *A Social History of Madness*, "*strangeness* has typically been the key feature in the fractured dialogues that go on, or the silences that intrude, between the 'mad' and the 'sane.' Madness is a foreign country."

Schizophrenia, then, is not like a flood, where one can imagine all one's possessions being washed away. Nor like a cancer, where one can imagine a slowly growing tumor, relentlessly spreading from organ to organ and squeezing life from your body. No, schizophrenia is madness. Those who are afflicted act bizarrely, say strange things, withdraw from us, and may even try to hurt us. They are no longer the same person— they are *mad!* We don't understand why they say what they say and do what they do. We don't understand the disease process. Rather than a steadily growing tumor, which we can understand, it is as if the person has lost control of his/her brain. How can we sympathize with a person who is possessed by unknown and unseen forces? How can we sympathize with a madman or a madwoman?

The paucity of sympathy for those with schizophrenia makes it that much more of a disaster. Being afflicted with the disease is bad enough by itself. Those of us who have not had this disease should ask ourselves, for example, how we would feel if our brain began playing tricks on us, if unseen voices shouted at us, if we lost the capacity to feel emotions, and if we lost the ability to reason logically. As one individual with schizophrenia noted: "The worst thing imaginable is to be terrified of one's own mind, the very matter that controls all that we are and all that we do and feel." This would certainly be burden enough for any human being to have to bear. But what if, in addition to this, those closest to us began to avoid us or ignore us, to pretend that they didn't hear our comments, to pretend that they didn't notice what we did? How would we feel if those we most cared about were embarrassed by our behavior each day?

Because there is little understanding of schizophrenia, so there is little sympathy. For this reason it is the obligation of everyone with a relative or close friend with schizophrenia to learn as much as possible about what the disease is and what the afflicted person is experiencing. This is not merely an intellectual exercise or a way to satisfy one's curiosity but rather the means to make it possible to sympathize with the person. For friends and relatives who want to be helpful, probably the most important thing to do is to learn about the inner workings of the brain of a person with schizophrenia. One mother wrote me after listening to her afflicted son's descriptions of his hallucinations: "I saw into the visual hallucinations that plagued him and frankly, at times, it raised the hair on my neck. It also helped me to get outside of *my* tragedy and to realize how horrible it is for the person who is afflicted. I thank God for that painful wisdom. I am able to cope easier with all of this."

With sympathy, schizophrenia is a personal tragedy. Without sympathy, it becomes a family calamity, for there is nothing to knit people together, no balm for the wounds. Understanding schizophrenia also helps demystify the disease and brings it from the realm of the occult to the daylight of reason. As we come to understand it, the face of madness slowly changes before us from one of terror to one of sadness. For the sufferer, this is a significant change.

The best way to learn what a person with schizophrenia experiences is to listen to someone with the disease. For this reason I have relied heavily upon patients' own accounts in describing the signs and symptoms. There are some excellent descriptions scattered throughout English literature; the best of these are listed at the end of this chapter. By contrast, one of the most widely read books, Hannah Green's *I Never Promised You a Rose Garden*, is not at all helpful, as is explained in appendix A. It describes a patient who, according to one analysis, should not have even been diagnosed with schizophrenia but rather with hysteria (now often referred to as somatization disorder).

When one listens to persons with schizophrenia describe what they are experiencing and observes their behavior, certain abnormalities can be noted:

1. Alterations of the senses
2. Inability to sort and interpret incoming sensations, and an inability therefore to respond appropriately
3. Delusions and hallucinations
4. Altered sense of self
5. Changes in emotions
6. Changes in movements
7. Changes in behavior
8. Decreased awareness of illness

No one symptom or sign is found in all individuals; rather, the final diagnosis rests upon the total symptom picture. Some people have much more of one kind of symptom, other people another. Conversely, there is no single symptom or sign of schizophrenia that is found exclusively in that disease. All symptoms and signs can be found at least occasionally in other diseases of the brain, such as brain tumors and temporal lobe epilepsy.

ALTERATIONS OF THE SENSES

In Edgar Allan Poe's "The Tell-Tale Heart" (1843), the main character, clearly lapsing into a schizophrenia-like state, exclaims to the reader, "Have I not told you that what you mistake for madness is but over-acuteness of the senses?" An expert on the dark recesses of the human mind, Poe put his finger directly on a central theme of madness. Alterations of the senses are especially prominent in the early stages of breakdown in individuals with schizophrenia and can be found, according to one study, in almost two-thirds of all patients. As the authors of the study conclude: "Perceptual dysfunction is the most invariant feature of the early stage of schizophrenia." It can be elicited from patients most commonly when they have recovered from a psychotic episode; rarely can patients who are acutely or chronically psychotic describe these changes.

Alterations of the senses as a hallmark of schizophrenia were also noted by Poe's professional contemporaries. In 1862 the director of the Illinois State Hospital for the Insane wrote that insanity "either entirely reverses or essentially changes the mind in its manner of receiving impressions. The light, so pleasurable to the healthy eye, becomes an unendurable irritant when thrown upon an inflamed surface. Those emotions that give pleasure to the healthy mind, are even more injurious when the mind is diseased, than is a flash of sunlight upon an inflamed retina." The alterations may be either enhancement (more common) or blunting; all sensory modalities may be affected. For example, Poe's protagonist was experiencing predominantly an increased acuteness of hearing:

> True!—nervous—very, very dreadfully nervous I had been and am!
> but why will you say that I am mad? The disease had sharpened my
> senses—not destroyed—not dulled them. Above all was the sense of

hearing acute. I heard all things in the heaven and in the earth. I heard many things in hell. How, then, am I mad? Harken! and observe how healthily—how calmly—I can tell you the whole story.

Another described it this way:

During the last while back I have noticed that noises all seem to be louder to me than they were before. It's as if someone had turned up the volume. . . . I notice it most with background noises—you know what I mean, noises that are always around but you don't notice them. Now they seem to be just as loud and sometimes louder than the main noises that are going on. . . . It's a bit alarming at times because it makes it difficult to keep your mind on something when there's so much going on that you can't help listening to.

Visual perceptual changes are even more common than auditory changes. One patient described it as follows:

Colours seem to be brighter now, almost as if they are luminous paint- ing. I'm not sure if things are solid until I touch them. I seem to be noticing colours more than before, although I am not artistically minded. The colours of things seem much clearer and yet at the same time there is something missing. The things I look at seem to be flatter as if you were looking just at a surface. Maybe it's because I notice so much more about things and find myself looking at them for a longer time. Not only the colour of things fascinates me but all sorts of little things, like markings in the surface, pick up my attention too.

And another noted both the sharpness of colors as well as the transfor- mation of objects:

Everything looked vibrant, especially red; people took on a devilish look, with black outlines and white shining eyes; all sorts of objects— chairs, buildings, obstacles—took on a life of their own; they seemed to make threatening gestures, to have an animistic outlook.

In some instances the visual alterations improved the appearance:

Lots of things seemed psychedelic; they shone. I was working in a restaurant and it looked more first class than it really was.

In other cases the alterations made the object ugly or frightening:

> People looked deformed, as if they had had plastic surgery, or were
> wearing makeup with different bone structure.

> People were pulling hideous faces.

> People were deformed, squarish, like in plaster.

Colors and textures may blend into each other:

> I saw everything very bright and rich and pure like the thinnest line
> possible. Or a shiny smoothness like water but solid. After a while
> things got rough and shadowed again.

Sometimes both hearing *and* visual sensations are increased, as happened to this young woman.

> These crises, far from abating, seemed rather to increase. One day,
> while I was in the principal's office, suddenly the room became
> enormous, illuminated by a dreadful electric light that cast false
> shadows. Everything was exact, smooth, artificial, extremely tense;
> the chairs and tables seemed models placed here and there. Pupils
> and teachers were puppets revolving without cause, without objec-
> tive. I recognized nothing, nobody. It was as though reality, attenu-
> ated, had slipped away from all these things and these people.
> Profound dread overwhelmed me, and as though lost, I looked
> around desperately for help. I heard people talking, but I did not
> grasp the meaning of the words. The voices were metallic, without
> warmth or color. From time to time, a word detached itself from the
> rest. It repeated itself over and over in my head, absurd, as though
> cut off by a knife.

Closely related to the overacuteness of the senses is the flooding of
the senses with stimuli. It is not only that the senses become more
sharply attuned but that they see and hear everything. Normally our
brain screens out most incoming sights and sounds, allowing us to concentrate on whatever we choose. This screening mechanism appears to
become impaired in many persons with schizophrenia, releasing a veritable flood of sensory stimuli into the brain simultaneously.

This is one person's description of flooding of the senses with auditory stimuli:

> Everything seems to grip my attention although I am not particularly interested in anything. I am speaking to you just now, but I can hear noises going on next door and in the corridor. I find it difficult to shut these out, and it makes it more difficult for me to concentrate on what I am saying to you. Often the silliest little things that are going on seem to interest me. That's not even true: they don't interest me, but I find myself attending to them and wasting a lot of time this way.

And with visual stimuli:

> Occasionally during subsequent periods of disturbance there was some distortion of vision and some degree of hallucination. On several occasions my eyes became markedly oversensitive to light. Ordinary colors appeared to be much too bright, and sunlight seemed dazzling in intensity. When this happened, ordinary reading was impossible, and print seemed excessively black.

Frequently these two things happen together.

> I can probably tell you as much or more about what really went on those days than lots of people who were sane: the comings and goings of people, the weather, what was on the news, what we ate, what records were played, what was said. My focus was a bit bizarre. I could do portraits of people who were walking down the street. I remembered license numbers of cars we were following into Vancouver. We paid $3.57 for gas. The air machine made eighteen dings while we were there.

> An outsider may see only someone "out of touch with reality." In fact we are experiencing so many realities that it is often confusing and sometimes totally overwhelming.

As these examples make clear, it is difficult to concentrate or pay attention when so much sensory data is rushing through the brain. In one study, more than half of people who had had schizophrenia recalled impairments in attention and in keeping track of time. One patient expressed it as follows:

Sometimes when people speak to me my head is overloaded. It's too much to hold at once. It goes out as quick as it goes in. It makes you forget what you just heard because you can't get hearing it long enough. It's just words in the air unless you can figure it out from their faces.

Sensory modalities other than hearing and vision may also be affected in schizophrenia. Mary Barnes in her autobiographical account of "a journey through madness" recalled how "it was terrible to be touched. . . . Once a nurse tried to cut my nails. The touch was such that I tried to bite her." A medical student with schizophrenia remembered that "touching any patient made me feel that I was being electrocuted." Another patient described the horror of feeling a rat in his throat and tasting the "decay in my mouth as its body disintegrated inside me." Increased sensitivity of the genitalia is occasionally found, explained by one patient as "a genital sexual irritation from which there was no peace and no relief." I once took care of a young man with such a sensation who became convinced that his penis was turning black. He countered this delusional fear by insisting that doctors—or anyone within sight— examine him every five minutes to reassure him. His hospitalization was precipitated by his having gone into the local post office where a girl-friend worked and asking her to examine him in front of the customers.

Another aspect of the overacuteness of the senses is a flooding of the mind with thoughts. It is as if the brain is being bombarded both with external stimuli (e.g., sounds and sights) and with internal stimuli as well (thoughts, memories). One psychiatrist who has studied this area extensively claims that we have not been as aware of the internal stimuli in persons with schizophrenia as we should be.

My trouble is that I've got too many thoughts. You might think about something, let's say that ashtray, and just think, oh! yes, that's for put-ting my cigarette in, but I would think of it and then I would think of a dozen different things connected with it at the same time.

My concentration is very poor. I jump from one thing to another. If I am talking to someone they only need to cross their legs or scratch their heads and I am distracted and forget what I was saying. I think I could concentrate better with my eyes shut.

And this person describes the flooding of memories from the past:

Childhood feelings began to come back as symbols, and bits from past conversations went through my head. . . . I began to think I was hypnotized so that I would remember what had happened in the first four and a half years of my life. . . . I thought that my parents had supplied information about the nursery school teacher and pediatrician to someone—perhaps my husband—with the hope that I would be able to straighten myself out by remembering the early years.

Perhaps it is this increased ability of some patients to recall childhood events that in the past mistakenly led psychoanalysts to assume that the recalled events were somehow causally related to the schizophrenia. There is no scientific evidence to support such theories, however, and much evidence to support contrary theories.

A variation of flooding with thoughts occurs when the person feels that someone is inserting the flood of thoughts into his/her head. This is commonly referred to as thought insertion and when present is considered by many psychiatrists to be an almost certain symptom of schizophrenia.

All sorts of "thoughts" seem to come to me, as if someone is "speaking" them inside my head. When in any company it appears to be worse (probably some form of self-consciousness), I don't want the "thoughts" to come but I keep on "hearing" them (as it were) and it requires lots of will power sometimes to stop myself from "thinking" (in the form of "words") the most absurd and embarrassing things. These "thoughts" do not mean anything to me and cause "lack of concentration" in whatever I am doing at work, etc.

In college, I "knew" that everyone was thinking and talking about me and that a local pharmacist was tormenting me by inserting his thoughts into my head and inducing me to buy things I had no use for.

With this kind of activity going on in a person's head, it is not surprising that it would be difficult to concentrate.

I was invited to play checkers and started to do so, but I could not go on. I was too much absorbed in my own thoughts, particularly those regarding the approaching end of the world and those responsible for the use of force and for the charge of homicidal intent. By nightfall my head was all in a whirl. It seemed to be the Day of Judgment and all humanity came streaming in from four different directions.

Concentrating on even as simple a task as walking from one building to another may become impossible.

Fear made me ill; just the same I ran out to visit a friend who was staying at a nearby sanatorium. To get there, a way led through the woods, short and well marked. Becoming lost in the thick fog, I circled round and round the sanatorium without seeing it, my fear augmenting all the while. By and by I realized that the wind inspired this fear; the trees, too, large and black in the mist, but particularly the wind. At length I grasped the meaning of its message: the frozen wind from the North Pole wanted to crush the earth, to destroy it. Or perhaps it was an omen, a sign that the earth was about to be laid waste. This idea tormented me with growing intensity.

Esso Leete, who has written many useful articles from a consumer's point of view, describes a similar experience in the early stages of her illness:

It was evening and I was walking along the beach near my college in Florida. Suddenly my perceptions shifted. The intensifying wind became an omen of something terrible. I could feel it becoming stronger and stronger; I was sure it was going to capture me and sweep me away with it. Nearby trees bent threateningly toward me and tumbleweeds chased me. I became very frightened and began to run. However, though I knew I was running, I was making no progress. I seemed suspended in space and time.

When all aspects of overacuteness of the senses are taken together, the consequent cacophony in the brain must be frightening, and it is so described by most patients. In the very earliest stage of the disease, however, before this overacuteness becomes too severe, it may be a pleasant experience. Many descriptions of the initial days of developing schizophrenia are descriptions of heightened awareness, commonly called "peak experiences"; such experiences are also common in manic-depressive illness and in getting high on drugs. Here is one patient's description:

Suddenly my whole being was filled with light and loveliness and with an upsurge of deeply moving feeling from within myself to meet and reciprocate the influence that flowed into me. I was in a state of the most vivid awareness and illumination. What can I say of it? A cloud-less, cerulean blue sky of the mind, shot through with shafts of exqui-site, warm, dazzling sunlight.

Many patients interpret such experiences within a religious frame-work and believe they are being touched by God.

Before last week, I was quite closed about my emotions; then finally I owned up to them with another person. I began to speak without think-ing beforehand and what came out showed an awareness of human beings and God. I could feel deeply about other people. We felt con-nected. The side which had been suppressing emotions did not seem to be the real one. I was in a higher and higher state of exhilaration and awareness. Things people said had hidden meaning. They said things that applied to life. Everything that was real seemed to make sense. I had a great awareness of life, truth, and God. I went to church and suddenly all parts of the service made sense. My senses were sharp-ened. I became fascinated by the little insignificant things around me. There was an additional awareness of the world that would do artists, architects, and painters good. I ended up being too emotional, but I felt very much at home with myself, very much at ease. It gave me a great feeling of power. It was not a case of seeing more broadly but deeper. I was losing touch with the outside world and lost my sense of time. There was a fog around me in some sense, and I felt asleep. I could see more deeply into problems that other people had and would go directly into a deeper subject with a person. I had the feeling I loved everybody in the world.

In view of such experiences it is hardly surprising to find excessive religious preoccupation listed as a common early sign of schizophrenia.

Sensations can be blunted, as well as enhanced, in schizophrenia. Such blunting is more commonly found late in the course of the disease, whereas enhancement is often one of the earliest symptoms. The blunt-ing is described "as if a heavy curtain were drawn over his mind; it resembled a thick deadening cloud that prevented the free use of his senses." One's own voice may sound muted or faraway, and vision may be wavy or blurred: "However hard I looked it was as if I was looking through a daydream and the mass of detail, such as the pattern on a car-pet, became lost."

One sensation which may be blunted in schizophrenia is that of pain. Although it does not happen frequently, when such blunting does occur it may be dramatic and have practical consequences for those who are caring for the person. It is now in vogue to attribute such blunting to medication, but in fact it was clearly described by Dr. John Haslam as early as 1798 in his book *Observations on Insanity*. In older textbooks, for example, there are many accounts of surgeons being able to do appendectomies and similar procedures on some patients with schizophrenia with little or no anesthesia. One of my patients did not realize she had a massive breast abscess until the fluid from it seeped through her dress; although this is normally an exceedingly painful condition, she insisted she had felt no pain whatsoever. Nurses who have cared for patients with schizophrenia over many years can recite stories of fractured bones, perforated ulcers, or ruptured appendixes the patients said nothing about. Practically, it is important to be aware of this possibility so that medical help can be sought for persons if they look sick, even if they are not complaining of pain. It is also the reason that some people with schizophrenia burn their fingers when they smoke cigarettes too close to the end.

It may well be that there is a common denominator for all aspects of the alterations of the senses discussed thus far. All sensory input into the brain passes through the limbic area in the lower portion of the brain. It is this area that is most suspect as being involved in schizophrenia, as will be discussed in chapter 6. The limbic system and thalamus filter this sensory input, and it is likely that disease of this part of the brain accounts for many or most symptoms. Norma MacDonald, a woman who published an account of her illness in 1960, foresaw this possibility in a particularly clear manner several years before psychiatrists and neurologists understood it, and she wrote about her conception of the breakdown in the filter system.

> At first it was as if parts of my brain "awoke" which had been dormant, and I became interested in a wide assortment of people, events, places, and ideas which normally would make no impression on me. Not knowing that I was ill, I made no attempt to understand what was happening, but felt that there was some overwhelming significance in all this, produced either by God or Satan, and I felt that I was duty-bound to ponder on each of these new interests, and the more I pondered the worse it became. The walk of a stranger on the street could be a sign to me which I must interpret. Every face in the windows of a passing streetcar would be engraved on my mind, all of them concen-

trating on me and trying to pass me some sort of message. Now, many years later, I can appreciate what had happened. Each of us is capable of coping with a large number of stimuli, invading our being through any one of the senses. We could hear every sound within earshot and see every object, hue, and colour within the field of vision, and so on. It's obvious that we would be incapable of carrying on any of our daily activities if even one-hundredth of all these available stimuli invaded us at once. So the mind must have a filter which functions without our conscious thought, sorting stimuli and allowing only those which are relevant to the situation in hand to disturb consciousness. And this filter must be working at maximum efficiency at all times, particularly when we require a degree of concentration. What had happened to me in Toronto was a breakdown in the filter, and a hodge-podge of unrelated stimuli were distracting me from things which should have had my undivided attention.

INABILITY TO INTERPRET AND RESPOND

In normal people the brain functions in such a way that incoming stimuli are sorted and interpreted; then a correct response is selected and sent out. Most of the responses are learned, such as saying "thank you" when a gift is given to us. These responses also include logic, such as being able to predict what will happen to us if we do not arrive for work at the time we are supposed to. Our brains sort and interpret incoming stimuli and send out responses hundreds of thousands of times each day. The site of this function is also thought to be the limbic system, and it is intimately connected with the screening function referred to above.

A fundamental defect in schizophrenia is a frequent inability to sort, interpret, and respond. Textbooks of psychiatry describe this as a thought disorder, but it is more than just thoughts that are involved. Visual and auditory stimuli, emotions, and some actions are misarranged in exactly the same way as thoughts; the brain defect is probably similar for all.

We do not understand the human brain well enough to know precisely how the system works; but imagine a telephone operator sitting at an old plug-in type of switchboard in the middle of your limbic system. He or she receives all the sensory input, thoughts, ideas, memories, and emotions coming in, sorts them, and determines those that go together. For example, normally our brain takes the words of a sentence and converts them automatically into a pattern of thought. We don't have to concentrate on the individual words but rather can focus on the meaning of the whole message.

Now what would happen if the switchboard operator decided not to do the job of sorting and interpreting? In terms of understanding auditory stimuli, two patients describe this kind of defect:

> When people are talking I have to think what the words mean. You see, there is an interval instead of a spontaneous response. I have to think about it and it takes time. I have to pay all my attention to people when they are speaking or I get all mixed up and don't understand them.

> I can concentrate quite well on what people are saying if they talk simply. It's when they go on into long sentences that I lose the meanings. It just becomes a lot of words that I would need to string together to make sense.

One pair of researchers described this defect as a receptive aphasia similar to that found in some patients who have had a stroke. The words are there but the person cannot synthesize them into sentences, as explained by this person with schizophrenia:

> I used to get the sudden thing that I couldn't understand what people said, like it was a foreign language.

Difficulties in comprehending visual stimuli are similar to those described for auditory stimuli.

> I have to put things together in my head. If I look at my watch I see the watchstrap, watch, face, hands and so on, then I have got to put them together to get it into one piece.

> Everything is in bits. You put the picture up bit by bit into your head. It's like a photograph that's torn in bits and put together again. If you move it's frightening. The picture you had in your head is still there but broken up. If I move there's a new picture that I have to put together again.

One patient had similar problems when she looked at her psychiatrist, seeing "the teeth, then the nose, then the cheeks, then one eye and the other. Perhaps it was this independence of each part that inspired such fear and prevented my recognizing her even though I knew who she was."

It is probably because of such impairments in visual interpretation that some persons with schizophrenia misidentify someone and say he or she looks like someone else. My sister with schizophrenia does this frequently, claiming to have seen many friends from childhood who I know in fact could not have been present. Another patient with schizophrenia added a grandiose flair to the visual misperception:

> This morning, when I was at Hillside [Hospital] I was making a movie. I was surrounded by movie stars. The X-ray technician was Peter Lawford. The security guard was Don Knotts . . .

In addition to difficulties in interpreting individual auditory and visual stimuli in coherent patterns, many persons with schizophrenia have difficulty putting the two kinds of stimuli together.

> I can't concentrate on television because I can't watch the screen and listen to what is being said at the same time. I can't seem to take in two things like this at the same time especially when one of them means watching and the other means listening. On the other hand I seem to be always taking in too much at the one time and then I can't handle it and can't make sense of it.

> I tried sitting in my apartment and reading; the words looked perfectly familiar, like old friends whose faces I remembered perfectly well but whose names I couldn't recall; I read one paragraph ten times, could make no sense of it whatever, and shut the book. I tried listening to the radio, but the sounds went through my head like a buzz saw. I walked carefully through traffic to a movie theater and sat through a movie which seemed to consist of a lot of people wandering around slowly and talking a great deal about something or other. I decided, finally, to spend my days sitting in the park watching the birds on the lake.

These persons' difficulties in watching television or movies are very typical. In fact, it is striking how few patients with schizophrenia on hospital wards watch television, contrary to what is popularly believed. Some may sit in front of it and watch the visual motion, as if it were a test pattern, but few of them can tell you what is going on. This includes patients of all levels of intelligence and education, among them college-educated persons who, given little else to do, might be expected to take advantage of the TV for much of the day. On the contrary, you are more likely to find them sitting quietly in another corner of the room, ignoring the TV; if you ask them why, they may tell you that they cannot follow what is going on, or they may try to cover up their defect by saying they are tired. One of my patients was an avid New York Yankees baseball fan prior to his illness, but he refused to watch the game even when the Yankees were on and he was in the room at the time, because he could not understand what was happening. As a practical aside, the favorite TV programs and movies of many persons with schizophrenia are cartoons and travelogues; both are simple and can be followed visually without the necessity of integrating auditory input at the same time.

But the job of the switchboard operator in our brain does not end with sorting and interpreting the incoming stimuli. The job also includes hooking up the stimuli with proper responses to be sent back outside. For example, if somebody asks me, "Would you like to have lunch with me today?" my brain focuses immediately on the overall content of the question and starts calculating: Do I have time? Do I want to? What excuses do I have? What will other people think who see me with this person? What will be the effect on this person if I say no? Out of these calculations emerges a response that, in a normal brain, is appropriate to the situation. Similarly, news of a friend's death gets hooked up with grief, visual and auditory stimuli from a funny movie are hooked up with mirth, and a new idea regarding the creation of the universe is hooked up with logic and with previous knowledge in this area. It is an orderly, ongoing process, and the switchboard operator goes on, day after day, making relatively few mistakes.

The inability of patients with schizophrenia to not only sort and interpret stimuli but also select out appropriate responses is one of the hallmarks of the disease. It led Swiss psychiatrist Eugen Bleuler in 1911 to introduce the term "schizophrenia," meaning in German a splitting of the various parts of the thought process. Bleuler was impressed by the inappropriate responses frequently given by persons with this disease; for example, when told that a close friend has died, a person with schizophrenia may giggle. It is as if the switchboard operator not only gets bored and stops sorting and interpreting but becomes actively malicious and begins hooking the incoming stimuli up to random, usually inappropriate, responses.

The inability to interpret and respond appropriately is also at the core of patients' difficulties in relating to other people. Not being able to

put the auditory and visual stimuli together makes it difficult to understand others; if in addition you cannot respond appropriately, then interpersonal relations become impossible. One patient described such
difficulties:

> During the visit I tried to establish contact with her, to feel that she was
> actually there, alive and sensitive. But it was futile. Though I certainly
> recognized her, she became part of the unreal world. I knew her name
> and everything about her, yet she appeared strange, unreal, like a
> statue. I saw her eyes, her nose, her lips moving, heard her voice and
> understood what she said perfectly, yet I was in the presence of a
> stranger. To restore contact between us I made desperate efforts to
> break through the invisible dividing wall but the harder I tried, the less
> successful I was, and the uneasiness grew apace.

It is for this reason that many persons with schizophrenia prefer to
spend time by themselves, withdrawn, communicating with others as little as possible. The process is too difficult and too painful to undertake
except when absolutely necessary.

Just as auditory and visual stimuli may not be sorted or interpreted
by the person's brain and may elicit inappropriate responses, so too may
actions be fragmented and lead to inappropriate responses. This will be
discussed in greater detail in a subsequent section, but it is worth noting
that the same kind of brain deficit is probably involved. For example,
compare the difficulties this patient has in the simple action of getting a
drink of water with the difficulties in responding to auditory and visual
stimuli described above:

> If I do something like going for a drink of water, I've got to go over
> each detail—find cup, walk over, turn tap, fill cup, turn tap off, drink it.
> I keep building up a picture. I have to change the picture each time.
> I've got to make the old picture move. I can't concentrate. I can't hold
> things. Something else comes in, various things. It's easier if I stay
> still.

It suggests that there may be relatively few underlying brain deficits
leading to the broad range of symptoms the disease of schizophrenia
comprises.

When schizophrenia thought patterns are looked at from outside, as
when they are being described by a psychiatrist, such terms as "discon-

nectedness," "loosening of associations," "concreteness," "impairment of logic," "thought blocking" and "ambivalence" are used. To begin with disconnectedness: one of my patients used to come into the office each morning and ask my secretary to write a sentence on paper for him. One request was "Write all kinds of black snakes looking like raw onion, high strung, deep down, long winded, all kinds of sizes." This patient had put together several apparently disconnected ideas that a normally functioning brain would not have joined. Another patient wrote:

> My thoughts get all jumbled up, I start thinking or talking about some-
> thing but I never get there. Instead I wander off in the wrong direction
> and get caught up with all sorts of different things that may be con-
> nected with the things I want to say but in a way I can't explain. Peo-
> ple listening to me get more lost than I do.

Sometimes there may be a vague connection between the jumbled thoughts in schizophrenia thinking; such instances are referred to as loose associations. For example, in the sentence about black snakes above, it may be that the patient juxtaposed onions to black snakes because of the onionlike pattern on the skin of some snakes. On another occasion I was drawing blood from a patient's arm and she said, "Look at my blue veins. I asked the Russian women to make them red," loosely connecting the color of blood with the "Reds" of the former Soviet Union. And the great Russian dancer Vaslav Nijinsky wrote the follow-ing as he was developing schizophrenia, jumping from the round shape of a stage to his eye:

> I am not artificial. I am life. The theatre is not life. I know the customs
> of the theatre. The theatre becomes a habit. Life does not. I do not like
> the theatre with a square stage. I like a round stage. I will build a the-
> atre which will have a round shape, like an eye. I like to look closely in
> the mirror and I see only one eye in my forehead.

Occasionally the loose association will rest not upon some tenuous logical connection between the words but merely upon their similar sound. For example, one young man presented me with a written poem:

> *I believe we will soon*
> *achieve world peace. But*
> *I'm still on the lamb.*

He had confused the lamb associated with peace with the expression "on the lam," the correct spelling of which he apparently did not know. There is no logical association between "lamb" and "lam" except for their similar sound; such associations are referred to as clang associations.

Another characteristic of schizophrenia thinking is concreteness. This can be tested by asking the person to give the meaning of proverbs, which require an ability to abstract, to move from the specific to the general. When most people are asked what "People who live in glass houses shouldn't throw stones" means, they will answer something like: "If you're not perfect yourself, don't criticize others." They move from the specific glass house and stones to the general concept without difficulty.

But the person with schizophrenia frequently loses this ability to abstract. I asked a hundred patients with schizophrenia to explain the proverb above; less than one-third were able to think abstractly about it. The majority answered simply something like "It might break the windows." In many instances the concrete answer also demonstrated some disconnected thinking.

> Well, it could mean exactly like it says 'cause the windows may well be broken. They do grow flowers in glass houses.

> Because if they did they'd break the environment.

> Because they might be put out for the winter.

A few patients personalized it:

> People should always keep their decency about their living arrangements. I remember living in a glass house but all I did was wave.

> Because it might bust the wall and people could see you.

Others responded with totally irrelevant answers that illustrated many facets of the thinking disorder in schizophrenia.

> Don't hit until you go—coming or going.

> Some people are up in the air and some in society and some up in the air.

A few patients were able to think abstractly about the proverb, but in formulating their reply incorporated other aspects of thinking typical of schizophrenia.

People who live in glass houses shouldn't forget people who live in stone houses and shouldn't throw glass.

If you suffer from complexities, don't talk about people. Don't be agile.

The most succinct answer came from a quiet, chronically ill young man who pondered it solemnly, looked up and said, "Caution."

Concrete thinking can also occur during the everyday life of some persons. For example, one day I was taking a picture of my sister who has schizophrenia. When I said, "Look at the birdie," she immediately looked up to the sky. Another patient, passing a newspaper stand, noticed a headline announcing that a star had fallen from a window. "How could a big thing like a star get into a window?" he wondered, until he realized it referred to a movie star.

An impairment of the ability to think logically is another facet of thinking characteristic of schizophrenia, as illustrated in several of the previous examples. Another example was a patient under my care who, in psychological testing, was asked, "What would you do if you were lost in a forest?" He replied, "Go to the back of the forest, not the front." Similarly, many patients lose the ability to reason causally about events. One, for example, set his home on fire with his wheelchair-confined mother in it; when questioned carefully he did not seem to understand the fact that he was endangering her life.

In this kind of impaired thinking, opposites can coexist.

I was extremely unhappy, I felt myself getting younger; the system wanted to reduce me to nothing. Even as I diminished in body and in age, I discovered that I was nine centuries old. For to be nine centuries old actually meant being not yet born. That is why the nine centuries did not make me feel at all old; quite the contrary.

Given this impairment of causal and logical thinking in many persons with this disease, it is not surprising that they frequently have difficulty with daily activities, such as taking a bus, following directions, or planning meals. It also explains the fantastic ideas that some patients offer as facts. One of my patients, for example, wrote me a note about "a spider that weighs over a ton" and "a bird which weighs 178 pounds and makes 200 tracks in the winter and has only one foot." The writer was college-educated.

In addition to disconnectedness, loosening of associations, concreteness, and impairment of logic, there are other features of the thought processes in individuals with schizophrenia. Neologisms—made-up words—are occasionally heard. They may sound like gibberish to the listener, but to those saying them they are a response to their inability to find the words they want.

> The worst thing has been my face and my speech. The words wouldn't come out right. I know how to explain myself but the way it comes out of my mouth isn't right. My thoughts run too fast and I can't stop the train at the right point to make them go the right way. Big magnified thoughts come into my head when I am speaking and put away words I wanted to say and make me stray away from what was in my mind. Things I am speaking just fade away and my head gets very heavy and I can't place what I wanted to say. I've got a lot to say but I can't focus the words to come out so they come out jumbled up. A barrier inside my head stops me from speaking properly and the mind goes blank. I try to concentrate but nothing comes out. Sometimes I find a word to replace what I wanted to say.

Another uncommon but dramatic form of thinking in schizophrenia is called a word salad; the person just strings together a series of totally unrelated words and pronounces them as a sentence. One of my patients once turned to me solemnly and asked, "Bloodworm Baltimore frenchfry?" It's difficult to answer a question like that!

Generally it is not necessary to analyze the thought pattern in detail to know that something is wrong with it. The overall effect on the listener is both predictable and indicative. In its most common forms, it makes the listener feel that something is fuzzy about the thinking, as if the words have been slightly mixed up. John Bartlow Martin wrote a book about mental illness called *A Pane of Glass*, and Ingmar Bergman portrayed the recurrence of the symptoms of schizophrenia in his *Through a Glass Darkly* (see chapter 14). Both were referring to this opaque quality in speech and thinking. The listener hears all the words, which may be almost correct, but at the end of the sentence or paragraph realizes that it doesn't "make sense." It is the feeling evoked when, puzzled by something, we squint our eyes, wrinkle our forehead, and smile slightly. Usually we exclaim "What?" as we do this. It is a reaction evoked often when we listen to people with schizophrenia who have a thinking disorder.

> I feel that everything is sort of related to everybody and that some people are far more susceptible to this theory of relativity than others because of either having previous ancestors connected in some way or other with places or things, or because of believing, or by leaving a trail behind when you walk through a room you know. Some people might leave a different trail and all sorts of things go like that.

There can, of course, be all degrees of these thinking disorders in patients. Especially in the early stages of illness there may be only a vagueness or evasiveness that defies precise labeling, but in the full-blown illness the impairment usually is quite clear. It is an unusual patient who does not have some form of thinking disorder. Some psychiatrists even question whether schizophrenia is the correct diagnosis if the person's thinking pattern is completely normal: they would say that schizophrenia, by definition, must include some disordered thinking. Others claim that it is possible, though unusual, to have genuine schizophrenia with other symptoms but without a thinking disorder.

A totally different type of thinking disorder is also commonly found in persons with schizophrenia: blocking of thoughts. To return to the metaphor of the telephone operator at the switchboard, it is as if she suddenly dozes off for a few moments and the system goes dead. The person is thinking or starting to respond and then stops, often in midsentence, and looks blank for a brief period. John Perceval described this as long ago as 1840:

> For instance, I have been often desired to open my mouth, and to address persons in different manners, and I have begun without premeditation a very rational and consecutive speech . . . but in the midst of my sentence, the power had either left me, or words have been suggested contradictory of those that went before: and I have been deserted, gaping, speechless, or stuttering in great confusion.

Other people have given these accounts:

I may be thinking quite clearly and telling someone something and suddenly I get stuck. You have seen me do this and you may think I am just lost for words or that I have gone into a trance, but that is not what happens. What happens is that I suddenly stick on a word or an idea in my head and I just can't move past it. It seems to fill my mind and there's no room for anything else. This might go on for a while and suddenly it's over.

If I am reading I may suddenly get bogged down at a word. It may be any word, even a simple word that I know well. When this happens I can't get past it. It's as if I am being hypnotized by it. It's as if I am seeing the word for the first time and in a different way from anyone else. It's not so much that I absorb it, it's more like it is absorbing me.

Sometimes I commit brief disappearances—my mind pauses and closes down for a short while, like falling asleep suddenly.

Everyone who has spent time with persons with schizophrenia has observed this phenomenon. James Chapman claims it occurs in 95 percent of all patients. Some of the patients explain it by saying the thoughts are being taken out of their head. This symptom—called thought withdrawal—is considered by many psychiatrists to be strongly suggestive of a diagnosis of schizophrenia when it is present.

Ambivalence is another common symptom of thinking in schizophrenia. Although now a fashionable term used very broadly, it was originally used in a narrower sense to describe patients with schizophrenia who were unable to resolve contradictory thoughts or feelings, holding opposites in their minds simultaneously. A person with schizophrenia might think: "Yes, they are going to kill me and I love them." One woman described the contradictory thoughts as follows:

I am so ambivalent that my mind can divide on a subject, and those two parts subdivide over and over until my mind feels like it is in pieces and I am totally disorganized.

Sometimes the ambivalence gets translated into actions as well. For example, one of my patients frequently left the front door of the building, turned right, then stopped, took three steps back to the left and stopped, turned back and started right, sometimes continuing in this way for a full five minutes. It is not found as dramatically in most patients but is of sufficient frequency and severity for Bleuler to have named it as one of the cardinal symptoms of schizophrenia. It is as if the ability to make a decision has been impaired. Normally our brain assesses the incoming thoughts and stimuli, makes a decision, and then initiates a response. The brains of some persons with schizophrenia are apparently impaired in this respect, initiating a response but then immediately countermanding it with its opposite, then repeating the process. It is a truly painful spectacle to observe.

DELUSIONS AND HALLUCINATIONS

Delusions and hallucinations are probably the best-known symptoms of schizophrenia. They are dramatic and are therefore the behaviors usually focused on when schizophrenia is being represented in popular literature or movies. The person observed talking to himself or to inanimate objects is almost a *sine qua non* for schizophrenia; it is the image evoked in our minds when the term "crazy" or "mad" is used.

And certainly delusions and hallucinations are very important and common symptoms of this disease. However, it should be remembered that they are not essential to it; indeed no *single* symptom is essential for the diagnosis of schizophrenia. There are many people with schizophrenia who have a combination of other symptoms, such as a thought disorder, disturbances of affect, and disturbances of behavior, who have never had delusions or hallucinations. It should also be remembered that delusions and hallucinations are found in brain diseases other than schizophrenia, so their presence does not automatically mean that schizophrenia is present.

Finally, it is important to realize that most delusions and hallucinations, as well as distortions of the body boundaries, are a direct outgrowth of overacuteness of the senses and the brain's inability to interpret and respond appropriately to stimuli. In other words, most delusions and hallucinations are logical outgrowths of what the brain is experiencing. They are "crazy" only to the outsider; to the person experiencing them they form part of a logical and coherent pattern. This was clearly illustrated by John Nash, who won the 1994 Nobel Prize in economics and who also had schizophrenia, when he was being queried by Professor George Mackey regarding his delusional beliefs:

> "How could you," began Mackey, "how could you, a mathematician, a man devoted to reason and logical proof . . . how could you believe

that extraterrestrials are sending you messages? How could you believe that you are being recruited by aliens from outer space to save the world? How could you . . . ?"

Nash looked up at last and fixed Mackey with an unblinking stare as cool and dispassionate as that of any bird or snake. "Because," Nash said slowly in his soft, reasonable southern drawl, as if talking to himself, "the ideas I had about supernatural beings came to me the same way that my mathematical ideas did. So I took them seriously."

Delusions are simply false ideas believed by the patient but not by other people in his/her culture and which cannot be corrected by reason. They are usually based on some kind of sensory experience that the person misinterprets. This may be as simple as brief static on the radio or a flicker of the television screen that the person interprets as a signal. Family members often wonder where the delusional ideas in the affected person came from. Here is an example:

I went to the door of my small room and peered into the hall. Men and women with unstylish clothes and expressionless eyes paraded back and forth past my door.

"Where do I know you from?" I asked a hefty woman with a tiny face. The woman's short curly hair circled her pudgy face in ringlets. I thought I knew her.

"In a cottage by the sea," said the woman, squinting austerely at me, "I was you and you were me."

This enigmatic message must be a piece to the puzzle. I pondered it. Grandma, before she had died, had lived by the sea. Suddenly I knew the woman was my grandma.

One simple form of a delusion is the conviction that random events going on around the person all relate in a direct way to him or her. If you are walking down the street and a man on the opposite sidewalk coughs, you don't think anything of it and may not even consciously hear the cough. The person with schizophrenia, however, not only hears the cough but may immediately decide it must be a signal of some kind, perhaps directed to someone else down the street to warn him that the person is coming. The schizophrenia sufferer *knows* this is true with a certainty that few people experience. If you are walking with such a person and try to reason him/her past these delusions, your efforts will probably be futile. Even if you cross the street, and in the presence of the same person question the man about his cough, the individual will probably just decide that you are part of the plot. Reasoning with people about their delusions is like trying to bail out the ocean with a bucket. If, shortly after the cough incident, a helicopter flies overhead, the delusion may enlarge. Obviously the helicopter is watching the person, which further confirms suspicions about the cough. And if in addition to these happenings, the person arrives at the bus stop just too late to catch the bus, the delusional system is confirmed yet again; obviously the person who coughed or the helicopter pilot radioed the bus driver to leave. It all fits together into a logical, coherent whole.

Normal persons would experience these events and simply curse their bad luck at missing the bus. The person with schizophrenia, however, is experiencing different things so the events take on a different meaning. The cough and the helicopter noise may be very loud to him/her and even the sound of the bus may be perceived to be strange. While the normal person responds correctly to these as separate and unrelated events, similar to the stimuli and events of everyday life, the person with schizophrenia puts them together into a pattern. Thus, both overacuteness of the senses and impaired ability to logically interpret incoming stimuli and thoughts may lie behind many of the delusions experienced by afflicted minds. To them the person who *cannot* put these special events together must be crazy, not the other way around.

There are many excellent examples of delusional thinking in literature. Chekhov, in his well-known "Ward No. 6," described it as follows:

> A policeman walking slowly passed by the windows: that was not for
> nothing. Here were two men standing still and silent near the house.
> Why? Why were they silent? And agonizing days and nights followed
> for Ivan Dmitritch. Everyone who passed by the windows or came into
> the yard seemed to him a spy or a detective.

Another good example was written by a patient:

> I got up at seven A.M., dressed and drove to the hospital. I felt my
> breathing trouble might be due to an old heart lesion. I had been told
> when I was young that I had a small ventricular septal defect. I decided
> that I was in heart failure and that people felt I wasn't strong enough to
> accept this, so they weren't telling me. I thought about all the things
> that had happened recently that could be interpreted in that light. I
> looked up heart failure in a textbook and found that the section had

been removed, so I concluded someone had removed it to protect me.
I remembered other comments. A friend had talked about a "walkie-
talkie," and the thought occurred to me that I might be getting medicine without my knowledge, perhaps by radio. I remembered someone
talking about a one-way plane ticket; to me that meant a trip to Houston and a heart operation. I remembered an unusual smell in the lab
and thought that might be due to the medicine they were giving me in
secret. I began to think I might have a machine inside me which
secreted medicine into my bloodstream. Again I reasoned that I had a
disease no one could tell me about and was getting medicine for it
secretly. At this point, I panicked and tried to run away, but the attendant in the parking lot seemed to be making a sign to motion me back.
I thought I caught brief glimpses of a friend and my wife so I decided
to go back into the hospital. A custodian's eyes attracted my attention;
they were especially large and piercing. He looked very powerful. He
had to be "in on it," maybe he was giving medicine in some way. Then
I began to have the feeling that other people were watching me. And,
as periodically happened throughout the early stages, I said to myself
that the whole thing was absurd, but when I looked again the people
really were watching me.

A young man with paranoid schizophrenia expressed the anguish of
his own delusions in a poem:

Anxiety:
like metal on metal in my brain
Paranoia: it is
making me run
away, away, away
and back again quickly
to see if I've been caught
Or lied to
Or laughed at
Ha ha ha. The ferris wheel
in Looney Land is not so funny.

In many cases the delusions become more complex and integrated.
Rather than simply being watched, the person becomes convinced that
he/she is being controlled by other persons, manipulated, or even hypnotized. Such persons are constantly on the alert for confirmatory evidence

to support their beliefs; needless to say, they always find it from among the myriad visual and auditory stimuli perceived by all of us each day. A good example of this was a kind, elderly Irish lady who was a patient on my ward. She believed that she had been wired by some mysterious foreign agents in her sleep and that through the wires her thoughts and actions could be controlled. In particular she pointed to the ceiling as the place from which the control took place. One morning I was dismayed to come onto the ward and discover workmen installing a new fire alarm system; wires were hanging down in all colors and in all directions. The lady looked at me, pointed to the ceiling, and just smiled; her delusions had been confirmed forever!

Delusions of being wired or radio-controlled are relatively common. Often it is the FBI or the CIA that is the suspected perpetrator of the scheme. One patient was convinced that a radio had been sewn into his skull when he had had a minor scalp wound sutured and had tried to bring legal suit against the FBI innumerable times. Another man, at one time a highly successful superintendent of schools, became convinced that a radio had been implanted in his nose. He went to dozens of major medical centers, even to Europe, seeking a surgeon who would remove it. He even had an X-ray of his nose showing a tiny white speck that he was convinced was the radio.

Friends of the unfortunate people often try to reason them out of their delusions. Rarely is this successful. Questions about why the FBI would want to control them are deftly brushed aside as irrelevant; the important point is that they do, and the person is experiencing sensations (such as strange noises) that confirm the fact. Reasoning a person with schizophrenia out of a delusion is hampered by the distorted stimuli he/she is perceiving and also by the fact that the thinking processes may not be logical or connected. A further impediment is the fact that delusions frequently become self-fulfilling. Thus, someone who believes others are spying on him/her finds it logical to act furtively, perhaps running from corner to corner and peering anxiously into the faces of passersby. Such behavior inevitably invites attention and leads to the delusional person's actually being watched by other people. As the saying goes, "I used to be paranoid but now people really *are* watching me."

Delusions in which the person is being watched, persecuted, or attacked are commonly called paranoid delusions. Paranoia is a relative concept; everybody experiences bits and pieces of it from time to time. In some places a little paranoia even has survival value; the fellow who works across the hall may really be stealing your memos, because he wants your job. Paranoid thinking by itself is not schizophrenia; it is only when it becomes a frank delusion (unaffected by reason) that it *may* be. Even then, however, it must be remembered that paranoid delusions can occur in brain diseases other than schizophrenia.

Paranoid delusions may on occasion be dangerous. "During the paranoid period I thought I was being persecuted for my beliefs, that my enemies were actively trying to interfere with my activities, were trying to harm me, and at times even to kill me." The paranoid person may try to strike first when the threat is perceived as too close. Facilities for the criminally insane in every state include among their inmates a large number of persons with schizophrenia who have committed a crime in what they believed to be self-defense. It is this subgroup that has produced the general belief that people with schizophrenia as a whole are dangerous. As will be discussed in chapter 11, when we take into consideration all persons with schizophrenia, this subgroup is very small. Most persons with schizophrenia are not dangerous at all, and I would far rather walk the halls of any mental hospital than walk the streets of any inner city.

Delusions may be of many types other than paranoid; grandiose delusions are quite common: "I felt that I had power to determine the weather, which responded to my inner moods, and even to control the movement of the sun in relation to other astronomical bodies." This often leads to a belief by the person that he/she is Jesus Christ, the Virgin Mary, the president, or some other exalted or important person. One admission in our hospital believed himself to be Mao Ze-dong. We began him on medication and, by the next day, knew he was getting better because he had become only the brother of Mao Ze-dong. Other individuals with grandiose delusions may believe that they are starring in a movie:

> I once believed that I was in the process of making a gigantic film of which I was the star. Everywhere I went in London there was a hidden camera and microphone and everything that I said and did was being recorded.

Grandiose delusions can on occasion be dangerous. People who believe that they can fly, or stop bullets with their chest, may place themselves in a position to demonstrate the truth of their belief with predictably tragic consequences.

There is one particular type of grandiose delusion that, although not seen commonly, is so distinctive that it has acquired its own name. It is the delusion that another person, usually famous, is deeply in love with the patient. Such cases, originally called *psychoses passionnelles* by Dr. Gaëtan G. de Clerambault, a French psychiatrist, now often bear the designation of de Clerambault syndrome, or erotomania. One of my patients, who believed that Senator Edward Kennedy was in love with her, spent all her time and money following him around but always staying at a distance; she produced a multitude of incredible reasons why he could not acknowledge her presence. Another patient believed she was engaged to a man whom she had met once casually several years before, and spent all day walking the city streets looking for him. Most patients with such delusions have schizophrenia, although a few may have manic-depressive illness. These patients have a pathos to their lives that is unusually affecting.

A relatively common delusion is that a person can control other people's minds. One young woman I saw had spent five years at home because each time she went into the street she believed that her mind compelled other people to turn and look at her. She described the effect of her mind as "like a magnet—they have no choice but to turn and look." Another patient believed he could change people's moods by "telepathic force": "I eventually felt I could go into a crowded restaurant and while just sitting there quietly, I could change everyone's mood to happiness and laughter." Here is a variant on this delusion:

> I like talking to a person but not in audible words. I try to force my thoughts into someone. I concentrate on how they move. I think of a message and concentrate in my head. It's thought you're passing over. I send the messages by visual indication. Sometimes the shoulder, sometimes my whole body.

Another variant is the delusional belief that one's thoughts are radiating out of one's head and being broadcast over radio or television; this is called thought broadcasting and is considered to be an almost certain indication of schizophrenia. Occasionally such individuals call or go to the radio or television station and ask them to stop broadcasting their thoughts. A 1999 study of radio and television stations reported that such contacts are relatively common.

In evaluating delusions, it is very important to keep in mind that their content is culture-bound. It is not the belief per se that is delusional but how far the belief differs from the beliefs shared by others in the same culture or subculture. A man who believes he is being influenced by others who have "worked roots" (put a hex) on him may be completely normal if he grew up in lowland South Carolina, where "working roots" is a widespread cultural belief. If he grew up in affluent Scarsdale, New York, on the other hand, his belief in being influenced by "worked roots" is more likely to suggest schizophrenia. Minority groups in particular may have a culturally induced high level of paranoid belief, and this belief may be based on real discrimination and real persecution. In other subcultural groups it may be difficult to assess the pathological nature of delusional thinking, for instance regarding grandiose delusions among the deeply religious and paranoid delusions among employees of the intelligence community. Imagine, for example, the dilemma of a Mother Superior in evaluating a novice who claims to have a special relationship with the Virgin Mary or a supervisor at the CIA who is told by one of his undercover employees that he is being watched all the time. Beliefs of persons suspected of having schizophrenia must *always* be placed within a cultural context and regarded as only one facet of the disease.

Occasionally individuals come to attention who have odd thoughts, but it may be very difficult to decide whether these thoughts constitute true delusions. Such an individual, apparently, is John Hinckley, who in 1981 attempted to assassinate President Ronald Reagan. According to court testimony, Hinckley had a fantasy relationship with Jodie Foster, a movie actress, and spent much of his time and energy trying to engage her attention; the assassination attempt was said to be Hinckley's ultimate effort to prove his love for Jodie Foster. At his trial, psychiatrists for the defense and the prosecution differed sharply on whether such thinking constituted a true delusion. Subsequent events, however, strongly supported the belief that Hinckley does indeed suffer from schizophrenia.

One other aspect of delusions is important to note. Delusions may be fixed and static in some individuals with schizophrenia, but in others the delusions may be labile and held with varying degrees of conviction. I recall one patient, for example, who believed that another patient was trying to kill him. On one day he would avoid the feared person completely, on the next day he would socialize with him pleasantly, and on the following day he would avoid him again. This lack of consistency was also noted in 1890 by Dr. Pliny Earle, whose patient believed she had "millions and billions of children . . . and that persons are constantly engaged in murdering them. . . . Yet this woman is always quiet and gentle, makes no outward show of grief or unhappiness, and never attempts to force or find her way into the presence of her imaginary children."

This lack of consistency in response to delusional thinking is difficult to understand for families of individuals with schizophrenia.

Hallucinations are very common in schizophrenia and are the end of that spectrum that begins with overacuteness of the senses. To take vision as an example: the spectrum has overacuteness of vision at one end of it, that is, lights are too bright, colors take on a more brilliant hue. In the middle of the spectrum are gross distortions of visual stimuli (also called illusions), such as a dog that takes on the appearance of a tiger. And at the far end of the spectrum are things that are seen by the person with schizophrenia when there is nothing there; this is a true hallucination. The experiences described by patients are usually a mixture of different points on the spectrum.

Gross distortions of visual or auditory stimuli are not uncommon experiences in schizophrenia.

> I was sitting listening to another person and suddenly the other person became smaller and then larger and then he seemed to get smaller again. He did not become a complete miniature. Then today with another person, I felt he was getting taller and taller. There is brightness and clarity of outline of things around me. Last week I was with a girl and suddenly she seemed to get bigger and bigger, like a monster coming nearer and nearer. The situation becomes threatening and I shrink back and back.

> This phenomenon can perhaps best be depicted by a description of the first time I experienced it. I was one of four men at a bridge table. On one of the deals, my partner bid three clubs. I looked at my hand: I had only one small club. Though my hand was weak, I had to bid to take him out. My bid won. When my partner laid down his cards, he showed only two small clubs in his hand. I immediately questioned why he had bid three clubs. He denied having made such a bid. The other two men at the table supported him. There was no opportunity and no reason for the three clubs despite the fact that I had distinctly heard him do so. Not only had the hallucination included a spatial component synchronized with the man's position, but it had also duplicated exactly the vocal tones of the man. Furthermore, the man had actually declared a different bid at the time I had heard him bidding three clubs. This bid I had not heard. Somewhere along the line of my nervous system the words which he had actually spoken were blocked and the hallucinatory words substituted.

In both instances there was a stimulus of some kind, but the person saw or heard it in a grossly distorted way. It is as if the person's brain is playing tricks.

Even worse tricks are played in forming true hallucinations, in which there is no initial stimulus at all. The brain makes up what it hears, sees, feels, smells, or tastes. Such experiences may be very real for the person. A person who hallucinates voices talking to him may hear the voices just as clearly as, or even more clearly than, the voices of real people talking to him, and people with schizophrenia frequently talk back to the voices. There is a tendency for people close to patients to scoff at the "imaginary" voices, to minimize them and not believe the persons really hear them. But they do, and in the sense that the brain hears them, they are real. The voices are but an extreme example of the malfunctioning of the sufferer's sensory apparatus.

Auditory hallucinations are by far the most common form of hallucination in schizophrenia. They are so characteristic of the disease that a person with true auditory hallucinations should be assumed to have schizophrenia until proven otherwise. They may take a variety of forms. They may be a simple swishing or thumping sound, such as the beating of the heart in Poe's famous short story:

No doubt I now grew very pale;—but I talked fluently, and with a heightened voice. Yet the sound increased and what could I do? It was a low, dull, quick sound—much such a sound as a watch makes when enveloped in cotton. I gasped for breath—and yet the officers heard it not. I talked more quickly—more vehemently; but the noise steadily increased. Why would they not be gone? I paced the floor to and fro with heavy strides, as if excited to fury by the observation of the men—but the noise steadily increased.

They may be a single voice: "Thus for years I have heard daily in hundredfold repetition incoherent words spoken into my nerves without any context, such as 'Why not?' 'Why, if,' 'Why, because I,' 'Be it,' 'With respect to him.' "

Or they may be multiple voices or even a choir:

There was music everywhere and rhythm and beauty. But the plans were always thwarted. I heard what seemed to be a choir of angels. I thought it the most beautiful music I had ever heard. Two of the airs I kept repeating over and over until the delirium ended. One of them

I can remember imperfectly even now. This choir of angels kept hovering around the hospital and shortly afterward I heard something about a little lamb being born upstairs in the room just above mine.

The hallucinations may be heard only occasionally or they may be continuous. When occasional, the most common time for them, in my clinical experience, is at night when going to sleep.

For about almost seven years—except during sleep—I have never had a single moment in which I did not hear voices. They accompany me to every place and at all times; they continue to sound even when I am in conversation with other people, they persist undeterred even when I concentrate on other things, for instance read a book or a newspaper, play the piano, etc.; only when I am talking aloud to other people or to myself are they of course drowned by the stronger sound of the spoken word and therefore inaudible to me. But the well-known phrases recommence at once, sometimes in the middle of a sentence, which tells me that the conversation had continued during the interval, that is to say that those nervous stimuli or vibrations responsible for the weaker sounds of the voices continue even while I talk aloud.

I have taken care of people with similar manifestations. One unfortunate woman had heard voices continuously for 20 years. They became especially loud whenever she tried to watch television, so she couldn't watch it at all.

In the vast majority of cases, the voices are unpleasant. They are often accusatory, reviling the victims for past misdeeds, either real or imagined. Often they curse them, and I have had many people refuse to tell me what the voices say to them because they were embarrassed by it. In a minority of cases the voices may be pleasant, as in the example with lovely music cited above. Occasionally they are even helpful, as with a woman who announced to me one day that she was getting well: "I know I am, because my voices told me so."

The precise mechanism of auditory hallucinations is not well understood. The most plausible explanation is that the schizophrenia disease process selectively affects auditory centers in the brain, thereby producing auditory hallucinations. There are several different auditory centers in the brain, some of which are contiguous with temporal lobe and frontal lobe areas thought to be involved in schizophrenia. In one study, an increase in

blood flow to a major language area was demonstrated to occur in schizophrenia during auditory hallucinations. Another study showed that "auditory hallucinations involve language regions of the cortex in a pattern
similar to that seen in normal subjects listening to their own voices,"
which may explain why auditory hallucinations sound so real to the person hearing them. Studies of brain structures in individuals with schizophrenia have also shown that auditory hallucinations are more common in
patients who have larger third ventricles, one of the fluid-filled spaces in
the brain. As technology improves for measuring brain structures, it is
likely that additional correlations will be found between symptoms such
as auditory hallucinations and specific abnormalities of brain structures. It
is also of interest that individuals who are born deaf and who later develop
schizophrenia can experience auditory hallucinations.

Visual hallucinations also occur but less frequently. One patient
described the variety of these hallucinations:

> At an early stage the appearance of colored flashes of light was com-
> mon. These took the form either of distant streaks or of nearby round
> glowing patches about a foot in diameter. Another type, which took
> place five or six times, was the appearance of words or symbols on
> blank surfaces. Closely connected with this was the occasional substi-
> tution of hallucinatory matter for the actual printed matter in books
> which I have been reading. On these occasions, the passage which I
> have been seeing has dissolved while I have been looking at it and
> another and sometimes wholly different passage has appeared in its
> place. . . . A further form of visual hallucinations that happened on
> two occasions was the appearance on a wall of the pictures of the
> heads of young women as though projected from a projection
> machine. These pictures were of women whom to the best of my
> knowledge I had never met.

Visual hallucinations usually appear in conjunction with auditory
hallucinations. When only visual hallucinations appear, it is unlikely that
schizophrenia is the cause. Many other brain diseases, notably drug
intoxications and alcohol withdrawal, cause purely visual hallucinations
and are the more likely diagnosis in such cases.

Like delusions, hallucinations must always be evaluated within their
cultural context. In medieval times and today among some religious
groups, visual hallucinations are not uncommon and do not necessarily
suggest mental illness. Dr. Silvano Arieti attempted to distinguish the

hallucinations of the profoundly religious from those of schizophrenia by proposing the following criteria:

A. Religious hallucinations are usually visual, while those in schizophrenia are predominantly auditory.
B. Religious hallucinations usually involve benevolent guides or advisers who issue orders to the person.
C. Religious hallucinations are usually pleasant.

Hallucinations of smell or taste are unusual but do occur. One patient gave this description of hallucinations of smell:

On a few occasions, I have experienced olfactory hallucinations. These have consisted of the seeming smelling of an odor as though originating from a source just outside the nose. Sometimes this odor has had a symbolical relationship with the thoughts-out-loud, as for instance, the appearance of an odor of sulphur in connection with a threat of damnation to hell by the thoughts-out-loud.

Another patient illustrated the same phenomenon of associating a smell with a thought:

During the time I was getting sick again, I began to think about the abortions I had before I was married. I was feeling guilty about them again. In those days you always tried to abort yourself first by taking quinine. When I was taking a shower and thinking about the past, I suddenly noticed the unmistakable smell of quinine. Soon after that, my mother and I were talking and she said something about oranges. I immediately began to smell oranges.

Hallucinations of taste usually consist of familiar food tasting differently. I have had patients with paranoid schizophrenia, for example, who decided that they were being poisoned when their food began tasting "funny." Certainly if one's food suddenly starts changing in taste, it is logical to suspect that somebody is adding something to it.

Hallucinations of touch are also found among individuals with schizophrenia although not commonly. I provided care for one woman who felt small insects crawling under the skin on her face; it is an understatement to say that this was very upsetting to her. Another patient experienced hallucinatory pain.

To the person who experiences hallucinatory pains, the pains feel identical with actual pains. There is no difference between the sensation of hallucinatory and the sensation of actual pain. The person who experiences it can distinguish it only by its lack of normal cause and its interrelations with other hallucinatory phenomena. The person who feels it undergoes real suffering. . . . To give some specific data concerning hallucinatory pains that I have experienced, it may be stated that they have varied considerably in intensity, in duration, and in locus. In intensity, they have ranged from a fraction of a second up to ten minutes or so. In locus, they have ranged over all parts of the body. In type, they have included smarting, burning, aching.

ALTERED SENSE OF SELF

Closely allied with delusions and hallucinations is another complex of symptoms that is characteristic of many patients with schizophrenia. Normal individuals have a clear sense of self; they know where their bodies stop and where inanimate objects begin. They know that their hand, when they look at it, belongs to them. Even to make a statement like this strikes most normal persons as absurd because they cannot imagine its being otherwise.

But many persons with schizophrenia can imagine it, for alterations in their sense of self are not uncommon in this condition. Such alterations are frequently associated with alterations in bodily sensations, such as was described by one man with schizophrenia who wrote to me:

My body has the same forms of distortions as my vision and these are manifested throughout my anatomy. My body feels like there are indentations, ridges, and agonizing disfigurements all over. Strands of hair falling down on my forehead feel much larger, heavier, and more noticeable. My body feels dry like it is brittle. My skin and underlying fat feels deadish like when you get novocaine, except you still have sensation. Eyes feel hollow, like they extend further back in the skull. Appendages frequently feel different shapes, narrower or fuller or curved in opposite directions. Hands, arms, and legs sometimes feel an inch to the side of where they really are at. Fingers at times feel and look longer or shorter than usual. My face can feel twice as long as it is.

Alterations of the self may range from such somatic perceptual distortions to, on the other end of the spectrum, confusion in distinguishing oneself from another person, as described by Marguerite Sechehaye in her biography:

> Sometimes I did not know clearly whether it was she or I who needed something. For instance if I asked for another cup of tea and Mamma answered teasingly, "But why do you want more tea; don't you see that I have just finished my cup and so you don't need any?" Then I replied, "Yes, that's true, I don't need any more," confusing her with myself. But at bottom I did desire a second cup of tea, and I said, "But I still want some more tea," and suddenly, in a flash, I realized the fact that Mamma's satiety did not make me sated too. And I was ashamed to let myself be thus trapped and to watch her laugh at my discomfiture.

Another patient described a similar experience in which

> I saw myself in different bodies. . . . The night nurse came in and sat under the shaded lamp in the quiet ward. I recognized her as me, and I watched for some time quite fascinated; I had never had an outside view of myself before. In the morning several of the patients having breakfast were me. I recognized them by the way they held their knives and forks.

A patient's body parts may develop lives of their own, as if they have become disassociated and detached. One patient described this feeling:

> I get shaky in the knees and my chest is like a mountain in front of me, and my body actions are different. The arms and legs are apart and away from me and they go on their own. That's when I feel I am the other person and copy their movements, or else stop and stand like a statue. I have to stop to find out whether my hand is in my pocket or not. I'm frightened to move or turn my head. Sometimes I let my arms roll to see where they will land. After I sit down my head clears again but I don't remember what happened when I was in the daze.

Sechehaye also describes confusion regarding where her body stopped and the rest of the world began: "This was equally true in body functions. When I urinated and it was raining torrents outside, I was not at all certain whether it was not my own urine bedewing the world, and I was gripped by fear."

Confusion about one's sexual characteristics is also not uncommon among people with schizophrenia, as in this man who believed his body was acquiring a feminine appearance:

> My breast gives the impression of a pretty well-developed female bosom; this phenomenon can be *seen* by anybody who wants to observe me *with his own eyes.* . . . A brief glance would not suffice. The observer would have to go to the trouble of spending ten or fifteen minutes near me. In that way anybody would notice the periodic swelling and diminution of my bosom.

The altered sense of self may be further aggravated if hallucinations of touch or delusions about the body are also present. One possible example of this is Kafka's famous story "The Metamorphosis," in which Gregor awakens in the morning and slowly realizes that he has been transformed into a huge beetle. Such passages in Kafka have led some scholars to speculate that Kafka himself may have had schizophrenia at times.

The origin of this altered sense of self in persons with schizophrenia is unknown. Normally our sense of self is formed by a complex set of tactile and visual stimuli through which we can feel and see the limits of our body and by which we differentiate it from the objects around us. It is likely that the same disease process that alters the senses and the thinking process is also responsible for the altered sense of self.

CHANGES IN EMOTIONS

Changes in emotions—or affect, as it is often called by professionals—are one of the most common and characteristic changes in schizophrenia. In the early stages of the illness depression, guilt, fear, and rapidly fluctuating emotions may all be found. In the later stages flattening of emotions is more characteristic, often resulting in individuals who appear to be unable to feel emotions at all. This in turn makes it more difficult for us to relate to them, so we tend to shun them even more.

Depression is a very common symptom early in the course of the disease but is often overlooked. In a 1994 study it was reported that "81 percent of the patients . . . presented a well defined episode of depressive mood." In half of the patients, the symptoms of depression preceded the onset of delusions or hallucinations. Most such depression is biologically based, caused by neurochemical changes in the brain as part of the disease process, although some of it may also be a reaction of the person to the realization that he/she is becoming sick. One of the tragic and not uncommon sequelae of such depression is suicide, which is discussed in chapter 11.

Early in the course of illness the person with schizophrenia may also feel widely varying and rapidly fluctuating emotions. Exaggerated feelings of all kinds are not unusual, especially in connection with the peak experiences described previously.

> During the first two weeks of my psychosis, religious experience provided that dominant factor of the psychotic phenomena. The most important form of religious experience in that period was religious ecstasy. The attempts of the thoughts-out-loud to persuade myself to adopt a messianic fixation formed the hallucinary background. In affective aspects, a pervasive feeling of well-being dominated the complex. I felt as though all my worries were gone and all my problems solved. I had the assurance that all my needs would be satisfied. Connected with this euphoric state, I experienced a gentle sensation of warmth over my whole body, particularly on my back, and a sensation of my body having lost its weight and gently floating.

Guilt is another commonly felt emotion in these early stages:

> Later, considering them appropriate, I no longer felt guilty about these fantasies, nor did the guilt have an actual object. It was too pervasive, too enormous, to be founded on anything definite, and it demanded punishment. The punishment was indeed horrible, sadistic—it consisted, fittingly enough, of being guilty. For to feel oneself guilty is the worst that can happen, it is the punishment of punishments. Consequently, I could never be relieved of it as though I had been truly punished. Quite the reverse, I felt more and more guilty, immeasurably guilty. Constantly, I sought to discover what was punishing me so dreadfully, what was making me so guilty.

And fear is frequently described by patients, often a pervasive and nameless fear that exists without any specific object. It is well described by a young man with schizophrenia:

I sat in my basement with a fear that I could not control. I was totally afraid—just from watching my cat look out the window.

Exaggerated feelings usually are not found in patients beyond the early stages of the disease. If they are, they should raise questions as to whether schizophrenia is the correct diagnosis. It is the *retention* of such feelings and emotions that is one of the sharpest dividing lines between schizophrenia and manic-depressive illness (see chapter 3). If the person retains exaggerated feelings to a prominent degree beyond the early stages of the disease, it is much more likely that the correct diagnosis will turn out to be manic-depressive illness.

In addition to the exaggerated emotions that are experienced by individuals with schizophrenia, there is also evidence that some people affected with this disease have difficulties in assessing emotions in other people. A review of studies in this area asserted that "there has been a growing literature suggesting that schizophrenics differ substantially from controls in processing emotional communication." One research technique used to demonstrate this is to ask individuals with schizophrenia to describe the emotions of people in photographs, which is frequently a difficult task for them. This impaired ability to judge emotions in others is a major reason why many people with schizophrenia have trouble in social communications and forming friendships.

The most characteristic changes in emotions in schizophrenia are inappropriate emotions or flattened emotions. It is an unusual patient who does not have one or the other—and sometimes both—by the time the disease is full-blown.

Inappropriate emotions are to be expected in light of the previous analogy of the telephone operator at the switchboard. Just as he/she hooks up the wrong thoughts with incoming stimuli, so she also hooks up wrong emotions. The incoming call may carry sad news but she hooks it up with mirth and the patient laughs. In other instances a patient responds with an inappropriate emotion because of the other things going on in his/her head that cause laughter.

Half the time I am talking about one thing and thinking about half a dozen other things at the same time. It must look queer to people when I laugh about something that has got nothing to do with what I am talking about, but they don't know what's going on inside and how much of it is running round in my head. You see I might be talking about something quite serious to you and other things come into my head at the

same time that are funny and this makes me laugh. If I could only concentrate on the one thing at the one time I wouldn't look half so silly.

These inappropriate emotions produce one of the most dramatic
aspects of the disease—the victim suddenly breaking out in cackling
laughter for no apparent reason. It is a common sight to those who have
worked or lived with people with this disease.

The flattening of emotions may be subtle in the earlier stages of the
disease. Chapman claims that "one of the earliest changes in schizophrenic experience involves impairment in the process of empathy with
other people." The person with schizophrenia loses the ability to put
him/herself in the other person's place or to feel what the other person is
feeling. As the disease progresses this flattening or blunting of the emotions may become more prominent: "During my first illness I did not
feel the emotions of anger, rage, or indignation to nearly as great an
extent as I would have normally. Attitudes of dislike, estrangement, and
fear predominated."

Emotions may become detached altogether from specific objects,
leaving the victim with a void, as poignantly described by this patient:

> Instead of wishing to do things, they are done by something that seems
> mechanical and frightening, because it is able to do things and yet
> unable to want to or not to want to. All the constructive healing parts
> that could be used healthily and slowly to mend an aching torment
> have left, and the feeling that should dwell within a person is outside,
> longing to come back and yet having taken with it the power to return.
> Out and in are probably not good terms, though, for they are too black
> and white and it is more like gray. It is like a constant sliding and shift-
> ing that slips away in a jelly-like fashion, leaving nothing substantial
> and yet enough to be tasted.

And Michael Wechsler summarized it neatly in a statement to his
father: "I wish I could wake up feeling really bad—it would be better
than feeling nothing."

In the advanced stage of flattening of the emotions, there appear to
be none left at all. This does not happen frequently, but when it does it is
an unforgettable experience for those who interact with the victims. I
have had two such patients in whom I was unable to elicit *any* emotion
whatsoever under any circumstances. They were polite, at times stub-
born, but never happy or sad. It is uncannily like interacting with a robot.

One of these patients set fire to his house, then sat down placidly to watch TV. When it was called to his attention that the house was on fire he got up calmly and went outside. Clearly the brain damage in these cases has seriously affected the centers mediating emotional response. Fortunately, most persons with schizophrenia do not have such complete damage to this area of the brain.

One must be cautious, however, in assuming that a person with schizophrenia who apparently is experiencing no emotions *really* is experiencing no emotions. A 1993 study of individuals with schizophrenia who were videotaped while watching emotion-laden films found that the individuals "reported experiencing as much positive and negative emotion" despite the fact that they expressed much less of the emotion. Ms. Jean Bouricius, the mother of a young man with schizophrenia, published excerpts from her son's writings that demonstrated that he was experiencing intense, although unexpressed, emotions at the same time that mental health professionals were rating him as being emotionally very flat. His writings included: "Loneliness needs a song, a song of love and pain, sweet release and hope for the future," and "I close my eyes softly and become that part of midnight winds where emotion is choked and no cries can emerge." It is becoming increasingly apparent that some individuals with schizophrenia, who on the surface appear to be experiencing no emotions, are inwardly feeling intense emotions.

Often associated with a flattening of emotions are apathy, slowness of movement, underactivity, lack of drive, and a paucity (usually called poverty) of thought and speech. This composite picture is frequently seen in patients who have been sick for many years and is frequently referred to as the "negative" symptoms of schizophrenia, as will be discussed in chapter 3. These patients appear to be desireless, apathetic, seeking nothing, wanting nothing. It is as if their will had eroded, and indeed something like that probably does happen as part of the disease process.

It is fashionable nowadays to believe that much of the flattening of emotions and apathy common in patients with schizophrenia are side effects of the drugs used to treat the disease. In fact, there is only a little truth to this. Many of the drugs used to treat schizophrenia do have a calming or sedative effect (see chapter 9). Most of the flattening of emotions and weakening of motivation, however, are products of the disease itself and not of the drug effects. This can easily be proved by reviewing descriptions of patients in the literature prior to the introduction of these drugs. Emotional flattening and apathy are just as prominent in those early descriptions as they are today.

CHANGES IN MOVEMENTS

In recent years changes in movements have been closely linked in people's minds with the side effects of drugs used to treat schizophrenia. And indeed the antipsychotic drugs and lithium may cause changes in movements, varying from a fine tremor of the fingers to gross jerky movements of the arms or trunk.

But it is important to keep in mind that the schizophrenia disease process can also cause changes in movements, and that these were clearly described in accounts of the disease for many years before modern drugs became available. One study of changes of movements in schizophrenia found that they occur "in virtually all cases of conservatively defined schizophrenia" and concluded that they were consequences of the disease process and not of the medication being taken by the patients. In another study half the patients in remission remembered changes in their movements. In some cases their movements appeared to speed up, while in others they slowed down. A feeling of awkwardness or clumsiness is relatively common, and persons with this disease may spill things, or stumble while walking, much more commonly than before they became sick.

Another change in movement is decreased spontaneity, and the person may be aware of this. One recalled: "I became the opposite of spontaneous, as a result of which I became very diffident, very labored." Some patients with schizophrenia have decreased spontaneous swinging of their arms when they walk, a finding that has led some researchers to theorize that the cerebellum or basal ganglia portions of the brain may be affected in this disease.

Repetitious movements such as tics, tremors, tongue movements, and sucking movements are also seen. In the majority of patients in whom they occur, these are side effects of the medication being given the patient, but in a minority they will not be due to the medication but rather to the disease process. Even subtle body movements like eye blinking may be affected in schizophrenia. Some patients with the disease blink much less often than normal people. Drugs can account for some of this decrease but not for all of it. Balzac noted it in a patient in the early years of the nineteenth century: "[He] stood, just as I now saw him, day and night, with fixed eyes, never raising or lowering the lids, as others do."

The most dramatic change of movements in schizophrenia, of course, is catatonic behavior. A patient may remain motionless for hours, and if the person's arm is passively moved the arm will often remain in its new position for an hour or longer. Catatonic forms of schizophrenia were seen more commonly in the earlier years of this century but have become much less common; the availability of antipsychotic medication may be one reason for this, as catatonic symptoms usually respond promptly to medication.

CHANGES IN BEHAVIOR

Changes in behavior are usually secondary rather than primary symptoms of schizophrenia; that is, the behaviors shown by persons with this illness are most often a response to other things occurring in their brains. For example, if the person with schizophrenia is beset by overacuteness of the senses and an inability to synthesize incoming stimuli, it makes perfect sense for him/her to withdraw into a corner. Many of the other behaviors seen in this disease can be similarly and logically explained.

Withdrawing, remaining quietly in one place for long periods, and immobility are all common behaviors in this illness. The extreme versions of such behaviors are catatonia, where the person remains rigidly fixed in one position for long periods of time, and mutism, where the person does not speak at all. Catatonia and mutism are part of a continuum that includes the less blatant forms of withdrawal and immobility so commonly seen in the disease.

A person with schizophrenia may withdraw and remain silent for any one of a number of reasons. Sometimes this occurs when the person becomes lost in deep thought:

> When I am walking along the street it comes on me. I start to think deeply and I start to go into a sort of trance. I think so deeply that I almost get out of this world. Then you get frightened that you are going to get into a jam and lose yourself. That's when I get worried and excited.

Or it may be adopted in order to slow down the incoming sensory stimuli so the brain can sort them out:

> I don't like moving fast. I feel there would be a breakup if I went too quick. I can only stand that a short time and then I have to stop. If I carried on I wouldn't be aware of things as they really are. I would just

be aware of the sound and noise and the movements. Everything would be a jumbled mass. I have found that I can stop this happening by going completely still and motionless. When I do that, things are easier to take in.

Unexpected sensory stimuli can also result in a slowing.

> I get stuck, almost as if I am paralysed at times. It may only last for a minute or two but it's a bit frightening. It seems to happen even when something unexpected takes place, especially if there's a lot of noise that comes on suddenly. Say I am walking across the floor and someone suddenly switches on the wireless: the music seems to stop me in my tracks, and sometimes I freeze like that for a minute or two.

The movements may also be slowed so as to allow them to be integrated into a whole in exactly the same way that visual and auditory stimuli may need to be integrated.

> I am not sure of my own movements any more. It's very hard to describe this but at times I am not sure about even simple actions like sitting down. It's not so much thinking out what to do, it's the doing of it that sticks me. . . . I found recently that I was thinking of myself doing things before I would do them. If I am going to sit down, for example, I have got to think of myself and almost see myself sitting down before I do it. It's the same with other things like washing, eating, and even dressing—things that I have done at one time without even bothering or thinking about at all. . . . All this makes me move much slower now. I take more time to do things because I am always conscious of what I am doing. If I could just stop noticing what I am doing, I would get things done a lot faster.

Other unusual behaviors are also found in persons with schizophrenia. Ritualistic behaviors are not uncommon. Some patients repeatedly walk in circles, and I had one who walked through all doors backwards. There are reasons why they do such things, as explained by this woman who felt compelled to beat eggs a certain way when making a cake:

> As the work progressed, a change came. The ingredients of the cake began to have a special meaning. The process became a ritual. At certain stages the stirring must be counter-clockwise; at another time it

was necessary to stand up and beat the batter toward the east; the egg whites must be folded in from the left to the right; for each thing that had to be done there were complicated reasons. I recognized that these were new, unfamiliar, and unexpected, but did not question them. They carried a finality that was effective. Each compelling impulse was accompanied by an equally compelling explanation.

Another example of ritualistic behavior is the following:

The state of indifference reigning until now was abruptly replaced by inner and outer agitation. At first I felt obliged to get up and walk; it was impossible to stay in bed. Singing a requiem without pause, I marched three steps forward and three steps back, an automatism that wearied me exceedingly and which I wished someone would help me break. I could not do it alone, for I felt forced to make these steps and if I stopped from exhaustion, even for a moment, I felt guilty again. Moreover, when any behavior became automatic, I felt guilty in interrupting it. But no one could believe that I wanted to stop, for as soon as they made me give up some stereotyped procedure, I began anew.

Certain gestures may be repeated often, for reasons that are quite logical to the person doing them but that appear bizarre to the onlooker. One patient shook his head rhythmically from side to side to try and shake the excess thoughts out of his mind. Another massaged his head "to help to clear it" of unwanted thoughts. It is because of such ritualistic and repetitive behaviors that occasional patients with schizophrenia may be misdiagnosed with obsessive-compulsive disorder. Obsessions and compulsions are indeed frequently present in schizophrenia; however, a person with true obsessive-compulsive disorder will not have the thought disorder, delusions, hallucinations, or other symptoms that are also present in schizophrenia.

Specific postures may also be adopted by persons with schizophrenia. One of my patients marched endlessly up and down the sidewalk with his left hand placed awkwardly on his left shoulder. It appeared to be uncomfortable, but he invariably returned to it for reasons I was never able to ascertain. Another posture was described in 1838 by John Perceval:

There were two or three other delusions I laboured under of which I hardly recollect how I was cured—one in particular, that I was to lean

on the back of my head and on my feet in bed, and twist my neck by
throwing my body with a jerk from side to side. I fancy that I never
attempted this with sincerity, because I feared to break my neck.

Occasionally a person with schizophrenia will repeat like a parrot
whatever is said to him/her. In psychiatric language this is called
echolalia. Chapman believes that repeating the words probably is useful
to the patient because it allows time to absorb and synthesize what was
said. Much rarer is the occurrence of behavior that is parroted, called
echopraxia. When it occurs it may be the consequence of a dissolution of
boundaries of the self so that the person does not know where his/her
body leaves off and where the body of the other person begins.

Most worrisome to friends and relatives of individuals with schizophrenia, for obvious reasons, are socially inappropriate behaviors. Fortunately, most patients who act inappropriately on hospital wards may act
quite appropriately when taken out of the hospital on trips. It is always
impressive to see patients from even the most regressed hospital wards
go to public places; they are usually more distinguishable by their dress
(characteristically poorly fitting) than by their behavior. A small number
of patients are so ill that they continue inappropriate behaviors (such as
random urination, open masturbation, spitting on others) even in public,
but such patients are comparatively rare. Some—but not all—of them
can be improved by proper medication or conditioning techniques.

It should always be remembered that the behavior of persons with
schizophrenia is internally logical and rational; they do things for reasons that, given their disordered senses and thinking, make sense to
them. To the outside observer the behavior may appear irrational,
"crazy," "mad," the very hallmark of the disease. To the ill person, however, there is nothing "crazy" or "mad" about it at all. Here, for example,
is an account of a woman who broke two pairs of glasses worn by her
nurses, an action that must have seemed inexplicable ("crazy") to those
who observed it.

My feelings about excessive light and truth were shown in ideas I had
about glasses. I was afraid of people who wore glasses, and thought
that I was being deliberately persecuted by doctors and nurses who
refracted an excessive amount of light into my eyes by wearing
glasses. At the same time glasses symbolized false or literary vision, a
barrier between the individual and the direct apprehension of life. I
myself normally wear glasses (slightly tinted, as my eyes are normally

somewhat oversensitive to light). I grabbed and broke two pairs of glasses worn by nurses.

A woman with schizophrenia who believed that a pharmacist was controlling her mind decided "the only way I could escape his influence and radiation was to walk a circuit a mile in diameter around his drugstore."

Similarly Daniel P. Schreber, in his autobiographical account of his illness, described sleeping with his feet out the window and clinging to icy trees with his hands until they were almost frozen in order to accomplish an important goal—such exposure to cold was the only way he could successfully divert the "rays" that afflicted him away from his head. Even bizarre behavior like taking one's clothes off in public may be done for logical reasons. One man with schizophrenia wrote me that he did so in an effort to be pure, like Adam and Eve when they first entered the Garden of Eden.

This same point can be made about everything a person with schizophrenia says and does. It is "crazy" only to the outsider who sits on the sidelines and observes from afar. To someone who will take the time to listen, a person with schizophrenia is not "crazy" at all if by "crazy" one means irrational. The "craziness" has its roots in the disordered brain function that produces erroneous sensory data and disordered thinking.

DECREASED AWARENESS OF ILLNESS

Some people with schizophrenia are aware of the misfunctioning of their brain; this is what is called awareness of illness, or insight. A few of them even tell those around them in the early stages of illness that something is going wrong with their head. One mother remembered her son holding his head and pleading: "Help me, Mom, something is wrong in my head." John Hinckley wrote a letter to his parents (but never sent it), in which he said: "I don't know what's the matter. Things are not going well. I think there's something wrong with my head." One of the most poignant stories I have ever heard concerned a very bright teenage boy who realized that something was going wrong with his brain in the earliest stages of the disease and then spent months in the local medical libraries researching the illness before his symptoms became too severe. In another instance a parent told me that her son "had diagnosed himself as having schizophrenia" before anyone in the family fully realized that he was sick.

Such awareness of illness in the early stages is often lost as the disease becomes fully manifest. This is not surprising since it is the brain that is malfunctioning and it is also the brain that we use to think about ourselves. In fact, I am always surprised at the many patients with schizophrenia who have awareness of their illness. Even in the stage of chronic illness an occasional person with schizophrenia will exhibit surprising insight. One woman, afflicted by schizophrenia for many years, wrote me that she would gladly "sacrifice my right arm to make my brain work." Another woman who had had severe schizo-phrenia for seven years, when I asked her what she was asking for at Christmas, looked at me sadly, paused for a moment, and then replied: "A mind."

Decreased awareness of illness is also found in other diseases of the brain. In Alzheimer's disease, for example, the affected individual is often aware of the illness when it first begins but then loses awareness as it progresses. Former president Ronald Reagan publicly announced his illness when it began, but as the disease progressed he lost all awareness and was even unable to identify members of his family. Decreased awareness of illness is also seen in other forms of dementia and in some individuals following strokes. Some poststroke victims will even deny that their arm or leg is paralyzed, despite the obvious visible evidence that it is. Decreased awareness of illness is officially referred to in neu-rological terms as anosognosia.

It is known that decreased awareness of illness is caused by damage to specific parts of the brain, especially portions of the frontal lobe, cin-gulate, and areas in the right cerebral hemisphere. Thus, some individu-als with schizophrenia have complete awareness of their illness, others have partial awareness, and some have no awareness, depending on the specific brain areas affected. It is also known that awareness of illness may fluctuate in some individuals over time; during periods of remis-sion, when the disease process is quiescent, the person may have good awareness, but during relapses, when the disease process is active, this awareness may be lost.

Decreased awareness of illness in individuals with schizophrenia has been observed for many years but only recently studied. In 1869 the *American Law Review* noted: "Generally, insane persons do not regard themselves as insane, and, consequently, can see no reason for their confinement other than the malevolent designs of those who have deprived them of their liberty." In the 1990s there was an outpouring of research on awareness of illness in schizophrenia; many of these are summarized in the book *Insight and Psychosis*, listed at the end of this chapter. Scales to assess such awareness have been developed and have revealed that approximately half of all individuals with schizophrenia have either moderately or severely impaired awareness of their illness.

The consequences of decreased awareness of illness for individuals with schizophrenia are legion. On the positive side, it has been shown that those with decreased awareness of their illness are less depressed and probably have a lower incidence of suicide, as one would expect. On the negative side, lack of awareness of illness is the largest single cause of the need for involuntary hospitalization and medication, major problems that are discussed in chapter 11.

THE BLACK-RED DISEASE

Schizophrenia, then, is a disorder of the brain. The distinguished neurologist C. S. Sherrington once referred to a normal brain as "an enchanted loom," taking the threads of experience and weaving them into the fabric of life. For persons whose brains are afflicted with schizophrenia the loom is broken, and in some cases appears to have been replaced by a Waring blender that produces jumbled thoughts and loose associations. Given the resulting cerebral cacophony, is it any wonder that patients with this disease often describe their life as like being in the Twilight Zone?

Imagine what it would be like to have the alterations of the senses, the inability to interpret incoming stimuli, the delusions and hallucinations, changes in bodily boundaries, emotions, and movements that are described above. Imagine what it would be like to no longer be able to trust your brain when it told you something. As one very articulate woman with schizophrenia explained to me, the problem is one of "a self-measuring ruler"—that is, you must use your malfunctioning brain to assess the malfunction of your brain. Is it any wonder that people with this disease get depressed? Is it any wonder that they frequently feel humiliated by their own behavior? If a worse disease than schizophrenia exists, it has not come to light. One young man with the disease captured its essence in a poem entitled "Lost":

Gigantic tides have overwhelmed me
I don't see anymore
Swept to the bottom of the
oceans floor.
The great pull has drawn me beneath
to the bottom
I can't hear anymore
What had he said?
I may never see home again
It feels that way
down here
Dead on the oceans floor
I'm so sad
I can't pull against the tow
I'm trapped
I'm gone
I'll never relive again
Somebody has pressed a pillow
against my face and
I can't breathe

How can family and friends of persons with schizophrenia understand what they are going through? Taking mind-altering drugs will produce alterations of the senses and even delusions that may resemble schizophrenia briefly, but it is not recommended that families use these drugs. A better way to understand the experience of having schizophrenia is to take a walk by yourself through an art museum and pretend that you are inside some of the pictures. (It is better not to tell your friends that you are doing this; they may worry about *your* mental status.) Some of the works described below are reproduced on the following pages.

Begin with works by Vincent van Gogh painted in late 1888 and 1889 when he was undergoing a psychosis; "The Starry Night" and "Olive Grove with White Cloud" especially illustrate van Gogh's distorted perception of light, colors, and texture. Van Gogh was especially insightful about his illness. In describing his painting "The Garden of St. Paul's Hospital," done in 1889 while he was hospitalized, he wrote:

You will realize that this combination of red-ocher, of green gloomed over by gray, the black streaks surrounding the contours, produces something of the sensation of anguish, called "noir-rouge," from which certain of my companions in misfortune frequently suffer.

This, then, is the "noir-rouge," or black-red disease.

Many other artists, although they themselves were not psychotic, included in their artistic creations elements that are reminiscent of the perceptions of people with schizophrenia. Joan Miró, for example, in paintings such as "Portrait IV, 1938," "Head of a Woman, 1938," and "Head of a Catalan Peasant," shows facial features as grossly distorted and disjointed. The viewer of a painting such as "Nude Woman" by Pablo Picasso is faced with the perplexing task of synthesizing the individual pieces into a whole, a task not unlike that faced every day by some individuals with schizophrenia. Marcel Duchamp's "Nude Descending a Staircase" suggests the jerky movements, lack of coordination, and clumsiness complained of frequently by persons with schizophrenia; this painting was specifically cited by one woman with schizophrenia symptoms from viral encephalitis to illustrate to the doctor how she felt.

Distorted emotions are evoked in several paintings of Henri Rousseau. Imagine yourself in "The Dream," for example, with eyes staring at you and unnamed terrors lurking behind every bush. Move on to lithographs or paintings by Edvard Munch, such as "The Scream," which mirrors the depression, despair, and loneliness of schizophrenia; the woman in the picture is covering her ears just as some patients do to try to shut out the auditory hallucinations. Finally, end your tour of the art museum at Hieronymus Bosch's "Garden of Earthly Delights." Study the tortures designed by Bosch for the "Hell" portion of the triptych, and think about the fact that the experience of having schizophrenia is much worse than anything Bosch ever imagined.

In summary, schizophrenia is a disease in which the brain, the essence of being, plays cruel tricks on the person affected. Kathy Bick, in the earliest stages of what was to become severe schizophrenia, poignantly captured that strangeness in her diary: "Something inside me is going thru this funny, alien state, a sense of being at the mercy of some strange force, and this pathetic scarecrow figure inside me at the mercy of other forces." Given the disordered brain function as a starting point, many persons with schizophrenia are heroic in their attempts to keep a mental equilibrium. And the proper response of those who care about the unfortunate persons with this disease is patience and understanding. Perhaps nowhere is this better illustrated than by Balzac's heroine in "Louis

Vincent van Gogh, "Starry Night," painted in 1889 while he was intermittently psychotic, shows distortions of textures, light, and color as perceived by some individuals with schizophrenia. (The Museum of Modern Art, New York. Acquired through the Lillie P. Bliss Bequest. Oil on canvas, 29" × 36".)

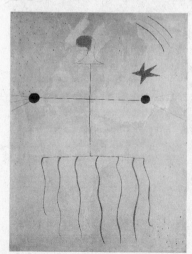

Joan Miró, "Head of a Catalan Peasant," painted in 1924, shows facial features grossly disjointed and distorted. (National Gallery of Art, Washington, D.C., gift of the Collectors Committee, 1981.)

Pablo Picasso, "Nude Woman," a work from 1910, presents the viewer with the perplexing task of synthesizing the pieces into a coherent whole; this is not unlike the task faced every day by some persons with schizophrenia. (National Gallery of Art, Washington, D.C., Alisa Mellon Bruce Fund.)

Marcel Duchamp, "Nude Descending a Staircase," painted in 1912, illustrates the disjointed perceptions and lack of coordination that often accompany schizophrenia. (Philadelphia Museum of Art, Louise and Walter Arensberg Collection. Oil on canvas, 58" × 35".)

Henri Rousseau, "The Dream," painted in 1910, evokes the dreamlike, other-worldly quality of life expressed by some patients, as well as the unnamed terrors of watching eyes described in paranoid schizophrenia. (The Museum of Modern Art, New York, gift of Nelson A. Rockefeller. Oil on canvas, 6' 8" × 9' 9".)

Edvard Munch, lithograph "The Scream" was created in 1895 as an expression of anxiety and fear. It also mirrors the despair, depression, and bewilderment of auditory hallu-cinations experienced so often in schizophrenia. (National Gallery of Art, Washington, D.C., Rosenwald Collection.)

Lambert," a young woman who married a man who developed schizophrenia. She then dedicates her life to caring for him:

> "No doubt Louis appears to be 'insane,'" she said, "but he is not so, if
> the word insanity is applied only to those whose brain, from unknown
> causes, becomes vitiated, and who are, therefore, unable to give a rea-
> son for their acts. The equilibrium of my husband's mind is perfect. If
> he does not recognize you corporeally, do not think that he has not
> seen you. He is able to disengage his body and to see us under another
> form, I know not of what nature. When he speaks, he says marvellous
> things. Only, in fact often, he completes in speech an idea begun in the
> silence of his mind, or else he begins a proposition in words and fin-
> ishes it mentally. To other men he must appear insane; to me, who lives
> in his thought, all his ideas are lucid. I follow the path of his mind; and
> though I cannot understand many of its turnings and digressions, I
> nevertheless reach the end with him. Does it not often happen that
> while thinking of some trifling matter, we are drawn into serious
> thought by the gradual unfolding of ideas and recollections? Often,
> after speaking of some frivolous thing, the accidental point of depar-
> ture for rapid meditation, a thinker forgets, or neglects to mention the
> abstract links which have led him to his conclusions, and takes up in
> speech only the last rings in the chain of reflections. Common minds
> to whom this quickness of mental vision is unknown, and who are
> ignorant of the inward travail of the soul, laugh at dreamers and call
> them madmen if they are given to such forgetfulness of connecting
> thoughts. Louis is always so; he wings his way through the spaces of
> thought with the agility of a swallow; yet I can follow him in all his
> circlings. That is the history of his so-called madness."

Such dedication and understanding, unachievable except in fiction,
is a worthy ideal. It exists to some degree in many families and among
some professionals who must care for such individuals on the wards of
mental hospitals or in outpatient clinics. As Louis Lambert's wife illustrates, compassion follows understanding. It is therefore incumbent on
us to understand as best we can; the burden of disease will become
lighter for all.

RECOMMENDED FURTHER READING

Amador, X. F., and A. S. David, eds. *Insight and Psychosis*. New York: Oxford University Press, 1998.

Chapman, J. "The Early Symptoms of Schizophrenia." *British Journal of Psychiatry* 112 (1966): 225–51.

Cutting, J., and F. Dunne. "Subjective Experience of Schizophrenia." *Schizophrenia Bulletin* 15 (1989): 217–31.

DeVries, M. W., ed. *The Experience of Psychopathology*. Cambridge: Cambridge University Press, 1992.

Dworkin, R. H. "Pain Insensitivity in Schizophrenia: A Neglected Phenomenon and Some Implications." *Schizophrenia Bulletin* 20 (1994): 235–48.

Freedman, B. J. "The Subjective Experience of Perceptual and Cognitive Disturbances in Schizophrenia: A Review of Autobiographical Accounts." *Archives of General Psychiatry* 30 (1974): 333–40.

Kaplan, B., ed. *The Inner World of Mental Illness*. New York: Harper and Row, 1964.

Kring, A. M., S. L. Kerr, D. A. Smith, and J. M. Neale. "Flat Affect in Schizophrenia Does Not Reflect Diminished Subjective Experience of Emotion." *Journal of Abnormal Psychology* 102 (1993): 507–17.

McGhie, A., and J. Chapman. "Disorders of Attention and Perception in Early Schizophrenia." *British Journal of Medical Psychology* 34 (1961): 103–16.

North, C. *Welcome Silence: My Triumph over Schizophrenia*. New York: Simon and Schuster, 1987.

Sechehaye, M. *Autobiography of a Schizophrenic Girl*. New York: Grune & Stratton, 1951. Paperback by New American Library. Part 2 of the book, a psychoanalytic interpretation of the woman's symptoms, should be skipped.

Sommer, R., J. S. Clifford, and J. C. Norcross. "A Bibliography of Mental Patients' Autobiographies: An Update and Classification System." *American Journal of Psychiatry* 155 (1998): 1261–64.

3

DEFINING SCHIZOPHRENIA: VIEW FROM THE OUTSIDE

To one who is mad, the world is still real, but it has a new meaning; people are real too, close and powerful and perhaps dangerous, but among them all the individual is alone. That is the central feature when we penetrate insanity. Not that the world is less with us, but that another world pervades it too, and we, seeing and experiencing life upon a different plane, are cut off from communication with the sane around us: the sane and blinkered folk who do not see and must not know or would never believe the vast, vital, urgent and perhaps cataclysmic truths of which we, alone among them, are aware.

—Morag Coate, 1965

The definition of most diseases of mankind has been accomplished. We can define typhoid fever by the presence of the bacteria that cause it, kidney failure by a rise in certain chemicals in the blood, and cancers by the appearance of the cells under the microscope. In most diseases there is something that can be seen or measured, and this can be used to define the disease and separate it from nondisease states.

Not so with schizophrenia! Although there are numerous abnormalities in brain structure and function, there is no single thing that can be measured and from which we can then say: Yes, that is schizophrenia. Because of this, the definition of the disease is a source of continuing debate. This situation is exacerbated because of the probability that schizophrenia includes more than one disease entity.

Since we do not yet have any definitive measures for schizophrenia, we must define it by its symptoms. This may be misleading, however, for different diseases may cause the same symptoms. For example, a pain in the abdomen is a symptom, but the diseases that may cause this symptom number well over one hundred. Thus, to use symptoms to define diseases is risky. Such is the state of the art with schizophrenia; yet precise diagnosis is of utmost importance. It both determines the appropriate treatment for the patient and provides the patient and family with an informed prognosis. It also makes research on the disease easier because it allows researchers to be certain they are talking about the same thing.

OFFICIAL CRITERIA FOR DIAGNOSIS

Although there is no single symptom that is found only in schizophrenia, there are several that are found very uncommonly in diseases other than schizophrenia. When these are present they should elevate the index of suspicion considerably. Eugen Bleuler, a Swiss psychiatrist, believed that

SCHNEIDER'S FIRST RANK SYMPTOMS FOR SCHIZOPHRENIA

1. Auditory hallucinations in which the voices speak one's thoughts aloud
2. Auditory hallucinations with two voices arguing
3. Auditory hallucinations with the voices commenting on one's actions
4. Hallucinations of touch when the bodily sensation is imposed by some external agency
5. Withdrawal of thoughts from one's mind
6. Insertion of thoughts into one's mind by others
7. Believing one's thoughts are being broadcast to others, as by radio or television
8. Insertion by others of feelings into one's mind
9. Insertion by others of irresistible impulses into one's mind
10. Feeling that all one's actions are under the control of others, like an automaton
11. Delusions of perception, as when one is certain that a normal remark has a secret meaning for oneself

loosening of associations in the thinking process was central to the disease. Similarly, Kurt Schneider, a German psychiatrist, proposed a list of symptoms that he called "first rank" symptoms, meaning that when one or more of them are present they point strongly toward schizophrenia as the diagnosis.

These symptoms are used informally in European countries for the diagnosis of schizophrenia, but less so in the United States. Studies have shown that at least three-quarters of patients with schizophrenia have one or more of these symptoms. However, they cannot be considered as

---

DSM-IV CRITERIA FOR SCHIZOPHRENIA

1. Symptoms of illness have been present for at least six months.
2. There has been some deterioration of functioning from previous levels in such areas as work skills, social relations, and self-care.
3. The disease symptoms do not suggest organic mental disorders or mental retardation.
4. The disease symptoms do not suggest manic-depressive illness.
5. Either a, b, or c must be present:
   a. Two of the following for a significant portion of time for at least a one-month period:
      • delusions
      • hallucinations
      • disorganized speech (e.g., frequent loose associations or incoherence)
      • grossly disorganized or catatonic behavior
      • negative symptoms (e.g., emotional flattening, severe apathy), *or*
   b. Bizarre delusions that other people in the individual's subculture regard as totally implausible, e.g., the belief that thoughts are being taken out of a person's head and broadcast over the radio, or
   c. Prominent auditory hallucinations consisting of voices keeping up a running commentary on a person's behavior, or two or more voices conversing with each other.

definitive for schizophrenia because they are also found in at least one-quarter of patients with manic-depressive illness.

Until 1980, the term "schizophrenia" was used much more loosely and broadly in the United States than in most European countries. In fact, the only other country in the world where schizophrenia was diagnosed as loosely was the former Soviet Union, where it was abused as a label to discredit and stigmatize opponents of the government.

American psychiatry took a major step forward in 1980 when it adopted a revised system of diagnosis and nomenclature in the third edition of the *Diagnostic and Statistical Manual of Mental Disorders*, usually referred to as *DSM-III*. This was followed by revisions in 1987 (known as *DSM-III-R*) and then by further revisions in 1994 (*DSM-IV*). Under this system a diagnosis of schizophrenia can be made only when specific criteria have been fulfilled. The official diagnostic criteria used in European countries are those found in the *International Classification of Diseases*, 10th edition (*ICD-10*), which differs only slightly from *DSM-IV*.

The *DSM-IV* criteria for schizophrenia have achieved wide acceptance in the United States and may be utilized by families who are seeking a definition of the disease. If these criteria are not met, an official diagnosis of schizophrenia should not be made.

Lists of symptoms such as the above give the impression that schizophrenia is relatively easy to diagnose. In its fully developed form it usually is, but in the earlier stages it may be difficult to diagnose with certainty. The symptoms may appear intermittently or may be relatively mild, and the affected individual may be able to cover up some manifestations of the disease. It is therefore quite common for mental illness professionals to write "rule out schizophrenia" on their initial encounter with a patient, which simply means that their diagnosis is tentative until the clinical picture is clearer.

Requiring that symptoms be present for at least six months before schizophrenia can be diagnosed is a sharp departure from traditional American practice. It is a useful advance, however, for schizophrenia is a serious diagnosis and should not be applied indiscriminately to someone with any schizophrenia-like symptom, however brief, as happened frequently in the past. For persons with schizophrenia-like symptoms of less than six months' duration, the *DSM-IV* recommends the use of schizophreniform disorder as a diagnosis. If the duration is less than one month, a diagnosis of brief psychotic disorder is used.

Although the *DSM-IV* criteria have been valuable in clarifying the diagnosis of schizophrenia, problems persist. Diagnosis continues to be based on the psychiatrist's subjective evaluation of patients' behavior and what patients say they are experiencing. What is clearly needed, and may be available before many years, are objective measures for diagnosis, such as laboratory tests of blood and cerebrospinal fluid. Until that time, criteria for the diagnosis of schizophrenia will continue to be debated and will require skilled clinical judgment.

A highly publicized experiment carried out by Dr. David L. Rosenhan, a psychologist at Stanford University, in 1973 illustrates some of the ongoing diagnostic problems. Rosenhan had volunteers go to psychiatric hospitals seeking admission and claiming to be hearing voices that had lasted for three weeks. Auditory hallucinations of any kind are unquestionably important and common symptoms of schizophrenia, with the majority of patients experiencing them at some point in the course of their illness. They are so important as symptoms that most psychiatrists take their presence as an indication of schizophrenia until proven otherwise. Thus, it should not have been surprising that all the volunteers were admitted as genuine patients. Rosenhan used this study to mock psychiatrists and their ability to diagnose patients, but this is erroneous. It would have been much *more* disturbing if these volunteers, who said they were being greatly troubled by the voices, had *not* been admitted for further investigation. Auditory hallucinations are to schizophrenia what abdominal pain is to appendicitis or vomiting blood is to a peptic ulcer. They are all danger signs suggesting that more definitive studies need to be done. The late Dr. Seymour Kety illustrated the fallacy of the Rosenhan study nicely:

> If I were to drink a quart of blood and, concealing what I had done, come to the emergency room of any hospital vomiting blood, the behavior of the staff would be quite predictable. If they labeled and treated me as having a bleeding ulcer, I doubt that I could argue convincingly that medical science does not know how to diagnose that condition.

SUBTYPES OF SCHIZOPHRENIA

During the last half of the nineteenth century different subtypes of what we now call schizophrenia were described as separate diseases. Thus, paranoid psychosis was initially characterized in 1868, hebephrenia in 1871, and catatonia in 1874. These three were grouped together in 1896 by Emil Kraepelin and called dementia praecox (dementia of early life). Bleuler changed the name to schizophrenia in 1911 and added the simple schizophrenia subtype as well.

Since that time these subtypes of schizophrenia have continued to be widely used. Their differentiation is based exclusively on the symptoms of the illness. Thus, paranoid schizophrenia is characterized by delusions and/or hallucinations with a predominantly persecutory or, less commonly, a grandiose content. Hebephrenic schizophrenia, called the "disorganized type" in the *DSM-IV* nomenclature, has as its predominant symptoms disorganized speech, disorganized behavior, and flat or inappropriate affect. Catatonic schizophrenia is diagnosed when the outstanding features of the disease are behavioral disturbances, such as posturing, rigidity, stupor, and often mutism. And simple schizophrenia, not included as a separate entity under *DSM-IV,* is characterized by an insidious loss of interest and initiative, withdrawal, blunting of emotions, and the absence of delusions or hallucinations.

The validity and utility of these subtypes are very questionable despite their widespread usage. Few patients fall cleanly into one subtype or another, with most having some mix of symptoms. Of greater concern is the fact that persons with schizophrenia often show a shift in their symptoms over time, so that initially the person may appear to be a catatonic subtype but a few years later may have symptoms of a hebephrenic nature. Even the old psychiatric axiom "Once a paranoid, always a paranoid" has been found not to hold up; I have seen many patients who present initially classic paranoid schizophrenia symptoms and five years later may have a quite different constellation of symptoms. For these reasons there has been an increasing tendency among psychiatrists in recent years to diagnose most patients as having the "undifferentiated type," which simply means that their symptoms are mixed, and to rely less on the traditional four-part division.

Another method of subtyping schizophrenia that has been used by researchers divides patients into those with predominantly "positive" symptoms and those with predominantly "negative" symptoms. Although the use of "positive" as an adjective for any symptoms seems like a contradiction of terms, it denotes those symptoms that are present but should be absent (e.g., delusions, hallucinations, thinking disorders such as loose associations). "Negative" symptoms, on the other hand, describe the absence of characteristics that should be present (symptoms include apathy, social withdrawal, poverty of thoughts, blunting of emotions, slowness of movement, lack of drive). This division has been elaborated into type I (those with predominantly "positive" symptoms) and type II (those with predominantly "negative" symptoms) by some researchers who claim that these are separate diseases. Whether or not this is so remains to be ascertained.

DELUSIONAL DISORDERS

What are the outer boundaries of the schizophrenia disease spectrum? This is an ongoing and hotly debated question, and there are, in fact, few murkier diagnostic lands to enter than the shadowy terrain lying at the borderlands of schizophrenia. Travelers to this region must have a high tolerance for ambiguity.

Delusional disorders are said to occur in individuals who have delusions but who do not meet the full criteria for schizophrenia. Such delusions may be paranoid delusions (e.g., the belief that you are being followed), delusions of jealousy (e.g., the belief that your spouse is being unfaithful), delusions of erotomania (e.g., the belief that a famous person is in love with you), or somatic delusions (e.g., the belief that you have a fatal disease). The hallmark of a delusional disorder is that the delusion is untrue but not unreasonable, that apart from the delusion the person's functioning is not impaired, and that hallucinations are either absent or not prominent.

The precise relationship of delusional disorders to schizophrenia is still to be determined. Most clinicians and researchers suspect that delusional disorders are a less developed form of schizophrenia, but this is not proven.

SCHIZOTYPAL, SCHIZOID, PARANOID, AND BORDERLINE PERSONALITY DISORDERS

Schizotypal Personality Disorder

These individuals were in the past said to have such things as borderline schizophrenia, ambulatory schizophrenia, pseudoneurotic schizophrenia, latent schizophrenia, subclinical schizophrenia, and schizophrenic character. They have oddities and eccentricities of perception, thinking, speech, and behavior. To meet criteria for this diagnosis under *DSM-IV* the individual should have at least five of the following:

- ideas of reference, meaning that the person frequently thinks that other people are talking about him/her

- odd beliefs or magical thinking that influence behavior and are inconsistent with subcultural norms (e.g., superstitiousness, belief in clairvoyance, telepathy, or "sixth sense"; in children and adolescents, bizarre fantasies or preoccupations)

- unusual perceptual experiences, including bodily illusions

- odd thinking and speech (e.g., vague, circumstantial, metaphorical, over-elaborate, or stereotyped)

- suspiciousness or paranoid ideation

- inappropriate or constricted affect

- behavior or appearance that is odd, eccentric, or peculiar

- lack of close friends or confidants other than first-degree relatives

- excessive social anxiety that does not diminish with familiarity and tends to be associated with paranoid fears rather than negative judgments about self

Schizoid Personality Disorder

These individuals are loners and have virtually no friends. They avoid social situations and seek employment in which they do not have to interact with others (e.g., forest ranger, computer programmer). Schizoid men rarely marry. Such individuals appear incapable of experiencing feelings for others, either those of affection or those of hostility, and are relatively indifferent to praise or criticism. Some also appear to be detached from their environment as if in a perpetual fog.

Paranoid Personality Disorder

These individuals are known for their hypersensitivity, mistrust, and suspiciousness of other people's motivations. They are always on guard, easily slighted, and quick to take offense. They believe that others are trying to trick or harm them, and will go to great lengths to prove it. They question the loyalty of others and often see plots where nobody else can see them. They are often rigid, argumentative, and litigious. Many are interested in electronics and mechanical devices that can be used for spying. They appear to have few tender feelings, disdain weak people, and lack any sense of humor. The dividing line between a paranoid personality disorder and a paranoid delusional disorder is a very narrow one, with the latter having a fully developed delusion.

Borderline Personality Disorder

Borderline personality disorder is a most unfortunate term, since it is invariably confused with the older term *borderline schizophrenia,* now categorized as schizotypal personality disorder. Individuals with borderline personality disorder are unstable in their behavior, relationships, and moods. Their behavior is often impulsive and unpredictable in such areas as money management, sex, alcohol and drug abuse, gambling, shoplifting, fights, reckless driving, and suicide gestures. Their relationships are intense but shift markedly over short periods of time. Their mood also shifts unpredictably and often includes temper tantrums or outbursts.

Controversy continues regarding the validity of these personality disorders and their relationship to schizophrenia. It is widely acknowledged that the personality disorders overlap and that many individuals have combinations of these traits. Studies of families of individuals with schizophrenia have found more relatives with schizotypal and paranoid personality disorders, suggesting that they are probably genetically related to schizophrenia. They can, in a theoretical sense, be considered a mild form of the disease. This possibility, generally referred to as the "spectrum concept" of schizophrenia, implies that there may be individuals at all points on the spectrum between mild personality disorders and severe schizophrenia. The concept has received support from the finding that many individuals with schizotypal personality disorder feel better and function better on low doses of antipsychotic drugs. On the other hand, there is no evidence that borderline personality disorder is related to schizophrenia. Studies of the family history of those with borderline personality disorder suggest that it may be related to major depression or manic-depressive illness.

The definitive word on the relationship of these various personality disorders to true schizophrenia will depend on the development of objective, laboratory criteria for making the diagnosis. Until that time, it is advisable to restrict the diagnosis of schizophrenia to individuals who meet the full criteria. Claiming that everyone with eccentricities or unusual thinking has "mild schizophrenia" is a slippery slope that the former Soviet Union slid down when it used schizophrenia as a label for its political dissidents and involuntarily hospitalized them in psychiatric hospitals. Recent studies in the Netherlands and Australia reported that schizotypal personality traits are more common than was expected among the general population. This is clearly an area where it is wise to err on the conservative side in our attempts to determine the outer boundary of schizophrenia.

SCHIZOAFFECTIVE DISORDER AND MANIC-DEPRESSIVE ILLNESS

Among psychiatric researchers, the relationship of schizophrenia to schizoaffective disorder and manic-depressive illness is just as controversial as the diagnostic borderlands discussed above.

The division of the psychoses into dementia praecox (now called schizophrenia) and manic-depressive illness was proposed by Emil Kraepelin in 1896 and has continued to be widely accepted in psychiatry. In 1980 the American Psychiatric Association under *DSM-III* proposed changing the name of manic-depressive psychosis to bipolar disorder, but the new term offers no significant advantages, and many of us have resisted giving up the older term.

Manic-depressive illness is approximately one-half as prevalent as schizophrenia. It has a modest predilection for women over men and is thought to be disproportionately common in higher socioeconomic groups for unknown reasons. It usually begins before age 30 but, unlike schizophrenia, later onsets are not unusual. Research on the causes of the disease is proceeding along the same lines as that for schizophrenia. A genetic predisposition is clearly established, with some researchers arguing that it is an inherited disease. Biochemical dysfunction in the brain of individuals with manic-depressive illness is also established, with interest centered on serotonin and its metabolites rather than on dopamine. Most biological abnormalities found in schizophrenia (e.g., ventricular enlargement on MRI scans, neurological abnormalities) are also found in manic-depressive illness, although they usually are not as marked.

The major clinical characteristic of manic-depressive illness is episodes of mania, depression, or some combination thereof. Manic episodes consist of an elevated (or occasionally irritated) mood, during which time the person is excessively cheerful, talkative, sociable, expansive, grandiose, energetic, and hypersexual, and often needs little sleep. The person's speech may be rapid (pressured), with ideas thrown out faster than the listener can sort through them (flights of ideas). Grandiosity may proceed to a delusional state (e.g., belief that one is the president), dress may turn flamboyant, and behavior may become dangerous and inappropriate (e.g., buying sprees, foolish investments). Depressive episodes consist of a sad ("dysphoric") mood with hopelessness, poor appetite, sleep disturbances (either insomnia or excessive sleeping), loss of interest in usual activities, loss of sexual desire, loss of energy, slowed thinking, feelings of guilt or worthlessness, and often suicidal ideas. To qualify for these diagnoses under current *DSM-IV* diagnostic standards, a manic episode must last at least one week (or require hospitalization) and a depressive episode must last at least two weeks.

Although the public stereotype of manic-depressive illness is a person who swings from one extreme to the other and back again, this is found only rarely. Some affected persons have a series of manic episodes, some have a series of depressive episodes, while others have the two in every conceivable combination. Many months or even years may separate episodes; between episodes the person is characteristically normal. There are, of course, all gradations of mood swings in either direction within the general population; some people have great energy and cheerfulness as part of their personality, others are chronically self-deprecating and depressed. A person who falls just short of being fully manic is referred to as hypomanic. If a person has numerous mood swings that fail to meet the full criteria for manic-depressive illness, the psychiatric diagnosis used is cyclothymic disorder. Approximately 15 percent of persons with manic-depressive illness commit suicide.

In its classic form, then, manic-depressive illness is easy to differentiate from schizophrenia; the predominant clinical symptoms involve disorders of *mood* rather than disorders of *thought*. Patients with manic-depressive illness may have delusions or hallucinations, but when they occur they accompany and are congruent with the elevated or depressed mood. Most important, manic-depressive illness occurs in discrete episodes with a return to normal functioning between episodes being the rule; schizophrenia rarely occurs in such discrete episodes and residual disability is the rule. Because of their recovery, it is common to find people with manic-depressive illness holding important jobs in government, industry, and the entertainment field, and some traits of the hypomanic (e.g., high energy, inflated self-esteem, decreased need for sleep) lead to greater productivity and success in such fields.

Textbooks of psychiatry and psychology usually imply that patients with psychosis fall neatly into either the schizophrenia or the manic-depressive category and that the two can be readily distinguished. Unfortunately, that is not always the case, as a large percentage of patients have symptoms of both diseases. Furthermore, it is not rare to find patients whose symptoms change over time, appearing initially as a textbook case of schizophrenia or manic-depressive illness, and a year or two later clearly exhibiting symptoms of the other disease. It has been facetiously suggested that either we need to insist that patients read the psychiatric textbooks and choose the disease they wish to have or we must become more flexible in our psychiatric thinking. I personally have seen patients with virtually every possible combination of symptoms of schizophrenia and manic-depressive illness.

The resolution of the problem within the psychiatric establishment has been the creation of an intermediate disease category called *schizoaffective disorder*. Prior to *DSM-III* it was officially included as a subtype of schizophrenia. *DSM-III* classified it independently and noted that "at the present time there is no consensus on how this category should be defined." *DSM-IV* defined schizoaffective disorder as the occurrence of symptoms of major depression or mania concurrent with the symptoms of schizophrenia, but there must be at least a two-week period in which the symptoms of schizophrenia have been present without the depression or mania.

If this sounds like arguments among psychiatrists about how many angels can dance on the head of a pin, to a large extent it is. For patients and families, however, it is often confusing because they think that schizophrenia and schizoaffective disorder are different diagnoses. In fact, they are two aspects of a diagnostic spectrum. At a practical level the diagnosis of schizoaffective disorder implies statistically a somewhat better prognosis than classical schizophrenia, although this may not be true for any given patient. Other than that, the treatments of schizoaffective disorder and schizophrenia are virtually identical, with the same medication being used in both cases.

"MANICDEPHRENIA"

What, then, is the relationship of schizoaffective disorder and manic-depressive illness to schizophrenia? In brief, the answer is not known. In recent years, suggestions have been made increasingly that perhaps Kraepelin was wrong, and that schizophrenia and manic-depressive illness are two ends of a spectrum of a single disease rather than two separate diseases. Perhaps the specific symptoms (e.g., more schizophrenia-like or more manic-depressive-like) are determined by *which specific areas of the brain* are predominantly affected in that person, or by precisely *when in the course of development* the initial brain damage took place.

Geneticists who believe that schizophrenia and manic-depressive illness are genetically caused diseases would like families with these diseases to "breed true," that is, families with schizophrenia should give birth to individuals with schizophrenia and families with manic-depressive illness should give birth to individuals with manic-depressive illness. Often this is the case, but sometimes it is not. Recent studies have shown that families with schizophrenia also give birth to more individuals with manic-depressive illness than would be expected, and that families with manic-depressive illness give birth to more individuals with schizophrenia than would be expected, especially if the person with manic-depressive illness has psychotic symptoms such as delusions or hallucinations. Such cases cause great angst among the geneticists who would like these disorders to fall into a tidy genetic pattern.

The following list summarizes ways in which schizophrenia and manic-depressive illness are alike and ways in which they are different.

ARE SCHIZOPHRENIA AND MANIC-DEPRESSIVE ILLNESS ONE DISEASE OR TWO?

A. How are the two alike?
- both disorders have an excess of people affected who were born in the winter and spring
- both disorders have an excess of admissions and readmissions in the summer
- both disorders have an excess of perinatal complications and dermatoglyphic abnormalities, suggesting an *in utero* origin of some cases
- genes on similar chromosomes (e.g., 10, 13, 18, 22) are suspected of being involved in both disorders
- both disorders show increased developmental abnormalities in some individuals, including delayed motor and language milestones, educational problems, and neurological signs such as poorer coordination, although these are more marked in schizophrenia
- on MRI studies, both show enlarged cerebral ventricles and basal ganglia abnormalities, although these are generally more marked in schizophrenia
- both conditions may have prominent psychotic features such as delusions and hallucinations
- both conditions respond to antipsychotic medication

B. How are the two different?
- schizophrenia is approximately twice as prevalent
- manic-depressive illness is more prevalent in upper socioeconomic groups
- schizophrenia affects men earlier and more severely, whereas manic-depressive illness has a slight predilection for women
- genetic factors are more prominent in manic-depressive illness
- individuals with manic-depressive illness are found more commonly in families with other members so diagnosed, and individuals with schizophrenia are found more commonly in families with other members so diagnosed, but exceptions to this rule are also found

- geographic, perhaps genetic, clustering of cases is more prominent in manic-depressive illness
- schizophrenia produces more marked and more generalized neuropsychological dysfunction, especially on tests of memory and frontal lobe function
- many people with manic-depressive illness have achieved fame for their creativity in the arts
- on MRI, schizophrenia shows greater decrease in brain volume and specific decrease in medial temporal lobe structures (e.g., hippocampus), whereas manic-depressive illness has more white matter hyperintensities
- although neurotransmitters are believed to be involved in both disorders, manic-depressive illness is thought to involve serotonin more prominently and schizophrenia is thought to involve dopamine more prominently
- clinically, manic-depressive illness is much more likely to have a relapsing and remitting course with periods of normality
- affective (mood) symptoms (e.g., depression, mania) are much more common in manic-depressive illness
- manic-depressive illness can be successfully treated by mood stabilizers (e.g., lithium), often with no other medication, but this is not true for schizophrenia
- ECT is more effective for manic-depressive illness
- calcium channel blockers (e.g., verapamil) often improve the symptoms of manic-depressive illness but may make the symptoms of schizophrenia worse

As can be seen, the two disorders share many *antecedents*, including seasonality of birth and admissions, excess perinatal complications and developmental abnormalities, some MRI findings, some clinical symptoms, and response to antipsychotic medications. On the other hand, the two disorders differ significantly in their *expression*, especially on neuropsychological abnormalities, some MRI findings, prominence of affective symptoms, clinical course, and response to mood stabilizers such as lithium.

There are many theoretical schemas that could be put forward to account for these similarities and differences. One, which I personally favor, is to assume that approximately 25 percent of cases of manic-depressive illness and 10 percent of cases of schizophrenia are true genetic diseases, while the remaining cases of both disorders form a continuum ("manicdephrenia"), with the specific symptoms being determined by some combination of genetic predisposition, timing of the etiological insults, and part of the brain primarily affected. In this schema, schizoaffective disorder becomes the name for those cases in the middle of the spectrum. The bottom line, however, is that we are all merely making guesses. When the causes of schizophrenia and manic-depressive illness become clear, we will be better able to definitively determine the relationship of what are presently considered to be two diseases.

RECOMMENDED FURTHER READING

Diagnostic and Statistical Manual of Mental Disorders: DSM-IV. 4th ed. Washington, D.C.: American Psychiatric Association, 1994.

Dickey, C. C., R. W. McCarley, M. M. Voglmaier, et al. "Schizotypal Personality Disorder and MRI Abnormalities of Temporal Lobe Gray Matter." *Biological Psychiatry* 45 (1999): 1393–1402.

Duke, P., and G. Hochman. *A Brilliant Madness: Living with Manic-Depressive Illness*. New York: Bantam Books, 1992.

Jamison, K. R. *An Unquiet Mind: A Memoir of Moods and Madness*. New York: Vintage Books, 1995.

Kendler, K. S., M. C. Neale, and D. Walsh. "Evaluating the Spectrum Concept of Schizophrenia in the Roscommon Family Study." *American Journal of Psychiatry* 152 (1995): 749–54.

Mondimore, F. M. Bipolar Disorder: *A Guide for Patients and Families*. Baltimore: Johns Hopkins University Press, 1999.

Papolos, D., and J. Papolos. *Overcoming Depression*. 3rd ed. New York: HarperCollins, 1997.

Slater, E., and M. Roth. *Clinical Psychiatry*. Baltimore: Williams and Wilkins, 1969. This is the best textbook description of schizophrenia by a wide margin.

Soares, J. C., and S. Gershon, eds. *Bipolar Disorders: Basic Mechanisms and Therapeutic Implications*. Vol. 15 of the series *Medical Psychiatry*. New York: Marcel Dekker, 2000.

Taylor, M. A. "Are Schizophrenia and Affective Disorder Related? A Selected Literature Review." *American Journal of Psychiatry* 149 (1992): 22–32.

Torrey, E. F., and M. B. Knable. "Are Schizophrenia and Bipolar Disorder One Disease or Two? Introduction to the Symposium." *Schizophrenia Research*

39 (1999): 93–94. The entire September 1999 issue of *Schizophrenia Research* (vol. 39, no. 2) is devoted to articles on this subject.

Tyrer, P. "Borderline Personality Disorder: A Motley Diagnosis in Need of Reform." *Lancet* 354 (1999): 2095–96.

Vallés, V., J. Van Os, R. Guillamat, et al. "Increased Morbid Risk for Schizophrenia in Families of In-patients with Bipolar Illness." *Schizophrenia Research* 42 (2000): 83–90.

4

CONDITIONS SOMETIMES CONFUSED
WITH SCHIZOPHRENIA

What consoles me is that I am beginning to consider madness as an illness like any other, and that I accept it as such.

Vincent van Gogh, 1889, in a letter to his brother, Theo

One way to understand a disease is to describe what it is, which was the task of the last chapter. The alternative is to describe what it is not. In the case of schizophrenia this is especially important to do, for in the past the term has been used broadly and imprecisely both in popular culture and in medicine. If we hope to move forward in our understanding of this disease, then we must first be clear what we are talking about.

A "SPLIT PERSONALITY"

Schizophrenia is not a multiple or "split personality," although many people mistakenly believe that it is. A "split personality," as in *Sybil* or *The Three Faces of Eve*, is officially called a dissociative disorder. It is much less common than schizophrenia, occurs almost exclusively in women, and is thought in most cases to be a reaction to sexual or physical abuse in childhood.

In recent years, "dissociative disorder" has become a trendy diagnosis among a few psychiatrists and has been applied to individuals with a wide variety of symptoms. I am even aware of a few patients with clear signs and symptoms of true schizophrenia who have been mistakenly rediagnosed with dissociative disorder. This represents the ultimate confusion for patients and their families: We tell them that schizophrenia is *not* a "split personality," then turn around and mistakenly tell them that some patients who appear to have schizophrenia really have a "split personality." Is it any wonder that families and patients get confused?

PSYCHOSIS CAUSED BY STREET DRUGS

It is a well-recognized fact that many drugs that are abused for their psychic effects may produce symptoms similar to schizophrenia. Even after ingesting a comparatively mild drug like marijuana, the user may experience strange bodily sensations, loss of body boundaries, and paranoid delusions. There is even a subgroup of people who give up using marijuana because it produces an unpleasant paranoid state after each usage. Stronger drugs, such as LSD and PCP, regularly produce hallucinations (although these are more likely to be visual than auditory), delusions, and disorders of thinking. Occasionally these symptoms become so severe that the person must be hospitalized and, if the history of drug abuse is not known, the person may be diagnosed with schizophrenia by mistake. Amphetamines (speed) in particular are well known for producing transient symptoms that may look identical to those of schizophrenia.

The question naturally arises whether drug abuse can *cause* schizophrenia. It is a question asked frequently by families and relatives of patients with this disease. There is now abundant evidence that chronic and repeated usage of many of the mind-altering drugs can damage the brain, impairing intellectual functions and memory. There is virtually no evidence, however, that the use of these drugs can actually *cause* schizophrenia in a person who is not already in the process of getting it.

Why, then, is it so common to see schizophrenia begin after a person has used mind-altering drugs? The answer is probably twofold. First, both drug abuse and the onset of schizophrenia occur in the same age range of the late teens and early twenties. The percentage of people in this age range who have at least smoked a few "joints" is very high. Assuming there is no connection whatsoever between drug abuse and schizophrenia, it would still be expected that a considerable number of people developing schizophrenia would also have tried mind-altering drugs.

Second, and more important, is the common sequence of people developing the early symptoms of schizophrenia and then turning to mind-altering drugs to provide a rationalization for what they are experiencing. Hearing voices for the first time in your life, for example, is a very frightening experience; if you then begin using hashish, PCP, or some similar drug, it provides you with a persuasive reason for hearing the voices. Drug use can put off the uncomfortable confrontation with yourself that tells you something is going wrong—very wrong—with your mind. You are, quite literally, losing it. Drugs, and alcohol as well, may also partially relieve the symptoms. In these cases persons can be said to be medicating themselves; this will be discussed in chapter 11.

The best study of the relationship of street drug use to the onset of schizophrenia was carried out by Drs. Hambrecht and Häfner in Germany. In examining 232 individuals who were experiencing their first episode of schizophrenia, they found that 14 percent had used street drugs, predominantly marijuana. Among those who had used street drugs, 27 percent had used drugs prior to any symptom of schizophrenia, 35 percent had started using street drugs in the same month in which their symptoms began, and 38 percent had not used street drugs until at least one month after the onset of their illness.

The families of persons who are developing schizophrenia are often not aware of the earliest symptoms of the disease. Not knowing what their relative is experiencing, all they see is him/her turning to increasingly heavy drug abuse. Three to six months later, the person is diagnosed with schizophrenia and the family immediately concludes that it was caused by the drug abuse. Such reasoning also relieves any burden of guilt on their part by making it clear that they had nothing to do with causing it. This may be especially attractive to relatives if they are faced with a mental health professional who implies that problems of child rearing or problems of family communication contributed to the genesis of the disease. In these cases, relatives will often seize on drug-abuse-causes-schizophrenia as a defense against the professional.

Ted was a promising college student who had his life well planned. Midway through his sophomore year he began having episodes of euphoria, strange bodily sensations, and ideas that he had been sent to save the world. His grades dropped sharply, he began going to church every day, and then began using LSD. Prior to that time he had used marijuana only occasionally at parties. His roommate, college authorities, and finally his parents became alarmed about his turn to drugs. Within one month he was admitted to the local hospital with symptoms of overt schizophrenia. His parents believe it was caused by his drug use and have never been persuaded otherwise.

PSYCHOSIS CAUSED BY PRESCRIPTION DRUGS

Our society is a drug-using society; young adults abuse street drugs, while older adults use extraordinary numbers of prescription drugs. One only has to open a medicine cabinet in any American home to realize the number of prescription drugs available for ingestion.

Many of these drugs can cause psychiatric symptoms as side effects, ranging from confusion to depression to paranoid delusions or hallucinations. In the majority of cases the hallucinations will be exclusively visual, suggesting that the symptoms are due to drugs or other organic medical conditions. Occasionally the hallucinations may be auditory and the patient may appear to have a sudden onset of classical schizophrenia. For any first episode of psychosis, therefore, the physician should always ask the question: "What medications are you taking?"

Prescription drugs that cause symptoms of psychosis as a side effect almost always do so when they are first started. The psychotic symptoms will go away, sometimes immediately and in other cases more slowly, as soon as the drug is stopped. Many of these drugs cause such symptoms more commonly in elderly individuals and/or at higher doses.

Medications that sometimes cause delusions or hallucinations and may therefore produce a clinical picture that could be confused with schizophrenia are listed in the box. There are undoubtedly others, and just because a specific drug is not listed here does not mean that it cannot cause such symptoms. The interaction of two or more drugs can also produce such symptoms. This list is taken from *the Medical Letter* (volume 40, Feb. 13, 1998) and lists drugs generically with a common trade name in parentheses. Many of these drugs have additional trade names.

MEDICATIONS THAT SOMETIMES CAUSE DELUSIONS OR HALLUCINATIONS

Acyclovir (*Zovirax*)
Alprazolam (*Xanax*)
Amantadine (*Symmetrel*)
Amitriptyline (*Elavil*)
Amphetamine-like drugs
Anabolic steroids
Anticholinergics and
   atropine
Anticonvulsants
Antidepressants, tricyclic
Antihistamine H^1-blockers
Asparaginase (*Elspar*)
Atropine
Baclofen (*Lioresal*)
Barbiturates
Benzodiazepines
Beta-adrenergic blockers
Bromocriptine (*Parlodel*)
Buprenorphine (*Buprenex*)
Bupropion
   (*Wellbutrin; Zyban*)
Caffeine
Captopril (*Capoten*)
Carbamazepine (*Tegretol*)
Cephalosporins
Chlorambucil (*Leukeran*)
Chloroquine (*Aralen*)
Cimetidine (*Tagamet*)
Ciprofloxacin (*Cipro*)
Clomipramine (*Anafranil*)
Clonazepam (*Klonopin*)
Clonidine (*Catapres*)
Cloazepate (*Tranxene*)
Clozapine (*Clozaril*)
Cocaine
Codeine
Corticosteroids
   (prednisone, cortisone,
   ACTH, others)
Cycloserine (*Seromycin*)

Dapsone
Deet (*Off*)
Desipramine *(Norpramin)*
Diazepam *(Valium)*
Digitalis glycosides
Diltiazem (*Cardizem*)
Disopyramide (*Norpace*)
Disulfiram (*Antabuse*)
Dronabinol (*Marinol*)
Erythropoietin (*Epogen*;
   Procrit)
Famotidine (*Pepcid*)
Fenfluramine (*Pondimin*)
Ganciclovir (*Cytovene*)
Histamine H^2-receptor
   antagonists
HMG-CoA reductase
   inhibitors ("statins")
Ifosfamide (*Ifex*)
Interleukin-2
Isoniazid (*INH*)
Levodopa (*Dopar*)
Lidocaine (*Xylocaine*)
Lorazepam (*Ativan*)
Lovastatin (*Mevacor*)
Maprotiline (*Ludiomil*)
Mefloquine (*Lariam*)
Meperidine (*Demerol*)
Methadone (*Dolophine*)
Methandrostenolone
   (*Dianabol*)
Methyldopa (*Aldomet*)
Methylphenidate (*Ritalin*)
Methyltestosterone
Methysergide (*Sansert*)
Metrizamide (*Amipaque*)
Morphine
Nalorphine
Narcotics
Nifedipine (*Procardia*)

Nizatidine (*Axid*)
Norfloxacin (*Noroxin*)
Nortriptyline (*Aventyl*)
Ofloxacin (Floxin)
Oxandrolone (*Anavar*)
Oxymetholone (*Anadrol*)
Penicillin G procaine
Pentazocine (*Talwin*)
Pergolide (*Permax*)
Phentermine (*Fastin*)
Phenylpropanolamine
   (*Dexatrim*)
Phenytoin (*Dilantin*)
Pravastatin (*Pravachol*)
Primidone (*Mysoline*)
Procaine derivatives
Propafenone (*Rythmol*)
Propoxyphene (*Darvon*)
Propranolol (*Inderal*)
Pseudoephedrine
   (in *Actifed*)
Quinidine
Ranitidine (*Zantac*)
Salicylates
Scopolamine
Selegiline (*Eldepryl*)
Simvastatin (*Zocor*)
Sulfonamides
Thiabendazole
   (*Mintezol*)
Tizanidine (*Zanaflex*)
Trazodone (*Desyrel*)
Triazolam (*Halcion*)
Trihexyphenidyl (*Artane*)
Trimethoprim-sulfa-
   methoxazole (*Bactrim*)
Valproic acid (*Depakene*)
Verapamil (*Isoptin*)
Vincristine (*Oncovin*)
Zolpidem (*Ambien*)

PSYCHOSIS CAUSED BY OTHER DISEASES

There are several diseases of the body that can produce symptoms similar to schizophrenia. In most cases there is no ambiguity because the disease is clearly diagnosable; in a few cases, however, there may be some confusion, especially in the early stages of the disease.

There is considerable dispute about how often other diseases mimic schizophrenia and go undetected. In a widely quoted study, Hall and his associates in Texas examined 38 hospitalized patients with schizophrenia and found that 9 percent of them had a medical illness that "caused or exacerbated" the schizophrenia. On the other hand, Koran and his colleagues in California thoroughly studied 269 patients with schizophrenia and found only one patient whose disease (temporal lobe epilepsy) had been missed and was apparently causing the schizophrenia-like symptoms. One English study of 318 hospital admissions with a diagnosis of schizophrenia found 8 percent "with antecedent organic cerebral disorders." Another English study of 268 first admissions with schizophrenia found fewer than 6 percent with relevant organic disease findings. A postmortem study of 200 patients with schizophrenia "found organic cerebral disease thought to be causally related in 11 percent." What is clear is that there is a small subgroup of patients with schizophrenia who have other medical diseases that are causing their symptoms, and that some of these other diseases are treatable.

The most important diseases that may produce symptoms of schizophrenia are as follows.

Brain Tumors

Tumors of the pituitary gland are especially likely to cause symptoms of schizophrenia, but other tumors (e.g., a meningioma of the temporal lobe) may also do so. These are usually detectable on MRI scan and often curable by surgery in their early stages.

Viral Encephalitis

It has been known for many years that viral encephalitis can produce schizophrenia-like symptoms following the encephalitis. What is becoming increasingly clear is that encephalitis occasionally mimics schizophrenia in the early stages of illness, before other signs and symptoms of encephalitis become apparent; how often this occurs is unknown. A recent review of 22 such cases identified a variety of viruses as capable of doing this, including herpes simplex, Epstein-Barr virus, cytomegalovirus, measles, coxsackie, and equine encephalitis. If suspected, most such cases can be diagnosed by lumbar puncture and EEG. It is likely that viral encephalitis also causes many cases of brief psychotic disorders, schizophrenia-like syndromes that last for only a few days. Additional discussion regarding the possible relationship of viruses to schizophrenia can be found in chapter 7.

Temporal Lobe Epilepsy

The relationship between epilepsy and schizophrenia has been a controversial issue for many years. There is agreement, however, that one type of epilepsy—that of the temporal lobe—frequently produces symptoms like schizophrenia. One study found that 17 percent of patients with temporal lobe epilepsy had some symptoms of schizophrenia.

Cerebral Syphilis

Although not seen so much as in the past, syphilis should never be forgotten as a possible cause of schizophrenia-like symptoms. A routine blood test will alert one to its possibility, and a lumbar puncture will confirm the diagnosis.

Multiple Sclerosis

Depression and intellectual deterioration are commonly found in the early stages of multiple sclerosis. Occasionally symptoms of schizophrenia may also occur, with one report of a woman who had symptoms of "paranoid schizophrenia" for 10 years before her multiple sclerosis became fully manifest.

Huntington's Disease

Schizophrenia is said to be "a common initial diagnosis" and "the most frequent persisting mis-diagnosis" in Huntington's disease, a genetic disease beginning in midlife. Once choreiform movements begin in the patient, the correct diagnosis becomes clear.

AIDS

This is the newest addition to the list of diseases that may present with symptoms resembling schizophrenia. It has been clearly established that AIDS may occasionally manifest itself with symptoms of either schizophrenia or manic-depressive illness because of the effect of the human immunodeficiency virus (HIV) on the brain. With the incidence of AIDS increasing, a test for HIV should be included in all routine first admission diagnostic workups for serious mental illness.

Other Diseases

A large number of other diseases have been recorded as occasionally presenting with symptoms similar to schizophrenia. They include the following:

Wilson's disease

acute intermittent porphyria

metachromatic
    leukodystrophy

lupus erythematosus

congenital calcification of
    basal ganglia

adrenal disease

hepatic encephalopathy

pellagra

sarcoidosis

pernicious anemia

metal poisoning
    (e.g., lead,
    mercury)

progressive supranuclear
    palsy

aqueductal stenosis

normal pressure
    hydrocephalus

cerebral vascular accident
    (stroke)

narcolepsy

thyroid disease

insecticide poisoning (e.g.,
    organophosphorus
    compounds)

leptospirosis

tropical infections (e.g.,
    trypanosomiasis,
    cerebral malaria)

For those interested in diseases that may mimic schizophrenia, see the publications by Coleman and Gillberg, Davison, and Lishman listed at the end of this chapter.

PSYCHOSIS CAUSED BY HEAD TRAUMA

Whether or not head injuries can cause psychosis has been hotly debated for over 200 years. In 1800 James Hadfield, who was psychotic and had shot at King George in a failed assassination attempt, was acquitted as insane because he had suffered a severe head injury six years previously. The jury was invited to look at the outer covering of Hadfield's brain, still visible through a hole in his skull.

Major changes in personality, including the onset of psychosis, were clearly documented in studies of penetrating head injuries during the Franco-Prussian and the Russo-Finnish wars. Still unresolved, however, is how often head trauma causes psychosis, how severe the trauma must be, what parts of the brain are affected, and how long the period can be between the trauma and the onset of psychosis.

As a general rule, it is extremely unlikely that head trauma could cause psychosis unless the person had been unconscious for at least several hours following the trauma. In addition, most injuries that are likely to produce psychosis will involve the frontal and especially the temporal lobes. An MRI study of three individuals with a schizophrenia-like psychosis reported that all three had abnormalities in the left temporal lobe.

The main problem arises in trying to assess whether the head trauma is related to the onset of the psychosis. Head trauma and schizophrenia are both more common in young adults and so will occur coincidentally from time to time. Most young adults can recall some instance of head trauma, and associating the trauma with the schizophrenia has an appeal to relatives who may be looking for an explanation for the sickness. Further complicating this assessment is the fact that individuals developing early symptoms of schizophrenia may do irrational things that produce head trauma; the family may not have been aware of the early symptoms and so may associate the onset of the schizophrenia with the trauma. Finally there is the confounding issue of whether the trauma produces the psychosis by direct injury to the brain or by acting as a severe stressor, the straw that broke the camel's back.

PSYCHOSIS WITH MENTAL RETARDATION

Mental retardation is an impairment of cognitive functions measured by the intelligence quotient (IQ). Depending on the person's IQ, mental retardation is divided into mild (50 to 70), moderate (35 to 49), severe (20 to 34), and profound (below 20). It may be caused by chromosomal abnormalities (e.g., Down's syndrome), metabolic diseases (e.g., phenylketonuria), or brain damage from any cause either prior to or after birth. Most individuals with schizophrenia show a mild loss of IQ as measured by their impaired functioning on tests of cognitive skills; their innate IQ is not necessarily impaired, but their ability to demonstrate their IQ is impaired (see chapter 13).

Occasional individuals may have both schizophrenia and mental retardation. Each may arise independently, with the combination merely occurring by chance, or both may be related to a common cause of brain damage. When this occurs it is virtually impossible to get adequate care for the person because treatment facilities are organized either for people with mental illness or mental retardation. In most states such individuals are passed back and forth from one agency to another, each agency disclaiming ultimate responsibility, with the individual made to feel like a leper's leper. Families of such individuals often achieve heroic heights providing services at home with little or no assistance from mental health officials.

The best-known example of co-occurring mental retardation and psychosis was Rosemary Kennedy, sister to John, Robert, and Edward Kennedy. She was mildly retarded in childhood, eventually reaching a fifth-grade level of achievement. At age 21, however, she had the onset of a schizophrenia-like psychosis that alarmed her family. Since antipsychotic medications were not yet available in 1941, she was given a surgical lobotomy. The results of the lobotomy were a disaster, causing severe retardation and brain damage, and she has been confined to a private nursing convent ever since.

INFANTILE AUTISM

Infantile autism, a brain disease of infancy, appears to be unrelated to schizophrenia. This syndrome, beginning within the child's first two and one-half years, is characterized by severe social withdrawal (e.g., the child resists being held or touched), retarded language development, abnormal responses to sensory stimuli (e.g., sounds may overwhelm the child), and a fascination with inanimate objects (e.g., a faucet, the child's own shadow) or repetitive routines (e.g., spinning). It occurs in approximately 4 children per 10,000 and thus is one-twentieth as common as schizophrenia. At one time it was said that autism was more common in higher socioeconomic groups, but that has been disproved. It occurs four times more often in males than in females.

Autism is almost certainly a collection of diseases rather than a single disease. Rett's disorder is a milder form, occurring only in girls. Asperger's disorder is another milder form in which there is normal language development. Autism-like behavior may also be observed in children with the fragile X syndrome, phenylketonuria, viral encephalitis, and other diseases. Epilepsy commonly accompanies autism; approximately one-half of children with autism may have some degree of mental retardation; and a higher than expected percentage of children with autism also have blindness or deafness.

Like schizophrenia, the evidence that autism has biological causes has become overwhelming in recent years; older psychogenic theories such as Kanner's "refrigerator mother" now are completely discredited. There definitely appears to be a genetic component to autism: neuropathological abnormalities occur in the brains of these children, especially in the cerebellum. MRI abnormalities have been found in some studies but not in others. Abnormalities in endocrine function and blood chemistry have also been found. One of the most interesting findings that may relate to the causes of autism is that mothers who give birth to children with autism report having had an unusually high frequency of bleeding during pregnancy, compared with controls. In addition to being found in retrospective studies, the increased bleeding has also been found in a prospective study in which information was collected on a large group of mothers and only later was the data analyzed on those who gave birth to the children with autism.

A variety of medications have been used to treat autism but so far with only modest success. As the child gets older, a small percentage improve and function well. An example of the latter is Temple Grandin, who earned a doctorate and is an assistant professor in the Department of Animal Science at Colorado State University; she documented her illness in her book *Thinking in Pictures*. The majority, however, take on the characteristics of adult schizophrenia with an emphasis on "negative" symptoms (e.g., withdrawal, flattened emotions, poverty of thoughts) rather than "positive" symptoms (e.g., delusions, hallucinations).

Differentiation of infantile autism from childhood schizophrenia is in most cases not difficult. Autism almost always begins before age two and one-half, while schizophrenia is rare before 5 and uncommon before age 10. The child with autism will have prominent withdrawal, language retardation, and repetitive routines, while the child with schizophrenia will have delusions, hallucinations, and thinking disorders. Half the children with autism will be retarded, but far fewer of the children with schizophrenia will be. Finally, children with schizophrenia may have a family history of schizophrenia, but children with autism almost never have such a family history.

ANTISOCIAL PERSONALITY DISORDERS AND SEXUAL PREDATORS

There really should not be confusion between antisocial personality disorders, sexual predators, and schizophrenia, but, because of recent court decisions, there is. Individuals with antisocial personality disorder have a pervasive disregard for other individuals as demonstrated by lying, cheating, breaking laws, injuring others, and feeling no remorse for their actions. They are also referred to as sociopaths, psychopaths, and common criminals. A subset of individuals with antisocial personality disorders also have sexual problems, leading them to rape or to prey on children (pedophilia). They are usually called sexually violent predators, or SVPs.

In 1994 the state of Kansas passed a law allowing the indefinite incarceration of sexually violent predators in public psychiatric hospitals. This law was upheld by the U.S. Supreme Court in 1997 and is usually referred to as the Hendricks decision. In the past, sexually violent predators were handled in the criminal justice system and sentenced to prison, but now they are being sentenced to psychiatric hospitals. At the same time, as described in chapter 1, many individuals with schizophrenia who have been discharged from psychiatric hospitals but who are not receiving treatment may commit crimes as a consequence of their illness and are sentenced to prison. This turnabout of putting prisoners into psychiatric hospitals and psychiatric patients into prisons has led many people to conclude that the system is more insane than most of the patients.

There is no relationship between antisocial personality disorder, sexually violent predators, and schizophrenia. And a study reported that the incidence of antisocial personality disorder among the relatives of individuals with schizophrenia was no higher than among the general population. Whether or not individuals with antisocial personality disorder and sexually violent predators have damage to their brains remains to be demonstrated; if they do, it will be different from the damage that occurs in schizophrenia.

CULTURALLY SANCTIONED PSYCHOTIC BEHAVIOR

Occasionally confusion will arise between schizophrenia and culturally induced or hysterical psychosis. This is an altered state of consciousness usually entered into voluntarily by an individual; while in this altered state of consciousness the person may exhibit symptoms that superficially look like schizophrenia. For example, the person may complain of altered bodily sensations and hallucinations and may behave in an excited and irrational manner. In the United States these conditions are seen most commonly in connection with fundamentalist religious services. In other cultural groups and in other countries, these conditions are known by such names as moth craziness (Navajo Indians), windigo (Cree and Ojibwa Indians), zar (Middle East), koro (China), susto (Latin America), latah (Southeast Asia), and amok (worldwide).

> Cecelia led a perfectly normal life except for the monthly all-night worship service at her fundamentalist church. During the service she claimed to hear voices talking to her, often spoke in tongues, and occasionally behaved in a wild and irrational way so that others had to restrain her. Other members of the congregation regarded her with both fear and awe, suspecting that she was possessed by spirits.

People like Cecelia should not be labeled as having schizophrenia unless there are other symptoms of the disease. Occasionally persons who have schizophrenia will be attracted to fundamentalist religious groups or religious cults, however, since such groups often value hearing voices or "speaking in tongues."

RECOMMENDED FURTHER READING

Achté, K. A., Hillbom, E., and Aalberg, V. "Psychoses Following War Brain Injuries." *Acta Psychiatrica Scandinavica* 45 (1969): 1–18.

Coleman, M., and C. Gillberg. *The Biology of the Autistic Syndromes*. New York: Praeger, 1985.

Coleman, M., and C. Gillberg. *The Schizophrenias: A Biological Approach to the Schizophrenia Spectrum Disorders*. New York: Springer, 1996.

Davison, K. "Schizophrenia-like Psychoses Associated with Organic Cerebral Disorders: A Review." *Psychiatric Developments* 1 (1983): 1–34. An earlier version of the article, widely referenced, was published by Davison and C. R. Bagley as "Schizophrenia-like Psychoses Associated with Organic Disorders of the Central Nervous System" in *Current Problems in Neuropsychiatry*, edited by R. N. Herrington. Ashford, England: Headley Brothers, 1969.

Grandin, T. *Thinking in Pictures*. New York: Vintage Books, 1996.

Hambrecht, M., and Häfner, H. "Substance Abuse and the Onset of Schizophrenia." *Biological Psychiatry* 40 (1996):1155–63.

Lishman, W. A. *Organic Psychiatry: The Psychological Consequences of Cerebral Disorder*. Oxford: Blackwell Science, 1998.

Torrey, E. F. "Functional Psychoses and Viral Encephalitis." *Integrative Psychiatry* 4 (1986): 224–36.

5

ONSET, COURSE, AND PROGNOSIS

Such a disease, which disorders the senses, perverts the reason and breaks up the passions in wild confusion—which assails man in his essential nature—brings down so much misery on the head of its victims, and is productive of so much social evil—deserves investigation on its own merits, by statistical as well as other methods. . . . We may discover the causes of insanity, the laws which regulate its course, the circumstances by which it is influenced, and either avert its visitations, or mitigate their severity; perhaps in a later age, save mankind from its inflictions, or if this cannot be, at any rate ensure the sufferers early treatment.

Dr. William Farr, 1841

When diagnosed with schizophrenia for the first time, the person and his/her family have many questions. Were there predictors of the illness in childhood? Did they miss the earliest symptoms? What are the chances for complete recovery? How independent is the person likely to be 10 years later, or 30 years later? What are the chances of the person spending most of his or her life in a mental hospital or group home? These are important questions, for the answers to them will determine how the family of the person with schizophrenia plans for the future.

CHILDHOOD PRECURSORS

The idea that the earliest manifestations of schizophrenia begin in childhood is not a new one. John Hawkes, a prominent English physician, noted in 1857 that "it is only too probable that, from a much earlier period than the actual manifestation of disease, the fuel has been laid." Similarly, Emil Kraepelin observed in 1919 that "in a considerable number of cases definite *psychic peculiarities* have come under observation in our patients from childhood up."

Formal studies of childhood precursors of schizophrenia date to the 1930s. Within the last decade, however, there has been an outpouring of information on this subject. Many of the best studies have included large groups of children born at a particular time who were intensively studied and tested as children. Many of these children have now reached the age of risk for schizophrenia and so it is possible to examine the childhood records and compare the records of those who do and those who do not have the disease. The largest such birth cohort included 55,000 children born in the United States between 1959 and 1966 (the National Collaborative Perinatal Study), but smaller birth cohorts have been similarly studied in England, Sweden, Finland, Denmark, and Israel.

What these studies show is that there is a subset of children, approximately one-quarter or one-third of those who later develop schizophrenia, who are different as children. These differences include:

1. Delayed developmental milestones in infancy, e.g., slower to walk and talk
2. More language and speech problems
3. Poorer coordination, e.g., not as good at sports, lower grades in physical education
4. Poorer academic achievement
5. Poorer social functioning and fewer friends

It should be emphasized that these childhood precursors are merely *statistical associations* and *not predictors for individual cases*. The majority of individuals who develop schizophrenia are not different in childhood, and in fact one recent study in Finland even found that a disproportionate number of the children who developed schizophrenia had done especially well in school. Conversely, most children who have delayed milestones, language and speech problems, and poor coordination, grades, and social skills will not develop schizophrenia.

Childhood precursors of schizophrenia have also been studied in the offspring of mothers who have schizophrenia (these are so-called "high risk" studies, because it is known that approximately 13 percent of the children will later develop schizophrenia) and among identical twins. In a twin study carried out by the author, for example, among 27 identical twin pairs in which one had schizophrenia and the other twin was well, seven of the twins who later developed schizophrenia were clearly different from the well twin by age 5. Among one pair, for example, both twins could tie their shoes at age 4, but a year later one of them had lost that ability and had also developed an odd gait. Although nothing was found on examination at that time, it was that twin who developed schizophrenia at age 26.

ONSET AND EARLY SYMPTOMS

One of the questions most frequently asked by families is how to identify the early symptoms of schizophrenia. This question is different from that of relapse of the disease, which is discussed in chapter 12. The question is asked by families who are raising difficult teenage children and are wondering if they might be developing schizophrenia. It is also asked by families in which an older child has been diagnosed with schizophrenia and the parents are worried about the younger children.

In thinking about the early symptoms of schizophrenia it is helpful to remember that this disease has a strikingly narrow age of onset. In the United States, three-quarters of those who get schizophrenia do so between ages 17 and 25. Having an initial onset before age 14 or after age 30 is unusual.

Why the onset of schizophrenia occurs in this particular age group is unknown. It should be pointed out, however, that other chronic brain diseases, such as multiple sclerosis and Alzheimer's disease, have particular age ranges of onset and we do not understand the reasons in these diseases either. There are also suggestions that the average age of onset of schizophrenia may be younger in the United States than it is in Europe, that the age of onset for paranoid schizophrenia is older than for the other subtypes, and that the average age of onset in the United States is younger now than it was in the nineteenth century.

There are some individuals for whom it is impossible to date the onset of the disease. As noted above, the family says things such as: "She was always different from the other children" or "Throughout childhood his teachers noticed he was eccentric and told us to get him evaluated." The suggestion in such cases is that the disease process began early in life despite the fact that the full-blown thinking disorder, delusions, and hallucinations did not begin until the late teens or early twenties.

This raises the question of when families with an eccentric child should worry. It is known that the majority of individuals who develop schizophrenia have normal childhoods and are not identifiable in their early years. And it is also known that the vast majority of eccentric children will not develop schizophrenia; many, in fact, grow up to be leaders. The problem of separating the eccentricities of normal childhood from the early symptoms of schizophrenia is especially difficult in adolescence, approximately ages 11 to 13, when the norms of behavior are very strange indeed. Overacuteness of the senses is a common symptom of schizophrenia, yet how many adolescents have not had some such experiences? Moodiness, withdrawal, apathy, loss of interest in personal appearance, perplexity, the belief that people are watching one, preoccupation with one's body, and vagueness in thoughts may all be harbingers of impending schizophrenia, but they may also be just normal manifestations of early adulthood and its accompanying problems. For this reason families should *not* worry about every quirk in their children, but rather should assume they are normal until proven otherwise. This can be particularly difficult for a parent who has already had one child diagnosed with schizophrenia and who is expecting the worst for the younger children, but it is important. A 15-year-old has enough to worry about without being told things like "Don't daydream. That's what your brother did and it got him sick and into the hospital."

At what point *should* parents begin to worry that something may be wrong? When do the normal psychological vicissitudes of early adulthood cross the line and enter the realm of early symptoms of schizophrenia? Researchers in Germany and Canada questioned large numbers of individuals in the first stages of schizophrenia and their families to ascertain the earliest symptoms. The results, together with those from other researchers and my own clinical experience, are summarized in the adjacent box. The most important word in this summary is "changes"—in social behavior, sleep or eating patterns, self-care, school performance, or emotional relationships. Parents may say things such as: "John has become a different person over the last six months" or "None of Jennifer's friends come around anymore, and she doesn't seem to want to see anyone." Such changes may of course be caused by things other than schizophrenia; the use of street drugs must always be considered as a possibility in this age group.

> ## THE MOST COMMON EARLY SYMPTOMS OF SCHIZOPHRENIA AS OBSERVED BY THE FAMILY
>
> - depression
> - changes in social behavior, especially withdrawal
> - changes in sleep or eating patterns
> - suspiciousness or feelings that people are talking about him/her
> - changes in pattern of self-care
> - changes in school performance
> - marked weakness, lack of energy
> - headaches or strange sensations in head
> - changes in emotional relationships with family or close friends
> - confused, strange, or bizarre thinking

It should be emphasized that this list of early symptoms contains those observed by the family. The individual who is in the early stages of schizophrenia may be experiencing things that are not visible to family members, including anxiety, restlessness, difficulty in concentration, and decreased self-confidence. They may also be hearing voices (auditory hallucinations) for weeks or months before family members become aware of it.

CHILDHOOD SCHIZOPHRENIA

It is generally believed that childhood schizophrenia is simply an early version of the adult disease, although much rarer. Approximately two males are affected for every female. Only about 2 percent of individuals with schizophrenia have the onset of their disease in childhood, although that percentage varies depending on where one fixes the childhood–adult line. Schizophrenia beginning before age 5 is exceedingly rare (see section on infantile autism, chapter 4), and between ages 5 and 10 it increases slowly. From age 10, schizophrenia increases in incidence until age 15, when it begins its sharp upward peak as the adult disease.

The symptoms of childhood schizophrenia are very similar to those of adult schizophrenia with the predictable exception that their content is age-related. For example, one study of young children with schizophrenia reported that the source of auditory hallucinations was frequently believed to be pet animals or toys and that "monster themes were common. . . . As age increased, both hallucinations and delusions tended to be more complex and elaborate." The other distinguishing feature of childhood schizophrenia is that the affected child also often has one or more of the following: seizures, learning disabilities, mild mental retardation, neurological symptoms, hyperactivity, or other behavioral problems. In an attempt to resolve this confusion the American Psychiatric Association deleted "childhood schizophrenia" from its official nomenclature and suggested instead using schizophrenia with onset in childhood or "childhood-onset pervasive developmental disorder," a catchall term for many poorly defined brain disorders of childhood.

Like adult schizophrenia, childhood schizophrenia is thought to have some genetic roots, although their relative importance is unclear. It is also known that these children have an excess number of minor physical anomalies and mothers' history of having had excess pregnancy and birth complications. The fact that childhood schizophrenia is a brain disease has been demonstrated by findings of MRI and EEG abnormalities. Recent MRI studies have shown that individuals with childhood-onset schizophrenia continue to have progressive brain changes related to their disease during adolescence.

Childhood schizophrenia is treated with the same antipsychotic medication used for adult schizophrenia. A follow-up of 10 children with this disease from 14 to 34 years after its onset found them still diagnosed with schizophrenia but with relatively few delusions or hallucinations. Instead they tended to be quiet and withdrawn, with poverty of thought and lack of drive. A minority of children with schizophrenia will recover and do quite well as adults, but what percentage this constitutes is uncertain. In general it is thought that the earlier the age of onset of schizophrenia, the worse the outcome is likely to be, but there are major exceptions to this rule. A fictional description of the onset of schizophrenia in a 12-year-old boy was written by Conrad Aiken in "Silent Snow, Secret Snow" (see chapter 14). Louise Wilson, in *This Stranger, My Son,* provides a good account of what it is like to live with a child with this illness.

POSTPARTUM SCHIZOPHRENIA

Some degree of depression in mothers following childbirth is relatively common and on occasion may be severe. Much less common, occurring approximately once in every thousand births, are symptoms of psychosis that develop in the mother. These usually begin between three and seven days postpartum and may include delusions (e.g., the mother believes her baby is defective or has been kidnapped) or hallucinations (the mother hears voices telling her to kill the baby). Because of the unpredictability of such patients, the baby is usually separated from the mother until she improves.

The vast majority of such cases of postpartum psychosis are eventually diagnosed with manic-depressive illness or major depression with psychotic features. A minority will be diagnosed as having schizophrenia. In a recent large study in Denmark, 9 percent of the women with postpartum psychosis were diagnosed with schizophrenia. These women had a poor prognosis; 50 percent were rehospitalized within one year of their initial illness, and 98 percent had relapsed within 10 years.

It is likely in such cases that the childbirth precipitated schizophrenia that would have developed sooner or later. Childbirth is accompanied by massive hormonal changes, and it is known that some women with schizophrenia are especially sensitive to hormonal fluctuations and become more symptomatic just prior to their menstrual period.

LATE-ONSET SCHIZOPHRENIA

Just as there is a form of schizophrenia that begins early in childhood, so there is also a form that begins later in life. Late-onset schizophrenia is variously defined as beginning after the age of 40 or 45. Its precise incidence is unclear, but it is not rare. Many studies of it have been done by Europeans, with less interest having been shown by American researchers. That fact is especially pertinent since the mean age of onset of schizophrenia in general is almost invariably reported as being older in European studies compared to American studies. It seems possible, therefore, that late-onset schizophrenia is of more interest to European researchers because it occurs more commonly there for reasons that are unknown.

Clinically, late-onset schizophrenia is similar to the earlier onset variety except for having a predominance of females affected, having more schizoid and paranoid personality traits in the person before he/she becomes sick, having more paranoid delusions and more visual, tactile, and olfactory (smell) hallucinations, and having fewer "negative" symptoms or thinking disorders. Neuropsychological tests and MRI scans show deficits similar to other forms of schizophrenia.

PREDICTORS OF OUTCOME

Over the years it has been noted that some persons afflicted with schizophrenia recover completely, others recover partially, and some do not recover at all. This observation has led many professionals to review the clinical data taken at the time of the original hospital admission to determine which factors might have predicted a good outcome and which might have predicted a poor outcome. The result of these efforts has been a series of predictive factors, each of which taken by itself has limited usefulness but which taken together may be very useful. From this a subtyping of schizophrenia into good outcome (good prognosis) and poor outcome (poor prognosis) has emerged and is becoming widely used. It is probably the most valid way to classify the disease that has been found to date.

Patients who are more likely to have a good outcome are those who were considered to be relatively normal prior to getting sick. Thus, if as children they were able to make friends with others, did not have major problems with delinquency, and achieved success levels in school reasonable for their intelligence level, their outcome is more likely to be good. Conversely, if they are described by relatives as "always a strange child," had major problems in school or with their peers, were considered delinquent, or were very withdrawn, they are more likely to fall into the poor outcome group.

It has now been clearly established that women with schizophrenia have a more favorable outcome than men. Patients with the best outcome also have no history of relatives with schizophrenia. The more close relatives who have schizophrenia, the poorer the outcome becomes. If there is a history of depression or manic-depressive psychosis in the family, the person is more likely to have a good outcome. Thus, a good outcome is suggested by a family history with no mental disease or only depression and/or manic-depressive illness. A poor outcome is suggested by a family history of schizophrenia.

In general, the younger the age at which schizophrenia develops, the poorer the outcome. A person who is first diagnosed with schizophrenia at age 15 is likely to have a poorer outcome than a person with the onset at age 25. Persons who are first diagnosed with schizophrenia in older age groups, especially over age 30, are more likely to fall into the good outcome group.

The type of onset is an important predictor of recovery, with the best outcomes occurring in those patients whose onset is the most sudden. A relative who describes the gradual onset of the person's symptoms over a period of many months is painting a bleak picture, for it is much more likely that the person will fall into the poor outcome group. Conversely, as a practicing psychiatrist I am very happy when a relative tells me that "John was completely normal up until about a month ago," for I know that such a history bodes well for the future. Awareness of one's illness (insight) is a very good sign, whereas lack of awareness is a bad sign.

The clinical symptoms that are more compatible with a good outcome are predominantly "positive" symptoms, especially paranoid delusions and catatonic behavior. Conversely, predominantly "negative" symptoms, such as withdrawal, apathy, and poverty of thoughts are bad. The presence of normal emotions is good, whereas flattening of emotions is bad. Obsessive and compulsive symptoms are also said to indicate a poor prognosis. If a diagnostic CT or MRI scan is done and it is normal, that is a good sign. If it shows enlargement of the ventricles in the brain and/or atrophy of brain tissue, that is a bad sign. The initial response of the person to antipsychotic medication is a strong indicator of prognosis: the better the response, the better the outcome is likely to be.

It should be emphasized again that each of these factors *by itself* has limited predictive value. It is only when they are all put together that an overall prognosis can be assigned. Many patients will, of course, have a mixture of good and poor outcome signs, whereas others will fall quite clearly into one category or the other.

It should also be remembered that *all predictors are only statistical assertions of likelihood*. There is nothing in the least binding about them. All of us who regularly care for patients with schizophrenia have seen enough exceptions to these guidelines to make us humble about any predictions. Thus, I have seen a patient with a normal childhood, no family history of the disease, a rapid onset at age 22, and initial catatonic symptoms who never recovered from even his initial illness and whose outcome is poor. More optimistically, I have seen patients with virtually every poor prognostic sign go on to almost complete recovery.

PREDICTORS OF OUTCOME

Good outcome	Poor outcome
Relatively normal childhood	Major problems in childhood
Female	Male
No family history of schizophrenia	Family history of schizophrenia
Older age at onset	Younger age at onset
Sudden onset	Slow onset
Paranoid or catatonic symptoms	Predominantly "negative" symptoms
Presence of normal emotions	Flattening of emotions
Good awareness of illness	Poor awareness of illness
Normal CT or MRI	Abnormal CT or MRI
Good initial response to medication	Poor initial response to medication

MALE-FEMALE DIFFERENCES

Although textbooks of psychiatry claim that schizophrenia occurs in equal incidence among men and women, there are suggestions that this may not be accurate and that men may be more commonly affected. Most striking is the earlier age of onset for men, which in the United States occurs three to four years earlier than in women. An analysis of a group of 17- or 18-year-old individuals with schizophrenia will reveal four or five males for every female.

Schizophrenia is also a more serious disease in men than it is in women. Men do not respond as well to antipsychotic drugs, they require higher doses of the drugs, they have a higher relapse rate, and their long-term adjustment—measured by such indices as social life, marriage, work record, suicide rate, and level of function—is not nearly so good as women's. There are, of course, many women with schizophrenia who have had a severe course and many men who have done well, but statistics clearly establish that schizophrenia occurs earlier and in a more severe form in the male.

The reasons for such gender differences, still unknown, provide one of the many questions about schizophrenia needing to be researched. It should be noted that both infantile autism and childhood schizophrenia also have a strong predominance for males, and that male fetuses generally are known to be more susceptible to environmentally caused problems such as infections. The fact that males get schizophrenia both at a younger age and more severely, then, may simply be another reflection of Mother Nature's dictum that in many ways men are the weaker sex. Another speculation about why schizophrenia might be more severe in males is the possibility that female sex hormones (estrogens) may exert an antipsychotic effect and be protective. This possibility has led to some promising trials of estrogen as an add-on medication to treat women with schizophrenia (see chapter 9). It is also possible, although unlikely, that schizophrenia resembles diabetes in having two major subgroups: an early-onset, more severe variety that affects mostly men, and a later-onset, less severe variety more apt to afflict women.

POSSIBLE COURSES: 10 YEARS LATER

For individuals hospitalized with schizophrenia for the first time, the outlook at the end of one year is reasonably optimistic. Dr. Jeffrey Lieberman and his colleagues completed a study of 70 such patients, and at the end of one year 74 percent of them "were considered to be fully remitted" and 12 percent were "partially remitted." For those who went into remission, the mean time for those with a diagnosis of schizophrenia was 42 weeks and for schizoaffective disorder 12 weeks.

The extended prognosis for schizophrenia is less optimistic than this one-year outcome. From the early years of this century, it has been said that there is a rule of thirds determining the possible courses in schizophrenia: a third recover, a third are improved, and a third are unimproved. Recent long-term follow-up studies of persons with schizophrenia both in Europe and in the United States suggest that this rule is simplistic and out of date. It is clear, for example, that the course of the disease over 30 years is better than it is over 10 years. The use of medications has probably improved the long-term course for many patients, while the positive effect of deinstitutionalization has been to decrease dependency on the hospital and increase the number of patients able to live in the community. On the other hand, it is also clear that the mortality rate, especially by suicide, for persons with schizophrenia is very high and apparently increasing.

The best summary of possible courses of schizophrenia was done by J. H. Stephens, who analyzed 25 studies in which there was follow-up for at least 10 years. The percentage of patients "recovered," "improved," or "unimproved" varied widely from study to study depending on the initial selection of patients, e.g., inclusion of large numbers with acute reactive psychosis increased the percentage of fully recovered patients. Utilizing all studies done to date, the ten-year course of schizophrenia can be seen in the chart and more nearly approximates a rule of "quarters" rather than a rule of "thirds":

THE COURSE OF SCHIZOPHRENIA

10 years later

25% completely recovered	25% much improved, relatively independent	25% improved, but requiring extensive support network	15% hospitalized, unimproved	10% dead (mostly suicide)

30 years later

25% completely recovered	35% much improved, relatively independent	15% improved, but requiring extensive support network	10% hospitalized, unimproved	15% dead (mostly suicide)

TWENTY-FIVE PERCENT RECOVER COMPLETELY

This assumes that all patients with symptoms of schizophrenia are part of the analysis, including those who have been sick for less than six months with schizophreniform disorders. If only patients with narrowly defined schizophrenia are included (i.e., "continuous signs of the illness for at least six months"), then the percentage of completely recovered will be under 25 percent. Patients who recover completely do so whether they are treated with antipsychotic medication, wheat germ oil, Tibetan psychic healing, psychoanalysis, or yellow jellybeans, and all treatments for schizophrenia must show results better than this spontaneous recovery rate if they are to be accepted as truly effective. Those who recover also do so within the first two years of illness and usually have had no more than two discrete episodes of illness.

> Andrea became acutely psychotic during her second year of college and was hospitalized for six weeks. She recovered slowly, with medication and supportive psychotherapy over the following six months while living at home, and was able to resume college the following year. She has never had a recurrence. She believes she got sick because of a failed romance and her family, when they refer to the illness at all, talk vaguely of a "nervous breakdown."

Such families often deny that their family member had schizophrenia and rarely join family support groups such as NAMI.

TWENTY-FIVE PERCENT ARE MUCH IMPROVED

These patients usually have a good response to antipsychotic medication, and as long as they take it they continue to do well. They can live relatively independently, can have a social life, may marry, and often are capable of working part- or full-time.

> Peter had a normal childhood and successful high school career. He then married and joined the army to get training and travel. There was no family history of mental illness. At age 21, while assigned to Germany, he began to have strange feelings in his body and later to hear voices. He started drinking heavily, which seemed to relieve the voices, then turned to the use of hashish and cocaine. His condition deteriorated rapidly, and he was arrested for hitting an officer who he believed was trying to poison him. He was hospitalized and eventually discharged from the army with a full service-connected disability. Over the next three years he was hospitalized three more times.

Peter responded slowly to very high doses of medication and was released from the hospital almost completely well. He returned faithfully for an injection of medicine every week, lived in his own apartment, and visited his family (including his divorced wife and children) and friends during the day. He clearly was capable of holding a job, but declined to do so for fear that it would jeopardize his monthly VA disability check. His only remaining symptoms were voices that he heard late in the day that he was able to ignore.

TWENTY-FIVE PERCENT ARE MODESTLY IMPROVED

These patients respond less well to medication, often have "negative" symptoms, and have a history of poorer adjustment prior to the onset of their illness. They require an extensive support network; in communities where this is available they may lead satisfactory lives, but where it is not they may be victimized and end up living on the streets or in public shelters.

Frank was a loner as a child but had considerable musical ability and received a college scholarship. In his third year of college his grades slowly dropped as he complained of continuous auditory hallucinations. Hospitalization and medication produced a modest improvement so that he could eventually be placed in a halfway house in the community. He is supposed to attend a day program but usually walks the street talking to himself or composing music on scraps of paper. He stays completely to himself and needs to be reminded to change his clothes, brush his teeth, and take his medicine.

FIFTEEN PERCENT ARE UNIMPROVED

These are the treatment-resistant patients for whom until recently we had little to offer. Some have responded to second-generation antipsychotic drugs such as clozapine (see chapter 9). Those who do not respond are candidates for long-term asylum care in a sheltered setting. When released into the community, often against their will, the results are frequently disastrous.

Dorothy was known as a quiet child who attained straight As in school. Her mother was hospitalized for schizophrenia for two years during Dorothy's childhood, and a brother was in an institution for the mentally retarded. She was first hospitalized at age 15 for one month;

information on this hospitalization was not obtainable except for a diagnosis of "transient situational reaction of adolescence." Following this, Dorothy dropped out of school, went to work as a domestic, married, and had three children. She apparently remained well until age 22, at which time she believed people were trying to kill her, believed people were talking about her, and heard airplanes flying overhead all day. She neglected her children and housework and simply sat in a corner with a fearful expression on her face. On examination she had a marked thinking disorder and catatonic rigidity and was noted to be very shy and withdrawn.

Over the ensuing fifteen years Dorothy has been hospitalized most of the time and has responded minimally to medication. During the earlier years she was returned to her home for brief periods, with homemaker services; and in more recent years she lived for several months in a halfway house. There she was invariably victimized by men and was judged not to be capable of defending herself. She remains in the hospital, sitting quietly in a chair day after day. She answers politely but with absolutely no emotion and shows marked poverty of thought and of speech.

TEN PERCENT ARE DEAD

Almost all of these die by suicide or accident; other factors will be discussed at greater length below.

POSSIBLE COURSES: 30 YEARS LATER

It has been clearly established in recent years that the 30-year course of schizophrenia is more favorable for the average patient than the 10-year course. This directly contradicts a widespread stereotype about the disease that dates to Kraepelin's pessimistic belief that most patients slowly deteriorate. A major reason for this better long-term prognosis is that aging ameliorates the symptoms of schizophrenia in most people. Symptoms of this disease tend to be most severe when the person is in his/her 20s and 30s, then become somewhat less severe in the 40s, and significantly less severe in the 50s and 60s. We do not understand why this is so and there are, of course, many exceptions, but schizophrenia represents one of the few conditions in life for which aging is an advantage.

The definitive work on the long-term course of schizophrenia has come from studies carried out by Dr. Manfred Bleuler, Dr. Luc Ciompi and his colleagues, Dr. Gerd Huber and his colleagues in Europe, and by Dr. Courtenay Harding and her colleagues on patients deinstitutional-ized from the Vermont State Hospital. Some patients followed up by these groups were as much as 40 years older than when they became ill, and the agreement between the results of the different studies is impres-sive. As summarized by Ciompi for patients followed for an average of 36 years: "About three-fifths of the schizophrenic probands have a favor-able outcome; that is, they recover or show definite improvement." And for patients with chronic schizophrenia in Vermont, followed up by Harding and her colleagues 20 to 25 years after leaving the hospital, "the current picture of the functioning of these subjects is a startling contrast to their previous levels described during their index hospitalization." Approximately three-quarters of the Vermont patients required little or no help in meeting their basic daily needs.

In most patients with schizophrenia, the "positive" symptoms of hallucinations, delusions, and thinking disorders decrease over the years. A person who was severely incapacitated at age 25 by these symptoms may have only residual traces of them at age 50. It is almost as if the dis-ease process has burned itself out over time and left behind only scars from its earlier activity. Patients also learn how to live with their symp-toms, ignoring the voices and not responding to them in public.

The residual phases of schizophrenia are often referred to in psychi-atric literature as a chronic defect state and are described as follows in a standard textbook:

> The patient, living in an institution or outside, has come to an *arrange-ment with his illness*. He has adapted himself to the world of his mor-bid ideas with more or less success, from his own point of view and from that of his environment. Compared with the experiences during the acute psychosis, his positive symptoms, such as delusions or hallu-cinations, have become colorless, repetitive, and formalized. They still have power over him but nothing is added and nothing new or unex-pected happens. Negative symptoms, thought disorder, passivity, cata-tonic mannerisms and flattening of affect rule the picture, but even they grow habitual with the patient and appear always in the same inveterate pattern in the individual case. There is a robotlike fixity and petrification of attitude and reactions which are not only due to poverty of ideas but also to a very small choice of modes of behavior.

As with all rules, there are exceptions, so this final course can vary. Occasional patients retain their more florid symptoms all their lives. For example, I had under my care a 75-year-old man who hallucinated all day every day and had been doing so for 50 years. His illness was virtually unaffected by medications. These kinds of patients are certainly exceptional, but they do exist.

It is currently popular among Scientologists and other anti-psychiatry activists to attribute many of the symptoms of chronic schizophrenia to drug effects. The truth is that exactly the same clinical picture was described for 50 years before the drugs were introduced. Drugs used in schizophrenia may certainly produce some sedation, especially in older patients, but such effects account for a very small portion of the total clinical picture on a properly run hospital ward. Similarly, these late symptoms are often blamed on the effects of chronic institutionalization; this also accounts for only a small portion of the picture. The late symptoms may be attributed to depression and hopelessness in a patient who is chronically ill and sees no possibility of leaving the hospital; this too may account for a small portion. The vast majority of the late clinical symptoms seen in patients with chronic schizophrenia have been shown to be a direct consequence of the disease and its effects on the brain.

As seen in the chart, only 10 percent of patients with schizophrenia will require hospitalization (or a similar total-care facility such as a nursing home) 30 years later. The vast majority are able to live in the community, with about 15 percent of them requiring an extensive support network.

One of the mysteries that has perplexed mental illness professionals in recent years is where all the persons with schizophrenia have gone. Comparisons of past hospitalization rates with the number of patients receiving care as outpatients invariably find that approximately half of the expected number of patients are missing. The answer is that most of the missing patients are living in the community, usually taking no medication, with varying degrees of adjustment. A community survey in Baltimore, for example, found that half the persons with schizophrenia in the community were receiving no ongoing care or medication from any psychiatric clinic. An example of such a patient follows:

A 72-year-old recluse was forcibly evicted from his rural decaying house by the police. He had been hospitalized for schizophrenia twice in his twenties, worked briefly as a clerk, then returned to live with his aging parents. After they died he had continued to live in the house for thirty years on Social Security disability checks. The house had no electricity or running water and the rooms were packed to the ceiling with piles of newspapers. He cooked over a sterno stove, did not bother anybody, and asked nothing except to be left alone.

The fierce independence and ability to live with his disease in such cases is commendable. The sad aspect, however, is how much better a life he might have led had he been on medication and had well-organized rehabilitation services been available.

Many questions about the long-term course of schizophrenia are as yet unanswered. Do more episodes of schizophrenia cause progressively more damage to the brain? How much can the long-term course be affected by rehabilitation programs that provide jobs and social interaction? The most important new question about the long-term course of schizophrenia, however, is whether the new, second-generation antipsychotics will improve it. The pharmaceutical companies, eager to justify their high prices, imply that the new antipsychotics will produce better outcomes, but to date there is no evidence to support that. A recently published nine-month follow-up of patients taking various second-generation antipsychotics, for example, showed improved symptoms and living skills but little or no change in the patients' behavior or overall function.

CAUSES OF DEATH: WHY DO PEOPLE WITH SCHIZOPHRENIA DIE AT A YOUNGER AGE?

It has been clearly established that individuals with schizophrenia die at a younger average age than do individuals who do not have schizophrenia. Between 1989 and 1991, three studies were published estimating the overall mortality in schizophrenia to be "about twice that of the general population," "nearly a threefold increase in overall mortality," and "5.05 times greater than expected" for males and "5.63 times greater" for females. A 1999 study in Massachusetts reported that men who are seriously mentally ill live 14.1 fewer years and women who are seriously mentally ill 5.7 fewer years than the general population.

The largest single contributor to this excess mortality is suicide, which is 10 to 13 times higher in schizophrenia than in the general population, as will be discussed in chapter 11. In addition to suicide, however, there are other contributors to the excess mortality. These include accidents, diseases, unhealthy lifestyles, inadequate medical care, and homelessness.

- *Accidents:* Although individuals with schizophrenia do not drive as much as other people, studies have shown that they have double the rate of motor vehicle accidents per mile driven. A significant but unknown number of individuals with schizophrenia are also killed as pedestrians by motor vehicles; for example, one patient under my care accidentally stepped off a curb into the path of an oncoming bus. Confusion, delusions, and distraction by auditory hallucinations all contribute to such deaths. In 1995, for example, Margaret King, who had schizophrenia and believed that she was Jesus Christ, was mauled to death by lions after she climbed into their enclosure at the National Zoo in Washington, D.C. An analysis of excess deaths in schizophrenia estimated that 12 percent of the excess was due to accidents.

- *Diseases:* There is some evidence that individuals with schizophrenia have more infections, heart disease, type II (adult onset) diabetes, and female breast cancer, all of which might increase their mortality rate. Partially offsetting this increased mortality is the likelihood that individuals with schizophrenia have a lower than expected incidence of lung cancer, prostate cancer, type I (juvenile onset) diabetes, and rheumatoid arthritis (to be discussed in chapter 6). The prostatic cancer data are especially interesting because one study found a relationship between having been treated with higher doses of antipsychotic medication and having a lower rate of prostate cancer.

- *Unhealthy lifestyles:* It has long been known that individuals with schizophrenia smoke heavily (see chapter 11). A recent study in England of 102 individuals with schizophrenia also reported that they ate a diet higher in fat and lower in fiber than the general populations, and that they exercised very little.

- *Inadequate medical care:* Individuals with schizophrenia who become sick are less able to explain their symptoms to medical personnel, and medical personnel are more likely to disregard their complaints and assume that the complaints are simply part of the illness. As noted in chapter 2, there is also evidence that some persons with schizophrenia have an elevated pain threshold, so that they may not complain of symptoms until a disease has progressed too far to be treatable. Even when diagnosed, individuals with schizophrenia are less likely to be offered standard medical or surgical care. For example, a recent study of cardiac catheterizations for people who had had a heart attack reported that individuals diagnosed with schizophrenia were 41 percent less likely to undergo this procedure.

- *Homelessness:* Although it has not been well studied to date, it appears that homelessness increases the mortality rate of individuals with schizophrenia by making them even more susceptible to accidents and diseases. A study in England followed 48 homeless seriously mentally ill individuals for 18 months; at the end of that time three had died of diseases (heart attack, suffocation during epileptic seizure, and ruptured aneurysm), one had been killed by a car, and three others had disappeared without taking their belongings with them. Scattered reports from around the United States suggest that homeless mentally ill individuals may have a very high mortality rate. For example, in Oklahoma, a woman who was released from a psychiatric hospital in January sought shelter in an old chicken coop, where she froze to death and was not found for two years. In Houston, a homeless woman with schizophrenia and her young son were killed when a car hit them while she was pushing a shopping cart along a street. In Santa Ana, California, a woman with schizophrenia was killed by a train when the shopping cart she was pushing with her dog in it got stuck on the train tracks. It is likely that when we finally do a careful study of mortality rates among homeless individuals with schizophrenia in the United States, the results will show a shockingly high mortality rate.

RECOMMENDED FURTHER READING

Cannon, M., P. Jones, M. O. Huttunen, et al. "School Performance in Finnish Children and Later Development of Schizophrenia: A Population-Based Longitudinal Study." *Archives of General Psychiatry* 56 (1999): 457–63.

Ciompi, L. "Aging and Schizophrenic Psychosis." *Acta Psychiatrica Scandinavica* (supp. 319), 71 (1985): 93–105.

Hambrecht, M., H. Häfner, and W. Löffler. "Beginning Schizophrenia Observed by Significant Others." *Social Psychiatry and Psychiatric Epidemiology* 29 (1994): 53–60.

Harding, C. M., J. Zubin, and J. S. Strauss. "Chronicity in Schizophrenia: Revisited." *British Journal of Psychiatry* (supp. 18), 161 (1992): 27–37.

Harris, A. E. "Physical Disease and Schizophrenia." *Schizophrenia Bulletin* 14 (1988): 85–96.

Harris, M. J., and D. V. Jeste, "Late-Onset Schizophrenia: An Overview." *Schizophrenia Bulletin* 14 (1988): 39–55.

Howard, R., Rabins, P. V., Seeman, M. V., et al. "Late-onset Schizophrenia and Very-late-onset Schizophrenia-like Psychosis: An International Consensus." *American Journal of Psychiatry* 157 (2000): 172–78.

Lewis, S. "Sex and Schizophrenia: Vive la Difference." *British Journal of Psychiatry* 161 (1992): 445–50.

Malmberg, A., G. Lewis, A. David, and P. Allebeck. "Premorbid Adjustment and Personality in People with Schizophrenia." *British Journal of Psychiatry* 172 (1998): 308–13.

Peschel, E., R. Peschel, C. W. Howe, and J. W. Howe, eds. *Neurobiological Disorders in Children and Adolescents*. San Francisco: Jossey-Bass, 1992.

Torrey, E. F., A. E. Bowler, E. H. Taylor, et al. *Schizophrenia and Manic-Depressive Disorder*. New York: Basic Books, 1994. See chapter 5.

Wilson, L. *This Stranger, My Son*. New York: Putnam, 1968. Paperback by New American Library.

6

RESEARCH FINDINGS ON THE CAUSES OF SCHIZOPHRENIA

Something has happened to me—I do not know what. All that was my former self has crumbled and fallen together and a creature has emerged of whom I know nothing. She is a stranger to me—and has an egotism that makes the egotism that I had look like skimmed milk; and she thinks thoughts that are—heresies. Her name is insanity. She is the daughter of madness—and according to the doctor, they each had their genesis in my own brain.

Lara Jefferson, *These Are My Sisters*

Research on schizophrenia in the 1990s, the congressionally consecrated Decade of the Brain, made major steps forward. Information regarding specific brain abnormalities in this disease amounted to a virtual explosion, and this is continuing into the twenty-first century. In 1999 the biennial International Congress on Schizophrenia attracted over 1,500 researchers; 15 years previously, it had attracted only 150.

This chapter will summarize research findings relevant to the causes of schizophrenia. The following chapter will discuss specific theories regarding the cause of schizophrenia, that is, how the research findings fit together. The reader should keep in mind that research on schizophrenia is currently progressing so rapidly that anything written on it will be somewhat dated even as it is being published.

THE NORMAL BRAIN

Before proceeding to a discussion of abnormalities in the brains of persons with schizophrenia, however, let us consider the normal brain—a three-pound, mushroomlike organ with a stem narrowing into the spinal cord, which runs down the back. The bulk of the brain consists of four arbitrarily defined lobes (frontal, parietal, temporal, and occipital), which are divided in half by a deep vertical cleft. At the bottom of the cleft is the corpus callosum, a thick band carrying nerve fibers back and forth between the two halves of the brain. The four major lobes perform functions such as muscle coordination, thinking, memory, language, hearing, and vision. It is now established that the two halves of the brain are not identical; in most persons the left half has more control over language skills and conceptual thinking, whereas the right half has more responsibility for spatial skills and intuitive thinking.

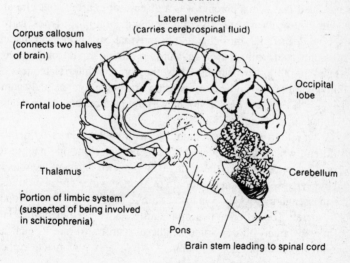

THE LOCATION OF THE LIMBIC SYSTEM IN THE BRAIN

Lateral ventricle (carries cerebrospinal fluid)

Corpus callosum (connects two halves of brain)

Occipital lobe

Frontal lobe

Thalamus

Cerebellum

Portion of limbic system (suspected of being involved in schizophrenia)

Pons

Brain stem leading to spinal cord

The four lobes come together at the base of the brain beneath the corpus callosum. There lie the thalamus, hypothalamus, pituitary gland, limbic system, basal ganglia, midbrain, and brain stem tapering into the spinal cord. It is this area that controls all vital functions (e.g., heart, respiration, eating, and the body's endocrine [hormone] system) and that acts as a gatekeeper for all incoming and outgoing stimuli to and from the major lobes. Attached to the back of this area, as if by afterthought, is the cerebellum, which until recently was thought to function exclusively to coordinate muscle function; it is now thought to have other functions as well.

The entire brain is housed in the vaultlike bony skull and surrounded by a layer of cerebrospinal fluid for further protection. The fluid circulates around the brain and goes through the center of the brain by a series of canals that widen into ventricles. It is because the brain is so well protected that we understand comparatively little about it or its diseases. It has been facetiously suggested that if we could persuade the brain to change places with the liver we might then understand its functioning and what causes schizophrenia.

The actual work of the brain is performed by approximately 100 billion neurons and 10 times 100 billion glia. Another way to conceptualize the number of brain cells is to say that there are more neurons and glia in one brain than there are days since the world began. Until recently, it was assumed that schizophrenia was a disease of neurons, but glia are now prime suspects as well. The glia are divided into four types: astrocytes, oligodendroglia, miroglia, and ependymal cells. The neurons are all interconnected, with an average neuron receiving input from between 1,000 and 10,000 other neurons. Thus, the complex interrelatedness of the human brain is beyond comprehension. As one scholar astutely summarized it: "If the brain was so simple we could understand it, we would be so simple that we couldn't."

The way that neurons communicate with each other is by neurotransmitters, which are chemical messengers sent from one neuron to another. The space between the arms (axons) of two adjacent neurons is called the synapse and is one millionth of an inch wide. The neurotransmitter messengers cross the synapse at a rate of up to 600 per second. Approximately 100 different neurotransmitters have been identified, but there may be many more. Some of these neurotransmitters, such as dopamine, norepinephrine, serotonin, GABA, and glutamate, are of great interest to schizophrenia researchers.

THE BRAIN WITH SCHIZOPHRENIA

Given the complexity of the brain and the fact that it is hidden away in a relatively inaccessible skull, it is hardly surprising that until recently we knew so little about schizophrenia. That is rapidly changing. What we now know about schizophrenia includes the following:

THE BRAIN WITH SCHIZOPHRENIA: A SUMMARY OF FINDINGS RELATED TO ITS CAUSE

1. The disease is familial.
2. There may be neurochemical changes.
3. There are structural and neuropathological changes.
4. There are neuropsychological deficits.
5. There are neurological abnormalities.
6. There are electrical abnormalities.
7. There are immunological and inflammatory abnormalities.
8. Individuals with schizophrenia are born disproportionately in the winter and spring.
9. Individuals with schizophrenia are born and/or raised disproportionately in urban areas.
10. Other abnormalities: pregnancy and birth complications, minor physical anomalies, and an absence of rheumatoid arthritis.

---

1. *The disease is familial.* To say that a disease is familial is merely to say that it runs in families; it does not tell you why it does. The fact that schizophrenia tends to run in families has been known for at least 200 years. As noted in chapter 13, when one child in a family has schizophrenia, the chance of a second child becoming ill is approximately 9 percent, or 9 times the chance of a person without a sibling with schizophrenia becoming ill. Twin studies have demonstrated not only that schizophrenia is familial but also that genes play some role in this; in nonidentical (dizygotic) twin pairs, the chance of the second twin being affected is approximately 9 percent, the same as for siblings, whereas in identical (monozygotic) twin pairs, the chance is approximately 28 percent. Finally, studies of adopted children have also demonstrated that schizophrenia is

familial, since the adopted-away children of mothers with schizophrenia have at least a fourfold greater chance of later developing schizophrenia than the adopted-away children of mothers without schizophrenia. What these findings mean in terms of genetic theories of schizophrenia will be discussed in chapter 7.

2. *There may be neurochemical changes.* Despite the prominence of the dopamine theory and other neurochemical theories of schizophrenia (to be discussed in chapter 7) and a large amount of research data, there is little agreement on how neurochemistry is actually altered. Studies of various neurochemicals have been carried out on blood, cerebrospinal fluid, and postmortem brain tissue, and in living patients with schizophrenia using neuroimaging techniques, but the results have been decidedly mixed. One major impediment to this research is that antipsychotic medications used for treating schizophrenia also affect many neurochemicals; thus, most of the initial positive research findings have turned out to be the effects of medication. Another major problem is that there are definite brain regional differences in these neurochemicals, so that many regions may have to be sampled to establish an abnormality.

The major neurochemicals that have been investigated are neurotransmitters and their receptors, especially dopamine, serotonin, noradrenaline, glutamate, and GABA. Dopamine has received the most attention in the past, but recent research has focused more on glutamate and serotonin. Also of interest are neuropeptides, especially cholecystokinin, neurotensin, and somatostatin.

In summary, there are almost certainly neurochemical differences in the brains of individuals with schizophrenia, especially in the hippocampus and frontal lobe, but much work still needs to be done to differentiate these changes from medication effects and other confounding variables such as concurrent drug abuse.

3. *There are structural and neuropathological changes.* Structural changes in the brains of individuals with schizophrenia are among the most solidly established lines of evidence that schizophrenia is a brain disease. Over 100 MRI studies have shown that the cerebral ventricles, which carry cerebrospinal fluid throughout the brain, are on average approximately 15 percent larger in individuals with schizophrenia. An additional 50 studies have been done on structures of the limbic system using MRI and neuropathological exami-

nation of postmortem brain tissue; these studies have shown volume loss, cell loss, and changes in the architecture of the cells in the hippocampus, amygdala, parahippocampal gyrus, entorhinal cortex, and cingulate. In most studies, the differences between individuals with schizophrenia and normal controls is subtle, in the range of 5–10 percent, and there is some overlap between individuals in the two groups. What this means on a practical level is that the brain changes are not specifically diagnostic for schizophrenia, that is, they cannot be used by themselves to say that a person either has, or does not have, the disease.

Other brain areas have also been shown to have structural abnormalities in schizophrenia. The thalamus, which lies adjacent to the main limbic system structures, has been shown by MRI to be smaller and to have a loss of cells in some of its nuclei. Structural changes have also been reported in the prefrontal cortex, cerebellum, brain stem, superior temporal gyrus, and inferior parietal lobule, although the number of studies on these areas is smaller.

In contrast to many of the neurochemical studies discussed above, the structural and neuropathological changes in schizophrenia are clearly established to be present prior to exposure to antipsychotic medications. Studies done on individuals with schizophrenia who have never received medication report the same findings as those on individuals who have been medicated. The one exception to this statement are reports of increased volume in the basal ganglia, especially the caudate, which are at least partially due to increased blood supply secondary to the medication. The other structural changes described above are thought to be due to the disease process itself.

4. *There are neuropsychological deficits.* The neuropsychological deficits of schizophrenia are among the most impressive abnormalities found in this disease and have been described in literally hundreds of studies. In an early review of cognitive impairment, for example, it was found that "three-quarters of the schizophrenic patients exhibited moderate to severe dysfunction."

Four types of cognitive function are especially impaired in this disease: attention, certain types of memory, executive function (planning, problem solving, abstracting, etc.), and awareness of illness. The deficits in attention are demonstrable on tests that measure vigilance and concentration. Individuals with schizophrenia are

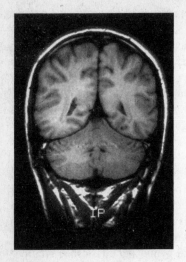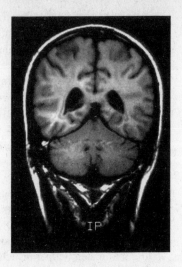

MRIs from 28-year-old identical male twins in which the one with schizophrenia has markedly enlarged posterior ventricles, suggesting the loss of brain tissue associated with the disease.

often distracted, and in fact "distracted" was another commonly used term for insanity in the early nineteenth century.

The memory deficits in schizophrenia are most prominent in short-term, or "working," memory. For example, many patients have difficulty remembering three objects for five minutes. Long-term memory, on the other hand, is usually intact and the person's ability to recollect events from the period prior to the onset of his/her disease is often excellent.

Executive function deficits are apparent in tasks such as abstracting proverbs (see chapter 2). Another common way to measure executive function is by a test called the Wisconsin Card Sort, in which the person must match cards by shape or color at the same time that the rules for matching the cards are constantly changing; individuals with schizophrenia find it difficult to change how they are matching the cards to accommodate the changing rules.

The fourth type of neuropsychological deficit commonly found in schizophrenia is impaired awareness of illness. This was discussed in chapter 2 and, as was noted, can be measured. Impaired awareness of illness is of great practical importance in the treatment of this disease, as will be discussed in chapter 11 under "medication noncompliance."

The neuropsychological deficits in schizophrenia are inherent in the disease process itself and are not due to medication. Studies that have compared never-medicated patients with those on medication have reported very similar results. The neuropsychological deficits also change surprisingly little in individuals with schizophrenia between when they are symptomatic and in remission.

It should be emphasized that the neuropsychological deficits in schizophrenia affect only selected brain functions. Many other brain functions are normal, or nearly normal, including such things as knowledge of commonplace information, verbal language skills, and visual spatial abilities.

5. *There are neurological abnormalities.* Neurological abnormalities in individuals with schizophrenia have been regularly noted since the middle of the nineteenth century. Since 1960 there have been approximately 40 studies, and virtually all reported more neurological abnormalities in individuals with schizophrenia compared to normal controls.

Neurological abnormalities may be of two types. "Hard"

neurological signs include things such as the patellar tendon reflex ("knee jerk") or the grasp reflex (found normally in infants) and usually indicate impaired function of a specific brain area. "Soft" neurological signs include such things as double simultaneous stimulation (being unable to feel two simultaneous touches), agraphesthesia (being unable to identify numbers on the palm of the hand), and confusion about the right and left sides of the body; these usually indicate impaired function of a neuron network. "Soft" sign abnormalities are much more common in schizophrenia than are "hard" sign abnormalities. A 1988 review of such studies concluded that between 50 and 60 percent of individuals with schizophrenia have neurological abnormalities.

Neurological abnormalities of the eye have also received much attention in schizophrenia research. The abnormality that has received the most attention is rapid eye movements, which are almost imperceptible to observers but can be measured by a special machine. Abnormal eye reflexes and abnormal blink rates (either frequent blinking or almost no blinking) have also been observed in some patients.

An important consideration in neurological studies of schizophrenia is the effect of antipsychotic medication. Since it is well known that these medications may cause tremors, movement disorders, and other neurological abnormalities in some patients, it is frequently assumed that all neurological abnormalities in individuals with schizophrenia are probably caused by medications. Against this belief is the finding in several studies that individuals off medications had just as many neurological abnormalities as those on medications. Especially significant was the 1992 study by Schroder et al. that included 17 patients with schizophrenia who had never received antipsychotic medications and who had just as many neurological abnormalities as those who had received medications. Thus, it is clear that the majority of neurological abnormalities seen in individuals with schizophrenia are inherent in the disease process, with the remainder being probable side effects of the medications.

6. *There are electrical abnormalities.* One method the brain uses to send information from one area to another is by electrical impulses, and these have been shown to be abnormal in many patients with schizophrenia. This is true when the electrical impulses are meas-

ured as evoked potentials, a special electrical impulse elicited by auditory, visual, or sensory input; abnormal evoked potentials (especially the P-300 component) have been reported in schizophrenia since the early 1970s. It is also true when electrical activity is recorded on electroencephalograms (EEGs); approximately one-third of persons with schizophrenia have abnormal EEGs. Abnormal EEGs in schizophrenia are twice as common as among persons with mania, and four times as common as among persons with depression. A review article summarizing electrical abnormalities in schizophrenia concluded that "a broad interpretation of the EEG and EP [evoked potential] findings supports the presence of brain disease in many patients with this disorder."

7. *There are immunological and inflammatory abnormalities.* Immunological and inflammatory abnormalities have been described in individuals with schizophrenia since the early 1900s. In 1942, for example, it was reported that patients with schizophrenia had diminished skin reactions to a protein injected beneath the skin. This and other immune abnormalities were clearly in evidence well before the introduction of antipsychotic medications.

In more recent years, there has been a continuing series of reported immunological and inflammatory markers in schizophrenia. The most prominent findings have been increases in various cytokines, especially interleukin-6 and its receptor. There have also been many reports of abnormalities in lymphocytes and in immunoglobulin subfractions. These markers of immune function and inflammation are known to be altered in infectious and in autoimmune diseases.

A major impediment to research on immunological and inflammatory abnormalities in schizophrenia is the fact that antipsychotic medications also affect them. Thus, it is often difficult to know whether the observed abnormalities are disease-related or caused by medications. The vast bulk of evidence suggests that both are true, since studies done on untreated patients with schizophrenia report similar abnormalities.

8. *Individuals with schizophrenia are born disproportionately in the winter and spring.* Over 100 studies have been done on the birth pattern of individuals with schizophrenia, covering almost half a million individuals in 34 countries. The findings of these studies are

remarkably consistent in showing a 5–8 percent excess of births in the winter and spring months (December through April) compared to the birth pattern of individuals who do not have schizophrenia. The birth pattern for schizophrenia is, in fact, one of the most consistently replicated and statistically significant aspects of this disease. It should be emphasized that this is a statistical finding based on thousands of births and is not predictive for any single individual.

Many possibilities have been proposed to explain this birth pattern, including the seasonal effect of genes, seasonal pregnancy and birth complications, toxins, nutrition, temperature and light fluctuations, and infectious agents. It is also not known whether the agent causing the increased winter-spring births occurs only at that time, in which case the 5–8 percent of births would represent a subgroup of the disease, or whether the agent occurs all year but merely peaks at that time, in which case the 5–8 percent excess would be part of a much larger group.

9. *Individuals with schizophrenia are born and/or raised disproportionately in urban areas.* Within the past decade, seven separate studies have been published reporting that being born or raised in an urban area is a risk factor for later developing schizophrenia. The increased risk for urban birth/rearing is approximately twofold over rural areas, with suburban areas being intermediate in risk. For many years, it was thought that there were more individuals with schizophrenia in urban areas merely because they selectively migrated there. That is true, but it is only part of the answer; the other part is that more individuals with schizophrenia were born and/or raised there.

The cause of the urban risk is unknown. The magnitude of it, however, is appreciable. A recent study in Denmark, for example, reported that for people with schizophrenia, the attributable risk for being born in a city was much greater than the attributable risk for having a family history of schizophrenia.

10. *Other abnormalities: pregnancy and birth complications, minor physical anomalies, and an absence of rheumatoid arthritis.* Reports that individuals with schizophrenia had more complications during their mothers' pregnancies and during the subjects' births have regularly surfaced since the first such study in 1966.

Over 20 such studies have now been published, with most reporting increased pregnancy and birth complications compared to control groups.

No single complication has been prominent across studies. Those that have been reported most often include slightly premature birth (prior to 37 weeks of pregnancy) or slightly underweight; evidence of anoxia and need for resuscitation; and increased number of infections in the period immediately following birth. There is also a report that mothers who give birth to individuals who develop schizophrenia have an unusually high number of miscarriages during other pregnancies.

Could the pregnancy and birth complications themselves cause the schizophrenia later in life? Some researchers argue that they could. Others have suggested that the pregnancy and birth complications are merely manifestations of infections or other complications occurring earlier in pregnancy that cannot be measured but which are the true cause of both the later schizophrenia and the birth complications.

There have also been at least 20 studies showing that individuals with schizophrenia have more minor physical anomalies. These anomalies are nonobvious but measurable physical features of the head, hands, and feet and are thought to be produced by disturbances to the developing fetus during pregnancy, especially early in pregnancy. Examples of such minor physical anomalies include low-set ears, a high, steepled palate (roof of the mouth), and unusual fingerprint and palm-print patterns (dermatoglyphics). Occasional minor physical anomalies are found in many normal people and in other conditions (e.g., autism), but the modest increase in schizophrenia suggests that for some individuals there has been a disturbance of unknown nature during pregnancy.

Another curious but clearly established research finding about schizophrenia is an inverse association with rheumatoid arthritis. Individuals with schizophrenia almost never get this type of arthritis. Since 1936, 18 studies of this association have been done, with 14 of them reporting a lower-than-expected incidence of rheumatoid arthritis in individuals with schizophrenia. Among the three studies that were methodologically the best, no individuals with rheumatoid arthritis were found among 111 and 301 inpatients with schizophrenia in two of the studies, and a very low incidence was found in the third.

There are many similarities between schizophrenia and rheumatoid arthritis that make this inverse correlation even more interesting. Neither disease was clearly described until the beginning of the nineteenth century. Both diseases have a lifetime incidence of approximately 1 percent and a pairwise concordance rate in identical twins of approximately 30 percent (i.e., when one twin gets it, the second twin also gets it approximately 30 percent of the time). Both diseases are said to be more common in urban than in rural areas. A major difference between the diseases is that rheumatoid arthritis is more common in women than in men by a ratio of three to one.

Several theories have been proposed to explain this inverse correlation but none has been proven. It is possible that there are genetic factors that render a person susceptible to schizophrenia and at the same time resistant to rheumatoid arthritis. Biochemical factors, including prostaglandins, essential fatty acids, beta-endorphins, and tryptophan, have all been hypothesized as playing a role by some researchers. Viruses could explain it if both diseases were caused by closely related types; becoming infected with one virus might confer immunity to the second virus. The most intriguing challenge is that if we are able to understand the causes of one of these diseases, then it may help to understand the other as well.

In summary, what can be said about the brains of individuals with schizophrenia? It can be said that schizophrenia is firmly and unequivocally established to be a brain disease, just as surely as multiple sclerosis, Parkinson's disease, and Alzheimer's disease are established as brain diseases. As Dr. Henry Griesinger said more than 100 years ago: "Psychiatry and neuropathology are not merely two closely related fields; they are but one field in which only one language is spoken and the same laws rule." The dichotomy used in the past, whereby schizophrenia was classified as a "functional" disorder as distinct from an "organic" disorder, is now known to be inaccurate; schizophrenia has impeccable credentials for admission to the organic category.

WHAT PARTS OF THE BRAIN ARE AFFECTED?

Researchers argue endlessly about what parts of the brain are primarily affected in schizophrenia. In the early twentieth century, when scientists began looking at autopsies for abnormalities in the brains of individuals with schizophrenia, they looked mostly in the outer layer of the brain. At that time it was believed that most of the important functions of the brain were closest to the surface. It is now known that areas in the center of the brain are more critical for the brain functions impaired in schizophrenia and that is where most of the research is focusing.

The majority of research has been done on the limbic system, known to be the gate through which most incoming stimuli must pass. It has "selective, integrative, and unifying functions by which raw experience is harmonized into reality and coherent activity is organized." According to Dr. Paul MacLean, the modern father of limbic system research, it is "able to correlate every form of internal and external perception."

All of this takes place in an area that is anatomically very small. It is composed of contiguous portions of the frontal and temporal lobes, and its main structures include the amygdala, hippocampus, hypothalamus, nucleus accumbens, ventral septum, mammillary bodies, stria terminalis, and olfactory area. However, its size is deceptive, for the limbic system has direct connections to all areas of the brain, including the frontal lobe, parietal lobe, thalamus, upper brain stem, and cerebellum. Increasingly it has been realized that the brain works as a functionally interdependent and intricate system, and an abnormality anywhere within it can throw the whole system off. It is analogous to an electrical system with a short circuit in it; the short circuit may occur at any one of several places, but the result will be the same.

Evidence that the limbic system is the site of pathology for some, if not most, cases of schizophrenia is strong. Abnormalities in this system in animals may produce profound changes in emotion, inappropriate behavior, and an impairment in the animal's ability to screen out multiple visual stimuli. Abnormalities in the limbic system in human beings may produce, in addition to the above effects, distortions of perception, illusions, hallucinations, feelings of depersonalization, paranoia, and catatonic-like behavior. In short, the symptoms of schizophrenia described in chapter 2 are a logical consequence of impaired limbic system dysfunction, given what we know about it.

Diseases of the brain that affect the limbic system are also known to produce schizophrenia-like symptoms. This is seen, for example, with brain tumors located in the limbic system. Cases of encephalitis that produce schizophrenia-like symptoms have been found in several studies to involve the limbic system, and epilepsy, when it originates in the limbic area, is more likely to be accompanied by schizophrenia-like symptoms.

The strongest evidence linking the limbic system to schizophrenia has come from studies of electrical activity in this area. The late Robert Heath and his coworkers in New Orleans found abnormal limbic electrical activity in patients with schizophrenia; these findings were replicated by three other groups of researchers. One group found abnormal electrical impulses in the limbic area of 61 out of 62 patients tested, and as the electrodes were moved away from the limbic area, the abnormalities became less frequent. Another group was able to correlate the occurrence of abnormal electrical activity and bizarre behavior in a patient.

Looking back over the research findings from the brains of individuals with schizophrenia, the structural and neuropathological changes described to date also point strongly to the limbic system. The enlarged ventricles are probably caused by the loss of brain tissue in limbic system structures lining the ventricles. Specific abnormalities have also been described in limbic system structures, especially the hippocampus, amygdala, entorhinal cortex, and cingulate.

Looking exclusively at functional abnormalities in schizophrenia, especially the neuropsychological findings, it seems clear that parts of the frontal cortex, including the prefrontal area, are also involved in the disease process. The prefrontal area has strong connections to the limbic system, so it is probably not a matter of either-or but rather both. The thalamus also is closely connected to parts of the limbic system and to the prefrontal cortex, so abnormalities in that structure are also not unexpected. It is increasingly clear that schizophrenia is not a disease of a single brain structure but rather variably affects all of these structures, either by a primary disease process or secondarily through interconnections.

There is one other curious fact about the anatomical location of schizophrenia. In recent years there have been several studies suggesting that the left side of the brain is primarily affected in schizophrenia much more often than the right side of the brain. Patients with temporal lobe epilepsy, for example, are more likely to have schizophrenia-like symptoms if the epilepsy is in the left temporal lobe. Similarly, studies of visual evoked potentials, abnormal EEGs, lateral eye movements, auditory discrimination, galvanic skin response, information processing, and neurological signs all suggest that the major problem may lie in the left hemisphere.

Progress on resolving the anatomy of schizophrenia should come rapidly in the next few years. In 1995, the Stanley Foundation began a postmortem brain collection and Neuropathology Consortium. The Consortium consists of 60 brains, 15 each with diagnoses of schizophrenia, manic-depressive illness, severe depression, and normal controls. Sections of the 60 Consortium brains have been sent to researchers in more than 80 laboratories worldwide, each studying different abnormalities. The research is all carried out coded, so the researchers are blind to the diagnosis of each brain until they complete their research. The results from these researchers are being synthesized, which should produce a more complete picture of the brain abnormalities.

In summary, where are we presently in our quest to identify the parts of the brain primarily affected in schizophrenia? To translate the research discussions into geographical terms, imagine that the brain is the equivalent of the United States. Most researchers are convinced that schizophrenia is caused by dysfunction in the greater New York area, although a few believe it is in Baltimore and occasional proponents can be found arguing for Cleveland or Detroit. Within the New York area, many researchers have favorite sites that they are researching; these may be as large as Queens, Bergen, or Suffolk counties or the size of towns like Hicksville, New Rochelle, or Paterson. Although the area under investigation is still relatively large, many other areas of the country (e.g., the northwest and southwest) have been effectively eliminated from consideration. In schizophrenia research, as in geography, it is obvious that the more researchers you have looking for something, the greater the chances are of finding it.

WHEN DOES THE BRAIN DAMAGE BEGIN?

The question of when the brain damage of schizophrenia begins has provoked lively controversy among researchers in recent years and has led to the neurodevelopmental theory (see chapter 7). It is an important question, because it has implications for the prevention of the disease.

What is increasingly clear is that, at least for one-third of cases of schizophrenia, the brain changes leading to the disease begin early in life, even though the actual symptoms of the disease do not begin until the person's late teenage years or twenties. The evidence pointing toward early brain changes includes the studies of pregnancy and birth complications, minor physical anomalies, the winter and spring excess of births, the urban risk factor for birth or early rearing, and, finally, some microscopic changes found in some brains postmortem that suggest changes that took place during the brain's development.

Do all individuals with schizophrenia have brain changes that date to early in life, or is that true merely for a subgroup? We do not yet know the answer to this. What we do know is that the early brain changes occur in approximately one-quarter of individuals with schizophrenia. This was shown, for example, by our study of identical twins in which one had schizophrenia and the other did not. When we looked for neurological or behavioral differences between the twins before the age of 5, in 7 out of 27 pairs (26 percent), there clearly were differences even though the symptoms of schizophrenia in the affected twin did not begin until many years later.

It remains to be ascertained whether this group of individuals with early changes is a clinical subgroup, that is, do they have a different cause for their disease? Or do all individuals with schizophrenia have a disease process that dates to early in life but cannot be measured yet? This is one of the most important research questions currently facing schizophrenia researchers.

RECOMMENDED FURTHER READING

Arnold, S. E., and J. Q. Trojanowski. "Recent Advances in Defining the Neuropathology of Schizophrenia," *Neuropathology* 92 (1996): 217–31.

Bogerts, B. "The Neuropathology of Schizophrenic Diseases: Historical Aspects and Present Knowledge." *European Archives of Psychiatry and Clinical Neuroscience* 249 (1999): Supp. 4, 2–13.

Geddes, J. R., H. Verdoux, N. Takei, et al. "Schizophrenia and Complications of Pregnancy and Labor: An Individual Patient Data Meta-analysis." *Schizophrenia Bulletin* 25 (1999): 413–23.

Goldberg, T., J. D. Ragland, E. F. Torrey, et al. "Neuropsychological Assessment of Monozygotic Twins Discordant for Schizophrenia." *Archives of General Psychiatry* 47 (1990): 1066–72.

Harrison, P. "The Neuropathology of Schizophrenia: A Critical Review of the Data and Their Interpretation." *Brain* 122 (1999): 593–624.

Helmchen, H., and F. Henn, eds. *Biological Perspectives of Schizophrenia*. Chichester, England: John Wiley, 1987.

Hirsch, S. R., and D. R. Weinberger, eds. *Schizophrenia*. Oxford: Blackwell Science, 1995.

Knable, M. B., J. E. Kleinman, and D. R. Weinberger. "Neurobiology of Schizophrenia." In A. F. Schatzberg and C. B. Nemoroff, eds., *Textbook of Psychopharmacology*, 2nd ed. Washington, D.C.: American Psychiatric Association Press, 1998, pp. 589–607.

McNeil, T. "Perinatal Risk Factors and Schizophrenia: Selective Review and Methodological Concerns." *Epidemiologic Reviews* 17 (1995): 107–12.

Mortensen, P. B., C. B. Pedersen, T. Westergaard, et al. "Effects of Family History and Place and Season of Birth on the Risk of Schizophrenia." *New England Journal of Medicine* 340 (1999): 603–8.

Müller, N., M. Riedel, M. Ackenheil, et al. "The Role of Immune Function in Schizophrenia: An Overview." *European Archives of Psychiatry and Clinical Neuroscience* 249 (1999): Supp. 4, 62–68.

Nasrallah, H. A., and D. R. Weinberger, eds. *The Neurology of Schizophrenia.* Amsterdam: Elsevier, 1986.

Oken, R. J., and M. Schulzer. "At Issue: Schizophrenia and Rheumatoid Arthritis: The Negative Association Revisited." *Schizophrenia Bulletin* 25 (1999): 625-38.

Torrey, E. F., A. E. Bowler, E. H. Taylor, and I. I. Gottesman. *Schizophrenia and Manic-Depressive Disorder: The Biological Roots of Mental Illness as Revealed by the Landmark Study of Identical Twins.* New York: Basic Books, 1994.

Torrey, E. F., J. Miller, R. Rawlings, et al. "Seasonality of Births in Schizophrenia and Bipolar Disorder: A Review of the Literature." *Schizophrenia Research* 28 (1997): 1–38.

7

THEORIES ABOUT THE CAUSES
OF SCHIZOPHRENIA

It [insanity] is no longer regarded as a disgrace, or as a disease resulting from some criminal offence. It is now considered a physical disorder, a disease of the brain . . .

Amariah Brigham, 1837

One of the most remarkable facts about schizophrenia is that researchers
in the mid–nineteenth century were closer to the truth regarding its causes
than were researchers in the mid–twentieth century. By the 1830s, in both
England and the United States, there was a consensus among most mental illness professionals that insanity was a brain disease. In England, for
example, William A. F. Browne stated that "insanity, then, is . . . produced by an organic change in the brain." Researchers, looking for abnormalities, assiduously examined the postmortem brains of insane
individuals, but the results were contradictory since the available techniques were inadequate to find them. In 1867 Henry Maudsley recognized that the "important molecular or chemical changes may take place
in those inner recesses to which we have not yet gained access . . . [and]
to conclude from the non-appearance of change to the non-existence
thereof would be just as if the blind man were to maintain that there were
no colors, or the deaf man to assert that there was no sound."

Incredibly, one hundred years after Brigham, Browne, Maudsley,
and their colleagues were discussing insanity as a brain disease, their
psychiatric offspring were investigating insanity as a product of bad
mothering or mislabeling. In no other area of medicine—perhaps in all
of science—did research go backwards for as far or as long as it did in
psychiatry.

Beginning in the last quarter of the twentieth century, research on schizophrenia finally got back on track, as was summarized in the last chapter. The present challenge is to synthesize the rapidly accumulating data into a coherent theory and then prove it to be correct. One is reminded of Edna St. Vincent Millay's sonnet that described "a meteoric shower of facts" that "lie unquestioned, uncombined":

> *Wisdom enough to leech of our ill*
> *Is daily spun, but there exists no loom*
> *To weave it into fabric.*

A major impediment to weaving the facts about schizophrenia into a coherent theory is the question of heterogeneity: is schizophrenia one disease or many diseases? Most researchers assume the latter, but that is not established as fact. A case can be made for the opposite approach— that schizophrenia may turn out to have a single major cause. Dr. Lewis Thomas pointed out that syphilis, tuberculosis, and pernicious anemia were all conditions with a bewildering variety of manifestations that few scientists thought could constitute a single illness, yet in each case a single cause (spirochete, tubercle bacillus, and vitamin deficiency) was eventually found to be the primary cause. That this may be true for schizophrenia (and possibly for manic-depressive illness as well) is not beyond the realm of possibility.

This chapter will summarize theories about the cause of schizophrenia, including theories that are currently at the center of research as well as those now considered to be obsolete. The reader should keep in mind that many of these theories are not mutually exclusive, and the final answer may involve some combination of them.

GENETIC THEORIES

Genetic theories of schizophrenia have been prominent since the 1960s and have been heavily supported by NIMH. Much contemporary interest has been spurred by the mapping of the human genome. Genetic theories of schizophrenia include the following:

(a) A single gene causes schizophrenia.
(b) Multiple interacting genes cause schizophrenia.
(c) Genes do not *cause* schizophrenia but rather are *predisposing*

factors that determine whether the specific causal factor (e.g.,
trauma during the development of the brain, an infectious agent,
a nutritional deficiency, stress, etc.) will or will not cause the
disease.

Virtually all schizophrenia researchers agree that genes play *some*
role in the development of schizophrenia, but precisely what role
remains in dispute. Current genetics research has focused primarily on
(b), above. The search for the genes thought to cause schizophrenia has
proceeded along two lines. The first involves linkage studies, in which
blood is obtained from many families having more than one family
member affected. The genes are then examined to detect a genetic abnormality shared by those family members with the disease. The second
research approach is a search for candidate genes, which are genes that
might be involved (e.g., genes controlling the production of dopamine).

Despite the expenditure of large amounts of NIMH research funds
over the past decade, genetic studies of schizophrenia have so far been
disappointing. Linkage studies reporting positive findings to genes on
chromosomes 1, 5, 6, 8, 13, 15, and 22 have raised hopes, only to be discredited later by failures to replicate the results. Some genetics
researchers claim that the problem is the need for larger sample sizes;
others say it is heterogeneity, that is, that schizophrenia has many different subgroups.

There are additional reasons to doubt whether schizophrenia is primarily a genetic disease. The fact that a second identical twin has only a
28 percent chance of developing the disease (pairwise concordance rate)
means that nongenetic factors are very important. It is also known that
inbreeding (i.e., marriage among close relatives) does not increase the
rate of schizophrenia. Genetic theories of schizophrenia are also difficult
to fit into the epidemiological findings noted in chapter 6, especially the
excess of winter and spring births. Most damaging to genetic hypotheses,
however, is the fact that from the early nineteenth century to the
mid–twentieth century, most individuals with schizophrenia in Europe
and the United States were confined in psychiatric hospitals and their rate
of reproduction was extremely low. During that time, the incidence of
schizophrenia did not decrease, and some researchers believe that it
increased substantially. It is certainly an unusual genetic disease that does
not decrease when the putative causal genes are not being passed on.

Increasingly, many geneticists are wondering whether genes may be
predisposing factors for schizophrenia rather than *causal* factors. This

would put schizophrenia into the same category as rheumatoid arthritis, insulin-dependent diabetes, breast cancer, bowel cancer, and many other diseases. In each case the person is genetically predisposed to get the disease *if* they are exposed to the causative agent, but the diseases are not truly genetic diseases because the disease itself is not transmitted on genes.

NEUROCHEMICAL THEORIES

The dopamine theory has dominated neurochemical research on schizophrenia for three decades despite the fact, as noted in chapter 6, that supporting research evidence is sparse. The theory, however, is compelling. For example, amphetamine, which releases dopamine, also causes schizophrenia-like symptoms. Similarly, when L-dopa, a drug that the body may turn into dopamine, is given to persons with schizophrenia, it often makes them worse. Finally, it is known that many drugs that are effective in schizophrenia block dopamine action. For all of these reasons, many researchers suspect that an excess of dopamine is one of the causes of schizophrenia.

Similar theories have been developed for many of the other neurotransmitters. Increasingly, however, it has been realized that neurotransmitters interact in a complex manner with each other, and recent theorists have therefore focused on such interactions.

The main limitation to neurochemical theories of schizophrenia is that there is so little research evidence to support them. It is also increasingly apparent that our original neurotransmitter theories were simplistic and that most antipsychotic medications affect a large number of neurotransmitters. Finally, it should be noted that the dopamine theory and other neurochemical theories of schizophrenia are not really theories of causation but rather theories of the pathophysiology, or *process*, of the disease. If altered dopamine is the cause of schizophrenia, how did it become altered? Possible answers are a genetic defect, stress, a virus, etc., but some other theory must be invoked to explain the altered dopamine.

DEVELOPMENTAL THEORIES

Developmental theories of schizophrenia are both elegant and fashionable. They are based on the hypothesis that something goes wrong during the period of brain development. During fetal life, neurons are being made at a rate of 250,000 per minute. They then have to migrate to the part of the brain where they belong and differentiate into a particular type of neuron. Finally, a pruning process of excess neurons begins during fetal life and continues until at least three years after birth. Clearly, there are many chances for something to go wrong in this extended and complex process.

Developmental theories of schizophrenia do not focus on *what* causes schizophrenia but rather *when* the disease begins. According to developmental researchers, any one of a number of agents could theoretically cause developmental problems. Such agents might include genes, infectious agents, alcohol, chemicals, medications, radiation, malnutrition, or very stressful experiences. As summarized by Dr. Daniel Weinberger, a major proponent of developmental theories, possible agents include "a hereditary encephalopathy or predilection to environmental injury, an infection or postinfectious state, damage from an immunologic disorder, perinatal trauma or encephalopathy, toxin exposure early in development, a primary metabolic disease, or other early developmental events." Once the original insult has taken place at a critical stage of brain development, the damage is done. In most cases, however, its effects would not be immediately noticeable, except perhaps for nonspecific signs such as lack of coordination or behavioral problems in childhood. Once the brain matured, according to developmental theory, the signs and symptoms of schizophrenia would appear.

Developmental theories of schizophrenia are consistent with findings such as minor physical anomalies, pregnancy and birth complications, and an excess of winter and spring births, as described in chapter 6. Developmental theorists also point to animal models wherein damage is intentionally done to vital brain structures (e.g., hippocampus, prefrontal cortex) while the animal is still a fetus and then the animal is found to behave abnormally when it reaches puberty. In the Weinberger et al., animal model, the hippocampal-damaged rat is also said to respond abnormally to chemicals that increase dopamine, thus tying a developmental theory to the dopamine theory. The most important evidence supporting developmental theories, however, are the reports of neuronal disorganization in schizophrenia, which could only have taken place during fetal development.

Despite their elegance, developmental theories have many limitations. Evidence to support the cornerstone of those theories, neuronal disorganization, is far from solid and is in need of replication. The animal models have been criticized as not relevant; what, for example, are equivalent symptoms of schizophrenia in rats? It can also be argued that if the disease process of schizophrenia really begins during fetal life in most cases, why don't we see more minor physical anomalies and mental retardation? Finally, developmental theories, like neurochemical theories, are theories of the pathophysiology or *process* of the disease and leave the identity of the specific cause unanswered.

INFECTIOUS AND IMMUNE THEORIES

As noted in chapter 6, inflammatory and immune abnormalities that are consistent with an infectious cause of schizophrenia have been reported for many years. In recent years, infectious theories have become more prominent, focusing especially on viruses. Viruses are known to attack very specific areas of the brain while leaving other areas untouched; for example, the rabies virus and the herpes zoster virus attack primarily only one kind of cell in one part of the central nervous system. Viruses may also alter the function of brain cells without altering their structure; cell enzymes, for example, may be permanently disrupted by a viral infection, yet the cell itself will continue to live and show no evident damage. This means that viruses could conceivably cause schizophrenia and leave no trace of their damage visible under a microscope.

Another intriguing fact about viruses as a possible cause of schizophrenia is that they may remain latent for many years at a time. This is true for some well-known viruses, such as those in the herpes family, but it is also true for a group of viruses called "slow" viruses, which may not cause disease for 20 years or more after they originally infect the person. Thus, persons with schizophrenia could theoretically become infected while still in the uterus or shortly after birth and yet not show symptoms of the disease until their twenties or thirties.

If viruses are involved in the causation of schizophrenia, it may be that the timing of the original infection is critical. There are known viral diseases that cause brain damage if introduced at one stage of fetal brain development but not at another stage. German measles (rubella) is the best-known example of this, causing mental retardation and heart and other defects if it infects the baby in the first three months of pregnancy but often causing no damage if infection takes place a few months later.

The evidence supporting viruses as a cause of schizophrenia has, until recently, been mostly circumstantial. It has been clearly shown that several different viruses can infect the brain and occasionally produce symptoms that mimic schizophrenia. Some studies have reported that women who are pregnant, especially those in mid-pregnancy, during an influenza epidemic are more likely to give birth to a child who will later develop schizophrenia, but other studies have not found this to be so. Some promising findings have emerged from the Stanley Division of Developmental Neurovirology at Johns Hopkins Medical Center, where elevations in antibodies to some herpes viruses and some retroviruses have been reported in the cerebrospinal fluid of individuals recently diagnosed with schizophrenia.

Findings have also been reported from the Johns Hopkins Laboratory suggesting that antibodies to toxoplasmosis, a parasite carried by cats, are also increased in individuals with schizophrenia. This finding is supported by two other studies, which reported that individuals with schizophrenia have had greater exposure to cats during their childhood than matched controls have had. If these recent findings can be replicated, they will represent a very promising line of research.

Infectious agents are attractive candidates as a cause of schizophrenia. Since many viruses are seasonal, they could account for the seasonality of births in this disease. Viruses are also known to cause minor physical anomalies, alterations in fingerprint patterns, and pregnancy and birth complications, which might explain the increased occurrence of these phenomena in schizophrenia. Some viruses also affect dopamine metabolism. And some antipsychotic medications that are effective in schizophrenia are also effective in suppressing viruses; thus, that could conceivably be their true mode of action. Furthermore, a genetic predisposition to viral infections has clearly been established. For diabetes, for example, Abner Notkins and his colleagues at the National Institutes of Health developed a strain of mice that, when injected with a particular virus, develop diabetes. Another strain of mice is completely resistant and never develops diabetes. It is clear that the first strain has a genetic predisposition toward reacting with the virus in such a way as to produce diabetes. The mice do not inherit the diabetes but rather the predisposition. Another possible virus-gene model for schizophrenia is the transmission of a virus on a gene, which is known to occur for retroviruses.

The shortcomings of a viral theory of schizophrenia include the fact that no specific virus has yet been positively identified. Past studies of viral antibodies, antigens, genomes, cytopathic effect, and animal transmission experiments have yielded mixed and frequently contradictory results. Another shortcoming is that there is little or no proliferation of glial cells (called gliosis) in postmortem brain specimens in schizophrenia; if there were an active, ongoing infectious process, one would expect to see gliosis.

NUTRITIONAL THEORIES

Nutritional theories of schizophrenia have had adherents since it was discovered that beriberi, pellagra, and pernicious anemia, all of which may have psychiatric symptoms, were vitamin deficiency diseases. Researchers have searched for a wide variety of nutritional deficiencies and food allergies with relatively little success, although it must be acknowledged that most of the studies have been methodologically poor. In the 1950s, Drs. Humphrey Osmond and Abram Hoffer began treating patients with schizophrenia with high doses of niacin, other vitamins, and minerals and claimed remarkable success. Their claims have not been substantiated. Treating schizophrenia with vitamins and minerals became known as orthomolecular psychiatry, and an organization of families, the American Schizophrenia Association, was formed.

At this time most schizophrenia researchers do not regard nutrition and food allergies as promising avenues for research. For many people, orthomolecular psychiatry has merged with food faddists and cultists and is not considered scientifically respectable. This is unfortunate because there are occasional individual patients who appear to be helped by specific nutritional regimens and there may indeed be small subgroups of individuals with schizophrenia whose disease has a nutritional basis.

ENDOCRINE THEORIES

Interest in endocrine dysfunction as a possible cause of schizophrenia is linked to observations that severe hypothyroidism, hyperthyroidism, and hyperfunction of the adrenal gland (Cushing's syndrome) may all produce psychiatric symptoms that resemble schizophrenia. A related observation is that maternal psychosis following childbirth is thought to be triggered by massive hormonal changes that occur postpartum. Such observations have led some researchers to question whether more subtle endocrine dysfunction may contribute to the causation of schizophrenia.

One finding that points in this direction is the occurrence of compulsive water drinking (polydypsia) among some individuals with schizophrenia. Water intake is related to hormones in the posterior pituitary gland. The anterior pituitary has also been provisionally linked to schizophrenia in some patients who show altered response to growth hormone when given apomorphine, a dopamine-stimulating drug. There have also been claims that reproductive hormones (FSH and LH), which come from the anterior pituitary, are abnormal in individuals with schizophrenia. The interruption of menstrual periods in some female patients is well known. The fact that insulin coma produced brief remissions in some individuals with schizophrenia led to interest in insulin metabolism, and there have been claims that schizophrenia is less common than expected in type I (insulin-dependent) diabetics and more common than expected in type II (noninsulin-dependent) diabetics. There has also been extensive research in melatonin and the pineal gland in schizophrenia, although the current consensus is that these are not abnormal.

The precise meaning of endocrine dysfunction in schizophrenia is unclear. It could represent an endocrine response to the stress of the illness or an effect of antipsychotic drugs. The endocrine dysfunction may also be another aspect of the disease process; if so, it would not be surprising since the hypothalamus, which controls much endocrine function, is both proximate to and closely connected with the limbic system.

STRESS THEORIES

Stress theories are occasionally invoked as a possible causative cofactor by geneticists and developmental defect proponents. The belief that stress may cause schizophrenia has a long history, and in fact "disappointment in a love affair" and similar stressors were regularly cited as causes of mental illness in the nineteenth century. Stress theories received additional impetus during recent wars when it was noted that occasional soldiers, when under the extreme stress of battle, had the sudden onset of a brief psychotic disorder that transiently resembled schizophrenia.

Since Brown and Birley published their 1968 study claiming that life stresses were important causes of schizophrenia, at least 13 other studies have been carried out. Three of these studies provided some support for the Brown and Birley findings, but the remainder did not. As early as 1980 Rabkin claimed that "no study found more events reported by schizophrenics than by other patient groups." In 1985 Tennant stated categorically that "there is no good evidence that life stress is causally related to episodes of schizophrenia." In 1993 Norman and Malla concurred: "There is no evidence for schizophrenia being related to higher levels of life event stressors than other psychiatric disorders."

The studies that reported an association between stressful events and schizophrenia have a major methodological flaw. In the early stages of schizophrenia, when the person is first becoming ill, the person often acts in unusual ways, thereby precipitating crises of one kind or another. The studies reporting a positive association viewed such crises as the cause of schizophrenia rather than being one of its early effects. This distinction was perceptively noted by Dr. Eugene Bleuler in his classic 1911 book on *Dementia Praecox*:

> In cases in which we have excellent anamneses [histories], one regularly notes that signs of disease existed before the suspected psychic trauma so that it becomes difficult to impute to such trauma any causal significance. In the majority of cases, it is also quite evident without much searching that the unfortunate love affair, demotion from office, etc., were consequences and not causes of the disease if there was any connection between them at all.

Epidemiological observations also make it unlikely that stress is more than a very minor factor—perhaps the straw that broke the camel's back—in causing schizophrenia. For example, if stress is important, why do epidemics not occur in prisons or concentration camps? Why was the schizophrenia rate not high during the Inquisition or the French Revolution? Why did the incidence of schizophrenia appear to go down, not up, during World War II? In summary, it appears likely that stress is no more than a very minor cause of schizophrenia, if indeed it plays any role at all. In contrast to stress as a *cause* of schizophrenia, stress *may* play a role in the *relapse* of the disease, as will be discussed in chapter 12.

OBSOLETE THEORIES

As knowledge evolves in every field of scientific enquiry, new theories arise to explain the observations. At the same time, older theories that no longer fit the facts are set aside and eventually discarded. All areas of science have dusty shelves full of discarded theories and schizophrenia research is no exception. Some of the more unusual discarded theories are as follows.

Masturbation

Masturbation was widely believed to be a cause of schizophrenia and other forms of insanity throughout the nineteenth century. Since many people were thought to masturbate and many people were afflicted with schizophrenia, it was theorized that the two were causally related. Only later was it realized that most people who masturbate do not get schizophrenia, and that some people who get schizophrenia do not masturbate. When it became clear that there was no scientific support for the masturbation theory, it simply died.

Bad Mothers

Bad mothers were widely believed to be a cause of schizophrenia for much of the twentieth century. Since many people were thought to have had bad mothers and many people were afflicted with schizophrenia, it was theorized that the two were causally related.

The strongest proponents of the bad mothering theory were psychoanalytic followers of Sigmund Freud. Freud himself knew virtually nothing about schizophrenia. In 1907 he acknowledged in a letter that "I seldom see dements [dementia praecox or schizophrenia] and hardly ever see other severe types of psychosis." In 1911 Freud published his analysis of a man, Daniel Schreber, who had paranoid schizophrenia. Freud concluded that Schreber had had a "conflict over unconscious homosexuality" that produced an inverted Oedipus complex. Incredibly, Freud never actually examined Schreber but merely read his memoirs. Freud later wrote to a friend that "I do not like these patients [with schizophrenia]. . . . I feel them to be so far distant from me and from everything human. A curious sort of intolerance, which surely makes me unfit to be a psychiatrist."

Freud's lack of interest in schizophrenia did not dissuade his followers from applying his theories to this disease. By the 1940s and 1950s, Freudian theories of schizophrenia were widely believed in the United States. For example, in 1949, when Dr. Trude Tietze published her widely cited study of 25 mothers of individuals with schizophrenia, she concluded that "all mothers were overanxious and obsessive, all were domineering. . . . The mothers' own warped psychosexual development and their own distorted ideas about sex were reflected in their attitude toward their children's sexual development." Like most studies of Freudian theory, Tietze used no controls in her study.

Bad Families

Following World War II, the bad mothering theory of schizophrenia was broadened to include the entire family constellation. The theorists who believed that family interaction caused schizophrenia were almost all psychoanalysts who had been trained in Freudian theory.

Foremost among them was Dr. Theodore Lidz at Yale University. In 1952, Lidz and his colleagues began a study of 16 families of individuals with schizophrenia. No controls were used. Lidz et al. concluded that approximately half of the mothers were "strange, near-psychotic or overtly schizophrenic" but said that the fathers could also exert "an extremely noxious or pathogenic influence upon the family and the patient."

In 1956 the "double-bind" was born, destined to become the cornerstone of family interaction theorists. Basically it postulated that schizophrenia arises when parents give their children heads-I-win-tails-you-lose messages. The lead author of the original paper describing this theory was Gregory Bateson, an anthropologist who had undergone Jungian psychoanalysis; Don Jackson, Jay Haley, and John Weakland were also authors. According to a later essay by Bateson, the inspiration for the "double-bind" came from his studies of communications theory, cybernetics, rituals among natives in Papua New Guinea, the communications of dolphins, and Lewis Carroll's *Through the Looking Glass*. No control studies were done, and Bateson freely acknowledged that "this hypothesis has not been statistically tested." In fact it never was, and in retrospect the single most important antecedent of the theory appears to have been the thinking of Lewis Carroll.

Family interaction theories of schizophrenia, like psychoanalytic theories, have by now been discarded and for many of the same reasons. Not only did they lack a scientific base, but when controlled studies were done on families of patients with schizophrenia by other researchers, the family interaction theories failed to hold up. As early as 1951, for

example, Prout and White compared the mothers of 25 men with schizophrenia with the mothers of 25 normal men and reported no significant
differences; several subsequent studies found the same results. The other
major problem with family interaction theories is that they fail to distinguish family interactions that cause schizophrenia from those *caused by*
schizophrenia. Clinicians experienced in dealing with schizophrenia are
acutely aware of the disruptions to normal family life, including family
communications, that can result from having a family member with this
disease.

In addition to lacking any scientific basis, both the bad mothers and
bad families theories of schizophrenia fell victim to common sense. Any
parent who has raised a child knows that parents are not powerful
enough to cause a disease like schizophrenia simply by favoring one
child over another or giving the child inconsistent messages. Furthermore, families in which one child had developed schizophrenia usually
contained one or more other children who were perfectly normal; they
stood as the final refutation of these theories.

Bad Cultures

In addition to bad mothers and bad families, a few individuals have proposed that bad cultures may cause schizophrenia. This idea was first
developed by anthropologists Margaret Mead and Ruth Benedict in the
1930s. In more recent years it has found expression among occasional
intellectuals, most of whom have become enamored with sociology,
socialism, or both.

One such writer was Christopher Lasch, who in his 1979 *The Culture of Narcissism*, claimed that psychoses are "in some sense the characteristic expression of a given culture." He also quoted Jule Henry, who
wrote that "psychosis is the final outcome of all that is wrong with a culture." Another example of this theory is included in the 1984 book *Not in
Our Genes* by R. C. Lewontin, Steven Rose, and Leon Kamin who, in
the preface, claim that "we share a commitment to the prospect of the
creation of a more socially just—a socialist—society." After disparaging
biological research on schizophrenia, the authors write: "An adequate
theory of schizophrenia must understand what it is about the social and
cultural environment that pushes some categories of people toward manifesting schizophrenic symptoms." The social and cultural environment,
they believe, produce biological changes in the brain that "might be the

reflections or correspondents of that schizophrenia with the brain." Such theorizing, atavistic in view of contemporary knowledge, is now heard only rarely.

Thomas Szasz

Dr. Szasz, a psychoanalyst in Syracuse, New York, became well known not for his theory of schizophrenia but rather for his theory of nonschizophrenia. According to Szasz, schizophrenia and other mental disorders are simply semantic artifacts and do not really exist. This will certainly be welcome news to the individuals afflicted with this disease and to their families. People with schizophrenia, says Szasz, have a "fake disease," which is simply "the sacred symbol of psychiatry." To be a true disease, Szasz claims, "it must somehow be capable of being approached, measured, or tested in a scientific fashion."

Szasz's theories deserve refutation only because they have been so widely circulated and because they are often cited by Scientologists and other anti-psychiatrists (see chapter 15). Szasz himself conducts a traditional psychoanalytic practice for individuals with problems of living; there is nothing in his writings to suggest that he has any experience with or ever treats patients with schizophrenia. Moreover, schizophrenia is now regularly "approached, measured, or tested in a scientific fashion" and the evidence that schizophrenia is a brain disease is overwhelming. The theories of Thomas Szasz about schizophrenia, therefore, have been relegated to the shelf of quirks of medical history.

Ronald Laing

Perhaps the most bizarre and puzzling of all obsolete theories of schizophrenia were those of British psychoanalyst Ronald Laing. He promoted the idea that schizophrenia was a sane response to an insane world and may even be a growth experience, a romantic if nonsensical idea that appealed to many 1960s radicals. Laing's ideas grew out of Freudian and family interaction theories. As expressed by Dr. Joseph Berke, one of his closest followers: " 'Mental illness' reflects what is happening in a disturbed and disturbing group of people, especially when internalized in and by a single person. More often than not, a person diagnosed as 'mentally ill' is the emotional scapegoat for the turmoil in his or her fam-

ily or associates, and may, in fact, be the 'sanest' member of this group."
Laing's ideas about schizophrenia take on a poignant air when it is realized that his eldest daughter was diagnosed with schizophrenia and hospitalized for many years.

Laing founded Kingsley Hall, a house in London in which people
with schizophrenia were allowed to experience their psychosis amidst
friends who were loving and understanding. He refused to treat patients
with medication unless they requested it. Kingsley Hall failed and ultimately closed, and Laing became increasingly disillusioned and alcoholic
as he grew older. In 1982 he commented to an interviewer: "I was looked
to as one who had the answers but I never had them." He died in 1989.

RECOMMENDED FURTHER READING

Buckley, P. F., and J. L. Waddington, eds. *Schizophrenia and Mood Disorders:
The New Drug Therapies in Clinical Practice*. Boston: Butterworth Heinemann, 2000.

Carlson, A. "The Dopamine Theory Revisited." In S. R. Hirsch and D. R. Weinberger, eds. *Schizophrenia*. Oxford: Blackwell Science, 1995.

Ferrier, I. N. "Endocrinology and Psychosis." *British Medical Bulletin* 43
(1987): 672–88.

Garver, D. L. "Neuroendocrine Findings in the Schizophrenias." *Endocrinology
of Neuropsychiatric Disorders* 17 (1988): 103–9.

Gottesman, I. I. *Schizophrenia Genesis: The Origins of Madness*. New York:
W. H. Freeman, 1991.

Hawkins, D., and L. Paulding, eds. *Orthomolecular Psychiatry*. San Francisco:
W. H. Freeman, 1973.

Hirsch, S., P. Cramer, and J. Bowen. "The Triggering Hypothesis of the Role of
Life Events in Schizophrenia." *British Journal of Psychiatry* 161 (suppl.
18) (1992): 84–87.

Lieberman, J., and R. Murray, eds. *Comprehensive Care of Schizophrenia*. London: Martin Dunitz Publishers, 2000.

Owen, F., and M. D. C. Simpson. "The Neurochemistry of Schizophrenia." In
S. R. Hirsch and D. R. Weinberger, eds. *Schizophrenia*. Oxford: Blackwell
Science, 1995.

Tennant, C. C. "Stress and Schizophrenia: A Review." *Integrative Psychiatry* 3
(1985): 248–61.

Torrey, E. F. "Are We Overestimating the Genetic Contribution to Schizophrenia?" *Schizophrenia Bulletin* 18 (1992): 159–70.

Torrey, E. F., and R. H. Yolken. "Familial and Genetic Mechanisms in Schizophrenia." *Brain Research Reviews* 31 (2000): 113–17.

Torrey, E. F., R. Rawlings, and R. H. Yolken. "The Antecedents of Psychoses." *Schizophrenia Research*. Forthcoming.

Torrey, E. F., A. E. Bowler, E. H. Taylor, and I. I. Gottesman. *Schizophrenia and Manic-Depressive Disorder: The Biological Roots of Mental Illness as Revealed by the Landmark Study of Identical Twins.* New York: Basic Books, 1994.

Weinberger, D. R. "Schizophrenia as a Neurodevelopment Disorder." In S. R. Hirsch and D. R. Weinberger, eds. *Schizophrenia.* Oxford: Blackwell Science, 1995.

Yolken, R. H., and E. F. Torrey. "Viruses, Schizophrenia, and Bipolar Disorder." *Clinical Microbiology Reviews* 8 (1995): 131–45.

Yolken, R. H., H. Karlsson, F. Yee, et al. "Endogenous Retroviruses and Schizophrenia." *Brain Research Reviews* 31 (2000): 193–99.

8

THE TREATMENT OF SCHIZOPHRENIA: NONMEDICATION ASPECTS

To lighten the affliction of insanity by all human means is not to restore the greatest of the divine gifts; and those who devote themselves to the task do not pretend that it is. They find their sustainment and reward in the substitution of humanity for brutality, kindness for maltreatment, peace for raging fury; in the acquisition of love instead of hatred; and in the acknowledgment that, from such treatment improvement, and hope of final restoration, will come if hope be possible.

Charles Dickens, *Household Words*, 1852

Contrary to the popular stereotype, schizophrenia is an eminently treatable disease. That is not to say it is a curable disease, and the two should not be confused. Successful treatment means the control of symptoms, whereas cure means the permanent removal of their causes. Curing schizophrenia will not become possible until we understand its causes; in the meantime we must continue improving its treatment.

The best disease model to explain schizophrenia is diabetes, a disease that has many similarities. Both schizophrenia and diabetes have childhood and adult forms, both probably have more than one cause, both have relapses and remissions in a course that often lasts over many years, and both can usually be well controlled, but not cured, by drugs. Just as we don't talk of curing diabetes but rather of controlling its symptoms and allowing the person with diabetes to lead a comparatively normal life, so we should also do with schizophrenia.

HOW TO FIND A GOOD DOCTOR

There is no easy solution to the problem of finding a good doctor, a task that usually falls to the friends and relatives of the person with schizophrenia. There are relatively few doctors in the United States who either know anything about, or have any interest in, treating schizophrenia. This is both shocking and sad, since it is one of the most important chronic diseases in the world. In Europe it is somewhat easier to find a good doctor.

Since schizophrenia is a true biological disease, and since drugs are the mainstay of treatment, there is no avoiding the doctor-finding issue. If schizophrenia is to be properly treated, sooner or later a doctor will need to be involved. He or she will be needed not only to prescribe the proper drugs but also to do an initial diagnostic workup, including laboratory tests, in order to rule out other diseases that may be masquerading as schizophrenia. Before the schizophrenia is treated, one had better be certain that it is not really a brain tumor or herpes encephalitis in disguise. Only a doctor can ascertain this.

The best way to find a good doctor for schizophrenia or any other disease is to ask others in the medical profession whom they would send their own family to if they had a similar problem. Doctors and nurses know who the good doctors are and pass the information freely among themselves; often they will tell you if you ask. If your brother-in-law has a sister who is a nurse, all the better. Use every contact and every relative you have, however distant, to locate and identify competent doctors who may know something about schizophrenia. It is an appropriate time to cash in all your IOUs, for the information is invaluable and may save you months of searching.

Another way to find a good doctor is through other families who have a family member with schizophrenia. They can often provide a quick rundown of the local resources and save weeks of hunting and false starts. Sharing this information is one of the most valuable assets of local chapters of NAMI and is an important reason to join. (Local and state chapters of NAMI can be contacted through NAMI, as listed in appendix D.)

Distinctly *un*helpful in searching for a good doctor are referral lists maintained by local medical societies or the local chapters of the American Psychiatric Association. Anyone can call these organizations and obtain three names. The names, however, are taken from a rotating list of those doctors who are looking for additional patients. Since any doctor who wishes to pay the annual dues can belong to these organizations, there is no screening or ascertainment of quality of any kind. Even those doctors who are under investigation for malpractice will continue to be listed by such organizations until they are specifically removed from membership, which is an all-too-rare occurrence. Thus, referral lists from medical and psychiatric societies are really no better than picking a name at random from the physicians' list in the Yellow Pages.

What should one look for in a good doctor who can treat schizophrenia? Ideally he/she should combine technical competence with an interest in the disease and empathy with its sufferers. Training in psychiatry or neurology is helpful but not mandatory; there are some internists and family practitioners who have an interest in schizophrenia and can treat it very competently. As a general rule younger physicians who have been trained recently are more likely to view schizophrenia as a biological disease. However, there are major exceptions to this rule: some older practitioners who will tell you, "I've said all along it was a real disease," and a few younger practitioners who still know remarkably little about it.

Another important quality possessed by doctors who are good in treating schizophrenia is an ability to work with the family and with other members of the treatment team. Psychologists, psychiatric nurses, social workers, case managers, rehabilitation specialists, and other members of the team are all part of the therapeutic process. Physicians who are reluctant to work with the family or as team members are not good doctors for treating schizophrenia no matter how skilled they may be in psychopharmacology.

In trying to find a good doctor it is perfectly legitimate to ask questions such as "What do you think causes schizophrenia?" "What has been your experience with clozapine?" "What do you think about risperidone (or any other new drug)?" "How important is psychotherapy in treating schizophrenia?" Such open-ended questions will quickly elicit the relative biological orientation of the doctor as well as some sense of how well the person is keeping up with new treatments. As families and consumers become increasingly knowledgeable and sophisticated about the treatment of schizophrenia, it is becoming common to find that they know as much (or more) than some of the treating doctors. The ultimate goal in looking for a good doctor, then, is to find one who is knowledgeable and who also views individuals with schizophrenia, in the words of one psychiatrist, "as a suffering patient, not a defective creation of abstruse, mystical, psychic body parts."

How important is it for the physician to be "board eligible" or "board certified" in his/her specialty? "Board eligible" means that the physician has completed an approved residency program in that specialty. "Board certified" means that the physician has taken and passed an examination in the specialty. Such board examinations are completely optional and are not required for licensure or for membership in any professional organization. They simply mean that the doctor had the theoretical knowledge required to be competent in that specialty at the time he/she took the examination. They do not indicate whether or not the doctor has kept up-to-date since the examination, and for that reason there is relatively little relationship between board certification and competency. All medical specialists should be required to become recertified by examination every five years. Until that time comes, families should give relatively little weight to selecting a "board certified" psychiatrist over a "board eligible" one unless all other things are equal.

What about international medical graduates? Psychiatry has attracted more international medical graduates than any other medical specialty in the United States, and in many states these psychiatrists constitute a majority of all psychiatrists in mental health centers and state hospitals. A 1996 survey reported that international medical graduates were almost twice as likely as American medical graduates to work in public psychiatric settings (42 percent vs. 22 percent) and that they saw almost twice as many patients with psychosis (20 percent vs. 11 percent). International medical graduates are therefore the backbone of American public psychiatry, and without them the disaster of deinstitutionalization would have been even worse than it has been.

On the plus side, some international medical graduates are among the most caring and competent psychiatrists I have known. On the minus side, other international medical graduates range from being mediocre to incompetent. The two foreign medical schools that have contributed the greatest number of psychiatrists to American state hospitals both have had very low pass rates on the Education Council for Foreign Medical Graduates (ECFMG) examination. Some of the international graduates who cannot pass basic licensing exams are given special exemptions by the state to practice only in the state institutions. In essence, the state is saying that it does not consider them competent to treat the "worried well" in private practice but will accept them if they treat the truly sick in the state hospitals.

The most disturbing aspect of utilizing large numbers of international medical graduates to treat patients with schizophrenia is the inevitable difficulty in communication. Verbal language skill is only one part of this; beyond it are many other levels of communication that involve nonverbal language, shared ideals and values, and other components of what is called culture. Communication between a psychiatrist and a person with schizophrenia is difficult enough even when they share a common language and culture; when they do not share these things, communication becomes virtually impossible. Delusions must be assessed in the context of the patient's culture. Affect that may appear appropriate within one culture context may be inappropriate within another. The evaluation of subtle disorders of thinking assumes a complete command of the idioms and metaphors of a language. One psychiatrist, for example, argued for an increase in medication for a patient who complained about "butterflies in her stomach." Another used as evidence of a patient's delusions the fact that she had talked of "babies coming from birds." "Do you mean storks?" asked the psychologist present. "Yes, that's the one," exclaimed the psychiatrist. "Isn't that crazy!" Still another foreign-trained psychiatrist was observed asking a patient the following proverb during a diagnostic interview: "What does mean, a stitch in time gathers no moss?" That kind of question inspires neither confidence nor clarity of thought in a person with schizophrenia.

What about using nonphysicians to treat schizophrenia? In fact psychologists, nurses, social workers, case managers, rehabilitation specialists, and other nonphysicians treat people with schizophrenia regularly and are often the primary contact on the treatment team. It is not uncommon to have the physician on the team merely be the manager of medication and play a relatively small role in the overall treatment plan.

The other aspect of using nonphysicians to treat schizophrenia is using them to prescribe medication. In many states physician assistants and nurse practitioners are already licensed to prescribe medications. Psychologists are currently lobbying for similar privileges that, not surprisingly, are being vigorously opposed by psychiatrists. With proper training in the use of medications and appropriate supervision, any one of these nonphysician groups can competently treat routine cases of schizophrenia while referring difficult diagnostic or therapeutic problems on to a supervising psychiatrist. It is extremely difficult to attract psychiatrists to work in state mental hospitals or public clinics, or in rural areas. Utilizing these nonphysician groups is one reasonable solution to the chronic shortage of psychiatrists in these settings.

To those looking for a good doctor to treat schizophrenia, one final word of caution. Doctors are human beings and, as such, run a wide range of personality types. Throughout the medical profession can be found occasional physicians who are dishonest, mentally ill, addicted to alcohol or drugs, or sociopathic, or who have some combination of the above. I have a sense that psychiatry attracts more than its share of such physicians, often because the physician has become interested in his/her own mental aberrations. Thus, one should not make an absolute assumption that physicians who treat persons with schizophrenia are themselves beyond question. If the physician seems strange to you, move on quickly to another. There are occasional strange birds in the psychiatric aviary.

WHAT IS AN ADEQUATE DIAGNOSTIC WORKUP?

In its full-blown stages, most cases of schizophrenia are not difficult to diagnose. Auditory hallucinations and/or delusional thinking are among the commonest and most prominent symptoms, and more than three-quarters of all patients will have one or the other. Various kinds of thinking disorders become evident in simple conversation (e.g., thought blocking) or on asking the patient to give the meaning of proverbs (e.g., inability to think abstractly). Emotions may be blunted or inappropriate, and the individual's behavior may vary from unusual to catatonic to bizarre.

For a person with the symptoms of schizophrenia who has become ill for the first time, what kind of diagnostic tests and procedures are appropriate? Most public psychiatric hospitals, and many private ones as well, offer cursory diagnostic workups, and there is no question that some patients are diagnosed with schizophrenia who have the diseases described in chapter 4. Given this fact, what should be done diagnostically to maximize the chances of uncovering all potentially reversible diseases masquerading as schizophrenia? The following diagnostic workup is what I would personally want to happen if I or a member of my family were admitted to a hospital with symptoms of schizophrenia for the first time.

History and Mental Status Examination

These are routinely done for all psychiatric admissions but often incompletely so. Visual hallucinations, headaches, and recent head injury should be specifically asked about. A general review of organ systems other than the central nervous system may turn up diseases masquerading as schizophrenia (e.g., abdominal pains suggesting acute intermittent porphyria, urinary incontinence suggesting normal pressure hydrocephalus). Perhaps the single most important question the examining physician can ask is: "What drugs are you using?" It is a two-pronged question intended to elicit information about street drug use, which may be producing or exacerbating the psychiatric symptoms, as well as prescription drug use, which may be producing psychiatric symptoms as a side effect (see chapter 4). Since acutely psychotic patients often cannot give a coherent history, family members and friends play an essential role in providing the needed information.

Physical and Neurological Examinations

These are also often done superficially, with the consequence that many medical and neurological diseases are missed. A careful neurological examination of patients with schizophrenia will elicit abnormal findings in a significant number of them (see chapter 6). A useful part of the neurological exam, which can be taught to nonphysicians who must screen psychiatric patients, is a series of pencil-and-paper tests such as write-a-sentence and draw-a-clock; as Dr. Robert Taylor describes in *Distinguishing Psychological from Organic Disorders*, such tests can help identify patients with other brain diseases, such as brain tumors or Huntington's disease, who may initially present with schizophrenia-like symptoms.

Basic Laboratory Work: Blood Count, Blood Chemical Screen, and Urinalysis

These are also routine everywhere, but abnormal results are sometimes not noticed or followed up. The blood count may elicit unexpected findings suggesting such diseases as pernicious anemia, AIDS, or lead intoxication. Blood chemical screens have become widespread and do many different tests on a single sample of blood. These normally include tests that may screen endocrine or metabolic imbalances. If a thyroid function test is not included in the routine blood chemical screen, it should be ordered separately. A routine test to screen for syphilis should also be included. Urinalysis should include screening tests to detect street drugs in the urine. A useful and cost-effective diagnostic algorithm for detecting physical disease in psychiatric patients has been developed by Dr. Harold Sox and colleagues. It is also useful at this time to get a baseline electrocardiogram (EKG); since some drugs used to treat schizophrenia affect the heart, having a baseline EKG done prior to starting medication may be helpful in future assessments of such side effects.

Psychological Tests

The choice of psychological tests varies from hospital to hospital and depends on the psychologist. Such tests can be extremely useful in making the diagnosis of schizophrenia in early or borderline cases and can also point the examiner away from schizophrenia and toward other brain diseases. Acutely agitated patients frequently are unable to concentrate long enough to do psychological tests.

MRI Scan

Magnetic resonance imaging (MRI) scans are now widely available and, with improving technology, should become less expensive. Computerized tomography (CT) scans can also be used if MRI scans are not available but are much less sensitive for detecting most brain pathology. An MRI scan should be done on every individual who presents with psychosis for the first time. Diseases that mimic schizophrenia and that may be detected by MRI scans include brain tumors, Huntington's disease, Wilson's disease, metachromatic leukodystrophy, sarcoidosis, subdural hematomas, Kuf's disease, viral encephalitis, and aqueductal stenosis. For a person who has had symptoms of schizophrenia for many years, a scan probably is not justified diagnostically, for the diseases the procedure is capable of detecting would have become evident over the years because of other signs or symptoms.

Lumbar Puncture

Despite the stereotype to the contrary, lumbar punctures are simple procedures producing little more discomfort than the drawing of blood. Cerebrospinal fluid is withdrawn by a needle from a sac in the lower back; since the sac is connected to fluid channels in the brain, examination of the cerebrospinal fluid often provides clues (e.g., antibodies to viruses) about events in the brain. Lumbar punctures are routinely used in the diagnosis of brain diseases, such as multiple sclerosis, and probably will become routine for schizophrenia in the future. They are capable of detecting a variety of diseases, especially viral diseases of the central nervous system. Indications for their use in patients admitted for a first episode of schizophrenia include the following.

INDICATIONS FOR LUMBAR PUNCTURE IN FIRST-EPISODE SCHIZOPHRENIA

A. Patient complains of headache (20 percent do) or stiff neck with nausea or a fever
B. Rapid onset of psychotic symptoms
C. Fluctuations in patient's orientation (e.g., patient knows where he is one day but does not know the next day)
D. Visual or olfactory (smell) hallucinations
E. Neurological signs or symptoms suggesting central nervous system disease other than schizophrenia (e.g., nystagmus of the eyes in which the gaze moves rapidly from side to side)
F. Concurrent or recent history of flu or fever

Lumbar punctures in patients with schizophrenia are relatively free of side effects, persons with schizophrenia being especially immune to getting post–lumbar puncture headaches that occur in approximately one-third of people who do not have schizophrenia. The utility of routine diagnostic use of lumbar puncture and CT scans was illustrated by a German study of 130 newly admitted patients with symptoms of schizophrenia; 12 cases of neurological diseases were found among the 130 patients, including three cases of AIDS encephalitis, two cases of encephalitis caused by other viruses, two cases of cerebral syphilis, one case of Lyme disease, and one case of multiple sclerosis.

Electroencephalogram (EEG)

The indications for an EEG are virtually identical to those for lumbar puncture, and in fact the two are often ordered together. I personally believe that both the lumbar puncture and EEG should be routinely included in the diagnostic workup of any young adult presenting with symptoms of psychosis for the first time. An EEG should always be ordered if there is a history of meningitis or encephalitis, birth complications, or severe head injury; it should be mandatory for any patient who has had episodic attacks of psychosis with a sudden onset. An EEG may detect temporal-lobe epilepsy, which sometimes mimics schizophrenia.

To be most useful an EEG should be done using nasopharyngeal leads (electrodes are put into the mouth as well as on the scalp) and be done after the person has been kept up all night (sleep-deprived); the diagnostic rewards for doing this more sophisticated type of EEG are appreciable. EEGs are completely harmless procedures that simply measure electrical impulses in the brain; there are no known side effects or harmful effects of any kind.

Other

Other diagnostic tests may be indicated by specific findings but are not routine. Newer brain scans can be done in a variety of ways (e.g., functional MRI scans, PET scans), but their use is still experimental. The dexamethasone suppression test (DST) was at one time thought to be useful to differentiate certain kinds of patients, but it has not proven to be so. As technology improves, the diagnostic workup of schizophrenia will become increasingly complex and sophisticated.

HOSPITALIZATION: VOLUNTARY AND INVOLUNTARY

In most cases persons *acutely* ill with schizophrenia need to be hospitalized. Such hospitalization accomplishes several things. Most important, it enables mental health professionals to observe the person in a controlled setting. Laboratory tests can be performed to rule out other medical illnesses that may be causing the symptoms, psychological testing can be done, and medication can be started in an environment in which trained staff can watch for side effects. In addition, the hospitalization often provides the family with a respite from what have often been harrowing days and nights leading up to the acute illness.

Hospitalization is also frequently necessary to protect patients. Some will try to injure themselves or others because of their illness (e.g., their voices tell them to do so). Ben Silcock, a young man with schizophrenia who, while acutely psychotic, jumped into the London zoo's lion enclosure and was almost killed, stated it as follows: "The hospital becomes a good place to be; for after being so shaken up it's vital to be in a situation where there is some protection." For this reason most hospitals utilize a locked ward for acutely agitated patients, and its use is often needed. Even in a locked setting the person occasionally may be dangerous and require additional restraints. These may include wrist or ankle restraints (usually made of leather), a special jacket that keeps the arms next to the body (the famous straitjacket of popular lore), or a seclusion room. None of these measures should be necessary for more than a few hours if the person is being properly medicated. It is currently fashionable to condemn locked wards and all use of restraints as "barbaric" and antiquated; the people who make such statements have usually never been faced with the task of providing care for persons with acute schizophrenia. Someday we will arrive at the point where medications are instantly effective in acutely disturbed patients and restraint is not necessary, but we have not reached that nirvana yet.

There are ancillary benefits of hospitalization for persons with schizophrenia. Well-functioning psychiatric units have group meetings for the patients; this often allows each of them to see that his or her experience is not unique. Occupational therapy, recreational activities, and other forms of group interaction often accomplish the same thing. For someone who has been acutely ill and who has experienced many of the disturbances described in chapter 2, it is usually a relief to learn that other people have experienced them too. None of the above activities are likely to be of much benefit, however, unless the person is also being properly medicated to relieve his or her acute symptoms.

There are several different types of hospitals available in which people can be treated for schizophrenia. State psychiatric hospitals were used most commonly in the past, but that has changed dramatically. A study in Oregon, for example, showed that between 1981–1984 and 1991–1994 the use of state hospitals for hospitalizations of individuals with schizophrenia decreased from almost 100 percent to 40 percent. The driving force behind the phasing-out of state psychiatric hospitals, as noted in chapter 1, has been the federal Institution for Mental Disease (IMD) Medicaid exclusion, whereby states are not eligible for federal reimbursement for most state hospital patients. The states therefore shut down state hospitals and force the patients to seek admission in general hospitals and other "semihospital" facilities that are eligible for federal Medicaid reimbursement. This effectively shifts the fiscal burden from the state government to the federal government.

This game of musical psychiatric beds may be good for states economically, but it is not necessarily good for patients clinically. Many general hospitals are not staffed to be able to care for individuals acutely ill with schizophrenia, with predictable untoward consequences. Care in private hospitals also runs a broad gamut, from very good to abysmal; many private hospitals run by for-profit hospital chains are notorious for keeping patients for whatever length of time their insurance benefits permit, then declaring them well and summarily discharging them.

In looking for a hospital for someone with schizophrenia, then, shop carefully. The most important factor by far is the competence of the treating psychiatrist. State hospitals, Veterans Administration (VA) hospitals, general hospitals, university hospitals, and private hospitals all may vary from very good to very bad. One of the finest hospitals I have been in is the New Hampshire State Hospital at Concord, and one of the hospitals with the poorest care for schizophrenia is a very expensive prestigious private hospital. In contrast to most other diseases, paying more money does not necessarily buy you better care for schizophrenia.

A measure of hospital quality that previously was considered to be useful was accreditation by the Joint Commission on Accreditation of Health Care Organizations (JCAHO). At the invitation of a hospital, JCAHO sends a survey team to evaluate it, as well as provide consultation and education. The survey focuses on patient care and services but also includes such related issues as the therapeutic environment, safety of the patient, quality of staffing, and administration of the hospital. The survey team then recommends that the hospital receive full three-year accreditation, full accreditation with a contingency (which may necessitate a follow-up inspection to ensure that the contingency has been corrected), or no accreditation. Full accreditation by JCAHO at one time was thought to signify that the hospital was a good one, although, since the accreditation was for the hospital as a whole, individual wards in an accredited hospital still may have been below standard. In more recent years, JCAHO accreditation has itself been discredited because of what one federal report labeled the "cozy relationship" between the hospitals and the privately run JCAHO. Hospitals pay many thousands of dollars for the survey and they expect to be accredited; JCAHO consequently accredits many hospitals despite evidence of poor patient care. JCAHO accreditation can therefore no longer be relied on as a measure of quality.

One aspect of hospitalization that has changed markedly in recent years is the length of hospitalizations. In the past, hospitalizations for schizophrenia were usually measured in weeks or even months. However, with the pressure of managed care and insurance companies, the average length of stay has decreased dramatically and is now measured in days. In the Oregon study cited above, for example, the average length of hospitalization for individuals with schizophrenia decreased from 124 to 65 days between the early 1980s and early 1990s. It is now 30 days or less in most hospitals. This has become a tremendous problem for both patients and their families because the patients are often being discharged prematurely.

Ideally, people with schizophrenia will recognize when they are becoming sick and then voluntarily seek treatment for their sickness. Unfortunately, as described in chapter 2, this is often not the case. Schizophrenia is a disease of the brain, the body organ charged with the responsibility of recognizing sickness and the need for treatment—the same organ that is sick. Out of this unfortunate circumstance arises the frequent need for persons to be committed to psychiatric treatment settings against their will. Inpatient commitment will be discussed here, and outpatient commitment, another and less restrictive form of assisted treatment, in chapter 11.

All laws governing commitment of psychiatric patients are state laws, not federal laws. Therefore commitment laws vary from state to state, especially those governing long-term commitment. Between 1970 and 1980 there was a broad shift in the United States to change state laws to make it more difficult to involuntarily hospitalize individuals with psychiatric illnesses. The effect of this shift was to make it virtually impossible in many states to hospitalize an individual with schizophrenia unless that person was shown to be an immediate danger to self or others. Because of the problems produced by these stringent laws, there is growing sentiment to modify the laws so that such persons can be involuntarily hospitalized and treated.

Legally there are two rationales for the commitment of mental patients. The first is referred to as *parens patriae*, which is the right of the state to act as parent and protect a disabled person; it arose from the belief that the king was the father of all his subjects. This may be invoked when people are so disabled that they do not recognize their own need for treatment or cannot provide for their own basic needs because of the symptoms of their illness. The second legal justification for commitment is the right of the state to protect other people from a person who is dangerous. This is used when persons, because of their mental illness, are dangerous to others.

There are also two kinds of commitment—emergency and long-term. The basic purpose of commitment laws is to, when appropriate, place persons who are psychiatrically ill in treatment in order to provide them with needed care and to prevent harm to themselves or others. This can be done as follows.

1. A petition for emergency commitment of the person thought to be psychiatrically ill must be initiated. In most states this can be done by one of several persons; for example, Tennessee allows petitions to be filed by "the parent, guardian, spouse, or a responsible adult relative of the individual or by any licensed physician or licensed psychologist or by any health or public welfare officer, or by the head of any institution in which the individual may be, or by any officer authorized to make arrests in Tennessee." In many states, any person can initiate a petition for emergency commitment.

2. The person initiating the petition asks a physician (not necessarily a psychiatrist) to examine the person for whom commitment is sought. Some states require two physicians to be examiners while others allow psychologists. If the examiner(s) concludes that the person is mentally ill and meets the grounds for commitment in that state, then the examiner's report is attached to the petition and it is filed. In many states, an affidavit from a physician who has recently examined the person may be substituted for this examination.

3. The examination may take place anywhere, including in the person's home.

4. If the person for whom commitment is sought refuses to be examined, many states have a provision for the petitioner to file a sworn written statement or petition. In Nevada, for example, this says, "such person is mentally ill and, because of such illness, is likely to harm himself or others, or is gravely disabled."

5. Once the petition has been filed, the person must appear for examination by a physician. If the person refuses, a law enforcement official can bring him or her to a hospital for the examination.

6. Alternatively, if any person is acting strangely in public, a police officer, sheriff, mental health crisis team, etc., can bring the person to the hospital for examination by a physician.

7. The examining physician at the hospital decides on the basis of his/her examination whether the person meets the criteria for commitment in that state. If the person does, emergency commitment is effected and the person is kept at the hospital. If not, the person is released.

8. An emergency commitment lasts for 72 hours in most states, not including weekends and holidays. At the end of that period the person must be released unless either the director of the hospital or the family has filed a petition with the court asking for longer term commitment. If this has been filed, then the person can be held until the hearing.

9. The hearing for long-term commitment may be held in a room in the hospital or in a courtroom. In most states, the person alleged to be mentally ill is expected to be present unless a physician testifies that the person's presence would be detrimental to his/her mental state. The person is represented by a lawyer appointed by the state if necessary; normal judicial rules of evidence and due process apply, although such hearings are often less formal than other court proceedings. Testimony may be taken from the examining physician, from family members, and from the person alleged to be mentally ill.

10. The hearing is held before a mental health commission, judge, or similar judicial authority depending on the state. In many states the person has the right to a jury trial if he/she so wishes.

The major differences in commitment procedures among states are the grounds that are used for commitment and the standard of proof. In states that utilize only dangerousness to self or others and define dangerousness stringently, it is generally more difficult to get a commitment than in states that define dangerousness vaguely (for example, until recently, Texas law said a mentally ill person could be committed "for his own welfare and protection or the protection of others"). Similarly, in states in which "gravely disabled" or "in need of treatment" are grounds for commitment by themselves, it should be easier to get a person with a severe mental illness committed for treatment.

Probably the most important variables in determining how easy or difficult it is to obtain a legal commitment to get a mentally ill person into treatment are the specific judge involved and the local community standards. As lawyers well know, laws are written one way but can be interpreted in many ways, and this is especially true for laws concerning psychiatric commitment. Thus, in the same state one judge may interpret dangerousness much more stringently than another. Similarly, what for one judge is "clear and convincing evidence" might not be at all persuasive for another. Community standards vary as well, with some localities more inclined to "lock up all those crazies" whereas others in the same state may be reluctant to commit people unless absolutely necessary. Also important is the current local milieu. For example, if a former psychiatric patient has recently been accused of murder in the local newspaper, the tendency may be to commit everyone with acute symptoms. If, on the other hand, the local newspaper is doing an exposé on the poor conditions in the state hospital, the tendency may be to not commit anybody unless absolutely necessary.

Individual horror stories abound of clearly psychotic persons who could not be involuntarily placed in treatment because of the stringent interpretation given to "dangerousness to self or others" by law enforcement and judicial officials. In 1984 in the District of Columbia, I personally examined a homeless woman who was blatantly hallucinating and had been carrying an axe around town; the police refused to take her to a hospital for possible commitment because they said she had not *yet* done anything to demonstrate dangerousness. In Wisconsin "a man barricaded himself in his house and sat with a rifle in his lap muttering 'Kill, kill, kill.' A judge ruled that the man was not demonstrably violent enough to qualify for involuntary commitment."

At another commitment hearing in Wisconsin, a man with schizophrenia, already mute and refusing to eat food or bathe, was observed to be eating feces while being held in jail. He was released because such behavior did not qualify as dangerous. The dialogue at the commitment hearing included the following:

Public defender: "Doctor, would the eating of fecal material on one occasion by an individual pose a serious risk of harm to that person?"

Doctor: "It is certainly not edible material. . . . It contains elements that are considered harmful or unnecessary."

Public defender: "But, Doctor, you cannot state whether the consumption of such material on one occasion would invariably harm a person?"

Doctor: "Certainly not on one occasion."

The public defender then moved to dismiss the action on the grounds that the patient was in no imminent danger of physical injury or dying, and the case was dismissed.

It is such absurd and inhumane legal decisions as these that have spurred a growing movement toward broadening grounds for commitment. The State of Washington was one of the first to move in this direction in 1979, and since then several others have begun to follow. Currently, about one-half of the states have incorporated some form of need for treatment or deteriorating clinical condition as criteria for involuntary treatment.

In 1983 the American Psychiatric Association proposed a model commitment statute that would allow psychiatrically ill persons to be placed in treatment if their behavior indicated "significant deterioration" of their psychiatric state and they were clearly in need of treatment. I believe it is a good model for state laws. It permits the treatment of a relapsing patient *before* the person has had to demonstrate dangerousness. Waiting to treat those affected with severe mental illnesses until they become dangerous to themselves or others ensures that many will become exactly that.

What does all this mean for a family with a member who is in need of treatment and who refuses to go to the hospital? It means that the family must first learn the commitment procedures and criteria that apply in their state. The quickest way is to contact the admission unit of the nearest psychiatric hospital or the clerk of the local court, whose personnel are usually experts in this area. Other potential resources for this information are the Treatment Advocacy Center, the local or state chapter of

NAMI, psychiatrists in your area, the local or state Department of Mental Health, the public defender, or the police. A good state-by-state summary of standards for commitment and assisted treatment can be found at the Treatment Advocacy Center website, www.psychlaws.org. The family must also learn what kinds of evidence are necessary and admissible to prove dangerousness. For instance, are threats to other people sufficient, or does the person actually have to have injured someone? The answer depends on what your state law is and how it is applied. Families who wish to can usually testify at the commitment hearing. Their knowledge of what proof is necessary often determines whether a person with schizophrenia gets the treatment he or she needs. Indeed, many family members of people with schizophrenia end up becoming amateur lawyers in order to survive!

The long-term consequences of involuntarily hospitalizing a person with schizophrenia are quite variable. On one end of the spectrum are individuals who, following an involuntary hospitalization, refuse to have anything to do with their families. Some may even run away from home. The more radical consumer groups of so-called "psychiatric survivors" (see chapter 15) appear to be primarily made up of individuals who were once involuntarily hospitalized and who then decided to turn their resentment into a career. Such individuals adopt their illness as their identity.

On the other end of the spectrum are those who retrospectively regard their involuntary hospitalization very positively because it got them into treatment. In one of the few studies done on this question, Dr. John Kane and his colleagues in New York interviewed 35 involuntarily admitted patients shortly after their admission and again just prior to discharge approximately two months later. They found that most patients had "significant changes toward recognition of the original need for involuntary treatment." Most other studies have reported similar results. I have personally participated in an involuntary commitment hearing in which a woman with schizophrenia told her daughter, who was testifying for the commitment, that she would never speak to her again; a year later, on medication and in complete remission, the woman expressed profound thanks to her daughter for being the only family member who had had the courage to get her the treatment she needed.

ALTERNATIVES TO HOSPITALIZATION

Hospitalization is usually necessary for patients with schizophrenia who are sick for the first time, for the reasons described above. For those who have already been clearly diagnosed and who have relapsed (often because they have stopped taking their medicine), hospitalization can sometimes be avoided. There are several possible alternatives.

One such alternative is the use of drugs given by injection in an emergency room or clinic. A skilled physician can dramatically reduce the psychotic symptoms in approximately half of patients with schizophrenia within six to eight hours, thereby allowing the person to return home. One problem with this technique, however, is that frequently the family members are so worn out by the person's recent behavior that *they* need the rest and understandably are not prepared to accept the person home again immediately.

Another increasingly popular alternative to hospitalization is the use of mobile treatment teams that go to the individual's home, assess the situation, and frequently begin treatment on the spot. This can effectively decrease the use of hospitalization but is effective only where there is also skilled and coordinated follow-up.

Another recent development is the increasing use by states and counties of psychiatric beds for short-term hospitalization in institutions other than hospitals, primarily because such beds are less expensive. These institutions, referred to in chapter 1 as "semihospitals," have different names in different places, such as IMDs (Institutions for Mental Diseases) or crisis homes. Some IMDs in California have over 200 beds and are similar to state mental hospitals in everything except name.

Another alternative is the treatment of the patient at home, using public health nurses or, rarely, physicians to make home visits. This technique is used much more often in England, with apparent success. It was also demonstrated to be feasible in a study done in Louisville, Kentucky, by Dr. Benjamin Pasamanick and his colleagues, who concluded that "the combination of drug therapy and public health nurses' home visitation is *effective* in preventing hospitalization, and that home care is at least as good a method of treatment as hospitalization by any or all criteria, and probably superior by most." I utilized this method once when practicing in a rural village, when the family expressed a wish to keep the person at home if possible; it required home visits for injections twice a day for a week, but it was successful.

The use of partial hospitalization is another good alternative. Day hospitals, in which the patient goes to the hospital for the day and returns home at night, and night hospitals, in which the patient goes to the hospital only to sleep, can both be effective in selected cases. Since both cost less than full hospitalization they may be useful in communities in which they are available. They are usually affiliated with a full-time institution. Unfortunately, both are much less available than they should be in the United States.

PAYMENT FOR TREATMENT AND INSURANCE PARITY

Selecting the optimal place for hospitalization and follow-up psychiatric care is usually constrained by the reality of costs. These can be astronomical, with hospitalization in a general or private hospital costing $500 to $1,000 a day, private psychiatrists charging $150 an hour or more, and the cost of newer antipsychotic medications approaching parity with the price of gold (see chapter 9). Even the wealthiest families have learned to sit down before opening bills for psychiatric care.

Like other Americans, a large number of individuals with schizophrenia have no medical insurance. A 1998 study of 525 individuals with psychosis being admitted to hospitals for the first time reported that 44 percent had no insurance, 39 percent had private insurance, 15 percent had Medicaid or Medicare, and 2 percent were covered by the Veterans Administration. For those with private insurance, there are often stricter limits on the number of hospital days and outpatient visits allowed for psychiatric diagnoses than there are for other medical or surgical diagnoses. This has led to a major push for insurance parity for psychiatric coverage, and since 1990 the majority of states have passed legislation mandating parity.

Resistance to insurance parity for psychiatric conditions has come primarily from insurance companies, who have to pay the bills. This resistance is based on the fact that psychiatrists have a reputation for gaming the insurance system and inflating costs. A 1985 study reported that "psychiatrists form a disproportionately large segment of the total" physicians who were suspended from the Medicaid and Medicare programs because of fraud and abuse. And psychiatrists played major roles in the private psychiatric hospital insurance scams of the early 1990s (see Joe Sharkey's description of this in *Bedlam: Greed, Profiteering, and Fraud in a Mental Health System Gone Crazy*).

Resistance to insurance parity for psychiatric conditions also arises from the vague outer limits of psychiatric diagnoses as defined by the American Psychiatric Association. Almost anybody can qualify for one or another diagnosis and therefore theoretically become eligible for insurance benefits for psychotherapy or hospitalization. This problem was summarized in December 1999 in an editorial in the *Wall Street Journal*:

> The reason "parity" doesn't exist is that, beyond treatment of obvious disorders, "mental health" is a vague and open-ended term. The difficulty has been abuse of mental-health insurance by both individuals and the "provider network" who gamed insurance plans to make endless payments for dubious benefits of apparently marginal problems, all the while lobbying to gain coverage for an ever-expanding definition of mental illness.

The obvious solution to the insurance problem is to limit parity to those psychiatric conditions for which there is convincing evidence that they are indeed diseases. This would include schizophrenia and would go a long way toward alleviating the restricted coverage faced by so many families.

For individuals with schizophrenia who are not covered by private insurance, establishing eligibility for Medicaid benefits is the most important thing to do. The easiest way to do this is to become eligible for Supplemental Security Insurance (SSI), since recipients of SSI are automatically eligible for Medicaid. Applying for SSI is discussed in chapter 10.

OUTPATIENT TREATMENT AND MANAGED CARE

With psychiatric hospitalizations becoming increasingly brief, most individuals with schizophrenia receive most of their treatment from community facilities. The quality of such outpatient care varies as widely as does inpatient care—from excellent to abysmal.

There are three important variables that determine the quality of outpatient psychiatric care:

Competency of the Professionals

Psychiatrists, psychologists, social workers, and psychiatric nurses run a very broad spectrum of competency. Most training programs, unfortunately, continue to train these professionals to be mental *health* professionals rather than mental *illness* professionals. There are a handful of good programs in which the professionals are being well trained to treat mental illness, but such programs stand out as exceptions rather than the rule.

Targeting the Seriously Mentally Ill as First Priority

Psychiatric outpatient services are obviously a finite resource for an almost infinite series of demands that may be placed on such services. Married couples having problems, poor or minority groups with no jobs and low self-esteem, elderly persons who are lonely, and children underachieving in school because of emotional problems are only a few of the groups that may view local psychiatric outpatient services as a primary solution to their problems. The needs of these groups are both worthy and compelling, yet if psychiatric resources are utilized for them in large numbers, soon no resources are left for the seriously mentally ill. This is precisely what has happened in many mental health centers in the United States. It is, in short, a choice between promoting "mental health" or treating mental illness.

The allocation of public psychiatric resources is ultimately an ethical question. Which group is most worthy? Which group needs the services more? Which group can utilize the services best? What is the benefit to society of providing psychiatric services to each group? Dr. J. R. Elpers, in a discussion of this question, argued that the seriously mentally ill have fewer alternative resources and are also sicker, and on these grounds require first priority. What has become abundantly clear in recent years is that states like New Hampshire and cities like Vancouver, British Columbia, which have targeted the seriously mentally ill as having priority for psychiatric services, have much better programs than states and cities that have not done so.

Continuity of Care

Although frequently given lip service, continuity of care for individuals with schizophrenia is rarely achieved in the United States. Sadly typical is an appalling lack of continuity, such as was experienced by Sylvia Frumkin, the focus of Susan Sheehan's book *Is There No Place on Earth for Me*, who over an eighteen-year period had twenty-seven separate admissions to eight different hospitals with a total of forty-five changes in treatment settings.

It may well be that the key element in continuity of care is continuity of the caregiver. In other words, a single individual or team should be responsible for the psychiatric care of a person with serious mental illness, no matter where that person goes within a defined geographic area. A description of such an arrangement was provided by Dr. Mary Ann Test, one of the nation's acknowledged leaders on the organization of psychiatric services, who defined continuity of caregiver as taking "responsibility for seeing to it that a chronically mentally ill person's needs are met. . . . The team members do not necessarily meet all the client's needs themselves (they may involve other persons or agencies). However they never transfer this obligation to someone else. The buck stops with the team . . . the team remains responsible for the client no matter what his or her behavior is. This fixed point of responsibility means that the client always has a consistent resource." Elsewhere I have called such an arrangement a "continuous treatment team."

Continuity of caregivers is logical in theory, considering the needs of the patients. People with schizophrenia often have great difficulties in establishing human relationships, and to expect them to transfer their trust from one treatment team to another is exceedingly unrealistic. Continuity of caregivers also has many advantages from the point of view of mental illness professionals, allowing them to get to know patients in depth, assessing their medication history and potentials for rehabilitation, and working with their family. Continuity of caregivers is nicely exemplified by continuous treatment teams that are patterned after the widely praised PACT (Program of Assertive Community Treatment) in Madison, Wisconsin. Continuous treatment teams have been widely used in Wisconsin, Michigan, Rhode Island, New Hampshire, and Delaware and are being implemented in 19 other states.

It is clear, therefore, that we know how to provide quality outpatient services for individuals with schizophrenia. So why don't we do it? The answer is twofold. First, we have structured the fiscal aspects of outpatient services in a way that virtually guarantees failure. This problem is related to the larger problem of how we fund medical care in the United States. We spend over $4,000 per person on health care, which is $1,500 *more* than the next highest country (Switzerland), and yet millions of people are not covered by any kind of health insurance. For outpatient psychiatric services, Medicaid and private insurance will reimburse for some kinds of specific services but not for others; there are no fiscal incentives to utilize continuous treatment teams or to keep patients from relapsing. Indeed, it is often said that the present system for funding psychiatric outpatient services is more thought-disordered than most of the patients it is designed to treat.

The other reason why quality outpatient services for people with schizophrenia do not exist in most places is managed care. Managed care is actually a misnomer; it is really only managed costs. It was implemented in the 1990s to help stem the tide of rapidly escalating medical costs. It has indeed accomplished that, but by injecting a profit motive without tying profits to patient outcomes, it has virtually guaranteed poor care for chronic diseases, including schizophrenia.

Imagine how different psychiatric services would be if managed care companies were reimbursed on the basis of decreased relapses, fewer medication side effects, and improved quality of life because of fewer symptoms. Instead, the companies make greater profits by minimizing the care they provide for individuals with schizophrenia, hiring the least expensive staff, which guarantees high turnover, using less expensive medications when more expensive medications may be indicated, making it virtually impossible to hospitalize patients until they have completely relapsed, and discharging them prematurely. The incentive structure is completely wrong for providing quality services. Most managed care companies are doing well financially, but most patients are doing poorly clinically. The product is managed costs but mangled care.

SERVICES FOR CHILDREN

Children with schizophrenia require the same treatment and rehabilitation services as adults with this disorder but, in addition, have special needs. Schizophrenia almost never begins before age five and increases slowly in incidence between five and 16, at which time its incidence rises sharply.

One special problem with schizophrenia in childhood is clarifying the diagnosis. Children with schizophrenia may also have behavioral problems, drug or alcohol abuse, severe depression, or neurological problems such as seizures and are sometimes mislabeled with these other conditions. For this reason it has become common in the United States to label children as "seriously emotionally disturbed," or SED, rather than specifying a specific condition. In recent years the term "neurobiological disorders," or NBD, has also been used to encompass schizophrenia, autism, severe depression, manic-depressive illness, obsessive-compulsive disorder, Tourette's syndrome, and other known brain diseases of childhood.

Another problem peculiar to childhood schizophrenia is that over half of the states encourage or require parents to give up custody of their child in order to be eligible for state residential services. The reason for this draconian practice is purely fiscal: Federal Medicaid under Title IV-E (the Adoption Assistance and Foster Care Act) will pay much of the cost for residential services for children who are under state custody but not for those who are not under state custody. Therefore, to save state funds and shift the cost to the federal government, states encourage, and sometimes require, parents to give up custody of their child with schizophrenia as a condition for receiving residential services. The fact that this is allowed to occur—indeed, encouraged by government—in a civilized society is a sad measure of the bankruptcy of the mental illness treatment system.

A third aspect of childhood schizophrenia that is not found in the adult variety is that, until recently, the majority of states sent large numbers of these children to other states to be treated in private facilities rather than provide the treatment themselves. For example, in 1990 Maryland sent 680 seriously emotionally disturbed children out of state for treatment, some as far as Vermont and Florida, at a cost to the state of $31.5 million. This practice is slowly becoming less common in most states.

Finally, children with schizophrenia, unlike adults, have not completed their education. Therefore, schools must be involved in such children's overall treatment plan. Most school systems are not effective in handling children with disabilities and avoid doing so whenever possible. Parents must therefore develop expertise in federal laws that protect such children's rights, including section 504 of the Rehabilitation Act of 1973, which mandates educational help for students with disabilities, the

Individuals with Disabilities Education Act (IDEA), and the Americans with Disabilities Act (ADA). Many states have additional statutes that mandate educational services for children with disabilities. The goal is to develop an Individualized Education Plan (IEP) for each child with schizophrenia.

There are three important principles that should be incorporated into services for children with schizophrenia or other neurobiological disorders.

1. Treatment must be integrated with education and job skills training. Model programs such as Kaleidoscope and Thresholds in Chicago have demonstrated how this can be done.

2. The child should continue to live at home whenever possible unless there is some contraindication. The Homebuilders program in Tacoma, Washington, is considered to be a model for such services.

3. Services must be flexible and well coordinated. A variety of services may be required, including residential group homes, foster care, day programs, wilderness camps, and transition services when the person graduates to adult services. Services for children with schizophrenia often involve a variety of local, county, and state agencies, including education, juvenile justice, social services, and child welfare as well as mental health; the coordination of these services can be a bureaucratic nightmare. The Alaska Youth Initiative and Ventura County, California, have been widely praised as ambitious attempts to coordinate such services.

SERVICES IN RURAL AREAS

Treatment and rehabilitation services for individuals with schizophrenia who live in rural areas are very deficient. Long distances, bad roads, and few mental illness professionals or facilities make the provision of good services an ongoing challenge. It *is* possible to provide quality services, however, utilizing some of the following principles.

1. A family physician, internist, physician assistant, nurse practitioner, or public health nurse can be utilized as the primary person to

prescribe and monitor medication. In order to do so, this person must be given some training, periodic continuing education, and consultation back-up by a psychiatrist who is available by telephone 24 hours a day. In Canada, the province of Saskatchewan has utilized family physicians and public health nurses very successfully to provide ongoing care for individuals deinstitutionalized from the provincial hospital. Similarly, in British Columbia family physicians provide extensive psychiatric services in rural hospitals and are visited on a monthly basis by psychiatrists from Vancouver. The feasibility of using public health nurses to provide primary care for individuals with schizophrenia living in the community was demonstrated more than 30 years ago by Dr. Benjamin Pasamanick and his colleagues in Louisville, Kentucky. More recently such nurses have been successfully used to follow elderly mentally ill persons in rural Iowa.

2. Brief psychiatric hospitalizations can be done utilizing the medical wards of general hospitals as well as crisis beds in nursing homes or other medical or social service facilities. Reading and Maguire demonstrated the effective use of general hospital beds for acute psychiatric admissions in rural upstate New York.

3. Continuity of care is just as important in rural areas as in urban areas. In South Carolina, it was shown that continuity of care could be achieved in a rural area using the PACT model, as described above.

4. Mobile clinics, which go to a different town each day, are very useful in rural areas. Mobile day programs, which cover five areas, each for one day a week, have also been successfully utilized.

5. Given the paucity of mental illness professionals in most rural areas, it is even more important to train local and state police, emergency medical technicians, and ambulance personnel on the proper management of individuals with acute psychosis. A good model for this is the training courses run by Dartmouth Medical School for rural areas in New Hampshire and Vermont.

6. With interactive video technology advancing rapidly, it should soon be economically feasible to utilize telepsychiatry, with video units placed in rural general hospitals and connected to a central psychiatric facility. Pilot programs have been carried out in Nebraska,

Ontario, and elsewhere, but to date it has been found to be too expensive. This should soon change as the technology improves.

COUNSELING, OR SUPPORTIVE "PSYCHOTHERAPY"

An integral part of outpatient psychiatric services is counseling, or supportive "psychotherapy," which can be helpful for individuals with schizophrenia, especially if the person providing these services is the same person for long periods of time. I put the term "psychotherapy" in quotations to differentiate it clearly from insight-oriented psychotherapy, discussed below, which for schizophrenia is a discredited and even harmful mode of treatment.

Counseling, or supportive "psychotherapy," on the other hand, may provide a patient with friendship, encouragement, practical advice such as access to community resources or how to develop a more active social life, vocational advice, suggestions for minimizing friction with family members, and, above all, hope that the person's life may be improved. Discussions focus on the here-and-now, not the past, and on problems of living encountered by the patient as he or she tries to meet the exigencies of life, despite a handicapping brain disease. The opening approach I took with my own patients was something like the following: "Look, I'm sorry you have this lousy brain disease, which is not your fault, but let's see what we can do to help you live better with it." It is exactly the same approach one might take with a patient with multiple sclerosis, polio, chronic kidney disease, severe diabetes, or any other long-term disease.

The person who provides counseling or supportive "psychotherapy" can be the physician who is overseeing the medication or it can be any other mental illness professional or paraprofessional who is on the care team. "Case manager" has become a popular term in recent years, although it is not clear to me how a case manager's job differs from what psychiatrists, psychologists, social workers, and psychiatric nurses are supposed to have been doing all along. The term "case manager" has the added disadvantage of implying that individuals with schizophrenia are "cases" who need to be "managed," when in fact a collaborative relationship between patient and mental illness professional is the goal. An additional disadvantage is that "case manager" is a term also used by insurance companies to manage insurance benefits. Thus, it is not uncommon to have an insurance company's case manager telling the mental health center's case manager what reimbursements will be allowed. Not surprisingly this is frequently confusing to patients and their families.

Case managers on psychiatric care teams may play a variety of roles. They may be the person's primary counselor, provide education about the illness, assist with applying for benefits and housing, provide transportation for clinic appointments, and make arrangements for rehabilitation programs. The effectiveness of a case manager depends in part on his or her personality characteristics but also on the quality of the available benefits and programs. All too often in the United States case managers are employed by psychiatric care programs that offer meager housing, rehabilitation programs, or other benefits, and they are "managers" in name only.

The frequency of meetings between the person with schizophrenia and the counselor may vary from once a week or more to once a year. Regarding the last, Dr. Werner M. Mendel once related the story of a man whose schizophrenia was in good remission but who always carried a small vial of antipsychotic medication because the rattling of the pills was reassuring to him. After about a year the pills became powder, the rattling stopped, and the man would return to Dr. Mendel for a refill.

There is scientific evidence that such a supportive relationship, when it is used *in addition to drug therapy*, is helpful in reducing the rehospitalization rate for schizophrenia. In one study patients were followed for one year after release from the hospital and offered one of four modes of follow-up: (1) placebo alone (a placebo is an inert or dummy medication with no physiological action), (2) placebo plus supportive "psychotherapy," (3) drugs alone, and (4) drugs plus supportive "psychotherapy." At the end of the year the rehospitalization rates were:

Treatment	Percentage of Patients Hospitalized
Placebo alone	72
Placebo plus supportive "psychotherapy"	63
Drugs alone	33
Drugs plus supportive "psychotherapy"	26

The "psychotherapy" used in this study included social services and vocational counseling provided by someone who was predictably available to the patients. The results suggest again that drugs are the single most important element in preventing rehospitalization but that a supportive relationship provides a measure of additional prevention.

INSIGHT-ORIENTED PSYCHOTHERAPY

Several studies have now demonstrated that insight-oriented psychotherapy is of no value for schizophrenia. Probably the best-known of these studies was done by Dr. Philip R. A. May and his colleagues at Camarillo State Hospital in California. May randomly assigned 228 patients with schizophrenia to five separate wards where they were treated by (1) insight-oriented psychotherapy alone, (2) psychotherapy plus drugs, (3) drugs alone, (4) milieu alone, and (5) electroconvulsive therapy. The patients who did best were those treated by drugs alone or psychotherapy plus drugs, and there were virtually no differences between the two groups; the patients who did worst were those treated by insight-oriented psychotherapy alone or milieu alone. The inescapable conclusion was that insight-oriented psychotherapy added nothing to the treatment regimen in this study. These patients were followed up for from three to five years after the initial treatment and the results did not change: "Analysis of variance indicated an extremely significant effect from drug [therapy and] . . . , no significant effect from psychotherapy."

May's study was criticized by some for utilizing insight-oriented psychotherapy which was not "intensive" enough and for having it done by psychotherapists who were relatively inexperienced. Another study was therefore designed to treat patients with schizophrenia with explicitly psychoanalytically oriented psychotherapy (two hours a week for two years), using highly experienced psychotherapists. At the end of the study period the outcome was said to be that "psychotherapy alone (even with experienced psychotherapists) did little or nothing for chronic schizophrenic patients in two years." Such studies were summarized by Donald Klein, a respected research psychiatrist: "There is no scientific basis for the affirmation of clinical benefit from the individual psychotherapy of schizophrenic patients."

There is some evidence that psychoanalysis and insight-oriented psychotherapy may be not only useless for treating schizophrenia but in fact harmful. In the May study, for example, the "outcome for patients who received only psychotherapy was significantly worse than the outcome in the no-treatment control group." In other words, getting no treatment at all led to better outcomes than being treated with insight-oriented psychotherapy alone. This correlates with the individual experience of many psychotherapists who have given up treating such patients with insight-oriented psychotherapy because many of their patients seemed to get worse. In following up Freud's original formulation about unconscious homosexual impulses being the cause of paranoid schizophrenia, one psychiatrist "checked the therapeutic successes of psychoanalysts and found to our surprise that it is common experience, frequently admitted and often implied, that not only are 'paranoid' patients not improved by homosexual interpretations, but even made worse."

Given what we now know about the brains of persons with schizophrenia, it should not be surprising to find that insight-oriented psychotherapy makes them sicker. Such persons are being overwhelmed by external and internal stimuli and are trying to impose some order on the chaos. In the midst of this, an insight-oriented psychotherapist asks them to probe their unconscious motivations, a difficult enough task even when one's brain is functioning perfectly. The inevitable consequence is to add insult to injury, unleashing a cacophony of repressed thoughts and wishes into the existing internal maelstrom. To do insight-oriented psychotherapy on persons with schizophrenia is analogous to directing a flood into a town already ravaged by a tornado. Or, to use another comparison from a review entitled "The Adverse Effects of Intensive Treatment of Chronic Schizophrenia," insight-oriented psychotherapies are "analogous to pouring boiling oil into wounds because they ignore the chronic schizophrenic's particular vulnerability to over-stimulating relationships, intense negative affects, and pressures for rapid change."

It is remarkable how many people (including even some mental illness professionals) still believe that insight-oriented psychotherapy is effective for treating schizophrenia. I still regularly talk to wealthy families who have paid exorbitant sums—$100,000 to $200,000 a year—to have their son or daughter treated by psychoanalysis or insight-oriented psychotherapy in a private hospital. This is one of the last areas of American medicine where a laetrile-type treatment—not only useless but probably harmful—may be legally purchased.

Recognition of the harmful role played by insight-oriented psychotherapy in patients with schizophrenia is not new. In a 1976 study of harmful effects of psychotherapy, Hadley and Strupp noted that "psychotic breaks resulting from psychotherapy were also frequently mentioned as a clear-cut negative effect . . . an occurrence would most typically be due to ego disintegration brought on by therapy." In 1978, the President's Commission on Mental Health observed that "there is some evidence that suggests that certain chronic schizophrenic patients respond adversely to psychological treatments." Shortly thereafter Dr. Gerald Klerman, at that time the highest ranking government psychiatrist and a respected researcher, also acknowledged that "recent evidence suggests that high intensity psychotherapy may actually have negative effects in schizophrenia."

What, then, is the proper role for insight-oriented psychotherapy in the treatment of schizophrenia? It has none, and should be explicitly avoided. As summarized by Dr. T. C. Manschreck in a 1981 article in the *New England Journal of Medicine:* "To offer traditional psychotherapy as the only treatment for schizophrenic disorder is generally regarded as inadequate and possibly negligent. Psychoanalysis and other insight-oriented psychotherapies have little demonstrated value in this illness." Given what is now known about schizophrenia, to treat it by utilizing these approaches is not only negligent, it is malpractice. Mental illness professionals who advocate such treatment should be regarded as interesting relics of the past, much as we regard the last survivors of World War I and other past eras.

COGNITIVE BEHAVIORAL THERAPY

Beginning in the 1990s, there was increasing interest in cognitive behavioral therapy, another form of psychotherapy, as a treatment for schizophrenia. Most of the studies have been carried out in Europe, especially in England, although interest in the United States is increasing.

Cognitive behavioral therapy initially became popular as a treatment for depression, panic disorder, and other types of anxiety. It is a psychological "talking" form of treatment in which the therapist instructs the patient how to use various psychological mechanisms to relieve symptoms and/or improve functioning. It utilizes a variety of techniques and targets specific symptoms; thus, cognitive behavioral therapy is really cognitive behavioral *therapies*.

One form of cognitive behavioral therapy targets delusional thinking. The patient is given a verbal challenge and encouraged to view a delusional belief as only one of multiple possible interpretations of the events. In another approach, the patient is encouraged to create an experiment in which the delusional belief can be conclusively proven or disproven.

Auditory hallucinations have also been targets for cognitive behavioral therapy. One method involves an analysis of the voices, so that gradually the patient comes to realize that the voices are internal and not coming from some outside source. Another method involves the development of distracting stimuli so that the patient pays less attention to the voices. A common denominator in all types of cognitive therapy is to give the patient greater control over his/her symptoms and a sense of mastery over the disease.

The relative efficacy of cognitive behavior therapy is under debate. A large, multi-center study of its efficacy in first-episode schizophrenia patients is in process in Europe (the Socrates Study), while other studies are targeting specific subgroups of patients, such as those who are medication-resistant or prone to frequent relapses. The preliminary data suggest that cognitive behavior therapy effectively reduces some delusional thinking and also makes some patients less bothered by their auditory hallucinations (though it may not reduce the hallucinations).

However, such results must be considered preliminary since there are many methodological problems with such studies. These include controlling for the effects of medications, small numbers of patients tested, and controlling for nonspecific effects of the therapy, e.g., the patient's personal relationship with the therapist leads him/her to take medication more frequently so the observed improvement is really an effect of the medication, not the therapy. A major limitation of cognitive behavioral therapy is that it is useful only for patients who have awareness of their illness and are thus willing to participate in such therapy.

The ultimate role of cognitive behavioral therapy in the treatment of schizophrenia is still to be determined. Even if it shows some effect, will it be economically cost-effective? A good recent review of cognitive behavioral therapy by Dr. Faith Dickerson is cited in the list of recommended further reading.

ELECTROCONVULSIVE THERAPY (ECT)

Electroconvulsive therapy (ECT) has a modest but definite role to play in the treatment of schizophrenia despite the adverse publicity it has received. It is a favorite whipping boy for Scientologists and anti-psychiatry advocates and was even banned from use in Berkeley, California, in 1982 by a local referendum. In European countries it has been used more widely for the treatment of schizophrenia than in the United States.

Indications for use of ECT in schizophrenia were summarized in 1993 in the *New England Journal of Medicine* as being "when the onset is acute and confusion and mood disturbance are present; and catatonia from almost any underlying cause." It may also be useful in some treatment-resistant cases, although it should be used in conjunction with an antipsychotic in such cases. Modern ECT is done using unilateral electrodes over the nondominant lobe to minimize memory loss. Some memory loss may nevertheless occur and is the major side effect of the procedure. Despite Scientologist claims to the contrary, there is no evidence that ECT causes any damage to the brain. Some patients respond to as few as 12 ECT treatments, whereas others need 20 or more. Max Fink, an expert on ECT, recommended in his recent book that "a minimum course of ECT for effective relief of psychosis is one that continues for at least six months." For individuals who respond well to ECT but rapidly relapse, it is possible to use monthly maintenance treatments, and these are quite commonly used in Europe.

NUTRITIONAL TREATMENTS

Throughout this century various kinds of nutritional treatments have been proposed as being helpful for schizophrenia. The one that has been researched most extensively is a gluten-free diet that contains no milk or meat. Unfortunately, most of the nutritional studies were done with small samples and so the results have been statistically inconclusive. The fact that only a small percentage of patients with schizophrenia may be improved by such diets makes research very difficult because very large numbers of patients would have to be used in order to demonstrate a statistical difference.

Nutritional treatments emphasizing various vitamins and multiple vitamin and mineral regimens have also been advocated. In 1990, a study was published showing significant clinical improvement in 17 individuals with schizophrenia who were given methylfolate supplements for six months. To date this study has not been replicated.

At this time there is no solid data supporting the use of any particular nutritional treatments for schizophrenia. Good eating habits and a healthy diet will help people with schizophrenia to feel better just as they will help anybody to feel better.

EXPERIMENTAL TREATMENTS

Efforts are ongong to find alternative treatments for schizophrenia, especially for those patients who do not respond to antipsychotic medication.
Two recently developed experimental treatments are transcranial magnetic stimulation (TMS) and vagal nerve stimulation (VNS).

Transcranial Magnetic Stimulation (TMS)

Introduced in the early 1990s as an experimental psychiatric treatment
for depression, TMS consists of the application of an electromagnetic
coil to the outside of the skull and thus is both painless and noninvasive.
Applications differ regarding precisely where the magnet is applied
(e.g., frontal or temporal areas, left or right), how frequently it is applied,
and the strength of the electromagnet. If the frequency of the electromagnetic wave is greater than one per second, it is called repetitive
TMS, usually written rTMS.

TMS is being tried as a treatment for depression, manic-depressive
illness, obsessive-compulsive disorder, anxiety disorder, and post-trau-
matic stress disorder as well as for schizophrenia. Like ECT, it is not
known precisely how TMS works. Initial trials have shown some effectiveness in reducing auditory hallucinations in some patients, but it is too
early to assess its long-term effectiveness as an alternate form of therapy.

Vagal Nerve Stimulation (VNS)

First developed as a treatment for refractory epilepsy, VNS has been
available for that purpose in the United States since 1997. The treatment
consists of the surgical implantation of a small generator (approximately
the size of a pocket watch) in the chest and is thus similar to the implantation of a cardiac pacemaker. The VNS generator is attached to the
vagus nerve, which goes directly to the brain, and can be programmed to
stimulate the nerve. It is not known how this stimulation of the brain
improves symptoms. The implantation procedure can be done as outpatient surgery and costs between $12,000 and $25,000.

VNS is being used experimentally for some cases of severe depression, manic-depressive illness, and schizophrenia. It is too early to tell
what role, if any, VNS will play in treatment.

RECOMMENDED FURTHER READING

Allness, D. J., and W. H. Knoedler. *The PACT Model of Community-Based Treatment for Persons with Severe and Persistent Mental Illnesses: A Manual for PACT Start-up.* Arlington, Va.: National Alliance for the Mentally Ill, 1998.

Cadet, J. L., K. C. Rickler, and D. R. Weinberger. "The Clinical Neurologic Examination in Schizophrenia." In H. M. Nasrallah and D. R. Weinberger, eds. *The Neurology of Schizophrenia.* Amsterdam: Elsevier, 1986.

Dickerson, F. "Cognitive Behavioral Psychotherapy for Schizophrenia: A Review of Recent Empirical Studies." *Schizophrenia Research* 43 (2000): 71–90.

Dincin, J., ed. *A Pragmatic Approach to Psychiatric Rehabilitation: Lessons from Chicago's Thresholds Program.* San Francisco: Jossey-Bass, 1995. No. 68 in the *New Directions for Mental Health Services* series.

Fink, M. *Electroshock: Restoring the Mind.* New York: Oxford University Press, 1999.

Flannery, M., and M. Glickman. *Fountain House: Portraits of Lives Reclaimed from Mental Illness.* Center City, Minn.: Hazelden, 1996.

Hawkins, D., and L. Pauling, eds. *Orthomolecular Psychiatry: Treatment of Schizophrenia.* San Francisco: W. H. Freeman, 1973.

Liberman, R. P., ed. *Psychiatric Rehabilitation of Chronic Mental Patients.* Washington, D.C.: American Psychiatric Press, 1988.

Peschel, E., R. Peschel, C. W. Howe, et al. *Neurobiological Disorders in Children and Adolescents.* San Francisco: Jossey-Bass, 1992.

Stevens, A., N. Doidge, D. Goldbloom, et al. "Pilot Study of Televideo Psychiatric Assessments in an Underserviced Community." *American Journal of Psychiatry* 156 (1999): 783–85.

Taylor, R. *Distinguishing Psychological from Organic Disorders: Screening for Psychological Masquerade.* New York: Springer Publishing, 2000.

Torrey, E. F. "Continuous Treatment Teams in the Care of the Chronic Mentally Ill." *Hospital and Community Psychiatry* 37 (1986): 1243–47.

Torrey, E. F. "Economic Barriers to Widespread Implementation of Model Programs for the Seriously Mentally Ill." *Hospital and Community Psychiatry* 41 (1990): 526–31.

Torrey, E. F. *Out of the Shadows: Confronting America's Mental Illness Crisis.* New York: John Wiley, 1997. Paperback edition 1998.

Wagenfeld, M. O., ed. *Perspectives on Rural Mental Health.* San Francisco: Jossey-Bass, 1981. No. 9 in the *New Directions for Mental Health Services* series.

9

THE TREATMENT OF SCHIZOPHRENIA: MEDICATIONS

Lunacy, like the rain, falls upon the evil and the good, and although it must forever remain a fearful misfortune, yet there may be no more sin or shame in it than there is in an ague fit or a fever.

Inmate of the Glasgow Royal Asylum, 1860

Once a competent doctor has been located and the intricacies of hospitalization have been mastered, then the treatment of schizophrenia becomes comparatively simple. Drugs are the most important treatment for schizophrenia, just as they are the most important treatment for many physical diseases of the human body. Drugs do not *cure*, but rather *control*, the symptoms of schizophrenia—as they do those of diabetes. The drugs we now have to treat schizophrenia are far from perfect, but they work for most of the people with the disease if they are used correctly.

The main drugs used to treat schizophrenia are usually called antipsychotics. They have also been called neuroleptics and major tranquilizers, but the best term is "antipsychotic" because that is what they are. They frequently do not produce tranquilization, so that term is a misnomer. The antipsychotic drugs were discovered in 1952 by French psychiatrist Pierre Deniker. He had heard about a new tranquilizer that his anesthesiology colleagues were using to sedate patients during surgery and decided to try it on psychiatric patients; the drug was chlorpromazine (Thorazine, Largactil).

Antipsychotics can be divided into two classes: first-generation and second-generation. Those are commonly referred to, respectively, as "typical" and "atypical," based on the previously widespread belief that the effectiveness of "typicals" was related to their ability to block dopamine receptors, whereas the effectiveness of the "atypicals" was related to their action on other neurotransmitter receptors. Associated with the dopamine blockade are certain side effects found commonly in first-generation antipsychotics but rarely in second-generation antipsychotics. These side effects are usually abbreviated EPS (extrapyramidal signs) and consist of Parkinsonian-like symptoms, acute dystonic reactions, and akathisia (see below). Researchers are now less certain that dopamine blockade is the primary reason why the first-generation antipsychotics are effective, and in fact there is considerable overlap in receptor activity of "typical" and "atypical" antipsychotics. It is therefore more accurate simply to classify antipsychotics into first-generation (beginning with the introduction of chlorpromazine in 1952) and second-generation (beginning with the introduction of clozapine in the United States in 1990). Such a division is admittedly America-centric, since clozapine was used in some European countries in the 1970s and 1980s.

FIRST-GENERATION ANTIPSYCHOTICS

There are five different chemical families of antipsychotic drugs, listed in the accompanying table of generic and trade (brand) names.

FIRST-GENERATION ANTIPSYCHOTICS

Chemical Family	Generic Name	Trade (brand) Names
Phenothiazines	chlorpromazine	Thorazine, Largactil, and others
	thioridazine	Mellaril
	mesoridazine	Serentil
	fluphenazine	Prolixin, Permitil
	trifluoperazine	Stelazine and others
	perphenazine	Trilafon
	prochlorperazine	Compazine
Thioxanthines	thiothixene	Navane
Butyrophenones	haloperidol	Haldol
	pimozide	Orap
Dibenzoxazepines	loxapine	Loxitane
Dihydroindolones	molidone	Moban

The first-generation antipsychotic drugs are roughly divided into high, intermediate, and low potency, depending on how high a dose is required to produce an equivalent effect. Thus, chlorpromazine (Thorazine) and thioridazine (Mellaril) are categorized as low potency because it takes 20 milligrams to produce the same effect as 1 milligram of fluphenazine (Prolixin) or haloperidol (Haldol), which are categorized as high potency. In other words, milligram-for-milligram fluphenazine and haloperidol are 20 times as strong as chlorpromazine and thioridazine. Molidone (Moban) and loxapine (Loxitane) are examples of antipsychotic drugs that are intermediate in potency.

Antipsychotic drugs are usually given as tablets or liquid. Tablets can be taken once a day and are more effective if taken on an empty stomach. If ingested at the same time as antacids containing aluminum or magnesium (information that appears on the lists of ingredients on their labels), their effectiveness is reduced. Some people believe that the first-generation antipsychotic medications should not be taken with coffee, tea, or cola drinks because the caffeine will reduce their effectiveness. This is probably true for the liquid form of these medications but not for the tablet form. For the second-generation antipsychotics, however, caffeine definitely has an effect on their efficacy, as noted later in this chapter. The tablets may also be crushed for ease of administration. The liquid form may be mixed with juices (other than apple juice) and used in individuals in which there is doubt whether the person is swallowing his/her tablets; however, the liquid form is more expensive than the tablet form. Many of these drugs can also be given as a short-acting intramuscular injection, and two (fluphenazine and haloperidol) can be given as long-acting injections that need to be given only every one to six weeks. Such long-acting injections are extremely useful for individuals who find it difficult (or refuse) to take pills; they have to return to the clinic for another injection only once every few weeks in order to stay well. Injections are usually given in the buttocks, although they may be given in the arm if preferred.

Do They Work?

The efficacy of antipsychotic drugs is well established. Studies show that approximately 70 percent of patients with schizophrenia clearly improve on these drugs, 25 percent improve minimally or not at all, and

5 percent get worse. This is approximately the same level of effectiveness that penicillin exerts in pneumonia or streptomycin in tuberculosis. Antipsychotic drugs reduce symptoms of the disease, shorten the stay in the hospital, and reduce the chances of rehospitalization dramatically. Whereas persons with schizophrenia entering a psychiatric hospital used to stay for several weeks or months, the average stay with these drugs is now reduced to days. And the data on their preventing rehospitalization are even more impressive. John Davis, for example, reviewed 24 scientifically controlled studies testing whether antipsychotic drugs were effective. All 24 studies found that persons with schizophrenia who took antipsychotic drugs were less likely to have to return to the hospital than those who did not take these drugs. The differences between the two groups were highly significant, especially for persons with chronic schizophrenia. On the average, a person who takes the drugs has a 3-out-of-5 chance (60 percent) of not being rehospitalized by the end of one year, whereas the person who does not take the drugs has only a 1-out-of-5 chance (20 percent) of not being rehospitalized.

When studies have been done on the long-acting, injectable form of antipsychotics (where compliance in taking the drug is assured), the results are even more impressive. In one study of chronic patients, only 8 percent of the patients who were taking the drug relapsed within one year, but 68 percent of those not taking the drug relapsed. In another study of patients taking long-acting, injectable antipsychotics, 80 percent relapsed within two years when the drug was stopped. What all this means is that though taking the drugs does not guarantee you will *not* get sick again, and not taking the drugs does not guarantee you *will* get sick again, their use improves the odds toward staying out of the hospital tremendously. The data on the effectiveness of drugs are so clear that any physician or psychiatrist who fails to try them on a person with schizophrenia is probably incompetent. It is not that drugs are the *only* ingredient necessary to treat schizophrenia successfully; they are just the most essential ingredient.

Antipsychotic drugs are not equally effective for all the symptoms of schizophrenia. They are most effective at reducing delusions, hallucinations, aggressive or bizarre behavior, thinking disorders, and the symptoms having to do with the overacuteness of the senses—the so-called "positive" symptoms. For example, against auditory hallucinations, one of the most common and disabling symptoms of schizophrenia, antipsychotic drugs are 80 to 90 percent effective in being able to relieve the hallucinations, usually making them disappear altogether. The drugs have less efficacy against symptoms such as apathy, ambivalence, poverty of thought, and flattening of the emotions—the "negative" symptoms.

Do They Change the Brain?

Some opponents of the use of antipsychotics have alleged that because these medications change the brain, that means they are dangerous and should not be used. Antipsychotic medications do, of course, change the brain—that is why they are effective. Medications used to treat epilepsy, Parkinson's disease, and other brain diseases also change the brain. And medications used to treat diseases in other organs, such as the heart and joints, may bring about structural changes to those organs as well.

The brain changes produced by antipsychotic drugs are relatively minor. The main changes that have been claimed to date are an increase in density of glial cells in the frontal cortex, an increase in synapses (connections between neurons), and changes in the properties of the synapses. There is no evidence that antipsychotic drugs cause the loss of neurons. Much research is ongoing in this area, since understanding the nature of these changes may help us understand how these drugs work, why they cause side effects, and who will respond to which drug.

Can We Predict Who Will Respond and Which Drug They Will Respond To?

The current answer to both questions is no. People who do not respond to medications are more likely to have been sick longer, to have more neurological abnormalities, and to have more evidence of organic brain damage on neuropsychological testing, but such predictors are relatively weak. And there is currently no way to predict which drug is best for which person with schizophrenia; the only way to find out is by trial and error. Three clues to predicting response should be noted, however. First, if a person responds well to a certain drug one time, then he/she is likely always to respond well to that drug. Second, if another person in the same family has been psychiatrically ill and responded well to a certain drug, then other members of the same family who become ill will probably respond well to that drug. This suggests that there is a genetic predisposition to how well one responds to these drugs. Third, at least two groups of investigators have shown that if the person with schizophrenia has a very unpleasant subjective reaction (called a dysphoric effect) to the first dose of the medication, then the chances of the person's ultimately responding favorably to this medication are low.

It is likely that in the future we will be able to predict who will respond and which drug they will respond to. One example of research on this problem is the use of electroencephalographic (EEG) patterns of brain waves. In one such study reported in 1994, EEG patterns recorded six hours following the initial dose of haloperidol correctly predicted at a high level of certainty which patients would respond to the drug. Another example is by analyzing a person's genetic pattern, which may predict drug response (pharmacogenetics).

At a practical level, every person with schizophrenia or the family members should keep a list of drugs tried, dosage level (i.e., how many milligrams), and response. This can be extremely helpful and save weeks of trial-and-error medications in future treatment.

High Dose, Low Dose, No Dose

It has become clear in recent years that people require widely varying doses for these drugs to be effective. This is probably a genetic trait and is not surprising in view of how differently our bodies handle other chemical compounds. One ounce of alcohol will make one person intoxicated and will not even be felt by another. Similarly, when 20 milligrams a day of fluphenazine was given to a group of patients with schizophrenia and then the blood level of the drug was measured, the difference between the lowest and highest blood level was *fortyfold*. The absorption and excretion of antipsychotic drugs vary widely from person to person, so that one patient requires 10 milligrams and another patient 400 milligrams to achieve identical blood levels. In another experiment on the same phenomenon, some patients with schizophrenia proved to need *32 times* more fluphenazine than other patients to produce a similar blood level of the drug.

One cause of dose variability in antipsychotic medication is race. Because there are some racial group differences in the distribution of enzymes that metabolize antipsychotic drugs, some individuals need a higher dose of medication than other individuals do to achieve the same effect. Studies to date suggest that whites and African Americans require approximately the same dose, while Hispanic patients require a lower dose, and Asian Americans the lowest of the four racial groups. These are merely statistical generalizations, of course, and not predictive of the needs of any given individual, because of inter-individual variation in enzyme levels.

The practical implication of this dose variability is that both physicians and patients must be flexible in thinking about dosage. Minidoses may suffice for some patients, with as little as 1 milligram a day of fluphenazine, haloperidol, or thiothixene keeping them well. And long-acting injectable fluphenazine doses as low as 1.25 milligram every two weeks have proved effective in some patients. On the other end of the spectrum, some patients with schizophrenia require megadoses of antipsychotic drugs in order to achieve a blood level that will be effective. Daily megadoses of 270 mg haloperidol, 480 mg thiothixene, and 500 mg loxapine are described in the psychiatric literature, and I personally have had patients who failed to respond at daily doses of less than 150 mg fluphenazine or 3,000 mg chlorpromazine. One well-known psychiatric researcher in New York claims to have had a patient take as much as 1,200 mg a day of fluphenazine by mouth—and the patient continued working as a taxi driver! The one first-generation antipsychotic that has an absolute upper limit of safety is thioridazine (Mellaril); doses over 800 mg per day may cause damage to the eyes.

For long-acting injectable fluphenazine, Dr. Sven Dencker in Sweden used weekly injectable doses of 900 mg on rare treatment-resistant patients with good results; he followed such patients for over 10 years and reported no more side effects from the megadoses than from standard doses. Dr. Dencker's top dose is *over 1,400 times* the minidoses found to be effective in other patients. The findings on dose variability also suggest that many patients who received drugs failed to respond because the drug was administered in too low a dosage. This information conflicts with a presently popular stereotype that portrays most patients as being over-medicated.

But stereotypes die slow deaths, and the image of the over-medicated, "zonked out," "zombied" patient is a very strong one. It has its principal origin in the fact that the *symptoms* of schizophrenia are often confused with the *effects* of the drugs used in its treatment. Thus, when families see their relatives with schizophrenia sitting lethargically, apathetic, ambivalent, and suffering poverty of thought, they assume that the drugs made them that way. All one has to do to prove this is not so is to talk with anyone who had to care for patients *before* antipsychotic drugs were introduced in the 1950s; you will invariably be told that *more* patients were "zonked out" in the old days.

This is not to say that antipsychotic drugs are never abused or that patients are not sometimes over-medicated for the convenience of the hospital staff who want to calm them down. These things certainly do happen. But stereotypes to the contrary, this problem is relatively minor in the treatment of schizophrenia, compared with the number of patients who have never been given an adequate trial of available medications.

In the 1980s there was considerable interest in an intermittent "no dose" strategy, in which medication was stopped until the person began to relapse, at which time it was restarted. Two American and two European research groups did controlled trials using intermittent medication and showed that for most individuals with schizophrenia the intermittent strategy was not effective and resulted in a much higher rehospitalization rate than did continuous medication.

How Long Should Antipsychotic Drugs Be Continued?

Given the wide variation in blood levels in different individuals who take the same dose of medication, it is not surprising to find that their rate of response also varies widely. On one end of the clinical spectrum are individuals who respond dramatically within 48 hours of being started on medication, whereas on the other end are individuals who respond very slowly over several months. Dr. Jeffrey Lieberman and his colleagues studied the treatment response in newly admitted, first-episode patients with schizophrenia and reported that the mean interval between beginning medication and achieving the maximum clinical improvement was 35 weeks, although half the patients had achieved it by 11 weeks. This means that a few patients respond rapidly but the remainder may take much longer. Patience is indeed a virtue when treating schizophrenia.

Once started, how long should the medications be continued? If a person has had an initial episode of schizophrenia and recovered, it is known that approximately one-quarter of such individuals will not get sick again and will not need medication. There is currently no way to identify for certain which patients fall into that group. Within a few months following recovery, therefore, medication should be slowly decreased and then discontinued.

The three-quarters who eventually relapse will again be treated with medication. For this group, medication should probably be continued for one to two years after recovery. If patients relapse a third time, then it is known that they will need the medication indefinitely, and I encourage them to think of themselves as similar to a person with diabetes who needs insulin. In summary, then: first episode, continue medications for several months; second episode, for one to two years; and third episode, indefinitely.

As persons with schizophrenia age, can they reduce and eventually discontinue their medication? Some can do so in their fifties, and many can do so by their sixties. Usually the older a person gets, the lower the required dose of antipsychotic medication.

Are Antipsychotic Drugs Addicting?

The abuse of antipsychotic drugs to achieve a "high" is extremely rare and has been reported only for loxapine. Antipsychotic drugs do not produce a pleasant or euphoric effect on normal people. I have had streetwise patients try to sell them and I always tell them: "If you can find somebody who will buy these from you, tell them I'll gladly give them an additional supply free because they undoubtedly need them."

In terms of addiction to antipsychotic drugs, this is unknown. The person's body does not slowly get used to them and therefore require higher and higher doses, and the stopping of these drugs does not usually cause withdrawal symptoms other than a recurrence of the person's psychotic symptoms. Antipsychotic drugs for schizophrenia are exactly the same as insulin for diabetes or digitalis for heart failure—they are drugs needed by the body to restore the functioning of the respective organs (brain, pancreas, and heart) to more normal levels.

Does Early Treatment Help?

Some studies have suggested that early treatment may lead to a better clinical outcome in schizophrenia and, conversely, that delayed treatment may lead to a worse outcome. Dr. Richard Wyatt of the National

Institute of Mental Health reanalyzed 22 studies on the course of schizophrenia and concluded that "early intervention with neuroleptics in first-break schizophrenic patients increases the likelihood of an improved long-term course." An analysis of the Lieberman et al. study of individuals undergoing their first episode of schizophrenia similarly concluded that "greater duration of illness [prior to beginning treatment] was found to predict increased time to remission" in younger but not in older patients. An Irish study of untreated patients with schizophrenia also found that "untreated psychosis in schizophrenia appears to have a progressive and, ultimately, a profoundly debilitating effect on long-term outcome." The implication of these studies is that the failure by mental illness professionals to treat individuals with schizophrenia with antipsychotic medications as early in the course of their illness as possible may produce a worse outcome. Other recent studies have not found this to be true, and this is an area of ongoing research. Until it is clarified, it should be assumed that treatment should begin as early in the course of the disease as possible.

ADVERSE EFFECTS

"The antipsychotic agents," says Dr. Ross J. Baldessarini, "are among the safest drugs available in medicine." As one of the foremost experts on these drugs, Dr. Baldessarini should know, yet his claim is at variance with popular stereotypes of the drugs. It is widely believed that the first-generation antipsychotic drugs have terrible adverse effects, are dangerous, and almost invariably produce tardive dyskinesia (involuntary muscle movements) and other irreversible conditions that may be worse than the original schizophrenia.

Dr. Baldessarini is in fact correct, and the popular stereotype is wrong. Antipsychotic drugs, compared with drugs used to treat other diseases, are relatively safe. It is almost impossible to commit suicide with them by overdosing, and their serious adverse effects are comparatively rare.

Then why is there such a strong misperception and fear of these drugs? Much of the reason can be traced to theories of causation of the disease. As we have noted, it is only in recent years that the evidence for schizophrenia's being a real biological disease has become clear. The resistance to this idea among mental illness professionals trained in the psychogenic belief systems has been impressive. And one of the ways this resistance is shown is by strongly opposing the use of drugs; implicitly, if the drugs are too dangerous to be used, then patients will again have to rely on psychotherapy and other nondrug modes of treatment. For this reason, occasional mental illness professionals—who should be better informed—still warn patients with schizophrenia about all kinds of terrible calamities that will befall them if they take antipsychotic drugs. Additional opposition to antipsychotic drug use comes from the Church of Scientology, whose founder, L. Ron Hubbard, was virulently anti-psychiatry, as well as from "consumer survivors," as discussed in chapter 15.

This is *not* to say that antipsychotic drugs are perfectly safe and have no adverse effects whatsoever. They do have adverse effects, sometimes so severe that the drug must be stopped. The adverse effects have on occasion even been fatal, but this is very rare. One of the main goals of the current search for second-generation antipsychotic drugs is to find effective compounds that will continue to suppress psychotic symptoms while producing minimal undesirable adverse effects. But it is important to repeat that the point to be remembered is that antipsychotic drugs, as a group, are one of the safest groups of drugs in common use and are the greatest advance in the treatment of schizophrenia that has occurred to date.

The adverse effects of first-generation antipsychotic drugs can be discussed as a group. Some adverse effects are more common with particular drugs, but the differences are not great. And, like adverse effects to all drugs used in medicine, it is not possible to predict with any accuracy which person is likely to get which adverse effect.

Common

Among the most common adverse effects of antipsychotic medications are the following:

> *Sedation:* This occurs most commonly with chlorpromazine, thioridazine, and mesoridazine. It occurs much less often with fluphenazine, haloperidol, and thiothixene. It usually decreases as the person takes the drug for a longer period of time. Taking the drug at bedtime will minimize this side effect.

Dry mouth, blurred vision, and constipation: This occurs most commonly with high-potency drugs such as haloperidol and fluphenazine. It usually decreases as the person takes the drug over a longer period of time.

Acute dystonic reaction: This adverse effect, which consists of the stiffening of muscles on one side of the neck and jaw, is frightening for patients and their families. It usually occurs within the first few days after beginning antipsychotic drug therapy and is more common in younger people and in men. Usually the neck becomes rigid so it cannot turn, talking becomes difficult because of stiffening of the tongue, and occasionally it also affects the eye muscles, causing the eyes to look upward. This side effect can be reversed within minutes by giving the patient an anticholinergic drug such as benztropine (Cogentin), biperiden (Akineton), procyclidine (Kemadrin), or trihexyphenidyl (Artane) or by giving diphenhydramine (Benadryl) or diazepam (Valium). Dystonic reactions can also be prevented by giving anticholinergic drugs prophylactically. Although frightening, acute dystonic reactions cause no permanent damage.

Stiffness and tremor: These adverse effects are grouped together because they usually occur together and are similar to the symptoms of Parkinson's disease. They may be accompanied by slowed body movements, loss of facial expression owing to stiffness of the facial muscles, and drooling. A tremor can be very annoying, especially if the person has a job that requires writing or other fine hand movements. These adverse effects can often be improved using the anticholinergic drugs mentioned above or bromocriptine (Parlodel). It should also be emphasized that stiffness and tremor may occur as part of the disease process in addition to being adverse effects of the medication. One study of individuals with schizophrenia who had never been treated with antipsychotic drugs reported that 29 percent of them had some stiffness and 37 percent had a tremor.

Akinesia or decreased spontaneity: This adverse effect is not usually noticed until several weeks after beginning antipsychotic drugs. It often occurs in the same persons who have stiffness and tremors. It is an especially difficult adverse effect to evaluate because decreased spontaneity may also be a symptom of the person's schizophrenia or a symptom of the depression that often accompanies schizophrenia. Decreased spontaneity that is caused by the medication can often be successfully reversed with the anticholinergic drugs mentioned above.

Akathisia or restlessness: This is one of the most uncomfortable adverse effects of antipsychotic drugs and occurs in approximately 25 percent of all patients. It consists of feelings of restlessness, jumpiness, and a need to keep moving. Individuals experiencing it will sometimes shift from one foot to the other or pace back and forth. It may begin within three days of starting the antipsychotic drug and is a major reason why some individuals refuse to continue taking their drugs. It can be successfully treated in many individuals with propranolol or other beta blockers. If these do not work, then a benzodiazepine can be tried, such as lorazepam or clonazepam. In some individuals it may be necessary to change to another antipsychotic.

WHAT IS EPS?

EPS is a widely used abbreviation that stands for extrapyramidal signs. These are the adverse effects, thought to be caused by blockade of dopamine receptors, that are found very commonly in first-generation antipsychotics but uncommonly in most second-generation antipsychotics. The presence or absence of EPS is thus a major dividing line between the older and newer agents. EPS includes:

1. Parkinsonian-like symptoms: stiffness, tremor, slowed movements, loss of facial expression
2. Acute dystonic reactions: stiffening of muscles of neck or eyes
3. Akathisia: restlessness

Weight gain: This is also a serious and moderately common adverse effect of first-generation antipsychotic medication but is an even greater problem in second-generation antipsychotics, as noted later in the chapter. The precise mechanism is not well understood but in some individuals involves increased appetite. The weight gain caused by the medication is also exacerbated by weight gain caused by the decreased activity and depression that are often part of the disease process. As the person gains weight he/she may exercise less, producing still further weight gain. The best ways to combat weight gain in individuals with schizophrenia are the same as in individuals who do not have schizophrenia—control of diet and exercise. There is also some evidence that, among the first-generation antipsychotics, molindone and pimozide are less likely to cause weight gain; individuals for whom this is a problem should probably be given a trial on these or the second-generation antipsychotic ziprasadone.

Uncommon

Among the less common adverse effects of antipsychotic drugs are the following:

Impaired sexual function: Impairments in sexual functioning definitely occur as an adverse effect of antipsychotic drugs, but both their frequency and their seriousness are matters of dispute. Decreased sexual desire may be found in both sexes and impotence or retrograde ejaculation may occur in men; the latter occurs especially with thioridazine (Mellaril). It is difficult to evaluate how many of these effects are due to the drugs, how many are due to the schizophrenia, and how many antedated the disease altogether. For example, impotence is a common condition among men, and it is obviously inaccurate to blame all impotence in men who take antipsychotic drugs on these medications. There is a general consensus among clinicians that thioridazine (Mellaril) is most likely among first-generation antipsychotics to cause sexual problems as an adverse effect, and some belief (although unproven) that molindone (Moban) and loxapine (Loxitane) are least likely to do so.

It is similarly difficult to evaluate the seriousness of these symptoms since sexual functioning varies so widely in people who do not have schizophrenia. For some people with comparatively little interest in sex, the decreased libido from antipsychotic drugs may not even be noticed. For others it may be a disaster of monumental proportions and they may insist on stopping the drugs for that reason. I had one patient, for example, who definitely was impotent when he took antipsychotic drugs and who became acutely psychotic whenever he did not. He was faced with a painful dilemma; the role of the physician in such cases should be to outline the choices and consequences as clearly as possible and then support the person's choice.

Menstrual changes: Missed menstrual periods commonly occur in women taking first-generation antipsychotic drugs, because these drugs elevate prolactin levels. Consequently, it is more difficult to get pregnant while taking these drugs. Missed periods may also occur because of the schizophrenia disease process; this phenomenon was well described prior to the introduction of antipsychotic drugs and therefore may be caused either by the medications or by the disease process itself.

Breast discharge: This may occur in either women or men and is a result of the effect of the medication on prolactin and the pituitary gland.

Urinary retention: This may occur in older patients, especially in men who have enlarged prostate glands.

Fast heartbeat or fainting: These occur more commonly in people with heart disease or problems with blood pressure.

Photosensitivity: Photosensitivity is an increased susceptibility to sunburn. It can be prevented by the liberal use of sunscreens and wide-brimmed hats.

Liver damage: This was seen more commonly when chlorpromazine was first introduced in the 1960s but now is rarely seen.

Eye damage: Damage to the retina may occur with thioridazine (Mellaril) when high doses are used. For this reason, thioridazine should never be given in doses of more than 800 mg per day.

Tardive dyskinesia

Tardive dyskinesia is the single most important adverse effect of first-generation antipsychotic drugs. Much of the fear of using these drugs is in fact linked to this adverse effect, and it has become a banner regularly waved by anti-psychiatry zealots. Tardive dyskinesia is certainly a serious problem, but it is not nearly as common as the apostles of hysteria have claimed.

Tardive dyskinesia consists of involuntary movements of the tongue and mouth, such as chewing movements, sucking movements, pushing the cheek out with the tongue, and smacking of the lips. Occasionally these are accompanied by jerky, purposeless movements of the arms or legs or, rarely, even the whole body. It usually begins while the patient is taking the drug but, rarely, may begin shortly after the drug has been stopped. Occasionally it persists indefinitely, and no effective treatment has been found to date.

The incidence of tardive dyskinesia is difficult to ascertain because it may occur as part of the disease process as well as being a side effect of medication. A study of the records of over 600 patients admitted to an asylum in England between 1845 and 1890 found an "extraordinary prevalence of abnormal movements and postures. . . . Movement disorder, often equivalent to tardive dyskinesia, was noted in nearly one-third of schizophrenics." A recent study of spontaneous dyskinesia in individuals with schizophrenia who had never been treated with antipsychotic medication reported it to be present in 12 percent of individuals below age 30 and in 25 percent of individuals aged 30 to 50. Most estimates of the incidence of tardive dyskinesia have assumed that all such cases are drug-related when in fact a substantial percentage are not. In a study of this problem aptly titled "Not All That Moves Is Tardive Dyskinesia," Khot and Wyatt concluded that the true incidence of drug-related tardive dyskinesia was less than 20 percent. This also falls within the 10 to 20 percent range estimated by the American Psychiatric Association's 1980 task force on the subject.

Much current research is taking place in an attempt to identify which persons with schizophrenia are most likely to get tardive dyskinesia. It is clear that the older the person, the more susceptible he or she is. It is also clearly established that women are more susceptible than men and that patients with more affective symptoms (for example, depression or mania) are more susceptible. Many other risk factors are being investigated including ethnicity (higher in Jews, lower in Asians), dose of medication, duration of medication, use of depot injectable medication, use of anticholinergic drugs, concurrent diabetes, concurrent alcohol or drug abuse, concurrent evidence of organic brain disease, and concurrent Parkinsonian-like symptoms, but none of them has yet been clearly established. There is also no firm evidence that any particular first-generation antipsychotic is more or less likely to cause tardive dyskinesia.

Previously, most people believed that once the symptoms of tardive dyskinesia began they would almost always get worse if the person continued taking the antipsychotic medication. This put many individuals with schizophrenia into a cruel bind, needing the medication to remain well but not wishing to worsen the early symptoms of tardive dyskinesia. A 10-year follow-up of 44 patients with tardive dyskinesia who remained on the same antipsychotic medication found that in 30 percent the tardive dyskinesia got worse, in 50 percent it remained the same, and in 20 percent the tardive dyskinesia actually improved. In another 10-year follow-up study it was reported that approximately 5 percent of existing cases of tardive dyskinesia disappeared each year *even in individuals continuing to take their antipsychotic medications*.

According to Dr. Daniel Casey, a leading researcher on tardive dyskinesia, 20 patients out of every 100 with schizophrenia will get tardive dyskinesia; among these, five patients will have their tardive dyskinesia completely disappear and five others will have at least a 50 percent improvement. Casey then added: "Of the 10 remaining TD [tardive dyskinesia] patients, almost all of them will have mild to moderate symptoms. Severe TD is a very uncommon syndrome that probably occurs in approximately 1 in 100 to 1 in 1,000 TD patients."

The best treatment for tardive dyskinesia is to switch the person to a second-generation antipsychotic, especially clozapine. All patients taking first-generation antipsychotics should be watched for early signs such as tongue movements. The use of the Abnormal Involuntary Movement Scale (AIMS) is useful for measuring the progression of tardive dyskinesia. For fully developed cases of tardive dyskinesia there is no known effective treatment, although trials of levodopa, vitamin E, oxypertine, sodium valproate, and tiapride have shown some promise.

Neuroleptic Malignant Syndrome

While rare, this adverse effect of antipsychotic medication merits serious study. Its prevalence appears to be less than 1 in 500 patients; men are affected twice as often as women. It may occur at any time while taking antipsychotic drugs, even in a person who has been taking them for several years, but in most cases it begins within 10 days of starting medication. The symptoms come on slowly over a period of one to three days and consist of rigidity of the muscles, fever, confusion or coma, pallor, sweating, and rapid heart rate. Laboratory tests show elevations of the white blood cell count and of the blood creatine phosphokinase level.

The precise mechanism causing the neuroleptic malignant syndrome is unknown, other than being a kind of toxic reaction to the drug. There is no evidence that one type of antipsychotic drug causes it more than another, and it has been documented as also occurring with some second-generation antipsychotics. Between 5 and 10 percent of those affected die, although this can be reduced by using specific drugs for treating the syndrome (dantrolene, bromocriptine). It is not yet clear what relationship the neuroleptic malignant syndrome has to malignant hyperthermia, a rare but potentially fatal allergic reaction to anesthetic agents used in medicine. The neuroleptic malignant syndrome may also appear similar to lethal catatonia, a very rare but often fatal development in some patients with schizophrenia, in which the person's temperature becomes extremely high. Lethal catatonia was clearly described before antipsychotic medications began to be used and is presumably a complication of the schizophrenia itself on the brain center controlling temperature regulation.

SECOND-GENERATION ANTIPSYCHOTICS

The second-generation antipsychotics have profoundly changed the prescribing patterns of clinical psychiatrists in North America and Europe. A 1997 study in the United States reported that over half of patients with schizophrenia who were taking antipsychotic medication were taking second-generation drugs. It is unclear at this time how much of this shift from first-generation to second-generation antipsychotics is due to their greater efficacy or fewer adverse effects and how much is due to the skilled marketing of pharmaceutical companies, but both appear to have played a role.

Assessing the true effectiveness and adverse effects of the second-generation antipsychotics has become increasingly difficult. The reasons are threefold:

- Most of the studies on these drugs have been funded by the drug companies, which then permit the publication of only the good news.

- Many of the most prominent psychiatric spokespersons who discuss the relative merits of these drugs at psychiatric meetings or NAMI meetings have accepted large amounts of money or other gifts from the pharmaceutical companies and thus may not be truly objective.

- Until very recently, the National Institute of Mental Health (NIMH) had abdicated all responsibility for drug trials, leaving the field to the pharmaceutical companies. The companies had understandably not been interested in studying aspects of their drugs that might put their products in a bad light.

OBJECTIVE INFORMATION ON ANTIPSYCHOTIC DRUGS

The best source of objective information on antipsychotic drugs is the website "eLetter on Drugs for Severe Psychiatric Illnesses" at www.citizen.org/eletter/. This website is a joint project of Public Citizen's Health Research Group and the Treatment Advocacy Center. It is privately funded; unlike many organizations that maintain websites on drugs and health, neither organization supporting this website accepts any support from pharmaceutical companies. I serve on the advisory board of this website.

Truly objective data on the second-generation antipsychotics is therefore limited. What can be said is the following:

1. *We do not know how they work.* As noted previously, the term "atypical antipsychotic" is not a good term, because we do not yet know how a "typical" antipsychotic works. It is clear that the second-generation antipsychotics affect a different portfolio of neurotransmitters and receptors than do the first-generation antipsychotics, and the second-generation agents vary widely among themselves. It is widely assumed that their efficacy is related to their neurotransmitter and receptor effects, but this remains an assumption and has not been established. It is also known that many second-generation antipsychotics are effective antiviral agents and also alter the immune system, so theoretically this might also be a mechanism of their action.

2. Clozapine is the only second-generation antipsychotic that has clearly established effectiveness for treatment-refractory patients. The other second-generation antipsychotics also appear to have some effectiveness for treatment-refractory patients, but the evidence is less impressive than that for clozapine.

3. Clozapine is the only antipsychotic that may be effective against the negative symptoms of schizophrenia, although the evidence is less than convincing. Although it has been widely claimed that the others also decrease negative symptoms, there is as yet no convincing evidence that they do so.

4. The second-generation antipsychotics have markedly fewer EPS (extrapyramidal signs, specifically Parkinsonian-like symptoms, acute dystonic reactions, and akathisia, as explained earlier in this chapter). For this reason, for many patients, they are better tolerated and more likely to be taken regularly. Thus, one would expect that individuals taking second-generation antipsychotics should have lower rates of rehospitalization, and studies support this.

5. Caffeine appears to markedly affect the serum levels of clozapine and olanzapine. Caffeine affects a liver enzyme, CYP1A2, which is also responsible for metabolizing clozapine and olanzapine. When a person taking these medications also uses caffeine, for example in coffee, tea, or cola drinks, the serum level of clozapine and olanzapine is increased. This interaction was reported in 1994, and in 1998 Carrillo et al. published a study showing that the modest use of caffeine (e.g., two cups of coffee a day) caused the serum level of medication to be

approximately twice as high, and the heavy use of caffeine (e.g., 15 cups of coffee a day) caused the serum level to be five times as high. The higher serum levels may cause the person to be more liable to the side effects of these medications, including sedation and, in the case of clozapine, seizures.

6. *The second-generation antipsychotics are very expensive.* This will be discussed below under "Drug Prices and the Use of Generics" and is a major limitation to the availability and use of these drugs. The pharmaceutical companies have undertaken a massive campaign to try to prove that these drugs are cost-effective, but since virtually all the studies on this question have been funded by the drug companies themselves, the data are suspect.

ADVERSE EFFECTS

Despite the many positive attributes of second-generation antipsychotics, they also have adverse effects that are troublesome and that have often been downplayed by the companies making them. Among these are:

Weight gain: This is a very important problem, with some patients gaining 60 to 100 pounds. Its mechanism is unknown but may involve increased appetite and/or effects on leptin, a hormone important for fat metabolism. Most disturbing is data suggesting that weight gain and the efficacy of the drug may be related, i.e., you have a choice between being fat and nonpsychotic or thin and psychotic. Weight gain has been called the tardive dyskinesia of second-generation antipsychotics. Weight gain occurs most with clozapine and olanzapine, less with risperidone and quetiapine, and least or not at all with ziprasidone (not yet approved for use in the United States). Thus, among antipsychotics in general, molindone and pimozide (first-generation) and ziprasidone (second-generation) have been least associated with weight gain. The person's baseline weight should be recorded before starting a second-generation antipsychotic and then rechecked every three months. Individuals taking clozapine or olanzapine should be referred to a dietitian to help them minimize weight gain by eating a balanced diet with fewer calories. The addition of sibutramine

(Meridia) or topirimate (Topamax), a mood stabilizer that is sometimes used as an adjunctive medication for schizophrenia and that also promotes weight loss, may also be useful.

Risk of unwanted pregnancy: Most of the first-generation antipsychotics elevate prolactin, which often causes women to not menstruate (amenorrhea) and thus to not be able to conceive. First-generation antipsychotics are thus reasonably effective contraceptives for many women. Most second-generation antipsychotics do not elevate prolactin, and therefore the woman may become pregnant. There have been multiple reports of women becoming pregnant after switching from a first-generation to a second-generation antipsychotic. This is most likely to happen when switching to clozapine, olanzapine, quetiapine, or ziprasidone (all of which do not elevate prolactin) and unlikely to happen when switching to risperidone.

Hyperglycemia: Clozapine, olanzapine, and quetiapine elevate the blood sugar and may even cause non-insulin-dependent diabetes.

Cardiac problems: Clozapine is known to have caused cases of myocarditis, some of which have proven fatal. Ziprasidone produces changes in cardiac electrical impulses (the Q-Tc interval) as measured by EKG, but the relative importance of these changes is not yet known.

Sedation: This is a major problem for second-generation antipsychotics except risperidone and ziprasidone. The degree of sedation is similar to that caused by such drugs as chlorpromazine and thioridazine (low-potency, first-generation) and is much worse than that seen in such drugs as fluphenazine or haloperidol (high-potency, first-generation).

Considered individually, the most important facts about each of the second-generation antipsychotics are as follows:

Clozapine (Clozaril, Leponex)

Clozapine has been used in Europe since the 1970s and was introduced in the United States in 1990. It comes in 25 mg and 100 mg tablets only. The usual dose is 300–700 mg per day.

The good news:

- It is the only antipsychotic that has definitely been proven to be effective in treatment-refractory schizophrenia.

- Approximately 10 percent of patients show dramatic improvement, most often those with persistent hallucinations and delusions without significant negative symptoms.

- It is effective against some negative symptoms.

- It is effective against some symptoms of hostility and violence.

- It produces some improvement in cognitive function and social function.

- In some patients, it decreases the desire to smoke.

- Preliminary studies suggest that it may decrease alcohol use in individuals with schizophrenia who have concurrent alcohol abuse.

- It has a very low incidence of EPS and akathisia.

- It produces almost no tardive dyskinesia and is often used as the drug of choice for patients developing, or with developed, tardive dyskinesia.

The bad news:

- It decreases white blood cells (agranulocytosis) in some patients (less than 1 percent); therefore, in the United States, blood counts must be done every week for six months, then every two weeks indefinitely. Agranulocytosis may be fatal, and deaths due to agranulocytosis have been reported in patients taking clozapine, although this should not occur if the white blood cell count is being monitored.

- It may cause cardiac problems (myocarditis) within the first month on the drug, and several deaths have been reported.

- Excessive salivation is common when starting clozapine or increasing the dosage.

- Sedation is a major problem, so it should be taken at bedtime.

THE TREATMENT OF SCHIZOPHRENIA: MEDICATIONS 233

- Seizures are common, especially at higher doses. At 900 mg per day, for example, the incidence of seizures is approximately 6 percent.

- Weight gain is a major problem.

- It may increase the blood sugar and even cause diabetes.

- It causes urinary incontinence in some patients, especially women.

- Pregnancy may occur in women being switched from first-generation antipsychotics.

- It should not be given with carbamazepine (Tegretol), which can also decrease white blood cells. Some antibiotics and other medications may also decrease white blood cells, so physicians treating the person for other conditions should always be informed that the person is taking clozapine.

- Starting it on patients who are taking benzodiazepines should be done only in the hospital, because of possible severe reactions.

- It may take many months to work; some psychiatrists believe that you should not give up until at least six months or 600 mg per day is achieved, whereas others believe that eight weeks is sufficient as a trial. Some physicians have found clozapine blood levels to be useful indicators for deciding how long to continue the trial.

- It is very expensive.

Olanzapine (Zyprexa)

Olanzapine was introduced in the United States in 1996. It comes in 2.5 mg, 5 mg, 7.5 mg, and 10 mg tablets. There is also a wafer-like preparation (Zyprexa Zydis) that dissolves on contact with saliva for patients who are inclined to hide tablets in their cheek and then spit them out. The usual dose is 10–20 mg per day, although it is used in doses up to 40 mg per day in treatment-resistant patients. The company is in the early stages of developing a once-weekly transdermal patch and a once-monthly, long-acting depot preparation.

The good news:

- It appears to be effective in some cases of treatment-refractory schizophrenia, but this is not as clearly established as with clozapine.

- It has a very low incidence of EPS and akathisia.

- Preliminary data suggest that it has a low incidence of tardive dyskinesia.

- There is some evidence for modest improvement of negative symptoms.

- It may have some mood stabilizing effectiveness and has been approved by the FDA for the treatment of mania.

The bad news:

- Sedation is a major problem, so it should be taken at bedtime.

- Weight gain is a major problem.

- Pregnancy may occur in women being switched from first-generation antipsychotics.

- It may increase the blood sugar and even cause diabetes.

- It is very expensive.

Risperidone (Risperdal)

Risperidone was introduced in the United States in 1994. It comes in 0.25 mg, 0.5 mg, 1 mg, 2 mg, 3 mg, and 4 mg tablets and in liquid form. The company is in the late stages of developing a long-acting depot preparation. The usual dose is 1–8 mg per day.

The good news:

- It has a low incidence of EPS, but this may be dose-related, i.e., EPS appears to be a problem at higher doses.

- It increases prolactin levels, so unwanted pregnancies are less likely than on some other second-generation antipsychotics.

- A liquid form is available, and a long-acting depot preparation is in the late stages of development.

The bad news:

- Some clinicians believe that its effectiveness as a second-generation antipsychotic has been oversold.

- It affects the hepatic P450 enzyme system, so drug interactions are more likely.

- Weight gain is a problem.

- Sexual adverse effects (e.g., amenorrhea, decreased libido) may be a problem.

- It is very expensive.

Quetiapine (Seroquel)

Quetiapine was introduced in the United States in 1997. It comes in 25 mg, 100 mg, 200 mg, and 300 mg tablets. The usual dose is 300–750 mg per day, although it is being used up to 1,000 mg per day for treatment-resistant patients.

The good news:

- It has a very low incidence of EPS.

- It may be effective against the symptoms of agitation and hostility, but data are very preliminary.

- It appears to have a very low incidence of sexual adverse effects.

The bad news:

- It must be taken twice a day.

- An eye exam is recommended when starting it and periodically thereafter to make sure that cataracts are not developing. To date, this does not appear to be a major problem.

- Weight gain is a problem.

- Sedation is a problem, especially since it must be taken twice a day.

- It affects the hepatic P450 enzyme system, so drug interactions are more likely.

- Pregnancy may occur in women being switched from first-generation antipsychotics.

- It is very expensive.

Ziprasidone (Geodon)

Ziprasidone is approved for use in Sweden and is expected to become available in the United States. In July 2000, an FDA Advisory Committee recommended that it be approved, but official FDA approval was still pending at the end of the year. It comes in 20 mg, 40 mg, and 80 mg capsules and also in a short-acting, intramuscular injectable form. The usual dose is 80–160 mg per day.

The good news:

- It is the only second-generation antipsychotic that is claimed to cause no weight gain.

- It has a low incidence of EPS.

- It may be effective for negative symptoms, but data are very preliminary.

- It may have an antidepressant effect.

The bad news:

- It produces changes in cardiac electrical impulses (the Q-Tc interval), which could in some patients cause irregular heartbeats. The relative importance of this cardiac effect is still being evaluated.

- It must be taken twice a day.

- Pregnancy may occur in women being switched from first-generation antipsychotics.

- It may cause sedation when first started, but this is not as severe as for many of the other antipsychotics.

- It is very expensive.

WARNING REGARDING ZIPRASIDONE (GEODON)

Ziprasidone (Zeldox) is a new antipsychotic that may be useful for some individuals who do not respond to other antipsychotics and for some individuals for whom weight gain is a major problem. However, ziprasidone interferes with heart rhythms by prolonging the Q-Tc interval; this might lead to cardiac arrhythmias. Ziprasidone should therefore *not be used* at the same time as other drugs that are also known to prolong the Q-Tc interval, since the effect may be additive, thereby increasing the chances of cardiac arrhythmias. The following drugs are known to prolong the Q-Tc interval and therefore should not be used at the same time as ziprasidone:

Drugs used for psychiatric conditions:

amitriptyline (Elavil)	imipramine (Tofranil)
chlorpromazine (Thorazine)	pimozide (Orap)
desipramine (Norpramin)	quetiapine (Seroquel)
doxepin (Sinequan)	risperidone (Risperdal)
fluoxetine (Prozac)	thioridazine (Mellaril)
haloperidol (Haldol)	venlafaxine (Effexor)

Drugs used for other conditions:

amiodarone (Cordarone)	flecainide (Tambocor)
azelastine (Astelin)	foscarnet (Foscavir)
bepridil (Vascor)	fosphenytoin (Cerebyx)
clarithromycin (Biaxin)	halofantrine (Halfan)
clemastine (Tavist)	ibutilide (Corvert)
disopyramide (Norpace)	indapamide (Lozol)
dofetilide (Tikosyn)	isradipine (Dynacirc)
erythromycin (EES)	itraconazole (Sporanox)
felbamate (Felbatrol)	ketoconazole (Nizoral)

levomethadyl (Orlaam)   salmeterol (Serevent)
moexipril/HCTZ (Uniretic)   sotalol (Betapace)
moxifloxacin (Avelox)   sparfloxacin (Zagam)
naratriptan (Amerge)   sumatriptan (Imitrex)
nicadipine (Cardene)   tacrolimus (Prograf)
octreotide (Sandostatin)   tamoxifen (Nolvadex)
pentamidine (NebuPent)   tizanidine (Zanaflex)
probucol (Lorelco)   trimethoprim/sulfamethoxazole
procainamide (Procan)   (Bactrim)
quinidine (Quinaglute)   zolmitriptan (Zomig)

THE BOTTOM LINE: WHICH ANTIPSYCHOTIC
SHOULD YOU TRY?

The questions of which antipsychotic to use, in which order, on what type of patient, and at what dosage level continue to be among the most controversial issues in psychiatry. A major reason for this is that most of the studies that purport to answer these questions were done by the drug companies themselves and are both contradictory and self-serving.

There *is* consensus on one issue: most individuals with schizophrenia are not receiving optimal pharmacologic care. This was demonstrated in 1998 by the publication of the Schizophrenia Patient Outcomes Research Team (PORT) survey of 719 patients. However, deciding what is "optimal pharmacologic care" is another matter. *A Practice Guideline for the Treatment of Patients with Schizophrenia* was published by the American Psychiatric Association in 1997, and "The Expert Consensus Guideline Series on the Treatment of Schizophrenia" was published in the *Journal of Clinical Psychiatry* in 1999. In addition, since 1995 the Texas Department of Mental Health and Mental Retardation, in conjunction with academic institutions, has been developing a medication algorithm to advise public-sector psychiatrists in that state which antipsychotic to use when. In England in early 2000, the Royal College of Psychiatrists issued an important review of these issues, "The Management of Schizophrenia: Pharmacologic Treatments."

Over the next few years, it is likely that consensus will be found on these pharmacologic questions. This will arise both from the experience of clinicians over time and as the result of research sponsored by the National Institute of Mental Health (NIMH), such as the Clinical Antipsychotic Trials of Intervention Effectiveness (CATIE), a large study of schizophrenia treatment undertaken in 2000 by the University of North Carolina.

In selecting an antipsychotic for an individual with schizophrenia, it is important to consider many questions. If the patient has been treated before, what was his/her response to the antipsychotics tried, what were the adverse effects, and what is the person's preference? For some individuals, adverse effects such as hand tremor or sedation may be unacceptable, while for others weight gain may be unacceptable. The risk of pregnancy in women is also important to consider. If awareness of illness and compliance are issues, should an antipsychotic that has a long-acting depot preparation be chosen? Is the person averse to having his/her blood drawn regularly, as is necessary for clozapine? Which antipsychotic truly improves the person's quality of life the most? Who will pay for the medication? This is an especially important consideration given the marked price differential between the first-generation and the second-generation antipsychotics.

If the person has never been treated before, the main question is whether to start with a first-generation or a second-generation antipsychotic. Although most American guidelines recommend starting with a second-generation antipsychotic, I personally agree with the Royal College of Psychiatrists guideline, which states that current evidence is insufficient to recommend second-generation antipsychotics as the drugs of choice for first-onset schizophrenia. It seems reasonable to begin with a first-generation antipsychotic and then move to the second-generation category only after a trial or two of the first-generation agents have been unsuccessful, either because of emergent side effects or lack of clinical improvement. At this point in time, there are insufficient data to determine in which order to use the second-generation antipsychotics. Clozapine appears to be underutilized in the United States because of the necessity of having blood tests. For patients with evidence of developing tardive dyskinesia, there appears to be a consensus that clozapine is the antipsychotic of choice.

All of these conclusions are, of course, subject to change as new information becomes available and will be further influenced as new antipsychotic medications are introduced. So far, surprisingly little has been clearly established regarding the proper dose of these newer mediations or how long a trial should be continued before switching to another medication. It is hoped that in the future it will become possible to predict which individual will respond to which drug, either by doing blood tests (e.g., genetic markers) or by neuroimaging (e.g., magnetic resonance spectroscopy), but to date such research has not yielded much useful information.

INTERACTIONS OF ANTIPSYCHOTICS WITH OTHER MEDICATIONS

Antipsychotic medications may not only cause side effects by them-selves but also interact with other drugs as well. Physicians prescribing antipsychotic medications and individuals taking them should be aware of interactions that have been reported to occur between antipsychotics and other drugs. Many of these interactions are rare, but if they occur in *you*, they do not seem insignificant from your viewpoint. They do not necessarily mean that the two drugs should not be given at the same time, but only that caution should be used. Many of these drug interac-tions are due to the fact that antipsychotic drugs are metabolized in the liver by various subunits of the P450 enzyme system; other drugs that are also metabolized by this enzyme system may therefore interfere with metabolism of the antipsychotics.

Interactions between an antipsychotic and another drug may affect the antipsychotic by decreasing the serum level (thus making it less effective) or by increasing it (thus making side effects more likely). Other drug interactions have little or no effect on the antipsychotic drug but instead cause generalized effects (e.g., the combination of an antipsychotic and a barbiturate may cause severe sedation). Still other interactions have no effect on the antipsychotic but instead cause changes in the effect of the other drug, e.g., some antipsychotics taken with Coumadin may cause a further increase in the clotting time of blood.

The following list shows the major drug interactions described between antipsychotics and other medications. Anyone taking an antipsychotic and one of these other medications should make sure that his or her physicians are aware of the other medications. If the person is going to have surgery, the anesthetist should also be informed. There are tremendous differences between individuals for drug interactions. And just because a suspected drug interaction is not listed here does not mean that it is not occurring; new interactions are being reported regularly.

POSSIBLE INTERACTIONS OF ANTIPSYCHOTICS WITH OTHER MEDICATIONS (*INDICATES ESPECIALLY IMPORTANT)

1. Antidepressants

    selective serotonin reuptake inhibitors (SSRIs):
    fluoxetine (Prozac)
    *fluvoxamine (Luvox)
    paroxetine (Paxil)
    sertraline (Zoloft)
    citalopram (Celexa)

    tricyclics
    amitriptyline (Elavil)
    imipramine (Tofranil)
    desipramine (Norpramin)
    doxepin (Sinequan)
    maprotiline (Ludiomil)
    nortriptyline (Aventyl)
    protriptyline (Vivactil)
    trimipramine (Surmontil)
    clomipramine (Anafranil)

    monoamine oxidase (MAO) inhibitors
    tranylcypromane (Parnate)
    phenelzine (Nardil)

2. Anticonvulsants and mood stabilizers
    *carbamazepine (Tegretol)
    divalproex sodium (Depakote)
    valproic acid (Depakene)
    phenytoin (Dilantin)
    phenobarbital

3. Antihypertensives
    beta blockers, e.g., propranolol (Inderal) and others
    guanethidine (Esimil, Ismelin)

> methyldopa (Aldomet)
> captopril (Capoten)
> enalapril (Vasotec)
> clonidine (Catapres)
> indomethacin (Indocin)
>
> 4. Other medications
>   cimetidine (Tagamet)
>   erythromycin (Erythrocin)
>   griseofulvin (Grifulvin, Grisactin, Grivate, others)
>   insulin (Humalog, Humulin, Iletin, others)
>   isoniazid (INH)
>   levodopa (Larodopa, Sinemet)
>   theophylline (Sustaire, Theo-Dur, others)
>   warfarin (Coumadin)

In addition to the interactions between antipsychotics and other medications as listed, the possibility should also be kept in mind that an antipsychotic might interact with an over-the-counter herb preparation being taken by the individual. The use of medicinal herbs has become increasingly common in recent years; individuals assume that since these are "natural" preparations, they can do no harm. This is not true. For example, evening primrose, a herb preparation sometimes used for schizophrenia, may react adversely with phenothiazine antipsychotics. And betel nut, taken in many tropical countries for a variety of complaints, may exacerbate the extrapyramidal signs (EPS) of many antipsychotic drugs. Individuals who are taking herb preparations should therefore inform their physicians.

OTHER DRUGS TO TRY IF ANTIPSYCHOTICS FAIL

What should be done if antipsychotics have been tried and do not adequately control the symptoms of schizophrenia? One common approach is to try combinations of two antipsychotics, most often one from the first-generation group and one from the second-generation group. Less often, two second-generation antipsychotics, such as clozapine and risperidone, are tried. The use of more than one antipsychotic at the same time, usually referred to as polypharmacy, is surprisingly common. However, virtually no studies have been done on it, so its potential risks and benefits are unknown. It should be kept in mind, however, that the more medications a person is taking, the greater are the chances of experiencing adverse medication interactions.

In addition to polypharmacy, the other strategy commonly used to enhance antipsychotic drug effectiveness is adding a second medication from another type (i.e., not an antipsychotic) to the antipsychotic medication. This is called adjunctive (add-on) treatment. The most commonly used types of medication as adjunctive treatment for schizophrenia are the following:

Anticholinergics

The anticholinergics are a class of drugs that include benztropine (Cogentin), biperiden (Akineton), procyclidine (Kemadrin), and trihexyphenidyl (Artane), among others. They have been used in schizophrenia since shortly after the first generation of antipsychotic drugs were introduced, because of the known ability of anticholinergics to block dystonic reactions. They are also used to treat tremors and akathisia caused by antipsychotic drugs.

The use of long-term anticholinergics in schizophrenia, concurrent with first-generation antipsychotics, continues to be controversial. Some psychiatrists claim that anticholinergics do more than simply block side effects and may *enhance* the effect of antipsychotic medication in some patients. Other psychiatrists are convinced that the anticholinergics *decrease* the effect of antipsychotic medication but may increase the chances of getting tardive dyskinesia.

Anticholinergic drugs may interact with amantadine (Symmetrel) to cause confusion and hallucination, so the two should be used cautiously together. They may also decrease the effectiveness of cimetidine (Tagamet) used to heal ulcers. There have been reported instances of occasional patients with schizophrenia getting a mild "high" from anticholinergics; I had one patient who was known in every emergency room in the city of Washington for his ability to mimic the symptoms of an acute dystonic reaction in his nightly quests for an injection of benztropine (Cogentin).

Benzodiazepines

Benzodiazepines have been used as adjunctive treatment for schizophrenia, primarily with the first-generation antipsychotics, for patients with anxiety and agitation. Lorazepam (Ativan), diazepam (Valium), and clonazepam (Klonopin) have been used most often because they can be injected as well as taken by mouth. Some studies have described modest clinical benefits, but overall the results are not impressive. *The benzodiazepines should not be given simultaneously to any individual taking clozapine except under strict medical supervision, because of the danger of a severe, even fatal, drug interaction.* The benzodiazepines also have the disadvantage of being addicting if taken over several months and of causing withdrawal symptoms such as seizures if stopped abruptly.

Lithium

Lithium has been used as an adjunctive treatment for schizophrenia. The results have been mixed, with some clinicians claiming that it is helpful in reducing symptoms, especially depression, agitation, and impulsivity, while other clinicians claim that it is of no value.

Lithium is available as tablets or liquid. Previously it was thought that lithium must be given in divided doses two or three times a day, but recent studies have suggested that it can be given once daily or even every other day. Before starting lithium, the patient should have a blood test for kidney and thyroid function (usually a TSH and creatinine), and women should certainly have a pregnancy test; lithium may harm the fetus and should not be given in the first three months of pregnancy except in very unusual circumstances. Women on lithium should also bottle-feed rather than breast-feed their babies.

Lithium differs from the antipsychotic drugs in being potentially much more dangerous if taken in overdose. For this reason blood must be drawn for lithium level testing initially every few days, then in decreasing frequency as the person becomes stabilized on the drug. Blood tests should also be done approximately every six to twelve months to check thyroid and kidney function. The therapeutic blood level of lithium is 0.6–1.2 meq. (milliequivalents) per liter, although a few patients can be maintained successfully in the 0.4–0.6 meq. range and a few require a 1.2–1.6 meq. range to be effective. To get a therapeutic blood level may require two or three tablets a day in one patient, six or eight tablets in another. Older patients need lower doses.

Side effects of lithium in a normal dose range may include thirst, frequent urination, a tremor of the fingers or hands, diarrhea, fluid retention (edema) of the hands or lower legs, weight gain, altered hair texture, acne, or the worsening of psoriasis if the person has it. Two of the most troublesome side effects are tremor and frequent urination, especially at night. If the person is clearly responding to the lithium, then the tremor can often be treated using beta blocker drugs (e.g., propranolol) and the frequent urination with amiloride or other diuretics; the use of diuretics with lithium, however, may be risky in some cases and should be done only by physicians who are familiar with these drugs.

If the lithium level goes too high, it can be a serious, even life-threatening situation. Symptoms of toxicity include vomiting, diarrhea, weakness, confusion, stupor, staggering, incoordination, slurred speech, dizziness, blurred vision, convulsions, and coma. Lithium should *never* be given to a patient with any of these symptoms without first checking with a doctor. Even if the person has only vomiting or diarrhea from a suspected gastrointestinal upset, stop the lithium until the person is better. Lithium levels also tend to rise in very hot weather when the person is sweating heavily, and fluid intake should be increased.

Lithium interacts unfavorably with many other drugs. There has even been controversy regarding the advisability of using lithium with antipsychotic drugs, as is useful in schizophrenia, because of rare reports of serious toxicity between lithium and haloperidol. The general consensus is that using lithium in combination with antipsychotic drugs is safe as long as a physician is involved in following the patient. Many other drugs interact with lithium by increasing the lithium blood level and thus increasing the chances of lithium toxicity.

Carbamazepine and Other Mood Stabilizers

Carbamazepine (Tegretol) is widely used to treat some forms of epilepsy and has also been found to be effective in treating manic-depressive illness (bipolar disorder), either in place of, or in conjunction with, lithium. It has also been used as an adjunctive drug to treat schizophrenia, especially for reducing aggression, violence, and paranoia, with modest effectiveness. It should be considered an adjunctive drug for any patient with schizophrenia who has an abnormal electroencephalograph

(EEG). There is some evidence that it may decrease the effectiveness of haloperidol when both drugs are taken simultaneously. One of carbamazepine's most serious side effects is agranulocytosis, and for this reason *it should not be given with clozapine, which also may cause agranulocytosis.*

Valproic acid (Depakene) and divalproex sodium (Depakote) are related mood stabilizers that are also occasionally used as adjunctive treatments for schizophrenia, but no careful studies of their efficacy have been carried out. Some of the newer mood stabilizers are also being tried as adjunctive medications, including lamotrigine (Lamictal), gabapentin (Neurontin), and topiramate (Topamax), but it is too early to tell whether they will be useful. The last is especially interesting because it is claimed to promote weight loss and thus might reverse one of the most troubling side effects of many second-generation antipsychotics.

Antidepressants

Individuals with schizophrenia often have depression as part of their illness or as a reaction to their illness. It is seen especially frequently in those cases that fall within the schizoaffective clinical spectrum. The symptoms of depression may be confused with other symptoms of schizophrenia, such as withdrawal and anergia, and the depression may make all the symptoms of schizophrenia seem more severe. The relatively high incidence of depression in schizophrenia is attested to by the fact that at least 10 percent of individuals with schizophrenia commit suicide.

Antidepressants have been used for schizophrenia specifically to treat the concurrent depression as well as adjunctive medications to ameliorate the symptoms of schizophrenia. Most commonly used are the selective serotonin reuptake inhibitors (SSRIs), such as fluoxetine (Prozac), sertraline (Zoloft), paroxetine (Paxil), fluvoxamine (Luvox), and citalopram (Celexa). Some clinicians have claimed that these drugs improve negative symptoms other than depression, but that has not been demonstrated in a controlled trial. The SSRIs increase the blood level of many antipsychotics, so that might also be their mechanism of effectiveness.

Other Adjunctive Medications

A variety of other medications have been, and are being, tried as adjunctive medications for schizophrenia. High-dose propranolol (Inderal) and other beta blocker antihypertensives have been tried with some success. Calcium channel blockers such as verapamil (Calan, Verelan, Isoptin) have also been tried. Reserpine, originally introduced as an antipsychotic and antihypertensive, has shown some promise. Recent studies of adjunctive estrogen in women have also shown some reduction in the symptoms of schizophrenia. And of course electroconvulsive therapy (ECT) should also be considered, as discussed in chapter 8.

NEW ANTIPSYCHOTICS ON THE HORIZON

The economic success of antipsychotics such as clozapine, olanzapine, risperidone, and quetiapine has produced a marked increase in interest of drug manufacturers in developing additional antipsychotics. This interest has been further fueled by anticipated payoffs of the human genome project, from which some researchers hope that schizophrenia-predisposing genes will be identified as targets for new drugs. The development of new antipsychotics has also been stimulated by improving brain-imaging technology, which permits the visualization of specific neurotransmitters and receptors in living individuals.

The development of new drugs in the United States is regulated by the Food and Drug Administration (FDA). Following preliminary trials done mostly in laboratory animals, a drug must pass through three phases of FDA-required trials to establish its safety and optimal dosage. Phase 1 trials are usually carried out on a small number of healthy volunteers; phase 2 trials involve a larger number of patients with the disease; and phase 3 trials include hundreds of patients with the disease. Most drugs that reach phase 3 are eventually approved for marketing. All three phases of trials combined may take several years.

Most antipsychotics being developed in the United States and Europe target neurotransmitters. Whereas earlier drugs targeted a single neurotransmitter, most newer drugs target several. Various dopamine and serotonin neurotransmitters are the most common targets, but histamine, noradrenalin, nicotine, acetylcholine, and glutamate are increasingly included as well. Some antipsychotic medications being investigated by pharmaceutical companies at this time include:

- *iloperidone (Zomaril):* Currently in phase 3 trials, it targets a combination of dopamine and serotonin receptors.

- *aripiprazole:* Currently in phase 3 trials, it appears to be promising in initial studies.

- *M100907:* Currently in phase 3 trials, this drug specifically targets the serotonin 5-HT2A receptor and has little direct effect on dopamine receptors. Initial claims include a lack of weight gain.

- *ORG 5222:* Currently in phase 2. This targets a combination of dopamine and serotonin receptors.

- *U-101387:* Currently in phase 2. This drug targets dopamine receptors.

- *SR-31742:* Currently in phase 2. This drug targets sigma receptors.

Drug trials are also underway involving novel agents as antipsychotics or as adjunctive agents that do not necessarily target neurotransmitters. Much of this research is being supported by the Stanley Foundation Research Programs. Among trials of antipsychotic efficacy underway at the time of the writing of this book were trials of secretin (a pancreatic protein), EPA (fish oil), hydroxychloroquine (anti-inflammatory), famciclovir (antiviral), sulfadoxine and pyrimethamine (Fansidar, antiprotozoal), and tamoxifen (antineoplastic). Research was also underway to develop an implantable antipsychotic that could be placed beneath the skin and then slowly released over many months, similar to implantable contraceptives for women.

In addition to these antipsychotic medications in various stages of development, several antipsychotics are available in other countries that are not marketed in the United States. The reasons for this are many, including lack of approval by the FDA and the failure of the pharmaceutical company to apply for FDA approval. It is usually not possible to ascertain why a pharmaceutical company decides not to market a product in the United States, as these companies are highly competitive and secretive about marketing decisions. The list of antipsychotics available in other countries but not in the United States includes the following.

amisulpiride   oxyprotipine   terguride
clopenthixol   penfluridol   timiperone
flupenthixol   pipamperone   zotepine
isofloxythepin   pipotiazine   zuclopenthixol
oxyprothepin   sulpiride

Some of these medications may be useful as alternate antipsychotics. For example, penfluridol can be given orally just once a week. Pipotiazine, zuclopenthixol, and flupenthixol have long-acting intermuscular depot forms and therefore would be useful alternatives to intermuscular depot haloperidol and fluphenazine.

DRUG PRICES AND THE USE OF GENERICS

The price of second-generation antipsychotic drugs is one of the scandals of American medicine. These drugs cost two to three times more in the United States than in most other countries. A 1998 survey comparing costs to pharmacists of antipsychotic medications in the United States and 16 other countries reported that clozapine costs six times more in the United States than in Spain, olanzapine costs four times more than in Spain, and risperidone costs twice as much as in France.

COSTS TO PHARMACISTS IN 1998 OF A 30-DAY SUPPLY* (in U.S. dollars)				
	Spain	**Finland**	**Canada**	**United States**
Clozapine (Clorazil)	51.94	64.39	271.08	317.03
Olanzapine (Zyprexa)	76.87	157.68	158.09	324.08
Risperidone (Risperdal)	142.29	132.86	135.95	248.86

*Costs to patients are typically at least 40 percent higher.

The reason for these gross discrepancies is simple: all other countries either cap the profit margin of the pharmaceutical companies (e.g., England allows a 20 percent profit) or they negotiate the price by buying in bulk for their national health service. In the United States, there is no limit to how much pharmaceutical companies can mark up drugs. Consequently, in 1998 *Fortune* magazine ranked the pharmaceutical business as "the most profitable of all industries . . . measured on returns on equity, sales and assets." The American pharmaceutical companies rationalize their profits by claiming that the profits are needed to develop the new drugs. In fact, both clozapine and risperidone were developed in Europe, and the majority of expenditures of American pharmaceutical companies are spent on advertising and not on drug development.

Antipsychotic drugs are big business. According to the *Wall Street Journal*, sales of antipsychotic medications almost quadrupled between 1995 and 1999. In 1999 it was estimated that Eli Lilly's sales of Zyprexa reached $2 billion, and in 2000 its sales surpassed those of Prozac. In 1999 Johnson and Johnson's Risperdal had total estimated sales of $1.2 billion. The enormous profits generated by these drugs are one reason why in 1999 Sidney Taurel, the CEO of Eli Lilly, was paid $6.0 million in salary, bonus, and other compensation, plus $6.9 million more in stock options. Ralph Larsen, the CEO of Johnson and Johnson, was paid $4.3 million in salary, bonus, and other compensation, plus $7.6 million in stock options. Antipsychotic drugs are thus not only big business, they are also a very profitable business.

Patients who respond well to first-generation antipsychotics are much better off in financial terms. Generic haloperidol, for example, costs patients approximately 10 cents a day, and generic thiothixene costs patients approximately $1 a day. By contrast, clozapine, olanzapine, or risperidone cost patients approximately $15 to $20 per day, which translates into $5,500 to $7,300 per year without including other costs such as the mandatory blood tests for clozapine or other drugs the person may be taking. Many states cover the costs of the medications, but that in turn has put great fiscal pressure on their budgets. More pharmaceutical costs mean fewer clubhouses or other rehabilitation programs.

To counteract the high cost of antipsychotic medications, patients and families can do the following:

1. *Buy larger size tablets and cut them.* For example, if a person is taking olanzapine (Zyprexa) 2.5 mg each day, don't buy 2.5 mg tablets.

Instead, buy 5 mg 7.5 mg, or 10 mg tablets and cut them in half, thirds, or quarters. The cost savings are remarkable. A recent study recommending this practice noted that a 2.5 mg Zyprexa tablet cost $5.37, while the 5 mg tablet cost $6.34; thus, by buying the larger tablet and cutting it in half, the cost of a daily 2.5 mg dose would be reduced from $5.37 to $3.17. Cutting tablets is easiest when the tablets are scored (i.e., they have a ridge), but a sharp knife is effective if they are not. Do not worry if the pieces are not precisely equal; blood levels of most antipsychotics will stay reasonably even as long as the person ingests the entire tablet in pieces over two to four days so that the combined dose equals what has been prescribed.

2. *Use generic drugs whenever possible.* When a pharmaceutical company markets a new drug, it is protected by a patent for several years and only that company can market the drug. When the patent expires, any company can apply to the Food and Drug Administration (FDA). The FDA inspects the company's manufacturing facilities and ascertains that the company's generic is therapeutically equivalent to the original product. The FDA publishes a list of approved generic drugs, *Approved Drug Products with Therapeutic Equivalence Evaluations*, under its website, www.fda.gov/cder/ob/default.htm (search by active ingredient).

Virtually all first-generation antipsychotics are available as generics. In 1997 the patent on clozapine expired, and it is now available as a generic from Mylan, Zenith Goldline, and Geneva Pharmaceuticals. In general, the cost of generic medications is 10 to 40 percent less than the brand name, and for older medications, the savings may be even greater.

When switching from a brand name to a generic drug, watch for any possible changes in the therapeutic response. The strength (bioequivalency) of generic medications may legally vary by as much as 20 percent, although in most cases the variation is only 2 to 3 percent. The manufacturers of brand name drugs would have patients and families believe that switching to generic drugs is risky; they have an economic interest in promoting such misinformation. The only medication used to treat schizophrenia for which problems of efficacy have been reported is carbamazepine, and problems of efficacy have also been reported for Tegretol, the brand name version.

The biggest problem in switching to generic formulations of antipsychotic drugs is confusion for patients. If a person has been taking a tablet of a particular color and shape for many months, it may take much explanation to help the person understand that a tablet of another color and shape is the same drug.

3. *Buy wisely.* The cost of antipsychotic medications may vary widely among pharmacies in a single city. The use of the Internet makes pharmaceutical price shopping much easier. Many patients and families are increasingly buying medications in other countries where they are much less expensive. This is especially true in states adjacent to the Canadian and Mexican borders, but it is also true for European countries. Indeed, one can fly to Spain first class, buy a year's supply of clozapine, and still save money!

**HOW TO SAVE MONEY BUYING
ANTIPSYCHOTIC MEDICATIONS**

- Buy larger tablets and cut them up.
- Use generics whenever possible.
- Shop around and use the Internet to find the best price. If possible, buy the medication in other countries.

MEDICATIONS FOR EARLY TREATMENT OR PREVENTION

In the late 1990s, substantial interest evolved in the early treatment and possible prevention of developing schizophrenia. This is a research area that is still evolving and is therefore difficult to evaluate.

The one thing almost everyone agrees on is that it is desirable to begin medication for the treatment of schizophrenia as early in the course of the disease as possible. There is some evidence that beginning treatment early may improve the long-term course of the disease, but the evidence is not yet convincing. On humanitarian grounds alone, however, early treatment is desirable.

The controversy begins when one tries to define "early." Does early mean starting medication on teenagers who have become withdrawn and have some findings consistent with schizophrenia on neuropsychological testing? Does early mean starting medication on children who have constellations of traits that markedly increase the chances of later being diagnosed with schizophrenia? Or does early mean treating younger brothers and sisters of individuals with schizophrenia, knowing that they have an increased risk of developing the disease?

These kinds of questions are being asked increasingly frequently, but they in turn raise other questions. Does early treatment really make any difference? What is the effect of treating with low-dose antipsychotics individuals who would not have developed the disease? What is the effect of labeling such individuals as schizophrenia-prone? Can we really tell who is in the earliest stages of the disease or which traits are predisposing with any reasonable degree of reliability? This last question is especially troubling; one study showed that efforts to detect college students who were schizophrenia-prone by using questionnaires on magical thinking was virtually worthless, and a retrospective study of schizophrenia prediction by high school teachers of their students "would have been hopeless, barely better than chance."

Research on the early treatment and possible prevention of schizophrenia is underway at several sites, especially under Dr. Patrick McGorry and colleagues in Melbourne, Australia, and under Dr. Tom McGlashan and colleagues in New Haven. Since the prevention of schizophrenia is, like motherhood, a universally accepted worthy goal, these efforts have won wide support. Whether or not they will make any difference, however, is yet to be determined.

THE MEDICATION-SAVVY CONSUMER AND FAMILY

Smart consumers and their families quickly learn what Edward Francell teaches—that medication is "the foundation of recovery." Francell, a social worker who has been diagnosed at various times as having schizophrenia and manic-depressive illness, says that his improvement really began when he shifted from "passive recipiency" of whatever psychiatrists told him to do to active, informed involvement. "Recovery began," said Francell, "when I got off the bench and became an active player in the treatment game," shifting from spectator to player.

The first step in being medication-savvy is to become as knowledgeable as possible. Read up on the available medications, their doses, their adverse effects, and their possible drug interactions. The list of recommended reading at the end of this chapter is a good place to begin. The goal for each consumer and family is to know at least as much about the medications as the treating psychiatrist knows. Indeed, a measure of your success is when you can (politely) tell the psychiatrist something that he/she did not know.

The second step in being a medication-savvy consumer and family is to keep a list of all medications taken, the length of time they were taken, the dose, and the adverse effects. This continuously updated list should be given to any new treating psychiatrist encountered in the course of the illness. If you see a psychiatrist for only 15 minutes every three months, it is also helpful to give the psychiatrist a list of your present medications and adverse effects; with limited time, it helps him/her to focus on the important issues. Consumers who have had a very bad reaction to a medication or who are taking medications with potentially severe drug interactions (e.g., clozapine and benzodiazepines) should also wear a Medic Alert bracelet, so that if they are unconscious or very psychotic, they will not be given the wrong medication. Medic Alert bracelets and necklaces can be purchased by calling 800-432-5378.

The final step in being a medication-savvy consumer (and family) is to keep a list of things you wish you could do but which the illness prevents you from doing. These are essentially the goals you wish to achieve by taking medication and participating in other forms of recovery and rehabilitation. The list reminds you *why* you are taking medication and *why* you are willing to try new medications as they become available to possibly ameliorate your symptoms. The list should, of course, be realistic and consistent with your abilities prior to your illness, e.g., be able to read a book, be able to go into a crowded room without panicking, be able to hold a job at least half-time, be able to have a boyfriend, etc. It should not include items such as "be a concert pianist" if you have never played the piano!

RECOMMENDED FURTHER READING

Bodenheimer, T. "Uneasy Alliance: Clinical Investigators and the Pharmaceutical Industry." *New England Journal of Medicine* 342 (2000): 1539–43.

Buckley, P. F., and J. L. Waddington, eds. *Schizophrenia and Mood Disorders: The New Drug Therapies in Clinical Practice.* Boston: Butterworth Heinemann, 2000.

Cohen, C. I., and S. I. Cohen. "Potential Cost Savings from Pill Splitting of Newer Psychotropic Medications." *Psychiatric Services* 51 (2000): 527–29.

Diamond, R. J. *Instant Psychopharmacology: A Guide for the Nonmedical Mental Health Professional.* New York: Norton, 1998.

Fenton, W. S. "Prevalence of Spontaneous Dyskinesia in Schizophrenia." *Journal of Clinical Psychiatry* 61 (suppl. 4) (2000): 10–14.

Francell, E. G., Jr. "Medication: The Foundation of Recovery." *Innovations and Research* 3 (1994): 31–40.

Gorman, J. M. *The Essential Guide to Psychiatric Drugs*. 3rd ed. New York: St. Martin's Press, 1997.

Handbook of Adverse Drug Interactions. New Rochelle, N.Y.: Medical Letter, 1999.

Siegfried, S. L., W. Fleischhacker, and J. Lieberman. "Pharmacological Treatment of Schizophrenia." In J. Lieberman and R. Murray, eds. *Comprehensive Care of Schizophrenia*. London: Martin Dunitz Publishers, 2000. Chapter 4.

Weiden, P. J., P. L. Scheifler, R. J. Diamond, et al. *Breakthroughs in Antipsychotic Medications: A Guide for Consumers, Families, and Clinicians*. New York: Norton, 1999.

Wong, A. H. C., M. Smith, and H. S. Boon. "Herbal Remedies in Psychiatric Practice." *Archives of General Psychiatry* 55 (1998): 1033–44.

ZumBrunnen, T. L., and M. W. Jann. "Drug Interactions with Antipsychotic Agents: Incidence and Therapeutic Implications." *CNS Drugs* 9 (1998): 381–401.

10

THE REHABILITATION
OF SCHIZOPHRENIA

Expecting the chronically ill patient to use the current mental health
system is like expecting a paraplegic to use stairs.

J. Halpern, et al., *The Illness of Deinstitutionalization*, 1978

The basic concept that underlies the rehabilitation of schizophrenia was
clearly articulated by Dr. Werner M. Mendel, a psychiatrist who spent
over 40 years treating patients with this disease in both the private and
the public sector. In his book *Treating Schizophrenia*, Mendel likens an
individual with schizophrenia to an individual with a physical disability:

> If, for example, someone has a paralyzed right arm that cannot be
> fixed, we then provide her with a brace to help with function. We may
> modify her car so that she can drive and work the controls with only
> one hand. We may retrain her to use her left hand for all the things she
> used to do with her paralyzed right hand. We may also give her psy-
> chological support for accepting herself with the defect and help focus
> on what she can do rather than what she cannot do.

Treating individuals who have schizophrenia with medication
alone, then, is not sufficient. A complete treatment program includes
rehabilitation as well. Although patients vary widely in their rehabilitation needs depending on the severity of their symptoms, all of them have
to address the basic problems of money, food, housing, employment,
friendship, and medical care.

Before addressing these specific problems, it should be noted that
one concept underlies all rehabilitation efforts—hope. If the individual

with schizophrenia has hope, then rehabilitation efforts are likely to succeed. If the person has no hope, these efforts are likely to fail. This was shown in a recent Swiss study of 46 individuals with schizophrenia in which poor rehabilitation outcomes were predicted by "pessimistic outcome expectancies . . . and depressive-resigned coping strategies," in short, "whether the patient has already given up or not." Treatment and rehabilitation programs will succeed, therefore, only insofar as they also engender hope.

MONEY AND FOOD

For over a century, most individuals with schizophrenia were locked away in state psychiatric hospitals, usually for many years at a time. If they got out at all it was to live with their families. It was not until the advent of antipsychotic medication and deinstitutionalization that money, food, and housing became major problems for the hundreds of thousands of individuals who were subsequently released from the hospitals.

Some persons with schizophrenia can work part-time or full-time and are self-supporting. The vast majority, however, must rely on their families or on two government programs, Supplemental Security Income (SSI) and Social Security Disability Insurance (SSDI), for the money to pay for their food and housing.

SSI, a program to provide income for needy aged, blind, and disabled persons, is administered by the Social Security Administration. It defines disability as "an inability to engage in any substantial gainful activity by reason of any medically determined physical or mental impairment which . . . has lasted, or can be expected to last, for a continuous period of not less than twelve months." SSDI is a similar program, except that to be eligible the person must have worked prior to becoming ill and accumulated sufficient credit under Social Security. Benefits from the two programs vary; SSDI varies according to how long the person had worked before becoming ill, while SSI varies from state to state depending upon how much that state supplements the federal SSI payment; approximately half of the states provide some supplement. SSDI and SSI are the most important sources of financial support for individuals with schizophrenia in the United States. As noted in chapter 1, in 1999 a total of 1.3 million people were receiving SSDI because of mental impairment (not including mental retardation), and 1.4 million more were receiving

SSI for the same reason. These 2.7 million people were 27 percent and 31 percent of all recipients of SSDI and SSI, respectively, and this category (mental impairment not including mental retardation) was the single largest category of medical disability for both SSDI and SSI.

During the early 1980s, considerable public attention focused on the SSI and SSDI programs when officials in the Reagan administration decided to tighten the criteria for eligibility for such payments. In 1981 and 1982 it was estimated that almost one-half million disabled persons were dropped from the program, including many persons with schizophrenia. Court challenges to these changes followed, and in 1986 the U.S. Supreme Court ruled in favor of the disabled, and the majority of those who had been cut off the SSI and SSDI programs were reinstated.

Applications to establish disability and receive SSI and SSDI funds should be made at the local Social Security office. The person's assets and other income are taken into consideration in computing eligibility. If the person has savings worth more than $2,000, he/she may not be eligible; in computing assets, a home, car, and basic household goods do not count toward the $2,000. The application for SSI or SSDI is evaluated by a team consisting of a disability examiner and a physician; they may request additional medical information or request an examination of the applicant in selected cases. In evaluating the application, they pay special attention to evidence of a restriction of daily activities and interests, deterioration in personal habits, marked impairment in relating to other people, and the inability to concentrate and carry out instructions necessary to hold a job. Thus, you should submit whatever medical records are pertinent to establishing this at the time you submit your application. Assessing eligibility for SSI and SSDI is necessarily a subjective task, and studies have reported disagreement among reviewers as much as 50 percent of the time. A decision on your initial application usually takes three to six months; approximately half of all initial applications are denied.

If the applicant is denied SSI or SSDI, he/she has the right to appeal. This must be done within 60 days of the denial, and additional evidence of disability can be included at that time. The initial reconsideration of the appeal occurs in the local Social Security office and results in approval only 15 percent of the time. However, the applicant may appeal again, and this time the hearing is before an administrative law judge of the Bureau of Hearings and Appeals of the U.S. Department of Health and Human Services. At this level a higher percentage of appeals are approved. Further appeals are possible to the Appeals Council Review

Board and then to a U.S. district court. It is clear that persistence in pressing a legitimate claim for SSI or SSDI benefits will often result in success.

For applicants who are approved for SSI or SSDI benefits, payments are made retroactively from the date of the initial application. Since the appeals process can take a year or longer, it is not unusual for SSI and SSDI recipients to receive, as their initial payment, a check for thousands of dollars. For individuals who are not capable of managing their own funds, especially those with concurrent substance abuse, it is customary for the Social Security Administration to appoint a representative payee who may be a family member, case manager, or other person (see chapter 11, "Assisted Treatment").

People with schizophrenia usually require assistance with SSI and SSDI applications and, when necessary, with the appeals processes. Social workers who are doing these on a regular basis are often very helpful, especially in ensuring that the correct clinical information is included so that the person's degree of disability can be assessed fairly. Persons applying for SSI or SSDI for psychiatric disability for the first time would be wise to utilize the services of a knowledgeable social worker. Application forms and appeals processes are confusing even for persons whose brains are working perfectly; to a person with schizophrenia they must appear completely Kafkaesque.

SSI payments, but not SSDI payments, are reduced when the disabled recipient lives with his/her family. In theory this takes account of the room and board the person receives, but in fact it penalizes people with schizophrenia for living at home. Many families resent this discriminatory living aspect of the SSI program and claim that they have expenses for the person just as surely as a boarding house operator does. SSI payments are also stopped if a person is hospitalized for more than 90 days. A portion of the SSI monthly payment is intended for the disabled person to use as spending money for clothes, transportation, laundry, and entertainment. The amount of spending money varies by state.

It is important for persons with schizophrenia to establish eligibility for SSI or SSDI benefits if they can. Even if they have other income, thereby reducing the monthly SSI or SSDI check to a very small amount, it is still worthwhile. The reason is that eligibility for SSI or SSDI also establishes eligibility for other assistance programs that can be worth much more than the SSI or SSDI benefits by themselves. Such programs include Medicaid, Medicare, vocational rehabilitation services, food stamps, and some housing and rental assistance programs of the Department of Housing and Urban Development. In some states, eligibility for SSI or SSDI automatically confers eligibility for the other programs, while in other states a separate application must be submitted.

In January 2000, the federal monthly payment for SSI was increased to $512 for an individual and $769 for a married couple; approximately half of all states provide a state supplement to this. Individuals on SSI can earn up to $65 per month without losing any SSI income. For persons earning more than $65 per month, their SSI benefits are reduced by $1 for each additional $2 earned. Also in early 2000, Congress passed legislation making it possible for SSI and SSDI recipients who are trying to return to full-time employment to retain their Medicaid and Medicare benefits; previously these benefits were automatically lost, thereby presenting a major disincentive for SSI and SSDI recipients to return to work.

Individuals with schizophrenia who do not receive support from their families or from the SSI and SSDI programs must rely on other income. Many of them, especially those living in public shelters, utilize public assistance or welfare checks. Individuals who were in the military at the time they first became ill often qualify for disability payments from the Veterans Administration; these are often very generous and may total over $2,000 a month when all benefits are included.

Food stamps are another supplementary source of support for persons with schizophrenia and are underutilized. To be eligible, a person must have an income below the poverty level; this level includes most persons with schizophrenia. The amount of food stamps a person can receive varies by state and with income. It also varies with the cost of food and so has been rising as food prices have been rising. Food stamps can be obtained through local welfare or social services offices.

HOUSING

Housing for individuals with schizophrenia includes facilities with varying degrees of supervision, independent living, and living at home.

Professional Supervision

This type of housing has professionally trained persons who provide supervision for most or all of the 24-hour day. It includes crisis houses, halfway houses, quarter-way houses, and similar facilities. An excellent description of one such home can be found in Michael Winerip's 1994 book, *9 Highland Road.*

Nonprofessional Supervision

These facilities have a supervisor in residence part or all of the time, but the supervisor has no training. These include foster homes, board-and-care homes, boarding houses, group homes, congregate care homes, and similar facilities that go by different names in different locales.

Intermittent Supervision

These residences include apartments and group homes set up for persons with schizophrenia to live basically on their own. Usually a case manager or other mental health professional stops by periodically (e.g., once a week) to make certain that there are no major problems.

The quality of supervised housing for persons with schizophrenia varies widely. On one end of the spectrum are small foster homes where each patient has a room, the food is adequate, and the foster home sponsors watch over and worry about their charges as if they were their own children. A larger version of this may be a renovated hotel where the manager hires staff that organizes social activities for the residents, checks to be sure they are taking their medicine, reminds them of dentist appointments, and helps them fill out applications for food stamps.

But at the other extreme are foster homes with sponsors who provide insufficient heat, blankets, and food, steal the patients' meager funds, use them as cheap labor, and sometimes even rape them or pimp for them. The larger versions of these homes are old hotels that provide no services other than a rundown room and carry out similar kinds of exploitation.

Supervision in many homes for released psychiatric patients often exists on paper only. In a group home in Baltimore, which was licensed as a "graduated independent living program" with 24-hour supervision, the staff failed to discover a young man with diabetes until three days after he had died in his room. And in New York City "the police found the decaying corpse of a former patient lying undisturbed in one home inhabited by six other residents."

Because the living facilities are so poor in many places, the professionals in charge of discharging patients from state hospitals are frequently caught in an ethical dilemma. Is the patient really better off in the community than in the hospital? Are the living conditions and exposure to potential victimization really an improvement? I am always surprised to find how many patients with schizophrenia express satisfaction with their living conditions in the community when I know how shoddy the living conditions are. In one study of patients living in board-and-care homes in Los Angeles, 40 percent claimed to be content or reasonably content. I suspect the contentment is in comparison to being back in the hospital or having to live in public shelters or on the streets.

What are the common denominators of good supervised housing for patients living in the community? There are four characteristics that can be identified. First, the people living there are treated with dignity and warmth, not simply as sources of income. Second, the best housing appears to set a maximum of 15 to 20 persons living in a single facility. Boarding homes or congregate care homes for 50, 100, or even more released patients almost invariably become mental hospital wards called by another name; this is transinstitutionalization rather than deinstitutionalization.

Third, good community housing for psychiatric patients should exist in a coordinated continuum whereby a person can be moved to a residence with more or less supervision depending on the needs of the person. Because schizophrenia is a disease of remissions and relapses, it is unrealistic to expect a patient to remain in the same kind of facility indefinitely.

Finally, community housing for patients with schizophrenia is most useful where it is integrated with other activities of the patients. An excellent example of this principle is the Fairweather Lodges, in which patients live together and contract for jobs as a group. Such facilities have been deemed to be very successful where they have been tried and are well described in John Trepp's *Lodge Magic*, listed at the end of this chapter.

There are a handful of excellent housing programs for individuals with schizophrenia and other severe psychiatric disorders. Many of them are affiliated with clubhouses, such as Fountain House in New York, the Green Door in Washington, D.C., and Thresholds in Chicago. The last, for example, has units for more than 700 individuals; furthermore, the housing units exist with many levels of supervision so that individuals can move to a more appropriate level as their clinical condition improves or deteriorates. Other outstanding housing programs, such as Project H.O.M.E. in Philadelphia and the St. Francis Residences in New York, target the most severely ill patients. Many smaller cities and towns also have model housing programs, such as Pine Tree Gardens in Davis, California, and the group homes on the grounds of the Chilton-Shelby Mental Health Center in Calera, Alabama. I will admit to some partiality, however, in recommending a model halfway house in Haverford, Pennsylvania (Torrey House), and an excellent independent living complex in Bartlesville, Oklahoma (Torrey Place).

A practical problem that frequently arises with community housing for psychiatric patients is the issue of zoning and community resistance to such housing. Everybody applauds the placement of patients in the community, it is said, as long as the placement is not in their neighborhood. In some towns and cities in the United States, local fights over this issue have been very bitter. There have now been 40 studies done on the effect of residential group homes for the mentally ill and mentally retarded on the surrounding neighborhood. A review of these studies found that "the presence of group homes in all the areas studied has *not* lowered property values or increased turnover, *not* increased crime, *not* changed the character of the neighborhood." Persons with schizophrenia in fact make very good neighbors. This assumes, of course, that they are being followed for their illness and supervised for medication by responsible mental illness professionals.

Independent Living

A large and growing number of individuals with schizophrenia live independently, either by themselves or with other people. In recent years this has been referred to as supported housing, implying that the mental illness professionals will support the choice of housing made by the consumers. Independent living may run a wide range in quality from rundown SROs (single-room-occupancy hotels) to nicely furnished apartments or homes. A major problem for individuals with schizophrenia living independently is social isolation; in one recent study, 59 percent of consumers and 71 percent of their families indicated that this was a problem. Some individuals with schizophrenia, especially those with limited awareness of their illness, cannot live independently.

Living at Home

A large number of individuals with schizophrenia live at home or with relatives. For some patients and their families this may be a perfectly satisfactory arrangement and cause minimal problems. For many others, however, living at home is quite unsatisfactory and this is especially true for men. This is not surprising since most grown individuals who do not have schizophrenia also encounter problems living at home. For those who do live at home, some suggested strategies are discussed in chapter 12.

EMPLOYMENT

People with schizophrenia extend over the same broad range as persons without schizophrenia regarding their interest in working. At one end of the spectrum are individuals who will do anything to work and will often continue working even when not being paid; individuals at the other end will do anything to avoid work. The only difference in work attitudes between persons with and without schizophrenia is that those with the disorder often have problems working closely with other people, thereby making work more difficult for them. Passage of the Americans with Disabilities Act in 1990 was intended to protect mentally ill workers from discriminatory practices and theoretically should result in increased job opportunities for those who want to work.

The majority of persons with schizophrenia have residual disabilities, such as thinking disorders and auditory hallucinations, that are sufficiently severe that full-time employment is impossible. Some can do part-time jobs, however. Estimates of the number of persons with schizophrenia capable of full-time work range as low as 6 percent; from my own experience I would estimate that approximately 15–20 percent of people with schizophrenia can work full-time and 20 percent more can work part-time *if* proper medication maintenance and rehabilitation programs are available and disincentives to losing medical benefits are removed. Past employment is the best single predictor of future employment for a person with schizophrenia; a person who becomes sick after having had a job is more likely to find work than a person who becomes sick without ever having worked.

Work provides several potential benefits for people, not the least of which is additional income. Improved self-esteem is equally important, for to hold a job is evidence that one is like other people. England's Douglas Bennett, one of the few mental illness professionals who has fought for vocational opportunities for persons with schizophrenia, says that a job magically transforms a patient into a person. Patients will often work very hard to control their psychiatric symptoms in work situations because work is so important to them. It has been observed, for example, that "in the morning at the day center, the same person is fulfilling the role of patient and acts like a patient, exhibiting symptoms and bizarre behavior never seen in the workshop the same afternoon." Work also provides people with a daily structure, a reason to get out of bed in the morning, an identity, and an extended social network.

It is ironic that the civil rights efforts that led to the release of so many patients from psychiatric hospitals also led to sharply decreased availability of jobs for them. In the past, many of these patients had worked on the hospital farms, on the grounds, and on housekeeping and kitchen details. Undoubtedly there was some abuse of this captive work force, and civil rights lawyers went to court with claims of "peonage." The result was a pendulum that swung too far in efforts to correct the situation; hospitals became reluctant to employ patients at all because they could not afford to pay them the minimum wage and other employee benefits. The consequence is thousands of patients in hospitals and in the community who are capable of, and enjoy, working for brief periods but who are not capable of full-time employment. The part-time jobs of the past that were often tailored to their needs are now gone.

The largest impediment to vocational opportunities for persons with schizophrenia is stigma, as will be discussed in chapters 14 and 15. Employers, like most people in our society, do not understand what schizophrenia is and so react negatively when asked if they would consider employing persons with this disease. "I can't have any psychos working in my place" is a common visceral reaction. Another major impediment is that government rehabilitation programs and sheltered workshops have traditionally shunned the mentally handicapped in favor of the physically handicapped. Vocational rehabilitation in the United States is still stuck in the polio era, and if you don't have a visible physical disability you need not apply. The failure of traditional vocational rehabilitation to serve individuals with schizophrenia was documented in a scathing 1997 report, *The Legacy of Failure*, by John Nobel et al. (see "Recommended Further Reading"). Some other countries do a much better job of providing job opportunities for psychiatric patients;

Sweden, England, and the Netherlands all have a greater availability of sheltered workshops for long-term partial employment.

There are several kinds of vocational rehabilitation programs for individuals with serious mental illnesses:

Sheltered Employment

These are sheltered workshops in which the person is not necessarily expected to graduate to competitive employment. In the United States, Goodwill Industries operates many of them. The most impressive example of a sheltered workshop that I have seen is the Broadway Industries, part of the Greater Vancouver Mental Health Services in Vancouver, British Columbia. It accommodates about 70 individuals per month and has developed more than 600 product design lines to allow one or more severely disabled individuals to be involved in production. Its high-quality crafts are sold at several locations in the city.

Transitional Employment

This model of vocational rehabilitation was developed by Fountain House, a clubhouse in New York City, and is used in many other clubhouses. Consumers are assigned to real jobs in commercial establishments and accompanied by a rehabilitation specialist. Two consumers will often divide a single job (e.g., each working half-time) as they learn the job. The graduation rate from transitional employment to competitive employment is impressive, and a 1991 study of transitional employment showed it to be highly cost-effective.

Supported Employment

In this model, the individual is encouraged to select the employment of his/her choice, then is trained intensively in job and related social skills before starting the job. An example of supported employment is the Access program affiliated with the Boston University Center for Psychiatric Rehabilitation. The person attends pre-employment classes for 15 hours a week for seven weeks, then is given a job coach and extensive support in the initial months on the job.

Job Skills Training

This model utilizes commercial establishments that are specifically set up to train individuals with serious mental illnesses in job skills. An impressive example was a restaurant in Hayward, California, called the "Eden Express," in which consumers did all jobs including food preparation, catering, aide to cook, busing, waiting on tables, hostessing, cashiering, dishwashing, and janitorial. Between 1980 and 1985 a total of 315 persons, or 80 percent of those who enrolled, completed the 15-week training program. Approximately 25 trainees were enrolled at any given time, and several job counselors made up the training staff. The staff also taught trainees how to interview for jobs at the completion of their training, and 94 percent of the graduates were able to obtain jobs. The "Eden Express" was largely self-supporting and served over 4,000 customers each month. Salaries for the job counselors were derived primarily from training funds from the California State Departments of Rehabilitation and Education. Other job skills programs have developed modules specifically designed to teach mentally ill workers how to keep their jobs once employed.

Competitive Employment

Some people with schizophrenia can return to competitive employment but not necessarily at the level they would have achieved if they had not become ill. An especially interesting example of competitive employment is the use of people with schizophrenia to be consumer case managers for others with this illness, as described in chapter 12.

FRIENDSHIP AND SOCIAL SKILLS TRAINING

Friendship is needed by persons with schizophrenia, just as it is by everyone without schizophrenia. For the person with schizophrenia, however, there are often barriers to friendship, including the symptoms and brain dysfunction associated with the disorder.

One young man I provided care for recovered from most of his symptoms and was living at home. He attempted to return to his social group of peers, going to taverns and drinking with them as he had done prior to his illness. He found this very difficult, however, complaining that "I can't make out their words, I don't know what to say. It's just not like it used to be." Another patient complained that in social situations "I get lost in the spaces between words in sentences. I can't concentrate, or I get off into thinking about something else." In view of such difficulties it is not surprising that many people with schizophrenia often respond inappropriately in social situations and eventually withdraw. Studies of patients living in the community report that approximately 25 percent are very isolated, 50 percent are moderately isolated, and only 25 percent lead active social lives. Almost half have no recreational activity whatsoever, other than watching television.

In addition to their brain dysfunction that may interfere with social relationships, individuals with schizophrenia must also contend with the stigma that accrues to their illness, as discussed in chapters 14 and 15. One older man, who returned to the hospital because the stigma encountered was so pervasive, expressed it well:

> I just can't make it out there. I know who I am and they know who I am—most of the people out there won't come near me or they spit me in the eye. I'm just like a leper in their eyes. They treat most of us like that. They're prejudiced, you know. They are either afraid or hate us. I've seen it a thousand times. I don't feel good on the outside. I don't belong. They know it and I know it.

There are several possible solutions to the need for friendship among individuals with schizophrenia. One is consumer self-help groups, which are discussed in chapter 12. Another is the Compeer Program that was begun in Rochester, New York, in 1981 and that has spread to more than 300 cities. Compeer volunteers who are not mentally ill are matched with individuals who have schizophrenia or other serious mental illnesses on a one-to-one basis. The two people then get together once a week to shop, go to a movie, go to dinner, play checkers, or share some common interest. (Contact Compeer at 259 Monroe St., Rochester, NY 14607, phone 716-546-8280, or visit their website, http://www.compeer.org/1/n2.asp.)

Still another solution to the friendship problem is offered by the Friendship Network in New York, which is run by the Queens Nassau NAMI chapter and is a dating service set up specifically for persons who have schizophrenia or manic-depressive illness. (Contact the Friendship Network, 1983 Marcus Ave., Suite C-103, Lake Success, NY 11042, or visit their website, www.echo.net/~friends/.) I have personally been very impressed by how much support two individuals with severe mental illnesses can give each other and the strength of the bond that comes from sharing these disorders. Some of the relationships are, of course, disasters, but others are the most important thing that has happened to the people involved; as such, they essentially mirror the range of relationships found among people who do not have severe mental illnesses.

Another approach to friendship is to improve the person's social skills through didactic instruction and supervised group interaction. Social skills training is built into many of the vocational rehabilitation programs mentioned in the previous section, but such training may also be done on its own. Some social skills training programs for individuals with schizophrenia are highly structured programs to make the person more aware of social cues, facial expressions, and the subtleties of normal social interactions, e.g., the person is taught to make eye contact when speaking to others. One of the most widely used such programs is the UCLA Skills Training Modules, created by Dr. Robert Liberman and his colleagues, which since 1981 has provided skills training for over 3,000 mentally ill individuals at the West Los Angeles Veterans Administration Medical Center as well as at many other facilities. It consists of 10 training modules, each of which has a trainer's manual, patient's workbook, user's guide, and videocassette. Such educational methods can be extremely useful in helping consumers function better socially and thereby better survive schizophrenia. (Contact Psychiatric Rehabilitation Consultants, P.O. Box 2867, Camarillo, CA 93011, phone 805-484-5663, fax 805-484-0735, E-mail DROPER@concentric.net, website www.npi.ucla.edu/irc/.)

One of the best solutions to the friendship problem are clubhouses. Modeled after Fountain House, which began in New York City in 1948, there are now over 200 clubhouses in the United States. Clubhouses are especially numerous in Virginia and Massachusetts because these states made their development an official policy of the state department of mental health. Clubhouses provide their "members," as the patients are called, not only with a location for friendship and social activities but with vocational, educational, and housing programs as well.

Clubhouses have also been shown to be cost-effective, because they decrease the rehospitalization rate of members. In studies done at Thresholds in Chicago and its allied program, The Bridge, the rehospitalization rate after nine months among members was 14 percent, compared with a rate of 44 percent for a control group that utilized existing community resources. For people with schizophrenia, who regularly go through the revolving door of community-hospital-community-hospital, it was found that the savings in treatment costs averaged $5,700 per member per year: "These findings imply that an outreach program like The Bridge can literally pay for itself while producing tangible benefits for the members it serves." One wonders how much better off persons with schizophrenia would be in the United States if the $3 billion in federal funds that were used to set up failed Community Mental Health Centers had been used instead to set up clubhouses.

Another aspect of friendship for a person with schizophrenia is the nonhuman variety. Pets often make excellent companions, just as they do for some persons without schizophrenia. Dogs are especially good, for they love indiscriminately, are not at all bothered by a person's thought disorders or auditory hallucinations, and are usually understanding when things are not going well. Providing pets for persons with schizophrenia can often bring them much pleasure; this has been discovered by families as well as by some psychiatric hospitals that have allowed the patients to keep pets or to utilize visiting "pets on wheels" programs.

MEDICAL CARE

Like everyone else, individuals with schizophrenia get sick with other illnesses and require medical care. Obtaining medical care may be difficult, however, for many reasons. Perhaps the most important one is that most people with schizophrenia do not have medical insurance and so must utilize Medicaid and Medicare. Medicaid benefits vary widely from state to state, and many physicians will not accept Medicaid patients.

Other impediments to obtaining medical care include the inability of some people with schizophrenia to give a coherent account of their symptoms to a physician or other health care practitioner, the higher pain threshold found in some individuals with schizophrenia leading to a delay in diagnosis (see chapter 2), and the difficulty that some people with schizophrenia have in understanding or following instructions for treatment. In addition, side effects of the person's antipsychotic medications may confuse the clinical picture, and the antipsychotic medication may interact with medication prescribed for the medical problems.

For all these reasons there is known to be a comparatively high incidence of untreated medical problems among persons with schizophrenia, with studies reporting such problems in 26 to 53 percent of patients. A 1991 study by Adler and Griffith concluded that "the treatment of the medically ill schizophrenic patient can be one of the most challenging tasks a physician will face." The failure to provide such treatment, however, is one reason why individuals with schizophrenia have a higher mortality rate, as discussed in chapter 5.

QUALITY OF LIFE MEASURES

In the 1990s, interest increased in assessing the outcome of treatment and rehabilitation for individuals with schizophrenia. One outcome measure is the quality of the person's life. Scales to measure this quality have been developed by Dr. Douglas A. Bigelow and colleagues at the University of Oregon Health Sciences Center and Dr. Anthony F. Lehman and colleagues at the University of Maryland Center for Mental Health Services Research, as well as others. They include such issues as the person's living situation, family relations, social relations, employment, health, finances, safety, and legal problems. Some quality-of-life surveys also include questions regarding the person's inner experiences, such as pleasure, self-reliance, and self-fulfillment.

To date these quality-of-life measures are little used by mental illness professionals. However, they may well be the wave of the future. Imagine how different services for mentally ill individuals would be if measures of the quality of their lives were included as a routine part of rehabilitation. Imagine, moreover, how different the service system would be if rehabilitation outcome measures were used to determine the compensation of the mental illness professionals.

Quality of life can be assessed either subjectively (by asking the person) or objectively (by having another person rate the quality of life). Both of these should be integral parts of all outcome measurements of treatment and rehabilitation for schizophrenia. Measurements can be done at any one of three levels: the person, the program, or the outcome from the family and community's point of view. This is schematically summarized in the following table.

METHODS OF MEASURING THE OUTCOMES OF TREATMENT AND REHABILITATION FOR INDIVIDUALS WITH SCHIZOPHRENIA

	Subjective Measures	Objective Measures
Person	Self ratings of quality of life	Interviewer ratings of the person's quality of life and severity of symptoms
Program	Consumer ratings of inpatient, outpatient, rehabilitation, housing and other services	Patient care indicators; JCAHO and other surveys and site visits, preferably unannounced
Family and community	Family satisfaction surveys; surveys of police and jail personnel, public shelter and soup kitchen managers	Quantitative information from family surveys; number of mentally ill persons using soup kitchens or sleeping in parks; number of police calls for cases related to mental illness

When measures such as these start being widely used, and when the compensation of the providers is tied to the outcomes, then mental illness services for individuals with schizophrenia and other severe psychiatric disorders will improve rapidly.

THE NEED FOR ASYLUM

When the deinstitutionalization of seriously ill psychiatric patients began in the early 1960s, most people assumed that some patients could be placed in the community but that many others would continue to need long-term hospitalization. By the early 1980s that assumption had been steadily eroded, and in some states (e.g., California, Vermont) there was serious talk of closing state hospitals altogether. Two decades later we have come back, full circle, to where we began, and most mental illness professionals who work with seriously ill patients believe that there is, and will continue to be, a need for state hospitals or their equivalents for some patients.

The kinds of patients who will continue to need state hospitals are those whose symptoms are the most severe and/or whose behavior makes placement in the community very difficult. They include the 10 to 20 percent of seriously mentally ill who respond minimally or not at all to antipsychotic drugs, those with a propensity toward aggression or violence, those with inappropriate behaviors such as setting fires or disrobing in public, and those who are so helpless and/or dependent that they need the protection of the institution. It would be nice if there were no such patients, but there are, and—until we learn the causes of brain diseases like schizophrenia—there will continue to be. Because of the push to close down hospitals and because of legal decisions mandating the placement of patients in the community as "the least restrictive setting," many patients are currently being returned to the community who should not be.

How big a group of patients is this? The answer will depend in large measure on the quality of outpatient psychiatric and rehabilitation services available. A county or state with good programs may be able to successfully maintain in the community all except 5–10 percent of the individuals with schizophrenia, whereas in an area with few services perhaps only half of all patients may be better off in the community. In every system there comes a point where you have to ask hard questions. Is this patient really better off living in the community than remaining in a long-term, sheltered environment? Is the quality of his/her life really going to be better? Is the community truly the "least restrictive setting" for this person? In our rush to return everybody to the community, we have avoided asking such questions, and many patients with schizophrenia have ended up in nursing homes, boarding homes, and public shelters worse than the hospital ward they left. In my eight years of placing patients in the Washington, D.C., community from St. Elizabeths Hospital, I would estimate that at least one-quarter of them were *worse* off, in terms of the quality of their lives, than they had been in the hospital. And such patients often told me that they would gladly return to the hospital if they had the opportunity.

We need to acknowledge, then, the need for some long-term psychiatric beds for the severely disabled. It is reviving the concept of asylum in the benevolent sense that the term was originally used—as protection for those who cannot protect themselves. We do not expect everyone who gets paralytic polio to necessarily be able to walk again, and we do not place them in boarding homes in the community if they are clearly unable to look after themselves. We maintain long-term hospital beds for patients with other severe brain diseases, such as multiple sclerosis and Alzheimer's disease, who are unable to care for themselves. Why shouldn't we do the same for schizophrenia?

RECOMMENDED FURTHER READING

Anthony, W., M. Cohen, and M. Farkas. *Psychiatric Rehabilitation.* Boston: Center for Psychiatric Rehabilitation, 1990.

Bond, G. R. "An Economic Analysis of Psychosocial Rehabilitation." *Hospital and Community Psychiatry* 35 (1984): 356–62.

Bond, G. R., R. E. Drake, K. T. Mueser, et al. "An Update on Supported Employment for People with Severe Mental Illness." *Psychiatric Services* 48 (1997): 335–46.

Carling, P. J. "Housing and Supports for Persons with Mental Illness: Emerging Approaches to Research and Practice." *Hospital and Community Psychiatry* 44 (1993): 439–48.

Dickerson, F. B., N. Ringel, and F. Parente. "Predictors of Residential Independence Among Outpatients with Schizophrenia." *Psychiatric Services* 50 (1999): 515–19.

Lamb, H. R. "The Need for Continuing Asylum and Sanctuary." *Hospital and Community Psychiatry* 35 (1984): 798–800.

Lehman, A. F. "Measures of Quality of Life Among Persons with Severe and Persistent Mental Disorders." *Social Psychiatry and Psychiatric Epidemiology* 31 (1996): 78–88.

Lehman, A. F. "Developing an Outcomes-Oriented Approach for the Treatment of Schizophrenia." *Journal of Clinical Psychiatry* 60 (supp. 19) (1999): 30–35.

Liberman, R. P., C. J. Wallace, G. Blackwell, et al. "Skills Training versus Psychosocial Occupational Therapy for Persons with Persistent Schizophrenia." *American Journal of Psychiatry* 155 (1998): 1087–91.

Marder, S. R., W. C. Wirshing, J. Mintz et al. "Two-Year Outcome of Social Skills Training and Group Psychotherapy for Outpatients with Schizophrenia." *American Journal of Psychiatry* 153 (1996): 1585–92.

Noble, J. H. "Policy Reform Dilemmas in Promoting Employment of Persons with Severe Mental Illnesses." *Psychiatric Services* 49 (1998): 775–81.

Noble, J. H., R. S. Honberg, L. L. Hall, et al. *A Legacy of Failure: The Inability of the Federal-State Vocational Rehabilitation System to Serve People with Severe Mental Illnesses.* Arlington, Va.: National Alliance for the Mentally Ill, 1997.

Randolph, F. L., P. Ridgway, and P. J. Carling. "Residential Programs for Persons with Severe Mental Illness: A Nationwide Survey of State-Affiliated Agencies." *Hospital and Community Psychiatry* 42 (1991): 1111–15.

Smith, G. R., R. W. Manderscheid, L. M. Flynn, et al. "Principles for Assessment of Patient Outcomes in Mental Health Care." *Psychiatric Services* 48 (1997): 1033–36.

Torrey, E. F., D. A. Bigelow, and N. Sladen-Dew. "Quality and Cost of Services for Seriously Mentally Ill Individuals in British Columbia and the United States." *Hospital and Community Psychiatry* 44 (1993): 943–50.

Torrey, E. F., K. Erdman, S. M. Wolfe, et al. *Care of the Seriously Mentally Ill: A Rating of State Programs.* Washington, D.C.: NAMI and Public Citizen Health Research Group, 1990.

Trepp, J. K. *Lodge Magic: Real Life Adventures in Mental Health Recovery.* Minneapolis: Tasks Unlimited, 2000.

Wasow, M. "The Need for Asylum for the Chronically Mentally Ill." *Schizophrenia Bulletin* 12 (1986): 162–67.

Winerip, M. *9 Highland Road.* New York: Pantheon, 1994.

Wing, J. K. "The Functions of Asylum." *British Journal of Psychiatry* 157 (1990): 822–27.

11

TEN MAJOR PROBLEMS

Although insanity is a disease to which every man is liable, a feeling prevails regarding it obviously different from any that prevails regarding most diseases. It is so incapacitating, and involves such complete dependence; its effects upon the civil and social condition of a man are so distinctive; and it is the subject of so much popular apprehension and horror, that it demands a consideration, especially if a cure is expected, that is peculiar to itself.

American Journal of Insanity, 1868

Having the misfortune to be afflicted with schizophrenia brings with it many problems, both for those affected and for their families. Of all those problems, 10 stand out as among the most common, the most persistent, and the most perplexing.

---

10 MAJOR PROBLEMS

- cigarettes and coffee
- alcohol and street drugs
- sex, pregnancy, and AIDS
- victimization
- confidentiality
- medication noncompliance
- assisted treatment
- assaultive and violent behavior
- arrest and jail
- suicide

CIGARETTES AND COFFEE

One cannot overstate the importance of cigarettes and coffee in the daily lives of many people with schizophrenia. They are a major focus of social interaction, expenditure of funds, accumulation of debt, and trading of favors. Some individuals with schizophrenia are so obsessed with obtaining cigarettes and coffee that it appears to dominate their daily activities.

Several studies have shown that between 80 and 90 percent of individuals with schizophrenia smoke cigarettes. This is significantly higher than the approximately 50 percent smoker rate among psychiatric patients with other diagnoses or the 30 percent rate in the general population. Studies have also shown that individuals with schizophrenia are more likely to be heavy smokers and to smoke high-tar cigarettes. Recent studies suggest that individuals on clozapine crave nicotine less and smoke less than those taking first-generation antipsychotics; clozapine thus is a good antipsychotic to use for patients who wish to reduce their smoking.

Many explanations have been proposed to account for heavy smoking among individuals with schizophrenia. Boredom from sitting on inpatient wards may account for some of it, but the incidence of heavy smoking among outpatients is almost as high as it is among inpatients. Nicotine reduces anxiety, reduces sedation, and improves concentration in some people, which might be a form of self-medication for the person with schizophrenia. The self-medication theory received support when a study of people with schizophrenia reported that smoking transiently improved specific brain functions (auditory sensory gating) that are known to be impaired in this disease. The self-medication theory received additional support from a study suggesting that rapid cessation of smoking leads to an exacerbation of schizophrenic symptoms. There are also two studies showing that smoking decreases the Parkinsonian-like stiffness and tremor that often occur as side effects of antipsychotic medication.

Nicotine is known to affect the receptors for many brain neurotransmitters and to promote the release of dopamine, serotonin, acetylcholine, and norepinephrine. There are also nicotine receptors in the brain, and it is possible that these might be related to schizophrenia. Nicotine has been shown in some studies to decrease the blood level of most antipsychotics by increasing excretion by the kidneys. Smokers with schizophrenia are known to require higher doses of antipsychotic medication than nonsmokers, but whether this is a result of the increased excretion is less certain. On the other hand, a study of Tourette's disease reported that nicotine potentiated the effects of haloperidol in decreasing tics.

Clozapine and olanzapine have a special relationship to smoking. Both drugs are metabolized in the liver by an enzyme, P450-CYP1A2, which is also activated by smoking. Thus, individuals taking clozapine or olanzapine who also smoke will have lower blood levels of the drug—approximately 40 percent lower in one study—than individuals taking these drugs who do not smoke. Conversely, if an individual taking these antipsychotic medications suddenly gives up smoking, the blood level of his/her antipsychotic medication may rise sharply and may therefore produce more side effects.

The consequences of smoking are well known. Individuals with schizophrenia have elevated death rates from pneumonia and heart disease, but it is not known how much of this is due to smoking and how much is due to the relatively poor medical care most of them receive. Smoking, especially in individuals who are mentally confused, can be dangerous, and serious fires in group homes caused by careless smoking are not uncommon. One study found an increased incidence of akathisia among individuals with schizophrenia who were smokers. Two studies reported that smoking also increased the risk for developing tardive dyskinesia, but a third study did not find this association. Smoking cessation programs have been tried for outpatients with schizophrenia with modest success, e.g., 12 percent had quit smoking at the end of six months. Nicotine patches or gum and sustained-release bupropion (Zyban, Wellbutrin SR) are worth trying.

One would also predict that individuals with schizophrenia should have a very high incidence of lung cancer. One of the intriguing mysteries about schizophrenia, however, is that the lung cancer rate in this disease appears to be *lower* than in the general population, not higher. There has been speculation that antipsychotic medication might in some way be protective and account for this, but this explanation seems unlikely since at least two studies reported a lower lung cancer rate in schizophrenia before antipsychotic drugs were introduced.

THE EFFECTS OF SMOKING AND CAFFEINE ON ANTIPSYCHOTIC BLOOD LEVELS

- Smoking *decreases* the blood level, and thus the effectiveness, of most antipsychotics.
- Smoking especially *decreases* the blood level of clozapine and olanzapine by as much as 40 percent.
- Caffeine markedly *increases* the blood level of clozapine and olanzapine by 100 percent or more, thereby increasing side effects.

Caffeine intake among individuals with schizophrenia is also very heavy but has not been quantified as precisely as has smoking. Patients have been documented drinking 30 or more cups of coffee each day as well as drinking many colas, which also contain caffeine; each cup of coffee contains approximately 80 mg of caffeine, and each cola approximately 35 mg. There are also occasional individuals with schizophrenia who buy instant coffee and eat it directly from the jar with a spoon. Like nicotine, it is not understood why individuals with schizophrenia are so strongly addicted to caffeine, although caffeine is known to affect adenosine receptors in the brain and, through them, the metabolism of dopamine, serotonin, GABA, glutamate, and norepinephrine. One study also suggests that caffeine may decrease Parkinsonian symptoms such as rigidity and tremor.

It is known that high caffeine intake in anyone can produce the symptoms of caffeine intoxication, including nervousness, restlessness, insomnia, excitement, flushing of the face, rapid heart beat, and muscle twitching. Studies of individuals with schizophrenia who ingest large amounts of caffeine have demonstrated that some patients have a worsening of their symptoms. It was previously thought that coffee, and especially tea, may interfere with the absorption of antipsychotic drugs, but this is now uncertain. Three controlled studies have been done in which psychiatric inpatient units were switched from caffeinated to decaffeinated coffee and tea to see what effect it would have on patients' symptoms. The first study reported an improvement in symptoms, but the other two studies reported no effect whatsoever.

Clozapine and olanzapine have a special relationship with caffeine.

Both drugs, as well as caffeine, are metabolized by the same liver enzyme, P450-CYP1A2. Thus, caffeine blocks the metabolism of these antipsychotic medications, thereby causing their blood levels to rise. In one recent study, patients taking clozapine had their serum levels measured while using caffeine and again after they had abstained from caffeine for five days. The clozapine levels while using caffeine were approximately twice as high as while not using caffeine. Thus, alterations in caffeine intake could markedly affect both the effectiveness of these medications and their side effects.

One thing that is clear about both smoking and caffeine intake among individuals with schizophrenia is that more studies are needed to clarify the consequences of the behavior. Until they are done, I would suggest the following.

1. Recognize the strength of these addictions in many individuals with schizophrenia. Obviously some reasonable maximum limits must be set, such as one pack of cigarettes and four cups of coffee or colas per day, but setting limits is different from trying to prohibit the behavior altogether. In my experience some mentally ill individuals who are strongly addicted to nicotine and caffeine will fight, sell their clothes, and even prostitute themselves to satisfy their addictions. Only masochists and martyrs pick fights they know they cannot win.

2. Be aware that smoking and drinking coffee are among life's most pleasurable activities for some individuals with schizophrenia. The fact that this is so is sad, but that does not change the reality. We should be careful about taking away such pleasures unless we are certain that the gains from doing so are worth it. The ban on smoking in hospitals by the Joint Commission on Health Care Organizations did not take into account the fact that for some individuals with schizophrenia these hospitals are their homes. It also does not take into account studies suggesting that the abrupt cessation of smoking may exacerbate the symptoms of schizophrenia.

3. Demand that individuals with schizophrenia who smoke do so in a safe manner (e.g., not in bed) and only in specified places. Nonsmokers have the right to not be exposed to the known dangerous effects of secondhand smoke. Establish clear penalties for not adhering to such rules, and enforce them.

4. Since cigarettes and coffee are very important to many individuals with schizophrenia, they can be used to reinforce other important behaviors, such as taking prescribed medication, as discussed below. This was once called bribery but is now called positive reinforcement. It works.

ALCOHOL AND STREET DRUGS

Alcohol and street drug abuse among individuals with schizophrenia is a large and apparently growing problem. A community study done in the early 1980s reported that 34 percent of individuals with schizophrenia abused alcohol, 26 percent abused street drugs, and altogether 47 percent abused one or both of these. Studies of this problem done in recent years strongly suggest that the incidence of substance abuse by individuals with schizophrenia has increased significantly. The severity of the problem may vary considerably, from an occasional episode of abuse to almost continuous abuse.

There are many reasons why individuals with schizophrenia abuse alcohol and drugs. Probably the most important one is the same reason why individuals who do *not* have schizophrenia abuse alcohol and drugs—it makes them feel good. Substance abuse is endemic in the general population, and there is no reason why individuals with schizophrenia should be exempt. It is important to realize, therefore, that many individuals with schizophrenia who are abusing alcohol and street drugs would also be doing so if they had never become sick.

There are other reasons for alcohol and drug abuse that are specific to schizophrenia. Substance abuse provides a social network and something to do for individuals who are often socially isolated and bored. There is also evidence that some individuals with schizophrenia are self-medicating with the alcohol or street drugs, resulting in decreased anxiety, decreased depression, and increased energy. One recent study reported that alcohol decreased depression and improved sleep in individuals with schizophrenia, but it also increased auditory hallucinations and paranoid delusions. It is also possible that there is a genetic connection between having a predisposition to schizophrenia and a predisposition to alcoholism, but the data on this question are not definitive.

Many of the consequences of alcohol and street drug abuse for individuals with schizophrenia are identical to the general population and include impaired family and interpersonal relations, job loss, loss of housing, financial debt, medical problems, and arrests and jailings. In addition it has been shown that individuals with schizophrenia who are substance abusers have many more symptoms, more frequent violent episodes, a higher use of emergency psychiatric services, lower compliance with antipsychotic medication, and a much higher relapse rate compared to non–substance abusers (see chapter 12). A large number of them end up among the homeless population.

The treatment of individuals with schizophrenia who also are severe substance abusers is quite unsatisfactory. Many are ping-ponged back and forth between the mental illness treatment system and the substance abuse treatment system, rejected on both sides. They are the patients nobody wants. Clozapine may be worth trying in individuals who are alcohol dependent, since one recent preliminary study suggested that it may decrease the person's drinking.

A limited number of model treatment programs have been created, usually referred to as MICA (Mentally Ill Chemical Abuser) programs. Of special note are the Continuous Treatment Teams set up by New Hampshire to promote integrated services and continuity of care, which have reported stable remissions from alcoholism in over half of the treated patients with schizophrenia.

A variety of treatment approaches have been tried. The Twelve-Step self-help methods of Alcoholics Anonymous (AA) and Narcotics Anonymous (NA) are effective for a minority of individuals with schizophrenia, although some do better with a lower-key modified Six-Step program. A disadvantage of some such groups is that they encourage total abstinence from all drugs, sometimes interpreted as including antipsychotic medications as well. Individuals with schizophrenia also do not do well in the confrontational groups promoted by some AA and NA chapters.

In some cases it is necessary to utilize compulsory monitoring techniques to decrease alcohol and drug abuse in individuals with schizophrenia. This is especially true for those patients who become violent or otherwise get in trouble when abusing alcohol or street drugs. Urine testing can be used to ascertain street drug use, and skin patches are being developed that change color if alcohol is ingested. Hair analysis can also be useful because it detects the use of amphetamines, barbiturates, cocaine, and heroin (but not marijuana) for up to three months after use. Alcohol abuse can sometimes be controlled by the use of disulfiram (Antabuse), which, if taken each day, makes the person physically ill if they then drink alcohol during the ensuing 24 hours. Disulfiram can be used in individuals with schizophrenia, but it tends to decrease blood levels of antipsychotics, so the person may need to take a higher dose of the antipsychotic while on disulfiram.

Families of individuals with schizophrenia who are abusing alcohol or street drugs need to be aware of how common this problem is and learn to recognize it. A useful clue is the disappearance of large amounts of the person's money that cannot be accounted for. Making the substance abuser aware of the effects and consequences of their substance abuse, setting and adhering to clearly defined limits, and utilizing compulsory treatment modalities (often mandated by the courts for individuals who have pending legal charges) are all important parts of a comprehensive treatment plan.

Should an individual with schizophrenia be allowed to drink at all? Many clinicians say no. I would agree with this if the person has a history of violent behavior or if alcohol appears to exacerbate the symptoms of their illness. However, if these are not factors and the person has had no tendency to abuse alcohol, I know of no reason why someone with schizophrenia should not have an occasional social drink if that is something they enjoy doing and is part of their culture. Having a beer at the end of the day with friends or having a glass of wine with dinner is for many people a pleasurable part of life. People who have had the misfortune to have been afflicted with schizophrenia should not be further penalized or deprived of small pleasures that are available to other people unless there is a clear reason to do so. At the same time I personally tell patients and their families to set clear limits on any alcohol intake (e.g., two cans of beer or two glasses of wine or one ounce of alcohol per day) and to be constantly alert for any signs of alcohol abuse.

Street drug use by persons with schizophrenia can be summed up in one word. NO. For many patients, even marijuana may set off psychotic symptoms in an unpredictable way, and it may take days to recover from them fully. One young man I treated remained virtually symptom-free on medication except when he smoked marijuana; he then became floridly psychotic for several days. Not every person with schizophrenia reacts so dramatically, of course, but there is no way to predict who will do so. Stronger drugs, especially PCP and amphetamines ("speed"), are like poison for anyone with schizophrenia. Families should discourage their use in every way possible, and should not allow a family member with schizophrenia in the home if street drug use is suspected. This rule is absolutely mandatory if the person has a history of assaultive or violent behavior; many of the homicides committed by those afflicted with schizophrenia appear to occur following use of street drugs. Draconian measures to discourage street drug use are perfectly legitimate, including requiring the person with schizophrenia to periodically submit to urine testing or hair analysis for street drug use as a condition of living at home, receiving support from the family, or remaining out of the hospital.

SEX, PREGNANCY, AND AIDS

Sex is an important issue for most men and women, and there is no reason to think that it should be any different for individuals with schizophrenia. Mentally ill individuals are commonly consigned to an asexual status in our imaginations, but that is a mistake. Individuals with schizophrenia run a wide range, from having virtually no interest in sex to being preoccupied with it, the same range found in individuals who do not have schizophrenia.

Studies suggest that approximately two-thirds of individuals with schizophrenia are sexually active in any given year. One study of women outpatients reported that 73 percent of them were sexually active; another study of men and women outpatients reported that 62 percent were sexually active, including 42 percent of the men and 19 percent of the women who had had multiple sexual partners within the past year. A study of individuals in a psychiatric admissions unit similarly found that 66 percent had been sexually active within six months, whereas a survey of long-term patients in a state psychiatric hospital noted that "sexual activity was extensive and far-ranging at the hospital." The reverse side of the picture is the group who is not sexually active; a recent study in England reported that more than one-third of adults with schizophrenia "had never had a sexual relationship."

Sexual activity for individuals with schizophrenia, however, is more difficult than for individuals who do not have schizophrenia. Imagine how complex sex would seem if you had delusions that the person was trying to harm you or you were hearing constant auditory hallucinations. Dr. M. B. Rosenbaum, in a sensitive article on the sexual problems of persons with schizophrenia, described one patient who "vividly described all the angels and devils in his bedroom telling him what and what not to do" while having intercourse. Dr. Rosenbaum concluded: "It is hard for most of us to 'get it together' sexually—how much harder for the schizophrenic with his or her many very real limitations!"

Antipsychotic medications may also interfere with the sex lives of individuals with schizophrenia. One study reported antipsychotic medication side effects affecting sexual function in 30 to 60 percent of individuals taking the medications. These effects included decreased libido, male impotence, orgasmic dysfunction, and female menstrual irregularities. Such side effects are a major reason why some patients discontinue taking their medications, although they usually do not verbalize this. In evaluating sexual side effects of antipsychotic medications, however, it must be remembered that some of the individuals reporting side effects had sexual dysfunction before they became sick or started taking medication, since sexual dysfunction is not uncommon in the general population. One recent study, for example, reported sexual side effects in 45 percent of individuals with schizophrenia taking antipsychotic medication but also in 17 percent of normal controls; thus, the true rate of sexual side effects due to the medication was 28 percent. A few individuals have had their sexual lives improved by antipsychotic medications; for example, one report described two heterosexual men who "would routinely engage in continuous sexual activity for two to six hours while taking the medication at a properly adjusted dose."

Another problem is how to assess whether the patient is a consenting adult or is being taken advantage of in the sexual situation. This usually applies to women, although occasionally men will be taken advantage of by homosexuals. Questions the family should ask itself include: Is she able to say no to men in nonsexual situations? Is her judgment reasonably good in other areas of her day-to-day functioning? Is she discreet, which suggests good judgment, in her sexual encounters? Is she trying to avoid men or is she seeking them out? Is she agreeing to sex primarily to obtain specific payment, most often cigarettes or food?

Consultation with the patient's psychiatrist and/or nursing staff at the halfway house or the psychiatric ward where the patient is known will often clarify the consent issue for the family. The family of one woman, for example, became upset when they found that she was having intercourse regularly at the halfway house and she told her parents she was being taken advantage of. Discussion with halfway house staff established that the woman was seeking out the sexual encounters, and her claim of being taken advantage of was designed to assuage the disapproval of her parents. If a woman really is being taken advantage of, however, increased supervision and restrictions in her activity may be indicated. Women who consent to intercourse merely to acquire cigarettes or food need a plan formulated by the families and psychiatric staff to provide these items reliably, so the person with schizophrenia will be less tempted to prostitute herself.

Protection against pregnancy is another problematic area for individuals with schizophrenia, since many such individuals have difficulties in planning ahead. According to one authority, "the rate of children born to psychotic women is estimated to have tripled since deinstitutionalization first began in the United States." Unplanned pregnancies are relatively common among women with schizophrenia; in one study 31 percent of the women had had induced abortions. As noted in chapter 9, it is also known that women being switched from a first-generation antipsychotic to clozapine, olanzapine, quetiapine, or ziprasidone have an increased risk of becoming pregnant unless they use contraceptives. The first-generation antipsychotics suppress prolactin and thus make ovulation less likely, whereas these second-generation antipsychotics do not suppress prolactin.

WARNING: INCREASED RISK OF PREGNANCY

Women have an increased risk of becoming pregnant when being switched from first-generation (typical) antipsychotics, such as haloperidol (Haldol) or fluphenazine (Prolixin), to clozapine (Clozaril), olanzapine (Zyprexa), quetiapine (Seroquel), or ziprasidone (Geodon). The use of contraceptives in such cases is strongly advised.

Condoms are the first choice for contraception because they provide protection against AIDS and other sexually transmitted diseases as well as against pregnancy; however, many men will not use them. Two methods of long-term contraception have been approved by the Food and Drug Administration and are now available for use by women. One is injections of medroxyprogesterone acetate (Depo-Provera), which need be given only every three months. The other is progestin implants beneath the skin (Norplant), which last for five years. Both methods can produce some menstrual irregularities but are highly effective and satisfactory contraceptives for many women.

Ethical aspects of contraception in women with schizophrenia can also pose major problems. Some women may not wish to use contraception for religious reasons. Others may not wish to do so because they want to become pregnant. It is easy to empathize with a 36-year-old woman who has just been released from the hospital after 15 years and wants to have a baby before it is too late; it is also easy to empathize with the infant who is born into such a situation and who is totally dependent for care on its mother. The genetic facts on a baby born to two persons with schizophrenia are harsh—an estimated 36 percent of these children will eventually develop schizophrenia (see chapter 13). It is also true that most people with schizophrenia have enough difficulties looking after their own needs without the burden of a dependent infant. A study of 80 female "chronic psychiatric outpatients" reported that only one-third of the 75 children they had borne were being reared by the mothers. Indeed, the loss of child custody by mothers with schizophrenia is very common because many of them are unable to care for the child. To assist in thinking through ethical issues regarding contraception in women with schizophrenia, some guidelines have been proposed by McCullough et al. at the Center for Ethics, Medicine and Public Issues at Baylor College of Medicine (see "Recommended Further Reading").

Once a baby has been conceived, the couple and their families are often caught between a rock and a hard place. Abortion and adoption should both be considered; responsible decisions frequently involve consultation with the psychiatrist, family physician, lawyer, religious adviser, and social worker. Often from such consultations a consensus will emerge on the best course of action, and this sharing of decision-making will alleviate the burden on both the patient and the patient's family. In the past, putting such children up for adoption was commonly done, and many families adopted children without being told that one or both parents had schizophrenia.

It is known that women with schizophrenia are less likely to seek prenatal care or to follow instructions for it. Some studies have claimed that women with schizophrenia have an excess number of complications of pregnancy and birth, while others have concluded that this is not so. A recent study from Denmark reported that women with schizophrenia had a higher than expected rate of preterm deliveries and low birth-weight babies. Especially disturbing was a preliminary report from Australia indicating that women with schizophrenia give birth to an increased number of children with mental retardation and an increased number who die before age one.

The major dilemma of pregnancy in women with schizophrenia is whether to take antipsychotic medications during the pregnancy. The safest advice regarding medications to give any pregnant woman is to not take anything, but that may be impossible for women with schizophrenia. Antipsychotic drugs have been used by thousands of women while pregnant and appear to be safe compared to many other drugs used in medicine. Recent studies, however, have shown that these drugs occasionally cause malformations or congenital anomalies to the growing fetus, so they should not be considered completely safe and should be taken only when absolutely necessary. The most critical time for such damage appears to be the first three months of pregnancy.

MEDICATIONS AND PREGNANCY

Given what is currently known, a reasonable plan for pregnant women with schizophrenia is the following:

1. Stop antipsychotic medication for the first three months of pregnancy if she can do so without a serious relapse.
2. Remain off medication for as much of the pregnancy as possible beyond three months unless symptoms start to recur.
3. If it is necessary to restart the medication, use whichever antipsychotic medication she has responded to in the past. There is insufficient data yet to say that one type of antipsychotic medication is more dangerous than another during pregnancy.
4. There are data, however, to suggest that carbamazepine (Tegretol) and valproic acid (Depakene), which are sometimes used as ancillary medications in schizophrenia, should be avoided during pregnancy.
5. Do not be heroic by avoiding medications at all costs. If the woman needs medication, use it. Having a pregnant woman who is acutely psychotic has risks of its own to both the woman and the fetus.
6. Discuss the issue of medication in detail before the pregnancy or as early in the pregnancy as possible. Be certain that the woman's family and all concerned understand the options. If the decision is made to stop medication, draw up a contract that specifies that the woman will resume medication if the doctor deems it advisable. The contract must be binding on the woman, even if she changes her mind because of her psychosis, so that she can be medicated involuntarily if necessary.

Regarding the taking of antipsychotic drugs while breast-feeding, this should not be done. Antipsychotic drugs are transmitted in the breast milk in small amounts, but because the baby's liver and kidneys are not mature the drugs may accumulate in the baby's body. Since a woman who needs medication has the option of bottle-feeding, it seems an unnecessary risk to take.

AIDS is an important threat to the health of individuals with schizophrenia. Surveys of the HIV positivity rate among admissions to state psychiatric hospitals have ranged from 1.6 percent in Texas to 5.5 percent in New York, but these surveys include patients with all diagnoses. The only survey done to date of HIV positivity of psychiatric admissions specifically with schizophrenia reported that 3.4 percent were positive in a university hospital in New York City. As expected in all such studies, it has been emphasized that concurrent substance abuse markedly increased the chance of becoming HIV positive.

Studies on individuals with schizophrenia regarding their knowledge about AIDS and its risk factors have reported a remarkably poor understanding. In one study of women with schizophrenia, 36 percent said that you can get AIDS by shaking hands, 58 percent said you can get it from a toilet seat, and 53 percent did not know that condoms help prevent AIDS. A 1993 study of condom use in the previous six months among individuals with schizophrenia found that condoms had been consistently used by only two of eight individuals who had had a single sexual partner and one of 15 individuals who had had multiple sexual partners. In another study, one-third of seriously mentally ill individuals had been treated for a sexually transmitted disease, a major risk factor for HIV transmission. Clearly, we are just seeing the beginning of a major AIDS problem among individuals with schizophrenia and other major psychiatric illnesses.

What can patients and families do about the problems connected with AIDS? Open discussion, education, and the use of condoms are obvious needs and should be given high priority. AIDS education programs for patients with serious mental illnesses have been developed by Dr. Robert M. Goisman and his colleagues at the Massachusetts Mental Health Center and by Dr. Jeffrey A. Kelly and his colleagues at the Medical College of Wisconsin (see "Recommended Further Reading"). The AIDS epidemic is upon us and will not exempt individuals with schizophrenia.

VICTIMIZATION

Individuals with schizophrenia are commonly victimized, although such events are only rarely reported. Many individuals with schizophrenia have impaired thought processes and mental confusion, making it difficult for them to keep track of money or personal belongings. It also results in their putting themselves into dangerous situations because they cannot assess the situation correctly. Criminals thus view individuals with schizophrenia as "easy marks"; this situation is exacerbated by the common practice of locating group homes in rundown neighborhoods in which criminals congregate. It is rather like placing unlocked rabbit hutches in the middle of a forest filled with foxes.

Theft and assault are the most common crimes perpetrated against individuals with schizophrenia. In a study of 278 residents living in a Los Angeles board-and-care home, of whom two-thirds had schizophrenia, one-third reported having been robbed or assaulted within the previous year. A study of 185 individuals with schizophrenia admitted to a psychiatric hospital in North Carolina found that 20 percent of them had been the victim of a nonviolent crime, and an additional 7 percent had been a victim of a violent crime, in the preceding four months. The danger is especially great for individuals with schizophrenia living in public shelters. In a New York shelter, for example: "The mentally ill are often preyed upon by criminals who come to the shelter straight from prison. Those who receive social security disability checks become targets for muggers."

For women with schizophrenia, rape is a constant danger. A study of 20 women with schizophrenia in New York reported that 10 of them had been raped, and half of those had been raped more than once. In Washington, D.C., among 44 women who had a serious psychiatric disorder and who were intermittently homeless, 30 percent had been physically assaulted and 34 percent had been sexually assaulted. In France, 14 out of 64 women with schizophrenia had been raped, and 9 of these had been raped multiple times. The director of a public women's shelter in San Francisco described the brutality of the streets: "I know one woman who has been raped 17 times. . . . She doesn't report it because it's just what happens out there."

Fewer than half of all individuals with schizophrenia bother to report to the police crimes such as assault, robbery, and rape. A study of the reporting of such crimes by individuals with severe psychiatric disorders found that approximately half the time the police responded with disbelief, rudeness, anger, or offered no help. It is also difficult for many individuals with schizophrenia who have a thinking disorder to construct a coherent narrative regarding the crime. The police, therefore, view them as a poor potential witness if the perpetrator of the crime should be brought to trial.

Several steps can be taken to improve the safety of individuals with schizophrenia. Most important is not placing group homes or other living facilities in high-crime neighborhoods. For individuals with schizophrenia who are living on their own, partially subsidized housing is needed because in many cities the only housing units that are affordable on SSI or SSDI are in high-crime areas. This is also a major reason why many people with schizophrenia have a better quality of life living in a small town rather than in a large city.

Another step that will improve the safety of individuals with schizophrenia is organized training sessions on self-defense, how to avoid being victimized, and how to report a crime to the police. Bringing members of the local police force to the group home, day program, clubhouse, or other gathering place would make such training sessions more effective as well as making both the police and the patients more comfortable with each other.

CONFIDENTIALITY

Issues of confidentiality are one of the most common and most irritatingly irrational problems faced by relatives of individuals with schizophrenia. Confidentiality between physicians and patients is governed by state laws, which differ somewhat from state to state. They are designed to protect the physician–patient relationship and have been extended to other mental illness professionals. However, these laws are not absolute and can be changed. They can also be justifiably breached when the interests of the patients or the public clearly take precedence. For example, when a person with schizophrenia (or any other mental disorder) confides to a mental illness professional a wish or plan to harm another person, at one time such communications were considered to be confidential and legally exempted from disclosure under physician–patient confidentiality. In 1976, however, courts in California ruled that mental illness professionals have a duty to warn the potential victim in such situations. This ruling, generally referred to as the Tarasoff decision, has been extended to many other states.

Abuse of confidentiality statutes is currently causing many problems not only for families but also for the public mental illness system generally. Relatives cannot get the information they need to provide appropriate care for their family member. Mental illness professionals in one sector of the mental illness care system (e.g., the psychiatric unit of the county jail) often cannot access the person's psychiatric records from another sector of the system (e.g., the community mental health center).

There are of course legitimate instances when confidentiality must be maintained. Such cases usually involve an individual with schizophrenia who has good awareness of his/her illness and who has expressly instructed the mental health professional to not share information with his/her relatives. The reasons may vary, and include anger at the relatives, a belief that they are overcontrolling, a wish to prevent disclosure of a recent abortion, etc.

Far more often, however, confidentiality is invoked in instances when the patient has little or no awareness of his/her illness and is clearly not competent to make an informed judgment regarding whether disclosure of information would be helpful to him/her. There is a Catch-22 quality to such situations, with the patient essentially saying: "I'm not sick, so you can't tell my relatives about my sickness because it doesn't exist."

In such situations the mental health professional will often return the relative's call with words such as: "I'm sorry, but I cannot answer your question because of confidentiality issues." If you then point out the logical absurdity of the situation, the mental health professional will become defensive. One of the most difficult aspects of solving the confidentiality problem is translating this phrase: "I'm sorry, but I cannot answer that because of confidentiality issues." Although the same words are used, the phrase may be translated into one of several different meanings, depending on the speaker. If you can make the proper translation, you will be on your way to solving the problem. The most common translations are the following (I have used male gender for convenience; such individuals are found equally among females):

Dr. Freud: "I personally think that you are part of the cause of your relative's schizophrenia, and the less you have to do with him/her, the better. So don't bother me again."

Mr. Milquetoast: "I would need permission from my supervisor to tell you anything, and besides, as an employee of this organization, I've learned that the less I say to anybody, the better."

Mr. Incharge: "I have information that you want and need, but I'm not going to share it, at least for now, until you have groveled a little and acknowledged my superiority."

Mr. Lawyer: "The less I tell you the better, because then you are less likely to sue me/my hospital, and besides, if I tell you too much, you will realize how badly we have botched the treatment of your relative."

The heights of absurdity to which the confidentiality problem may ascend was well illustrated by the mother of a young man with schizophrenia. She described how she attempted to get information about his condition during the six months he was committed to a psychiatric hospital in Boston:

> I was never told how he was doing. I was in complete darkness about his prognosis, whether positive or negative. Each time I questioned the social worker assigned to his case, which was almost daily, the answer would be, "Danny would not give us permission today to tell you how he was doing."
>
> This was the reply I received for the first month or so. Then one day, moved by pity because of the state of anxiety I was in, she replied to my inquiry, "Danny would not give us permission today to tell you how he was doing but the patients on the ward are doing well today."
>
> I grasped at her coded message with much relief. But after hearing that same coded message and only that for the remainder of his commitment, it became quite evident to me that the system was as ill as my son and needed much help.

The key to resolving the confidentiality problem is to recognize that, for many individuals with schizophrenia, the relatives are not *merely* relatives but are also essential members of the treatment team. Individuals with schizophrenia are no longer hospitalized for long periods of time; rather, they are treated in the community, often in the family's home. Relatives have become increasingly sophisticated about schizophrenia and its treatment and not infrequently now know at least as much as the mental illness professional. When the relatives are accepted as legitimate care providers, the issue of confidentiality becomes easier to resolve.

Pioneering work on the development of release-of-information forms, a protocol to guide confidentiality problems, and confidentiality staff training programs have been developed by the Department of Mental Health in Riverside County, California, and adopted in other counties. The protocol emphasizes the benefits of family involvement and the fact that mental illness professionals can (and should) accept information *from* the families at any time. If the individual with schizophrenia refuses to consent to any release of information, mental illness professionals can still provide much information to the family by speaking of hypothetical cases rather than the specific individual.

Families should also familiarize themselves with the confidentiality statutes governing the release of information in their states. If faced with uncooperative professionals such as Dr. Freud, Mr. Milquetoast, Mr. Incharge, or Mr. Lawyer, appeal first to the person's supervisor and, if necessary, to the supervisor's supervisor. Put your request in writing and send it by registered mail. Indicate your familiarity with your state's statute, and state that it does not apply in this case.

If that fails, have a lawyer friend send a letter on law firm stationery reiterating your request for information needed to provide adequate care for your relative. State clearly that you will hold the mental illness professionals and/or psychiatric care center legally responsible for any consequences of failed psychiatric care attributable to their failure to provide you with the necessary information. Most important, do not accept any less information than you would expect to be forthcoming from professionals if your family member had another brain disease, such as multiple sclerosis or Alzheimer's disease.

MEDICATION NONCOMPLIANCE

Medication noncompliance by individuals with schizophrenia is a major source of frustration for families and the single biggest cause of relapse and rehospitalization. It is extremely common, with studies showing that approximately 70 percent of patients are noncompliant with medication by the end of the second year following hospitalization. It is also extremely costly; one research group estimated that medication noncompliance for schizophrenia costs approximately $136 million per year. Medication noncompliance is also found in other medical conditions, such as hypertension, heart disease, rheumatoid arthritis, and tuberculosis, but it appears to be of greater magnitude in schizophrenia.

REASONS FOR MEDICATION NONCOMPLIANCE

1. Anosognosia: person unaware of illness (biological)
2. Denial: person aware of illness but wishes not to be ill (psychological)
3. Medication side effects
4. Poor doctor-patient relationship
5. Delusional beliefs regarding medication (e.g., that it is poison)
6. Cognitive deficits, confusion, disorganization
7. Fears of becoming medication dependent or addicted, or threats to masculinity

There are seven principal reasons for medication noncompliance in schizophrenia. The most important reason is anosognosia, the lack of awareness that one is sick. As described in chapter 2, such lack of insight is biological in origin, caused by damage to the frontal lobe, cingulate, and areas in the right cerebral hemisphere. One of the consequences of lack of awareness of illness is completely predictable—if a person does not believe he/she is sick, why take medication? In one study of schizophrenia, for example, the number of patients who were compliant with medication was twice as high among those with awareness of their illness as compared to those without such awareness. It is therefore not surprising that several studies have also reported an inverse correlation between awareness of illness and rehospitalization rates. Lack of awareness produces medication noncompliance, which leads to relapse and rehospitalization.

Anosognosia, or lack of awareness of illness, should be distinguished from denial. In denial, the person is aware that he/she is sick but wishes not to be. Taking medication is a daily reminder of one's illness; not taking medication is therefore an attempt to deny that the illness exists. Denial is often temporarily effective until the symptoms of the illness recur. Whereas anosognosia is biological in origin, denial is psychological in origin. A seriously mentally ill woman illustrated such thinking:

> I did not want to believe I was sick, falling to the false logic of medication. Instead of thinking, "I am sick; therefore I need medication," I thought, "I am taking medication; therefore I am sick, and if I stop taking medicine, I will be well."

A third major reason for medication noncompliance among individuals with schizophrenia is the side effects of the medication. As expressed by Esso Leete, who has schizophrenia: "Unfortunately the side effects of antipsychotic medications can often be more disabling than the illnesses themselves, and I have even experienced side effects from the pills I took to control the side effects of the antipsychotic medications."

Studies have shown that many psychiatrists are not clinically astute in their ability to diagnose side effects. In one study of psychiatrists, for example, "the major finding was a high rate of clinical underrecognition of all major extrapyramidal syndromes." Another study reported that "psychiatrists misjudged the bothersomeness to patients of 24 percent of side effects and 20 percent of symptoms." Among the most troubling side effects of antipsychotic medication are akathisia (feelings of restlessness), akinesia (decreased spontaneity), and sexual dysfunction. An early study of drug refusal by patients with schizophrenia found that "the reluctance to take antipsychotic medication was significantly associated with extrapyramidal symptoms—most notably a subtle akathisia." The author noted that the akathisia could change over time "so that a patient could be optimally medicated on one visit, and experience an akathisia or other EPI [extrapyramidal involvement] on the same dosage of phenothiazines two weeks later." Giving the patient an extra supply of antiparkinson drugs to take on an as-needed basis is a suggested solution. Akinesia is also especially difficult for clinicians to appreciate because it is primarily a subjective experience and may be confused with depression.

Another major cause of medication noncompliance in individuals with schizophrenia is a poor doctor-patient relationship. Arriving at the best antipsychotic medication and the right dose of that medication for any given individual should be a shared undertaking between the doctor and patient. Dr. Ronald Diamond, in a lucid paper on the subject, says that "it is still important to listen to what patients say and to take seriously their experience with their medication." Betty Blaska, writing from a consumer's point of view, makes the same point: "Many of the mistakes [of the psychiatrists] previously described come down to one thing: a refusal to see the consumer as an expert on his or her illness. The person with schizophrenia is *the* authority on *his* schizophrenia."

Instead, the norm for doctor-patient relationships in American psychiatry is complaints such as "I have this side effect but my doctor won't listen or take it seriously." One reason for this problem with doctor-patient relationships is that many of the psychiatrists in American public sector jobs were trained in other countries where the doctor is considered to be *the* authority and patients are not supposed to question his/her advice or judgment. Another reason is that the norm in many community mental health programs is for the psychiatrist to see the patient for 15 minutes every two or three months to check the medications; such a time frame precludes discussion of any except the most severe side effects (see chapter 9, "The Medication-Savvy Consumer and Family").

Still other patients refuse to take medication because of their delusions, which may be either grandiose (e.g., a belief that you are all-powerful and therefore do not need the medication) or paranoid (e.g., a belief that people are using the medication to poison you). Other patients do not take their medication because of confusion, disorganization, or other cognitive deficits. A few individuals do not comply with medication because of fears that they will become dependent on or addicted to it; such fears are found more frequently in men for whom taking medication may also impugn their masculinity.

What are the answers to medication noncompliance? It is important for families and mental illness professionals to recognize how common noncompliance is, including the high frequency of surreptitious noncompliance when others think the patient is taking his/her medicine. It is also important to ascertain the reasons for the noncompliance, because solutions to the problems of lack of awareness of illness, denial, medication side effects, a poor doctor-patient relationship, and other reasons such as delusional thinking are quite different.

Better education of the patient should be helpful in most cases. One recent study of psychiatric patients' knowledge of their medication at the time of hospital discharge found that 37 percent of the patients did not know why they were supposed to take their medication and 47 percent did not know when to take it. Part of this is undoubtedly owing to the cognitive impairment of the person secondary to the illness. Using pill containers that have separate compartments for each day and using once-daily dosing also simplifies medication taking. A variety of automated systems (e.g., the Medi-Monitor System) are also being developed that remind you which pill to take when; when attached to a computer or a telephone line, they also beep or send a message to your computer to allow feedback to the treating physician or clinic. Using injectable depot medications such as fluphenazine (Prolixin) or haloperidol (Haldol), which only have to be given every one to four weeks, can also be very helpful for individuals who respond to these medications.

The doctor-patient relationship can be improved if the psychiatrist is willing to accept the patient as a partner, not as an underling to carry out orders. Changes in medication or dose and attention to side effects are essential. Having the patient keep a daily diary of side effects and giving the patients some autonomy to increase or decrease medication dosage as needed can both be helpful. Medication should be approached as a joint venture with risks and benefits weighed against each other. The risks of medication noncompliance include rehospitalization, violence, jail, homelessness, and suicide, whereas the benefits include no medication side effects. The risks of medication compliance include side effects, whereas the benefits include living a more normal life and achieving a modified form of some of the person's original life goals.

For individuals who lack awareness of their illness, none of the above may be effective in persuading them to take medication. Positive reinforcement is always worth trying, and coffee and cigarettes are sometimes sufficient. A higher stakes positive reinforcement is to have

---

POSSIBLE SOLUTIONS TO IMPROVE MEDICATION COMPLIANCE

1. Educate the patient regarding the benefits of medication and the risks of noncompliance.
2. Improve the doctor-patient relationship or find a better doctor.
3. Change medications, reduce dose, and/or treat side effects.
4. Simplify the medication regimen, e.g., single daily dosing, use of compartmentalized pill containers, or automated pill-notification systems.
5. Use injectable, long-acting medications.
6. Use positive reinforcement, e.g., cigarettes, coffee, money, travel.
7. Make the treatment provider the payee for the person's SSI or other benefits check, then tie medication compliance to receiving the money.
8. Use assisted treatment, e.g., assertive case management, conditional release, outpatient commitment, conservatorship.

the clinic or case manager become the representative payee for the person's Supplemental Security Income (SSI) or other benefits, which will be discussed in the next section as one form of assisted treatment.

ASSISTED TREATMENT

Assisted treatment is necessary for many individuals with schizophrenia who lack awareness of their illness and, when unmedicated, are unable to provide for their needs or become a danger to themselves or others. Assisted treatment is used for conditions such as tuberculosis when patients refuse to take medication and, because of their untreated illness, are a danger to themselves or others. For schizophrenia, however, assisted treatment has become a lightning rod and has ignited opposition from civil libertarians, anti-psychiatry groups such as the Scientologists, and others who are dissatisfied with the psychiatric care system for other reasons (see chapter 15).

Assisted treatment has become increasingly necessary in the era of deinstitutionalization. In the past, when most individuals with schizophrenia were hospitalized, compliance with medication was not an issue. Now, however, most individuals with schizophrenia who previously would have been hospitalized are living in the community, and approximately half of them lack awareness of their illness. For many of these, assisted treatment, or the *threat* of assisted treatment, is necessary. This difference is, in fact, important because experience with assisted treatment programs has clearly demonstrated that the majority of individuals with schizophrenia will comply with medication based on the *threat* of assisted treatment alone and that assisted treatment programs such as outpatient commitment have to be actually implemented in only a very small number of cases. Possible options for assisted treatment are the following:

1. *Advance directives:* Increasingly used in all areas of medicine, individuals formulate directives at a time they are well regarding what they want to happen when they become sick. In a few states, individuals with severe psychiatric disorders, during a period of remission, can sign an advance directive instructing that they be treated (in which case it would be a form of assisted treatment) or that they may not be treated if they become sick again. Advance directives are

also known as "Ulysses contracts" after the Greek hero who, while sailing past the island of the deadly seductive Sirens, instructed his crew to bind him to the mast and "be strictly enjoined, whatever he might say or do, by no means to release him till they should have passed the Sirens' island."

The efficacy of advance directives as assisted treatment has not been studied. One possible problem is that advance directives could be signed by individuals who had no awareness of their illness at the time they signed. In states where advance directives must be certified by a psychiatrist, the certification could be done by psychiatrists who are unalterably opposed to assisted treatment under any circumstances. In such cases, advance directives would become an impediment to necessary treatment rather than being a form of assisted treatment. This has actually occurred in some cases in Ontario in Canada.

2. *Assertive case management:* Under assertive case management, case managers actively seek out at their homes or elsewhere in the community patients who do not follow up with appointments. The Program of Assertive Community Treatment (PACT or ACT teams) is the best-known example of this. Multiple studies have demonstrated that PACT teams decrease rehospitalization days. In a Baltimore study of homeless individuals with severe psychiatric disorders, 77 were assigned to a PACT team and compared with 75 others assigned to traditional outpatient treatment. During the following year, those treated by the PACT team had fewer hospital days (35 versus 67), fewer days living on the streets (10 versus 24), and fewer days in jail (9 versus 19). Those treated by the PACT team also had increased medication compliance (either intermittently or fully compliant) from 29 percent at the start to 55 percent after one year; however, "approximately one-third of the subjects were noncompliant at any given time point." Assertive case management would therefore appear to be an effective method of assisted treatment for some patients but not others.

3. *Representative payee:* To assist with money management, a patient's SSI, SSDI, or VA disability check can be assigned to the patient's family, case manager, or psychiatric clinic as the representative payee. Studies have shown that using a representative payee

reduces hospitalization days, substance abuse, and days spent homeless. No study has been done on the effect of using representative payees to improve medication compliance. Anecdotal information, however, suggests that this arrangement is not unusual, e.g., the patient must accept a depot antipsychotic injection as a condition for being given his/her monthly check. In a U.S. Third Circuit Court of Appeals ruling, the court ruled that a man with epilepsy and borderline mental retardation was not entitled to SSDI benefits unless he demonstrated compliance with his anti-epileptic medication.

4. *Conditional release:* Patients who have been legally committed to a hospital can be released on the condition that they are compliant with medication. Violation of the condition can result in rehospitalization. In most states the hospital director has the authority to do this without asking permission of the courts. Forty states have laws permitting conditional release. In the past, this form of assisted treatment was widely used for both civil and forensic (criminal) cases, but now it is used mostly for the latter.

New Hampshire is the leading state using conditional release for civilly committed patients; in 1998, 27 percent of patients released from the New Hampshire State Hospital were put on conditional release. In the only study of the effectiveness of conditional release on medication compliance reported to date, 26 severely psychiatrically ill patients were conditionally released from the New Hampshire State Hospital with assessment of various measures for the year prior to hospitalization and the two years following conditional release. The results were as follows.

EFFECTIVENESS OF CONDITIONAL RELEASE

	Year Prior to Hospitalization	First Year on Conditional Release	Second Year on Conditonal Release
Months of medication compliance	2.9	10.4	10.7
Episodes of violence (rated on a 7-pt. scale)	5.6	2.4	1.1

The patients on conditional release thus had markedly improved medication compliance (p < .001) and decreased episodes of violence (p < .001).

Among forensic (criminally committed) psychiatric patients, conditional release is much more widely used. The best-known example is Oregon's Psychiatric Security Review Board, which has been studied and reported to be highly effective in reducing future criminal behavior. Additional studies on the effectiveness of conditional release for insanity defense acquittees have been carried out in Maryland, Illinois, California, New York, and Washington, D.C.

5. *Outpatient commitment:* Outpatient commitment involves a court order for the patient to comply with treatment (usually including medication) as a condition for remaining in the community. Violation of the condition can result in rehospitalization. Some form of outpatient commitment is available in 41 states but is used in very few of them.

The effectiveness of outpatient commitment in decreasing hospital admissions has been clearly established. In Washington, D.C., admissions decreased from 1.81 per year to 0.95 per year before and after outpatient commitment. Similarly, in Ohio the decrease was from 1.5 to 0.4, and in Iowa from 1.3 to 0.3. In one study in North Carolina, admissions for patients on outpatient commitment decreased from 3.7 to 0.7 per 1,000 days. In another study in North Carolina, "subjects who underwent sustained periods of outpatient commitment beyond that of the initial court order had approximately 57 percent fewer readmissions and 20 fewer hospital days than control subjects." The only study that failed to find outpatient commitment effective in significantly reducing admissions was a Tennessee study; however, in that study it was evident that "outpatient clinics are not vigorously enforcing the law" and thus nonadherence had no consequences.

Outpatient commitment has also been shown to be effective as a form of assisted treatment in increasing treatment compliance. In North Carolina, only 30 percent of patients on outpatient commitment refused medication during a six-month period, compared to 66 percent of patients not on outpatient commitment. In Ohio, outpatient commitment increased patients' compliance with outpatient psychiatric appointments from 5.7 to 13.0 per year and with attendance at day treatment sessions from 23 to 60 per year. In Arizona, among patients who had been outpatient committed, "71 percent of the patients voluntarily maintained treatment contacts six months after their orders expired" compared to "almost no patients" who had not been put on outpatient commitment. And in Iowa "it appears as though outpatient commitment promotes treatment compliance in about 80 percent of patients while they are on outpatient commitment. After commitment is terminated about three-quarters of that group remain in treatment on a voluntary basis."

Most important, outpatient commitment has been shown to decrease violent behavior by individuals with schizophrenia and other severe mental illnesses. In a recent randomized trial of 262 individuals who were on court-ordered outpatient commitment for longer than six months, the authors reported that "the results were striking." Specifically, "the predicted probability of any violent behavior was cut in half from 48 percent to 24 percent, attributable to extended OPC [outpatient commitment] and regular outpatient services provision."

6. *Conservatorship:* Conservatorships and guardianships occur when a court appoints an individual to make treatment decisions for another individual who is believed to be mentally incompetent. They are used most frequently for individuals with mental retardation and with severe neurological diseases such as Alzheimer's disease; they

are used much less often for individuals with severe psychiatric illnesses. In one study done in California, "of the 35 patients who were placed on conservatorship, 29 (83 percent) remained stable as long as the conservatorship lasted," but for the 21 patients whose conservatorship was terminated, only 9 (43 percent) remained stable after termination."

7. *Substituted judgment:* This is closely related to outpatient commitment and conservatorship. In Massachusetts, which does not have an outpatient commitment statute, patients with severe psychiatric illnesses have the right to refuse medication. A mental health professional can take such an individual to court; if the court finds that the patient is incompetent, it may use a substituted judgment standard, appoint a guardian, and order the patient to take medication. In a six-month study of patients subjected to such a procedure, their admissions decreased from 1.6 to 0.6, and hospital days decreased from 113 to 44. Reflecting on substituted judgment, Dr. Jeffrey Geller noted: "In one of the more ironic outcomes of mental health law over the last two decades, the right to refuse treatment court decisions have become the basis in Massachusetts for involuntary community treatment orders."

8. *"Benevolent coercion":* This is Dr. Geller's term for threatening to institute legal proceedings to compel treatment for patients who do not comply with treatment. Geller reported that he informed his patients that "if the lithium level fell below 0.5 meq/liter, the patient would be involuntarily admitted to a state hospital." According to Geller, such "benevolent coercion" is an effective method of assisted treatment. Anecdotal evidence suggests that it is used widely but rarely discussed publicly.

9. *Threat of incarceration:* In one mental health center in upstate New York, prior to the passage of Kendra's Law permitting outpatient commitment, the staff had an informal working arrangement with the local judge. Patients with severe psychiatric disorders who were noncompliant with medication and who were considered to be potentially dangerous to themselves or others were picked up by the police on misdemeanor charges. On arraignment, the judge referred them to the mental health center and suspended sentence pending their compliance with treatment. If they did not comply, they could

be put in jail. There is no published account of such an arrangement, but anecdotal data suggest that it is not rare, especially in rural areas where a single judge may cover the entire population.

Assisted treatment for individuals with schizophrenia can therefore be achieved using several different options. In published accounts of these procedures, it is usually implied that only one such method is being used, but in fact more than one are often being used at the same time. For example, the PACT program of assertive case management is sometimes combined with the use of guardianship in Wisconsin. And many of the patients in the Baltimore PACT study of homeless individuals were given representative payees as well as assertive case managers.

Although all forms of assisted treatment appear to be effective for some patients with schizophrenia, efficacy for treatment compliance has only been clearly established for outpatient commitment. The paucity of research on the various forms of assisted treatment is surprising, given its importance.

A common problem for those supervising individuals with schizophrenia on assisted treatment is how to know whether the person is taking the medication. Using long-acting, injectable medications such as fluphenazine (Prolixin) or haloperidol (Haldol) is effective for individuals who respond to those medications. Research is also in progress to develop a slow-release antipsychotic capsule that could be implanted beneath the skin that would gradually release the medication over several months; it could be removed at any time by a physician. Many antipsychotics also come in liquid form that can be mixed with juice and the person can be observed swallowing it. Patients taking lithium pills can be monitored by taking blood samples and checking their lithium level. For individuals taking other kinds of pills or capsules, it is possible to mix substances such as riboflavin or isoniazid with the medication and then take urine samples to see whether the person is taking the medication. These measures have been used to assess medication compliance in other diseases, such as tuberculosis, but to date they have not been used to routinely monitor medication compliance in individuals with schizophrenia.

What is the effect on individuals with schizophrenia who lack awareness of their illness of being forced to take medication? Opponents of assisted treatment have alleged that the effects are devastating and drive those so treated permanently away. In fact, studies done on assisted treatment have found it to be remarkably benign in most cases. In one study, 27 outpatients who "had felt pressured or forced to take medications within the past year" were asked to express their feelings about the forced treatment. Among the 27, 9 were positive, 9 expressed mixed views, 6 said they had no feelings about it, and only 3 reported a negative effect. In another study, 30 patients who had been forcibly medicated during their psychiatric hospitalization were asked about it after being discharged. Retrospectively, 18 of them said that being forced to take medication was a good idea, 9 disagreed, and 3 were unsure.

For many mental illness professionals and other people, however, coercive treatment for individuals with schizophrenia is anathema. It contravenes our beliefs about civil liberties, the rights of individuals to privacy, and the freedom of speech and thought. The American Civil Liberties Union and the Bazelon Center for Mental Health Law in Washington, D.C., have staunchly opposed laws allowing forced treatment and have obtained court rulings in some states that have made such treatment virtually impossible.

What these well-meaning but misguided advocates have failed to understand is that approximately half of all individuals with schizophrenia have little awareness of their illness. When such individuals refuse medication they are doing so as part of illogical or irrational thought processes. The right to be free of the symptoms of a brain disease must be weighed against the individual's right to privacy. Safeguards to prevent abuse of forced treatment must, of course, be built into the system, and this can be done using public defenders and individuals who have been mentally ill themselves to monitor the system. As articulated by one observer, psychiatric patients "will suffer if a liberty they cannot enjoy is made superior to a health that must sometimes be forced on them." The rights of the individual must also be weighed against the needs of the person's family and society as a whole, especially in those individuals who become assaultive or violent when not taking medications.

In an effort to focus attention on the consequences of failing to treat large numbers of individuals with schizophrenia and other severe mental disorders, the Treatment Advocacy Center in Arlington, Virginia, was founded in 1998. Funded by private donations, the Center promotes the use of assisted treatment when needed and is working with many states to revise their outdated statutes. The Treatment Advocacy Center is the only national organization that has addressed the issue of assisted treatment. It can be accessed on the Internet at www.psychlaws.org and is also listed in appendix D.

ASSAULTIVE AND VIOLENT BEHAVIOR

Assaultive and violent behavior by some individuals with schizophrenia has become an increasing problem in recent years. Studies have made clear that *most* individuals with schizophrenia are not assaultive or violent but that a small number of them are. The common denominators of those who are assaultive and violent are abuse of alcohol or drugs and/or noncompliance with antipsychotic medication.

Two studies of families who belong to NAMI have demonstrated a high incidence of assaultive and violent behavior. In a 1986 survey, 38 percent of the families "reported that their ill relative was assaultive and destructive in the home either sometimes or frequently." A 1990 NAMI survey of 1,401 families reported that within the preceding year 10.6 percent of the seriously mentally ill individuals had physically harmed another person and an additional 12.2 percent had threatened harm.

These findings are consistent with other studies of assaultive and violent behavior among individuals with serious mental illnesses. Rabkin reviewed studies done in the 1960s and 1970s and reported that for patients discharged from public mental hospitals "arrest and conviction rates for the subcategory of violent crimes were found to exceed general population rates in every study in which they were measured." In another study, it was found that 15 of 20 individuals who were arrested for attempting to push people in front of subway trains in New York City had a diagnosis of schizophrenia. Steadman et al. also followed up patients discharged from mental hospitals and reported "that 27 percent of released male and female patients report at least one violent act within a mean of four months after discharge."

Other surveys of mentally ill individuals living in the community have reported similar findings. A methodologically excellent study by Link et al. in New York City found that former psychiatric patients were two to three times more likely than other community residents to have used a weapon or hurt someone badly and that most of the excess violence was committed by those individuals who were psychiatrically sickest and presumably not taking medication. Similarly, in the five-site Epidemiologic Catchment Area (ECA) study carried out by the National Institute of Mental Health, individuals with schizophrenia reported having used a weapon in a fight more than 20 times as often as individuals with no psychiatric disorder. There was also found to be a high correlation between violent behavior in schizophrenia and concurrent alcohol or drug abuse.

In reviewing many of these studies in 1992, Professor John Mona-han concluded: "The data that have recently become available, fairly read, suggest the one conclusion I did not want to reach: Whether the measure is the prevalence of violence among the disordered or the prevalence of disorder among the violent, whether the sample is people who are selected for treatment as inmates or patients in institutions or people randomly chosen from the open community, and no matter how many social and demographic factors are statistically taken into account, there appears to be a relationship between mental disorder and violent behavior." In a 1996 editorial reviewing such studies, Dr. Peter Marzuk added: "In the last decade, however, the evidence showing a link between violence, crime, and mental illness has mounted. It cannot be dismissed; it should not be ignored." And an April 2000 series in the *New York Times* on "rampage killers" reported that 48 of 100 killers studied "had some kind of formal diagnosis, often schizophrenia," and that "the incidence of these rampage killings appears to have increased" in the 1990s.

It should be emphasized that America is a violent society and, within this broad context, the contribution of individuals with schizo-phrenia to total violence is very small. It should also be reiterated that most individuals with schizophrenia are not assaultive or violent. How-ever, a minority of individuals with schizophrenia are assaultive or vio-lent, and the problem will not go away simply by repeating outdated mantras to the contrary.

The three best predictors of assaultive and violent behavior in indi-viduals with schizophrenia are concurrent alcohol or drug abuse, non-compliance with medication, and a past history of being assaultive or violent. Families that are faced with this problem must learn to recog-nize cues of impending violence and pay attention to them. If an individ-ual with schizophrenia becomes assaultive or violent it is best to stay calm (listen mostly, but respond in a calm and sympathetic manner), keep physically distant from the person, and call for help and/or the police as necessary.

Most assaultive and violent behavior can be prevented with plan-ning. If there have been one or more episodes in the past, the family should have safe-proofed the house (e.g., sharp knives are kept locked up), asked for a review of the person's medication, explored options for improving medication compliance (e.g., outpatient commitment), made an effort to reduce alcohol or drug abuse by controlling the person's funds, and conveyed very clearly to the person the precise consequences (e.g., the person will no longer be allowed to live at home) if assaultive or violent behavior recurs. If it does, then it is mandatory to carry out those consequences.

HOW TO RESPOND TO AN INDIVIDUAL WITH SCHIZOPHRENIA WHO IS POTENTIALLY VIOLENT

- Be aware that the three most important predictors of violence are a past history of violence, concurrent alcohol or drug abuse, and the failure to take antipsychotic medications.
- Make the person's treatment team aware of your concerns and of the person's past history of violence. This is more effective if done in writing.
- If the person has been violent, suggest to the treatment team that they consider using clozapine, carbamazepine, valproate, beta blockers, or other medications thought to decrease violent behavior.
- Safe-proof your house by removing all potential weapons. Put a good lock on the door of one room that you can use as a refuge if needed; this room should have a telephone.
- If threatened, stay calm, remain physically distant (give the person lots of space), do not look directly into his/her eyes, sympathize, try to find something on which you can both agree.
- Remain physically between the person and an open door; do not allow yourself to become trapped.
- Have the emergency response number posted next to the telephone and do not hesitate to call the police. If in doubt, call.
- Have a Crisis Information Form, already filled out for such emergencies, ready to hand to the police when they arrive. It should include the person's name, age, diagnosis, treating psychiatrist or clinic with telephone number, current medications, and summarized past history of violent behavior.

A family within which the patient has been assaultive or violent is particularly poignant and lives in a special circle of hell. Its members are often afraid of the patient yet at the same time feel sorry for him/her and recognize that the behavior is a product of abnormal brain function. The ambivalence inevitably felt by the family members is formidable; fear and love, avoidance and attraction, rest uneasily side by side. Afterward, no matter how well the patient gets, no matter how much time elapses, the memory of the past assault or violence never fully recedes.

ARREST AND JAIL

Being arrested and jailed has become a common, yet rarely discussed, experience for many individuals with schizophrenia. It is yet another sad measure of the failed mental illness treatment system. In the 1990 study of 1,401 randomly selected members of NAMI, the families reported that 20 percent of their severely mentally ill family members had been arrested within the previous five years and 40 percent had been arrested at some time in their lives. A 1985 Los Angeles study of homeless individuals who had been previously psychiatrically hospitalized found that 76 percent of them had been arrested. Going to jail for individuals with schizophrenia appears to be almost as much a part of their lives as is going to a psychiatric hospital.

The present situation is an inevitable consequence of deinstitutionalizing hundreds of thousands of individuals with severe psychiatric disorders without ensuring that they received the medication and aftercare necessary to remain well. As early as 1972 in California, psychiatrist Marc Abramson published data showing that the number of mentally ill persons in jails was increasing as deinstitutionalization got underway. Abramson coined the term "criminalization of mentally disordered behavior" and predicated accurately that the situation was going to get much worse.

By the 1980s it had become possible to track mentally ill individuals directly from psychiatric hospitals to jails. In Belcher's study of 132 patients discharged from Columbus State Hospital in Ohio, for example, within six months of discharge 32 percent of those with schizophrenia, manic-depressive illness, or severe depression had been arrested. The reason for arrest in most cases was behavior associated with a recurrence of their illness because of their failure to take medication, e.g., "walking in the community without clothes."

The vast majority of individuals with schizophrenia who are arrested are arrested on misdemeanor charges, usually associated with untreated illness. In the NAMI survey referred to above, only 2.6 percent of the 20 percent arrested had been arrested for "serious acts of violence or other felonies." Most were arrested on such charges as trespassing, disturbing the peace, destroying property, shoplifting, and being drunk and disorderly.

For most individuals with schizophrenia, the experience of being jailed varies from "unpleasant" to "a living hell." Being ridiculed by guards or other prisoners is the least problem; in some jails "mental cases" wear uniforms of a different color and so are readily identifiable. More serious are problems of assault, rape, suicide, and even homicide, all of which have been well documented. Jails require prisoners to follow rules, but following rules assumes that your brain is thinking logically. For many individuals with schizophrenia who are not on medication, logical thinking is impossible. Such individuals commit bizarre acts that cause problems for everyone. In California, a newspaper reported that mentally ill inmates in one jail "try to escape by smearing themselves with their own feces and flushing themselves down the toilet."

For families it is also painful to watch helplessly as a mentally ill family member is arrested and jailed. There is, of course, the stigma attached to it, but much worse is knowing that the person may be abused or assaulted.

For a small number of individuals with schizophrenia, however, the opposite is the case. Because it is so difficult to get psychiatric care for individuals with schizophrenia who are unaware of their illness and who refuse voluntary treatment, and because mentally ill individuals with legal charges pending often can be treated involuntarily, it has become increasingly common for public officials and families to have mentally ill persons arrested *solely as a means for getting them into treatment*. In Massachusetts, for example, one mother noted: "Rather than wait for the patient to become so psychotic that disaster occurs, many families bring charges against a patient for making threats or damaging property." The fact that families have to have their family member arrested in order to get treatment for the person's schizophrenia is indeed a pitiful commentary on our mental illness treatment system.

SUICIDE

The largest single contributor to the excess death rate in individuals with schizophrenia is suicide. A recent review of studies done on this subject concluded that "suicide is the number one cause of premature death among schizophrenics, with 10 to 13 percent killing themselves." This rate is just slightly lower than the 15 to 17 percent suicide rate reported in contemporary studies of manic-depressive illness. Among individuals in the general population the suicide rate is approximately 1 percent.

Depression represents the single most important cause of suicide among persons with schizophrenia, just as it does among persons without schizophrenia. The majority of patients will experience significant depression at some point during the course of their illness; this realization should lead psychiatrists to remain alert for depression and to treat it more aggressively with antidepressant medication. Depression may arise from the disease process itself (i.e., the schizophrenia affects the brain chemistry so as to cause depression), from the patients' realization of the severity of their illness (i.e., as a reaction to the disease), or occasionally as a side effect of medications used to treat schizophrenia. Depression must also be differentiated in schizophrenia from the slowed movements (akinesia) and slowed thought processes that may be symptoms of the disease.

Most persons with schizophrenia who commit suicide do so within the first 10 years of their illness. As might be expected, approximately three-quarters of them are men. Those at highest risk have a remitting and relapsing course, good insight (i.e., they know they are sick), a poor response to medication, are socially isolated, hopeless about the future, and have a gross discrepancy between their earlier achievements in life and their current level of function. Any patient with these characteristics *and* associated depression should be considered at high risk for suicide. The most common time for suicide is during a remission of the illness immediately following a relapse.

Recent data also suggest that the failure to adequately treat individuals with schizophrenia increases the risk of suicide. In a Finnish study of 92 individuals with schizophrenia who killed themselves, it was found that "the majority of victims (78 percent) were in the active illness phase, but among them over half (57 percent) were either not prescribed adequate neuroleptic [antipsychotic] treatment or were not using it." Similarly, a Belgian study of 63 individuals with schizophrenia who committed suicide reported that "there were seven times as many patients who did not comply with treatment in the suicide group as there were in the control group."

Occasionally persons with schizophrenia will commit suicide accidentally in a stage of acute psychosis, e.g., they may jump off a building because they think they can fly or because voices tell them to do so. Most suicides in schizophrenia are intended, however, and are often carefully planned by the person. Like all clinicians who have taken care of large numbers of patients with schizophrenia, I have known several who eventually committed suicide, and such deaths evoke great sadness.

There are other suicides, however, that evoke not only sadness but also anger. These are the preventable ones—the patient who is treated inadequately with medications and then told that nothing more can be done, or the patient who is doing nicely on medication until another doctor reduces it and begins insight-oriented psychotherapy. I wish I could say that these suicides were rare occurrences but they are not. The high suicide rate in schizophrenia is in part due to our inadequate care system (or, more accurately, nonsystem) on which these patients are forced to rely.

What can families and friends of individuals with schizophrenia do to minimize the risk of suicide? The most important thing is to be alert for it, especially in an individual who is depressed and who has recently recovered from a relapse. Past suicide gestures or attempts are an important predictor of future attempts. Expressions of guilt and worthlessness, hopelessness about the future, an unwillingness to make plans for the future, and putting one's affairs in order (e.g., giving away prized possessions or making a will) are all red flags that may indicate serious suicidal intent.

Families and friends should then *ask* and *act*. Ask the person if he/she is planning to commit suicide, e.g., "I know you have been depressed recently and I am very worried about you. Are you planning to harm yourself?" Some people are afraid to ask about suicide because they fear it will put the idea into the person's head. This is not true, and often the person is relieved to be able to talk about suicidal thoughts and plans. Most people who are planning to commit suicide have mixed feelings about it. Do not directly argue with the person about committing suicide but rather point out the reasons for not doing so. One excellent reason at this time is the promise of more effective medications with fewer side effects that are likely to become available in the next few years.

Act by taking away the person's planned modalities for committing suicide (e.g., a gun or pills) and similar weapons in the immediate environment. Act also by ensuring that the person's treating psychiatrist is aware of the person's suicidal intentions and urge him or her to aggressively treat the person's depression. If the psychiatrist is reluctant to act, put your advice and admonitions in a registered letter to the psychiatrist, if necessary, adding that you have consulted your lawyer about the case. The psychiatrist will get the message. In some cases involuntary commitment to a psychiatric unit may be necessary to ensure the person's safety until antidepressant medication can take effect.

Despite the best efforts of family and friends, however, some individuals with schizophrenia will commit suicide. If family and friends have done what they could do to help, they should not feel guilty or blame themselves. Suicide in schizophrenia is the final and ultimate measure of the tragedy of this disease.

RECOMMENDED FURTHER READING

Amador, X. *I Am Not Sick, I Don't Need Help!* Peconic, N.Y.: Vida Press, 2000.

Bogart, T., and P. Solomon. "Procedures to Share Treatment Information Among Mental Health Providers, Consumers, and Families." *Psychiatric Services* 50 (1999): 1321–25.

Caldwell, C. B., and I. I. Gottesman. "Schizophrenics Kill Themselves Too: A Review of Risk Factors for Suicide." *Schizophrenia Bulletin* 16 (1990): 571–89.

Caton, C. L. M., F. Cournos, and B. Dominguez. "Parenting and Adjustment in Schizophrenia." *Psychiatric Services* 50 (1999): 239–43.

Citrome, L., and J. Volavka. "Management of Violence in Schizophrenia." *Psychiatric Annals* 30 (2000): 41–52.

Cohen, J., and S. J. Levy. *The Mentally Ill Chemical Abuser: Whose Client?* New York: Lexington Books, 1992.

Diamond, Ronald. "Drugs and the Quality of Life: The Patient's Point of View." *Journal of Clinical Psychiatry* 46 (1985): 29–35.

Drake, R. E., C. Mercer-McFadden, K. T. Mueser, et al. "Review of Integrated Mental Health and Substance Abuse Treatment for Patients with Dual Disorders." *Schizophrenia Bulletin* 24 (1998): 589–608.

Empfield, M. D. "Pregnancy and Schizophrenia." *Psychiatric Annals* 30 (2000): 61–66.

Evans, K., and J. M. Sullivan. *Dual Diagnosis: Counseling for the Mentally Ill Substance Abuser*. New York: Guilford Press, 1990.

Goisman, R. M., A. B. Kent, E. C. Montgomery, et al. "AIDS Education for Patients with Chronic Mental Illness." *Community Mental Health Journal* 27 (1991): 189–97.

Gottesman, I. I., and C. S. Groome. "HIV/AIDS Risks as a Consequence of Schizophrenia." *Schizophrenia Bulletin* 23 (1997): 675–84.

Hatfield, A. "Coping with Aggressive Behavior." National Alliance for the Mentally Ill, 1992, pamphlet.

Hyde, A. P. "Coping with the Threatening, Intimidating, Violent Behaviors of People with Psychiatric Disabilities Living at Home: Guidelines for Family Caregivers." *Psychiatric Rehabilitation Journal* 21 (1997): 144–49.

Jamison, K. R. *Night Falls Fast: Understanding Suicide*. New York: Knopf, 1999.

Kelly, J. A., T. L. McAuliffe, K. J. Sikkema, et al., "Reduction in Risk Behavior Among Adults with Severe Mental Illness Who Learned to Advocate for HIV Prevention." *Psychiatric Services* 48 (1997): 1283–88.

Lehman, A. F., and L. B. Dixon, eds. *Double Jeopardy: Chronic Mental Illness and Substance Use Disorders*. Langhorne, Pa.: Harwood Academic Publishers, 1995.

Lyon, E. R. "A Review of the Effects of Nicotine on Schizophrenia and Antipsychotic Medications." *Psychiatric Services* 50 (1999): 1346–50.

McCullough, L. B., J. Coverdale, T. Bayer, et al. "Ethically Justified Guidelines for Family Planning Interventions to Prevent Pregnancy in Female Patients with Chronic Mental Illness." *American Journal of Obstetrics and Gynecology* 167 (1992): 19–25.

Miller, L. J. "Sexuality, Reproduction, and Family Planning in Women with Schizophrenia." *Schizophrenia Bulletin* 23 (1997): 623–35.

Minkoff, K., and R. E. Drake, eds. *Dual Diagnosis of Major Mental Illness and Substance Abuse*. San Francisco: Jossey-Bass, 1991.

Monahan, J. "Mental Disorder and Violent Behavior." *American Psychologist* 47 (1992): 511–21.

Swanson, J. W., M. S. Swartz, R. Borum, et al. "Involuntary Out-Patient Commitment and Reduction of Violent Behaviour in Persons with Severe Mental Illness." *British Journal of Psychiatry* 176 (2000): 224–31.

Swartz, M. S., J. W. Swanson, H. R. Wagner, et al. "Can Involuntary Outpatient Commitment Reduce Hospital Recidivism?: Findings from a Randomized Trial with Severely Mentally Ill Individuals." *American Journal of Psychiatry* 156 (1999): 1968–75.

Torrey, E. F. *Out of the Shadows: Confronting America's Mental Illness Crisis*. New York: John Wiley, 1997.

Torrey, E. F., J. Stieber, J. Ezekiel, et al. *Criminalizing the Seriously Mentally Ill: The Abuse of Jails as Mental Hospitals*. Washington, D.C.: Health Research Group and National Alliance for the Mentally Ill, 1992.

Torrey, E. F., and M. Zdanowicz. "Outpatient Commitment: What, Why, and for Whom?" *Psychiatric Services*. Forthcoming.

12

HOW CAN CONSUMERS AND FAMILIES SURVIVE SCHIZOPHRENIA?

The wretchedness of those families upon whom devolve the care and maintenance of the insane can be estimated only by those who, from personal observation, have become acquainted with its extent. Their peace is interrupted, their cares are multiplied, their time is engrossed, and their fortunes reduced or entirely dissipated in attempting to restore to reason one unfortunate member. . . . The misery which they suffer is communicated to a large circle of friends and the whole neighborhood is indirectly disturbed by the malady of one.

Samuel B. Woodward, 1821

Schizophrenia brings with it myriad practical problems. Other chronic diseases, such as polio, kidney failure, and cancer, may drain patients and families emotionally, physically, and sometimes financially. When the disease affects the person's brain, however, the management of the disease assumes Herculean dimensions. Whatever one does and however hard one tries, there is always the lingering feeling that it is not quite enough.

One of the main reasons why having schizophrenia is so problematic is that most people do not understand the disease. A mother of two sons illustrated this point poignantly. Her elder son, affected with muscular dystrophy, "gets emotional support everywhere he turns. His handicap is visible and obvious and the community, family, and friends open their hearts to him and go out of their way to make his life better." By contrast, her younger son, affected with schizophrenia, "is misunderstood by all. He is also terribly disabled, but his disability is not visible. He looks like a healthy, strong young man, . . . but the neighbors ignore him. . . . They don't understand him. All in all, they wish he'd go away."

THE RIGHT ATTITUDE

Developing the right attitude is the single most important thing an individual or family can do to survive schizophrenia. The right attitude evolves naturally once there is resolution of the twin monsters of schizophrenia—blame and shame. These lie just beneath the surface of many families, impeding the family from moving forward, souring relations between family members, and threatening to explode in a frenzy of finger pointing, accusations, and recriminations. Blame and shame are the Scylla and Charybdis of schizophrenia.

As should be clear from chapters 6 and 7, feelings of blame and shame are completely irrational. There is no evidence whatsoever that schizophrenia is caused by how people have been treated either as children or as adults; it is a biological disease of the brain, unrelated to interpersonal events of childhood or adulthood. But many people believe otherwise, and their feelings have often been based on what a mental health professional has said (or at least implied) to them. An excellent description of this process is recounted by Louise Wilson in *This Stranger, My Son:*

> Mother: "And so it is we who have made Tony what he is?"
> Psychiatrist: "Let me put it this way. Every child born, every mind, is a tabula rasa, an empty slate. What is written on it"—a stubby finger shot out, pointed at me—"you wrote there."

The consequences are predictable, with the mother lying awake at night remembering all the things she did that might have caused the schizophrenia.

> We had moved too often during his early years. . . . My tension during the prenatal period when his father was overseas . . . His father's preoccupation with his profession . . . No strong companionship and father image . . . A first child, and too many other children coming along too rapidly . . . Our expectations were too high . . . He had been robbed of his rightful babyhood, had grown up too fast . . . Inconsistent handling . . . Too permissive . . . Too much discipline . . . Oedipal fixation . . .

There is, of course, not a mother, father, brother, or sister in the world who has not done things he or she regrets in past relationships with other family members. We are, after all, rather imperfect human beings, and it is not surprising that at times we all speak or act impulsively out of jealousy, anger, narcissism, or fatigue. But fortunately we have resilient psyches, capable of absorbing random blows without crumbling or being permanently damaged. People do not cause schizophrenia; they merely blame each other for doing so.

Moreover, not only do the well family members blame each other for causing the schizophrenia in the family, but the person with schizophrenia may also do so. James Wechsler's son, in *In a Darkness*, once turned to him and angrily exclaimed, "You know, Dad, I wasn't *born* this way." And in *This Stranger, My Son*, Louise Wilson recounts the following conversation with her son:

> "I read a book the other day," Tony said. "It was in the drugstore. I stood there and read it all the way through."
>
> We waited, alarmed by the severity of his expression.
>
> "It told what good parents ought to be. It said that people get . . . the way I am . . . because their parents weren't qualified to be parents."
>
> "Oh Tony," I began, but Jack's signal silenced me.
>
> "I'm a miserable wreck, because both of you are, too. You're queers and you never should have had a child."
>
> "In what way are we queer?" Jack asked quietly.
>
> "You never played ball with me. All you ever wanted to do was tramp around looking at birds or read. Or work in the damned hospital."
>
> "Well, maybe it would have been more fun for you if I'd been an athlete. I can see that. But I really don't see why that should make me such a terrible father."
>
> "Read the book!" Tony exclaimed.
>
> "Tony, there are a lot of things written in books, a lot of opinions that are inaccurate, distorted, or just plain wrong. Besides, I'm sure the book—"
>
> "Listen, even the doctor that I've got here agrees! He says nobody's born with problems like mine!"

The blaming of one another for the illness magnifies the tragedy of schizophrenia manyfold. By itself it is a chronic disease of the brain and a personal and family disaster of usually manageable proportions. But when family members add blame to its burden, the disease spreads its roots beneath the whole family structure and becomes a calamity of boundless dimensions. The pain that blame causes in such circumstances must be seen to be believed. One woman wrote to me:

> My mother died twelve years ago, tormented by my sister's illness. After reading every book and article published on the subject, she decided that she was to blame. My father, who is in his seventies, brought my sister home from the state hospital for five years following my mother's death, in memory of my mother, trying to prove that she wasn't sick. My sister was so sick he finally had to return her to the hospital.

Few members of the mental health profession have focused on the amount of harm that has been done by the idea that parents and families cause schizophrenia. Psychiatrists especially, as members of the medical profession, see themselves as unlikely to cause harm. We now know that this is not so, and it is likely that in the twentieth century psychiatrists as a group did more harm than good to persons with schizophrenia. The harm was not done maliciously; indeed I know of few psychiatrists who could be characterized as mean-spirited. Rather the harm was done inadvertently because of prevailing psychodynamic and family interaction theories of the disease (see chapter 7). But it was harm nonetheless. William S. Appleton is one of the few professionals who have written about this and analyzed the undesirable consequences that follow when professionals blame the families for causing the disease:

> Badly treated families retaliate in ways that are detrimental to the patient. They become less willing to tolerate the problems he causes, are less agreeable to changing their behavior toward him, do not give much information when interviewed, and pay few visits to the hospital.

Occasionally, families are reluctant to give up the blame and guilt they feel. This may occur, for example, in a family where there are still young children; if the parents believe themselves to be responsible for the schizophrenia in their older child, then by changing their behavior they can theoretically prevent it in the younger children. If, on the other hand, they believe that schizophrenia is a random biological happening, as all the evidence suggests, then they are helpless to prevent it. Guilt in such families provides an illusion of control. Another type of family sometimes encountered that resists giving up guilt is one in which guilt is the family's way of life. Usually one or more members of such families are in long-term psychotherapy and the family seems to thrive on guilt, wallowing in it and blaming each other as their principal pastime. In such families, as one mother explained to me, "guilt is the gift which keeps on giving." I encourage individuals with schizophrenia who come from such families to minimize time spent within the family setting because it is detrimental to progress and to getting on with life despite a handicap.

The obverse of blame is shame. Inevitably, if families believe that they have somehow caused the schizophrenia, they will try to hide the family member affected, deny the illness to their neighbors, and otherwise dissociate themselves from the victim in a multiplicity of ways. Persons with schizophrenia sense this and feel more isolated than ever. It is not unusual for the patient then to react angrily toward the family, retaliating by making less effort to control bizarre behavior, and perhaps disrobing in front of elderly Aunt Agatha. Such behavior generates more shame in the family, producing more isolation and anger in the patient, and the downward spiral of shame and anger continues.

Education, as noted below, may resolve the problem of blame and shame. When family members come to understand that they did not cause the disease, the blame and shame felt by them are usually markedly reduced and the living situation for the person with schizophrenia improved. The question of who is responsible for the disease should be asked of all family members, and the person with schizophrenia should participate in the discussion if possible. Once this is opened up, the beliefs and fears that will sometimes emerge in the ensuing discussion are extraordinary. And once the issue of blame and shame is resolved and put to rest, schizophrenia becomes much easier to live with. One parent expressed it this way:

> Once you have unloaded your guilt, laid upon you by well-meaning professionals, the next step is easier. If you have done nothing wrong and have been doing the best you can, then you have nothing to be ashamed of. You can *come out of the closet*. The relief experienced by this act gives you strength to go on, and support starts coming out of the woodwork.

Once blame and shame have been put aside, the right attitude naturally evolves. The right attitude has four elements and can be called a SAFE attitude: Sense of perspective, Acceptance of the illness, Family balance, and Expectations that are realistic.

THE RIGHT ATTITUDE

Sensé of perspective

Acceptance of the illness

Family balance

Expectations that are realistic

Sense of Perspective: At first glance, a sense of perspective seems antithetical to schizophrenia. How can the most tragic disease known to mankind elicit perspective of any kind? And yet it is precisely because schizophrenia is such a tragic disease that a sense of perspective is mandatory. Without perspective the family burns out and loses its resiliency to handle the inevitable ups and downs inherent in the disease. The people I have seen who were most successful in coping with schizophrenia were those who had retained a sense of perspective and an appreciation of the absurd.

What do I mean by a sense of perspective? I certainly do not mean laughing at a person with this disease. Rather it is laughing *with* them. For example, one family in which the son relapsed each autumn and required rehospitalization had a standing family joke with the son that he always carved his pumpkins in the hospital. In another family, a woman went to a Halloween party dressed as a Cogentin tablet, a medication used for side effects in schizophrenia. In my own family, I once sent my sister with schizophrenia a new suit as a gift, and she replied, "The suit looks ghastly on me, and I gave it away." It is the kind of ingenuous reply that is often heard from individuals with schizophrenia, a reply stripped of the social graces to which we have become accustomed, a reply that we would all like to make on occasion but usually do not. Being able to laugh with a person with schizophrenia on such occasions is good therapy for everyone; becoming indignant is not.

Perhaps the best example of the sense of perspective so necessary in schizophrenia was told by researcher H. B. M. Murphy, while surveying a small Canadian village for individuals with schizophrenia:

One of our other informants learnt first of another case in a fashion which still less suggests shame or embarrassment. To use his own words, it happened that my wife had been making a social visit to them and she noticed a blanket over the parlour sofa as if some stuff had been covered up there. After a time, while they were having tea, it moved. She must have seemed a little startled, for they said: "Oh, that's just Hector. He always hides himself like that." Then they went on with tea!

Acceptance of the Illness: For both the patient and the family, this is the second important ingredient in the right attitude. Acceptance does not mean giving up, but rather an acknowledgment that the disease is real, that it is not likely to just go away, and that it will impose some limitations on the person's abilities. It is acceptance of things as they are, not things as you wish them to be.

Esso Leete, an articulate woman who has schizophrenia, described the problems she has had in accepting her disease as follows: "I am haunted by an evasive picture of what my life could have been, whom I might have become, what I might have accomplished." Once acceptance has been achieved, however, the person is freed up from a huge burden, as Judith Baum, another mentally ill woman, described: "There came the morning, sunny and bright and cold, when I accepted the fact that I had a mental illness. It was a stormy, angry and tearful time. But with acceptance came release."

Some parents experience prolonged grief in reaction to their child's schizophrenia and find acceptance very difficult to achieve. Rosalynn Carter, in her book *Helping Someone with Mental Illness*, quoted a letter from such a mother:

"I cry most every night before I go to sleep," she continued. "I cry when I see street people. I cry when I think that even if a 'miracle' drug is produced, Stephanie will still have lost a part of her life. I cry when I think she's never gone to a dance with a boy; that she'll never marry; never be a mother; never experience life in the way others do.

"I cry when my older daughter gets to travel the world as a representative of her law firm while Stephanie sits on her bed and rocks. I cry when my middle daughter published articles in our local newspapers and Stephanie smokes and listens to her 'voices.' "

Many individuals with schizophrenia and their families never learn to accept the disease. They go on, year after year, denying it and pretending it does not exist. When acceptance can be achieved it becomes easier for everyone. One mother wrote about her sick daughter's reaction when the daughter fully realized her diagnosis and that she had been the 1 in 100 to get the disease: "Well, I guess if it's percentage-wise it might as well be me. I have such a terrific family to hold my hand, and since I've been tagged someone else has escaped." Such an extraordinary attitude is an ideal to be striven for but rarely achieved, because such insight and kindness are so unusual.

More common, unfortunately, is anger in both the patient and the family. The anger may be directed at God for creating a world in which schizophrenia exists, at fate for dealing a bad hand, at the patient for becoming sick, or at each other for causing the illness. It varies from being a mild resentment bubbling to the surface when social activities must be curtailed because of the person with schizophrenia to a more virulent bitterness flowing beneath the surface of their daily activities like a caustic acid. Occasionally the anger does not achieve overt expression but rather turns inward; it is then seen as depression.

Whenever I encounter such families I wish I could send them to a Buddhist monastery for a month. There they might learn the Oriental acceptance of life as it is, an invaluable attitude in surviving this disease. Such acceptance puts schizophrenia into perspective as one of life's great tragedies but stops it from becoming a festering sore eating away at life's very core. As one mother told me, "You can't stop the bird of sorrow from flying over your head, but you can stop it from making a mess in your hair."

Family Balance: An important aspect of the right attitude in surviving schizophrenia is an ability to weigh the needs of the ill family member against those of others in the family. Families that selflessly sacrifice everything for the person with schizophrenia are usually doing so because they feel irrationally guilty about possibly having caused the disease. To provide care for a seriously disabled person living at home may be a job requiring 168 hours per week; furthermore, it is unpaid and offers few thanks. Who is to care for the caregiver, who more often than not is the mother? How are we to weigh the needs of other children? Or the needs of the parent or parents to get away periodically? It is important to weigh these conflicting needs calmly and rationally, recognizing that the person with schizophrenia does not always come first. It may be necessary, for example, to occasionally rehospitalize a person with schizophrenia for the needs of the family and not the needs of the patient; perceptive mental illness professionals recognize such dilemmas and support the family in such decisions.

Expectations That Are Realistic: Modifying assumptions about a person's future is difficult to accomplish but important to attempt, for it often follows directly from acceptance of the disease. It is especially difficult if the person with schizophrenia had been unusually promising prior to becoming ill. Such families tend to hang on to the hope, year after year, that the person with schizophrenia will someday become normal again and resume his or her career. Grossly unrealistic plans are made, money is saved for college or a big wedding, and family members fool each other with the shared myth of "when he gets well again."

The problem with the myth is that the ill person knows it is a myth, and it puts him/her in a no-win situation. There is nothing the person can do to please the family except to get well, and that is beyond his or her control. Several observers have noted this problem and have urged families to lower their expectations for the person. If this is done, the families themselves become happier. Creer and Wing noted in their interviews with such families:

> Several relatives mentioned that giving up hope had paradoxically been the turning point for them in coming to terms with their unhappiness. "Once you give up hope," one mother said, "you start to perk up." "Once you realise he'll never be cured you start to relax." These relatives had lowered their expectations and aspirations for the patient and had found that doing this had been the first step in cutting the problem down to manageable size.

Another parent said, "You've got to reach bedrock, to become depressed enough, before you are forced to accept the reality and the enormity of the problem. Having done that, you don't allow your hopes to become too high and thus leave yourself open to disappointment when they are not fulfilled."

This does not mean that families should have no expectations at all of the person with schizophrenia. H. Richard Lamb, one of the few psychiatrists who have worked assiduously on the rehabilitation of such patients, has said, "Recognizing that a person has limited capabilities should not mean that we expect nothing of him." Expectations must be realistic, however, and consonant with the capabilities of the person with schizophrenia. Just as the family of a polio victim should not expect the person's legs to return to complete normality, so too the family of a person with schizophrenia should not expect the person's brain to return to complete normality. Psychiatrist John Wing wrote:

> A neutral (not overemotional) expectation to perform up to *attainable* standards is the ideal. This rule, if difficult for the specialist to adopt, is a thousand times more difficult for relatives. Nevertheless, we should be humbled to recognize that a large portion of relatives, by trial and error, do come to adopt it, without any help from professionals.

The effect of lowering one's expectations is often to be able to enjoy and share things with the person for the first time in many years. Thus, if someone who was an accomplished flutist prior to becoming ill takes up the flute again to play simple pieces, both the person and the family can enjoy that accomplishment. It no longer is going to be seen, implicitly or explicitly, in the light of when-you-are-well-you'll-be-able-to-give-concerts-again-dear. Similarly, if the person is able to ride a bus for the first time alone or go to the store by himself or ride a bicycle, these accomplishments can also be celebrated for what they are—often magnificent accomplishments for a person whose brain is not functioning properly. The person with schizophrenia and the family need to be able to find joy in such accomplishments just as a polio victim finds joy in relearning to walk. Oliver Sacks, in his book *The Man Who Mistook His Wife for a Hat*, expresses this attitude well in his story about brain-damaged and deformed Rebecca who could still see beauty in life:

> Superficially she *was* a mass of handicaps and incapacities . . . but at some deeper level there was no sense of handicap or incapacity, but a feeling of calm and completeness, of being fully alive, of being a soul, deep and high, and equal to all others. . . . We paid far too much attention to the defects of our patients, as Rebecca was the first to tell me, and far too little to what was intact or preserved.

THE IMPORTANCE OF EDUCATION

Achieving the right attitude about schizophrenia becomes increasingly possible the more one learns about the disease. As Ed Francell, a consumer, succinctly put it: "My advice to consumers and families is to get your hands on anything and everything. . . . The more information you know, the better you can put the illness in perspective."

Much learning about schizophrenia takes place in local support groups for consumers and families. The monthly or bimonthly meetings of local groups throughout the United States sponsored by NAMI and analogous Canadian groups sponsored by the Schizophrenia Society of Canada have been the single most important contributions of these organizations. They provide a forum for individuals with schizophrenia and their families to learn about the disease and to learn from each other how to survive.

At a more formal level, the "Family-to-Family" 12-week education course developed by Joyce Burland and NAMI Vermont has been a great success. Under NAMI sponsorship it has been taught in 42 states to over 50,000 family members, and over 2,000 volunteer teachers have been certified. It is the first national peer program in family education and includes units on the causes and treatment of schizophrenia, manic-depressive illness, and depression, as well as units on problem solving, communications skills, and advocacy (contact NAMI; see appendix D).

A variety of other education courses have also been developed. "The Journey of Hope" is an eight-week education course developed by NAMI Louisiana and also taught in surrounding states (contact Journey of Hope, P.O. Box 1561, Baton Rouge, LA 70821, phone 225-343-6928). Education courses, such as "Pebbles in the Pond: Living with Chronic Neurobiological Disorders," developed by Larry Baker and Karen Landwehr of the Comprehensive Mental Health Center in Tacoma, Washington, are available through some public mental health centers. Many clubhouses, such as Fountain House in New York and Thresholds in Chicago, have also developed educational curriculums for their members.

In the private sector, Mary Moller, R.N., and her colleagues in Spokane, Washington, utilize videotapes to teach three courses: "Recovering from Psychosis: A Wellness Approach" (12 weeks), "Symptom Management" (9 weeks), and "Be Smart," a course for mentally ill individuals who have also been abused (12 weeks) (contact NurSeminars, 12204 W. Sunridge Dr., Nine Mile Falls, WA 99026, phone 509-468-9848). Another highly praised education program is that created by Christopher Amenson, a psychologist at Pacific Clinics Institute in Los Angeles who has taught consumers, families, and mental illness professionals about severe mental illnesses for many years. He has developed excellent courses lasting 6 to 12 sessions: "Schizophrenia: A Family Education Curriculum," "Schizophrenia: Family Education Methods," and "Family Skills for Relapse Prevention," each complete with syllabus and slides (contact Pacific Clinics Institute, 909 S. Fair Oaks Ave., Pasadena, CA 91105, phone 626-795-8471).

SURVIVAL STRATEGIES FOR CONSUMERS

For a person with schizophrenia, surviving the disease is often a major challenge. In recent years, however, a large number of suggestions have been put forward by individuals who are affected and by mental illness professionals. Such suggestions can make survival easier.

Most individuals with schizophrenia do better if they have a daily routine and a predictable schedule. This allows them to anticipate stresses and minimize surprises. One consumer, Esso Leete, believes that "a controlled environment is probably so important to me because my brain is not always manageable. Making lists organizes my thoughts."

Most individuals who successfully manage their schizophrenia also have specific plans for doing so. Identifying and coping with specific stressors is one aspect of this. For example, Leete describes her four-part approach as "recognizing when I am feeling stressed; identifying the stressor; remembering from past experience what action helped in the same situation or a similar one; and taking that action." Keeping a card in one's wallet or purse listing what to do when under stress may also be useful.

General coping strategies for surviving schizophrenia consist of activities such as exercise, good diet, and pursuing hobbies. A study of exercise in individuals with schizophrenia reported that it improved their sleep pattern, improved self-esteem, and decreased auditory hallucinations. Other approaches for dealing with auditory hallucinations include cognitive behavioral therapy, described in chapter 8, and a variety of self-developed methods summarized in the article "Patients' Strategies for Coping with Auditory Hallucinations," by Dorothy Carter et al., listed under "Recommended Further Reading" at the end of this chapter.

Specific coping strategies for other symptoms are both varied and imaginative. Esso Leete minimizes her paranoia by always choosing "a seat where I can face the door, preferably with my back to the wall instead of to other people" and by "asking the people I am with questions like who they are calling, where they are going, or whatever."

Dr. Frederick Frese, a psychologist who has been hospitalized on multiple occasions with paranoid schizophrenia, likens having schizophrenia to being a person in a foreign country where language, customs, and assumptions are alien. As such he recommends studying the "chronically normal persons," or CNPs, as he calls them, in order to become more aware of how their behavior differs. He says, for example, that CNPs usually look directly at persons to whom they are talking but "we are more easily distracted and if we look at others while we are talking we will see their facial reactions, making it more difficult to focus on what we are saying." Dr. Frese offers many practical suggestions, such as "don't talk with your voices where CNPs can see or hear you because it makes them very uncomfortable." Frese, who has never lost his sense of humor despite his schizophrenia, is also well known for handing out a card he carries with him to people who are being unpleasant to him:

Excuse me. I need to tell you that I am a person who suffers from Schizophrenia. When I am berated, belittled, insulted, or otherwise treated in an oppressive manner, I tend to become emotionally ill. Could I ask that you restate your concerns in a manner that does not tend to disable me?

One of the most important things that individuals with schizophrenia can do to survive is to join self-help groups. These go under a variety of names such as Recovery Inc., GROW, Schizophrenics Anonymous, On Our Own, and Psychosis Free. All such groups provide support and education and a place where, as one patient put it, "I can just be myself." Schizophrenics Anonymous, for example, was established in Michigan in 1985 by Joanne Verbanic, who has schizophrenia, to provide fellowship, to educate, and "to help restore dignity and sense of purpose for persons who are working for recovery from schizophrenia or related disorders." There are now over 40 Schizophrenics Anonymous chapters (contact Schizophrenics Anonymous, Mental Health Association, 15920 W. Twelve Mile Rd., Southfield, MI 48076, phone 800-482-9534, website www.sanonymous.org/). Many individuals with schizophrenia also join NAMI. Dr. Fred Frese, referred to above, has been a vice-president of the NAMI national board, and in 1990, another consumer, Thomas Posey, was president of the national board.

One of the most exciting recent developments among individuals with schizophrenia is the increasing role they are playing in providing mental illness services. In many communities they run drop-in centers for mentally ill persons. In San Francisco, consumers have been trained and hired as "peer counselors" on locked psychiatric inpatient units. And in San Mateo County, California, consumer "peer counselors" have been hired to do AIDS education and to provide support for other consumers who are being moved from psychiatric hospitals to apartment living. In Denver, consumers since 1986 have been trained in a six-month training program as case management aides and are playing an increasingly important role in the state's Community Mental Health Centers. The Denver consumer provider program has been replicated in Texas, Washington, and Massachusetts and logically should represent a wave for the future of mental illness services.

The development of consumer self-help groups, "peer counselors," and consumer provider programs has, unfortunately, proceeded much more slowly than should have been the case. The major reason for this is the "consumer survivor" movement, described in chapter 15. The small but highly vocal group of "consumer survivors" has frequently encouraged individuals with schizophrenia to stop taking their medication, and some "consumer survivors" even deny that schizophrenia exists as a brain disorder. This small group has widely discredited the much larger and respectable consumer movement in the eyes of many families and agencies who provide mental illness services.

Even worse, the small "consumer survivor" movement has been made to appear much more important than it really is because it has received substantial fiscal support from the federal Center for Mental Health Services, an agency afflicted with terminal political correctness. It is one of the strangest unwritten Washington stories that one federal agency, the National Institute of Mental Health, is spending money to develop better treatments for schizophrenia at the same time that another federal agency, the Center for Mental Health Services, is spending money to encourage patients not to use those treatments. This lack of logic mirrors the symptoms of schizophrenia itself.

SURVIVAL STRATEGIES FOR FAMILIES

In recent years, there has been an outpouring of studies documenting the burden for families of having a family member with schizophrenia living at home. One review article summarized 28 such studies, of which 17 were published in the 1990s. These studies described the family members' loss of personal time, decreased social relationships, poorer health, and decreased finances because someone had to stop working in order to be at home. The family is frequently asked to act as the ill person's case manager, psychotherapist, nurse, landlord, cook, janitor, banker, disciplinarian, and best friend. This impossible array of family tasks is relatively new, since, prior to the 1960s, the majority of people with schizophrenia were hospitalized at least intermittently. The frustrations that are inevitable in such situations were described by one mother as follows:

> Sometimes I feel like a social director. It is my job to think of stimulating things for my daughter to do and places for her to visit. I arrange outings and provide transportation and amiable companionship. It is not that I dislike my personal role in Carrie's life, but I admit to some frustration. I have a life of my own that I want to get back to, and I'm ready for Carrie to take more responsibility for hers.

Such families need support from mental illness professionals for their caregiving activities but often do not receive it. In an effort to improve the support of mental illness professionals for families, a group of families and professionals in Australia created a training program for the professionals. In the United States, the Riverside County Department of Mental Health in California created a position called "family advocate" to support the families and train the professionals; this idea is spreading to other counties in California.

Whether the family member with schizophrenia is living at home or not, the family must confront some basic questions. One that frequently comes up is how should the family members behave toward someone with schizophrenia? In general, people who get along best with individuals with schizophrenia are those who treat them most naturally. This can be verified by watching the nursing staff in any psychiatric hospital. The staff who are most respected by both professionals and patients treat the patients with dignity and as human beings, albeit with a brain disease. The staff who are least respected treat the patients in a condescending manner, frequently reminding them of their inferior status. Often this is because the staff member does not understand schizophrenia or is afraid of it. The simple answer, then, to the question "How should I behave toward a person with schizophrenia?" is: Kindly.

Beyond this, however, there are certain aspects of schizophrenia as a disease that do modify to some degree one's behavior toward a person who has it. These modifications arise directly and predictably out of the nature of the brain damage and the symptoms of the disease as described in chapter 2. Persons with schizophrenia have great difficulty in processing sensory input of all kinds, especially two or more simultaneous sensory stimuli. If this is kept in mind, then determining how to behave toward the person becomes much easier.

Make communications, for example, brief, concise, and unambiguous. As explained by one family member: "Look at the person. Talk in short, concise, adult statements . . . be clear and practical . . . give one set of directions at a time with no options."

Another mother described how she communicates with her adult son with schizophrenia:

> My son seemed to have difficulty dealing with all the stimuli around him. He responded slowly and said that he had difficulty with "everything coming at me." At those times it was important for me to speak in simple, slow sentences. Requests were made for one thing at a time. Keeping down complexity was very important. Strong emotion increased his difficulty in processing what I was saying. However much in a hurry I felt, there was no way to hurry him. Patience was absolutely necessary.
>
> I learned finally the futility of arguments. When S. was in more acute stages, it was easy to get into impossible rounds of arguments. Often he could not be reasoned with, but I didn't know how to back off. I learned to choose carefully what had to be done, plan ahead how I would handle the situation, and not respond to all the objections. For example, I might say in a clear, firm, simple statement, "You must be ready to leave at 8 o'clock." Then I stood expectantly, even handing him his coat, and opening the door.
>
> Sometimes leaving requests by way of memo or over the telephone seemed to work better than face to face—I am not sure why—sometimes he seemed to be overstimulated by my presence.

Ask the person with schizophrenia one question at a time. "Did you have a nice time, dear? Who went with you?" may seem like a straightforward two-part question for a normal person, but for a person with schizophrenia it may be overwhelming.

It is also counterproductive to try to argue people with schizophrenia out of their delusional beliefs. Attempts to do so often result in misunderstanding and anger, as described by John Wing:

Patients tended to develop sudden irrational fears. They might, for instance, become fearful of a particular room in the house. Maybe they would tell the family the reason for their fear. "There's a poisonous gas leaking into that room" or "There are snakes under the bed in that room." At first relatives are baffled by this. Some admitted they had grown frustrated with a patient's absolute refusal to abandon some idea, despite all their attempts to reason with him, and had lost their temper. But they found this only resulted in the patient becoming very upset, and in any case the idea continued to be held with as much conviction as ever.

Rather than arguing with the patient, simply make a statement of disagreement; this can be done without challenging or provoking him or her. Thus, a reasonable response to "There are snakes under the bed in that room" is "I know you believe there are snakes there, but I don't see any and I doubt that there are," rather than a peremptory "There are no snakes in that room." The patient has some reason for believing that there are snakes there—perhaps he/she heard them or even saw them. It is often useful for the family member to acknowledge the validity of the patient's sensory experiences without accepting the person's interpretation of the experiences. Such a statement might be "I know you have some reason to believe there are snakes there, but I think that the reason has to do with the fact that your brain is playing tricks on you because of your illness."

Family members and friends of patients are often tempted to deal with the patient's delusional beliefs in a sarcastic or humorous manner. The statement about snakes, for example, might be responded to as follows: "Oh yes, I saw them there too. And did you see the rattlesnakes in the kitchen as well?" Such statements are never useful and are often very confusing for the patient. It also reinforces their delusional belief and makes it more difficult for them to separate their personal experiences from reality. One patient, who believed he had a rat in his throat and asked the doctors to look at it, was told sardonically by the doctors that the rat was too far down to see. When the patient recovered he recalled, "I would have been grateful if they had stated quite plainly that they did not believe that there was a rat in my throat." This is good advice.

Another useful way to handle the delusional thinking of people with schizophrenia is to encourage them to express such thinking only in private. Talking about snakes being under the bed is not harmful within the context of family and friends, but if said in a crowded elevator or announced to the saleslady in a store, it can be embarrassing for everyone concerned. Discuss this frankly and straightforwardly with the person and it will often be appreciated. As Creer and Wing point out: "A more realistic aim is to try to limit the effect of such ideas upon the patient's public behavior. Many patients were well able to understand this and to limit odd behavior, such as talking to themselves, and the expression of odd ideas, to private occasions."

An impediment to communicating with persons with schizophrenia is their frequent inability to participate in normal back-and-forth conversation. "One patient returned home each evening from the day center, ate in complete silence the meal her aunt provided, and then went straight to her room. . . . Her aunt, who was lonely and elderly, would have been very glad for a chat in the evenings. She was puzzled by the patient's almost total lack of communication." Such patients often are aware of conversations around them but are unable to participate. "One young man generally sat in silence, or muttering to himself, while his parents were conversing about family matters. Later, however, they learned that he had quite often spoken to a nurse at the hospital about such topics of conversation at home and had clearly been taking in what was said despite all appearances to the contrary." Many such patients like to have other people around them but do not like to interact with them directly. "One lady said she had been surprised to hear from a friend that her nephew suffering from the disease liked to come and visit her. 'I would never have guessed it because when he comes he just sits in a chair and says absolutely nothing.' "

An analogous problem families have in their efforts to relate to persons with schizophrenia is their impaired ability to express emotions. Frequently the patient will relate to even close family members in what appears to be a cold and distant way. This emotional aloofness is quite normal for many persons with this disease and should be respected. Difficult though this coldness may be, do not take it personally. The patient may find it easier to express emotion or verbal affection toward a family pet, and it is sometimes a good idea to provide the person with a cat or dog for this purpose.

A common problem is how the family should behave toward a person with schizophrenia when he/she is withdrawn. It is important to recognize the need of many persons with this disease to withdraw. One mother wrote me that while chatting with her ill daughter as they were doing the dishes, the daughter turned and said: "Leave me alone now,

Mom, so I can enjoy my own world." Sometimes the withdrawal can be pronounced. I once had a patient who remained in her room at home for weeks at a time, coming out only during the night to eat.

It can be puzzling to know what to do in these cases of social withdrawal. Should you insist that the person emerge from the bedroom and interact socially, or should you leave him or her alone? The answer is, as a general rule, to leave the person alone. If the withdrawal seems excessive or too persistent, it is possible it may herald the recurrence of more severe symptoms and will require evaluation by the patient's psychiatrist. But in most cases the withdrawal is being used as a means for coping with the internal chaos in the patient's brain and is an appropriate response. Family members should remind themselves not to take such withdrawal as a personal rejection but should keep themselves available. As described usefully by one mother: "When our son was acutely ill we managed best by not being too intrusive, by not trying too hard to draw him out of his world and into ours, but by always being available at the times when he needed our support and tried to communicate."

In social situations it is important not to expect too much from persons with schizophrenia. Remember that they may be having problems assimilating sensory input or understanding what is being said. Minimize the number and scale of social events in the house in order to relieve pressure on the person. Patients can often handle one visitor at a time, but groups are usually overwhelming to them. Similarly, taking the person to group gatherings or parties outside the home is often a difficult and confusing experience for the person.

Experiment to find leisure time activities that are enjoyable. Those with a single (or dominant) sensory input are usually most successful. Thus, a person with schizophrenia will often enjoy cartoons or a travelogue on TV but will not be able to understand a show with a plot. A boxing match may be preferable to a baseball game. Visual spectacles, such as a circus or ice show, are often very enjoyable, while a play is often a total failure. Individuals are, of course, different in this regard, and it is necessary to explore different possibilities. The fact that people enjoyed something before they became ill does not mean that they necessarily will enjoy it after they become ill.

A common trap that families frequently fall into is to blame *all* the person's undesirable or unwanted behavior on the disease. It should be called "the disease trap." Every little shortcoming, including the person's failure to pick up dirty socks or replace the cap on the tube of toothpaste, is blamed on schizophrenia. Families need to remind themselves that human beings come with peccadilloes built in and that there are few around who have achieved perfection. Resist the temptation to blame everything on schizophrenia and ask how many mistakes you made in the last week. Along the same line, allow individuals with schizophrenia to have a bad day now and then, just as we allow those of us without schizophrenia to have a bad day. We all need such days since our neurochemical and neurophysiological machinery does not work perfectly all the time; extending the privilege of a bad day to individuals with schizophrenia is both common sense and common courtesy.

Above all, cultivate the art of being unflappable. Radiate quiet confidence that you can handle any idea, however strange, that your relative may come up with. If the person's auditory hallucinations are worse that morning, simply comment on it matter-of-factly, just as if you noticed that a person's arthritis is worse: "I'm sorry to see that the voices are bothering you more today." One parent said, "The most remarkable lesson I have learned about managing a schizophrenic person at home is to try to stay as calm as possible. The upsets and delusions have not been caused by me, and being calm keeps my son that way also. I might be heaving inside but my behavior on the outside is controlled." The epitome of unflappability was illustrated by Pliny Earle, one of the best-known nineteenth-century American psychiatrists. Earle described the superintendent of an insane asylum who went to the top of the hospital's tower accompanied by one of his patients:

> While admiring the extensive and beautiful prospect spread before them, the patient, with much excitement, suddenly seized the superintendent by the arm, and pressed him toward the edge of the tower, exclaiming, "Let's jump down, and thus immortalize ourselves!" The superintendent very coolly arrested the patient's attention, and replied: "Jump down! Why, any fool can do that. Let's go down and jump up!" The proposition struck the fancy of the patient, and thus the two were saved from their impending peril.

If the family member with schizophrenia lives at home, two things are essential—solitude and structure. A person with schizophrenia needs his or her own room, a quiet place that can be used for withdrawing. Families solve this problem in a variety of ways, including putting a small house trailer in the backyard. Structure is also helpful for most persons with schizophrenia, and they function better with regular meal hours, chores, and a predictable daily and weekly routine. One mother said:

I found structure was very important during the more difficult days. Things were done similarly each day and at designated times, and every day of the week had its individual character which was kept as consistent as possible. This seemed to give him a sense of order, that life was predictable, and also established a sense of time.

At the same time that routines are established, realize that the person with schizophrenia may deviate from them for no apparent reason. This is especially true of sleeping and eating routines. One father complained about his son, "My wife will cook a meal, and then he doesn't want it. Then two hours later he suddenly decides he does." An admirable solution to this kind of problem was outlined by this mother:

> The second practical suggestion concerns the schizophrenic's need for a sudden intake of food. At least in the case of our son, available wholesome snacks are very important. I've learned to keep yogurt, cheese, cold meat, etc., in the refrigerator; fruit on the table; and quick canned meals on the shelves. All this has seemed more important than a regular schedule of meals, although three good meals a day helps, too. The strict time doesn't matter. If Jim fixes himself a can of stew at four in the afternoon, I simply leave his dinner ready for him to heat up when he's ready.

Another thing needed for a family member with schizophrenia whether he/she is living at home or just visiting is a set of clearly defined limits regarding which behaviors are not acceptable. A failure to bathe for several weeks has consequences that affect all family members. No family should tolerate assaultive behavior (as discussed in chapter 11) or dangerous behavior (e.g., smoking in bed), and this message must be conveyed clearly and unambiguously. The consequences for such behaviors should also be spelled out in advance and the family must be willing to follow through on the consequences if it becomes necessary to do so.

Another problem that perplexes many families is the amount of independence and autonomy that can be given to a person with schizophrenia. The problem is similar to that faced by parents of adolescent children. As a general rule, persons should be given as much autonomy and independence as they can handle, and this should be done in a graduated series of steps. For example, a person who believes he or she should be able to travel alone to a concert and stay out late should be given the opportunity to demonstrate readiness by successfully going to the store regularly, traveling alone to the halfway house during the day, avoiding street drugs, and not getting into trouble in public because of bizarre behavior. I have known families who discreetly followed their family member on initial forays into the community to ensure that no harm befell the patient. When the patient asks for more autonomy, the family should set up a series of conditions that must be met before the autonomy can be granted; for example, a patient who asks to travel home alone from the halfway house might be told that this can be tried once the patient has demonstrated familiarity with the bus route and has successfully gone for two weeks without forgetting to lock the door of the house.

Chores are another means by which persons with schizophrenia may demonstrate their readiness for more independence. Sweeping, cleaning, doing the dishes, taking out the garbage, feeding the dog, and weeding are all examples of chores that may be appropriate to assign to the ill family member. Families are sometimes reluctant to assign such chores, fearing that any stress will cause a recurrence of the patient's symptoms. Patients who are lazy may encourage such fears, pleading illness whenever there is work to be done. One mother described the resentment that is an inevitable consequence of this situation: "It's so annoying when you've got lots of housework to do, and there he is, a fine healthy-looking young man, and he just sits there doing absolutely nothing." Doing chores will not cause a patient to become sicker, and such chores are used extensively in halfway house settings and clubhouse programs. They are an ideal way for patients to assume more independence and they increase the person's self-esteem at the same time. I have seen some extremely psychotic patients doing chores quite nicely and feeling better for having done so.

The management of the patient's money may cause the most difficulty of all. Most patients know that a portion of their SSI check is earmarked for their personal needs, and they believe they should have the right to spend it however they please. They should be reminded, however, that the personal portion of the check is intended to cover necessities, such as clothes, as well as cigarettes and sodas.

Occasionally persons with schizophrenia can take total responsibility for their money and can manage it with minimal difficulties. I knew one woman severely affected with paranoid schizophrenia, for example, who was very delusional much of the time but was able to take monthly trips to the bank and manage her funds. Predictably, she would not tell the doctors or nurses how much money she had. More common, however, is the person who cannot manage money at all; some patients, for example, will repeatedly give away any money they have to the first person who asks for it. For such persons it may be useful to link autonomy in money management to other behavior indicating independence. For example, if patients have difficulty with personal hygiene and grooming, it may be appropriate to agree to give them more money to spend as they wish every week that they successfully take a shower without being told. The successful performance of chores is another way that patients can demonstrate that they are ready for greater financial responsibility.

Issues of independence and money management may also cause problems for families because of the family's inability to understand that their family member is getting better. When one has lived with a severely psychotic individual who may have even needed help in dressing himself, it is often difficult to recognize a few weeks later that the person is now able to travel by bus alone and manage a weekly allowance. Families have often been both scared and scarred, and their ability to respond and adapt sometimes becomes constricted.

As discussed previously, education for families is extremely important in helping them to survive schizophrenia. Support groups, such as those organized by state and local NAMI organizations (see appendix D), are also very helpful.

For families who have their ill family member living at home, it is essential to periodically have some time off. One way to accomplish this is by respite care. For example the Palo Alto Veterans Administration Medical Center in California has a program whereby people with schizophrenia who are living at home can be readmitted to the hospital for two to seven days every two months to provide the family some respite. In South Carolina, the Alliance for the Mentally Ill, in conjunction with the South Carolina Department of Mental Health, began in 1990 a one-week summer camp respite program for individuals with serious mental illnesses to give the families a week off from their usual caregiving responsibilities.

THE RISE AND FALL OF EXPRESSED EMOTION

Since the early 1980s, one of the impediments for families attempting to cope with schizophrenia has been the concept of expressed emotion. The concept originated in England in the 1960s, when it was observed that some patients with schizophrenia relapsed when they returned home to live with their families. Out of this observation came a series of studies attempting to identify the family characteristics that were likely to produce relapse. These characteristics included being overly critical, hostile, overinvolved and overidentified with the ill family member, intrusive, and highly expressive of emotions. The mother in a high expressed-emotion (high EE) family says things like: "John, you look like a dirty slob. Why can't you ever change your clothes? It's very embarrassing to me." By contrast, the mother in a low EE family handles the same situation by saying things like: "John, you would probably feel much better if you put on some clean clothes."

The corollary that follows from high EE research is that families exhibiting such characteristics can be educated to be less critical, less involved, etc., and that when this occurs the family member with schizophrenia is less likely to relapse. As described by one of the major researchers in this field, the relapse rate can be lowered "by teaching the patients and their families better methods of coping with stressful events and by changing the attitudes of key family members in the direction of greater support, less destructive criticism, and less emotional overinvolvement."

At first glance, research on expressed emotion seems reasonable enough. On closer inspection, however, this research elicits some expressed emotions from me personally that can be summarized as follows.

Surprise: Given what is known about the difficulties people with schizophrenia have in sorting sensory stimuli and messages (see chapter 2), it would be surprising to find that they were not affected by overtly expressed criticisms, hostility, or overinvolvement by family members. The main thesis of EE research appears to be, in short, self-evident. It is therefore surprising to find so much attention and research resources devoted to demonstrating the obvious. In 1985 alone, for example, NIMH awarded grants totaling $687,000 for EE research, and during that year four new books deriving from this work were published, with such titles as *Expressed Emotion in Families, Working with Families of the Mentally Ill, The Family and Schizophrenia, and Family Management of Schizophrenia.*

Skepticism: Given the manpower and hours devoted to working with high EE families, teaching them to become more tolerant, etc., it is difficult to imagine that the findings of the studies on expressed emotion would ever be of more than academic interest. Compliance with medication-taking remains by far the single most important factor determining relapse rates; if half the energy devoted to educating families about high EE had been devoted instead to ensuring compliance with medications, the relapse rate of the patients would have decreased much more dramatically than anything demonstrated by EE. There were also many methodological problems with EE research that elicited skepticism of its importance; included are the well-known Hawthorn effect (things will change just because they are being closely studied) and the apparent confusion between cause and effect in many of the research projects (e.g., did the family's high expressed emotion cause the relapse or did the characteristics of the patient elicit the expressed emotion?).

Suspicion: Although most of the EE researchers seemed genuinely convinced that families did not cause schizophrenia in their family member, that is not true of all of them. Dr. Michael Goldstein of the University of California, Los Angeles, who was until his recent death one of the most prominent researchers in the EE field, carried out research on disturbed adolescent boys that he claimed "provides evidence that family attributes measured during adolescence are associated with the subsequent presence of schizophrenia or schizophrenia-related disorders in the offspring once they entered young adulthood." In other words, the family caused the schizophrenia. In the *New York Times*, Goldstein was quoted as claiming that "the parents of these kids engaged in character assassinations." Such assertions made families of people with schizophrenia justifiably suspicious of EE research. Was EE research merely the bastard offspring of Gregory Bateson's double-bind?

In recent years, the expressed emotion concept has lost favor and is no longer prominent. A major reason for this has been an increasingly widespread suspicion that expressed emotion does not cause the exacerbation of symptoms, but rather the exacerbation of symptoms produces expressed emotions. This suspicion has been fully supported by the research of Suzanne King at McGill University, who measured expressed emotions (critical comments and emotional overinvolvement) as well as the patients' symptoms in 28 families over a two-year period. What she found was that critical comments and emotional overinvolvement "are both influenced by the patient's total symptoms severity" and "appear to be more effect than cause."

Although the concept of expressed emotion has quietly passed away, does it have anything useful to teach us? People with schizophrenia do best in situations where people are calm and communicate clearly and directly. The attributes of the right attitude discussed above (sense of perspective, acceptance of the illness, family balance, and expectations that are realistic) are the antithesis of high expressed emotions; insofar as families are striving to achieve these, they should not worry about expressed emotion.

What about counseling or family "therapy" to help the family learn to live with the disease? If families wish to seek help from a counseling professional, that may be useful in some instances. Be very careful, however, that the professional has an educational approach and will help you learn ways to manage the family situation, not a psychoanalytic approach that will merely produce guilt and blame. Families with mentally ill family members need to be educated, not "treated," and to do everything they can to learn how to live with a difficult situation. This is precisely the same for families with members affected by multiple sclerosis, polio, severe diabetes, renal disease, or any other long-term disabling disease.

EFFECTS OF SCHIZOPHRENIA ON SIBLINGS, CHILDREN, AND SPOUSES

Although most family accounts of schizophrenia focus on the effects of the disease on mothers and fathers of ill individuals, schizophrenia is a problem for other family members as well. Brothers, sisters, sons, daughters, husbands, wives, uncles, aunts, grandfathers, and grandmothers may all be profoundly involved in the care of family members with schizophrenia. As such they have all of the same problems as do mothers and fathers. There are certain problems, however, that other family members confront frequently.

Shame and Embarrassment: Family members may be profoundly embarrassed by the psychotic behavior of their ill relative. Roxanne Lanquetot, whose mother had schizophrenia, recalls being "convinced that I would have been better off an orphan, I tried to hide my mother and deny her existence by pretending she didn't exist." Kathleen Gordon's ill mother would take her children "and sit us down on the side of a busy street and count trucks for hours on end. And write down the names of all the trucks that went by." One young woman I know almost literally stumbled over her mother, homeless and psychotic, in an airport as she was returning to college. And Meg Livergood, stopped for a red light in Miami, saw her homeless sister with schizophrenia shuffle across the street in front of her car but was too embarrassed to call out to her. One common reaction to such shame and embarrassment is to move as far away from the family home as possible.

Anger, Jealousy, and Resentment: Individuals with schizophrenia frequently occupy an inordinate amount of their family's energy and time, leaving little for other family members. Wendy Kelley recalled that when her sister developed schizophrenia "suddenly both my brother and I felt there was no time for us; everyone was consumed by what was going on with my sister." Jody Mozham, whose father had schizophrenia, remembers being "envious watching my friends have regular conversations with their fathers. . . . I had a father, yet I didn't." Anger and resentment may become exacerbated if large amounts of the family's financial resources, such as money set aside for college, must be used to pay for the ill person's treatment.

Depression and Guilt: When a person develops schizophrenia, other family members may lose a relationship. Ami Brodoff expressed this loss poignantly:

> That day, many days before it, and many days since, I've missed my older brother with the persistent ache and longing usually reserved for a loved one lost through death. Although grieving for someone who has died is painful, some sense of peace and acceptance is ultimately possible. However, mourning for a loved one who is alive—in your very presence and yet in vital ways inaccessible to you—has a lonely, unreal quality that is extraordinary painful.

One man whose wife developed schizophrenia described the loss of the relationship as follows:

> I feel such great sorrow towards my wife of twenty-five years. The person I knew died in 1985. I try to grieve, but it's complicated by the body that keeps reappearing. It looks like her, but it's not.

And a woman whose husband developed schizophrenia noted:

> My husband's schizophrenia is like a third member in our marriage. It is always there. Even with medication, we still deal with his paranoia, his isolation, and his need for my full attention on a daily basis.

The family members who did not develop schizophrenia may also develop survivor guilt, a common phenomenon in airplane accidents and other random tragedies. Paul Aronowitz described this when he announced to his brother, who was affected with schizophrenia, that he was getting married: "'It's funny,' my brother answered matter-of-factly. 'You're getting married, and I've never even had a girlfriend.'"

Pressure to Succeed: The siblings or children of individuals with schizophrenia often try to compensate for their ill family member by being as perfect as possible. In a study of the children of mentally ill parents, Kauffman et al. labeled the extremely competent offspring as "superkids."

Fear of Becoming Sick: Most siblings and children of individuals with schizophrenia are themselves haunted by a fear that they too will develop the disease. As Roxanne Lanquetot recalls: "Growing up with a mentally ill mother was oppressive and worrisome and it interfered with the development of my sense of self. I was terrified that I was like my mother and therefore had something wrong with me."

Forced to Play Unwanted Roles: Schizophrenia changes family relationships, often profoundly. Margaret Moorman in *My Sister's Keeper* described how difficult it was to change from being a younger sister to being, in essence, a mother for her older sister. Husbands and wives whose spouse becomes ill often must become their spouse's parent. Jody Mozham described the effect of her father's illness on her mother: "She once knew this dream man that turned into an invalid. No longer did she have the role of being a wife, she was his guardian." Kathleen Gordon, both of whose parents had schizophrenia, even at age four "was aware that I could not trust my parents in what they told me to do or in their behavior" and by age nine was the "virtual head of her household."

There are many things that family members can do to alleviate some of the burden of having a relative with schizophrenia. Education is most important, and this should always include even small children in the family whose ability to understand is much greater than most adults assume. Some articles and books targeting the problems of relatives of individuals with schizophrenia are listed at the end of this chapter under "Recommended Further Reading." Support groups can be extremely helpful, including groups specifically set up for other relatives. Julie Johnson, whose brother has schizophrenia, developed an eight-stage healing process for siblings as outlined in her book *Hidden Victims— Hidden Healers*. Acceptance of the inevitable role shifts comes slowly but is necessary because siblings often end up with at least some responsibility for their ill brother or sister once their parents have died.

Finally, many brothers, sisters, husbands, wives, sons, and daughters are learning to cope with schizophrenia by becoming advocates for better services and more research, working with organizations such as NAMI and the Treatment Advocacy Center. Advocacy, in fact, is one of the most useful and therapeutic means for coping by the unaffected family members, and many suggestions are listed in chapter 15. A corollary of this is that many schizophrenia researchers, including myself, began working in this field primarily because we had a family member affected with the disease. I also know many clinical psychiatrists, psychologists, psychiatric social workers, and psychiatric nurses whose work is motivated by the fact that someone in their family has schizophrenia. They tend to be among the best professionals.

MINIMIZING RELAPSES

One of the keys to surviving schizophrenia is to minimize relapses. The threat of relapse is a perpetual shadow hanging over individuals with schizophrenia and their families. Each minor deviation from the person's usual behavior is regarded as suspect. The question hangs in the air, often not expressed in words but rather as a sideways glance: "Is this the beginning of another episode?" "Should I/he/she take additional medicine?" "Should I say anything?"

As discussed in chapter 11, medication compliance is the single most important thing a person with schizophrenia can do to minimize relapses. Individuals who take their medication regularly will have far fewer relapses than those who are intermittently compliant or noncompliant. Substance abuse is another powerful predictor of relapse; in one study of 37 individuals with schizophrenia, all of whom were on long-acting injectable antipsychotic medication, those who were abusing alcohol or drugs had four times as many relapses as those who were not substance abusers.

In one of the largest studies of relapse in schizophrenia, 145 patients were questioned regarding the symptoms they experienced in the early stages of their relapses. The symptoms reported most frequently were being tense and nervous, eating and sleeping problems, trouble concentrating, enjoying things less, and restlessness. Marvin Herz, one of the study's authors, concluded that "it is extremely important to educate both patients and families" about the symptoms and signs of relapse, and that "family involvement is a crucial component in the treatment of schizophrenia."

In England, Max Birchwood and his colleagues have done studies to ascertain which symptoms are the best predictors of impending relapse. Out of this work has evolved a "Warning Signals Scale," which should be kept by all individuals with schizophrenia and their families. It includes eight questions that, if answered in the affirmative, may indicate an impending relapse.

WARNING SIGNALS SCALE

This questionnaire concerns *new or worsened* problems and complaints which you have experienced during the *last 2 weeks*.

	Yes	No
1. Sleep has been restless or unsettled	☐	☐
2. Feeling tense, afraid or unsettled	☐	☐
3. Having difficulty concentrating	☐	☐
4. Feeling irritable or quick tempered	☐	☐
5. Feeling unable to cope, difficulty in managing everyday tasks and interests	☐	☐
6. Feeling tired or lacking energy	☐	☐
7. Feeling depressed or low	☐	☐
8. Feeling confused or puzzled	☐	☐

In many cases the patient and/or family has learned over time which symptoms and signs heralded relapse. One woman who had had multiple episodes of schizophrenia described to me the things she looked for: "My main prodromal symptoms are quick irritability and anger and, when out-of-doors, thinking that everyone I see looks familiar although I do not know *whom* they remind me of." Another woman described her relapse as occurring in four stages:

In the first stage, I feel just a bit estranged from myself. From my eyes the world seems brighter and more sharply defined, and my voice seems to echo a bit. I start to feel uncomfortable being around people, and also uncomfortable in sharing my changing feelings.

In the second stage, everything appears a bit clouded. This cloudiness increases as does my confusion and fear, especially fear of letting others know what is happening to me. I try to make logical excuses and to get control over the details of my life, and often make frantic efforts to organize everything; cleaning, cataloging, and self-involved activity is high. Songs on the radio begin to have greater meaning, and people seem to be looking at me strangely and laughing, giving me subtle messages I can't understand. I start to misinterpret people's actions toward me, which increases my fear of losing control.

In the third stage, I believe I am beginning to understand why terrible things are happening to me: others are the cause of it. This belief comes with a clearing of sight, an increasing level of sound, and an increasing sensitivity to the looks of others. I carry on an argument with myself as to whether these things are true: "Is the FBI or the devil causing this? . . . No, that's crazy thinking. I wonder why people are making me crazy."

In the fourth and last stage, I become chaotic and see, hear, and believe all manner of things. I no longer question my beliefs, but act on them.

Each person with schizophrenia has their own particular symptom pattern when relapsing, and that pattern tends to be similar from relapse to relapse. Personally, I find changes in the person's sleep pattern an especially useful indicator, and I ask about this frequently.

How can relapses be minimized? First, everyone with schizophrenia should keep their own relapse symptom list, and it should be familiar to their family and friends. Individuals with schizophrenia should try to identify those things that tend to exacerbate relapses (e.g., the stress of social situations) and avoid them when necessary. For example, it may be possible to attend the wedding of a friend when things are going well, but it may be best to call and say you cannot come if you think that you might be in the early stages of a relapse. Spending more time alone, reducing work hours, and getting more exercise are all examples of strategies used by some people with schizophrenia to reduce stress.

Always keep in mind that the single most common cause of relapse is not getting enough medication. This may be because the person stopped taking it, or because the doctor reduced the dosage, or simply because the person needs more medication at this point in their illness. And extra medication in the early stages of relapse will frequently abort it and get the person back to baseline. For this reason I give many patients an extra supply of medication and allow them to increase it on their own if they feel that they need it. Physicians do this all the time with patients with diabetes who may need more insulin on some days and less on other days, and I find the same principle useful in schizo-phrenia.

All of this assumes, of course, a best-case scenario in which the person with schizophrenia has awareness of his/her illness and therefore can assess warning signs of relapse. As discussed in chapters 2 and 11, approximately half of individuals with schizophrenia have limited awareness. One possible strategy for minimizing relapses in such cases is to take videotapes of the persons when they are very psychotic, then to show them the videotapes when they are in remission. A preliminary study of this strategy reported some improvement in the person's aware-ness of illness. Whether such improvement is translated into fewer relapses is currently under study.

Finally, remember that schizophrenia has ups and downs for no apparent reason, just as multiple sclerosis and Parkinson's disease do, and most people have occasional relapses no matter how hard they try to avoid them. This is part of the disease process and must be accepted. For most people with schizophrenia, then, relapses can be reduced but they cannot be prevented altogether.

RECOMMENDED FURTHER READING

In the past decade, there has been an outpouring of articles and books written to help consumers and families survive schizophrenia. Many of these are listed below without annotation. Appendix A includes my selections of the most useful books, with annotation. Some of the books are out of print but may be available at your local library or used book-store (over the Internet, try www.bookfinder.com).

For Families in General

Adamec, C. *How to Live with a Mentally Ill Person.* New York: John Wiley, 1996.

Backlar, P. *The Family Face of Schizophrenia.* New York: Putnam, 1994. Paper-back by Tarcher, 1995.

Baronet, A.-M. "Factors Associated with Caregiver Burden in Mental Illness: A Critical Review of the Research Literature." *Clinical Psychological Review* 19 (1999): 819–41.

Bernheim, K. F., and A. F. Lehman. *Working with Families of the Mentally Ill.* New York: Norton, 1985.

Bernheim, K. F., R. R. J. Lewine, and C. T. Beale. *The Caring Family: Living with Chronic Mental Illness.* New York: Random House, 1982.

Busick, B. S., and M. Gorman. *Ill Not Insane.* Boulder, Colo.: New Idea Press, 1986.

Carter, R. *Helping Someone with a Mental Illness.* New York: Times Books, 1998.

Creer, C., and J. Wing. *Schizophrenia at Home.* London: Institute of Psychiatry, 1974.

Dearth, N. S., B. J. Labenski, E. Mott, et al. *Families Helping Families.* New York: Norton, 1986.

Deveson, A. *Tell Me I'm Here.* New York: Penguin, 1992.

Esser, A. H., and S. D. Lacey. *Mental Illness: A Homecare Guide.* New York: John Wiley, 1989.

Farhall, J., B. Webster, B. Hocking, et al. "Training to Enhance Partnerships Between Mental Health Professionals and Family Caregivers: A Comparative Study." *Psychiatric Services* 49 (1998): 1488–90.

Flach, F. *Rickie.* New York: Fawcett Columbine, 1990.

Garson, S. *Out of Our Minds.* Buffalo: Prometheus Books, 1986.

Hatfield, A. B. *Family Education in Mental Illness.* New York: Guilford Press, 1990. Paperback edition 1999.

Hatfield, A. B., ed. *Families of the Mentally Ill: Meeting the Challenge.* San Francisco: Jossey-Bass, 1987.

Hatfield, A. B., and H. P. Lefley. *Surviving Mental Illness: Stress, Coping and Adaptation.* New York: Guilford Press, 1993. Paperback edition 1999.

Hatfield, A. B., and H. P. Lefley, eds. *Families of the Mentally Ill: Coping and Adaptation.* New York: Guilford Press, 1987.

Hinckley, J., and J. A. Hinckley. *Breaking Points.* Grand Rapids, Mich.: Chosen Books, 1985.

Howe, G. *The Reality of Schizophrenia.* London: Faber and Faber, 1991.

Howells, J. G., and W. R. Guirguis. *The Family and Schizophrenia.* New York: International Universities Press, 1985.

Jeffries, J. J., E. Plummer, M. V. Seeman, and J. F. Thornton. *Living and Working with Schizophrenia.* Toronto: University of Toronto Press, 1990. (This is a revised edition of the book by M. V. Seeman et al.)

Johnson, J. *Hidden Victims—Hidden Healers.* New York: Doubleday, 1988. 2nd ed. paperback, by PEMA Publications, 1994.

Johnson, J. *Understanding Mental Illness.* Minneapolis: Lerner, 1989.

Keefe, R. and P. Harvey. *Understanding Schizophrenia.* New York: Free Press, 1994.

Lamb, H. R. *Treating the Long-Term Mentally Ill.* San Francisco: Jossey-Bass, 1982.

Lefley, H. P., and D. L. Johnson, eds. *Families as Allies in Treatment of the Mentally Ill.* Washington: American Psychiatric Press, 1990.

Marsh, D. T. *Families and Mental Illness: New Directions in Professional Practice.* New York: Praeger, 1992.

Marsh, D. T. *Serious Mental Illness and the Family.* New York: John Wiley, 1998.

McElroy, E., ed. *Children and Adolescents with Mental Illness: A Parents Guide.* Kensington, Md.: Woodbine House, 1988.

Mendel, W. *Treating Schizophrenia.* San Francisco: Jossey-Bass, 1989.

Mueser, K. T., and S. Gingerich. *Coping with Schizophrenia: A Guide for Families.* Oakland, Calif.: New Harbinger, 1994.

Rollin, Henry, ed. *Coping with Schizophrenia.* National Schizophrenia Fellowship. London: Burnett Books, 1980.

Secunda, V. *When Madness Comes Home.* New York: Hyperion, 1997.

Vine, P. *Families in Pain: Children, Siblings, Spouses, and Parents of the Mentally Ill Speak Out.* New York: Pantheon, 1982.

Walsh, M. *Schizophrenia: Straight Talk for Family and Friends.* New York: Morrow, 1985.

Wasow, M. *Coping with Schizophrenia: A Survival Manual for Parents, Relatives and Friends.* Palo Alto: Science and Behavior Books, 1982.

Wasow, M. *The Skipping Stone: Ripple Effects of Mental Illness in the Family.* Palo Alto: Science and Behavioral Books, 1995.

Wechsler, J. *In a Darkness.* Miami: Pickering, 1988. Originally published in 1972.

Wilson, L. *This Stranger My Son.* New York: New American Library, 1968.

Woolis, R. *When Someone You Love Has a Mental Illness.* New York: Perigee Books, 1992.

Consumers' Viewpoint

Barham, P., and R. Hayward. "In Sickness and in Health: Dilemmas of the Person with Severe Mental Illness." *Psychiatry* 61 (1998): 163–70.

Carter, D. M., A. MacKinnon, and D. L. Copolov. "Patients' Strategies for Coping with Auditory Hallucinations." *Journal of Nervous and Mental Disease* 184 (1996): 159–64.

"Consumer-Survivors Share Awakening Insights." *Journal of the California Alliance for the Mentally Ill* 7 (1996): 32–58.

Davidson, L., and D. Stayner. "Loss, Loneliness, and the Desire for Love: Perspectives on the Social Lives of People with Schizophrenia." *Psychiatric Rehabilitation Journal* 20 (1997): 3–12.

Davidson, L., M. Chinman, B. Kloos, et al. "Peer Support Among Individuals with Severe Mental Illness: A Review of the Evidence." *Clinical Psychology: Science and Practice* 6 (1999): 165–87.

Frese, F. J. "Twelve Aspects of Coping for Persons with Schizophrenia." *Innovations and Research* 2 (1993): 39–46.

"Self-Help." *Journal of the California Alliance for the Mentally Ill* 6 (1996).

Leete, E. "The Treatment of Schizophrenia: A Patient's Perspective." *Hospital and Community Psychiatry* 38 (1987): 486–91.

Leete, E. "How I Perceive and Manage My Illness." *Schizophrenia Bulletin* 15 (1989): 197–200.

Siblings' Viewpoint

Brodoff, A. S. "First Person Account: Schizophrenia Through a Sister's Eyes— The Burden of Invisible Baggage." *Schizophrenia Bulletin* 14 (1988): 113–16.

Conroy, P. *The Prince of Tides*. Boston: Houghton Mifflin, 1986. Paperback by Bantam Books, 1987.

Dickens, R. M., and D. T. Marsh, eds. *Anguished Voices: Siblings and Adult Children of Persons with Psychiatric Disabilities*. Boston: Center for Psychiatric Rehabilitation, 1994.

Gerace, L. M., D. Camilleri, and L. Ayres. "Sibling Perspectives on Schizophrenia and the Family." *Schizophrenia Bulletin* 19 (1993): 637–47.

Greenberg, J. S., H. W. Kim, and J. R. Greenley. "Factors Associated with Subjective Burden in Siblings of Adults with Severe Mental Illness." *American Journal of Orthopsychiatry* 67 (1997): 231–41.

Horwitz, A. V. "Siblings as Caregivers for the Seriously Mentally Ill." *Milbank Quarterly* 71 (1993): 323–39.

Hyland, B. *The Girl with the Crazy Brother*. New York: Franklin Watts, 1987.

Lamb, W. *I Know This Much Is True*. New York: Regan Books, 1998. Paperback by HarperPerennial, 1999.

Landeen, J., C. Whelton, S. Dermer et al. "Needs of Well Siblings of Persons with Schizophrenia." *Hospital and Community Psychiatry* 43 (1992): 266–69.

Marsh, D. T., N. F. Appleby, R. M. Dickens, et al. "Anguished Voices: Impact of Mental Illness on Siblings and Children." *Innovations and Research* 2 (1993): 25–34.

Marsh, D. T., R. M. Dickens, R. D. Koeske, et al. "Troubled Journey: Siblings and Children of People with Mental Illness." *Innovations and Research* 2 (1993): 13–23.

Moorman, M. *My Sister's Keeper*. New York: Norton, 1992.

Neugeboren, J. *Imagining Robert: My Brother, Madness and Survival*. New York: Morrow, 1997.

Saylor, A. V. "Nannie: A Sister's Story." *Innovations and Research* 3 (1994): 34–37.

Simon, C. *Mad House: Growing Up in the Shadow of Mentally Ill Siblings*. New York: Doubleday, 1997.

Swados, E. *The Four of Us: A Family Memoir*. New York: Farrar, Straus and Giroux, 1991. Paperback by Penguin Books, 1993.

Children of Parents with Schizophrenia Viewpoint

Caton, C. L. M., F. Cournos, A. Felix, et al. "Childhood Experiences and Current Adjustment of Offspring of Indigent Patients with Schizophrenia." *Psychiatric Services* 49 (1998): 86–90.

Crosby, D. "First Person Account: Growing Up with a Schizophrenic Mother." *Schizophrenia Bulletin* 15 (1989): 507–9.

Higgins, J., R. Gore, D. Gutkind, et al. "Effects of Child-Rearing by Schizophrenic Mothers: A 25-Year Follow-up." *Acta Psychiatrica Scandinavica* 96 (1997): 402–04.

Holley, T. E., and J. Holley. *My Mother's Keeper: A Daughter's Memoir of Growing Up in the Shadow of Schizophrenia*. New York: Morrow, 1997. Reprinted in paperback, 1998.

"Offspring." *Journal of the California Alliance for the Mentally Ill* 7 (1996).

Kauffman, C., H. Grunebaum, B. Cohler, et al. "Superkids: Competent Children of Psychotic Mothers." *American Journal of Psychiatry* 136 (1979): 1398–1402.

Lachenmeyer, N. *The Outsider: A Journey into My Father's Struggle with Madness*. New York: Broadway Books, 2000.

Lanquetot, R. "First Person Account: Confessions of the Daughter of a Schizophrenic." *Schizophrenia Bulletin* 10 (1984): 467–71.

Lanquetot, R. "First Person Account: On Being Daughter and Mother." *Schizophrenia Bulletin* 14 (1988): 337–41.

Olson, L. S. *He Was Still My Daddy*. Portland, Ore.: Ogden Howe, 1994.

Riley, J. *Crazy Quilt*. New York: Morrow, 1984.

Williams, A. S. "A Group for the Adult Daughters of Mentally Ill Mothers: Looking Backwards and Forwards." *British Journal of Mental Psychology* 71 (1998): 73–83.

Husband or Wife of Person with Schizophrenia Viewpoint

"First Person Account: Life with a Mentally Ill Spouse." *Schizophrenia Bulletin* 20 (1994): 227–29.

"Spouses." *Journal of the California Alliance for the Mentally Ill* 9 (1998).

Mannion, E. "Resilience and Burden in Spouses of People with Mental Illness." *Psychiatric Rehabilitation Journal* 20 (1996): 13–23.

Nasar, Sylvia. *A Beautiful Mind: A Biography of John Forbes Nash, Jr., Winner of the Nobel Prize in Economics, 1994.* New York: Simon and Schuster, 1998. Paperback by Touchstone Books, 1999.

13

COMMONLY ASKED QUESTIONS

There is no disease more to be dreaded than madness. For what greater
unhappiness can befall a man than to be deprived of his reason and
understanding.

Richard Mead, *Medical Precepts and Cautions*, 1751

Schizophrenia is like a movie that never ends. Even worse is the fact that
you are in the movie. Just when you think you have seen it all, a new
scene presents itself, with new questions.

The following are some of the questions patients and families frequently ask. For many, there are no simple answers, because each individual with schizophrenia and each family is a little different.

DOES SCHIZOPHRENIA CHANGE THE
UNDERLYING PERSONALITY?

Does schizophrenia change a person's underlying personality? For
many years, based on my experiences in observing my sister and in
working with hundreds of people afflicted with the disease, I suspected
that it did not but could find no scientific study to verify my suspicions.
For example, I remember one young man whose symptoms I helped to
get under control using a combination of antipsychotic medications.
His family, however, kept complaining that it was impossible to get him
up in the morning and urged me to try different medications. After
doing this for several months without success, I inquired whether the
family had had difficulty getting him up before he got sick. "Oh yes,"
they said, "he would never get up then either, just like he doesn't get up

now." That ended my medication changes and taught me a most useful lesson.

In the early 1990s, an opportunity arose to ascertain whether schizophrenia does or does not change the underlying personality. We studied identical twins in which one had schizophrenia and the other was well. Since personality traits of identical twins are remarkably alike, by testing the personality traits of twins in which one is sick and one is well it should theoretically be possible to tell how much a person's personality has been changed by having schizophrenia. A total of 27 identical twin pairs discordant for schizophrenia were tested.

The results were clear and unequivocal. On personality scales that measured traits such as happiness, nervousness, and satisfaction with social relationships, the twins with schizophrenia scored significantly lower, as would be expected from having the disease. However, on the remaining scales of personality traits there were remarkably few differences, and on many scales, such as adherence to traditional values and interest in risk-taking behavior, there were virtually no differences. A pair of quiet, pious women were both still quiet and pious even though one had severe schizophrenia. A pair of hell-raising, risk-taking young men were both still raising hell and taking risks, even though one had schizophrenia. The underlying, core personality of the person with schizophrenia had been only minimally altered.

The fact that schizophrenia alters a person's underlying personality relatively little has been noted by other observers. The mother of one of the most severely affected women I have treated expressed it as follows: "The daughter I would have had—were it not for this evil illness—exists in embryo in the daughter I do have." The disease and the person are not the same; they can, and should, be separated. Schizophrenia is an equal opportunity disease and randomly affects personality types from the most selfish and narcissistic to the most giving and altruistic. Once the person has schizophrenia, those underlying personality traits are still visible beneath the delusions, hallucinations, thinking disorders, and altered affect.

It is always tempting, of course, to attribute all undesirable personality traits in a person to the disease. I have known families who retrospectively idealized the personality of their family member before the person got schizophrenia when the reality was quite different. I have also known individuals with schizophrenia who used their disease as an excuse for all of their shortcomings and weaknesses when in fact they had had the same shortcomings and weaknesses prior to becoming sick.

It should be self-evident that schizophrenia also does not change the underlying personalities of mothers, fathers, brothers, or sisters. Family members come in all personality types and are not fundamentally changed by another family member having schizophrenia. Parents and siblings may be intrusive, helpful, rejecting, or loving, but such personality traits pre-exist the onset of schizophrenia in their family member. It was in fact the existence of undesirable personality traits in some parents of individuals with schizophrenia that formed the basis of family interaction theories of schizophrenia, reviewed in chapter 7; what these researchers failed to point out was that the undesirable personality traits in these families were neither more nor less common than they were in any other family. Schizophrenia is an equal opportunity disease for families as well as for individuals.

ARE PEOPLE WITH SCHIZOPHRENIA RESPONSIBLE FOR THEIR BEHAVIOR?

One of the most challenging problems for individuals with schizophrenia, their families, mental illness professionals, and judges and juries is to assess how much control a person with schizophrenia has over his/her symptoms and behavior. Most individuals have some control and can be held at least partly responsible, but the degree varies widely from individual to individual and, in a single individual, from week to week. Many patients, for example, can suppress with great effort their auditory hallucinations or bizarre behavior for brief periods but not for long periods. The dilemma of responsibility was expressed nicely by Dr. John Wing, a leading schizophrenia researcher in England:

> Part of the peculiar difficulty in managing schizophrenia is that it lies somewhere between conditions like blindness which, though severely handicapping, do not interfere with an individual's capacity to make independent judgments about his own future, and conditions like severe mental retardation, in which it is clear that the individual will never be able to make such independent judgments. There is frequently a fluctuating degree of insight and of severity.

What should be done, for example, when your son with schizophrenia insists on suddenly disrobing in front of visiting Aunt Agatha? In some cases he may be responding to command hallucinations that are telling him that if he does not do so the world will end and he will be responsible. In other cases his disrobing may represent a complex mixture of confused thinking and resentment against some real or imagined slight by someone who looks like Aunt Agatha. In still other cases his disrobing may represent a consciously hostile gesture toward Aunt Agatha or toward his family. Some individuals with schizophrenia, just like some individuals who do not have schizophrenia, are very skilled at using their symptoms to manipulate those around them to get what they want. Some patients who are placed where they do not want to live, for example, know exactly what to do behaviorally to ensure that they will be returned to the hospital or wherever they were living previously. And I have had many patients improve and tell me explicitly, "Doc, I'm a little better but I'm not well enough to go to work."

How can you tell how much responsibility the person with schizophrenia has for his or her behavior? Family members, friends, and mental illness professionals who have known the person for a long period of time are most capable of making such assessments because they know the person's underlying personality traits. In the case cited above, the family should sit down with the person after Aunt Agatha has gone and calmly review what happened, why it happened, how it might be prevented in the future, the consequences of such behavior for the person's living at home, and the legal consequences for disrobing in public. It is often useful to include the patient's psychiatrist, counselor, social worker, or case manager in such discussions.

The question of responsibility for behavior for persons with schizophrenia becomes even more convoluted when the person is charged with a crime. In such cases the person may be declared incompetent to stand trial and involuntarily committed to a mental hospital, or he/she may be brought to trial. In such cases the insanity defense is often invoked for persons with schizophrenia.

The insanity defense dates back to the thirteenth century, when it was known as the "wild beast test" (insofar as persons are like wild beasts they cannot be held accountable). In England in the nineteenth century it was modified in the M'Naghten case to the "right or wrong test" (insofar as persons do not know right from wrong they cannot be held accountable). In the United States in recent years this has been replaced in many states by the "product test" (insofar as their acts were a product of a mental disease, persons cannot be held accountable) or by various modifications and compromises between the "right or wrong test" and the "product test." Most of these incorporate a volitional element, stating that the person acted on an "irresistible impulse."

Among the arguments urging the insanity defense for persons accused of crimes is the fact that it protects them from being simply convicted and punished as if they had been fully responsible. Thus, a person with schizophrenia who steals a car with the key in it because he thought it was his car or because voices told him to do so is not treated in the same way as a car thief who steals it to sell to others.

Arguments against use of the insanity defense are impressive, and many people have suggested that it be abolished. Deciding whether a person's behavior is a "product" of his or her mental illness is an exceedingly difficult and subjective task. As one observer has noted, "Almost all crimes, by definition, involve transgressions of societal norms that could be called insane." And in terms of an "irresistible impulse" it has been noted that "the line between an irresistible impulse and an impulse not resisted is probably no sharper than that between twilight and dusk." Such judgments are made even more difficult by the fact that they are retrospective. Who can really know what was in a person's mind when a criminal act was being committed months before he or she came to trial?

Many proposals to change the insanity defense have included a two-part trial in which the issues of guilt for the crime and extenuating circumstances (including insanity) would be separated. In the first part the only question addressed would be whether or not the accused actually committed the crime. If the person was found guilty, *then* psychiatrists and other witnesses would be allowed to testify on the person's mental state and other extenuating circumstances; this testimony would be used to help decide where the person should be sent (prison or psychiatric hospital) and for how long.

If the second part of the trial specifically addressed the question of responsibility, such a system would be a definite improvement over the current legal quagmire engendered by the insanity defense. The insanity defense as currently practiced includes an assumption that persons are either responsible or not responsible for their actions. Sane persons are considered to be responsible, insane persons to be not responsible; it is an all-or-nothing determination. Such simplistic thinking, however, contradicts the experience of everyone who has ever lived with someone with schizophrenia. People with schizophrenia sometimes are fully responsible for their behavior and sometimes are not at all responsible; in the majority of cases, however, the truth is somewhere in between.

DOES SCHIZOPHRENIA AFFECT THE PERSON'S IQ?

Neuropsychological abnormalities occur commonly in individuals with schizophrenia, as was discussed in chapter 6. But one specific aspect of neuropsychological function—intelligence—is of special concern to both individuals afflicted with schizophrenia and their families. Ours is, after all, a society obsessed with IQ.

In discussing IQ and schizophrenia, it is important to remember what IQ measures. Most IQ tests measure some combination of reading, reasoning, and mathematical skills, which are assessments of specific types of brain function. IQ tests do not measure experience, common sense, or wisdom. And they certainly do not tell you how much of the person's IQ he/she uses on a day-to-day basis. I have a "normal" relative, for example, who has an IQ of 160; on most days, however, he appears to use about half of it and is virtually devoid of common sense and wisdom.

Recent studies of IQ and schizophrenia have established the following:

1. As a rule, many but not all, individuals with schizophrenia have a small loss of IQ (i.e., approximately 8 to 10 points), which occurs early in life, many years before they develop their illness. This has been demonstrated in European studies that measured the IQ of large numbers of children, then later ascertained which of the children developed schizophrenia. This loss of IQ is probably associated with the same brain damage that caused the schizophrenia.

2. There are major exceptions to this rule. In a study in Finland, for example, a disproportionate number of boys who had excellent school grades later developed schizophrenia. One also thinks of John Nash, who accomplished mathematical feats in his early twenties, for which he was later awarded a Nobel Prize, but who in his late twenties developed schizophrenia.

3. For individuals who develop schizophrenia in childhood, there is also a small loss of IQ because their illness interferes with learning and their ability to acquire new information.

4. Studies are inconclusive about whether or not, once a person has developed schizophrenia in adulthood, there is any additional loss of IQ. It probably depends on the severity of the schizophrenia. On average, however, such a loss of IQ in adulthood is very small.

SHOULD PEOPLE WITH SCHIZOPHRENIA
DRIVE VEHICLES?

Remarkably little has been written about whether individuals with schizophrenia should drive motor vehicles, despite the fact that patients, their families, and insurance companies face this problem regularly. In a 1989 study of this problem it was reported that only 68 percent of outpatients with schizophrenia drive compared to 99 percent of nonpsychiatrically ill controls. Even those patients who did drive did so far less than the controls. Most important, mile for mile, the drivers with schizophrenia had an accident rate that was twice as high as the controls. Two earlier studies had not found a higher accident rate among drivers with schizophrenia.

Should individuals with schizophrenia drive motor vehicles? Driving a vehicle utilizes three separate skills: (1) planning trips and making decisions about crowded roads and darkness; (2) tactical decisions involving judgment and paying attention, such as knowing when to pass another vehicle; and (3) operational coordination, such as being able to put on the brakes quickly. Individuals with schizophrenia are least likely to have problems with operational coordination, although some slowing of movements may be a side effect of antipsychotic drugs. However, some individuals with schizophrenia are clearly impaired in their planning and/or tactical decisions, and this should be self-evident from their planning, judgment, and ability to pay attention in other areas of their lives.

In summary, the majority of individuals with schizophrenia can and do drive. However, those whose planning and/or tactical decisions are clearly impaired should not drive. The assessment of which individuals with schizophrenia should drive and which should not is similar to the assessment made for individuals who are elderly. For some patients whose ability to drive is dependent on taking antipsychotic medication, it would seem reasonable to make their driving license conditional on taking medication, much as is done for some people with epilepsy.

HOW DO RELIGIOUS ISSUES AFFECT PEOPLE
WITH SCHIZOPHRENIA?

People with schizophrenia, like other people, have a need to relate to a god or philosophical worldview that allows them to place themselves and their lives within a larger context. For individuals with schizophrenia this can be particularly problematical for many reasons. For one thing, the onset of the disease often occurs during the same period of life when religious and philosophical beliefs are in great flux, thus making resolution extremely difficult. Another complicating factor is that many persons with this disease undergo intense heightened awareness, or "peak experiences" (as described in chapter 2), during the early stages of their illness and conclude that they have been specially chosen by God. When auditory hallucinations are experienced, these usually reinforce such a belief. Still another impediment to resolution of religious concerns is the person's inability to think metaphorically and in symbols, which most formalized religious belief systems require. It is therefore not surprising that religious concerns continue to be important for many persons with this disease throughout the course of their illness. One recent study, in fact, reported that 30 percent of individuals with schizophrenia reported "an increase in their religiousness after the onset of illness."

Delusions of a religious nature are extremely common, and can be found in almost half of all people with schizophrenia. It is also known that members of the clergy are frequently consulted by individuals with schizophrenia; in one study it was found that "the clergy are as likely as mental health professionals to be sought out by individuals from the community who have serious psychiatric disorders." Many clergy are knowledgeable and helpful in such situations. Unfortunately, however, many others are not current regarding what is known about serious mental illnesses and erroneously tell mentally ill persons or their families that the illness has been caused by sin. Such a message can, of course, be very destructive and make an already bad situation much worse. Various efforts are underway to educate the clergy about mental illness, including groups such as the Religious Outreach Network and Pathways to Promise, organized under NAMI; visit their website at www.pathways2promise.org. Another worthy effort at clergy education is *Strength for His People*, a book by Pastor Steven Waterhouse, who has a brother with schizophrenia (see "Recommended Further Reading" in this chapter).

Occasionally individuals with schizophrenia resolve their religious concerns by joining a religious cult of one kind or another. The variety of available cults is wide and includes the Unification Church ("Moonies"), Hare Krishna, Divine Light Mission, Jesus People, Scientology, and many smaller groups. A study reported that 6 percent of the members of the Unification Church and 9 percent of the members of the Divine Light Mission had been previously hospitalized for psychiatric problems. However, psychiatrists who have studied such groups believe that most of these previously hospitalized members were severely neurotic. The groups themselves tend to exclude seriously disturbed individuals as too disruptive to the closely cooperative living and working conditions demanded by the groups.

For individuals with schizophrenia who are accepted into these cults there may be some advantages. A highly structured belief system and lifestyle are inherent in such groups, as is also a sense of belonging and community. These in turn lead to increased self-esteem for the member. Some cults also value unusual religious experiences, and in such settings a person with schizophrenia may feel more comfortable with his/her "peak experiences" or auditory hallucinations.

The cults also pose potential dangers, however. Many such groups emphasize the desirability of not taking any drugs; patients who are doing nicely on maintenance medication may be encouraged to stop the drug, with resultant relapse. The groups may also encourage the person to deny the reality of his or her illness, casting problems such as delusional thinking and auditory hallucinations into the mold of spiritual shortcomings rather than acknowledging that they are products of a brain disease. Some groups may also encourage paranoid thinking in persons who are already inclined in that direction, as there is often a siege mentality in the cults, a "we-they" feeling that the world is out to persecute them as a group. Finally, a few religious cults may exploit the money or property of members with schizophrenia, as they sometimes do that of other members.

SHOULD YOU TELL PEOPLE THAT YOU HAVE SCHIZOPHRENIA?

The question of whether or not to tell people that you have schizophrenia is a difficult one, especially when the person is a prospective date or employer. Increasingly frequently, however, the answer is "yes." Some issues to consider in thinking about the problem are: Is the person likely to find out anyway? How sophisticated is the person likely to be about mental illness? If I withhold this information, will the person be able to trust me on other issues? How difficult is it for me to interact with the person knowing that I have not told him/her?

Since the early 1980s there has been a dramatic increase in open discussion of schizophrenia by both consumers and their families. The Americans with Disabilities Act affords some theoretical protection against discrimination by employers, but how effective this is in actuality is less clear. There are still occasions, however, when it is better not to disclose the fact that you have schizophrenia. On such occasions Dr. Frederick Frese, a psychologist who has schizophrenia, suggests "that you respond by saying you are a writer, an artist, a (mental health) consultant, or perhaps that you freelance, depending on how you have been spending your time. None of these responses are lies, per se, but they leave considerable latitude for interpretation and they do not require that you have a specific employer or work location."

GENETIC COUNSELING: WHAT ARE THE CHANCES OF GETTING SCHIZOPHRENIA?

Almost every brother, sister, son, daughter, nephew, or niece of a person with schizophrenia has at one time or another wondered about the chances of themselves or their children developing schizophrenia. Furthermore, since an increasing number of individuals with schizophrenia are now having children, genetic counseling is increasingly important.

One might suppose that information on the risk of developing schizophrenia in relatives of affected individuals would be accurate, widely available, and generally agreed upon by the experts. One would be wrong. As discussed in chapter 7, opinions regarding the relative importance of genetic factors in the causation of schizophrenia vary widely and inevitably color genetic counseling. A researcher who believes that genetic factors are the most important antecedents of schizophrenia will give comparatively conservative advice regarding reproduction among relatives, while a researcher who believes that genetic factors are less important will be likely to give less conservative advice.

In thinking about one's chances of getting schizophrenia, it is useful to keep in mind some general observations.

1. Genes certainly play some role, but the magnitude of that role is not nearly as clearly established as most geneticists would have you believe.

2. A majority of individuals who develop schizophrenia—63 percent—do not have any family history of schizophrenia in first-degree (parents and siblings) or second-degree (grandparents, aunts, and uncles) relatives.

3. The more relatives you have with schizophrenia, the higher your risk is of developing it. From a practical point of view this means that if your sister is your only close relative with schizophrenia, your own risk is very low. If, on the other hand, your uncle and sister both have schizophrenia, then your risk is higher. And if you are unfortunate enough to come from one of the relatively rare families that are heavily loaded with the disorder (e.g., mother, aunt, grandfather, and two siblings affected), then your own risk is substantially higher and you should give serious consideration to the question of having children.

4. Many risk figures that are found in psychiatric textbooks are worst-case scenarios and are based on older studies with questionable methodology. For example, the risk of developing schizophrenia if both parents are affected is usually said to be 46 percent. Two more recent studies, however, reported the risk to be 28 and 29 percent, and a consensus risk appears to be approximately 36 percent. Similarly, the risk of developing schizophrenia in the second twin of identical twins is traditionally said to be 48 percent, but that number depends on the use of selected twin samples and a type of double-counting called probandwise rates. When unselected twin samples and single-counting (pairwise) rates are used, the chances of the second identical twin developing schizophrenia is found to be only 28 percent.

5. The risks of developing schizophrenia can be viewed as a glass half empty or half full. For a brother or sister of an affected sibling the probability of developing schizophrenia is 9 percent, but the probability of *not* developing it is 91 percent. For a child when one parent is affected, the risk of developing schizophrenia is 13 percent but the probability of *not* developing it is 87 percent. Even for identical twins the probability of the second twin *not* developing schizophrenia is 72 percent.

6. Schizophrenia is only one of many disorders for which there is some genetic risk. Creating life is, and always has been, a genetic lottery. Knowing the odds in the game will not make the decision for you but will allow you to choose more intelligently.

WHAT ARE MY CHANCES OF GETTING SCHIZOPHRENIA?

If nobody in my family (first- or second-degree relative) has it . . . . 1 percent

If my half-brother or half-sister has it . . . . 4 percent

If my full brother or full sister has it . . . . 9 percent

If my mother or father has it . . . . 13 percent

If both my mother and father have it . . . . 36 percent

If my identical twin has it . . . . 28 percent

If my aunt or uncle has it . . . . 3 percent

If my grandfather or grandmother has it . . . . . . 4 percent

---

WHAT WILL HAPPEN WHEN THE PARENTS DIE?

One of the most troubling problems for families with a family member with schizophrenia is what will happen after the family members who are providing the person's care die. Typically it is a mother and father who provide much of the care needed by an ill son or daughter, although in other cases the same problem may arise for an aging or sick person who is providing care for an ill sibling. In the old days such care was transferred to the extended family or the state hospital. Now, however, the extended family has disappeared and the state hospital will simply discharge the person with schizophrenia to live in the community. The specter of their family member ending up living in public shelters and on the streets haunts many families.

Guardianship is one mechanism used by families to ensure care for the family member and safeguard his or her assets after the death of the well family members. The guardian may be either a relative or friend of the patient or, if none is available or appropriate, another person selected by the judge. The appointment of a guardian occurs most frequently when the patient owns large amounts of money or property or is likely to inherit some. Guardianship is a legal relationship authorizing one person

to make decisions for another and is based on the same *parens patriae*
tenet of English law that permits involuntary hospitalization. When the
guardian has jurisdiction only over the property of the patient, it is frequently referred to as a conservatorship. When both property and personal decisions are involved it is called a guardianship.

Guardianship (and conservatorship) laws are remarkably outmoded
in most states. In many instances no distinction is made between personal and property decisions, and a guardian automatically is granted
decision-making permission for both. Personal decisions affected by a
guardianship may include where the patient may reside, the right to
travel freely, and the right to consent to medical or psychiatric treatment;
property decisions may include the right to sign checks or withdraw
money from a bank account. Most guardianship laws are all-or-nothing
affairs and fail to take into account the ability of patients to manage
some areas of their lives but not others. The laws are often extremely
vague: the law in California, until recently changed, said that a guardian
could be appointed for any "incompetent person . . . whether insane or
not . . . , who is likely to be deceived or imposed upon by artful and
designing persons." This could include most of us! The actual appointment of a guardian is usually done without legal due process and without
the person present; nor is there periodic review to determine whether the
guardianship is still necessary.

Another mechanism used by some families to plan for the future are
nonprofit organizations founded by groups of families. These organizations will accept responsibility for the ill family member after the death
of the well family members. For many years, such organizations were
utilized by families with mentally retarded members; more recently,
groups under NAMI have been setting them up on a local level. For
example, in Virginia, Maryland, and several other states, there is the
Planned Life Assistance Network (PLAN), with family members serv-
ing on the organization's board of directors. A person who joins pays a
membership fee and annual dues, then develops a plan of care for the
family member with schizophrenia to be activated after the death of
other family members. At that time the professional staff and volunteers
of PLAN will assume the responsibilities previously provided by the
family, including visiting the person regularly, maintaining contact with
the person's doctor or case manager, paying the person's bills, acting as
payee for SSI payments, and assuming other fiscal or supervisory functions as needed.

Planning for the future of relatives with schizophrenia is essential both for their well-being and for your own peace of mind. However, understanding benefits, assets, wills, trusts, estate taxes, and everything that goes with them is a major undertaking for nonlawyers. Some state NAMI groups have prepared relevant material, e.g., a booklet by Jean Little entitled "Take Me to Your Lawyer," published by NAMI New York State in 1991. A very helpful publication is a book by attorney L. Mark Russell et al., *Planning for the Future: Providing a Meaningful Life for a Child with a Disability After Your Death* (see appendix A).

RECOMMENDED FURTHER READING

DiLalla, D. L., and I. I. Gottesman. "Normal Personality Characteristics in Identical Twins Discordant for Schizophrenia." *Journal of Abnormal Psychology* 104 (1995): 490–99.

Edlund, M. J., C. Conrad, and P. Morris. "Accidents Among Schizophrenic Outpatients." *Comprehensive Psychiatry* 30 (1989): 522–26.

Gottesman, I. I. *Schizophrenia Genesis: The Origins of Madness*. New York: W. H. Freeman, 1991.

Govig, S. D. *Strong at the Broken Places: Persons with Disabilities and the Church*. Louisville: Westminster, 1989.

Journal of the California Alliance for the Mentally Ill 8 (4). This entire issue is devoted to spirituality and mental illness.

Kirov, G., R. Kemp, K. Kirov, et al. "Religious Faith After Psychotic Illness." *Psychopathology* 31 (1998): 234–45.

Lefley, H. P., and A. B. Hatfield. "Helping Parental Caregivers and Mental Health Consumers Cope with Parental Aging and Loss." *Psychiatric Services* 50 (1999): 369–75.

Russell, A. J., J. C. Munro, P. B. Jones, et al. "Schizophrenia and the Myth of Intellectual Decline." *American Journal of Psychiatry* 154 (1997): 635–39.

Russell, L. M., A. E. Grant, S. M. Joseph, et al. *Planning for the Future: Providing a Meaningful Life for a Child with a Disability After Your Death*. 3rd ed. Evanston, Ill.: American Publishing, 1995.

Torrey, E. F. "Are We Overestimating the Genetic Contribution to Schizophrenia?" *Schizophrenia Bulletin* 18 (1992): 159–70.

Waterhouse, S. *Strength for His People: A Ministry for Families of the Mentally Ill*. Amarillo, Tex.: Westcliff Bible Church (Box 1521, Amarillo, TX 79105).

14

SCHIZOPHRENIA IN THE PUBLIC EYE

> But the brilliance, the versatility of madness is akin to the resourcefulness of water seeping through, over and around a dike. It requires the united front of many people to work against it.
>
> F. Scott Fitzgerald, *Tender Is the Night*, 1934

Schizophrenia has come out of the closet. Slowly, reluctantly, and shyly at first, the disease has increasingly entered the public arena. In 1960, many individuals with schizophrenia denied that anything was wrong except, perhaps, "a case of nerves." In 1980, individuals with schizophrenia would whisper to those they trusted that they had, indeed, been given this label. In 2000, individuals with schizophrenia regularly, even proudly, identified themselves in public meetings and on national television. It has been a remarkable change over the past 40 years.

The major breakthroughs into the public arena began in the early 1980s. The public television series *The Brain* included an excellent segment on schizophrenia produced by DeWitt Sage. Phil Donahue followed with three separate shows discussing the disease; this was the first time most people had heard the term "schizophrenia" mentioned on a major network or seen people who had schizophrenia discussing it. Now schizophrenia has become so commonplace on television that in 1998 Oprah Winfrey featured a book about schizophrenia, Wally Lamb's *I Know This Much Is True*, on her show. And in March 2000, a television series, *Wonderland*, featured individuals with schizophrenia in a psychiatric emergency room; the program generated considerable public controversy but survived just two episodes because of low viewership.

The progress in television has been mirrored by the movies. Except for Ingmar Bergman's films, such as his stunning 1961 *Through a Glass*

Darkly, almost no serious movies were made about schizophrenia until the 1990s. During that decade, several were released and are reviewed below.

In literature, there has been an occasional depiction of "insanity" by major writers over the past two centuries, but few people have connected these to the contemporary concept of schizophrenia. Many of these older portrayals deserve to be more widely known and are summarized below. With rare exceptions, such as Mark Vonnegut's 1975 *Eden Express*, there were almost no books written by individuals with schizophrenia or by their families until the 1980s. Now they are so numerous that it was difficult to select those to include for the annotated list in appendix A.

SCHIZOPHRENIA IN THE MOVIES

The serious depiction of schizophrenia in cinema is a recent phenomenon. There have, of course, been insane characters in movies for as long as movies have been made. These characters, however, were until recently merely caricatures, used as props for humor (e.g., *Dr. Dippy's Sanitarium* in 1906) or horror (e.g., *Maniac Barber* in 1902). As the century progressed and Hollywood fell increasingly under the spell of Freudian psychoanalysis, insane characters were also used as props to display the talents of omniscient and wise psychiatrists, as depicted in *David and Lisa* (1962). It was only later that Hollywood's psychiatrists fell from grace, as shown in such movies as in *Dressed to Kill* (1980) and *Frances* (1982).

Another common way of representing insane persons in films in the 1960s and 1970s was to depict them as not really insane at all but as rather more sane than the purportedly normal people around them. *King of Hearts* (1966) was an enormously popular film in which the inmates leave their asylum and take over a war-deserted town. Their sane behavior is contrasted with the insanity of the ongoing war, and in the end Alan Bates, as Private Plumpick, decides to leave the army and join the inmates.

The theme of *One Flew over the Cuckoo's Nest* (1975) was similar, with the inmates of the asylum shown as more normal than Nurse Ratched and her staff. Jack Nicholson as Randle McMurphy is finally defeated by a lobotomy but not before he has shown his fellow inmates the road to freedom. *Cuckoo's Nest* was, in the words of one reviewer, "the quintessential film for the counterculture: the mental institution as a metaphor for the abuse of authority."

Serious attempts to portray individuals with schizophrenia really only began with Ingmar Bergman's film *Through a Glass Darkly* in 1961, but such attempts were rare until recent years. The following are synopses of these films. Most are available for sale over the Internet, and some can be rented at your local video store. The best of them, in my opinion, are *Through a Glass Darkly; Clean, Shaven;* and *Angel Baby*.

Through a Glass Darkly, 1961. Directed by Ingmar Bergman. In Swedish with English subtitles. $25.95. B&W. This is a brilliant movie, one of Bergman's finest. Karin (Harriet Andersson), married to a physician (Max von Sydow), has returned from the hospital in a remission from her illness after having been treated with ECT. Gradually her schizophrenia returns, including symptoms of acuteness of hearing and auditory hallucinations. The depiction of her symptoms, as she finds herself repeatedly lured into an upstairs room where voices invite her to step behind the wallpaper and await the coming of God, and her description of her hallucinations to her teenage brother are very moving. The voices, she says, are not dreams but real, and she is exhausted from struggling against them: "Now I'm in one world, now the other, and I cannot prevent it." Showing considerable insight, she begs her father for compassion: "It's horrible to see your own confusion and understand it." Her family watches helplessly as she slowly deteriorates, and at the end of the film she returns to the hospital. Starkly filmed in black and white on a desolate seacoast, the film won an Academy Award for Best Foreign Language Film in 1961.

Birdy, 1984. Directed by Alan Parker. $14.95 VHS. This is a wonderful film about friendship, with moving performances by Nicholas Cage and Matthew Modine, but it has little to do with the reality of serious mental illness. Al Columbato (Cage) is a tough guy with a good heart, growing up on the south side of Philadelphia. Although he finds his neighbor (Modine) strange, the two become devoted friends and spend most of their time together—fixing up an old jalopy, escaping for a day at the beach, constructing an aviary for the pigeons "Birdy" hopes to train. Al tolerates Birdy's obsessions, first with the pigeons, then with canaries, and always with flying. They are separated when first Al, then Birdy, is sent to Vietnam. Upon his return, Al, who has suffered severe burns to his face, is sent for by a psychiatrist who needs help understanding Birdy, who has suffered deep psychological wounds following a month missing in action. During his daily visits to the ward, Al finds Birdy catatonic, either squatting on the floor like a canary or crouched naked by the toilet, staring upward at the window. The attending psychiatrist, Major Weiss (John Harkins), is an ineffectual bully who alternates between psychoanalyzing the two young men and, as Al puts it, pumping Birdy "so full of [drugs] that he doesn't know who he is anymore." Al pleads with Birdy to come to his senses before he's put away for good: "You think I don't know what you're doing, with all this squatting and sideways staring stuff. So you're really a bird. Big deal! If Weiss finds out, he's going to put you in a display case . . . [and] write papers on you forever." The movie's climax is a tribute to enduring friendship but, like *Cuckoo's Nest* and *King of Hearts*, leans heavily on the theories of Ronald Laing (see chapter 7).

Clean, Shaven, 1993. Directed by Lodge Kerrigan. $16.99 VHS. Spare, bleak, and mean, this film is not for the faint of heart. Film critic Roger Ebert calls it a "must see" for anyone with a serious interest in schizophrenia, and indeed, it is the most vivid cinematic portrait to date of the "view from the inside." Peter Winter (Peter Greene), just released from a psychiatric hospital, is desperate to find his daughter, who was given up for adoption by Peter's mother during his confinement. ("Do you know what it's like to see your son deteriorate?" Mrs. Winter explains. "When he was growing up, he was a quiet boy, but he was happy. Then all of a sudden he changed. I won't have that same thing happen to her.") Plagued by voices and fears that are palpable to the viewer, Peter smashes in or covers any glass that reflects his image or allows others to look in, including the rearview mirrors and side windows of his car. Haunted by memories that are presumably false, he frantically flees the siren of a police car that never materializes. In an effort to rid himself of the receiver he believes was implanted in the back of his head and the transmitter he believes is in his finger, he gouges his scalp with scissors and tears off a fingernail. Convinced he has extricated the transmitter, he explains: "I feel better. I think clearer. I still have to get the receiver out of my head. If I could just slow down a little bit, I know I could come up with a solution." The film raises troubling questions that its 80 minutes don't have time to answer: What was the course of Peter's illness, and what treatment did he receive? Is he still taking medication? How much of his paranoia is justified? He is, in fact, a suspect in a serial murder case, and his movements are being tracked by a detective. How many of the memories flashing through his mind are real? What are we to assume from his mother's distant behavior upon his return? A cacophony of sounds—buzzing wires, radio static, voices spewing profanity—and disordered images contribute to our uncertainty but also help us better understand the turmoil in Peter's brain. Winner of the Best First Feature Award for 1993 at the Chicago International Film Festival and presented at the 1994 Cannes Film Festival.

Benny and Joon, 1993. Directed by Jeremiah Chechik. $9.99 VHS. A beautifully filmed but unrealistic story about a brother who is the sole caretaker of his kid sister, who has schizophrenia. Benny (Aidan Quinn) owns an auto repair shop; Joon (Mary Stuart Masterson) stays at home and paints, except when the urge hits her to set fire to something or don scuba gear and direct traffic. Along the way, she loses a poker bet and "wins" another player's eccentric cousin Sam (Johnny Depp), whose whimsical pantomimes à la Buster Keaton and Charlie Chaplin charm her. While the film addresses such issues as noncompliance with medication and disputes over independent living arrangements, the bad times are never too severe or long-lasting. As film reviewers Mick Martin and Marsha Porter point out: "[Although] most viewers will enjoy this bittersweet comedy . . . folks coping with mental illness in real life will be offended by yet another film in which the problem is sanitized and trivialized."

The Saint of Fort Washington, 1994. Directed by Tim Hunter. $16.99 VHS. More about homelessness than schizophrenia per se, this film nevertheless touches on issues of importance to those cut off from their families and society by their symptoms. Matthew (Matt Dillon), a young man suffering from schizophrenia, is forced out of his cheap hotel room by a wrecker's ball. When Social Services directs him to the Fort Washington shelter for men, he finds himself vulnerable to the criminal elements residing there. Jerry (Danny Glover), a Vietnam vet who has gradually lost his business, his home, and his family, rescues Matthew, and together the two struggle to find work, food, and shelter on the street. The film falls far short in its depiction of Matthew's schizophrenia and attributes too much success to Jerry's attempts to talk Matthew out of his hallucinations. Furthermore, Matt Dillon seems unsure how an individual with schizophrenia should act. But the film does address some of the problems peculiar to the homeless mentally ill, including the vagaries of a mental health system that can't provide assistance to someone with no address.

Angel Baby, 1995. Directed by Michael Rymer. $12.99 VHS. The winner of seven Australian Film Institute awards for 1995, this film is a sensitive, realistic portrayal of love between two people with schizophrenia. Harry (John Lynch) is a regular at a local clubhouse. From the moment he sees Kate (Jacqueline McKenzie), he is smitten. He pursues and she responds. To the distress of his family, Harry moves out of his brother's home and Kate leaves her halfway house to move into an apartment together. Harry takes a job as a computer programmer and Kate does the neighbors' laundry, and their life is marginally successful until Kate becomes pregnant and they both stop taking their medication. Largely unnoticed in the United States,

this film deals frankly with many important issues affecting those who suffer from serious mental illness: sexual relations, independent living
arrangements, relationships with family members, noncompliance with
medication, pregnancy, stigma, and suicide. Since a copy of *Surviving
Schizophrenia* is shown in the movie, it ranks very high on my list!

Shine, 1996. Directed by Scott Hicks. $16.99 VHS. This highly successful
movie, which garnered seven Academy Award nominations, depicts Australian pianist David Helfgott, afflicted with a severe mental disorder not
named in the film but obviously schizophrenia. Geoffrey Rush as Helfgott
gives a sterling performance portraying a gifted artist with continuing
symptoms of his illness, and the movie is worth seeing for this alone.
Unfortunately, those making the movie were three decades behind in their
knowledge of the disease, and the movie implies that Helfgott's illness was
caused by his having been cruelly treated in childhood by his father (Armin
Mueller-Stahl), a charge that has been emphatically refuted by Helfgott's
older sister. Even worse, Helfgott's wife (portrayed in the film by Lynn
Redgrave), a consummate flaky astrologer, has been quoted as saying that
Helfgott does not need medication, because it would merely " 'adapt' him
to some arbitrary standard of normality, but then David would no longer be
David and, by destroying the individual, one would risk destroying his
magic." Following the film's success, Helfgott was taken on a recital tour of
the United States, which impressed some critics as pure exploitation. For
example, Terry Teachout of the *New York Daily News* wrote: "Two centuries
ago, nice people went to asylums on Sunday, and gawked at the inmates.
But times have changed. Today, we let the inmates out of the asylums and
encourage them to live 'normal' lives. Some preach strange religions on
street corners; others give concerts at Avery Fisher Hall, and nice people
pay $50 a head to watch them, and call it progress."

Mrs. Dalloway, 1998. Directed by Marleen Gorris. $16.99 VHS. Virginia Woolf
suffered from manic-depressive illness from the age of 13 until she committed suicide at the age of 59. Between episodes, she was a prolific and
gifted writer, and several of her novels depict her symptoms, although usually under the guise of a socially acceptable tropical fever or shell shock. In
Mrs. Dalloway, written in 1925, Septimus Warren Smith, home from the
battlefields of Italy, exhibits many of the classic features of schizophrenia.
Despite Woolf's efforts to camouflage the cause of his symptoms, the
beauty and poignancy of her writing make painfully clear her intimacy with
hallucinations and delusions. Although much of this is lost in the book's
translation to film (starring Vanessa Redgrave, Natascha McElhone, and
Rupert Graves), it is well worth watching, ideally in conjunction with

reading the book and exploring Malcolm Ingram's website on Woolf's psychiatric history (http://ourworld.compuserve.com/homepages/malcolmi/summary.htm).

Pi, 1998. Directed by Darren Aronofsky. $9.98 VHS. B&W. This disturbing film deals with the complex relationship between insanity and genius (see "Schizophrenia, Creativity, and Famous People," below). Max Cohen (Sean Gullette) is a brilliant, reclusive mathematician who earned his Ph.D. at age 20. Convinced that everything in nature can be explained by mathematical patterns, he becomes obsessed with a 216-digit series in the expansion of *pi* that he believes holds a secret about the universe. His work, however, is stymied by computer crashes that destroy his data and excruciating headaches that climax in auditory and visual hallucinations from which he can find no relief. Like *Clean, Shaven*, this film seeks to portray psychosis from the inside, leaving the viewer uncertain where Max's paranoia ends and reality begins. Even holed up in his apartment behind triple locks and a dead bolt, he is pursued by Wall Street brokers who are convinced he's found a pattern in the stock market, Jewish mystics who believe he can tell them the true name of God, and visions of his own brain on the steps of a subway station. Winner of the Sundance Film Festival's Directing Award for 1998.

SCHIZOPHRENIA IN LITERATURE

Descriptions of schizophrenia are now widely represented in both medical and popular literature. Medical journals, such as *Schizophrenia Bulletin* and *Psychiatric Services*, regularly carry accounts of the illness written by those who have been affected. Popular journals do likewise; Susan Sheehan's superb account of schizophrenia was originally carried in the *New Yorker* and later published as *Is There No Place on Earth for Me?* This book, and many other books on schizophrenia, are summarized in appendix A. The literature now available on schizophrenia includes an abundance of riches, providing many choices for those who wish to learn more about the disease.

This was not always the case. Until approximately 1980, the subject of schizophrenia was confined mostly to textbooks of psychiatry. Within general literature, however, there were also occasional descriptions of "mad" or "insane" persons who had symptoms of schizophrenia. Some of these descriptions are both instructive and entertaining, and a selection of them is included below. Most are from the English language, although others exist in other languages. Such accounts enrich our understanding of this disease.

One early example was Honoré de Balzac's short story "Louis Lambert," written in 1832 in French. Even in translation, it is an extraordinary story, and an excerpt from it is included at the end of chapter 2. Other selections from literature prior to 1950 that depict individuals with symptoms of schizophrenia include the following.

"Berenice," by Edgar Allan Poe, 1835. Poe's descriptions have been widely praised for their realism. In this short story, the narrator, Egaeus, suffers from schizophrenia characterized by a fixed delusion, previously called monomania. Even as a boy, he felt detached from his surroundings: "The realities of the world affected me as visions, . . . while the wild ideas of the land of dreams became, in turn, not the material of my every-day existence, but in very deed that existence utterly and solely in itself." As a young man, he would "muse for long unwearied hours with my attention riveted to some frivolous device on the margin, or in the typography of a book; . . . become absorbed for the better part of a summer's day, in a quaint shadow falling aslant upon the tapestry; . . . lose myself, for an entire night, in watching the steady flame of a lamp." When he becomes engaged to his cousin Berenice, he fixates on her teeth, believing that his possession of them will restore him to reason: "Then came the full fury of my *monomania*, and I struggled in vain against its strange and irresistible influence. In the multiplied objects of the external world I had no thoughts but for the teeth. For these I longed with a phrenzied desire. All other matters and all different interests became absorbed in their single contemplation. They—they alone were present to the mental eye, and they, in their sole individuality, became the essence of my mental life." In the end, as if in nightmare that he later only vaguely remembers, Egaeus, believing Berenice to be dead from an epileptic seizure, extracts her teeth and puts them in a box.

"A Madman's Manuscript," in *The Pickwick Papers*, by Charles Dickens, 1837. Charles Dickens was fascinated by insanity, was close friends with several prominent psychiatrists, had many medical books on insanity in his personal library, and visited asylums whenever he had the opportunity. "A Madman's Manuscript" is a strange tale, told in the first person by an asylum inmate who is being laughed at by visitors peering into his cell. Rather than being humiliated, he delights in his status:

> Yes!—a madman's! How that word would have struck to my
> heart, many years ago! How it would have roused the terror

that used to come upon me sometimes; sending the blood
hissing and tingling through my veins, till the cold dew of
fear stood in large drops upon my skin, and my knees
knocked together with fright! I like it now though. It's a fine
name. Show me the monarch whose angry frown was ever
feared like the glare of a madman's eye—whose cord and
axe were ever half so sure as a madman's grip. Ho! ho! It's a
grand thing to be mad! to be peeped at like a wild lion
through the iron bars—to gnash one's teeth and howl,
through the long still night, to the merry ring of a heavy
chain—and to roll and twine among the straw, transported
with such brave music. Hurrah for the madhouse! Oh, it's a
rare place!

Jane Eyre, by Charlotte Brontë, 1847. When Jane Eyre takes the position of gov-
erness at Thornfield Hall, she is both frightened and intrigued by noises she
hears coming from the attic. But it is not until her wedding day that she
actually sees Bertha Rochester, whose existence and insanity have been
kept a secret by her husband for 10 years. Brontë's description of Mrs.
Rochester is of a dangerous wild animal:

In the deep shade, at the farther end of the room, a figure ran
backwards and forwards. What it was, whether beast or
human being, one could not, at first sight, tell: it grovelled,
seemingly, on all fours; it snatched and growled like some
strange wild animal: but it was covered with clothing, and a
quantity of dark, grizzled hair, wild as a mane, hid its head
and face.

When Brontë was criticized for her brutish depiction of Mrs. Rochester, she
responded that she was merely reflecting the reality of some cases of madness "in which all that is good or even human seems to disappear from the
mind and a fiend-like nature replaces it."

David Copperfield, by Charles Dickens, 1850. When David runs away from
London to seek refuge with his Aunt Betsey in Dover, he is introduced to
her permanent houseguest, Mr. Dick, who clearly has symptoms of schizophrenia. His primary symptom is a belief that thoughts are being inserted
into his head, considered by many psychiatrists to be an almost certain sign
of this disease. Mr. Dick believes the thoughts have come from the head of
King Charles I and that they were transferred to him when the king was
beheaded in 1649. That the king's demise was so far in the past seems to
trouble Mr. Dick more than the motives of those inserting the thoughts:

" 'Well,' returned Mr. Dick, scratching his ear with his pen, and looking dubiously at me. ' . . . I don't see how that can be. Because, if it was so long ago, how could the people about him have made that mistake of putting some of the trouble out of his head, after it was taken off, into *mine?*' "

Bartleby the Scrivener, by Herman Melville, 1853. Bartleby's illness is a classic example of the type of schizophrenia in which the negative symptoms predominate. He has what used to be called "simple" schizophrenia. As the narrator notes, "his eccentricities are involuntary" and he "was the victim of [an] innate and incurable disorder." The man who hires him as a scrivener (law-copyist) and who tries unsuccessfully to help him finally concludes that "he is a little deranged." Bartleby's behavior slowly deteriorates as the story progresses, and he is overtaken by apathy and an inability to act. His affect is completely flat as he refuses all offers of help, repeating politely but firmly: "I would prefer not to make any change." At the end of the story, Bartleby is put in prison as a vagrant and there he dies, with "his knees drawn up, and lying on his side, his head touching the cold stones" of the prison wall.

Poems by Emily Dickinson, 1861–1864. Although she was completely reclusive by the time she was in her thirties, Emily Dickinson continued to correspond with friends and write poetry; over a thousand of her letters were preserved and more than 1,700 poems were found in a drawer after her death. As one critic noted, "Dickinson's letters . . . reveal a slow transformation of style during her 20's, from conventionally phrased well-wrought sentences to spare, gnomic, highly charged, idiosyncratic and often difficult phrasings punctuated by dashes, with capitalizations for emphasis." Dickenson almost certainly suffered from agoraphobia, and several of her poems also describe a fear of, or the experience of, madness:

"THE FIRST DAY'S NIGHT HAD COME" (1862):

> *My Brain—begun to laugh—*
> *I mumbled—like a fool—*
> *And tho' 'tis Years ago—that Day—*
> *My Brain keeps giggling—still.*
> *And Something's odd—within—*
> *That person that I was—*
> *And this One—do not feel the same—*
> *Could it be Madness—this?*

"I FELT A FUNERAL IN MY BRAIN" (1861):

I felt a Funeral, in my Brain,
And Mourners to and fro
Kept treading—treading—till it seemed
That Sense was breaking through—
And when they all were seated,
A Service, like a Drum—
Kept beating—beating—till I thought
My Mind was going numb

"I FELT A CLEAVING IN MY MIND" (1864):

I felt a Cleaving in my Mind—
As if my Brain had split—
I tried to match it—Seam by Seam—
But could not make them fit.
The thought behind I strove to join
Unto the thought before—
But sequence ravelled out of Sound
Like balls—upon a Floor.

"Ward No. 6," by Anton Chekhov, 1892. Chekhov's talents as a writer and a physician came together in his moving portrayal of Ivan Dmitritch, who suffers from paranoid schizophrenia. He is a lonely man with no family or friends, and as a teacher he has a hard time getting along with his colleagues and his students. One autumn day, he encounters convicts on the road. In the past, he felt compassion; now, paranoid thoughts begin: "At home he could not get the convicts or the soldiers with their rifles out of his head all day . . . at night he could not sleep, but kept thinking that he might be arrested, put into fetters, and thrown into prison. He did not know of any harm he had done, and could be certain that he would never be guilty of murder, arson, or theft in the future either; but was it not easy to commit a crime by accident, unconsciously, and was not false witness always possible, and indeed, miscarriage of justice? . . . Everyone who passed by the windows or came into the yard seemed to him a spy or a detective." In the spring, when the snow melts, an old woman and boy are found dead. Worrying that others will suspect him, Ivan hides in his landlady's cellar but runs away when workmen come to the house, fearing they are policemen in disguise. When he is stopped and brought home, his landlady calls for a doctor. Ivan is taken to the hospital, where he is put on the ward for patients with venereal disease. When he disturbs the other patients there, he is taken to Ward No. 6, the psychiatric ward.

Mrs. Dalloway, by Virginia Woolf, 1925. As noted above in the description of the movie, Virginia Woolf herself had manic-depressive illness, but Septimus Warren Smith in *Mrs. Dalloway* is depicted as having classic symptoms of schizophrenia. These include a heightening of the senses:

> Septimus heard [her] . . . close to his ear, deeply, softly, like a mellow organ, but with a roughness in her voice like a grasshopper's, which rasped his spine deliciously and sent running up into his brain waves of sound which, concussing, broke.

Alterations in one's bodily boundaries:

> But they beckoned; leaves were alive; trees were alive. And the leaves being connected by millions of fibres with his own body, there on the seat, fanned up and down; when the branch stretched he, too, made that statement. The sparrows fluttering, rising, and falling in jagged fountains were part of the pattern; the white and blue, barred with black branches. Sounds made harmonies with premeditation; the spaces between them were as significant as the sounds. A child cried. Rightly far away a horn sounded. All taken together meant the birth of a new religion—

And paranoid delusions:

> Septimus let himself think about horrible things. . . . He had grown stranger and stranger. He said people were talking behind the bedroom walls. . . . He would argue with her about killing themselves; and explain how wicked people were; how he could see them making up lies as they passed in the street. . . . [He] saw faces laughing at him, calling him horrible disgusting names, from the walls, and hands pointing round the screen.

Faced with separation from his wife and life in a "home," he climbs out the window of his boarding house, hesitates momentarily on the sill, and then flings himself down, impaling himself on the rusty spikes of the railing below.

The Waves, by Virginia Woolf, 1931. In this novel, one of Woolf's most experimental, each of six characters is revealed through a series of soliloquies. One character, Rhoda, like many individuals with schizophrenia, is unable to sort and interpret incoming stimuli and so often responds inappropriately. As a schoolgirl, she is confounded by arithmetic: "Now the terror is beginning . . . What is the answer? The others . . . look with understanding . . . But I . . . see only figures. . . . Look, the loop of the figure is beginning to fill with time; it holds the world in it. I begin to draw a figure and the world is looped in it, and I myself am outside the loop; which I now join—so—and seal up, and make entire. The world is entire, and I am outside of it, crying, 'Oh, save me, from being blown for ever outside the loop of time!' " She is similarly stymied in society: "Other people have faces; . . . they are here. . . . The things they lift are heavy. . . . They laugh really; they get angry really; while I have to look first and do what other people do when they have done it. . . . I attach myself only to names and faces; and hoard them like amulets against disaster. . . . Alone, I often fall down into nothingness. . . . Month by month things are losing their hardness; even my body now lets the light through; my spine is soft like wax near the flame of the candle." Interpersonal relations become impossible: "When I have passed through this drawing-room flickering with tongues that cut me like knives, making me stammer, making me lie, I find faces rid of features, robed in beauty. . . . I am not composed enough, standing on tiptoe on the verge of fire, still scorched by the hot breath, afraid of the door opening and the leap of the tiger, to make even one sentence. . . . Every time the door opens I am interrupted. I am not yet twenty-one. I am to be broken. I am to be derided all my life."

"Silent Snow, Secret Snow," by Conrad Aiken, 1932. Conrad Aiken's father and sister both developed insanity, and Aiken lived his entire life in the fear that he was destined for the same fate. "Silent Snow, Secret Snow" is an account of the onset of schizophrenia in a 12-year-old boy whose auditory and visual hallucinations entice him to withdraw from the world around him. Paul's symptoms begin with a muffling of sound, "a sense as of snow falling about him, a secret screen of new snow between himself and the world." Later, his illness takes on an aspect of paranoia and his hallucinations become more vivid: his mother's entrance into his room is seen as something alien and hostile, and the snow laughs and calls to him: "Lie down. Shut your eyes, now—you will no longer see much—in this white darkness who could see, or want to see? We will take the place of everything."

Save Me the Waltz, by Zelda Fitzgerald, 1932. Like her husband's novel Tender Is the Night, Zelda Fitzgerald's Save Me the Waltz is a thinly disguised description of her experience with schizophrenia and her family's reaction to her illness. Written in 1932, shortly after her second breakdown, the novel describes a young woman's delirium after she is hospitalized for what is said to be blood poisoning:

. The walls of the room slid quietly past, dropping one over

the other like the leaves of a heavy album. They were all
shades of gray and rose and mauve. There was no sound
when they fell. . . .

The doctors stood impersonally at the end of the
bed. . . .

"This afternoon, then, at three," said one of the men,
and left. The other went on talking to himself.

"I can't operate," she thought he said, "because I've got
to stand here and count the white butterflies to-day."

"And so the girl was raped by a calla lily," he said, "—
or, no, I believe it was the spray of a shower bath that did the
trick!" he said triumphantly.

He laughed fiendishly. . . .

Meaningfully the nurses laughed together and left her
room. The walls began again. She decided to lie there and
frustrate the walls if they thought they could press her
between their pages like a bud from a wedding bouquet.

Tender Is the Night, by F. Scott Fitzgerald, 1934. After the success of *The Great
Gatsby*, F. Scott Fitzgerald proposed a new idea to his editor. Even as he
started the new project, however, Zelda began showing signs of illness, and
in spring 1930 she had her first breakdown. Fitzgerald began anew, and the
result was *Tender Is the Night*, in which the main characters' lives—Nicole
Diver's illness and her husband, Dick's, reaction to it—so closely parallel
the Fitzgeralds' experiences that it is often difficult to separate the fictional
story from the real one. Scott writes to Zelda's doctor: ". . . my great worry
is that time is slipping by, life is slipping by. . . . If she were an anti-social
person who did not want to face life and pull her own weight that would be
one story, but her passionate love of life and her absolute inability to meet it
seems so tragic that it is scarcely to be endured." Zelda replies through
Nicole: "Think how you love me," she whispered. "I don't ask you to love
me always like this, but I ask you to remember. Somewhere inside me
there'll always be the person I am tonight." In the book, Dick tries to contain Nicole's illness but is unsuccessful. He says: "It was necessary to treat
her with active and affirmative insistence, keeping the road to reality always
open, making the road to escape harder going. But the brilliance, the versa-
tility of madness is akin to the resourcefulness of water seeping through,
over and around a dike. It requires the united front of many people to work
against it."

"I Am Lazarus," by Anna Kavan, 1940. Anna Kavan was twice confined to mental hospitals in Switzerland and England. In "I Am Lazarus," Thomas Bow,

25, is confined to a clinic where he has been receiving insulin shock treatment for "advanced dementia praecox." A visiting doctor finds him apparently cured but with an "inexpressive face and . . . curious flat look of the eyes." He takes no notice of those around him: "What had he to do with talking? All around the table were different colored shapes whose mouths opened and closed and emitted sounds that meant nothing to him." Inanimate objects, on the other hand, draw his attention: Moon daisies have yellow eyes that squint "craftily" at him; grasses respond to his touch, "like thin sensitive cats [that arch] themselves to receive the caress of his fingertips"; coats hanging in the washroom fill him "with deep suspicion." Only the cool leather of the pigskin belt he is making is a friend that can "assuage the hurt and anger inside his heart."

"The Headless Hawk," by Truman Capote, 1946. Truman Capote was only 22 when he wrote this short story about a young woman with schizophrenia. Vincent firsts meets D. J. when she tries to sell him her self-portrait: a figure dressed in a monk-like robe, reclining on a vaudeville trunk, with her severed head lying bleeding at her feet. Although he finds her odd, with lips that tremble "with unrealized words as though she had possibly a defect of speech" and a mind "like a mirror reflecting blue space in a barren room," he is attracted to her. In the end, however, he is overwhelmed by her paranoia, manifested in her fear of a man named Destronelli, who has pursued her as Doctor Gum, with his gray wig, pretending to be "real old and kind"; as a man with a little red car and cruel eyes; as a man in the movie theater; and as a man in a Philadelphia cafe. "*Sometimes he's not a man at all—*she'd told him . . . —*sometimes he is something very different: a hawk, a child, a butterfly . . . I knew he was going to murder me. And he will. He will.*"

SCHIZOPHRENIA, CREATIVITY, AND FAMOUS PEOPLE

An oft-debated question around firesides and pubs is whether there is a relationship between creativity and schizophrenia. John Dryden reflected the views of many people when he wrote 300 years ago, "Great wits are sure to madmen near allied." Since then we have moved a little closer to a definitive answer to this question.

It is known that the creative person and the person with schizophrenia share many cognitive traits. Both use words and language in unusual ways (the hallmark of a great poet or novelist), both have unusual views of reality (as great artists do), both often utilize unusual thought processes in their deliberations, and both tend to prefer solitude to the company of others. When creative persons are given traditional psychological tests, they manifest more psychopathology than noncreative persons, and creative persons are often viewed as eccentric by their friends. Conversely, when people with nonparanoid schizophrenia are given traditional tests of creativity they score very high (people with paranoid schizophrenia do not).

Several surveys have shown that highly creative persons are not themselves more susceptible to schizophrenia. However, one study has suggested that the immediate relatives of creative persons may be more susceptible to schizophrenia. As a case in point one thinks of Robert Frost, whose aunt, son, and perhaps daughter all developed schizophrenia. In addition, Albert Einstein's son developed schizophrenia, as did the daughters of Victor Hugo, Bertrand Russell, and James Joyce.

James Joyce is a particularly interesting study in psychopathology. A biography on him noted his "keen pleasure in sounds," his periods of depression, intermittent alcohol abuse, and at least one episode of mania during which "he could not sleep for six or seven nights . . . he felt as if he were wound up and then suddenly shooting out of water like a fish. During the day he was troubled by auditory hallucinations." A psychiatrist who studied Joyce's writings concluded that he was a schizoid personality with paranoid traits and claimed that "*Finnegans Wake* must ultimately be diagnosed as psychotic." Joyce's only daughter, Lucia, was diagnosed with classical schizophrenia at age 22, treated by Jung, and spent the rest of her life in mental hospitals. It was noted that "Joyce had a remarkable capacity to follow her swift jumps of thought, which baffled other people completely."

There is, however, one fundamental difference between the creative person and the person with schizophrenia. The creative person has his/her unusual thought processes under control and can harness them in the creation of a product. The person with schizophrenia, on the other hand, is at the mercy of disconnected thinking and loose associations which tumble about in cacophonic disarray. The creative person has choices, whereas the schizophrenia sufferer does not.

The list of creative individuals who are thought to have had schizophrenia or schizoaffective disorder is remarkably short; this is not surprising when one considers how thinking disorders interfere with a person's ability to work. Individuals who apparently suffered from schizophrenia include French writer Antonin Artaud, American painter Ralph Blakelock, English composer and poet Ivor Gurney, American mathematician John Nash, and Russian dancer Vaslav Nijinsky.

Antonin Artaud, a writer and actor, was a major figure in the French Surrealist movement from 1924 to 1927. He exhibited occasional symptoms of schizophrenia during those years, but in 1937, at age 41, he was hospitalized and spent much of his remaining life confined in Paris, Rouen, and Rodez. His *Letters from Rodez* describe his sickness, as in this 1943 letter to a friend:

> . . . this sickness has to do with the scandal of the horrible plot of which I am the victim and which you know about in the privacy of your soul and your conscience; for you have suffered from it horribly yourself. You have seen the hordes of demons which afflict me night and day, you have seen them as clearly as you see me. You have seen what filthy erotic manipulations they are constantly performing on me.

Ralph Blakelock was a prominent American landscape artist whose paintings just prior to World War I sold for more than had ever before been paid to a living American artist. By then, however, Blakelock had been diagnosed with dementia praecox and hospitalized for more than a decade in the state psychiatric hospital at Middletown, New York. He became known as the "American Van Gogh" because he was unable to sell any paintings until after he had become psychotic; he and his family lived much of their lives in poverty.

Blakelock's symptoms included paranoid and grandiose delusions (he claimed to be the Duke of York). He also threatened to kill members of his family. Late in life he wrote, mostly without punctuation: "If I am insane I am not conscious of it I am not a paranoiac I am not in the period of senility nor aged dotage. For I can whistle and sing." When he died in 1919, President Woodrow Wilson sent Blakelock's family a message of condolence.

Ivor Gurney was a promising English composer and poet when he was struck down by what most Gurney scholars have labeled as schizophrenia. A recent biography casts some doubt on this diagnosis and suggests that manic-depressive illness may have been the problem. He had studied under Ralph Vaughan Williams, but by age 23 was already complaining that "his brain won't move as he wishes it to." In 1917, at age 27, Gurney had his first psychotic break, during which he believed he was being visited by Beethoven: "I felt the presence of a wise and friendly spirit; it was old Ludwig van all right . . . Bach was there but does not care for me." Gurney recognized that he was becoming sick and reflected upon it:

> Misery weighed by drachms and scruples
> Is but scrawls on a vain page.
> To cruel masters are we pupils,
> Escape comes careless with old age.
>
> Oh why were stars so set in Heaven
> To desire greedily as gluttons do,
> Or children trinkets—May death make even
> So rough an evil as we go through.

His illness worsened and he became convinced that "electrical tricks" were being played on him. "He would sit with a cushion on his head to guard against electric waves coming from the wireless [radio] . . . He has had such pains in the head that he felt he would be better off dead." Finally, at age 32, he was permanently hospitalized in the London Mental Hospital in Kent and there he spent the next 15 years, continuing to write poetry, such as these lines from the poem "To God":

> Why have you made life so intolerable
> And set me between four walls, where I am able
> Not to escape meals without prayer, for that is possible
> Only by annoying an attendant. And tonight a sensual
> Hell has been put upon me, so that all has deserted me
> And I am merely crying and trembling in heart
> For Death, and cannot get it. And gone out is part
> Of sanity. And there is dreadful Hell within me.

At age 47, still hospitalized, he died from tuberculosis.

John Nash was awarded the Nobel Prize for Economics in 1994 for work he had done at age 21 on mathematical game theory. *Fortune* magazine had called him "America's young star" at that time. In his late twenties, however, he developed a type of schizophrenia characterized by paranoid and grandiose delusions. He believed that "his career was being ruined by aliens from outer space" and that "he was scheduled to become Emperor of Antarctica" as part of a new world government. For more than 20 years he wandered between hospitals and lived with family members, supported mostly by his wife. Then, in his fifties, Nash's condition improved. When he received the Nobel Prize, the White House invited him for a visit. His life and illness have been nicely chronicled by Sylvia Nasar in *A Beautiful Mind* (see appendix A).

Vaslav Nijinsky was the most famous dancer in the years preceding World War I and, some have said, the greatest dancer who ever lived. His leaps were astounding, as he was said to be the only dancer who could, while in the air, cross his feet back and forth ten times. At age 29, he was diagnosed with schizophrenia and was intermittently hospitalized for the remainder of his life. He was markedly delusional, catatonic, and at times exhibited a word-salad thought disorder. He was treated by Alfred Adler and Manfred Bleuler, and Nijinsky's wife also consulted Freud and Jung. Nijinsky was also among the first to be treated by insulin coma therapy. In his diary, he wrote:

> I love life and want to live, to cry but cannot—I feel such a pain in my soul—a pain which frightens me. My soul is ill. My soul, not my mind. The doctors do not understand my illness. I know what I need to get well. My illness is too great to be cured quickly. I am incurable. My soul is ill, I am poor, a pauper, miserable. Everyone who reads these lines will suffer—they will understand my feelings.

In Paris, at the height of his career, the newspapers had labeled Nijinsky "God of the Dance." Nijinsky signed his diary entry, "God and Nijinsky."

One additional artist who is sometimes said to have had schizophrenia was Vincent van Gogh. Van Gogh has been given many other retrospective diagnoses by medical historians, including manic-depressive illness, brain syphilis, porphyria, and heavy metal poisoning from his paints. His symptoms included paranoid delusions, auditory and visual hallucinations, mutism, depression, and periods of great energy. Although there is a tendency to romanticize his psychosis and view it as partially responsible for his great art, van Gogh's own letters make explicit how painful and unpleasant it was. He ultimately committed suicide after painting for just ten years. From St.-Rémy he wrote to his brother, Theo: "Oh, if I could have worked without this accursed disease—what things I might have done."

In contrast to schizophrenia, manic-depressive illness lends itself to creativity because of the high energy level and rapid thought processes experienced by many people with this disease. The list of people suspected of having manic-depressive illness among creative individuals includes Handel, Berlioz, Schumann, Beethoven, Donizetti, Gluck, Byron, Shelley, Coleridge, Poe, Balzac, Hemingway, Fitzgerald, Eugene O'Neill, and Virginia Woolf. Alcoholism is also common among creative individuals; the first five Americans who won a Nobel Prize for literature were all alcoholics or nearly so (Sinclair Lewis, O'Neill, Faulkner, Hemingway, and Steinbeck).

THE PROBLEM OF STIGMA

People with schizophrenia and their families have to live with an extraordinary amount of stigma. Schizophrenia is the modern-day equivalent of leprosy, and in the general population the level of ignorance about schizophrenia is appalling. A 1987 survey among college freshmen found that almost two-thirds mistakenly believed that "multiple personalities" were a common symptom of schizophrenia, whereas less than half were aware that hallucinations are a common symptom. A 1986 poll found that 55 percent of the public did not believe that mental illness existed, and only 1 percent realized that mental illness is a major health problem. Other surveys have reported that many people continue to believe that schizophrenia and other severe psychiatric disorders are caused by sin or weakness of character.

There is good news and bad news regarding stigma. The good news is that the emergence of schizophrenia into the public eye has had a marked overall effect on reducing stigma. In the 1950s, when 400 individuals representative of the general population were surveyed concerning their beliefs about insanity, they rated "an insane person" as being more dangerous, more unpredictable, and worse than "a leper," traditionally the most stigmatized figure in most societies. By contrast, in 1996, when 1,301 "mental health consumers" were surveyed about stigma, "a majority reported that they had seldom or never been discriminated against in obtaining jobs or housing." Compared to earlier years, there is much greater understanding now that schizophrenia is a brain disorder and that people with schizophrenia are not responsible for being sick and cannot "just snap out of it."

The bad news is that schizophrenia is associated with violent behavior in the minds of the public. A survey in California in 1984, for example, reported widespread belief that people with schizophrenia were more likely than other people to commit violent crimes. A 1996 survey of a "nationally representative sample" of adults found that 13 percent believed that people with schizophrenia were "very likely" to be violent, and an additional 48 percent believed they were "somewhat likely" to be violent; the remainder of those surveyed thought that people with schizophrenia were "not very likely" (31 percent) or "not likely at all" (8 percent) to be violent. Thus, 61 percent of people associated violent behavior with schizophrenia. In this same survey only 33 percent associated violent behavior with major depression, and only 17 percent associated it with being "a troubled person." The only people with whom violent behavior was more strongly associated than those with schizophrenia were those with alcoholism (71 percent) and those with drug addiction (87 percent).

The really bad news, however, is that the association between schizophrenia and violent behavior appears to be growing stronger. This was highlighted in the 1999 "Report on Mental Health of the United States Surgeon General," which noted that in 1996, more than twice as many people associated violence with severe mental illness than did so in the 1950s. The report concluded:

> Why is stigma so strong despite better public understanding of mental illness? The answer appears to be fear of violence: people with mental illness, especially those with psychosis, are perceived to be more violent than in the past. . . . In other words, the perception of people with psychosis as being dangerous is stronger today than in the past.

Other recent studies have confirmed the relationship between violent behavior committed by individuals with severe psychiatric disorders and increased stigma against all individuals with mental illnesses. For example, a study using university volunteers demonstrated that reading a newspaper article reporting a violent crime committed by a mental patient led to increased "negative attitudes toward people with mental illnesses." And in Germany, following highly publicized attacks on prominent officials by individuals with severe mental illnesses, there was a measurable "marked increase in desired social distance from mentally ill people immediately following [the] violent attacks." The increased social distance and consequent stigma slowly decreased over time but had not returned to baseline two years later. Furthermore, in the 1996 U.S. national survey referred to above, there was found to be a high correlation "between the belief that a person is likely to be violent and the desire to maintain social distance from that person."

Individuals with schizophrenia and their families are acutely and painfully aware that episodes of violence by mentally ill individuals increase the stigma against them all. For example, in 1999, when a man with schizophrenia killed two people in a church library in Salt Lake City, "within hours Valley Mental Health began getting calls from frightened clients. Clients were just sobbing," said a spokesperson. "They were afraid that the public would want to retaliate against them." Such events are said to "set back years" ongoing efforts to destigmatize mental illness in the minds of the public.

Suggestions for how such stigma can be effectively decreased will be discussed in chapter 15.

RECOMMENDED FURTHER READING

Journal of the California Alliance for the Mentally Ill 4 (1). This entire issue is on mental illness in the media.

Nasar, S. *A Beautiful Mind: A Biography of John Forbes Nash, Jr., Winner of the Nobel Prize in Economics, 1994.* New York: Simon and Schuster, 1998.

Pescosolido, B. A., J. Monahan, B. G. Link, et al. "The Public's View of the Competence, Dangerousness, and Need for Legal Coercion of Persons with Mental Health Problems." *American Journal of Public Health* 89 (1999): 1339–45.

Wahl, O. F. "Mental Health Consumers' Experience of Stigma." *Schizophrenia Bulletin* 25 (1999): 467–78.

15

ISSUES FOR ADVOCATES

And, once more, we may say, that we have reason to plead for this class, because they cannot plead for themselves. It is one of the evils of insanity, that it cannot gain a fair hearing, or make known its wants. It laughs in horrid mirth, while coals of fire are on its head. It shrinks and shudders before the phantoms of its own creation. It sits in morbid silence while disease is gnawing upon its life. The insane plead not for themselves, but will not every generous heart feel yet more for them, in remembrance of their forlorn condition?

Robert Waterston, 1843

They say, "Nothing can be done here!"
I reply, "I know no such word in the vocabulary I adopt!"

Dorothea Dix, 1848

Dorothea Dix was an extremely effective advocate for persons with serious mental illnesses. She went into the poorhouses and jails to witness the atrocious conditions. She emphasized that mentally ill persons are not hopeless cases but rather can function much better if given adequate care and humane living conditions. She testified before innumerable state legislatures and investigatory commissions, always emphasizing the consequences of poor psychiatric care for individuals. She confronted and embarrassed officials, from local clerks to governors, publicly accusing them of not doing their jobs. Most important, she never took "no" for an answer.

Dorothea Dix has much to teach us today. Although not every consumer and family member can achieve her stature as an advocate, we all can do some work to improve the lives of people with schizophrenia. In doing so it is useful to keep in mind the following four general principles.

THE FOUR PRINCIPLES OF ADVOCACY

1. Master the facts of the situation. Credibility comes from facts, not merely from emotions.
2. Many consumers make excellent advocates. When trying to improve services, there is no substitute for the credibility that comes from having had schizophrenia or another serious mental disorder.
3. Put everything in writing, including your summary of meetings with officials. Send copies to everyone concerned. Officials can deny ever hearing you say something, but it is much more difficult for them to deny having received your letter when you have a copy of it.
4. Be careful of being co-opted. Politicians are experts at verbally agreeing with people and then doing nothing. Judge public officials by what they do, not by what they say. Don't accept crumbs when what is needed is a seven-course meal.

CONGRESS, STATE GOVERNMENT, AND THE POLITICS OF NEGLECT

Improving services and research for people with schizophrenia necessitates understanding how the system works. Until the 1960s, almost all decisions for public services for mentally ill individuals rested at the state level. Since then, the decision making has become much more complex. As noted in chapter 1, the federal government has become a major player in funding services, mostly through Medicaid reimbursement. Many states, meanwhile, have attempted to shift their remaining responsibility for services to the counties or cities, although the state government is still ultimately responsible. Thus, advocacy efforts, to be effective, must often be carried out at all three levels—federal, state, and local.

Effective advocacy for individuals with schizophrenia did not begin until the 1980s. Prior to that time, the organizations that might have been

expected to provide leadership for individuals with schizophrenia neglected this patient population. This neglect is one of the most shameful
stories in the history of American medicine.

The American Psychiatric Association (APA) was an especially
good candidate for such leadership. It had been begun in the 1840s as an
association of superintendents of state psychiatric hospitals and, until
World War II, its major area of interest was the seriously mentally ill.
With the ascendance of psychoanalysis in the United States and the
1930s influx of psychoanalysts from prewar Europe, however, the pres-
tige and dominant interest of American psychiatry shifted sharply to private psychotherapy for the worried. well. Patients with serious mental
disorders were no longer viewed as interesting or desirable, and in fact
the more prestigious a psychiatrist was, the less likely it was that his/her
patients would have schizophrenia.

Lack of APA interest in the seriously mentally ill was clearly
demonstrated in the 1970s when Dr. John Spiegel, then president of the
organization, toured the country to discuss with groups of psychiatrists
the 10 most important problems facing American psychiatry. The last
problem on the list was that of the chronic mental patient. Dr. Spiegel
noted that "although audiences tended to respond to the other points vigorously, on this issue, except for a rare complaint that something ought
to be done about it by the leaders of psychiatry, there was a numbing
silence." A study at that time showed that only 11 percent of patients
seen by psychiatrists in private practice were diagnosed with schizophrenia, despite the fact that schizophrenia was by far the most serious problem facing America's psychiatrists.

By the mid-1980s, the APA had evolved into being merely a union
to protect the vested interests of the nation's private psychiatrists. Today,
the energy and resources of the organization are devoted to lobbying for
insurance coverage to pay psychotherapy fees for the worried well and
to keeping psychologists and psychiatric social workers from taking
away private patients. A small number of psychiatrists have done, and
are continuing to do, outstanding jobs in providing competent and
humane care for individuals with schizophrenia; NAMI has recognized
this fact by each year publicly commending such psychiatrists. A few
APA leaders, such as Drs. John Talbott, Richard Lamb, Carl Bell, Jeffrey
Geller, and Mark Munetz, have also exhorted their colleagues to take
more interest in patients with schizophrenia, and an occasional APA district branch (e.g., the California Psychiatric Association) has taken some
action. Such examples, however, are conspicuous by being so rare. Most

exhortations produce occasional spasms of institutional guilt, resulting in study groups or conferences but little else. Therefore, most of the time the APA continues to act simply as a union for the nation's privately practicing psychiatrists. As such, it is no more likely to provide leadership for individuals with schizophrenia than is the Brotherhood of Teamsters or the AFL-CIO.

The National Institute of Mental Health (NIMH), created in the late 1940s as a research institute for serious mental illnesses, also seemed a logical candidate to provide leadership for the seriously mentally ill. However, for many years NIMH was not interested in these patients. Instead it strove to become an institute of human behavior, with tentacles extending to all problems of society, from poverty and racism to campus unrest, urban blight, child-rearing practices, and divorce. Its name, the National Institute of Mental Health rather than the National Institute of Mental Illness, has been used to rationalize an interest in virtually every social problem in America except the problem of the seriously mentally ill. Whereas the problem of the seriously mentally ill should be the primary focus of NIMH, it has instead become a minor issue relegated to the back corridors and trotted out ceremonially for official occasions such as budget hearings. In such an atmosphere NIMH has been about as likely to provide leadership for individuals with schizophrenia as has the Smithsonian Institution. In the late 1990s, NIMH began expressing more interest in the problem of schizophrenia; whether this rhetoric will lead to any real change remains to be seen.

The National Mental Health Association (NMHA), an advocate group for the mentally ill, should theoretically have been another candidate to provide leadership for the seriously mentally ill. It had been, after all, founded in 1909 by Clifford Beers (who had himself been hospitalized with manic-depressive illness) with the express purpose of reforming care in state mental hospitals. By World War II, however, the Mental Health Association, like American psychiatry generally, had lost interest in individuals with severe psychiatric disorders. It had instead supported the private practice, problems-of-living model of American psychiatry, acting as a handmaiden for psychiatrists and other mental health professionals and strongly supporting NIMH. On issues such as the coverage of individual psychotherapy under health insurance, the Mental Health Association became very active, mobilizing volunteers to visit and write their congressmen and otherwise lobbying for the rights of the worried well. Much of its rhetoric has focused on the need for good mental health, a concept as nebulous as it is all-inclusive. "Have you hugged your kid today?" Mental Health Association posters ask. Like mother-hood and apple pie, it is difficult to be against hugging your kid, but if most of an organization's energy goes into hugging kids there is little energy left over to promote better services for individuals with schizo-phrenia or other severe mental illnesses.

At the local level in cities such as Pittsburgh, Philadelphia, Dallas, Los Angeles, and Honolulu, the Mental Health Association has worked hard on behalf of the seriously mentally ill. At the national level, how-ever, it has continued to champion the ephemeral concept of "mental health" and has shown little interest in the mentally ill. In 1977, in fact, the organization gave its annual research award to two researchers whose work was based on the thesis that families cause schizophrenia. In terms of the politics of mental illness, the National Mental Health Association has quietly slipped into oblivion, a relic of the past.

Effective public leadership for individuals with schizophrenia and other serious mental illnesses had to await the birth of NAMI, formerly called the National Alliance for the Mentally Ill. The roots of NAMI go back to 1976, when Dr. Richard Lamb, then working in San Mateo County, California, assisted some local families in organizing advocacy efforts to improve county services for their family members with schizo-phrenia. In 1978 this group published an article, "Schizophrenia Through the Eyes of Families," in a national psychiatric journal. At the same time, families elsewhere were beginning to organize themselves, and those in Wisconsin convened a national meeting in Madison in 1979 with 284 attendees. That meeting was the birth of NAMI, which has now grown to over 1,000 local chapters. NAMI provides invaluable education and support services for its members (as discussed in chapter 12) as well as effective lobbying at the federal level for increased research funding and improved services for individuals with severe psychiatric disorders. Information on NAMI can be found in appendix D and on the Internet at www.nami.org.

In 1998 a new advocacy organization, the Treatment Advocacy Cen-ter (TAC) came into being. TAC focuses on the consequences of failed services for individuals with schizophrenia and other severe mental ill-nesses, including the numbers of mentally ill persons who are homeless, in jails and prisons, being victimized, or committing violent acts because they are not being treated. TAC focuses on changing state laws so that individuals can be treated before they suffer the consequences of non-treatment, and in 1999 was instrumental in effecting the passage of an assisted treatment statute (Kendra's Law) in New York State. TAC is also working to ensure that a sufficient number of state psychiatric hospital beds continue to exist to provide for the needs of severely mentally ill individuals. Information on TAC can be found in appendix D and on the Internet at www.psychlaws.org.

SCIENTOLOGISTS, ANTIPSYCHIATRISTS, AND "CONSUMER SURVIVORS"

One impediment to improving services for individuals with severe psychiatric disorders is a small but vocal coalition of Scientologists, antipsychiatrists, and "consumer survivors." These disparate and often interdependent groups are united by a hatred of psychiatry. Many are intellectual descendents of the Szaszian (that schizophrenia does not exist) or Langian (that schizophrenia is a growth experience) rhetoric of the 1960s. These radical groups oppose any form of assisted treatment, even its use for individuals with schizophrenia who are not aware they are sick and are incarcerated because of actions caused by their illness or living on the streets. Many, if not most of the Scientologists, anti-psychiatrists, and "consumer survivors" are against the use of any psychiatric medications whatsoever.

The Scientologists channel their opposition to psychiatry through their Citizens Commission on Human Rights (CCHR), which proclaims on its letterhead "established by the Church of Scientology in 1969 to investigate and expose psychiatric violations of human rights." CCHR, not known for its subtlety, disseminates publications with titles such as "Betraying Women: Psychiatric Rape," "Psychiatry: Victimizing the Elderly," "Psychiatry's Role in the Creation of Crime," and "Psychiatry: Destroying Religion."

The efforts of CCHR are based on the teachings of L. Ron Hubbard, the founder of Scientology, whose main book was entitled *Dianetics: The Modern Science of Mental Health*. Scientologists see psychiatry as a rival that must be destroyed. According to one published account, "Hubbard taught that the psychotic person is a 'potential trouble source' who is connected to forces opposed to Scientology. People who behave as psychotics are 'unethical' and 'immoral.'" Hubbard also taught that the "forces" behind psychiatry are extraterrestrial. According to a recent published account, Hubbard claimed that "Earthlings are the pawns of aliens" and that "the psychiatric establishment—which always looked askance at his theories—was not just a present-day evil but a timeless one. In a distant galaxy, alien 'psychs' [as Hubbard called them] devised implants that would ultimately wreck the spiritual progress of human beings." Thus, psychiatrists were the Darth Vaders of Hubbard's universe.

All of this sounds like harmless nonsense until one realizes that many Scientologists actually believe it. Of even more concern, however, is that, by making financial demands on members and by recruiting celebrities such as John Travolta and Tom Cruise, the Scientologists have assembled enormous monetary resources to finance their anti-psychiatry crusade as well as provide support to other individuals and groups who oppose psychiatry. The Scientologists' opposition to psychiatric treatment also has occasional fatal consequences. For example, in 1995, when a woman Scientologist in Clearwater, Florida, developed acute mania, other Scientologists confined her and failed to seek psychiatric care, and she died 17 days later; a civil wrongful death suit filed against Scientology by the woman's estate is pending.

One prominent anti-psychiatrist who has been linked to Scientology's Citizens Commission on Human Rights is Dr. Thomas Szasz, discussed in chapter 7. The CCHR website lists Szasz as a "founder," and its letterhead lists him as a "Founding Commissioner," although Szasz himself has disavowed this relationship.

Another anti-psychiatrist who has been linked to Scientology is Dr. Peter Breggin, author of *The Psychology of Freedom* and *Toxic Psychiatry* (see appendix A, "The 15 Worst Books on Schizophrenia"). According to a published account, "Breggin admits that he was once an ally of the group [Scientologists] and that his wife was a member." Breggin, who trained under Szasz, has written that the main cause of mental illness is "stress in the family, community, and society," and that "people diagnosed schizophrenic often seem in crisis over the meaning of their lives and their personal identities." He has also written, in the context of mental illness, that "the difference in believing in the divinity of Christ and believing in oneself as Christ is merely a difference in religious point of view." In place of psychiatric medications, which Breggin has labeled "the worst plague of brain damage in medical history," he advocates the use of "therapy, empathy and love." Breggin's methods for promoting good mental health early in life are equally bizarre; he has written that "permitting children to have sex among themselves would go a long way toward liberating them from oppressive parental authority."

Szasz and Breggin are revered by the "consumer survivors," a small group of former psychiatric patients opposed to psychiatric medications and any form of assisted psychiatric treatment. Much of their rhetoric has a Scientology ring to it. "Mad Nation" proclaims itself to be "People Working Together for Social Justice and Human Rights in Mental Health." Another "consumer survivor" group is the Support Coalition. One of this group's codirectors, Janet Foner, is also the "main leader for Mental Health Liberation in the Re-Evaluation Counseling Communities." Re-Evaluation Counseling was founded by an ex-Scientologist and, like Scientology, presents its teachings as an alternative to psychiatry. As noted in chapter 12, much of the "consumer survivor" movement is funded by the federal Center for Mental Health Services, which certainly qualifies as one of the strangest existing misuses of federal money.

It is important for advocates to understand the position of Scientologists, anti-psychiatrists, and "consumer survivors" because these groups frequently oppose efforts to improve services or to provide treatment for those who need it most. Organized psychiatric advocacy groups are too often silent when confronted by the distortions and misinformation of the Scientologists and other anti-psychiatry groups. Some people are also reluctant to counter erroneous public statements by "consumer survivors," because of a misplaced belief that it is politically incorrect to argue with ex-patients. This is, of course, nonsense; for every "consumer survivor" there are a hundred other individuals with schizophrenia who are quietly working to provide support for others so afflicted and to improve psychiatric services. These "consumer survivors" speak for no one but themselves.

What you can do as an advocate:

- Counter the misinformation of Scientologists and other groups by writing letters-to-the-editor and making calls to call-in radio shows.

- Offer to testify at hearings at your city or county council or your state legislature regarding the necessity of treating people with schizophrenia, the importance of medications, and the necessity of improved psychiatric services.

- If you are a consumer, speak out against the distortions and misinformation disseminated by the "consumer survivors." Let people know that they do not represent you.

- Educate yourself about how laws can be changed so that individuals with severe mental illnesses can be treated. A good source of information is the Treatment Advocacy Center's website (www.psychlaws.org).

NIMH AND RESEARCH FUNDING

Increased federal research funding for schizophrenia has been one of the most successful of NAMI's accomplishments. Largely through the bipartisan support of senators Pete Domenici and Paul Wellstone as well as other members of Congress, funding for schizophrenia research at NIMH tripled between the late 1980s and the mid-1990s. That is the good news.

The bad news is that, despite such increases, NIMH still falls woefully short in allocating money to schizophrenia research. A study of 1997 NIMH research dollars, done *after* the improvement in research allocation from the late 1980s to the mid-1990s, reported that only 13.5 percent of all NIMH research funds was going to research that had any relationship to schizophrenia, and this included some basic neuroscience research whose relationship to schizophrenia was decidedly tenuous. Even more alarming was the fact that only one-fifth of the 13.5 percent, or 2.7 percent of the total NIMH funds, was being spent for clinical or treatment-related research on schizophrenia. Given the fact that the federal government is spending approximately *$10 billion* a year on federal SSI and SSDI subsidies alone for individuals with schizophrenia (see chapter 1), to allocate such a small share of federal research dollars to this disease is completely illogical on economic grounds alone. To be spending such a small portion of research funds on the treatment of such an important and costly disease is also morally unconscionable; to be doing so *after* NIMH has increased its spending in this area is scandalous.

What you can do as an advocate:

- Contact your representatives in Congress and ask them why they are permitting NIMH to spend such a small proportion of its budget on schizophrenia research. The Director of NIMH should have to answer that question each time he/she comes to Congress at budget time.

- Support the National Alliance for Research on Schizophrenia and Affective Disorders (NARSAD) by helping them raise funds for research. They can be contacted at NARSAD Research Fund, 60 Cutter Mill Road, Suite 404, Great Neck, NY 11021; their website is www.mhsource.com/narsad.html.

- Support efforts of researchers to maintain brain banks in which brains of persons who had serious mental illnesses are collected after death. These are exceedingly useful for research. A brain bank that specifically works with families is the Harvard Brain Tissue Resource Center. They can be contacted at McLean Hospital, 115 Mill Street, Belmont, MA 02178-9896, phone 800-BRAINBANK, website http://www.brainbank.mclean.org:8080.

- Support animal research. Animals are essential both for understanding the causes of schizophrenia and for developing better treatments. In recent years, some animal rights activists have lobbied to ban the use of animals for medical research. The public must be educated to realize that such a ban would seriously impair research efforts.

EDUCATING THE PUBLIC

One of the major reasons why services and research for schizophrenia have been so neglected is that most people do not understand this disease. The number of people who still believe that schizophrenia is a "split personality," for example, is shockingly high. We should not expect legislators or the public at large to support improved services or research unless we are willing to help educate them. Education, therefore, is one of the most important tasks for us all, and there are many different groups that need to be educated.

What you can do as an advocate:

- Develop a speakers' bureau and offer to talk to community service organizations (e.g., Kiwanis, Lions, Rotary), school assemblies, and local companies. Mr. and Ms. Ron Norris in Wilmington, Delaware, persuaded the Du Pont Corporation to fund the making of a film that can be used for such presentations. It is called "When the Music Stops" and is 20 minutes long. Many of the other videotapes listed in appendix C are also very useful as educational tools.

- Organize a local education campaign. For example, in the mid-1990s, Gregg and Sandra Miller organized an annual mental illness awareness campaign in St. Petersburg, Florida, called "End the Mystery." This initiative has been very successful and has been copied by several hundred other communities. For more information, contact Elliott Steele at 19236 Gulf Blvd., #501, Indian Shores, FL 33785, phone 727-596-2506.

- Another type of community education program is "Nothing to Hide: Mental Illness in the Family." This is an exhibit of photographs and interviews with 20 families affected by severe mental illnesses. It is available for booking in your community through Family Diversity Projects, Inc., c/o Chriscomm Management, P.O. Box 1493, Kingston, PA 18704, phone 570-675-4933, fax 570-675-4980, E-mail chriscom@familydiv.org, Internet address http://209.207.203.197/nothingtohide/.

- Create a local cable TV show. Local cable stations often allocate free studio time and free broadcast time to local organizations. NAMI/NYC started a cable show called "Mental Illness Update" that has been running for over six years. Once a month, a NAMI member goes to the cable company and records four half-hour interviews (often with another NAMI member) that are broadcast over the following four weeks. This is free and gets lots of new members for the chapter. Contact NAMI/NYC at 432 Park Avenue South, New York, NY 10016, phone 212-684-3264, website www.nami.org/about/naminyc/index.htm.

- Schools are an especially fertile ground for education. Several NAMI state affiliates have developed working groups that target the schools. For example, in 1993, NAMI New York State developed a lesson plan on mental illness for grades 4–6, 7–8, and 9–12, then sent it to the health coordinators in every school district in the state and urged local NAMI members to encourage the health coordinator to use it.

- There are 344,000 churches, synagogues, and mosques in the United States. The clergy are often the first people consulted by individuals with schizophrenia and their families, so the clergy are natural allies. Offer to give a talk on schizophrenia to the congregation; Mental Illness Awareness Week is a good time to do so. NAMI Maine developed a Religious Outreach Committee to educate all clergy in the state. Pathways to Promise, which started as part of NAMI St. Louis, has attempted to educate clergy on a national level; their address is 5400 Arsenal Street, St. Louis, MO 63129, and their website is www.pathways2promise.org. In some areas clergy still teach that mental illness is a sign of sin; *Strength for His People*, by Pastor Steven Waterhouse (see "Recommended

Further Reading," chapter 13), is a good educational tool in such instances. Religious groups are the main providers of care for the homeless mentally ill, since these groups operate most public shelters; they are therefore aware of the vast numbers of untreated individuals with schizophrenia and are potentially strong allies in your advocacy efforts.

- Establish contact with officials of local newspapers and radio and television stations. Encourage them to consider more coverage of the problems of the seriously mentally ill, e.g., an exposé of a run-down boarding house. Educate them about schizophrenia and manic-depressive illness. Ask them to speak at a meeting of your support group. Extensive information about how to work with the media is available in the "Advocacy" section of the NAMI/Metro NYC website, www.nami.org/about/naminyc/index.htm.

- Educate mental health professionals in training by offering to make presentations to local nursing schools, schools of social work, university departments of psychology, schools of medicine, and psychiatric residency training programs.

- Initiate a dialogue between your group and the local psychiatric society. Ask them to make a presentation to your group and ask to make one to their group. Both sides will emerge with a better understanding of each other's problems and with ideas on how you can be helpful to each other. The Northeast Ohio Alliance for the Mentally Ill in Cleveland has done this very effectively. Offer to write articles for the local or state APA newsletter, presenting your point of view on an issue for which you need their support.

- Educate lawyers and judges about schizophrenia. Request time to make a presentation to the monthly meeting of the local bar association and offer to teach a class at the law school.

- Offer to give a lecture to police trainees. Police officers come into frequent contact with individuals with schizophrenia on the street; the more education they have, the more humane will be the services they render.

- For all educational efforts, utilize informed consumers whenever possible. They have much more credibility with laypersons than do either family members or professionals. They should—they have been there.

DECREASING STIGMA

Decreasing the stigma associated with schizophrenia and other mental illnesses is a task for Sisyphus—every time you start to make some progress, the stone rolls back downhill and you must begin all over again. What repeatedly pushes the stone downhill are episodes of violence committed by individuals with schizophrenia or other severe psychiatric disorders.

As noted in chapter 14, research studies in both the United States and Europe have demonstrated that episodes of violence are the largest single cause of stigma against individuals with mental illness. Such studies suggest that it will be extremely difficult to decrease stigma against individuals with mental illnesses until the episodes of violence are decreased. This has not been widely recognized by some advocacy groups who prefer instead to deny that episodes of violence exist, or to suggest that the media not report them. This is the traditional stance of the ostrich, which does, indeed, keep the problem out of sight but simultaneously leaves important bodily areas exposed. In discussing this problem as early as 1981, Dr. Henry Steadman, who has done research on violence and mental illness, noted: "Recent research data on contemporary populations of ex-mental patients supports these public fears [of dangerousness] to an extent rarely acknowledged by mental health professionals. . . . It is [therefore] futile and inappropriate to badger the news and entertainment media with appeals to help destigmatize the mentally ill."

The single most important thing advocates can do to decrease stigma, therefore, is to support attempts to decrease violence. An important part of these attempts is the use of assisted treatment for individuals with severe mental illnesses who have limited awareness of their illness and who have demonstrated a propensity for violence (see chapter 11 and TAC in appendix D). Dr. Richard Lamb made this point in a recent editorial when he said: "We can reduce stigma by doing what needs to be done to ensure that persons with severe mental illness who resist treatment receive the treatment they so clearly need." To claim that you are working to decrease stigma but that you oppose all assisted treatment is simply to identify yourself as an admirer of Sisyphus.

In addition to reducing episodes of violence, there are many other things advocates can do to help reduce stigma. Virtually all educational efforts, as listed previously, decrease stigma; studies have shown that the more people understand about schizophrenia, the less likely they are to stigmatize persons who are affected.

What else you can do as an advocate:

- Organize a local advertising campaign to combat stigma. For example, the Ontario Friends of Schizophrenics and NAMI New York State funded a series of billboards and posters (e.g., on city buses), explaining what schizophrenia is and how widespread it is. A NAMI group in Ohio persuaded a local grocery chain to put on the grocery bags: "The brain is part of the body. It too can become ill. Schizophrenia and depressive disorder are *no fault* brain illnesses."

- Utilize materials prepared by NAMI's anti-stigma campaign (see "Stigma Alert Listings" at www.nami.org).

- Whenever possible, have responsible consumers give talks to community groups and schools. Studies have shown that personal contact with individuals who are mentally ill is one of the most effective means of decreasing the perception that they are dangerous.

IMPROVING SERVICES

As detailed in chapter 1, services for most individuals with schizophrenia in the United States, with few exceptions, vary from mediocre to abysmal. It has been said that individuals with schizophrenia "are not falling between the cracks—they are lost in the ravines."

What you can do as an advocate:

- Publish a resource book describing local resources for persons with schizophrenia and manic-depressive illness. Several NAMI groups that have done this can be used as models (e.g., NAMI Dupage County, Illinois; NAMI Washington; NAMI Colorado; NAMI Missouri; NAMI Connecticut; NAMI New Hampshire; NAMI North Carolina).

- Become an expert on low-cost housing. Visit existing units being used by persons with schizophrenia living in your community, take pictures, and show them to the county council, etc. Visit model housing projects and make people in your community aware of what can be done.

- Encourage the setting-up of group homes in decent neighborhoods by working against restrictive zoning ordinances.

- If there is a great lack of halfway houses in your community, work with the local agencies to set one up yourself. The Main Line Mental Health Group outside Philadelphia successfully did this, renovating a mansion adjacent to Haverford State Hospital into what is almost certainly the most elegant and comfortable halfway house in the United States.

- Become an expert on vocational training for individuals with serious mental illnesses. Visit model programs. Meet with state vocational training officials and explore possibilities. Go to the state legislature if necessary.

- Visit the nearest state-sheltered workshop. Ask the director why more persons with schizophrenia are not included. If, as in most such workshops, they are few and far between, organize a letter and telephone blitz of the state legislature to get the policy changed. Look at model workshops.

- Organize part-time jobs with local business and industry to be filled by persons with schizophrenia and manic-depressive illness.

- Organize a local clubhouse, using the Fountain House model in New York City. Encourage the state to fund such programs.

- Become an expert on SSI and SSDI regulations. Do a brief survey to ascertain how many people with schizophrenia and/or manic-depressive illness are eligible for, but not in fact receiving, their benefits. Meet with the local officials in charge of these programs. Ask consumers and families to bring to your attention instances where persons with these diseases have been rejected or cut off from benefits.

- Lobby to eliminate the Medicaid IMD exclusion (see chapter 1). For more information, visit the TAC website at www.psychlaws.org.

- Work to get responsible consumers and representatives of family support groups on all city, county, and state mental health boards and advisory commissions, on the boards of directors of Community Mental Health Centers (CMHCs), and on the boards of local Protection and Advocacy Programs.

- Become politically aware. Identify the legislators in your county and state who support the concerns of the mentally ill. Let these legislators know that you back them because of their stand. Organize political support for them in elections.

- Become an expert on the county and state mental health budget. Where is the money going? Who is getting services? Who is *not?* Attend the key subcommittee meetings. Offer to testify as a consumer or family member.

- Meet regularly with the director of the local CMHC. Push to raise serious mental illness to top priority for clinic services. Make sure that he/she understands that the failure to do so may result in decreased state funding for the CMHC.

- Lobby the state legislature to give greater priority to serious mental illness for the expenditure of state mental health dollars. Accomplishing this in some states (e.g., Colorado and Oregon) has proved helpful. Members of the legislature whose special concern is corrections and public safety will be especially responsive to your message, and these members should be targeted.

- Arrange for the introduction of legislation in your state to change the name of the state Department of Mental Health to the Department of Mental Illness. It will help people to focus on the real problems.

- Lobby for the establishment of a bill of rights guaranteeing minimum standards of service for individuals with serious mental illnesses. For a model of such a bill, write to the Deputy Commissioner for Mental Health, Iowa Department of Human Services, Des Moines, IA 50319.

- Set up a system of respite care among a group of families, with families covering for each other so they can get away on vacations. NAMI South Carolina did this. Suggest to local authorities that they support such services and provide some of the necessary manpower.

- Organize a plan for providing continuing care for individuals with serious mental illnesses after the other family members have died (e.g., Planned Lifetime Assistance Network [PLAN], described in chapter 13).

- Educate insurance companies about the necessity of covering schizophrenia and manic-depressive illness in exactly the same way multiple sclerosis is covered. They should be encouraged to differentiate these brain diseases from problems of living, for which insurance coverage is not practical since there is no logical cutoff to the need. Take an insurance executive to lunch, or have your NAMI group make a formal presentation to the company staff so that they will better understand the disease. Buy a single share in the company; this will entitle you to go to the company's annual meeting and publicly ask questions.

- Change state insurance laws to require insurance companies to cover schizophrenia and other serious mental illnesses in the same way they cover serious physical illnesses. NAMI has done this very successfully with their campaign for parity.

- Publish a booklet outlining commitment laws and procedures in your state, including the major impediments to obtaining hospitalization for individuals with serious mental illnesses. A brief synopsis of each state law is included on the TAC website, www.psychlaws.org.

- Combat the negligent release of patients by psychiatric inpatient units. If the patient scheduled to be released is known to be a danger to himself or others, send a letter such as the following by registered mail:

Dear _____ ,

You have under your care John Doe. I am informed that you intend to release John Doe. You should not do so. I know John Doe to be a danger to himself and to others. You already have information that puts you on notice of this fact. If there is any doubt, I now put you on notice.

   If, in spite of this information, you release John Doe and he causes injury to himself or others, you will be responsible because you were on notice that your release of John Doe would be the substantial factor in causing either harm to him or to others or both.

Better yet, have a lawyer send it.

- Sue mental illness professionals who endanger patients by negligently reducing medication to levels known to be too low, or who release patients from the hospital when it is clear that the patients cannot care for themselves.

- Work with the Treatment Advocacy Center to advocate the wider use of assisted treatment when necessary, including the use of outpatient commitment laws that permit patients to live in the community as long as they continue to take medication (see chapter 11 and visit www.psychlaws.org).

- Work with the state commissioner of mental health to set up quarterly meetings between responsible consumers, family groups, and mental illness professionals to discuss problems. In Maine such a program proved useful.

- Work with state mental health officials to devise innovative ways to recruit good mental illness professionals into the state system, as Maryland did. Let good mental illness professionals know that the families appreciate them.

- Establish public awards at the local and state levels for outstanding employees of the mental illness system and representatives of the media who have covered mental illness issues. Civil service systems do not reward excellence, so support groups must. Create a coalition with other community groups (e.g., Kiwanis, Rotarians, Elks, etc.) to form annual awards presentation ceremonies.

- Vigorously oppose the closing of state hospital beds until *after* adequate housing and outpatient services are in place. Do not believe future promises; the promising official will be long gone when the time comes to deliver. If necessary, bring legal suits against city and state governments, insisting that they provide psychiatric aftercare and shelter for released mental patients.

- Ascertain how many seriously mentally ill children are being sent to other states for inpatient treatment. Publicize the fact. Ask officials why they cannot be treated in your state.

- Ascertain whether families of seriously mentally ill children in your state are being asked to give up custody of their children as a condition for receiving services. If so, go to the media and ask them to publicize this medieval practice.

- Become an expert on the confidentiality laws in your state; then educate other families and the mental illness professionals.

- Advocate a mandatory service pay-back system in public facilities for all psychiatrists, psychologists, and psychiatric social workers who are trained with state funds.

- Advocate for changing state licensing laws to require, as a condition of licensure, two hours a week of pro bono services in public facilities (e.g., mental health centers, jails, shelters) for all psychiatrists, psychologists, and psychiatric social workers.

- Visit local nursing homes and get to know the administrators. Explore with them and with local officials how psychiatric care can be improved for the many persons with serious mental illnesses who are confined to nursing homes. Ask the administrator to make a presentation to your support group. Encourage the establishment of in-service education about serious mental illnesses to the nursing homes' staffs.

- Arrange for your NAMI group to visit the local jail to become educated about the problems of mentally ill individuals there. Invite a member of the media to come along. Get a copy of *Improving Mental Health Services in California's Local Criminal Justice System*, by Thomas E. Backer et al., 1997, which was largely written by NAMI California members (Human Interaction Research Institute, 1849 Sawtelle Blvd., Suite 102, Los Angeles, CA 90025).

- Organize regular unannounced inspections of public psychiatric inpatient units. A few state NAMIs have done this.

- Work with the psychiatric staff of the local Veterans Administration (VA) hospital. In Largo, Florida, a NAMI group called the Suncoast Community Support Auxiliary has worked closely with the Bay Pines VA Hospital to provide support, advocacy, and services through its Community Support Group. In Maine a

NAMI group formed a wives' support group at the Togus VA Hospital. The VA Hospital in West Haven, Connecticut, has a continuous treatment team (PACT model); ask why your VA hospital doesn't have one too. The VA hospital in Denver has an exemplary rehabilitation program (Bayaud Industries); ask why your VA doesn't have one too.

• If the inpatient psychiatric unit in your local hospital is deficient, notify the Joint Commission on Accreditation of Healthcare Organizations (JCAHO) at One Renaissance Boulevard, Oakbrook Terrace, IL 60181 (telephone 800-994-6610, E-mail: complaint@jcaho.org); additional information on JCAHO is available on the Internet at www.jcaho.org/. JCAHO inspects most such facilities every three years. You can ask to meet with the JCAHO accreditation team to make your concerns known when they next visit the hospital. Be sure to also send your concerns to JCAHO by registered letter. Although JCAHO has generally been an ineffectual watchdog, you can still use them to send a clear message to your local psychiatric unit.

• If the hospital flagrantly disregards the rights of patients, ask for an investigation by the Civil Rights Division, U.S. Department of Justice, Washington, DC 20530.

• In larger states, do a ranking of state hospitals and/or CMHCs on the quality of care they provide for individuals with serious mental illnesses. Publicize the rankings. NAMI North Carolina and NAMI Alabama have done this.

HOW TO ORGANIZE FOR ADVOCACY

Your advocacy efforts will be more effective if you have a well-organized and strong group. Numbers of members help, but in fact effective advocacy in most organizations is usually accomplished by a small number of its members. Consumers, siblings, children of mentally ill individuals, spouses, parents, grandparents, friends, and mental illness professionals who are interested can all play important roles. Considering the fact that there are 2.2 million persons with schizophrenia today in the United States, a coalition of them, their families, and friends should theoretically be able to accomplish almost anything. To do so, however, it is necessary to get more of them out of the closets and into the streets. Some suggestions for doing so are the following:

- Increase membership in your local support group. Leave brochures for your group with all local mental illness profession-als. Give brochures to drug salesmen who visit physicians. Leave leaflets on the windows of cars parked in the visitors lot of the state hospital. Put notices on community bulletin boards, in church bulletins, and in company and local newspapers. One NAMI group persuaded a grocery chain to print its name and telephone number on milk cartons. Another persuaded the telephone com-pany to include information on their group with telephone bills.

- Organize special support groups for siblings, children of mentally ill individuals, wives and husbands, the parents of seriously men-tally ill children, and individuals being treated in the VA system. These special support groups have been started by some state and local NAMI chapters.

- Enlist the help of the individuals who run the local homeless shel-ter and your local law enforcement officials. These people are acutely aware of the failure of public services for individuals with serious mental illnesses. They are potentially excellent allies.

- Enlist the assistance of local civic groups that are also concerned about problems of individuals with severe mental illnesses. For example, some Kiwanis Clubs have been helpful, and the League of Women Voters in Illinois undertook a major survey of services for mentally ill individuals.

- If *none* of the above suits your aptitudes or abilities and you still want to help, there is one thing left that you can do. As advocated in the movie *Network*, when fed up with existing conditions you should lean out your window and yell loudly: "I'm mad as hell and I'm not going to take it anymore!" After doing this you will be forced to explain to your neighbors what is going on, and sev-eral more families will thereby become educated about schizo-phrenia.

Services for individuals with schizophrenia and other serious men-tal illnesses are not likely to improve until enough individuals become angry and get organized. Persons with schizophrenia will continue to be fourth-class citizens, leading twilight lives, often shunned, ignored, and neglected. They will continue to be, in the words of President Carter's Commission on Mental Health, "a minority within minorities. They are the most stigmatized of the mentally ill. They are politically and economically powerless and rarely speak for themselves. . . . They are the totally disenfranchised among us." The mad will become liberated only when those of us fortunate enough to have escaped the illness show how mad we really are.

A

50 OF THE BEST AND 15 OF THE WORST BOOKS ON SCHIZOPHRENIA

THE ESSENTIAL SCHIZOPHRENIA LIBRARY

The following books are the best readings for becoming familiar with all phases of schizophrenia. Some of them, and several listed under "Other Good Books on Schizophrenia," are now out of print. However, almost all are available used over the Internet (www.bookfinder.com), and some may be available at your local library.

Amador, Xavier. *I Am Not Sick, I Don't Need Help*. Peconic, N.Y.: Vida Press, 2000. This is the first book that attempts to address the elephantine question running roughshod over families of individuals with schizophrenia: Why won't the sick person take his/her medicine? Amador, a psychologist who has a brother with schizophrenia, has pioneered research on awareness of illness, also known as insight or anosognosia, for the past decade and is an acknowledged authority on it. He blends clinical vignettes skillfully with his erudition, and the resulting mix is edifying. Most important, Amador provides families and mental illness professionals with a concrete, step-by-step plan to improve awareness of illness in the person who has schizophrenia. It will not work all the time but is well worth trying before having to utilize involuntary hospitalization and various forms of assisted treatment. This book fills a tremendous void in the schizophrenia literature.

Buckley, Peter F., and John L. Waddington, eds. *Schizophrenia and Mood Disorders: The New Drug Therapies in Clinical Practice*. Boston: Butterworth Heinemann, 2000. This is the best information available on the newest antipsychotics and mood stabilizers, along with summaries of the older medications. It is a dense compilation of 25 chapters by 50 different contributors, including many of the most knowledgeable persons in that field. The editors have cleverly combined an American and a non-American author for most chapters, so the reader is given a worldwide perspective. A series of chapters covers the treatment of special populations, e.g., children, the elderly, substance abusers, violent patients, and pregnant women, and each chapter includes an extensive list of references at the end. A deficiency of the book is identifying the drugs by their generic name only and not adding the trade names in parentheses, as is usually done. Nevertheless, this book will be widely used by professionals and will also be of interest to consumers and families using the newer medications.

Deveson, Anne. *Tell Me I'm Here*. New York: Penguin Books, 1992. This is a powerfully written account of a son's schizophrenia as seen through his mother's eyes. Deveson is a broadcaster and filmmaker, well known to the Australian public, and her account of her son's illness enabled many Australian families with a seriously mentally ill family member to come out of the closet. Because it is real, her story is more terrifying than the worst fictional horror story. Deveson skillfully captures the various shades and nuances of the tragedy we call schizophrenia.

Gorman, Jack M. *The Essential Guide to Psychiatric Drugs*, 3rd ed. New York: St. Martin's Press, 1997. This is a general guide to psychiatric drugs that has been popular with patients and families since the first edition was published in 1990. It includes not only a summary of each drug used for schizophrenia, manic-depressive illness, depression, and other psychiatric disorders but also chapters on issues of special interest, e.g., "Sex and Psychiatric Drugs" and "Psychiatric Drugs and Pregnancy." The book is user-friendly and well organized, making it easy to find what you are looking for.

Hatfield, Agnes B., and Harriet P. Lefley. *Surviving Mental Illness: Stress, Coping and Adaptation*. New York: Guilford Press, 1993. Eminently practical and well-written, this book will be useful for families trying to sort out the myriad problems confronting them when a family member becomes seriously mentally ill. Emphasis is put on the importance of understanding what the sick person is experiencing, so the book includes some useful personal accounts by Dr. Frederick Frese, Esso Leete, and Daniel Link.

Isaac, Rael Jean, and Virginia C. Armat. *Madness in the Streets*. New York: Free Press, 1990; Paperback published by the Treatment Advocacy Center, 2000. This is an important history of the "mental health" movement and how so many individuals with serious mental illnesses ended up homeless and on the streets. There is enough blame to go around for just about everyone involved in the "mental health" scene, but the lawyers with the American Civil Liberties Union and the Bazelon Center for Mental Health Law collect (and deserve) the largest share. It is a well-written and depressing history and essential to understand if we expect to improve things.

Marsh, Diane T., and Rex Dickens. *How to Cope with Mental Illness in Your Family: A Self-Care Guide for Siblings, Offspring, and Parents.* New York: Putnam, 1997. This is an excellent book on how severe psychiatric disorders affect other members of the family and, more important, what to do about it. The authors, a psychologist specializing in severe psychiatric disorders and a man whose mother and three siblings have been affected, have been active members of NAMI for many years. Their book is a synthesis of what they have been told by hundreds of families, including extended personal accounts that they published in an earlier book, *Anguished Voices.* The emphasis in this book is on self-help and coping skills. Most important, the authors emphasize the tremendous variability of the effect of having a family member with a severe psychiatric disorder. On one end is devastation, divorce, and what has been called "a funeral that never ends." On the other end is the young woman described by Marsh and Dickens who remembers "standing up in second grade and sharing the mental condition of my brother as my contribution to Show and Tell. I thought it was the most unique thing about my life and certainly better than any hamster!"

Russell, L. Mark, Arnold E. Grant, Suzanne M. Joseph, and Richard W. Fee. *Planning for the Future: Providing a Meaningful Life for a Child with a Disability After Your Death,* 3rd ed. Evanston, Ill.: American Publishing, 1995. For anyone who is trying to plan for the future for a mentally disabled family member, this is essential reading. The authors cover everything from SSI, SSDI, Medicaid, Medicare, and other government benefits to wills, trusts, estate planning, power of attorney, and nursing home expenses. The book is replete with detailed examples and includes sample letters of intent. It has been especially popular with parents who worry about what will happen to their mentally ill child after they are gone.

Sheehan, Susan. *Is There No Place on Earth for Me?* Boston: Houghton Mifflin, 1982. Paperback published by Random House, 1983. Susan Sheehan's superb study originally appeared in the *New Yorker* magazine. It provides the best available description of the course of a chronic schizophrenic illness, the difficulties encountered by a person with the disease, the frustrations for the family, and the mediocre care available at the state hospital. It is searingly accurate and mandatory reading for anyone who wants to understand the tragedy of this disease. The patient described has the schizoaffective subtype.

Torrey, E. Fuller. *Out of the Shadows: Confronting America's Mental Illness Crisis*. New York: John Wiley, 1997. Paperback ed., 1998. It seems like bad manners to recommend one's own book, but in fact the book has been very well received. It details the consequences of our failed mental illness treatment system, including individuals with schizophrenia and manic-depressive illness who are homeless, in jails and prisons, or victimized or who commit violent acts because they are not being treated. Much of the blame goes to the thought-disordered funding system and laws, and the book offers a blueprint for solving these problems. *Out of the Shadows* is, in some respects, a sequel to my *Nowhere to Go: The Tragic Odyssey of the Homeless Mentally Ill* (New York: Harper and Row, 1988), which gives more of the historical background of the disaster that we call contemporary mental illness services.

Wasow, Mona. *The Skipping Stone: Ripple Effects of Mental Illness on the Family*. Palo Alto: Science and Behavioral Books, 1995. This is a lyrical summary of 100 interviews done with family members of individuals with a serious mental illness. Mona Wasow is a social worker and the mother of a son with schizophrenia. "The ripple effect of mental illness on the entire family is enormous," she states, and proceeds to document this effect on the siblings, spouses, grandparents, and children of affected individuals. Her chapters on grief, coping, and hope are excellent, e.g., "trying to capture the essence of grief in writing is like trying to capture the wind in a box or the ocean in a glass." Her understanding of these illnesses is beautifully and brutally frank: "But let us be honest with ourselves: the tortures of hallucinations, the failure to connect with people, and the anxieties, desperate isolation, and loneliness of people with serious mental illness take a staggering toll."

Winerip, Michael. *9 Highland Road*. New York: Vintage Books, 1994. Michael Winerip, a respected reporter for the *New York Times*, spent two years hanging around a group home on Long Island. The result is an engaging, lively, and very well-written narrative that captures the home's ambience, including the struggles and joys of its residents diagnosed with schizophrenia and other severe psychiatric disorders. "Schizophrenia," writes Winerip, "is the most monstrous of the mental illnesses." And elsewhere: "Listening to Anthony's explanations when he was psychotic was like trying to understand one of your dreams the next morning." Perhaps the book's greatest contribution is to illustrate that individuals with schizophrenia need more than medication to reclaim their lives. They also need friends, guidance, support, and people who believe in them. A good group home, such as Winerip is describing, provides those things and is an optimal living situation for many people with this diagnosis. Oh, that there were more such places! The contrast between the warmth of the home at 9 Highland Road and the living situations of the majority of individuals with schizophrenia is enough to make you cry.

OTHER GOOD BOOKS ON SCHIZOPHRENIA

The following are other books that are recommended to learn more about schizophrenia.

Adamec, Christine. *How to Live with a Mentally Ill Person: A Handbook of Day-to-Day Strategies*. New York: John Wiley, 1996. This is a solid and practical how-to book by a professional writer whose daughter developed schizophrenia. It utilizes a positive, "cheerleading" approach "to energize you and give you the hope you need." Included are a multitude of practical suggestions, such as a model "Crisis Information Form" to be prepared ahead of time for emergency admissions or if you have to call the police. The author emphasizes the importance of accepting the illness and moving on, of not being bogged down by the "myth of the 'before' person" or the "ghost of patient past." She also emphasizes the importance of a sense of humor, exemplified by a woman with schizophrenia who "went to a Halloween party dressed as a Cogentin tablet, a medication to counter the side effects in antipsychotic medication." Above all, says Adamec, "never give in, never give in, never, never, never, never . . ."

Amador, Xavier F., and Anthony S. David, eds. *Insight and Psychosis*. New York: Oxford University Press, 1998. Although expensive, this is an important book for understanding the issue of insight, or awareness of one's illness, which forms the core of the debate about involuntary treatment. A chapter by Joseph McEvoy ("The Relationship Between Insight in Psychosis and Compliance with Medications") is excellent. The chapter by William Bara on the anatomy of insight and the first and last summary chapters by the editors are also first-class. This is not a page-turner to peruse in an airport lounge but rather a scholarly treatise for those who want to really understand a complex but critical issue.

Andreasen, Nancy. *The Broken Brain: The Biological Revolution in Psychiatry*. New York: Harper and Row, 1984. Despite the fact that some sections of this book are now quite out of date, it has been a favorite of families and consumers and is still one of the best accounts of brain research. Its especially clear description of the structure and function of the brain provides lay readers with everything they need to know to follow the current neuroscience revolution. It covers not only schizophrenia but manic-depressive psychosis, Alzheimer's disease, and anxiety disorders as well.

Backlar, Patricia. *The Family Face of Schizophrenia: Practical Counsel from America's Leading Experts*. Los Angeles: Tarcher, 1994. "Being a family member of someone with schizophrenia is a difficult job. No one ever applies for these jobs and there is no standard job description." This quite nicely summarizes this book, which includes seven true stories of schizophrenia, each followed by a commentary by a professional (two psychiatrists, two psychologists, a psychiatric nurse, a social worker, and a lawyer). It is an unusual format, but it works surprisingly well. The most extraordinary story is that in which Eric Morgan, suffering from paranoid schizophrenia, kills his psychiatrist in Portland, Oregon. If you have any lingering doubts whether the mental illness treatment system is broken, you won't have after you finish this story.

Bernheim, Kayla F., Richard R. J. Lewine, and C. T. Beale. *The Caring Family: Living with Chronic Mental Illness*. New York: Random House, 1982. Although this was one of the first books written for family members of someone with a severe mental illness, its message is as useful today as when it was published. The authors discuss such common reactions as guilt, shame, fear, anger, and despair and offer suggestions for resolving them. The book discusses "chronic mental illness" as a whole and does not focus specifically on schizophrenia, but its discussion of individual and family dynamics as a consequence of the illness is certainly applicable.

Button, Margo. *The Unhinging of Wings*. Lantzville, British Columbia, Canada: Oolichan Books, 1996. This is a remarkable collection of 66 poems written by Margo Button about her son, afflicted with schizophrenia, who committed suicide at age 27. Many of the poems had been previously published in literary journals, and the collection is a poignant and moving memorial.

> *Now I know there is no one to blame,*
> *but that impassive god*
> *who shoots stray bullets*
> *through the brain.*

The preface for the book is by Dr. Michael Smith, who won the 1993 Nobel Prize for Chemistry and donated his prize money to schizophrenia research.

Coleman, Mary, and Christopher Gillberg. *The Schizophrenias: A Biological Approach to the Schizophrenia Spectrum Disorders*. New York: Springer, 1996. This is a very good book for those who are interested in the many diseases that may mimic schizophrenia. In fact, there are so many of them, and they are covered in such detail, that the reader is left wondering whether there is anything called "schizophrenia" other than these mimicking diseases. That question is consistent with the conclusion of the authors, who contend that "schizophrenia forms a behavioral syndrome that represents the final common pathway of a number of different developmental, physical, enzymatic, infectious, and other injuries."

Cutting, John, and Anne Charlish. *Schizophrenia: Understanding and Coping with the Illness*. London: Thorsons, 1995. Written by a respected schizophrenia researcher and a journalist, this has been a popular book in England for families of schizophrenia sufferers. The descriptions of symptoms by patients themselves are especially noteworthy, e.g., "I seem to be empty inside. Nothing touches me anymore. It's as if I am an object without feelings, without the urge to do anything." The sections on the diagnosis of schizophrenia are also strong.

Frangou, Sophia, and Robin M. Murray. *Schizophrenia*. London: Martin Dunitz, 2000. Distributed in the United States by Blackwell Science. This is a handy summary of schizophrenia done in two colors with many boxes and graphs. It is visually appealing, easy to read, and can be carried in your pocket or purse for reading on the bus or train. It relies heavily on studies done in England since it is targeted primarily at an English market, but its message is universal.

Gottesman, Irving I. *Schizophrenia Genesis: The Origin of Madness*. New York: W. H. Freeman, 1991. Gottesman is one of the leading researchers on the genetics of schizophrenia, and in this book he summarizes the pertinent studies. He also weaves into the text personal accounts of individuals with schizophrenia, which makes the research data both more pertinent and more interesting.

Hall, Laura Lee, ed. *Genetics and Mental Illness: Evolving Issues for Research and Society*. New York: Plenum Press, 1996. This is a useful volume for those with a specific interest in the genetics of severe psychiatric disorders. There are good overviews of genetic research in general and of the nature-nurture controversy. The section on genetic counseling is especially thoughtful. The chapter on the inheritance of schizophrenia, by Dr. Irving Gottesman, summarizes information from his *Schizophrenia Genesis*. The research discussed in the book was current at the time it was written in the mid-1990s, but this is an area that is changing rapidly.

Hirsch, Steven R., and Daniel R. Weinberger, eds. *Schizophrenia*. Oxford: Blackwell Science, 1995. Revised ed. 2001. If your recently deceased Aunt Agatha left you a large bequest and you are having trouble spending it, this textbook on schizophrenia would be a worthy addition to your library. Its 31 chapters and 688 pages cover all clinical aspects of schizophrenia, including descriptive aspects, causes, and both pharmacological and psychosocial treatments. The authors are, almost without exception, respected authorities on their subjects and include a nice mix of Europeans and Americans. This textbook is being widely used by psychiatric trainees despite its cost of $165.

Holley, Tara E., and Joe Holley. *My Mother's Keeper: A Daughter's Memoir of Growing Up in the Shadow of Schizophrenia*. New York: Morrow, 1997. Reprinted in paperback, 1998. This is a good book, though with a skilled editor it could have been much better. A daughter's account of her mother's paranoid schizophrenia, the book chronicles the effects of the illness on the daughter and other family members and the daughter's ceaseless attempts to provide care for her mother. Despite Tara Holley's best efforts, however, her mother lives on the streets for long periods; as such, the book bears similarities to Margaret Moorman's *My Sister's Keeper* (sister with schizophrenia becomes homeless) and Nathaniel Lachenmeyer's *The Outsider* (father with schizophrenia becomes homeless). The book's strength is in its descriptions of the author's relationship to her mother's illness and her attempts to help. What do you do, for example, when you are walking down the street talking with one of your college professors and your homeless mother comes shuffling toward you along the sidewalk? The author's husband, a journalist, adds an articulate and sensitive prologue and epilogue. The book's weakness is that it is exceedingly long-winded, and the reader will lose little by skipping most of the first half. Despite this, the book will be of interest to anyone whose mother has become severely mentally ill.

Jeffries, J. J., E. Plummer, M. V. Seeman et al. *Living and Working with Schizophrenia*, 2nd edition. Toronto: University of Toronto Press, 1990. This is the second edition of a basic book on schizophrenia that has been especially popular with Canadian families. Although the section on medications is now out of date, the rest of the book continues to be helpful, especially for an individual or family confronting schizophrenia for the first time. It includes chapters specifically targeted toward consumers (e.g., "I Am a Schizophrenic") and also toward relatives (e.g., "How Relatives Can Help"). It is concise and well written.

Karp, David. *Burden of Sympathy: How Families Cope with Mental Illness*. New York: Oxford University Press, 2000. After reading works by Erving

420

APPENDIX A

Goffman, Thomas Schiff, and other sociologists who have studied mental illness, my expectations of another such work were virtually zero. What a pleasant surprise to be proven wrong! Karp, a professor of sociology at Boston College, himself suffered from severe depression. Based on 60 intensive interviews he did with family members of individuals with schizophrenia, manic-depressive illness, and severe depression, he has written an excellent book "about the social tango between emotionally ill people and those who try to help them." In examining the lives of the family members, he demonstrates that "sustaining an appropriate level of involvement with a mentally ill child, parent, sibling, or spouse is extraordinarily difficult." Karp writes well and, perhaps because of his own experience with depression, captures the essence of caring and caregivers.

Keefe, Richard S. E., and Philip D. Harvey. *Understanding Schizophrenia: A Guide to the New Research on Causes and Treatment*. New York: Free Press, 1994. Written by two respected research psychologists, this book has some major strengths but also some weaknesses. The section on symptoms is good, as is the brief section on skills training approaches. The index is extensive, and the authors have commendably donated their royalties to NARSAD. However, the title promises more than is actually delivered on either causes or treatment; the authors are only partially responsible for this, since things are moving so rapidly in the research arena.

Lachenmeyer, Nathaniel. *The Outsider: A Journey into My Father's Struggle with Madness*. New York: Broadway Books, 2000. Charles Lachenmeyer had a Ph.D. in sociology before he developed paranoid schizophrenia and ultimately became homeless. This story is his son's reconstruction of his father's life. It is painful and poignant, and all the more so because the father responded to medications when he took them for brief periods. The story also abounds in ironies, including the fact that the father had worked as an attendant in a state hospital while in college and had written his thesis on the double-bind theory of schizophrenia. The book is also a reminder of the number of Charles Lachenmeyers living on the streets today and the number of sons and daughters who wonder what has happened to them.

Lamb, Wally. *I Know This Much Is True*. New York: Regan Books, 1998. Paperback published by HarperPerennial, 1999. Would you believe that in 1998 a book of fiction about identical twins in which one has schizophrenia was number one on the *New York Times* bestseller list? That in itself is good news. And for the most part, the author gets the schizophrenia story right, complete with self-mutilation, suicide, and the consequences of deinstitutionalization. An especially nice touch is casting a psychologist from India as the most competent clinician in the story. But the story has no shortage of problems. The largest is the ambiguity left by the author regarding whether early childhood experiences contributed to the sick twin's illness. The portrayal of the relationship between the identical twins also badly misses reality. In addition, much of the book has the tedium of a never-ending soap opera, on and on, for 897 pages. Half as long would have been twice as good. But if you have a very long flight, say to Mongolia, it will fill the hours.

Lefley, Harriet P. *Family Caregiving in Mental Illness*. Thousand Oaks, Calif.: Sage Publications, 1996. This is the most recent of several good books Lefley has written to bridge the gulf of understanding between families (she is the mother of an individual with schizophrenia) and psychiatric professionals (she is also a psychologist). She is thus admirably qualified to help each side understand the problems faced by the other. Previously, she coedited *Families as Allies in Treatment of the Mentally Ill* (Washington: American Psychiatric Press, 1990) and *Helping Families Cope with Mental Illness* (New York: Harwood Academic Publishers, 1994). If the mental health professional with whom you are dealing does not understand the family burden of schizophrenia, Dr. Lefley's book would make a nice present.

Lieberman, Jeffrey, and Robin Murray, eds. *Comprehensive Care of Schizophrenia*. London: Martin Dunitz, 2000. This is an excellent and up-to-date textbook on the treatment of schizophrenia. Jeffrey Lieberman and Robin Murray are among the best-known experts on schizophrenia in the United States and England, respectively. Their approach to treatment is truly comprehensive, beginning with pharmacological approaches and proceeding to psychological (cognitive behavioral) approaches and rehabilitation. Special treatment problems receive individual attention, including patients who are suicidal, violent, substance abusers, or treatment-resistant. Patient compliance with treatment, a critical but oft-neglected subject in such books, is also allotted a chapter of its own. And the importance of listening to the patients and their families is emphasized in the chapter "Clinician Interactions with Patients and Families." The book includes many two-color illustrations and, except for the cost ($99.95 in the United States), would be a useful addition to the library of any serious student of this disease.

Marsh, Diane T. *Serious Mental Illness and the Family: The Practitioner's Guide*. New York: John Wiley, 1998. This is the best book available for mental illness professionals providing care for individuals with severe mental illnesses. The author, a psychologist who specializes in treating individuals with these illnesses and their families, also authored the useful *Families and Mental Illness: New Directions in Professional Practice*, published in 1992. As the author notes, *Serious Mental Illness and the Family* "is designed to assist practitioners in developing the competencies necessary for working with families." Although aimed at mental health professionals, families will find the sections on siblings, spouses, and off-spring of seriously mentally ill individuals especially useful. Marsh knows her business, and I had only one question after reading the book: Where are all those other knowledgeable professionals who practice as she does? Another very worthy book in this genre is Harriet P. Lefley and Dale L. Johnson, eds., *Families as Allies in Treatment of the Mentally Ill* (Washington, D.C.: American Psychiatric Press, 1990).

Mendel, Werner. *Treating Schizophrenia*. San Francisco: Jossey-Bass, 1989. This was the late Dr. Mendel's last book and is a tribute to his remarkable work. He followed 497 patients with schizophrenia for up to 35 years. The book is unusual in its longitudinal perspective on the disease and in emphasizing the importance of the relationship between the psychiatrist and the individual with schizophrenia in helping the latter to cope. At the time of his death, Dr. Mendel had retired from private practice and was working in a state psychiatric hospital. Oh that we had more such doctors!

Moorman, Margaret. *My Sister's Keeper*. New York: Norton, 1992. The effect on siblings of having a seriously mentally ill brother or sister has been little studied or written about. Moorman's account of her older sister's schizophrenia goes a long way toward filling that gap. She is especially articulate about the problems of role reversal as a younger sister who had to, in effect, become an older sister to her older sister. Part of the book was originally published in the *New York Times*, and Moorman also appeared on the *Oprah Winfrey Show* to discuss her experiences.

Mueser, Kim, and Susan Gingerich. *Coping with Schizophrenia: A Guide for Families*. Oakland, Calif.: New Harbinger Publications, 1994. Written by a psychologist and a social worker, this book has an excellent section, "Creating a Supportive Environment," that includes discussions of communicating, problem solving, managing stress, and establishing rules. Also included are abundant worksheets and practical ideas. The book is weaker and now dated in its presentation of medication, and it contains no index whatsoever, an inexplicable omission for a family manual. Overall, however, it is a useful book, especially for a family with someone with schizophrenia living at home.

Nasar, Sylvia. *A Beautiful Mind: A Biography of John Forbes Nash, Jr., Winner of the Nobel Prize in Economics, 1994*. New York: Simon and Schuster, 1998. Paperback published by Touchstone Books, 1999. This is a nicely written account of John Nash. A brilliant mathematician in his twenties, he then developed schizophrenia but partially recovered in his late fifties and was awarded the Nobel Prize for Economics in 1994 for his earlier work. The book describes clearly the early premorbid asociality and other symptoms of illness that precede the illness in approximately one-third of cases. It also provides a poignant account of the devastating effects of the illness on Nash's wife, sons, mother, and friends, as well as a good description of the confused etiological ambience of the early 1960s. Except for a few errors, such as overstating the risk of tardive dyskinesia and other possible adverse effects of antipsychotics, the author did her homework and exhibits a good understanding of the disease.

North, Carol. *Welcome, Silence: My Triumph over Schizophrenia*. New York: Simon and Schuster, 1987. This is the personal account of a young woman's fight against the symptoms of schizophrenia. Although her case is quite atypical in many ways, the book includes excellent descriptions of what it is like to experience auditory hallucinations and to fight the symptoms of the disease. North was one of the few patients who responded dramatically to renal dialysis as an experimental treatment, and she is today a fully trained psychiatrist who specializes in serious mental illness.

Preston, John D., et al. *Consumer's Guide to Psychiatric Drugs*. Oakland, Calif.: New Harbinger Publications, 1998. This guide to drugs used for treating schizophrenia and other psychiatric illnesses is similar to Gorman's *Essential Guide to Psychiatric Drugs*, with each book having different strengths. The first half of this book discusses general issues (e.g., "Managing Your Medications," "Seeking Treatment"), while the second half is an extensive description of each drug listed alphabetically along with a directory by brand names that makes it user-friendly. There is also a useful chapter, "Nonpharmaceutical Approaches," that includes such treatments as melatonin and St. John's wort.

Riley, Jocelyn. *Crazy Quilt*. New York: Morrow, 1984. An unusual children's book, this is the fictional account of a 13-year-old girl whose mother has schizophrenia. It is a poignant reminder of the effects of this disease on other family members and the fact that children need education and support just as siblings and parents need them. We need many more such books so that children, too, may understand. An earlier book by the same author, *Only My Mouth Is Smiling* (1982), is also good. Other worthy children's books are Betty Hyland, *The Girl with the Crazy Brother* (New York: Watts, 1987), in which a 16-year-old girl has to cope with the onset of schizophrenia in her brother, and Regina Hanson, *The Face at the Window* (New York: Clarion Books, 1997), set in rural Jamaica.

Schiller, Lori, and Amanda Bennett. *The Quiet Room: A Journey out of the*

Torment of Madness. New York: Warner Books, 1994. This is a brave book by a woman whose schizoaffective disorder began at age 17 with auditory hallucinations as the only symptom. The hallucinations remained her only symptom for several years, allowing her to complete college and start working; in this respect, her atypical course is similar to that described by Carol North in *Welcome, Silence*. Lori Schiller tells her story from the perspective of several other people (mother, father, brother) as well as from her own. She provides an especially good account of her use of cocaine as a form of self-medication as well as capturing the loss of a normal life because of her illness. Eventually, her illness evolves into full-blown psychosis until she begins clozapine, to which she responds very well.

Simon, Clea. *Mad House: Growing Up in the Shadow of Mentally Ill Siblings*. New York: Doubleday, 1997. What is it like, as an eight-year-old girl, to have your older brother and sister both develop schizophrenia? Clea Simon lived it and eloquently describes it. She is especially articulate in describing being caught between fear and guilt, the traditional Scylla and Charybdis of relatives of those afflicted. Simon, who writes for the *Boston Globe*, is an excellent writer and has created a lovely book about a very cruel disease.

Swados, Elizabeth. *The Four of Us: A Family Memoir*. New York: Farrar, Straus and Giroux, 1991. Paperback published by Penguin Books, 1993. This is an extraordinary account of how severe mental illness can devastate an entire family. The son is officially diagnosed with schizophrenia but appears to have the schizoaffective type or even bipolar disorder. The effects of the disease's malignant ripples are stunning, as the young man spirals downward to a failed suicide attempt, throwing himself beneath a subway train, then to homelessness. It is beautifully written, brutally honest, and profoundly depressing. Recommended for reading on sunny days in pleasant gardens.

Taylor, Robert. *Distinguishing Psychological from Organic Disorders: Screening for Psychological Masquerade*. New York: Springer, 2000. This is an updated, second edition of an excellent book. The author lays out a method for mental illness professionals to use to distinguish organic brain diseases (e.g., brain tumors) from schizophrenia, manic-depressive illness, and other psychiatric conditions. Taylor's method is lucid, eminently practical, and remarkably easy to implement, and any professional who reads this book will be a better clinician. If I were an insurance company executive, I would offer lower malpractice premiums to professionals who read this book, because they will have significantly reduced their chances of being sued. This book should also be required reading for all mental illness professionals in training.

Torrey, E. Fuller, Ann E. Bowler, Edward H. Taylor, and Irving I. Gottesman. *Schizophrenia and Manic-Depressive Disorder: The Biological Roots of Mental Illness as Revealed by a Landmark Study of Identical Twins*. New York: Basic Books, 1994. Paperback ed. 1996. This is the report of a study of 66 pairs of identical twins; in 27 pairs, one had schizophrenia and the other was well, and in 13 pairs, both had schizophrenia. The twins were intensively studied—their developmental history, minor physical anomalies, fingerprint patterns, PET scans, and neurological, neuropsychological, MRI, and blood studies—in an effort to identify nongenetic causes of the disease. As one twin researcher wrote, identical twins are " 'experiments' which nature has conducted for us, starting in each case with identical sets of genes and varying environmental factors." And as "experiments," they indeed are both interesting and useful.

Walsh, Maryellen. *Schizophrenia: Straight Talk for Families and Friends*. New York: William Morrow, 1985. This is one of the best accounts of schizophrenia from the point of view of the parent of a person afflicted. Articulate and angry, yet able to maintain a sense of humor, Walsh describes confrontations with the ignorance and the indignities faced by families. There is familiarity and comfort in sharing her ordeals, and hope in joining her fight to change the system.

Wechsler, James. *In a Darkness*. New York: Norton, 1972. Republished in Miami by Pickering Press, 1988. A product of the dark 1960s, when most families were told that they had caused the disease, this is an account of a son's schizophrenia written by his father, a distinguished journalist. It is an articulate and poignant account of 10 years of searching for a good psychiatrist and a cure, and of the family chaos caused by the illness. The family's agony of not knowing what to do is exceeded only by the pain of the son's eventual suicide.

Weiden, Peter J., Patricia L. Scheifler, Ronald J. Diamond, and Ruth Ross. *Breakthroughs in Antipsychotic Medications: A Guide for Consumers, Families and Clinicians*. New York: Norton, 1999. This book focuses primarily on the second-generation antipsychotics and includes valuable summaries of clozapine, risperidone, olanzapine, quetiapine, and ziprasidone. It also includes fact sheets on such adverse effects as weight gain, sedation, and sexual difficulties. The major drawback of the book is its uncritical enthusiasm for the newer drugs and implicit assumption that virtually everyone with schizophrenia should be switched from first-generation medication to these medications. As is becoming increasingly clear, the second-generation antipsychotics have their own set of problems, and many patients are better off with the older drugs.

Wyden, Peter. *Conquering Schizophrenia: A Father, His Son, and a Medical Breakthrough*. New York: Knopf, 1998. This is the story of a dedicated father, who died shortly after publication of the book, and his search for an effective treatment for the schizophrenia suffered by one of his sons. It provides a good history of antipsychotic drug development and focuses especially on olanzapine (Zyprexa), to which his son responded. The author was a professional writer, so the book is well written. The author's other son is the current U.S. senator from Oregon.

Woolis, Rebecca. *When Someone You Love Has a Mental Illness: A Handbook for Family, Friends, and Caregivers*. New York: Perigee Books, 1992. This is a handy book to have around because of its numerous "Quick Reference Guides" for such subjects as "Handling Your Relative's Anger," "Dealing with Bizarre Behavior," "Preventing Suicide," and "Rules for Living at Home or Visiting." It does not provide long discourses on the various subjects but instead tells you what to do. It is a practical book par excellence.

THE 15 WORST BOOKS ON SCHIZOPHRENIA

The following are nominations for the 15 worst books on schizophrenia. If you own any of them, don't throw them away; some day they may be worth money as intellectual curiosities. Your grandchild will ask, incredulously, "Did they *really* believe that then?"

Barnes, Mary, and Joseph Berke. *Mary Barnes: Two Accounts of a Journey Through Madness*. New York: Ballantine Books, 1973. This is the book that made Ronald Laing's approach to schizophrenia widely known. Schizophrenia, it says, is a "career" that is "launched with the aid and encouragement of one's immediate family." The family member with schizophrenia is often "the least disturbed member of the entire group." This assertion is preposterous in any context, but it becomes completely bizarre when one realizes that Laing's own daughter was diagnosed with schizophrenia. Moreover, the authors claim that suffering from schizophrenia can be a growth experience—"psychosis may be a state of reality, cyclic in nature, by which the self renews itself." There is no end to such absurd drivel in this book.

Bateson, Gregory, Don D. Jackson, Jay Haley, and John Weakland. "Toward a Theory of Schizophrenia." *Behavioral Science* 1 (1956): 251–64 and reprinted in several books, including *Beyond the Double Bind*, Milton M. Berger, ed. New York: Brunner Mazel, 1978. This paper gave birth to the double-bind, the heads-I-win-tails-you-lose method of family communication that the authors "hypothesize goes on steadily from infantile beginnings in the family situation of individuals who become schizophrenic." The authors admitted that "this hypothesis has not been statistically tested" and in fact it never was; nevertheless, it was adopted as fact by two generations of mental health professionals who proceeded to blame the family (especially the mother) for causing the disease. Schizophrenia, say the authors, is "a way of dealing with double-bind situations to overcome their inhibiting and controlling effect." What seems incredible in retrospect is that theoretically intelligent people could postulate the symptoms of schizophrenia as the product of such relatively innocuous family communications. The fact that psychiatrists, psychologists, and social workers bought it—untested—is a scathing indictment of their intelligence quotient.

Breggin, Peter R. *The Psychology of Freedom*. Buffalo, N.Y.: Prometheus Books, 1980. It is difficult to select the worst books about schizophrenia from the many Dr. Breggin has written, but this is one of my favorites. "Craziness," as Breggin refers to schizophrenia, "is a failure of nerve. . . . Insanity is cowardice; utter insanity is utter cowardice." Individuals who develop schizophrenia, says Breggin, are responsible for making themselves that way. "The individual makes himself or herself helpless" because he does not have the courage to face his own shortcomings. "People who are grossly deluded and hallucinating are grossly cowardly and have forfeited responsibility for the control of their own inner life. . . . It is the self-imposed crippling of the individual by himself or herself." This extraordinary drivel continues page after page; it is a wonder that people with schizophrenia haven't yet chased Breggin up a tree for his vitriolic attacks on them.

Breggin, Peter R. *Toxic Psychiatry*. New York: St. Martin's Press, 1991. It would have been difficult to imagine that Dr. Breggin could have written a worse book on psychiatric medications than his previous one, *Psychiatric Drugs: Hazards to the Brain*, but he has accomplished this considerable feat. Schizophrenia, Breggin tells us, is "a psychospiritual overwhelm" caused by child abuse and/or the drugs used to treat it. His style is a disjointed hysteria in which he grossly exaggerates the negatives and ignores the positives. For example, his opinion of antipsychotic drugs has not improved since 1986, when he wrote: "Psychiatry has unleashed a plague on the world with millions upon millions of permanently damaged patients. It's the worst doctor-induced catastrophe in the history of medicine." Rather than antipsychotic drugs, Breggin recommends psychotherapy, love, and empathy as the treatments of choice for schizophrenia. The book is truly a "psychospiritual" underwhelm, and St. Martin's Press should be ashamed to have its name on it.

Colbert, Ty C. *Broken Brains or Wounded Hearts: What Causes Mental Illness*. Santa Ana, Calif.: Kevco, 1996. There seems to be no end to the repackaging of traditional psychoanalytic theory and attempts to sell it as something new. Colbert, a California psychologist in private practice, would have us believe that "schizophrenia is not a brain disease" but rather merely the product of "an overload of emotional pain." He claims that "the mind *purposely* creates the defenses necessary to deal with that pain. Thus, the disorders of schizophrenia, depression, and other so-called mental illnesses are seen as the person's own strategy for adapting to the pain." The person *chooses* to have schizophrenia. If this isn't enough, Colbert reaches for new depths of absurdity by analyzing the childhoods of psychotic killers Charles Manson and Jeffrey Dahmer and claiming that their homicidal behavior was simply due to "wounded hearts" from disappointments in their childhoods. This book is an overload of something, and it's not emotional pain.

Cooper, David. *Psychiatry and Anti-Psychiatry*. New York: Ballantine Books, 1967. Another confused protégé of R. D. Laing, Cooper in this book romanticized the individual with schizophrenia as merely expressing the pathology of the family. Specifically he speculated that "in the 'psychotic' families the identified schizophrenic patient member by his psychotic episode is trying to break free of an alienated system and is, therefore, in some sense less 'ill' or at least less alienated than the 'normal' offspring of the 'normal' families." This is pure bunkum.

Goffman, Erving. *Asylums: Essays on the Social Situation of Mental Patients and Other Inmates*. Garden City, N.Y.: Anchor Books, 1961. Supported by funds from the National Institute of Mental Health, sociologist Erving Goffman spent a year at St. Elizabeths Hospital in Washington, D.C., observing the patients. He concluded that most of the patients' behavior was a reaction to being hospitalized, not a result of their illnesses. The logical corollary was that one needed only to open the gates of the hospital and let the patients go free, no strings (or medication) attached, and they would live happily ever after. *Asylums* was widely read and was an important influence on mental health administrators who decided to do exactly that. One only wishes today that Goffman could be given a mattress under a bridge or freeway in any American city so that he could observe how the experiment turned out.

Green, Hannah. *I Never Promised You a Rose Garden*. New York: Holt, Rinehart and Winston, 1964. If a prize were to be given to the book that has produced the most confusion about schizophrenia over the past 30 years, this book would win going away. The young woman with "schizophrenia" is helped to become well by psychoanalytic psychotherapy. In fact, the woman almost certainly never had schizophrenia; her symptoms were much more consistent with hysteria, and she went on to marry, have a family, write 15 books, and lecture all over the country—not exactly a typical course of schizophrenia. Furthermore, psychoanalytic therapy is about as likely to cure schizophrenia as it is likely to cure multiple sclerosis. The book belongs in the Kingdom of Ur with the young woman's fantasies.

Kesey, Ken. *One Flew over the Cuckoo's Nest*. New York: Signet Books, 1962. Made into a popular movie, this is a fictional version of the idea promoted by Erving Goffman in *Asylums* and by the movie *King of Hearts*. Randle McMurphy tries to mobilize the patients in the state hospital to challenge Big Nurse Ratched and the evil psychiatrists who work there. The patients are depicted as oppressed, not sick, and in the end Chief Broom escapes from the hospital to live happily ever after. In reality Chief Broom probably joined the legion of homeless mentally ill individuals living under some bridge, ended up in jail, was beaten up, or all of the above. Kesey was a guru of psychedelic drugs at the time, and his story also has an hallucinatory ring to it.

Lidz, Theodore. *The Relevance of the Family to Psychoanalytic Theory*. Madison, Conn.: International Universities Press, 1992. This book completes 45 years of pumpkin-headed publications by Dr. Lidz, a professor of psychiatry at Yale University. His career started in 1949 with "Psychiatric Problems in the Thyroid Clinic," which asserted that individuals with hyperthyroidism "had in childhood felt less wanted than a sibling." He then moved on to his study of 16 families in which one member had schizophrenia: "In each family at least one parent suffered from serious and crippling psychopathology, and in many both were markedly disturbed . . . the father appeared to be seriously disturbed just as often as the mother." Over the years Lidz and his colleagues evolved a two-part classification of families with a member with schizophrenia into "skewed" or "schismatic," and said that "they both revolve around the egocentricity of one or both parents." In his 1992 book Lidz still claims that "by now numerous investigators have found serious disorders of communication in all families of schizophrenia patients." It is the distant cry of the Yaleosaurus, thought to have been long extinct! It is doubtful if ever in the history of medicine so many papers and books have been published on so few patients in studies of such doubtful scientific merit.

Modrow, John. *How to Become a Schizophrenic: The Case Against Biological*

Psychiatry. Everett, Wash.: Apollylon Press, 1992. This is a pathetic book by a man who was once diagnosed with schizophrenia. "My fate had been sealed not by my genes, but by the attitudes, beliefs, and expectations of my parents [who] had serious psychological problems of their own." His symptoms, says Modrow, were merely the consequence of the stress his mother and father subjected him to. In one chapter he claims that "schizophrenia is largely caused by feeling of intense self-loathing." Elsewhere he reassures us that "there is no vast difference between schizophrenia and normalcy." "Psychiatry," says the author, "can be compared to the Ku Klux Klan and other racist or white supremacist organizations." One can sympathize, to some extent, with anyone with schizophrenia who is trying to make sense of this terrible affliction. It is much less easy to sympathize with the muddleheadedness of Drs. Thomas Szasz ("an impressive piece of work"), Theodore Lidz ("a very important contribution"), and Peter Breggin ("one of the best things I've read on the subject"), who provided cover endorsements for this sad tome.

Mosher, Loren R., and Lorenzo Burti. *Community Mental Health*. New York: Norton, 1989. If you have ever wondered why the National Institute of Mental Health (NIMH) exerted so little leadership for individuals with serious mental illnesses for so many years, this book may provide you with an answer. Dr. Loren Mosher was, for over a decade, the chief of NIMH's Center for Studies of Schizophrenia. Incredibly, he believes that schizophrenia is merely "disturbed and disturbing behavior," not a disease. He is staunchly anti-medication "because many psychotropics separate persons from their experience of themselves" and adds that "we do not believe in routine maintenance neuroleptic drug treatment for persons labeled schizophrenic." Instead, he believes "that madness is all too understandable, and that it can be effectively treated by psychosocial methods," mostly love, understanding, and a soft teddy bear. In the context of contemporary psychiatry, the book is a relic from the distant past.

Robbins, Michael. *Experiences of Schizophrenia*. New York: Guilford Press, 1993. This book may well become a collector's item as one of the last books written in which psychoanalysis and other forms of insight-oriented psychotherapy are recommended as the treatment of choice for schizophrenia. As such, it follows in the tradition of Boyer and Giovacchini's *Psychoanalytic Treatment of Schizophrenic, Borderline and Characterological Disorders* (1980) and Karon and Van den Bos' *Psychotherapy of Schizophrenia: Treatment of Choice* (1981). Robbins describes selected cases of schizophrenia that he treated with psychoanalysis for up to seven years. Like most psychoanalysts, Robbins blames families for causing schizophrenia, describing them as "quietly totalitarian and controlling, suppressive of the autonomy and potential for separation of individual members." Psychoanalysis is not the treatment of choice for schizophrenia; on the contrary, since it often makes the patient worse, it can be said to be the nontreatment of choice.

Rubin, Theodore I. *Lisa and David*. New York: Macmillan, 1961. This book is included because it became a movie (*David and Lisa*) and thus influenced a generation of thinking about schizophrenia. Lisa, a 13-year-old girl with "hebephrenic schizophrenia," and David, a 15-year-old boy with "pseudoneurotic schizophrenia," are eloquently described in their daily activities in a residential treatment center in 1959 and 1960. Unfortunately, the author is a psychoanalyst whose only plan for treatment for the two is continued psychotherapy until they can "become involved in problems of . . . neurotic defenses, sexuality, and family relations." The two case histories cry out for antipsychotic drug therapy, which was available in 1959 and 1960 but is nowhere to be seen. One only hopes that in the intervening years the families of Lisa and David have taken them out of such an anachronistic treatment facility and found them more up-to-date treatment.

Szasz, Thomas. *Schizophrenia: The Sacred Symbol of Psychiatry*. New York: Basic Books, 1976. Starting with *The Myth of Mental Illness* in 1961 and continuing with *The Manufacture of Madness* (1970), *Schizophrenia: The Sacred Symbol of Psychiatry* (1976) and *Psychiatric Slavery* (1977), Szasz has produced more erudite nonsense on the subject of serious mental illness than any writer alive. As a historian Szasz is first class, but as a psychiatrist he never moved beyond a strictly psychoanalytic approach to treating schizophrenia. He argues, for example, that schizophrenia is merely a creation of psychiatry and "if there is no psychiatry there can be no schizophrenics." What wonderful simplicity! One wonders whether he has ever seen a patient with this disease.

B

USEFUL WEBSITES ON SCHIZOPHRENIA

(This review was done with extensive assistance from Judy Miller.)

Two of the greatest benefits of the Internet are ready access to information and the opportunity to communicate with people with similar interests. These benefits are particularly important to individuals and families faced with a diagnosis of schizophrenia, who may find themselves overwhelmed with unanswered questions at the very time they feel most isolated from family and friends. It is especially helpful that the information can be accessed, and the contacts made, from a home computer.

However, surfing the Web for information on schizophrenia is like exploring an uncharted and rather primitive country. There are occasional gold mines hidden in the hills, but to find them you must pass through many arid regions, as well as dangerous swamps. In five years or so, explorers will have mapped this country and it should be much easier to locate the sites of special interest. For the time being, however, Web surfers should take along their own supply of water, virus repellent, and plenty of patience.

In our initial explorations, several points stood out.

1. The terrain is changing daily. Websites come and go. Links to other sites often go nowhere. In the coming months, some of the most prominent health websites are likely to merge, be bought by other companies, or cease to exist.
2. Keeping websites updated is a major job and is not being done very well. Even on some of the best websites, much of the information, especially on medications, is out of date.

3. There is no one best website to get information on schizophrenia. Those listed below are the most useful, but none of them cover all aspects of the disease.

4. There are more websites providing misleading and erroneous information about schizophrenia than there are websites providing reliable information. Websites with erroneous information include many maintained by governmental organizations. Especially to be avoided are websites maintained by anti-psychiatry groups such as the Citizens Commission on Human Rights (a part of Scientology, www.cchr.org) or "consumer survivor" groups (see chapter 15). Surprisingly, some otherwise respectable websites, including some of those recommended here, have links to the anti-psychiatry sites.

5. In general, websites run by nonprofit groups provide more accurate information than do websites run by for-profit groups. Some of the pharmaceutical companies (e.g., Janssen, Pfizer) support or maintain websites that include useful information on nonmedication aspects of schizophrenia, but the information on medication is, not surprisingly, biased toward their own product.

6. Several of the best websites for information on schizophrenia originate in Canada.

In addition to providing information, the Internet is also very useful for putting families and consumers in touch with each other through bulletin boards, mailing lists, and chat rooms. Much of the information exchanged in such formats is helpful but, as above, some of it is also erroneous.

The website bulletin boards, mailing lists, and chat rooms can also be used for advocacy purposes, e.g., organizing families and consumers to oppose the closing of a state psychiatric hospital before alternative services are in place. Some state departments of mental health also maintain websites where you can find the names, titles, and addresses of state mental health officials who can then be contacted so that you can press your advocacy issue.

Still another use of the Internet is to search for published articles about a specific topic and, in many cases, to then access the articles online. This is becoming increasingly easy to do. For example, the National Library of Medicine (NLM) website, http://www.nlm.nih.gov/databases/freemedl.html, offers two free systems to search MEDLINE, a database with references and abstracts from more than 4,300 biomedical journals, dating back to 1966. From the NLM website, click on either "PubMed" or "Internet Grateful Med" and enter a query term, with or without various limits. For example, if you enter the term "neuroleptic malignant syndrome," you will receive citations to over 1,300 articles. Further refining your search by entering "olanzapine" and specifying the years 1990 and 2000 will yield 28 articles, 15 of which have an abstract available by clicking on the author link (for PubMed) or "Full Citation"(for Internet Grateful Med). Full-text versions of several of the 28 articles are also available.

Articles not available online may be found at your local library and may also be ordered via NLM's Loansome Doc service (you must establish an agreement with a health science library in your area to use this service and you may be charged a fee).

The following are summaries of the 10 most useful Internet sites for information about schizophrenia as of the time of publication of this book. We visited approximately 40 websites, as might a person who has a family member newly diagnosed with schizophrenia and recently started on olanzapine (Zyprexa). We thus approached the websites with four specific questions in mind: (1) What is known about the causes of schizophrenia? (2) What are the adverse effects of olanzapine? (3) If my family member won't take the medication, what can I do? (4) What are the chances that the offspring of a person with schizophrenia will get the disease?

The following 10 websites were found to be the most useful for providing information that is relevant for a person diagnosed with schizophrenia:

www.schizophrenia.com
Sponsor: This is a private website maintained by Brian Chiko in memory of his deceased brother, John, who had schizophrenia. A small amount of its support comes from donations from pharmaceutical companies.

This is an excellent comprehensive website, one of the best sites to begin a search, and a lovely tribute by Mr. Chiko to his brother's memory. It is well organized, with a homepage that provides multiple headings (e.g., causes, medications, coping, support groups), and a powerful schizophrenia search engine that searches over 100 medical websites (e.g., "genetic" plus "risk" yields 999 titles, "olanzapine" yields 55 titles, and "noncompliance" yields 55 titles). It also includes one of the most useful message boards and chat rooms (e.g., "When I split a pill in half, do I get half the dose on each side, i.e., are pills always homogeneous?"). This website also includes "Schizophrenia Update," a free, periodic online newsletter containing research of interest.

www.mentalhealth.com
Sponsor: This is a private website maintained and personally funded by a Canadian psychiatrist, Phillip W. Long, M.D. Dr. Long became aware of the need for such a website following his 1994 survey of Japanese psychiatric facilities.

This is a very comprehensive website that is easily navigated and is one of the best sites to begin a search. The homepage allows you to select by diagnosis (e.g., schizophrenia) or medication (e.g., olanzapine) to reach information that is both detailed and specific. This is also one of the most up-to-date websites. Another strength of this website is that Dr. Long refuses to accept any corporate sponsors (see his editorial of July 2, 1998, "Why Not Have Corporate Sponsors?"). The website is therefore uncontaminated by information slanted by pharmaceutical companies. Note: Do not confuse this website with www.mentalhealth.org, which is a much less helpful website maintained by the Center for Mental Health Services under the U.S. Department of Health and Human Services.

www.chovil.com
Sponsor: This is a private website maintained by Ian Chovil, a Canadian who has schizophrenia.

This is another excellent website for familiarizing oneself with many aspects of schizophrenia. It is especially useful for individuals who have this disease, since its author enhances the information provided with excellent insight and personal perspective. Although there is no search engine, an index provides clear links to an overview of the disease; the author's own story of illness and "recovery"; essays on medication, early intervention, relapse prevention, housing, benefits, family relations, social support, and "meaningful activity"; and lists of recommended books, movies, and related websites. Last but not least is a guest book where visitors are invited to post comments, questions, and concerns. It is clear from these postings that the website's success is based in large part on Mr. Chovil's comments and perspective. For example, he writes:

> It can be a very isolating experience to have no job, no school, few friends, no romantic relationship, no money, and live in a room day in

and day out. It is very difficult to live alone and not stare at the four walls and wonder if life can get any worse.

It is very stressful to walk by somebody not sure if they are going to physically assault you, and I feel that all the time. It wears you down to always speak to other people over the phone as if the police are listening.

www.psychlaws.org
Sponsor: This is the website of the Treatment Advocacy Center and is privately funded by foundations and individual donations; funds from pharmaceutical companies are not accepted. (Note conflict of interest: I am president of the Board of the Treatment Advocacy Center.)

This unique website focuses specifically on problems associated with the failure to treat individuals with schizophrenia and other severe psychiatric disorders. It includes useful briefing papers (e.g., "Options for Assisted Treatment"), fact sheets (e.g., "Violence," "Homelessness"), reports, personal accounts, individual state mental illness treatment statutes, a model law, and a "preventable tragedies" database that may be searched by state and lists homicides and other tragedies consequent of the failure to treat. Most of the information on this website is not available elsewhere.

www.nami.org
Sponsor: This is the website of NAMI, formerly called the National Alliance for the Mentally Ill. NAMI is funded by dues and donations from its members and receives partial support from pharmaceutical companies.

This website provides a list of local NAMI support groups (under "Affiliates"), a useful consumer e-mail list (the "Know How List"), and abundant information on various advocacy efforts (e.g., decreasing stigma). The site also offers two useful newsletters, one on pending legislation and one on stigma. However, it is not recommended for general information on schizophrenia.

www.schizophrenia.ca
Sponsor: The Schizophrenia Society of Canada, which receives partial support from pharmaceutical companies.

This site includes a comprehensive, online, 200-page manual, *Learning About Schizophrenia: Rays of Hope*, both in PDF format for easy printing and in HTML format for easy keyword searching; a detailed table of contents also helps with searches. Among the many topics addressed, in addition to causes, adverse effects, medication non-compliance, and genetic risks, are sexuality, managing money, and independent living. This website also includes *A Handbook of Mental Health Resources Across Canada*, funded by Janssen-Ortho Inc., which lists support and treatment resources by province.

www.bcss.org
Sponsor: The British Columbia Schizophrenia Society, which receives support from the British Columbia Ministry of Health.

This is a useful, general information website that offers a booklet, "Schizophrenia: Youth's Greatest Disabler," which includes a wide array of information, e.g., early warning signs.

www.mhsource.com/narsad.html
Sponsor: The National Alliance for Research on Schizophrenia and Affective Disorders, which raises funds for research; partial support comes from pharmaceutical companies.

This website is not especially user-friendly, but if you have patience, you can find some useful things. There is an online pamphlet ("Understanding Schizophrenia") and a Medical Q & A that covers many topics, although the answers are often not up-to-date. This site also includes the NARSAD newsletter, which covers many research topics of interest, including medications that are being developed for treating schizophrenia.

www.citizen.org/eletter/
Sponsor: Public Citizen's Health Research Group and the Treatment Advocacy Center. Neither organization accepts pharmaceutical company support. (Note conflict of interest: I am on the advisory board of this website.)

This "eLetter on Drugs for Severe Psychiatric Illnesses" website provides unbiased, up-to-date information on medications used to treat schizophrenia and other severe psychiatric disorders. It includes an index of more than 50 drugs, with information about what they are designed to treat, their adverse effects, how to use the drugs, and a list of other drugs that may create dangerous interactions. Also included are instructions for reporting adverse drug reactions by phone or fax or via the Food and Drug Administration's MedWatch website, www.fda.gov/

MedWatch/. This website is especially useful for obtaining the latest information on reported adverse effects of these drugs.

www.healthscout.com
Sponsor: This is a commercial, for-profit, general medical website that sells medications and other health items.

This website is specifically useful for locating the most recent research and general news articles about schizophrenia (type in "schizophrenia" under Find, then indicate "all" under news type and specify period, e.g., past week, month, year, etc.). Be aware that the reliability and validity of schizophrenia research by the general news media is variable. This site also includes detailed information about all drugs (under "Look Up a Drug"), including contraindications, adverse reactions, dosage, and how supplied.

APPENDIX

C

USEFUL VIDEOTAPES
ON SCHIZOPHRENIA

(by Katie Petray, an active member of the National Alliance for
the Mentally Ill and Director of the NAMI Family-to-Family
Education Program in Illinois)

I have reviewed 40 videotapes on schizophrenia, including those shown
at the 2000 NAMI National Conference, in an attempt to identify those
that are most useful. Undoubtedly, some good videotapes of which I am
unaware have been missed. The 18 "favorites" listed are thought-pro-
voking videos designed not only to educate family members, consumers,
mental health professionals, and concerned citizens but also to deal with
the stigma that surrounds serious mental illness. Scientific advance-
ments in treatment over the last decade are revealed in video segments.

Many compelling videos contain personal accounts by consumers
and family members and provide insights into the problems of living
with schizophrenia that help us all to better understand what the ill person is experiencing and the impact this illness has on families. Such
videos also help encourage parents and their loved ones to seek treatment.

Two of these videos serve as an introduction to schizophrenia and
mental illness and the NAMI family movement. All videos are listed
alphabetically and may be purchased as indicated or are available at
local libraries and/or through NAMI affiliate lending libraries.

A Mother's Search 1996
A mother's extraordinary journey to rescue her son, Mark, who has
schizophrenia, is homeless, and is in need of medical attention. The
issues of medication noncompliance and involuntary treatment are

addressed. Designed especially for families, professionals, and law enforcement officers.

CBS Video: "48 Hours," 10–24–96. CBS, P.O. Box 2284, So. Burlington, VT 05407. 800-542-5621. 45-min. videotape, $29.95 + 7.13 shipping, $37.08.

Annick Hollister's Story 1997

Annick's story is about living with schizophrenia. Determined to face mental illness and overcome the obstacles to recovery, Annick and members of her family relate their experiences. A heartwarming video to inspire and encourage other consumers and families to seek help. The importance of research is emphasized.

CBS "60 Minutes" segment, 5–18–97. CBS, P.O. Box 2284, So. Burlington, VT 05407. 800-542-5621. (sM70518C) videotape, $29.95 + 7.13 shipping, $37.08.

Critical Connections 1997

From the perspective of individuals who have schizophrenia, the viewer learns that treatment is not just a matter of medications: the individual must take control and build relationships of trust with others. The message the video conveys is: "See the individual first, then the illness." Video cites progress in science and medications with fewer side effects. Suitable for families, consumers, mental health professionals, and concerned citizens.

American Psychiatric Association, Public Affairs, 1400 K Street NW, Washington, DC 20005. 28-min. videotape. Call 202-682-6325 to obtain free copy.

Families Coping with Mental Illness 1996

Families convey stories about their struggles and successes. A provocative tape that stimulates excellent discussions. Families will get a perspective that will help them to cope more effectively. This is a powerful learning tool for social workers and other mental health professionals to use in training and when attempting to help families cope with mental disease.

Bonnie Tapes. Mental Illness Education Project, 22-D Hollywood Avenue, Hohokus, NJ 07423. 201-652-1989. 22-min. or 43-min. videotape, $29.95 + 9.00 shipping, $38.95.

I'm Still Here. The Truth About Schizophrenia: A Non-Fiction Film **1996**
Real and compelling stories told by individuals struggling with schizophrenia but who are able to lead lives of extraordinary courage and accomplishment. College students, mental health professionals, and family members view this tape as moving, remarkable testimony.

Direct Cinema, P.O. Box 10003, Santa Monica, CA 90410. 800-525-0000, 310-636-8200. 67-min. videotape, $20.95 (includes shipping).

In a World Alone: Living with Schizophrenia **1997**
William M. Glazer, M.D., and Peter M. Weiden, M.D., discuss the history of deinstitutionalization, the history of treatment methods, and the advances in medications used today. The viewer is reminded that "stigma is caused by disease that cannot be precisely measured." Consumers express belief in recovery and cite importance of staying on meds.

Lisa Rosas, WLIW Health Chronicles, 1790 Broadway, 16th floor, New York, NY 10019. 212-974-2121, ext. 3825. 800-847-7793. 26-min. videotape, $24.95 + 3.00 shipping, $27.95.

Madness **(Part 7, "The Brain" series) 1984**
An excellent, detailed, informative, and interesting introduction to schizophrenia, used extensively by college students, professionals, and families to better understand schizophrenia.

Produced by PBS. Annenberg CPB Project, P.O. Box 2345, South Burlington, VT 05407. 800-LEARNER, fax: 802-864-9846. 60-min. videotape, $29.95 + 2.40 shipping, $32.35.

Mental Illness: Unraveling the Myths **1990**
An impressive and provocative panel discussion explores the origins of the stigma surrounding people with serious mental illness. Host is Rutgers professor Richard Heffner; panelists are Alexander D. Brooks, law professor; Patricia Deegan, psychologist; Joanne Verbanic, founder of Schizophrenics Anonymous; Phyllis Vine, author; and Otto Wahl, psychology professor.

Rutgers University, New Jersey, Electronic Communications, 6 Berrue Circle, Piscataway, NJ 08854. 732-445-3710, ext. 129. 60-min. videotape, $35.00 + 5.00 shipping, $40.00.

Negative Symptoms of Schizophrenia **1995**
Dr. Nancy Andreasen and the multidisciplinary team clearly put both the negative and positive symptoms of schizophrenia in perspective. Through descriptions, discussions, and interviews, a patient, a family member, and various treatment team members explain in interesting detail the disease of schizophrenia, its impact, treatment approaches, and current thinking. For consumers, caretakers, and health professionals.

Produced by Nancy Andreasen, M.D., Ph.D. Order: Wheeler Communications Group, Inc., P.O. Box 650, Honeoye, NY 14471. 60-min. videotape, $29.95 + 6.00 shipping, $35.95.

No More Shame: Understanding Schizophrenia **1995**
Videotape presents current findings and thinking in the area of research on schizophrenia. Symptoms of the illness and treatment options are brought to the forefront. Use of graphics and computer animations help to assist the viewer to better understand the brain, the neurotransmitters, and what actually happens at the level of the neuron. Schools, colleges, families, and professionals will learn from and enjoy this videotape.

Films for Humanities and Sciences, P.O. Box 2053, Princeton, NJ 08543. Cat.#5827. 800-257-5126. 20-min. videotape, $89.95 + 5.95 shipping, $95.90.

Recovering from Mental Illness **1996**
Bonnie is a young woman who talks openly about her schizophrenia and about learning to cope with its symptoms. She and her family discuss her progress and the process of recognizing "recovery." A video with compelling testimony to convince others to seek treatment.

Bonnie Tapes. Mental Illness Education Project Videos, 22-D Hollywood Avenue, Hohokus, NJ 07423. 800-343-5540, fax 201-652-1973. 27-min. videotape, $29.95 + 9.00 shipping, $38.95.

Schizophrenia **1996 (3-part series enjoyed by families and useful as teaching tools):**

Schizophrenia: Causation **1996 (30-min. videotape)**
The epidemiology of schizophrenia, studies on neurotransmitters, and information processing are discussed. Descriptions of structural

abnormalities and changes in metabolism and cerebral blood flow are included.

Schizophrenia: Symptomotology 1996 (30-min. videotape)
Learn how to differentiate between positive and negative symptoms in schizophrenia. Presentations offer techniques for communicating and interacting with individuals with delusions and hallucinations. *DSM-IV* criteria are discussed. The clinical course of schizophrenia is explored.

Schizophrenia: The Community's Response 1996 (41-min. videotape)
Video details a brief history of deinstitutionalization and its consequences. Learn about the problems individuals with mental illness encounter when incarcerated and the problems law enforcement officers face when dealing with a person who is mentally ill. Discover factors that contribute to a person's adapting successfully to community living and the elements of a successful continuity of care program.

Concept Media, P.O. Box 19542, Irvine, CA 92623-9542, 949-660-0727, fax 949-660-0206, E-mail: info@conceptmedia.com. $119.00 each, three for $357 (includes shipping).

Schizophrenia: Surviving in the World of Normals, and *A Love Story: Living with Someone with Schizophrenia* 1991
Frederick J. Frese, a psychologist and consumer, and his wife, Penny Frese, speak candidly about schizophrenia. Dr. Frese offers an insider's perspective and practical approaches to the problems surrounding the illness; Penny Frese speaks from the perspective of a spouse. An impressive and inspiring model for "openness" about mental illness. A favorite among consumers and families, college students, and professionals.

Wellness Reproduction, 23945 Mercantile Road, Beachwood, OH 44122-5924, 216-831-9209. 120-min. videotape, $49.95 + 5.95 shipping, $55.90.

The Cutting Edge Report (#701):Preventing Relapse in Schizophrenia 1996
Research psychiatrists examine schizophrenia and discuss what measures can be taken to prevent relapse and work toward helping individuals lead independent lives. Remarkable new treatments, such as clozapine and other new antipsychotics, when combined with support networks,

can help prevent relapse. Genetics is opening up a whole new research area and uncovering secrets of the brain not yielded easily.

The Cutting Edge Report (#401): Schizophrenia and Depression 1995
NIMH (National Institute of Mental Health) doctors and patients explore both positive and negative symptoms of schizophrenia and bring to the viewer recent advances in atypical medications to treat schizophrenia, specifically the introduction of clozapine. Presenters describe schizophrenia as "the most misunderstood illness, although the stigma attached appears to be on the decline."

NARSAD (National Alliance for Research on Schizophrenia and Depression), 60 Cutter Mill Road, Great Neck, NY 11021, 800-829-8289, 516-829-0091, E-mail: info@NARSAD.org. #701: 21-min. videotape; #401, 15-min. (of 30 min.) videotape, $10.00 each, plus 2.00 shipping, $12.00 each.

When the Music Stops 1987
An informative and effective introductory film that presents a clear, compassionate picture of mental illness. Dr. E. Fuller Torrey and other experts provide explanations about mental illness and mental illness research. This excellent video, which also includes an introduction to the NAMI family movement, continues to be widely used and enjoyed by NAMI family/consumer groups, high school and college students, and mental health professionals and is frequently shown to religious congregations.

Produced by Dupont Company. Order from NAMI, Colonial Place Three, 2107 Wilson Blvd., #300, Arlington, VA 22201-3042, 888-780-4167. 22-min. videotape #R506, $20.00 + 2.00 shipping, $22.00.

D

OTHER USEFUL RESOURCES ON SCHIZOPHRENIA

EDUCATION, ADVOCACY, AND RESEARCH

NAMI (formerly called the National Alliance for the Mentally Ill)
Colonial Place Three
2107 Wilson Blvd., Suite 300
Arlington, VA 22201-3042
703-524-7600
Helpline: 800-950-6264
www.nami.org

Begun in 1979, NAMI is the nation's largest advocacy organization for individuals with severe mental illnesses, including schizophrenia, bipolar disorder (manic-depressive illness), major depression, obsessive-compulsive disorder, and severe anxiety disorders. It is composed of people with serious mental illness and their families. Membership costs $25 and includes a subscription to the bimonthly *NAMI Advocate*, which has much helpful information. There are over 1,200 state and local affiliates, which provide excellent education and support; to contact the affiliate closest to you, click on "Affiliates" at the NAMI website, www.nami.org. NAMI has a toll-free Helpline that is an information and referral service about mental illness issues. The annual NAMI convention is also a good place to learn about schizophrenia. NAMI accepts donations.

Treatment Advocacy Center (TAC)
3300 N. Fairfax Drive, Suite 220
Arlington, VA 22201
703-294-6001
www.psychlaws.org

This legal advocacy organization was formed in 1998 to bring attention to and correct the consequences of the failing mental illness treatment system. TAC specifically focuses on people with mental illness who are homeless, in jails or prisons, being victimized, or at risk of suicide or committing violent acts because they are not being treated and works to reform legal systems that prevent them from getting treatment. The Center is a resource for individuals seeking to reform assisted treatment laws in their own states. Its free bimonthly newsletter (*Catalyst*) and its website, www.psychlaws.org, include much useful information; there is also a free online newsletter. From the website, subscribe to the newsletters by clicking on "Join Us" and completing the "TAC Network Form." TAC accepts donations but does not accept funding from pharmaceutical companies.

National Alliance for Research on Schizophrenia and Affective Disorders (NARSAD)
60 Cutter Mill Rd., Suite 404
Great Neck, NY 11021
516-829-0091
www.narsad.org

Begun in 1986, NARSAD is one of the two largest providers of funds for schizophrenia research outside of the federal government. It also funds research on other major psychiatric disorders. Its newsletter includes useful accounts of current research. NARSAD welcomes help in raising funds for research and accepts donations.

Stanley Foundation Research Programs/NAMI Research Institute
5430 Grosvenor Lane, Suite 200
Bethesda, MD 20814
301-571-0770
www.stanleyresearch.org

Begun in 1989, the Stanley Foundation Research Programs/NAMI Research Institute is one of the two largest providers of funds for schizophrenia research outside of the federal government. It also funds research on manic-depressive illness. It accepts donations.

Schizophrenia Society of Canada
75 The Donway West, Suite 814
Don Mills, Ontario M3C-2E9, Canada
416-445-8204
www.schizophrenia.ca

This organization serves the same purposes in Canada as NAMI does in the United States. Call or visit its website to locate the provincial or local affiliate closest to you. The Schizophrenia Society of Canada accepts donations.

USEFUL PUBLICATIONS

- *Schizophrenia Bulletin*, a quarterly publication of the Schizophrenia Research Branch of NIMH, contains useful summaries of evolving research. The cost is $20 per year. Order from the Superintendent of Documents, Government Printing Office, Washington, DC 20402, using the subscription form provided as a tear-out from the back of any issue. Forms can also be obtained from the Government Printing Office (phone 202-512-2250, fax 202-512-1800) or NIMH (fax 301-443-4279, E-mail: nimhinfo@nih.gov).

- *Schizophrenia Research*, published 18 times each year, contains current research and the abstracts from the two most important schizophrenia research meetings. The cost is $154 per year. Order from Elsevier Science, Regional Sales Office, Customer Support Department, P.O. Box 945, New York, NY 10159-0945 (phone 888-437-4636, fax 212-633-3680, E-mail usinfo-f@elsevier.com, website www.elsevier.nl/inca/publications/store/5/0/6/0/9/1/).

- *Hospital and Community Psychiatry*, a monthly publication of the American Psychiatric Association, is the best single source of information on services and treatment. The cost is $51 per year. Order from the APA, 1400 K St., NW, Washington, DC 20005 (phone 202-682-6000, fax 202-682-6850, E-mail: apa@psych.org).

NOTES

DEDICATION:

S. Norman, "Saving Grace." *Fly Rod and Reel*, July/October, 1994, pp. 46–70.

EPIGRAPHS:

Van Gogh letter quoted by J. Rewald, *Post-Impressionism: From van Gogh to Gauguin* (New York: Museum of Modern Art, 1962), p. 321.
M. Button, "With No Explanation," in *The Unhinging of Wings* (Lantzville, British Columbia: Oolichan Books, 1996), pp. 30–31.

CHAPTER 1

"Schizophrenia is": W. Hall, G. Andrews, and G. Goldstein, "The Costs of Schizophrenia," *Australian and New Zealand Journal of Psychiatry* 19 (1985): 3–5. **"one of the most sinister":** L. Wilson, *This Stranger, My Son* (New York: Putnam, 1968), p. 174. **Studies of homeless:** E. F. Torrey, *Out of the Shadows: Confronting America's Mental Illness Crisis* (New York: John Wiley, 1997; other data in this chapter are taken from this book unless otherwise indi-

cated. **16 percent of inmates:** P. M. Ditton, *Bureau of Justice Statistics Special Report: Mental Health and Treatment of Inmates and Probationers* (Washington, D.C.: Department of Justice, 1999). **29 percent:** E. F. Torrey, J. Steiber, J. Ezekiel, et al., *Criminalizing the Seriously Mentally Ill* (Washington, D.C.: National Alliance for the Mentally Ill and Public Citizen Health Research Group, 1992). **1991 survey:** D. M. Steinwachs, J. D. Kasper, E. A. Skinner, et al., *Family Perspectives on Meeting the Needs for Care of Severely Mentally Ill Relatives* (Arlington, Va.: NAMI, 1992). **1,000 homicides:** J. M. Dawson and P. A. Langan, *Murder in Families* (Washington, D.C.: Department of Justice, 1994). **In Los Angeles:** A. F. Lehman and L. S. Linn, "Crimes Against Discharged Mental Patients in Board-and-Care Homes," *American Journal of Psychiatry* 141 (1984): 271–74. **In New York:** S. Friedman and G. Harrison, "Sexual Histories, Attitudes, and Behavior of Schizophrenic and Normal Women," *Archives of Sexual Behavior* 13 (1984): 555–67. **In Des Moines:** T. Alex, "Summer in the City: Violent Crime in D. M.," *Des Moines Register,* August 3, 1989, p. 1. **the police removed:** "21 Ex–Mental Patients Taken from 4 Private Homes,"

New York Times, August 5, 1979, p. A-33. **in 1990:** S. Raab, "Mental Homes Are Wretched, A Panel Says," *New York Times,* August 6, 1990. **in Mississippi:** "9 Ex-Patients Kept in Primitive Shed," *New York Times,* October 21, 1982, p. A-21. **In Illinois:** R. Davidson, "A Mental Health Crisis in Illinois," *Chicago Tribune,* December 9, 1991. **In New York:** C. F. Muller and C. L. M. Caton, "Economic Costs of Schizophrenia: A Postdischarge Study," *Medical Care* 21 (1983): 92–104. **A study of readmissions:** J. L. Geller, "A Report on the 'Worst' State Hospital Recidivists in the U.S.," *Hospital and Community Psychiatry* 43 (1992): 904–8. **24,787 such calls:** E. Bumiller, "In Wake of Attack, Giuliani Cracks Down on Homeless," *New York Times,* November 20, 1999, p. 1. **only 3 percent:** M. Olfson, H. A. Pincus, and T. H. Dial, "Professional Practice Patterns of U.S. Psychiatrists," *American Journal of Psychiatry* 151 (1994): 89–95. **only 60 percent:** D. A. Regier, W. E. Narrow, D. S. Rae, et al., "The De Facto U.S. Mental and Addictive Disorders Service System," *Archives of General Psychiatry* 50 (1993): 85–94. **survey in Baltimore:** M. Von Korff, G. Nestadt, A. Romanoski, et al., "Prevalence of Untreated DSM-III Schizophrenia," *Journal of Nervous and Mental Disease* 173 (1985): 577–81. **in Wisconsin:** D. A. Treffert, "The Obviously Ill Patient in Need of Treatment," *Hospital and Community Psychiatry* 36 (1985): 259–64. **1.5 percent:** "Health Care Reform for Americans with Severe Mental Illnesses: Report of the National Advisory Mental Health Council," *American Journal of Psychiatry* 150 (1993): 1447–65. **study in Baltimore:** J. C. Anthony, M. Folstein, A. J. Romanoski, et al., "Comparison of the Lay Diagnostic Interview Schedule and a Standardized Psychiatric Diagnosis," *Archives of General* Psychiatry 42 (1985): 667–75. **Director of . . . (NIMH), testifying:** Testimony of Dr. Shervert H. Frazier before Committee on Appropriations, U.S. Senate, November 20, 1986. **A 1988 survey:** B. J. Burns and D. B. Kamerow, "Psychotropic Drug Prescriptions for Nursing Home Residents," *Journal of Family Practice* 26 (1988): 155–60. **A 1993 random:** P. N. Tariot, C. A. Podgorski, L. Blazina, et al., "Mental Disorders in the Nursing Home: Another Perspective," *American Journal of Psychiatry* 150 (1993): 1063–69. **"chronic mental patients":** B. W. Rosner and P. V. Rabins, "Mental Illness Among Nursing Home Patients," *Hospital and Community Psychiatry* 36 (1985): 119–28. **Illinois:** M. J. Berens, "With State Help, Nursing Homes Open Door to Mentally Ill," *Chicago Tribune,* September 27, 1998, p. 1. **recent survey of NAMI members:** D. M. Steinwachs, J. D. Kasper, and E. A. Skinner, *Family Perspectives on Meeting the Needs for Care of Severely Mentally Ill Relatives: A National Survey* (Arlington, Va.: NAMI, 1992). **Five separate studies:**

See M. Kramer, B. M. Rosen, and E. M. Willis, "Definitions and Distribution of Mental Disorders in a Racist Society," in C. V. Willie, B. M. Kramer, and B. S. Brown, eds., *Racism and Mental Health* (Pittsburgh: University of Pittsburgh Press, 1973); and M. Kramer, "Population Changes and Schizophrenia, 1970–1985," in L. Wynne et al., eds., *The Nature of Schizophrenia* (New York: Wiley, 1978). **careful study in Rochester:** *Report of the President's Commission on Mental Health* (Washington, D.C.: U.S. Government Printing Office, 1978). **in Texas and in Louisiana:** Kramer, Rosen, Willis. **Hispanic residents:** M. A. Burnam, R. L. Hough, J. I. Escobar, et al., "Six-Month Prevalence of Specific Psychiatric Disorders Among Mexican Americans and Non-Hispanic Whites in Los Angeles," *Archives of General Psychiatry* 44 (1987): 687–94. **study of Mexican-American residents:** E. G. Jaco, *The Social Epidemiology of Mental Disorders: A Psychiatric Survey of Texas* (New York: Russell Sage Foundation, 1960). **Hutterites:** J. W. Eaton and R. J. Weil, *Culture and Mental Disorders: A Comparative Study of the Hutterites and Other Populations* (Glencoe: Free Press, 1955). **schizophrenia elsewhere in the world:** Unless otherwise indicated, all studies mentioned in this section are reviewed in E. F. Torrey, *Schizophrenia and Civilization* (New York: Jason Aronson, 1980); and E. F. Torrey, "Prevalence Studies in Schizophre-

nia," *British Journal of Psychiatry* 150 (1987): 598–608. **Micronesia:** F. X. Hezel and A. M. Wylie, "Schizophrenia and Chronic Mental Illness in Micronesia: An Epidemiological Survey," *ISLA: A Journal of Micronesian Studies* 1 (1992): 329–54. **"insanity is a disease":** A. Halliday, *Remarks on the Present State of the Lunatic Asylums in Ireland* (London: John Murray, 1808). **Caribbean immigrants:** S. Wessely, D. Castle, G. Der, et al., "Schizophrenia and Afro-Caribbeans," *British Journal of Psychiatry* 159 (1991): 795–801. **Since 1985 similar:** R. E. Kendell, D. E. Malcolm, and W. Adams, "The Problem of Detecting Changes in the Incidence of Schizophrenia," *British Journal of Psychiatry* 162 (1993): 212–18. **In Baltimore:** R. Lemkau, C. Tietze, and M. Cooper, "Mental-Hygiene Problems in an Urban District," *Mental Hygiene* 25 (1941): 624–46; and 26 (1942): 100–19. **in New Haven:** A. B. Hollingshead and F. C. Redlich, *Social Class and Mental Illness* (New York: John Wiley, 1958). **high incidence of new cases:** A. Y. Tien and W. W. Eaton, "Psychopathologic Precursors and Sociodemographic Risk Factors for the Schizophrenia Syndrome," *Archives of General Psychiatry* 49 (1992): 37–46. **"schizophrenia has existed":** D. V. Jeste, R. del Carmen, J. B. Lohr, et al., "Did Schizophrenia Exist Before the Eighteenth Century?" *Comprehensive Psychiatry* 26 (1985): 493–503; see also N. M. Bark, "On the History of Schizophrenia," *New York State Journal of Medicine* 88 (1988): 374–83. **The other side:** E. F. Torrey, *Schizophrenia and Civilization* (New York: Jason Aronson, 1980). **Poor Mad Tom:** N. M. Bark, "Did Shakespeare Know Schizophrenia? The Case of Poor Mad Tom in *King Lear*," *British Journal of Psychiatry* 146 (1985): 436–38. **George Trosse:** Jeste et al., and E. Hare, "Schizophrenia Before 1800? The Case of the Revd George Trosse," *Psychological Medicine* 18 (1988): 279–85. **insanity was increasing:** Torrey, *Schizophrenia and Civilization,* and E. Hare, "Was Insanity on the Increase?" *British Journal of Psychiatry* 142 (1983): 439–55. **accompanying graph:** Data are from A. L. Stroup and R. W. Manderscheid, "The Development of the State Mental Hospital System in the United States: 1840–1980," *Journal of the Washington Academy of Sciences* 78 (1988): 59–68. **"insanity is an increasing disease":** E. Jarvis, "On the Supposed Increase in Insanity," *American Journal of Insanity* 8 (1852): 333. **"the successive reports":** Quoted in W. J. Corbet, "On the Increase of Insanity," *American Journal of Insanity* 50 (1893): 224–38. **"the insane have increased":** F. B. Sanborn, "Is American Insanity Increasing? A Study," *Journal of Mental Science* 40 (1894): 214–19. **Deinstitutionalization:** Most of the material in this section is from Torrey, *Nowhere to Go.* **"no convictions were had":** Hearings on the National Neuropsychiatric Institute, Subcommittee on Health and Education, United States Senate, March 6–8, 1946, pp. 167 and 169. **"in some of the wards":** A. Deutsch, *The Shame of the States* (New York: Harcourt Brace, 1948), p. 28. Kennedy's younger sister: See Torrey, *Nowhere to Go,* pp. 102–06. **"it has been demonstrated":** President Kennedy's 1963 special message to Congress, reprinted in H. A. Foley and S. S. Sharfstein, *Madness and Government* (Washington, D.C.: American Psychiatric Press, 1983). **federal CMHC program:** E. F. Torrey, S. M. Wolfe, and L. M. Flynn, "Fiscal Misappropriations in Programs for the Mentally Ill: A Report on Illegality and Failure of the Federal Construction Grant Program for Community Mental Health Centers" (Washington, D.C.: Public Citizen Health Research Group and National Alliance for the Mentally Ill, 1990). **number of lawyers:** L. Caplan, "The Lawyers Race to the Bottom," *Washington Post,* August 6, 1993, A-24. **A 1980 survey:** C. A. Taube, B. J. Bums, and L. Kessler, "Patients of Psychiatrists and Psychologists in Office-Based Practice: 1980," *American Psychologist* 39 (1984): 1435–47. **In 2000:** The Oregon example is taken from "No Housing, No Recovery," an editorial in the *Oregonian,* March 20, 2000, p. E12. **$636,000:** A. E. Moran, R. I. Freedman, and S. S. Sharfstein, "The Journey of Sylvia Frumkin: A Case Study for Policymakers," *Hospital and Community Psychiatry* 35 (1984): 887–93.

One study: D. P. Rice and L. S. Miller, "The Economic Burden of Schizophrenia," *Journal of Clinical Psychiatry* 60 (suppl. 1) (1999): 4–6. **other study:** R. J. Wyatt, I. de Saint Ghislain, M. C. Leary, et al., "An Economic Evaluation of Schizophrenia—1991," *Social Psychiatry and Psychiatric Epidemiology* 30 (1995): 196–205. **In Australia:** G. Andrews, W. Hall, G. Goldstein et al., "The Economic Costs of Schizophrenia," *Archives of General Psychiatry* 42 (1985): 537–43. **$180 billion:** R. J. Wyatt, "Science and Psychiatry," in J. T. Kaplan and B. J. Sadock, eds., *Comprehensive Textbook of Psychiatry*, 4th ed. (Baltimore: Williams and Wilkins, 1984), chapter 53, p. 2027. **"In whatever":** E. Jarvis, "Insanity and Idiocy in Massachusetts: Report of the Commission on Lunacy, 1855" (Cambridge: Harvard University Press, 1971), p. 104.

CHAPTER 2

"What then does": H. R. Rollin, *Coping with Schizophrenia* (London: Burnett Books, 1980), p. 162. **"Sympathy":** R. W. Emerson, *Journals* (1836). *"strangeness has":* R. Porter, *A Social History of Madness* (New York: Weidenfeld and Nicolson, 1987), p. 9. **"The worst":** P. J. Ruocchio, "First person account: the schizophrenic inside," *Schizophrenia Bulletin* 17: 357–60, 1991. *I Never Promised You a Rose Garden:* See C. North and R. Cadoret, "Diagnostic Discrepancy in Personal Accounts of Patients with 'Schizophrenia,'" *Archives of General Psychiatry* 38 (1981): 133–37. **"Perceptual dysfunction":** J. Cutting and F. Dunne, "Subjective Experience of Schizophrenia," *Schizophrenia Bulletin* 15 (1989): 217–31. **"either entirely":** N. Dain, *Concepts of Insanity in the United States, 1789–1865* (New Brunswick: Rutgers University Press, 1964), p. 226, quoting the 1861–62 *Reports of the Illinois State Hospital for the Insane.* **"During the last":** A. McGhie and J. Chapman, "Disorders of Attention and Perception in Early Schizophrenia," *British Journal of Medical Psychology*, 34 (1961): 103–16. **"Colours seem":** Ibid. **"Everything looked vibrant":** Cutting and Dunne. **"Lots of things":** Ibid. **"People looked deformed":** Ibid. **"I saw everything":** G. Burns, "An Account of My Madness," mimeo, 1983. **"These crises":** M. Sechehaye, *Autobiography of a Schizophrenic Girl* (New York: Grune and Stratton, 1951), p. 22. **"Everything seems":** McGhie and Chapman. **"Occasionally during":** Anonymous, "An Autobiography of a Schizophrenic Experience," *Journal of Abnormal and Social Psychology* 51 (1955): 677–89. **"I can probably":** M. Vonnegut, *The Eden Express* (New York: Praeger, 1975), p. 107. **"An outsider":** E. Leete, "Mental Illness: An Insider's View," presented at annual meeting of National Alliance for the Mentally Ill, New Orleans, 1985. **In one study:** Cutting and Dunne. **"Sometimes when people":** McGhie and Chapman. **"it was terrible":** M. Barnes and J. Berke, *Mary Barnes: Two Accounts of a Journey Through Madness* (New York: Ballantine, 1973), p. 44. **"touching any patient":** P. S. Wagner, "Life in the Closet," *Hartford Courant*, August 26, 1993. **"decay in my":** Rollin, p. 150. 64. **"a genital sexual":** Ibid, p. 150. **One psychiatrist:** See M. B. Bowers, *Retreat from Sanity: The Structure of Emerging Psychosis* (Baltimore: Penguin, 1974). **"My trouble is" and "My concentration is":** McGhie and Chapman. **"Childhood feelings":** Bowers, p. 152. **"All sorts of":** W. Mayer-Gross, E. Slater, and M. Roth, *Clinical Psychiatry* (Baltimore: Williams and Wilkins, 1969), p. 268. **"In College":** Wagner. **"I was invited":** A. Boisen, *Out of the Depths*, 1960. Quoted in B. Kaplan, ed., *The Inner World of Mental Illness* (New York: Harper and Row, 1964), p. 118. **"Fear made me":** Sechehaye, p. 26. **"It was evening":** E. Leete, "The Interpersonal Environment," in A. B. Hatfield and H. P. Lefley, *Surviving Mental Illness* (New York: Guilford Press, 1993), p. 117. **"Suddenly my whole":** M. Coate, *Beyond All Reason* (Philadelphia: Lippincott, 1965), p. 21. **"Before last week":** Bowers, p. 27. **"as if a heavy":** B. J. Freedman, "The Subjective Experience of Perceptual and Cognitive Disturbances in Schizophrenia," *Archives of General Psychiatry* 30 (1974): 333–40. **"However hard":** Rollin, p. 150. **One Sensation:** See E. F. Torrey, "Headaches After Lumbar Puncture and Insensitivity to Pain in Psychiatric Patients," *New England Journal of Medicine* 301 (1979): 110; G. D. Watson, P. C. Chandarana, and H. Merskey, "Relationship between Pain and Schizophrenia," *British Journal of Psychiatry* 138 (1981): 33–36; and L. K. Bickerstaff, S. C. Harris, R. S. Leggett, et al., "Pain Insensitivity in Schizophrenic Patients," *Archives of Surgery* 123 (1988): 49–51. **"At first it":** N. McDonald, "Living with Schizophrenia," *Canadian Medical Association Journal* 82 (1960): 218–21, 678–81. **"When people are":** McGhie and Chapman. **"I can concentrate":** Ibid. **"I used to get":** Cutting and Dunne. **"I have to":** J. Chapman, "The Early Symptoms of Schizophrenia," *British Journal of Psychiatry* 112 (1966): 225–51. **"Everything is in":** McGhie and Chapman. **"the teeth, then":** Sechehaye, foreword. **"This morning":** S. Sheehan, *Is There No Place on Earth for Me?* (Boston: Houghton Mifflin, 1982), p. 69. **"I can't concentrate":** McGhie and Chapman. **"I tried sitting":** B. O'Brien, *Operators and Things: The Inner Life of a Schizophrenic* (New York: Signet, 1976), pp. 97–98. **"During the visit":** Sechehaye, p. 28. **"If I do":** Chapman. **"My thoughts get":** McGhie and Chapman. **"I am not":** Nijinsky, quoted in Kaplan, p. 424. **"How could** a": O'Brien, p. 100. **"I was extremely"**: Sechehaye, pp. 66–67. **"The worst thing"**: Chapman. **"I feel that"**: Mayer-Gross, Slater, and Roth, pp. 281, 267. **"For instance, I"**: G. Bateson, ed., *Perceval's Narrative: A Patient's Account of His Psychosis 1830–1832* (1838, 1840) (New York: Morrow, 1974), p. 269. **"I may be"**: McGhie and Chapman. **"If I am"**: Ibid. **"Sometimes I commit"**: Burns. **Chapman claims**: See Chapman. **"I am so"**: Anonymous, "I Feel Like I Am Trapped Inside My Head, Banging Desperately Against Its Walls," *New York Times*, March 18, 1986, p. C-3. **"How could"**: S. Nasar, *A Beautiful Mind* (New York: Simon and Schuster, 1998), p. 11. **"I went to"**: Anonymous, "First Person Account: A Pit of Confusion," *Schizophrenia Bulletin* 16 (1990): 355–51. **"A policeman walking"**: A. Chekhov, "Ward No. 6," quoted in A. A. Stone and S. S. Stone, eds., *The Abnormal Personality Through Literature* (Englewood Cliffs, N.J.: Prentice-Hall, 1966), p. 5. **"I got up"**: Bowers, pp. 186–87. *"Anxiety like metal"*: Poem by Robert L. Nelson, now deceased, and published with the permission of his mother. **"During the paranoid"**: Anonymous, "Schizophrenic Experience." **"I felt that"**: Ibid. **"I once believed"**: R. Jameson, "Personal View," *British Medical Journal* 291 (1985): 541. **de Clerembault**: G. Remington and H. Book, "Case Report of de Clerembault Syndrome, Bipolar Affective Disorder and Response to Lithium," *American*

Journal of Psychiatry 141 (1984): 1285–88. **"telepathic force"**: Rollin, p. 132. **"I like talking"**: Chapman. **A 1999 study**: E. F. Torrey et al., *Threats to Radio and Television Station Personnel in the United States by Individuals with Severe Mental Illnesses* (Washington, D.C.: Public Citizen's Health Research Group and the Treatment Advocacy Center, 1999). **"millions and billions"**: P. Earle, "Popular Fallacies in Regard to Insanity and the Insane," *Journal of Social Science* 26: 107–17, 1890. **"I was sitting"**: Ibid. **"This phenomenon can"**: J. Lang, "The Other Side of Hallucinations," *American Journal of Psychiatry* 94 (1938): 1090–97. **"No doubt I"**: Poe, "The Tell-Tale Heart." **"Thus for years"**: D. P. Schreber, *Memoirs of My Nervous Illness* (1903), translated and with introduction by I. Macalpine and R. A. Hunter (London: William Dawson, 1955), p. 172. **"There was music"**: Boisen, quoted in Kaplan, p. 119. **"For about almost"**: Schreber, p. 225. **one study**: P. K. McGuire, G. M. S. Shah, and R. M. Murray, "Increased Blood Flow in Broca's Area during Auditory Hallucinations in Schizophrenia," *Lancet* 342 (1993): 703–6. **"auditory hallucinations"**: J. M. Cleghorn et al., "Toward a Brain Map of Auditory Hallucinations," *American Journal of Psychiatry* 149 (1992): 1062–69. **larger third ventricles**: J. Cullberg and H. Nyback, "Persistent Auditory Hallucinations Correlate with the Size of the Third Ventricle in Schizophrenic Patients," *Acta Psychiatrica Scandinavica* 86 (1992): 469–72. **born deaf:** E. M. R. Critchley, "Auditory Experiences of Deaf Schizophrenics," *Journal of the Royal Society of Medicine* 76 (1983): 542–44. **"At an early":** Lang. **Silvano Arieti:** *Creativity: The Magic Synthesis* (New York: Harper Colophon, 1976), p. 251. **"On a few":** Ibid. **"During the time":** Bowers. p. 37. **"To the person":** Lang. **"Sometimes I did":** Sechehaye, pp. 87–88. **"I saw myself":** Coate, pp. 66–67. **"I get shaky":** Chapman. **"This was equally":** Sechehaye, p. 87. **"My breast gives":** Schreber, p. 207. **"81 percent":** S. Bustamante, K. Maurer, W. Loffler, et al., "Depressive Symptoms in the Early Course of Schizophrenia," Abstract, *Schizophrenia Research* 11 (1994): 187. **"During the first":** J. Lang, "The Other Side of the Affective Aspects of Schizophrenia," *Psychiatry* 2 (1939): 195–202. **"Later, considering them":** Sechehaye, p. 35. **"I sat":** M. Stakes, "First Person Account: Becoming Seaworthy," *Schizophrenia Bulletin* 11 (1985): 629. **"there has been":** P. Cramer, J. Bowen, and M. O'Neill, "Schizophrenics and Social Judgment," *British Journal of Psychiatry* 160 (1992): 481–87. **"Half the time":** McGhie and Chapman. **"one of the":** Chapman. **"During my first":** Anonymous, "Schizophrenic Experience." **"Instead of wishing":** E. Meyer and L. Covi, "The Experience of Depersonalization: A Written Report by a Patient," *Psychiatry* 23 (1960): 215–17. **"I wish I":** J. A. Wechsler, *In a Darkness* (New York: Norton, 1972), p. 17. **"reported experiencing":** A. M. Kring, S. L. Kerr, D. A. Smith, et al., "Flat Affect in Schizophrenia Does Not Reflect Diminished Subjective Experience of Emotion," *Journal of Abnormal Psychology* 102 (1993): 507–17. **"Loneliness needs":** J. K. Bouricius, "Negative Symptoms and Emotions in Schizophrenia," *Schizophrenia Bulletin* 15 (1989): 201–7. **One study . . . found:** T. C. Manschreck et al., "Disturbed Voluntary Motor Activity in Schizophrenic Disorder," *Psychological Medicine* 12 (1982): 73–84; see also M. Jones and R. Hunter, "Abnormal Movements in Patients with Chronic Psychotic Illness," in G. E. Crane and R. Gardner, *Psychotropic Drugs and Dysfunctions of the Basal Ganglia*, publication no. 1938 (Washington, D.C. U.S. Public Health Service, 1969). **In another study:** Cutting and Dunne. **"I became":** Ibid. **eye blinking:** See J. R. Stevens, "Eye Blink and Schizophrenia: Psychosis or Tardive Dyskinesia," *American Journal of Psychiatry* 135 (1978): 223–26. **"[He] stood":** H. de Balzac, "Louis Lambert" (1832), in A. A. Stone and S. S. Stone, eds., *The Abnormal Personality Through Literature* (Englewood Cliffs, N.J.: Prentice-Hall, 1966), pp. 63–64. **"When I am":** McGhie and Chapman. **"I don't like":** Ibid. **"I get stuck":** McGhie and Chapman. **"I am not":** Ibid. **"As the work":** Kindwall and Kinder

(1940), quoted in C. Landis and F. A. Mettler, *Varieties of Psychopathological Experience* (New York: Holt, Rinehart, and Winston, 1964), p. 530. **"The state of":** Sechehaye, pp. 61–62. **"to help to":** Chapman. **"There were two":** *Perceval's Narrative*, quoted in Kaplan, p. 240. **Chapman believes:** Chapman. **"My feelings about":** Anonymous, "Schizophrenic Experience." **"the only way":** Wagner. **Schreber:** p. 146. **John Hinckley:** "Hinckley Sr. Seeks Support in Fight Against Mental Illness," *Psychiatric News*, November 16, 1984. **"Generally, insane":** "Confinement of the Insane," *American Law Review* 3 (1869): 215. **"an enchanted loom":** Quoted by O. Sacks, *The Man Who Mistook His Wife for a Hat* (New York: Summit Books, 1985), p. 140. **"self-measuring ruler":** Burns. **"Lost":** Nelson. **"You will realize":** *The Complete Letters of Vincent van Gogh,* vol. 3 (Boston: New York Graphic Society, 1978), p. 524. **cited by one woman:** A. Sobin and M. N. Ozer, "Mental Disorders in Acute Encephalitis," *Journal of Mt. Sinai Hospital* 33 (1966): 73–82. **"Something inside":** B. Bick, "Love and Resentment," *New York Times*, March 25, 1990. **"No doubt Louis":** Balzac.

Mellor, "First Rank Symptoms of Schizophrenia," *British Journal of Psychiatry* 117 (1970): 15–23. **patients with manic-depressive illness:** W. T. Carpenter, J. S. Strauss, and S. Muleh, "Are There Pathognomonic Symptoms in Schizophrenia?" *Archives of General Psychiatry* 28 (1973): 847–52. ***DSM-IV:* Diagnostic and Statistical Manual of Mental Disorders** (Washington, D.C.: American Psychiatric Association, 1994). **Rosenhan study:** D. L. Rosenhan, "On Being Sane in Insane Places," *Science* 179 (1973): 250–58; see also R. L. Spitzer, "More on Pseudoscience in Science and the Case for Psychiatric Diagnosis," *Archives of General Psychiatry* 33 (1976): 459–70. **"If I were":** S. S. Kety, "From Rationalization to Reason," *American Journal of Psychiatry* 131 (1974): 957–63. **"positive" symptoms:** This subtyping is reviewed in an entire issue of *Schizophrenia Bulletin* (vol. 11, no. 3, 1985) devoted to the subject; the articles by Drs. Crow and Andreasen are especially useful. **Recent studies:** V. Vallès, J. Van Os, R. Guillamat, et al., "Increased Morbid Risk for Schizophrenia in Families of In-patients with Bipolar Illness," *Schizophrenia Research* 42 (2000): 83–90.

CHAPTER 3

"To one": M. Coate, *Beyond All Reason* (Philadelphia: Lippincott, 1965), pp. 1–2. **Studies have shown:** C. S.

CHAPTER 4

"What consoles me": J. Rewald, *Post-Impressionism: From van Gogh to Gauguin* (New York: Museum of Modern Art, 1962), p. 320. **The best study:**

M. Harbrecht and H. Häfner, "Substance Abuse and the Onset of Schizophrenia," *Biological Psychiatry* 40 (1996): 1155–63. **widely quoted study:** R. C. W. Hall, E. R. Gardner, S. K. Stickney, et al., "Physical Illness Manifesting as Psychiatric Disease," *Archives of General Psychiatry* 37 (1980): 989–95. **Koran and his colleagues:** L. M. Koran, H. C. Sox, K. I. Marton, et al., "Medical Evaluation of Psychiatric Patients," *Archives of General Psychiatry* 46 (1989): 733–40. **One English study:** K. Davison, "Schizophrenia-like Psychoses Associated with Organic Cerebral Disorders: A Review," *Psychiatric Developments* 1 (1983): 1–34. **Another English study:** E. C. Johnstone, J. F. Macmillan, and T. J. Crow, "The Occurrence of Organic Disease of Possible or Probable Aetiological Significance in a Population of 268 Cases of First Episode Schizophrenia," *Psychological Medicine* 17 (1987): 371–79. **A postmortem study:** Davison. **Viral encephalitis:** E. F. Torrey, "Functional Psychoses and Viral Encephalitis," *Integrative Psychiatry* 4 (1986): 224–36. **One study:** Davison. **one report:** A. G. Awad, "Schizophrenia and Multiple Sclerosis," *Journal of Nervous and Mental Disease* 171 (1983): 323–24. **"a common":** Davidson. **AIDS:** N. Buhrich, D. A. Cooper, and E. Freed, "HIV Infection Associated with Symptoms Indistinguishable from Functional Psychosis," *British Journal of Psychiatry* 152 (1988): 649–53. **An MRI study:** P. Buckley, J. P. Stack, C. Madi-

gan, et al., "Magnetic Resonance Imaging of Schizophrenia-like Psychoses Associated with Cerebral Trauma: Clinicopathological Correlates." *American Journal of Psychiatry* 150 (1993): 146–48. **Rosemary Kennedy:** E. F. Torrey, *Nowhere to Go* (New York: Harper and Row, 1988), pp. 102–6. **study of relatives:** J. Rimmer and B. Jacobsen, "Antisocial Personality in the Biological Relatives of Schizophrenics." *Comprehensive Psychiatry* 21 (1980): 258–262.

CHAPTER 5

"Such a disease": Quoted in V. Norris, *Mental Illness in London* (London: Oxford University Press, 1959), p. 15. **"it is only":** J. Hawkes, "On the Increase of Insanity," *Journal of Psychological Medicine and Mental Pathology* 10 (1857): 508–21. **"in a considerable":** E. Kraepelin, *Dementia Praecox and Paraphrenia* (Huntington, N.Y.: Robert E. Krieger, 1971), pp. 236–37. **study in Finland:** M. Isohanni, I. Isohanni, P. Jones, et al., "School Predictors of Schizophrenia in the 1966 Northern Finland Birth Cohort," *Schizophrenia Research* 36 (1999): 44. **Researchers in Germany and Canada:** M. Hambrecht, H. Häfner, and W. Löffler, "Beginning Schizophrenia Observed by Significant Others," *Social Psychiatry and Psychiatric Epidemiology* 29 (1994): 53–60; J. Varsamis and J. D. Adamson, "Somatic Symptoms in Schizophrenia," *Canadian Psychiatric Association Journal* 21 (1976): 1–6. **"monster themes":** A. T. Russell, L. Bett, and C. Sammons, "The Phenomenology of Schizophrenia Occurring in Childhood," *Journal of the American Academy of Child and Adolescent Psychiatry* 28 (1989): 399–407. **Recent MRI studies:** J. L. Rapoport, J. N. Giedd, J. Blumenthal, et al., "Progressive Cortical Change During Adolescence in Childhood-Onset Schizophrenia," *Archives of General Psychiatry* 56 (1999): 649–54. **follow-up of 10:** J. G. Howells and W. R. Guirguis, "Childhood Schizophrenia 20 Years Later," *Archives of General Psychiatry* 41 (1984): 123–28. **Louise Wilson:** *This Stranger, My Son* (New York: Putnam, 1968). **study in Denmark:** I. M. Terp, G. Engholm, H. Moller, et al., "A Follow-Up Study of Postpartum Psychoses: Prognosis and Risk Factors for Readmission," *Acta Psychiatrica Scandinavica* 100 (1999): 40–46. **gender differences:** See M. V. Seeman, "Gender Differences in Schizophrenia," *Canadian Journal of Psychiatry* 27 (1982): 107–11; J. M. Goldstein, "Gender Differences in the Course of Schizophrenia," *American Journal of Psychiatry* 145 (1988): 684–89; and S. Lewis, "Sex and Schizophrenia: Vive la Difference," *British Journal of Psychiatry* 161 (1992): 445–50. **"were considered to be":** J. Lieberman et al., "Time Course and Biologic Correlates of Treatment Response in First-Episode Schizophrenia," *Archives of General Psychiatry* 50 (1993): 369–76. **best summary:** J. H. Stephens, "Long-term Prognosis and Follow-up in Schizophrenia," *Schizophrenia Bulletin* 4 (1978): 25–47. **"About three-fifths":** L. Ciompi, "Catamnestic Long-term Study of the Course of Life and Aging of Schizophrenics," *Schizophrenia Bulletin* 6 (1980): 606–16. **"the current picture":** C. M. Harding and J. S. Strauss, "The Course of Schizophrenia: An Evolving Concept," in M. Alpert, ed., *Controversies in Schizophrenia* (New York: Guilford Press, 1985), p. 347. **"The patient":** W. Mayer-Gross, E. Slater, and M. Roth, *Clinical Psychiatry* (Baltimore: Williams and Wilkins, 1969), p. 275. **community survey in Baltimore:** M. Von Korff, G. Nestadt, A. Romanoski, et al., "Prevalence of Treated and Untreated DSM-III Schizophrenia," *Journal of Nervous and Mental Disease* 173 (1985): 577–81. **nine-month follow-up:** K. H. Roberts, P. J. Tyson, and A. M. Mortimer, "The Influence of Atypical Antipsychotics on Social Outcomes: A Nine-Month Follow Up," *Schizophrenia Research* 41 (2000): 215. **"about twice":** P. Allebeck, "Schizophrenia: A Life-Shortening Disease," *Schizophrenia Bulletin* 15 (1989): 81–89. **"nearly a three-fold":** D. W. Black and R. Fisher, "Mortality in DSM-IIIR Schizophrenia," *Schizophrenia Research* 7 (1992): 109–16. **"5.05 times":** P. Corten, M. Ribourdouille, and M. Dramaix, "Premature Death Among Outpatients at a Community Mental Health Center," *Hospital and Community Psychiatry* 42 (1991): 1248–51. **A 1999 study:** B. P. Dembling, D. T. Chen, and L. Vachon, "Life Expectancy and Causes of Death in a Population Treated for Serious Mental Illness," *Psychiatric Services* 50 (1999): 1036–42. **double the rate:** M. J. Edlund, C. Conrad, and P. Morris, "Accidents Among Schizophrenic Outpatients," *Comprehensive Psychiatry* 30 (1989): 522–26. **12 percent of the excess:** S. Brown, "Excess Mortality of Schizophrenia," *British Journal of Psychiatry* 171 (1997): 502–8. *Diseases:* See A. E. Harris, "Physical Disease and Schizophrenia," *Schizophrenia Bulletin* 14 (1988): 85–96; and S. Mukherjee, D. B. Schnur, and R. Reddy, "Family History of Type 2 Diabetes in Schizophrenic Patients," *Lancet* 1 (1989): 495. **prostate cancer:** P. B. Mortensen, "Neuroleptic Medication and Reduced Risk of Prostate Cancer in Schizophrenic Patients," *Acta Psychiatrica Scandinavica* 85 (1992): 390–93. **102 individuals:** S. Brown, J. Birtwistle, L. Roe, et al., "The Unhealthy Lifestyle of People with Schizophrenia," *Psychological Medicine* 29 (1999): 697–701. **41 percent less:** B. G. Druss, D. W. Bradford, R. A. Rosenheck, et al. "Mental Disorders and Use of Cardiovascular Procedures After Myocardial Infarction," *Journal of the American Medical Association* 283 (2000): 506–11.

study in England: M. Marshall and D. Gath, "What Happens to Homeless Mentally Ill People? Follow Up of Residents of Oxford Hostels for the Homeless," *British Medical Journal* 304 (1992): 79–80. **in Oklahoma:** J. Cannon, "Remains Identified," *Norman Transcript*, December 21, 1990, p. 2. **In Houston:** S. K. Bardwell, "Services Saturday for Homeless Woman, Son Killed in Traffic Accident," *Houston Chronicle*, April 29, 1999, p. A-32. **In Santa Ana:** R. Hinch, "Woman Killed by Train Has Final Resting Place," *Orange County Register*, February 23, 2000, p. A-1.

CHAPTER 6

"Something has happened": L. Jefferson, *These Are My Sisters* (1948), quoted in B. Kaplan, ed., *The Inner World of Mental Illness* (New York: Harper and Row, 1964), p. 6. **"If the brain":** Lyall Watson, quoted in J. Hooper and D. Teresi, *The 3-Pound Universe* (New York: Macmillan, 1986), p. 21. **"three-quarters of the schizophrenic":** M. A. Taylor and R. Abrams, "Cognitive Impairment in Schizophrenia," *American Journal of Psychiatry* 141 (1984): 196–201. **A 1988 review:** D. W. Heinrichs and R. W. Buchanan, "Significance and Meaning of Neurological Signs of Schizophrenia," *American Journal of Psychiatry* 145 (1988): 11–18. **study by Schroder et al.:** J. Schroder, R.

Niethammer, F. J. Geider, et al., "Neurological Soft Signs in Schizophrenia," *Schizophrenia Research* 6 (1992): 25–30. **"a broad":** J. A. Grebb, D. R. Weinberger, and J. M. Morihisa, "Electroencephalogram and Evoked Potentials Studies of Schizophrenia," in H. A. Nasrallah and D. R. Weinberger, eds., *The Neurology of Schizophrenia* (Amsterdam: Elsevier, 1986), pp. 121–40. **In 1942:** H. B. Molholm, "Hyposensitivity to Foreign Protein in Schizophrenic Patients," *Psychiatric Quarterly* 16 (1942): 565–71. **study in Denmark:** P. B. Mortensen, C. B. Pedersen, T. Westergaard, et al., "Effects of Family History and Place and Season of Birth on the Risk of Schizophrenia," *New England Journal of Medicine* 340 (1999): 603–8. **number of miscarriages:** D. MacSweeney, P. Timms, and A. Johnson, "A Thyro-Endocrine Pathology, Obstetric Morbidity and Schizophrenia: Survey of a Hundred Families with a Schizophrenic Proband," *Psychological Medicine* 8 (1978): 151–55. **"Psychiatry and neuropathology":** H. Griesinger, cited by G. Zilboorg and G. W. Henry, *A History of Medical Psychology* (New York: Norton, 1941), p. 436. **"selective, integrative":** D. R. Roberts, "Schizophrenia and the Brain," *Journal of Neuropsychiatry* 5 (1963): 71–79. **"able to correlate":** P. D. MacLean, "Psychosomatic Disease and the Visceral Brain," *Psychosomatic Medicine* 11 (1949): 338–53. **limbic system dysfunction:** E. F. Tor-

rey and M. R. Peterson, "Schizophrenia and the Limbic System," *Lancet* 2 (1974): 942–46. **brain tumors:** N. Malamud, "Psychiatric Disorders with Intracranial Tumors of the Limbic System," *Archives of Neurology* 17 (1967): 113–23. **Cases of encephalitis:** J. R. Brierley et al., "Subacute Encephalitis of Later Life Mainly Affecting the Limbic Areas," *Brain* 83 (1960): 357–68. **epilepsy, when it originates:** N. Malamud, "The Epileptogenic Focus in Temporal Lobe Epilepsy from the Pathological Standpoint," *Archives of Neurology* 14 (1966): 190–95; M. A. Falconer, E. A. Serafetinides, and J. A. N. Corsellis, "Etiology and Pathogenesis of Temporal Lobe Epilepsy," *Archives of Neurology* 10 (1964): 233–48. **limbic electrical activity:** R. G. Heath, *Studies in Schizophrenia: A Multidisciplinary Approach to Mind-Brain Relationships* (Cambridge: Harvard University Press, 1954); R. G. Heath, "Correlation of Electrical Recordings from Cortical and Subcortical Regions of the Brain with Abnormal Behavior in Human Subjects," *Confina Neurologia* 18 (1958): 305–15.

CHAPTER 7

"It [insanity] is": A. Brigham, "Insanity and Insane Hospitals," *North American Review* 44 (1837): 91–121. **"insanity, then, is":** W. A. F. Browne, *What Asylums Were, Are, and Ought to Be* (Edinburgh: Black, 1837), p. 6.

"**important molecular**": H. Maudsley, *Physiology and Pathology of the Mind* (London: Macmillan, 1867), p. 367. "**a meteoric shower**": from Sonnet 137, in her 1934 collection, *Huntsman, What Quarry?: Poems by Edna St. Vincent Millay,* (New York: Harper and Brothers, 1939). "**a hereditary**": D. R. Weinberger, "Implications of Normal Brain Development for the Pathogenesis of Schizophrenia," *Archives of General Psychiatry* 44 (1987): 660–69. "**no study found**": J. G. Rabkin, "Stressful Life Events and Schizophrenia: A Review of the Research Literature," *Psychological Bulletin* 87 (1980): 408–25. "**there is no good**": C. C. Tennant, "Stress and Schizophrenia: A Review," *Integrative Psychiatry* 3 (1985): 248–61. "**There is no evidence**": R. M. G. Norman and A. K. Malla, "Stressful Life Events and Schizophrenia," *British Journal of Psychiatry* 162 (1993): 161–66. "**In cases**": E. Bleuler, *Dementia Praecox or the Group of Schizophrenias* (New York: International Universities Press, 1950), p. 345; first published in 1911. "**I seldom see**": Letter from Sigmund Freud to Karl Abraham in E. Jones, *The Life and Work of Sigmund Freud,* vol. 2 (New York: Basic Books, 1955), p. 437. "**I do not like**": Quoted in M. Shur, *The Id and the Regulatory Principle of Mental Functioning* (London: Hogarth, 1967), p. 21. "**all mothers were**": T. Tietze, "A Study of Mothers of Schizophrenic Patients," *Psychiatry* 12 (1949): 55–65. "**strange, near-psychotic**": T. Lidz, S. Fleck, and A. R. Cornelison, *Schizophrenia and the Family* (New York: International University Press, 1965), p. 327. "**an extremely noxious**": T. Lidz, B. Parker, and A. R. Cornelison, "The Role of the Father in the Family Environment of the Schizophrenic Patient," *American Journal of Psychiatry* 113 (1956): 126–32. "**double-bind**": G. Bateson, D. D. Jackson, J. Haley, et al., "Toward a Theory of Schizophrenia," *Behavioral Science* 1 (1956): 251–64. **later essay:** G. Bateson, "The Birth of a Matrix or Double Bind and Epistemology," in M. M. Berger, ed., *Beyond the Double Bind* (New York: Brunner Mazel, 1978). **As early as 1951:** C. T. Prout and M. A. White, "A Controlled Study of Personality Relationships in Mothers of Schizophrenic Male Patients," *American Journal of Psychiatry* 107 (1951): 251–56. **subsequent studies:** See, for example, J. Block, V. Patterson, J. Block, et al., "A Study of Parents of Schizophrenic and Neurotic Children," *Psychiatry* 21 (1958): 387–97. "**in some sense**": C. Lasch, *The Culture of Narcissism* (New York: Norton, 1979), p. 76. "**psychosis is the final**": Ibid. "**we share**": R. C. Lewontin, S. Rose, and L. J. Kamin, *Not in Our Genes* (New York: Pantheon Books, 1984), p. ix. "**An adequate**": Ibid. p. 231. "**fake disease**": T. Szasz, *Schizophrenia: The Sacred Symbol of Psychiatry* (New York: Basic Books, 1976). " '**Mental illness**' ": M. Barnes and J. Berke, *Mary Barnes:*

Two Accounts of a Journey Through Madness (New York: Ballantine Books, 1971), pp. 75–76. **"I was looked":** "Britain's Offbeat Psychoanalyst," *Newsweek,* November 1, 1982, p. 16.

CHAPTER 8

"To lighten": Charles Dickens, "A Curious Dance Around a Curious Tree," in *Household Words,* January 17, 1852. **"as a suffering":** W. J. Annitto, "Schizophrenia and Ego Psychology," *Schizophrenia Bulletin* 7 (1981): 199–200. **A 1996 survey:** C. Blanco, C. Carvalho, M. Olfson, et al., "Practice Patterns of International and U.S. Medical Graduate Psychiatrists," *American Journal of Psychiatry* 156 (1999): 445–50. **"What does mean":** B. J. Ennis, *Prisoners of Psychiatry* (New York: Harcourt Brace Jovanovich, 1972); for a more complete discussion of this problem see R. L. Taylor and E. F. Torrey, "The Pseudo-regulation of American Psychiatry," *American Journal of Psychiatry* 129 (1972): 658–62. **diagnostic algorithm:** H. C. Sox, L. M. Koran, C. H. Sox, et al., "A Medical Algorithm for Detecting Physical Disease in Psychiatric Patients," *Hospital and Community Psychiatry* 40 (1989): 1270–76. **German study:** B. von der Stein, W. Wittgens, W. Lemmer, et al., "Schizophrenia Mimicked by Neurological Diseases," presented at the International Conference on Schizo-

phrenia, Vancouver, July 1992. **"The hospital becomes":** B. Silcock, "Three Experiences of Madness," *Sane Talk,* Summer 1994, p. 5. **study in Oregon:** J. D. Bloom, M. H. Williams, C. Land, et al., "Changes in Public Psychiatric Hospitalization in Oregon over the Past Two Decades," *Psychiatric Services* 49 (1998): 366–69. **"cozy relationship":** "JCAHO Responds to Concern over Psychiatric Hospital Oversight," *Mental Health Weekly,* vol. 9, October 4, 1999, p. 1. **"a man barricaded":** C. Holden, "Broader Commitment Laws Sought," *Science* 230 (1985): 1253–55. **"Public defender":** D. A. Treffert, "The Obviously Ill Patient in Need of Treatment: A Fourth Standard for Civil Commitment," *Hospital and Community Psychiatry* 36 (1985): 259–64. **"significant changes":** J. M. Kane, F. Quitkin, A. Rifkin, et al., "Attitudinal Changes in Involuntarily Committed Patients Following Treatment," *Archives of General Psychiatry* 40 (1983): 374–77. **"the combination of drug":** B. Pasamanick, F. R. Scarpitti, and S. Dinitz, *Schizophrenics in the Community: An Experimental Study in the Prevention of Hospitalization* (New York: Appleton-Century-Crofts, 1967), p. ix. **A 1998 study:** J. Rabinowitz, E. Bromet, J. Lavelle, et al., "Relationship Between Type of Insurance and Care During the Early Course of Psychosis," *American Journal of Psychiatry* 155 (1998): 1392–97. **A 1985 study:** G. Geis, P. Jaslow, H. Pontell, et al.,

"Fraud and Abuse of Government Medical Benefit Programs by Psychiatrists," *American Journal of Psychiatry* 142 (1985): 231–34. **"The reason":** editorial, "Mind and Money," *Wall Street Journal,* December 17, 1999, p. A-14. **Dr. J. R. Elpers:** "Dividing the Mental Health Dollar: The Ethics of Managing Scarce Resources," *Hospital and Community Psychiatry* 37 (1986): 671–72. **45 changes:** A. E. Moran, R. I. Freedman, and S. S. Sharfstein, "The Journey of Sylvia Frumkin: A Case Study for Policymakers," *Hospital and Community Psychiatry* 35 (1984): 887–93. **Dr. Mary Ann Test:** "Continuity of Care in Community Treatment," in L. I. Stein, ed., *Community Support Systems for the Long-term Patient* (San Francisco: Jossey-Bass, 1979). **Elsewhere I have:** E. F. Torrey, "Continuous Treatment Teams," *Hospital and Community Psychiatry* 37 (1986): 1243–47. **give up custody:** R. Cohen, R. Harris, S. Gottlieb, et al., "States' Use of Transfer of Custody as a Requirement for Providing Services to Emotionally Disturbed Children," *Hospital and Community Psychiatry* 42 (1991): 526–30. **Maryland sent:** M. Moran, "Initiatives Throughout Country Bring Child MH Care Home," *Psychiatric News,* March 1, 1991, p. 9. **Saskatchewan:** C. M. Smith, "From Hospital to Community," *Canadian Journal of Psychiatry* 24 (1979): 113–20. **Louisville:** B. Pasamanick, F. R. Scarpitti, and S. Dinitz, *Schizophrenics in the Community: An Experimental Study in the Prevention of Hospitalization* (New York: Appleton-Century-Crofts, 1967). **Iowa:** K. C. Buckwalter, I. L. Abraham, M. Smith, et al., "Nursing Outreach to Rural Elderly People Who Are Mentally Ill," *Hospital and Community Psychiatry* 44 (1993): 821–23. **upstate New York:** G. R. Reding and B. Maguire, "Nonsegregated Acute Psychiatric Admissions to General Hospitals: Continuity of Care Within the Community Hospital," *New England Journal of Medicine* 289 (1973): 185–89. **South Carolina:** A. B. Santos, P. A. Deci, K. R. Lachance, et al., "Providing Assertive Community Treatment for Severely Mentally Ill Patients in a Rural Area," *Hospital and Community Psychiatry* 44 (1993): 34–39. **New Hampshire:** G. M. Barton, "The Practice of Emergency Psychiatry in Rural Areas," *Hospital and Community Psychiatry* 43 (1992): 965–66. **Dr. Werner M. Mendel:** "Managing Dependency in a Psychiatric Patient," *Audio-Digest* 6 (1977): 16. **In one study:** G. Hogarty and S. Goldberg, "Drug and Sociotherapy in the Post-Hospital Maintenance of Schizophrenia," *Archives of General Psychiatry* 24 (1973): 54–64. **best-known of these studies:** P. R. A. May, *Treatment of Schizophrenia: A Comparative Study of Five Treatment Methods* (New York: Science House, 1968). **"Analysis of variance":** P. R. A. May et al., "Schizophrenia: A Follow-up Study of the Results of Five Forms of Treatment," *Archives of*

General Psychiatry 38 (1981): 776–84. **"psychotherapy alone":** L. Grinspoon, J. R. Ewalt, and R. I. Shader, *Schizophrenia: Pharmacotherapy and Psychotherapy* (Baltimore: Williams and Wilkins, 1977), p. 154. **"There is no scientific":** D. F. Klein, "Psychosocial Treatment of Schizophrenia, or Psychosocial Help for People with Schizophrenia?" *Schizophrenia Bulletin* 6 (1980): 122–30. **"outcome for patients":** J. M. Davis et al., "Important Issues in the Drug Treatment of Schizophrenia," *Schizophrenia Bulletin* 6 (1980): 70–87. **"checked the therapeutic":** I. Macalpine and R. A. Hunter, in D. P. Schreber, *Memoirs of My Nervous Illness* (1903), translation and introduction by I. Macalpine and R. A. Hunter (London: William Dawson, 1955), p. 23. **"analogous to pouring":** R. E. Drake and L. I. Sederer, "The Adverse Effects of Intensive Treatment of Chronic Schizophrenia," *Comprehensive Psychiatry* 27 (1986): 313–26. **"psychotic breaks":** S. W. Hadley and H. H. Strupp, "Contemporary Views of Negative Effects in Psychotherapy," *Archives of General Psychiatry* 33 (1976): 1291–1302. **"there is some":** *Report of the President's Commission on Mental Health* (Washington, D.C.: U.S. Government Printing Office, 1978), vol. 4, p. 1766. **"recent evidence suggests":** G. L. Klerman, "Pharmacotherapy and Psychotherapy in the Treatment of Schizophrenia," paper presented at the Annual Meeting of the American Psy-

chiatric Association, San Francisco, 1980. **"To offer traditional":** T. C. Manschreck, "Current Concepts in Psychiatry: Schizophrenic Disorders," *New England Journal of Medicine* 305 (1981): 1628–32. **"when the onset":** W. Z. Potter and M. V. Rudorfer, "Electroconvulsive Therapy—A Modern Medical Procedure," *New England Journal of Medicine* 328 (1993): 882–83. **damage to the brain:** C. E. Coffey, R. D. Weiner, W. T. Djang, et al., "Brain Anatomic Effects of Electroconvulsive Therapy," *Archives of General Psychiatry* 48 (1991): 1013–21. **"a minimum course":** M. Fink, *Electroshock: Restoring the Mind* (New York: Oxford University Press, 1999), p. 62. **gluten-free diet:** D. S. King, "Statistical Power of the Controlled Research on Wheat Gluten and Schizophrenia," *Biological Psychiatry* 20 (1985): 785–87. **given methylfolate:** P. S. A. Godfrey, B. K. Toone, M. W. R Carney, et al., "Enhancement of Recovery from Psychiatric Illness by Methylfolate," *Lancet* 336 (1990): 392–97.

CHAPTER 9:

"Lunacy, like the rain": *The Philosophy of Insanity*, by an inmate of the Glasgow Royal Asylum for Lunatics at Gartnavel, 1860; used as an epigraph by Albert Deutsch, *The Shame of the States* (New York: Harcourt, Brace, 1948). **John Davis:** J. M. Davis, "Overview: Maintenance Therapy in Psychiatry: 1. Schizophrenia," *American Journal of Psychiatry* 132 (1975): 1237–45. **80 percent relapsed:** N. Capstick, "Long-Term Fluphenazine Decanoate Maintenance Dosage Requirements of Chronic Schizophrenic Patients," *Acta Psychiatrica Scandinavica* 61 (1980): 256–62. **two groups of investigators:** T. Van Putten, P. R. A. May, and S. R. Marder, "Response to Antipsychotic Medication: The Doctor's and the Consumer's View," *American Journal of Psychiatry* 141 (1984): 16–19; T. P. Hogan, A. G. Awad, and M. R. Eastwood, "Early Subjective Response and Prediction of Outcome to Neuroleptic Drug Therapy in Schizophrenia," *Canadian Journal of Psychiatry* 30 (1985): 246–48. **study reported in 1994:** S. Galderisi, A. Mucci, M. Maj, et al., "QEEG Mapping Changes after a Single Dose as Predictors of Clinical Response to Haloperidol in Schizophrenia," Abstract, *Schizophrenia Research 11* (1994): 189. **the difference between:** "Fluphenazine Levels—Short and Long," *Biological Therapies in Psychiatry* 4 (1981): 33–34. **racial group differences:** P. Ruiz, R. V. Varner, D. R. Small, et al., "Ethnic Differences in the Neuroleptic Treatment of Schizophrenia," *Psychiatric Quarterly* 70 (1999): 163–72. **Dr. Sven Dencker:** S. J. Dencker, P. Enoksson, R. Johansson, et al., "Late (4–8 Years) Outcome of Treatment with Megadoses of Fluphenazine Enanthate in Drug Refractory Schizophrenics," *Acta Psychiatrica Scandi-*

navica 63 (1981): 1–12; and also S. Steiner and C. Nagy, "Follow-up Study of 281 Schizophrenic Patients Treated with High Dosage Fluphenazine Decanoate," *International Pharmacopsychiatry* 16 (1981): 184–92. **intermittent medication:** A. G. Jolley, S. R. Hirsch, E. Morrison, A. McRink, and L. Wilson, "Trial of Brief Intermittent Neuroleptic Prophylaxis for Selected Schizophrenic Outpatients: Clinical and Social Outcomes at Two Years," *British Medical Journal* 301 (1990): 837–42. **Dr. Jeffrey Lieberman:** J. Lieberman, D. Mayerhoff, A. Loebel, et al., "Biologic Indices of Heterogeneity in Schizophrenia: Relationship to Psychopathology and Treatment Outcome," *Schizophrenia Research* 4 (1991): 289–90. **for loxapine:** L. Sperry, B. Hudson, and C. H. Chan, "Loxapine Abuse," *New England Journal of Medicine* 310 (1984): 598. **"early intervention":** R. J. Wyatt, "Neuroleptics and the Natural Course of Schizophrenia," *Schizophrenia Bulletin* 17 (1991): 325–51. **"greater duration":** A. Loebel, J. Lieberman, D. Mayerhoff, et al., "Correlates of Course of Outcome in First-Episode Schizophrenia," *Schizophrenia Research* 4 (1991): 290. **"untreated psychosis":** H. A. Youssef, A. Kinsella, and J. L. Waddington, "Extreme Negative Symptoms in Schizophrenia as a Correlate of Years of Untreated Psychosis Within a Rural Irish Population," *Schizophrenia Research* 9

(1993): 142. **"The antipsychotic agents":** R. J. Baldessarini, "The Neuroleptic Antipsychotic Drugs, *Postgraduate Medicine* 65 (1979): 108–28. **One study:** M. P. Caligiuri, J. B. Lohr, and D. V. Jeste, "Parkinsonism in Neuroleptic-Naive Schizophrenic Patients," *American Journal of Psychiatry* 150 (1993): 1343–48. **"extraordinary prevalence":** T. Turner, "Rich and Mad in Victorian England," *Psychological Medicine* 19 (1989): 29–44. **A recent study:** W. S. Fenton, "Prevalence of Spontaneous Dyskinesia in Schizophrenia," *Journal of Clinical Psychiatry* 61 (2000) (supp. 4): 10–14. **less than 20 percent:** V. Khot and R. J. Wyatt, "Not All That Moves Is Tardive Dyskinesia," *American Journal of Psychiatry* 148 (1991): 661–66. **10-year follow-up:** R. Yassa and N. P. V. Nair, "A 10-Year Follow-Up Study of Tardive Dyskinesia," *Acta Psychiatrica Scandinavica* 86 (1992): 262–66. **another 10-year:** G. Gardos, D. E. Casey, J. O. Cole, et al., "Ten Year Outcome of Tardive Dyskinesia," *American Journal of Psychiatry* 151 (1994): 836–41. **"Of the 10":** D. E. Casey, "Tardive Dyskinesia: Outcome with Typical and Atypical Neuroleptics," in H. Y. Meltzer and D. Nerozzi, eds., *Current Practices and Future Developments in the Pharmacotherapy of Mental Disorders* (Amsterdam: Elsevier, 1991), pp. 49–57. **A 1997 study:** P. S. Wang, J. C. West, T. Tanielian, et al., "Recent Patterns and Predictors of Antipsychotic Medication Regimens Used to

Treat Schizophrenia and Other Psychotic Disorders," *Schizophrenia Bulletin* 26 (2000): 451–57. **effective antiviral agents:** L. V. Jones-Brando, J. L. Buthod, L. E. Holland, et al., "Metabolites of the Antipsychotic Agent Clozapine Inhibit the Replication of Human Immunodeficiency Virus Type 1," *Schizophrenia Research* 25 (1997): 63–70. **alter the immune system:** M. Maes, L. B. Chiavetto, S. Bignotti, et al., "Effects of Atypical Antipsychotics on the Inflammatory Response System in Schizophrenic Patients Resistant to Treatment with Typical Neuroleptics," *European Neuropsychopharmacology* 10 (2000): 119–24. **in 1998:** J. A. Carrillo, A. G. Herraiz, S. I. Ramos, et al., "Effects of Caffeine Withdrawal from the Diet on the Metabolism of Clozapine in Schizophrenic Patients," *Journal of Clinical Psychopharmacology* 18 (1998): 311–16. **(PORT) survey:** A. F. Lehman, D. M. Steinwachs, and the Survey Co-Investigators of the PORT Project, "Patterns of Usual Care for Schizophrenia: Initial Results from the Schizophrenia Patient Outcomes Research Team (PORT) Client Study," *Schizophrenia Bulletin* 24 (1998): 11–20. *Practice Guideline:* **Practice Guideline for the Treatment of Patients with Schizophrenia**, Washington, D.C.: American Psychiatric Association, 1997. **"The Expert Consensus":** "The Expert Consensus Guideline Series on the Treatment of Schizophrenia 1999," *Journal of Clinical Psychiatry* 60 (supp. 11) (1999): 1–80. **Texas Department:** J. A. Chiles, A. L. Miller, M. L. Crismon, et al., "The Texas Medication Algorithm Project: Development and Implementation of the Schizophrenia Algorithm," *Psychiatric Services* 50 (1999): 69–74. **In England:** J. R. Gedder, N. Freemantle, P. Harrison, and P. E. Beddington, "Atypical Antipsychotics in the Treatment of Schizophrenia—Systematic Overview and Meta-Regression Analysis," *British Medical Journal* 321 (2000): 1371–76. **A 1998 Survey:** L. D. Sasich, E. F. Torrey, and S. M. Wolfe, *International Comparison of Prices for Antidepressant and Antipsychotic Drugs* (Washington, D.C.: Public Citizen's Health Research Group, 1998). *"Fortune magazine":* D. Cauchon, "Americans Pay More; Here's Why," *USA Today*, November 10, 1999, p. 1-A. **According to:** E. Tanouye, "For Drug Makers, High-Stakes Race Inside the Brain," *Wall Street Journal*, August 25, 1999, p. B-1. **A recent study:** C. I. Cohen and S. I. Cohen, "Potential Cost Savings from Pill Splitting of Newer Psychotropic Medications," *Psychiatric Services* 51 (2000): 527–29. **one study showed:** L. J. Chapman, J. P. Chapman, T. R. Kwapil, et al., "Putatively Psychosis-prone Subjects 10 Years Later," *Journal of Abnormal Psychology* 103 (1994): 171–83. **"would have been hopeless":** P. B. Jones and J. J. Van Os, "Predicting Schizophrenia in Teenagers: Pessimistic Results from the British 1946

Birth Cohort" [abstract], *Schizophrenia Research* 29 (1998): 11. **"Recovery began":** E. G. Francell, Jr., "Medication: The Foundation of Recovery," *Innovations and Research* 3 (1994): 31–40.

CHAPTER 10

"Expecting the": J. Halpern, P. R. Binner, C. B. Mohr, et al., *The Illusion of Deinstitutionalization* (Denver: Denver Research Institute, 1978). **"If, for example":** W. M. Mendel, *Treating Schizophrenia* (San Francisco: Jossey-Bass, 1989), p. 128. **"pessimistic outcome":** H. Hoffmann, Z. Kupper, and B. Kunz, "The Impact of 'Resignation' on Rehabilitation Outcome in Schizophrenia," *Schizophrenia Research* 36 (1999): 325–26. **"an inability to engage":** Social Security Administration, Department of Health and Human Services, *Supplemental Security Income Regulations* (these regulations are available in all Social Security offices). **SSDI and SSI:** The number of recipients with mental disabilities is from the *Annual Statistical Supplement to the Social Security Bulletin*, Social Security Administration, 1999. **"graduated independent":** "Diabetic Lay Dead at Group Home 3 Days," *Washington Post*, April 19, 1986, p. C-3. **"the police found":** "21 Ex–Mental Patients Taken from 4 Private Homes," *New York Times*, August 5, 1979, p. B-3. **In one study:** H. R. Lamb, "Board-and-Care Home Wanderers," *Hospital and Community Psychiatry* 32 (1981): 498–500. **Fairweather Lodges:** G. W. Fairweather, ed., *The Fairweather Lodge: A Twenty-Five-Year Retrospective* (San Francisco: Jossey-Bass, 1980). **"the presence of":** *There Goes the Neighborhood* (White Plains, N.Y.: Community Residences Information Services Program, 1986). **one recent study:** R. M. Friedrich, B. Hollingsworth, E. Hradek, et al., "Family and Client Perspective on Alternative Residential Settings for Person with Severe Mental Illness," *Psychiatric* Services 50 (1999): 509–14. **6 percent:** R. J. Turner, "Jobs and Schizophrenia," *Social Policy* 8 (1977): 32–40. **"in the morning":** H. R. Lamb and Associates, *Community Survival for Long-term Patients* (San Francisco: Jossey-Bass, 1976), p. 8. **"I get lost":** S. E. Estroff, *Making It Crazy: An Ethnography of Psychiatric Clients in an American Community* (Berkeley: University of California Press, 1981), p. 233. **"I just can't":** C. Smith, "Schizophrenia in the 1980s," presented at the Alberta Schizophrenia Conference, May 1986. **studies done at Thresholds:** J. Dincin and T. F. Witheridge, "Psychiatric Rehabilitation as a Deterrent to Recidivism," *Hospital and Community Psychiatry* 33 (1982): 645–50. **"These findings":** T. F. Witheridge and J. Dincin, "The Bridge: An Assertive Outreach Program in an Urban Setting," in L. I. Stein and M. A. Test, eds., *The Training in Community Living Model: A Decade of Experience* (San Francisco: Jossey-Bass, 1985). **26 to 53 percent:** R. P. Roca, W. R. Breakey, and P. J. Fisher, "Medical Care of Chronic Psychiatric Outpatients," *Hospital and Community Psychiatry* 38 (1987): 741–44. **"the treatment of":** L. E. Adler and J. M. Griffith, "Concurrent Medical Illness in the Schizophrenic Patient," *Schizophrenia Research* 4 (1991): 91–107. **Methods of Measuring:** This schema is taken from E. F. Torrey, *Out of the Shadows* (New York: John Wiley, 1997), p. 132.

CHAPTER 11

"Although insanity": Anonymous, "Admissions to Hospitals for the Insane," *American Journal of Insanity* 25 (1868): 74. **80 and 90 percent:** J. B. Lohr and K. Flynn, "Smoking and Schizophrenia," *Schizophrenia Research* 8 (1992): 93–102. **Recent studies:** E. R. Lyon, "A Review of the Effects of Nicotine on Schizophrenia and Antipsychotic Medications," *Psychiatric Services* 50 (1999): 1346–50. **among outpatients:** J. R. Hughes, D. K. Hatsukami, J. E. Mitchell, et al., "Prevalence of Smoking Among Psychiatric Outpatients," *American Journal of Psychiatry* 143 (1986): 993–97. **received additional support:** L. A. Adler, L. D. Hoffer, A. Wiser, et al., "Normalization of Auditory Physiology by Cigarette Smoking in Schizophrenic Patients," *American Journal* *of Psychiatry* 150 (1993): 1856–61. **exacerbation:** G. W. Dulack and J. H. Meador-Woodruff, "Smoking, Smoking Withdrawal and Schizophrenia: Case Reports and a Review of the Literature," *Schizophrenia Research* 22 (1996): 133–41. **smoking decreases:** D. C. Goff, D. C. Henderson, and E. Amico, "Cigarette Smoking in Schizophrenia: Relationship to Psychopathology and Medication Side Effects," *American Journal of Psychiatry* 149 (1992): 1189–94. **affect the receptors:** D. G. Kirch, A. M. Alho, and R. J. Wyatt, "Hypothesis: A Nicotine-Dopamine Interaction Linking Smoking with Parkinson's Disease and Tardive Dyskinesia," *Cellular and Molecular Neurobiology* 8 (1998): 285–91. **nicotine potentiated:** B. J. McConville, M. H. Fogelson, A. B. Norman, et al., "Nicotine Potentiation of Haloperidol in Reducing Tic Frequency in Tourette's Disorder," *American Journal of Psychiatry* 148 (1991): 793–94. **40 percent lower:** N. H. Seppälä, E. V. J. Leinonen, M. L. Lehtonen, et al., "Clozapine Serum Concentrations Are Lower in Smoking than in Non-Smoking Schizophrenic Patients," *Pharmacology and Toxicology* 85 (1999): 244–46. **incidence of akathisia:** Goff et al. 1992. **tardive dyskinesia:** Kirch et al. 1988; Goff et al. 1992. **12 percent:** J. Addington, "Group Treatment for Smoking Cessation Among Persons with Schizophrenia," *Psychiatric Services* 49 (1998): 925–28. **instant coffee:** J. I. Benson and J. J. David, "Coffee Eating in Chronic Schizophrenic Patients," *American Journal of Psychiatry* 143 (1986): 940–41. **adenosine receptors:** P. B. Lucas, D. Pickar, J. Kelsoe, et al., "Effects of the Acute Administration of Caffeine in Patients with Schizophrenia," *Biological Psychiatry* 28 (1990): 35–40. **caffeine may decrease:** S. R. Hirsch, "Precipitation of Antipsychotic Drugs in Interaction with Coffee or Tea," letter, *Lancet* 2 (1979): 1130–31. **worsening of their symptoms:** Lucas et al. 1990; M. O. Zaslove, R. L. Russell, and E. Ross, "Effect of Caffeine Intake on Psychotic In-Patients," *British Journal of Psychiatry* 159 (1991): 565–67. **interfere with the absorption:** F. Kulhanek, O. K. Linde, and G. Meisenberg, "Precipitation of Antipsychotic Drugs in Interaction with Coffee or Tea," letter, *Lancet* 2 (1979): 1130. **Three controlled studies:** B. DeFreitas and G. Swartz, "Effects of Caffeine in Chronic Psychiatric Patients," *American Journal of Psychiatry* 136 (1979): 1337–38; A. Koczapski, J. Paredes, C. Kogan, et al., "Effects of Caffeine on Behavior of Schizophrenic Inpatients," *Schizophrenia Bulletin* 15 (1989): 339–44; K. M. Mayo, W. Falkowski, and C. A. H. Jones, "Caffeine: Use and Effects in Long-Stay Psychiatric Patients," *British Journal of Psychiatry* 162 (1993): 543–45. **one recent study:** J. A. Cabarillo, A. G. Herraiz, S. I. Ramos, et al., "Effects of Caffeine Withdrawal from the Diet on the Metabolism of Clozapine in Schizophrenic Patients," *Journal of Clinical Psychopharmacology* 18 (1998): 311–16. **47 percent abused:** D. A. Regier, M. E. Farmer, D. S. Rae, et al., "Comorbidity of Mental Disorders with Alcohol and Other Drug Abuse," *Journal of the American Medical Association* 264 (1990): 2511–18. **has increased significantly:** B. J. Cuffel, "Prevalence Estimates of Substance Abuse in Schizophrenia and Their Correlates," *Journal of Nervous and Mental Disease* 180 (1992): 589–92. **One recent study:** C. A. Pristach and C. M. Smith, "Self-Reported Effects of Alcohol Use on Symptoms of Schizophrenia," *Psychiatric Services* 47 (1996): 421–23. **higher relapse rate:** R. E. Drake and M. A. Wallach, "Substance Abuse Among the Chronically Ill," *Hospital and Community Psychiatry* 40 (1989): 1041–46. **remissions from alcoholism:** R. E. Drake, G. J. McHugo, and D. L. Noordsy, "Treatment of Alcoholism Among Schizophrenic Outpatients: 4-Year Outcomes," *American Journal of Psychiatry* 150 (1993): 328–29. **Disulfiram can be used:** S. J. Kingsbury and C. Salzman, "Disulfiram in the Treatment of Alcoholic Patients with Schizophrenia," *Hospital and Community Psychiatry* 41 (1990): 133–34. **73 percent of them:** J. Coverdale, J. Aruffo, and H. Grunebaum, "Developing Family Planning Services for Female Chronic Mentally Ill Outpatients," *Hospital and Community Psychiatry* 43 (1992): 475–77. **62 percent were:** J. A. Kelly, D. A. Murphy, G. R. Bahr, et al., "AIDS/HIV Risk Behavior Among the Chronically Mentally Ill," *American Journal of Psychiatry* 149 (1992): 886–89. **66 percent had:** K. McKinnon, F, Courrios, H. F. L. Meyer-Bahlburg, et al., "Reliability of Sexual Risk Behavior Interviews with Psychiatry Patients," *American Journal of Psychiatry* 150 (1993): 972–74. **"sexual activity was":** D. Civic, G. Walsh, and D. McBride, "Staff Perspectives on Sexual Behavior of Patients in a State Psychiatric Hospital," *Hospital and Community Psychiatry* 44 (1993): 887–90. **"had never had":** K. Bhui, A. Puffet, and G. Strathdee, "Sexual and Relationship Problems Amongst Patients with Severe Chronic Psychoses," *Social Psychiatry and Psychiatric Epidemiology* 32 (1997): 459–67. **"vividly described":** M. B. Rosenbaum, "Neuroleptics and Sexual Functioning," *Integrative Psychiatry* 4 (1986): 105–06. **30 to 60 percent:** G. Sullivan and D. Lukoff, "Sexual Side Effects of Antipsychotic Medication: Evaluation and Interventions," *Hospital and Community Psychiatry* 41 (1990): 1238–41. **reported sexual side effects:** S. Smith, P. Mostyn, S. Vearnals, et al., "The Prevalence of Sexual Dysfunction in Schizophrenic Patients Taking Conventional Antipsychotic Medication," *Schizophrenia Research* 41 (2000): 218. **"would routinely engage":** D. D. Gold and J. D. Justino, " 'Bicycle Kickstand' Phenomenon: Prolonged Erections Associated with Antipsychotic

Drugs," *Southern Medical Journal* 81 (1988): 792–94. **"the rate of children":** M. V. Seeman, M. Lang, and N. Rector, "Chronic Schizophrenia: A Risk Factor for HIV?" *Canadian Journal of Psychiatry* 35 (1990): 765–68. **31 percent of the women:** J. H. Coverdale and J. A. Aruffo, "Family Planning Needs of Female Chronic Psychiatric Outpatients," *American Journal of Psychiatry* 146 (1989): 1489–91. **"chronic psychiatric outpatients":** Coverdale and Aruffo 1989. **guidelines have been proposed:** L. B. McCullough, J. Coverdale, T. Bayer, et al., "Ethically Justified Guidelines for Family Planning Interventions to Prevent Pregnancy in Female Patients with Chronic Mental Illness," *American Journal of Obstetrics and Gynecology* 167 (1992): 19–25. **study from Denmark:** B. E. Bennedsen, P. B. Mortensen, A. V. Olesen, et al., "Preterm Birth and Intra-Uterine Growth Retardation Among Children of Women with Schizophrenia," *British Journal of Psychiatry* 175 (1999): 239–45. **report from Australia:** A. Jablensky, S. Zubrick, V. Morgan, et al., "The Offspring of Women with Schizophrenia and Affective Psychoses: A Population Study," *Schizophrenia Research* 41 (2000): 8. **breast-feeding:** A. Buist, T. R. Norman, and L. Dennerstein, "Breastfeeding and the Use of Psychotropic Medication: A Review," *Journal of Affective Disorders* 19 (1990): 197–206. **1.6 percent in**

Texas: D. Gamino, "1 in 24 New Austin State Hospital Patients Has HIV," *Austin American-Statesman*, August 22, 1991. **5.5 percent in New York:** F. Cournos, M. Empfield, E. Horwath, et al., "HIV Seroprevalence Among Patients Admitted to Two Psychiatric Hospitals," *American Journal of Psychiatry* 148 (1991): 1225–30. **3.4 percent were positive:** M. Sacks, H. Dermatis, S. Looser-Ott, et al., "Seroprevalence of HIV and Risk Factors for AIDS in Psychiatric Inpatients," *Hospital and Community Psychiatry* 43 (1992): 736–37. **AIDS by shaking hands:** J. F. Aruffo, J. H. Coverdale, R. C. Chacko, et al., "Knowledge About AIDS Among Women Psychiatric Outpatients," *Hospital and Community Psychiatry* 41 (1990): 326–28. **A 1993 study:** F. Cournos, K. McKinnon, H. Meyer-Bahlburg, et al., "HIV Risk Activity Among Persons with Severe Mental Illness: Preliminary Findings," *Hospital and Community Psychiatry* 44 (1993): 1104–6. **In another study:** J. A. Kelley et al. 1992. **AIDS education programs:** R. M. Goisman, A. B. Kent, E. C. Montgomery, et al., "AIDS Education for Patients with Chronic Mental Illness," *Community Mental Health Journal* 27 (1991): 189–97; J. A. Kelly, T. L. McAuliffe, K. J. Sikkema, et al. "Reduction in Risk Behavior Among Adults with Severe Mental Illness Who Learned to Advocate for HIV Prevention," *Psychiatric Services* 48 (1997): 1283–88. **278 residents:** A. F. Lehman and L. S. Linn,

"Crimes Against Discharged Mental Patients in Board-and-Care Homes," *American Journal of Psychiatry* 141 (1984): 271–74. **185 individuals:** V. A. Hiday, M. S. Swartz, J. W. Swanson, et al., "Criminal Victimization of Persons with Severe Mental Illness," *Psychiatric Services* 50 (1999): 62–68. **"The mentally ill":** C. W. Dugger, "Big Shelters Hold Terrors for the Mentally Ill," *New York Times*, January 12, 1992, pp. 1 and 22. **20 women:** S. Friedman and G. Harrison, "Sexual Histories, Attitudes, and Behavior of Schizophrenic and 'Normal' Women," *Archives of Sexual Behavior* 13 (1984): 555–67. **In Washington:** L. A. Goodman, M. A. Dutton, and M. Harris, "Episodically Homeless Women with Serious Mental Illness: Prevalence of Physical and Sexual Assault," *American Journal of Orthopsychiatry* 65 (1995): 468–78. In France: J. -M. Darvez-Bornoz, T. Lemperiere, A. Degiovanni, and P. Grillard, "Sexual Victimization in Women with Schizophrenia and Bipolar Disorder," *Social Psychiatry and Psychiatric Epidemiology* 30 (1995): 78–84. **"I know one":** C. J. Cooper, "Brutal Lives of Homeless S. F. Women," *San Francisco Examiner*, December 18, 1988, p. A-1. **half the time:** J. A. Marley and S. Buila, "When Violence Happens to People with Mental Illness: Disclosing Victimization," *American Journal of Orthopsychiatry* 69 (1999): 398–402. **"I was never":** N. Dearth, B. J. Labenski, M. E. Mott, et al., *Families*

Helping Families (New York: Norton, 1986), p. 61. **Riverside County:** T. Bogart and P. Solomon, "Procedures to Share Treatment Information Among Mental Health Providers, Consumers, and Families," *Psychiatric Services* 50 (1999): 1321–25. **70 percent of patients:** P. J. Weiden, L. Dixon, A. Frances, et al., "Neuroleptic Noncompliance in Schizophrenia," in C. A. Tamminga and S. C. Schulz, eds., *Advances in Neuropsychiatry and Psychopharmacology*, vol. 1, *Schizophrenia Research* (New York: Raven Press, 1991), pp. 285–96. **$136 million per year:** P. J. Weiden and M. Olfson, "Measuring Costs of Rehospitalization in Schizophrenia," presented at the annual meeting of the American Psychiatric Association, San Francisco, California, May 1993. Costs averaged for first two years. **twice as high:** I. E. Lin, R. Spiga, and W. Fortsch, "Insight and Adherence to Medication in Chronic Schizophrenics," *Journal of Clinical Psychiatry* 40 (1979): 430–32. **"I did not want":** D. Minor, quoted in A. B. Hatfield and H. P. Lefley, *Surviving Mental Illness* (New York: Guilford Press, 1993), p. 134. **"Unfortunately the side":** E. Leete, "The Treatment of Schizophrenia: A Patient's Perspective," *Hospital and Community Psychiatry* 38 (1987): 486–91. **"the major finding":** P. J. Weiden, J. J. Mann, G. Haas, et al., "Clinical Nonrecognition of Neuroleptic-Induced Movement Disorders: A Cautionary Study," *American Journal of Psychiatry* 144 (1987):

1148–53. **"psychiatrists misjudged":** S. E. Finn, J. M. Bailey, R. T. Schultz, et al., "Subjective Utility Ratings of Neuroleptics in Treating Schizophrenia," *Psychological Medicine* 20 (1990): 843–48. **"the reluctance":** T. Van Putten, "Why Do Schizophrenic Patients Refuse to Take Their Drugs?" *Archives of General Psychiatry* 31 (1974): 67–72. **"it is still":** R. Diamond, "Drugs and the Quality of Life: The Patient's Point of View," *Journal of Clinical Psychiatry* 46 (1985): 29–35. **"Many of the mistakes":** B. Blaska, "The Myriad Medication Mistakes in Psychiatry: A Consumer's View," *Hospital and Community Psychiatry* 41 (1990): 993–98. **found that 37 percent:** C. Clary, A. Dever, and E. Schweizer, "Psychiatric Inpatients' Knowledge of Medication at Hospital Discharge," *Hospital and Community Psychiatry* 43 (1992): 140–44. **In a Baltimore study:** A. F. Lehman, L. B. Dixon, E. Kernan, et al., "A Randomized Trial of Assertive Community Treatment for Homeless Persons with Severe Mental Illness," *Archives of General Psychiatry* 54 (1997): 1038–43. **"approximately one-third":** L. Dixon, P. Weiden, M. Torres, et al., "Assertive Community Treatment and Medication Compliance in the Homeless Mentally Ill," *American Journal of Psychiatry* 154 (1997): 1302–4. **reduces hospitalization days:** D. J. Luchins, P. Hanrahan, K. J. Conrad, et al., "An Agency-Based Representative Payee Program and Improved Community Tenure of Persons with Mental Illness," *Psychiatric Services* 49 (1998): 1218–22. **substance abuse:** R. Rosenheck, J. Lam, and F. Randolph, "Impact of Representative Payees on Substance Use Among Homeless Persons with Serious Mental Illness and Substance Abuse," *Psychiatric Services* 48 (1997): 800–806. **days spent homeless:** M. R. Stoner, "Money Management Services for the Homeless Mentally Ill," *Hospital and Community Psychiatry* 40 (1989): 751–53. **the court ruled:** Brown v. Bowen, 845 F2d 1211, 3rd Circuit, 1988. **27 percent of patients:** P. Gorman, New Hampshire Department of Health and Human Services, personal communication, September 11, 1998. **In the only study:** C. O'Keefe, D. P. Potenza, K. T. Mueser, "Treatment Outcomes for Severely Mentally Ill Patients on Conditional Discharge to Community-Based Treatment," *Journal of Nervous and Mental Disease* 185 (1997): 409–11. **best-known example:** J. D. Bloom, M. H. Williams, J. L. Rogers, et al., "Evaluation and Treatment of Insanity Acquittees in the Community," *Bulletin of the American Academy of Psychiatry and Law* 14 (1986): 231–44. **Additional studies:** J. D. Bloom, M. H. Williams, and D. A. Bigelow, "Monitored Conditional Release of Persons Found Not Guilty by Reason of Insanity," *American Journal of Psychiatry* 148 (1991): 444–48. **Some form of outpatient commitment:** E. F. Torrey and R. J. Kaplan, "A National Survey of the

Use of Outpatient Commitment," *Psychiatric Services* 46 (1995): 778–84. **In Washington, D.C.:** G. Zanni and L. deVeau, "Inpatient Stays Before and After Outpatient Commitment," *Hospital and Community Psychiatry* 37 (1986): 941–42. **in Ohio:** M. R. Munetz, T. Grande, J. Kleist, et al., "The Effectiveness of Outpatient Civil Commitment," *Psychiatric Services* 47 (1996): 1251–53. **and in Iowa:** B. M. Rohland, "The Role of Outpatient Commitment in the Management of Persons with Schizophrenia," Iowa Consortium for Mental Health, Services, Training, and Research, May 1998. **In one study in North Carolina:** G. A. Fernandez and S. Nygard, "Impact of Involuntary Outpatient Commitment on the Revolving-Door Syndrome in North Carolina," *Hospital and Community Psychiatry* 41 (1990): 1001–4. **In another study:** M. S. Swartz, J. W. Swanson, H. R. Wagner, et al., "Can Involuntary Outpatient Commitment Reduce Hospital Recidivism?: Findings from a Randomized Trial with Severely Mentally Ill Individuals," *American Journal of Psychiatry* 156 (1999): 1968–75. **a Tennessee study:** B. Bursten, "Posthospital Mandatory Outpatient Treatment," *American Journal of Psychiatry* 143 (1986): 1255–58. **only 30 percent:** V. A. Hiday and T. L. Scheid-Cook, "The North Carolina Experience with Outpatient Commitment: A Critical Appraisal," *International Journal of Law and Psychiatry* 10 (1987): 215–32. **In Ohio, outpatient commitment:** Munetz, Grande, Kleist, et al., "The Effectiveness of Outpatient Civil Commitment." **"71 percent":** R. A. Van Putten, J. M. Santiago, and M. R. Berren, "Involuntary Outpatient Commitment in Arizona: A Retrospective Study," *Hospital and Community Psychiatry* 39 (1988): 953–58. **"it appears":** Rohland, "The Role of Outpatient Commitment." **"the results were striking":** J. W. Swanson, M. S. Swartz, R. Borum, et al., "Involuntary Out-Patient Commitment and Reduction of Violent Behaviour in Persons with Severe Mental Illness," *British Journal of Psychiatry* 176 (2000): 224–31. **"of the 35 patients":** H. R. Lamb and L. E. Weinberger, "Conservatorship for Gravely Disabled Psychiatric Patients: A Four-Year Follow-up Study," *American Journal of Psychiatry* 149 (1992): 909–13. **six-month study:** J. Geller, A. L. Grudzinskas, Jr., M. McDermett, et al., "The Efficacy of Involuntary Outpatient Treatment in Massachusetts," *Administration and Policy in Mental Health* 25 (1998): 271–85. **"In one of the more":** J. L. Geller, "On Being 'Committed' to Treatment in the Community," *Innovations and Research* 2 (1993): 23–27. **"if the lithium level":** J. L. Geller, "Rights, Wrongs, and the Dilemma of Coerced Community Treatment," *American Journal of Psychiatry* 143 (1986): 1259–64. **Baltimore PACT study:** A. F. Lehman, personal communication, October 12, 1998.

riboflavin: S. Kapur, R. Ganguli, R. Ulrich, et al., "Use of Random-Sequence Riboflavin as a Marker of Medication Compliance in Chronic Schizophrenics," *Schizophrenia Research* 6 (1992): 49–53. **isoniazid:** G. A. Ellard, P. J. Jenner, and P. A. Downs, "An Evaluation of the Potential Use of Isoniazid, Acetylisoniazid and Isonicotinic Acid for Monitoring the Self-Administration of Drugs," *British Journal of Clinical Pharmacology* 10 (1980): 369–81. **27 outpatients:** A. Lucksted and R. D. Coursey, "Consumer Perceptions of Pressure and Force in Psychiatric Treatments," Psychiatric Services 46 (1995): 146–52. **30 patients:** W. M. Greenberg, L. Moore-Duncan, and R. Herron, "Patients' Attitudes Toward Having Been Forcibly Medicated," *Bulletin of the American Academy of Psychiatry and the Law* 24 (1996): 513–24. **"will suffer if a liberty":** R. Michels, "The Right to Refuse Psychoactive Drugs," Hastings Center Report 3 (1973): 8–11. **"reported that their":** Cited in A. B. Hatfield, *Family Education in Mental Illness* (New York: Guilford Press, 1990), p. 124. **A 1990 NAMI:** D. M. Steinwachs, J. D. Kaspar, and E. A. Skinner, "Family Perspectives on Meeting the Needs for Care of Severely Mentally Ill Relatives: A National Survey" (Arlington, Va.: National Alliance for the Mentally Ill, 1992). **"arrest and conviction":** J. Rabkin, "Criminal Behavior of Discharged Mental Patients: A Critical Appraisal of the Research," *Psychological Bulletin* 86 (1979): 1–27. **15 of 20:** D. A. Martell and P. E. Dietz, "Mentally Disordered Offenders Who Push or Attempt to Push Victims onto Subway Tracks in New York City," *Archives of General Psychiatry* 49 (1992): 472–75. **"that 27 percent":** J. Monahan, "Mental Disorder and Violent Behavior," *American Psychologist* 47 (1992): 511–21. **study by Link et al.:** B. G. Link, H. Andrews, and F. T. Cullen, "The Violent and Illegal Behavior of Mental Patients Reconsidered," *American Sociological Review* 57 (1992) 275–92. **(ECA) study:** J. W. Swanson, C. E. Holzer, V. K. Ganju, et al., "Violence and Psychiatric Disorder in the Community: Evidence from the Epidemiologic Catchment Area Surveys," *Hospital and Community Psychiatry* 41 (1990): 761–70. **"The data":** J. Monahan, "Mental Disorder and Violent Behavior," *American Psychologist* 47 (1992): 511–21. **"In the last":** P. M. Marzuk, "Violence, Crime, and Mental Illness," *Archives of General Psychiatry* 53 (1996): 481–86. **"rampage killers":** F. Fessenden, "They Threaten, Seethe and Unhinge, Then Kill in Quantity," *New York Times,* April 9, 2000, p. A-1. **20 percent:** All references in this section, unless otherwise noted, are taken from E. F. Torrey, *Out of the Shadows,* chapter 3, pp. 25–42. **"suicide is the number":** C. B. Caldwell and I. I. Gottesman, "Schizophrenics Kill Themselves Too: A Review of Risk Factors for Suicide," *Schizophrenia Bulletin* 16 (1990): 571–89. **15 to 17 percent:** F. K. Goodwin and K. R. Jamison, *Manic-Depressive Illness* (New York: Oxford University Press, 1990), p. 230. **within the first 10 years:** C. P. Miles, "Conditions Predisposing to Suicide: A Review," *Journal of Nervous and Mental Disease* 164 (1977): 231–46. **Finnish study:** H. Heilä, "Suicide in Schizophrenia—A Review," *Psychiatria Fennica* 30 (1999): 59–79. **Belgian study:** M. De Hert, K. McKenzie, and J. Peuskens, "Risk Factors for Suicide in Young People Suffering from Schizophrenia: A Long-term Follow-up Study," forthcoming.

CHAPTER 12

"The wretchedness": H. M. Hurd, *The Institutional Care of the Insane in the United States and Canada*, vol. 2 (New York: Arno Press, 1973), p. 95, quoting S. B. Woodward; originally published in 1917. **"gets emotional support":** "Compassion and Love for One Son; Fear and Anger for Other," *Ontario Friends of Schizophrenics Newsletter*, Summer 1987; reprinted from the *Alliance for the Mentally Ill of Southern Arizona Newsletter*. **An excellent description:** L. Wilson, *This Stranger, My Son* (New York: Putnam, 1968). **"We had moved":** Ibid., p. 178. **"You know, Dad":** J. Wechsler, N. Wechsler, and H. Karpf, *In a Darkness* (New York: Norton, 1972),

p. 27. **"I read a book":** Wilson, *This Stranger, My Son*, pp. 123–24. **"My mother died":** M. C., personal communication, New York. **"Badly treated families":** W. S. Appleton, "Mistreatment of Patients' Families by Psychiatrists," *American Journal of Psychiatry* 131 (1974): 655–57. **"Once you have":** A. C., personal communication, Maryland. **Cogentin tablet:** C. Adamec, *How to Live with a Mentally Ill Person* (New York: John Wiley, 1996), p. 52. **"One of our":** H. B. M. Murphy, "Community Management of Rural Mental Patients," Final Report of USPHS Grant (Rockville, Md.: National Institute of Mental Health, 1964). **"I am haunted":** E. Leete, "The Treatment of Schizophrenia: A Patient's Perspective," *Hospital and Community Psychiatry* 38 (1987): 486–91. **"There came the morning":** J. Baum, "Mental Illness: Acceptance Is the Key," originally published in the *Alabama Advocate* and reprinted in the *Utah AMI Newsletter*, Oct./Dec. 1993, p. 4. **"I cry":** R. Carter, *Helping Someone with Mental Illness* (New York: Times Books, 1998), pp. 6–7. **"Well, I guess":** G. L., personal communication, Maryland. **Several observers have noted:** W. W. Michaux et al., *The First Year Out: Mental Patients After Hospitalization* (Baltimore: Johns Hopkins University Press, 1969). **"Several relatives mentioned":** C. Creer and J. K. Wing, *Schizophrenia at Home* (London: Institute of Psychiatry, 1974), p. 33.

"You've got to reach": Laffey, p. 40. "Recognizing that a person": H. R. Lamb and Associates, *Community Survival for Long-term Patients* (San Francisco: Jossey-Bass, 1976), p. 7. "A neutral": Wing, *Schizophrenia*, p. 29. "Superficially she was": O. Sacks, *The Man Who Mistook His Wife for a Hat* (New York: Summit Books, 1985), pp. 70–74. "My advice": E. Francell, "Medication: The Foundation of Recovery," *Innovations and Research* 3 (1994): 31–40. "a controlled environment": E. Leete, "How I Perceive and Manage My Illness," *Hospital and Community Psychiatry* 15 (1989): 197–200. "recognizing when": Leete, "The Treatment." study of exercise: G. Faulkner and A. Sparkes, "Exercise as Therapy for Schizophrenia: An Ethnographic Study," *Journal of Sport and Exercise Psychology* 21 (1999): 52–69. "a seat where": Leete, "How I." "we are more": F. J. Frese, "Twelve Aspects of Coping for Persons with Schizophrenia," *Innovations and Research* 2 (1993): 39–46, "don't talk": F. Frese, "Pointers for Persons Recovering from Mental Illness," *Newsletter of the Georgia Alliance for the Mentally Ill*, March 1992, p. 4. "to help restore": J. Walsh, "Schizophrenics Anonymous: The Franklin County, Ohio, Experience," *Psychosocial Rehabilitation Journal* 18 (1994): 61–74. "peer counselors": C. W. McGill and C. J. Patterson, "Former Patients as Peer Counselors on Locked Psychiatric Inpatient Units," *Hospital and Community Psychiatry* 41 (1990): 1017–20. case management aides: P. S. Sherman and R. Porter, "Mental Health Consumers as Case Management Aides," *Hospital and Community Psychiatry* 42 (1991): 494–98. 28 such studies: A.-M. Baronet, "Factors Associated with Caregiver Burden in Mental Illness: A Critical Review of the Research Literature," *Clinical Psychology Review* 19 (1999): 819–841. "Sometimes I feel": "Thoughts from a NAMI Mother," *NAMI Oklahoma News* 15 (1999), p. 1. in Australia: J. Farhall, B. Webster, B. Hocking, et al., "Training to Enhance Partnerships Between Mental Health Professionals and Family Caregivers: A Comparative Study," *Psychiatric Services* 49 (1998): 1488–90. "Look at the person": Anonymous, personal communication, Davis, California. "My son seemed": A. H., personal communication, Washington, D.C. "Patients tended to": Wing, *Schizophrenia*, p. 27. "I would have been": H. R. Rollin, ed., *Coping with Schizophrenia* (London: Burnett, 1980), p. 158. "A more realistic": Creer and Wing, p. 71. "One patient returned home": Ibid., p. 22. "One young man": Ibid., p. 11. "One lady said": Ibid., p. 8. "Leave me alone": B. B., personal communication, New York. "When our son was": L. Y., personal communication, San Jose, California. "The most remarkable lesson": L. M., personal communication, Florida. "While admiring": P. Earle, "Popular Fallacies in Regard to Insanity and the Insane," *Journal of Social Science* 26 (1890): 113. **"I found structure"**: A. H., personal communication, Washington, D.C. **"My wife will cook"**: Creer and Wing, p. 30. **"The second practical"**: Anonymous, personal communication, California. **"It's so annoying"**: Creer and Wing, p. 10. **respite care**: R. Geiser, L. Hoche, et al., "Respite Care for Mentally Ill Patients and Their Families," *Hospital and Community Psychiatry* 39 (1988): 291–97; see also the "Respite Program Technical Assistance Guide," NAMI South Carolina, Columbia, S.C. **"by teaching the patients"**: I. R. H. Falloon, J. L. Boyd, C. M. McGill, et al., "Family Management in the Prevention of Exacerbations of Schizophrenia," *New England Journal of Medicine* 24 (1982): 1437–40. **"provides evidence that"**: M. J. Goldstein and J. A. Doane, "Family Factors in the Onset, Course and Treatment of Schizophrenic Spectrum Disorders," *Journal of Nervous and Mental Disease* 170 (1982): 692–700. **"the parents"**: D. Goleman, "Schizophrenia: Early Signs Found," *New York Times*, December 11, 1984. **"are both influenced"**: S. King, "Is Expressed Emotion Cause or Effect in the Mothers of Schizophrenic Young Adults?" *Schizophrenia Research* 45 (2000): 65–78. **"convinced that"**: R. Lanquetot, "First Person Account: On Being Daughter and Mother," *Schizophrenia Bulletin* 14 (1988): 337–41. **"and sit us"**: M. Fichtner, "Children of Mad-

ness," *Miami Herald*, September 15, 1991, pp. J-1–4. **Meg Livergood**: M. Blais, "Trish," *Miami Herald Sunday Magazine*, May 24, 1987, pp. 7–16. **"suddenly both"**: W. Kelley, "Unmet Needs," *Journal of the California Alliance for the Mentally Ill* 3 (1992): 28–30. **"envious watching"**: J. Mozham, "Daddy and Me: Growing Up with a Schizophrenic," *Reflections of AMI of Michigan*, May/June 1991, pp. 18–19. **"That day"**: A. S. Brodoff, "First Person Account: Schizophrenia Through a Sister's Eyes—The Burden of Invisible Baggage," *Schizophrenia Bulletin* 14 (1988): 113–16. **"I feel such"**: M. Wasow, *The Skipping Stone* (Palo Alto: Science and Behavior Books, 1995), p. 72. **"My husband's"**: D. T. Marsh, *Serious Mental Illness and the Family* (New York: John Wiley, 1998), p. 239. **"It's funny"**: P. Aronowitz, "A Brother's Dreams," *New York Times Magazine*, January 24, 1988, p. 355. **"superkids"**: C. Kauffman, H. Grunebaum, B. Cohler, et al., "Superkids: Competent Children of Psychotic Mothers," *American Journal of Psychiatry* 136 (1979): 1398–1402. **"Growing up"**: Lanquetot. **Moorman**: M. Moorman, *My Sister's Keeper* (New York: Norton, 1992). **"She once knew"**: Mozham. **"was aware that"**: Fichtner. **Julie Johnson**: J. Johnson, *Hidden Victims—Hidden Healers* (New York: Doubleday, 1988). **in one study**: C. D. Swofford, J. W. Kasckow, G. Scheller-Gilkey, et al., "Substance

Use: A Powerful Predictor of Relapse in Schizophrenia," *Schizophrenia Research* 20 (1996): 145–151. **145 patients:** M. I. Herz and C. Melville, "Relapse in Schizophrenia," *American Journal of Psychiatry* 137 (1980): 801–05. **"it is extremely":** M. Herz, "Prodromal Symptoms and Prevention of Relapse in Schizophrenia," *Journal of Clinical Psychiatry* 46 (1985): 22–25. **In England:** M. Birchwood, J. Smith, F. MacMillan, et al., "Predicting Relapse in Schizophrenia: The Development and Implementation of an Early Signs Monitoring System Using Patients and Families as Observers," *Psychological Medicine* 19 (1989): 649–56. **"Warning Signals Scale":** P. Jørgensen, "Schizophrenic Delusions: The Detection of Warning Signals," *Schizophrenia Research* 32 (1998): 17–22. **"In the first stage":** M. Lovejoy, "Recovery from Schizophrenia: A Personal Odyssey," *Hospital and Community Psychiatry* 35 (1984): 809–12. **videotapes:** S. A. Davidoff, B. P. Forester, S. N. Ghaemi, et al., "Effect of Video Self-Observation on Development of Insight in Psychotic Disorders," *Journal of Nervous and Mental Disease* 186 (1998): 697–700.

CHAPTER 13

"There is": R. Mead, *Medical Precepts and Cautions* (London: J. Brindley, 1751). **identical twins:** D. L. DiLalla and I. I. Gottesman, "Normal Personality Characteristics in Identical Twins Discordant for Schizophrenia," *Journal of Abnormal Psychology* 104 (1995): 490–99. **"The daughter":** B. Bick, "Love and Resentment," *New York Times Magazine,* March 25, 1990, p. 26. **"Part of the":** J. K. Wing, *Schizophrenia and Its Management in the Community* (pamphlet published by National Schizophrenic Fellowship, 1977), pp. 28–29. **"Almost all crimes":** S. Brill, "A Dishonest Defense," *Psychology Today,* November 1981, pp. 16–19. **"the line between":** C. Holden, "Insanity Defense Reexamined," *Science* 222 (1983): 994–95. **small loss of IQ:** A. J. Russell, J. C. Munro, P. B. Jones, et al., "Schizophrenia and the Myth of Intellectual Decline," *American Journal of Psychiatry* 154 (1997): 635–39. **in Finland:** I. Isohanni, M.-R. Jarvelin, P. Jones, et al., "Can Excellent School Performance Be a Precursor of Schizophrenia? A 28-Year Follow-Up in the Northern Finland 1966 Birth Cohort," *Acta Psychiatrica Scandinavica* 100 (1999): 17–26. **in childhood:** J. S. Bedwell, B. Keller, A. K. Smith et al., "Why Does Postpsychotic IQ Decline in Childhood-Onset Schizophrenia?" *American Journal of Psychiatry* 156 (1999): 1996–97. **a 1989 study:** M. J. Edlund, C. Conrad, and P. Morris, "Accidents Among Schizophrenic Outpatients," *Comprehensive Psychiatry* 30 (1989): 522–26. **Two earlier studies:** L. E. Hollister, "Automobile Driving by Psychiatric Patients," letter, *American*

Journal of Psychiatry 149 (1992): 274; see also D. O'Neill, "Driving and Psychiatric Illness," letter, *American Journal of Psychiatry* 150 (1993): 351. **"an increase":** G. Kirov, R. Kemp, K. Kirov, et al., "Religious Faith After Psychotic Illness," *Psychopathology* 31 (1998): 234–45. **the clergy:** D. B. Larson, A. A. Hohmann, L. G. Kessler, et al., "The Couch and the Cloth: The Need for Linkage," *Hospital and Community Psychiatry* 39 (1988): 1064–69. **religious cult:** See M. Galanter, "Psychological Induction into the Large Group: Findings from a Modern Religious Sect," *American Journal of Psychiatry* 137 (1980): 1574–79; see also M. Galanter et al., "The 'Moonies': A Psychological Study of Conversion and Membership in a Contemporary Religious Sect," *American Journal of Psychiatry* 136 (1979): 165–70; for a particularly cogent analysis, see also S. V. Levine, "Role of Psychiatry in the Phenomenon of Cults," *Canadian Journal of Psychiatry* 24 (1979): 593–603. **there may be some advantages:** See S. V. Levine, "Role of Psychiatry." **"that you respond":** F. J. Frese, "Twelve Aspects of Coping for Persons with Schizophrenia," *Innovations and Research* 2 (1993): 39–46. **28 and 29 percent:** E. Kringlen, "Adult Offspring of Two Psychotic Parents, with Special Reference to Schizophrenia," in L. C. Wynne, R. L. Cromwell, and S. Matthysse, *The Nature of Schizophrenia* (New York: John Wiley, 1978), pp. 9–24; K. Modrzewska,

"The Offspring of Schizophrenic Parents in a Swedish Isolate," *Clinical Genetics* 17 (1980): 191–201. **only 28 percent:** E. F. Torrey, "Are We Overestimating the Genetic Contribution to Schizophrenia?" *Schizophrenia Bulletin* 18 (1992): 159–70.

CHAPTER 14

"But the brilliance": F. S. Fitzgerald, *Tender Is the Night* (New York: Scribner's, 1934), pp. 191–92. **"the quintessential film":** J. Mahler, "Fully Committed," *Talk,* March 2000, pp. 134–35. **a "must see":** Although he occasionally misses the mark, as in his review of *Shine*, Roger Ebert usually writes about mental illness with sensitivity and understanding; see www.suntimes.com/ebert/index.html *or Roger Ebert's Video Companion* (Kansas City: Andrews and McMeel, updated annually since 1986). **"[Although] most viewers":** M. Martin and M. Porter, *Video Movie Guide 2000* (New York: Ballantine Books, 1999). **" 'adapt' him":** T. Teachout, "The David Helfgott Show," *Commentary*, June 1997 (www.commentarymagazine.com/index.html). **"Two centuries ago":** T. Teachout, "The Music and the Mayhem," *New York Daily News*, March 20, 1997 (www.nydailynews.com). Thanks to Darlene Bakk for her article "David Helfgott—Poster Boy for the Mental Illness Myth," which was published in the *AMI Cooke County North Subur-*

ban Newsline in early 1998. **"Berenice"**: Quotes are taken from E. A. Poe, "Berenice," in *The Works of the Late Edgar Allan Poe,* vol. 1, N. P. Willis, J. R. Lowell, and R. W. Griswold, eds. (New York: J. S. Redfield, 1850), pp. 437–45. **"Yes!—a madman's!"**: C. Dickens, "A Madman's Manuscript," in *The Works of Charles Dickens: The Pickwick Papers* (New York: Books, Inc., 1868), pp. 134. **"In the deep shade"**: C. Brontë, *Jane Eyre* (New York: Penguin Books, 1982), p. 295. **"in which all"**: H. Small, *Love's Madness: Medicine, the Novel, and Female Insanity, 1800–1865* (New York: Oxford University Press), p. 165, quoting Brontë's letter of January 4, 1848. **" 'Well,' returned Mr. Dick"**: C. Dickens, *The Oxford Illustrated Dickens: The Personal History of David Copperfield* (London: Oxford University Press, 1966), p. 202. **Bartleby:** H. Melville, *Herman Melville: Four Short Novels* (New York: Bantam Books, 1959), pp. 3–41. **"one critic"**: Bill Gelson, http://metalab.unc.edu/cheryb/women/Emily-Dickinson-bio.html). **"The first Day's Night"**: Poem 410, stanzas 4 and 5, *The Poetry of Emily Dickinson,* vol. 1, Thomas H. Johnson, ed. (Cambridge: Harvard University Press, 1955). **"I felt a Funeral"**: Ibid., poem 280, stanzas 1 and 2. **"I felt a Cleaving"**: Ibid., poem 937. **"At home"**: Excerpted in A. A. Stone and S. S. Stone, eds., *The Abnormal Personality Through Literature* (Englewood Cliffs, N.J.: Prentice-Hall, 1966), p. 5. **"Septimus heard"**: V.

Woolf, *Mrs. Dalloway* (New York: Knopf, 1993), p. 22. **"But they beckoned"**: Ibid., p. 23. **"Septimus let himself"**: Ibid., p. 73. **"Now the terror"**: V. Woolf, *The Waves* (New York: Harcourt Brace, 1988), pp. 21–22. **"Other people"**: Ibid., pp. 43–45. **"When I have"**: Ibid., p. 107. **"a sense as of"**: C. Aiken, "Silent Snow, Secret Snow," in *The World Within: Fiction Illuminating Neuroses of Our Time,* Mary Louise Aswell, ed. (New York: McGraw-Hill, 1947), p. 241. **"Lie down"**: Ibid., p. 258. **"The walls of the room"**: Z. Fitzgerald, *Save Me the Waltz* (New York: Signet, 1968), p. 186. **"my great worry"**: Letter from F. S. Fitzgerald to Dr. J. Slocum, April 8, 1934 (www.poprocks.com/-zelda/scottletters; shfitz4.html). **"Think how"**: F. S. Fitzgerald, *Tender Is the Night* (New York: Scribner's, 1934), pp. 201. **"But the brilliance"**: Ibid., pp. 191–92. **"I Am Lazarus"**: A. Kavan, in *The World Within: Fiction Illuminating Neuroses of Our Time,* Mary Louise Aswell, ed. (New York: McGraw-Hill, 1947), pp. 270–81. **"The Headless Hawk"**: T. Capote, in *The World Within: Fiction Illuminating Neuroses of Our Time,* Mary Louise Aswell, ed. (New York: McGraw-Hill, 1947), pp. 283–311. **one study has suggested:** J. L. Karlson, "Genetic Association of Giftedness and Creativity with Schizophrenia," *Hereditas* 66 (1970): 177. **a biography:** R. Ellmann, *James Joyce: New and Revised Edition* (New York: Oxford University Press, 1982), p. 685. **A psychiatrist:** N. J. C.

Andreasen, "James Joyce: A Portrait of the Artist as a Schizoid," *Journal of the American Medical Association* 224 (1973): 67–71. **"Joyce had":** Ellmann, p. 650. **"this sickness":** *Antonin Artaud: Selected Writings* (New York: Farrar, Straus, and Giroux, 1976), p. 423. **"If I am":** A. A. Davidson, "The Wretched Life and Death of an American Van Gogh," *Smithsonian Magazine*, December 1987, pp. 80–91. **"his brain":** This and other quotes about Gurney are from M. Hurd, *The Ordeal of Ivor Gurney* (Oxford: Oxford University Press, 1978), pp. 43, 122, and 158. **"Drachms and scruples" and "To God":** From P. J. Kavanagh, ed., *Collected Poems of Ivor Gurney* (Oxford: Oxford University Press, 1982), pp. 91 and 156; reprinted by permission of the editor. **"his career":** These quotes are from S. Nasar, *A Beautiful Mind* (New York: Simon and Schuster, 1998), pp. 243 and 244. **"I love life":** R. Nijinsky, ed., *the Diary of Vaslav Nijinsky* (Berkeley: University of California Press, 1968), pp. 185–86. **"Oh, if I":** B. Schiff, "Triumph and Tragedy in the Land of 'Blue Tones and Gay Colors,' " *Smithsonian Magazine*, October 1984, p. 89. **college freshmen:** O. Wahl, "Public vs. Professional Conceptions of Schizophrenia," *Journal of Community Psychiatry* 15 (1987): 285–91. **A 1986 poll:** C. Holden, "Giving Mental Illness Its Research Due," *Science* 232 (1986): 1084–86. **400 individuals:** O. F. Wahl, *Telling Is Risky Business* (New Brunswick: Rutgers University Press, 1999), p. 14, quoting Jum Nunnally's study, published in 1961 as *Popular Conceptions of Mental Health*. **"a majority":** O. F. Wahl, "Mental Health Consumers' Experience of Stigma," *Schizophrenia Bulletin* 25 (1999): 467–78. **survey in California:** Wahl, *Telling Is Risky Business*, p. 15. **a 1996 survey:** B. A. Pesco-solido, J. Monahan, B. G. Link, et al., "The Public's View of the Competence, Dangerousness, and Need for Legal Coercion of Persons with Mental Health Problems," *American Journal of Public Health* 89 (1999): 1339–45. **"Why is stigma":** *Report on Mental Health of the United States Surgeon General* (Washington, D.C.: U.S. Department of Health and Human Services, 1999). **"negative attitudes":** J. A. Thorton and O. F. Wahl, "Impact of a Newspaper Article on Attitudes Toward Mental Illness," *Journal of Community Psychology* 24 (1996): 17–25. **"marked increase":** M. C. Angermeyer and H. Matschinger, "The Effect of Violent Attacks by Schizophrenic Persons on the Attitude of the Public Towards the Mentally Ill," *Social Science and Medicine* 43 (1996): 1721–28. **"between the belief":** B. G. Link, J. C. Phelan, M. Bresnahan, et al., "Public Conceptions of Mental Illness: Labels, Causes, Dangerousness, and Social Distance," *American Journal of Public Health* 89 (1999): 1328–33. **"within hours":** E. Jarvik, "Mental Health Clients Fear Growing Stigma," *Deseret News*, April 24, 1999, p. A-1.

CHAPTER 15

"And, once more": R. C. Waterston, "The Insane in Massachusetts," *Christian Examiner* 33 (1843): 338–52. **"They say, 'Nothing' ":** F. Tiffany, *Life of Dorothea Lynde Dix* (Ann Arbor: Plutarch Press, 1971), p. 134. **"although audiences tended":** Quoted in J. A. Talbott, ed., *The Chronic Mental Patient* (Washington, D.C.: American Psychiatric Association, 1978), p. xiii. **In 1977:** The National Mental Health Association (NMHA) McAlpin Research Achievement Award was given to Drs. Lyman Wynne and Margaret Singer for their work on communication among family members that may contribute to the development of schizophrenia; see *Research on Mental Health: Progress and Promise* (Washington, D.C.: NMHA, 1978). **an article:** H. R. Lamb and E. Oliphant, "Schizophrenia Through the Eyes of Families," *Hospital and Community Psychiatry* 29 (1978): 803–6. **"Hubbard taught":** "Hubbard's Teachings Guide Treatment of Mental Illness," *St. Petersburg Times,* November 14, 1998. **"Earthlings are":** R. Leiby, "John Travolta's Alien Notion," *Washington Post,* November 28, 1999, p. G-1. **"Breggin admits":** C. Gorman, "Prozac's Worst Enemy," *Time,* October 10, 1994, pp. 64–64. **"stress in the family":** J. Cornwall, *The Power to Harm* (New York: Viking Press, 1996), p. 176. **"people diagnosed":** P. Breggin, *Toxic Psychiatry* (New York:

St. Martin's Press, 1991), p. 22. **"the difference":** Cornwall, p. 191. **"the worst":** Breggin, p. 68. **"permitting children":** Cornwall, pp. 189–190. **Re-Evaluation Counseling:** M. D. O'Hartigan, "The Psychotherapy Conspiracy to Rule the World," *PDXS,* September 11–24, 1998, pp. 3–6. **"only 13.5 percent":** E. F. Torrey, M. B. Knable, J. M. Davis, et al., *A Mission Forgotten: The Failure of the National Institute of Mental Health to Do Sufficient Research on Severe Mental Illnesses* (Arlington, Va.: NAMI, 1999). **"Recent research":** H. J. Steadman, "Critically Reassessing the Accuracy of Public Perception of the Dangerousness of the Mentally Ill," *Journal of Health and Social Behavior* 22 (1981): 31–316. **"We can reduce":** H. R. Lamb, "Combating Stigma by Providing Treatment," *Psychiatric Services* 50 (1999): 729. **contact with individuals:** B. G. Link and F. T. Cullen, "Contact with the Mentally Ill and Perceptions of How Dangerous They Are," *Journal of Health and Social Behavior* 27 (1986): 289–303. **"are not falling":** M. Starin, "What Mental Illness Doesn't Destroy, the System Does," *Poughkeepsie Journal,* January 18, 1984, p. 5. **"a minority within minorities":** *Report of the President's Commission on Mental Health,* vol. 2 (Washington, D.C.: U.S. Government Printing Office, 1978), p. 362.

INDEX

INDEX 501

mental hospitals, 18–19; *See also type of hospital*
mental illness: misunderstanding about causes of, 21
mental retardation, 90, 114, 116, 124, 163, 286, 301, 303
mental status examination, 179–80
mentally ill: abuse of, 327
Mentally Ill Chemical Abuser (MICA) programs, 282
mesoridazine (Serentil), 220
metachromatic leukodystrophy, 112, 181
metal poisoning, 112
methylfolate, 207
Mexican Americans, 13
MICA (Mentally Ill Chemical Abuser) programs, 282
Middle Ages, 16
military service, 19, 260
Miller, Leonard, 26
minority groups, 60
Miró, Joan, 82, *83*
mislabeling: and causes of schizophrenia, 158; and childhood schizophrenia, 198
M'Naghten defense, 357
Moban, 212, 223, 230
mobile clinics, 200
mobile treatment teams, 192
molindone (Moban), 212, 223, 230
Moller, Mary, 327
Monahan, John, 308
money management, 256, 257–60, 283, 338–39
moods, 99, 234, 245–46. *See also* manic-depressive illness
Moorman, Margaret, 344
mortality. *See* death; suicide
mothering, 158, 168–69, 170
motivation, 72, 93, 94, 122, 124. *See also* apathy

motor vehicles; accidents and, 138; driving and, 360
movement/coordination, 120, 360; and causes of schizophrenia, 148, 162; and diagnosis, 94; and effects of antipsychotic drugs, 73, 74, 219, 221, 222, 225; and symptoms of schizophrenia, 32, 72, 73–74, 82, 84. *See also* akinesia; *type of schizophrenia*
movies. *See* films
Mozham, Jody, 343, 344
MRI scans, 115, 124, 126, 127, 128, 144–45, 146, 181, 183
Mrs. Dalloway (film), 373–74
Mrs. Dalloway (Woolf), 379
multiple sclerosis, 13, 111, 121, 152, 182, 274, 348, 406
Munch, Edvard, 82, 85
Munetz, Mark, 392
Murphy, H. B. M., 322–23
mutism, 74, 93

NAMI. *See* National Alliance for the Mentally Ill
narcolepsy, 112
Nasar, Sylvia, 386
Nash, John, 53–54, 359, 384, 385–86
National Alliance for the Mentally Ill (NAMI), 2, 10, 11, 175, 307, 339, 345, 394; and advocacy, 392, 394, 400, 401, 402, 403, 406, 408–9, 410; educational programs of, 327; and guardianship/conservatorship, 366, 367; jail and arrest study by, 310, 311; patients as members of, 329; and rehabilitation programs, 268–69; religious groups within, 361; support groups of, 131, 327; and treatment of schizophrenia, 190–91
National Alliance for Research on Schizophrenia and Affective Disorders (NARSAD), 398

vocational rehabilitation, 259–60, 404
voices in hallucinations. *See* auditory
    hallucinations
Vonnegut, Mark, 369

Ward, Mary Jane, 20
"Ward No. 6" (Chekhov), 55, 378–79
"Warning Signals Scale," 345–46
Waterhouse, Steven, 361, 400–401
Waterston, Robert, 390
The Waves (Woolf), 379–80
Weakland, John, 168
websites/Internet: and advocacy, 394,
    395, 397, 400, 401, 403, 404, 406,
    407, 409; and assisted treatment,
    306; for buying antipsychotic drugs,
    228, 251, 252; about rehabilitation
    programs, 269; and religion, 361
Wechsler, James, 319
Wechsler, Michael, 71
weight, 222–23, 230–31, 233, 234,
    235, 236, 237, 245, 248
Weinberger, Daniel, 162
welfare, 260
Wellstone, Paul, 398
Wilson, Louise, 124, 318, 319
Wilson's disease, 112, 181
Winerip, Michael, 261
Winfrey, Oprah, 368
Wing, John, 325, 326, 332–33, 334,
    342, 356
wish list, 254

withdrawal: alcohol, 64; and
    alternatives to antipsychotic drugs,
    246; from antipsychotic drugs, 218;
    from benzodiazepines, 244; and
    childhood schizophrenia, 124; and
    diagnosis, 89, 93, 94; and onset,
    122, 123; and predictors of
    outcome, 126, 127; and
    rehabilitation, 268; social, 46, 74,
    94, 122, 123, 126, 246, 268,
    334–35, 336; and survival, 334–35,
    336; and symptoms of
    schizophrenia, 46, 52, 74, 122, 123;
    thought, 52, 89
Wonderland (TV series), 368
Woodward, Samuel B., 317
Woolf, Virginia, 373–74, 379–80,
    387
word salad, 50–51
work. *See* employment
workshops: sheltered, 265, 266,
    404
workup, diagnostic, 175, 179–83
Wyatt, Richard, 26, 218–19

X syndrome, 115

ziprasidone (Geodon), 223, 230, 231,
    236–38, 285
Zoloft, 246
zuclopenthixol, 249
Zyprexa. *See* olanzapine

ABOUT THE AUTHOR

E. Fuller Torrey, M.D., is a clinical and research psychiatrist specializing in schizophrenia and manic-depressive illness. He is currently the Executive Director of the Stanley Foundation Research Programs, president of the Treatment Advocacy Center, and professor of psychiatry at the Uniformed Services University of the Health Sciences. He is the author or editor of seventeen books, including *The Roots of Treason,* which was nominated by the National Book Critics Circle as one of the five best biographies of 1983. He has lectured extensively and has appeared on *Donahue, Oprah, 60 Minutes, 20/20, Dateline,* and other programs. Dr. Torrey lives in Bethesda, Maryland.